Twentieth Century Russia

EIGHTH EDITION

TWENTIETH CENTURY RUSSIA

DONALD W. TREADGOLD

University of Washington

WESTVIEW PRESS
Boulder • San Francisco • Oxford

Copyright © 1987, 1990, 1995 by Westview Press, Inc. First edition published in 1959 by Rand McNally & Co.; copyright © 1959, 1964, 1972, and 1976 by Rand McNally & Co. Fifth edition published in 1981 by Houghton Mifflin Co.; copyright © 1981 by Houghton Mifflin Co.

Published in 1995 in the United States of America by Westview Press, Inc., 5500 Central Avenue, Boulder, Colorado 80301–2877, and in the United Kingdom by Westview Press, 36 Lonsdale Road, Summertown, Oxford OX2 7EW

Library of Congress Cataloging-in-Publication Data
Treadgold, Donald W., 1922–
    Twentieth century Russia / Donald W. Treadgold — 8th ed.
      p.   cm.
    Includes bibliographical references and index.
    ISBN 0–8133-1810–6 — ISBN 0–8133-1811–4 (pbk.)
    1. Former Soviet republics—History—20th century.   I. Title.
DK246.T65   1995
947.084—dc20

94-25860
CIP

Printed and bound in the United States of America

10   9   8   7   6   5   4   3   2   1

For Warren

Contents

PART 2   THE COMMUNISTS TAKE POWER

PART 4   THE POSTWAR PERIOD

Maps

Preface to the Eighth Edition

This book attempts to summarize what is known about the main lines of development of Russia and the Soviet Union from 1900 to 1994 and to establish a sound basis for further investigation and study.

The book is organized around the chief threads of political change, but considerable space is devoted also to the transformations that occurred in the economy, literature and the other arts, and religion. Mention is made of the major developments in the non-Russian borderlands. Attention is given to the growth of Russian Marxism and Marxist organization, to the role of Marxism-Leninism as the official ideology of the Soviet state, and to the Kremlin's use of foreign Communist parties in its efforts at expansion. I have briefly sketched the main lines of policy and practice of Communist parties that have come to power outside the USSR, with or without Soviet military support, particularly with the purpose of comparing them with Soviet policy and practice.

At the time of writing, Russia has discarded communism but still suffers from the effects of seven decades of Communist rule. Archives, with some exceptions and qualifications, are open after being closed or difficult to access for many years. Thus far much has been learned, but little of it startling to those who followed the reports of émigrés and defectors. Some archival materials have probably been destroyed and some certainly remain inaccessible, so may yet in the future yield dramatic revelations. I make bold to assert that the facts and judgments made in the first edition of this book (1959) remain generally valid, while critics of those judgments have been proven wrong over and over. In this edition I have sought to use the results of recent research and thought, but no one person can claim to have read all of the scholarly publications of the past few years, and I would appreciate corrections from any reader.

In preparing the first edition, I acknowledged special indebtedness to my mother (deceased) and my wife; to John A. Armstrong, Richard Pipes, John S. Reshetar, and George E. Taylor, who are alive, and Gladys Greenwood, Franz Michael, and Udo Posch, who are deceased. My intellectual obligations are great to the late Fr. Georges Florovsky, Michael Karpovich, and Karl A. Wittfogel—who were also my dear friends. I am grateful to my Russian and Soviet colleagues and friends, as well as those of Russian birth and extraction, who have helped me understand the history of their country (or country of origin).

The eighth edition appears after events that some of us thought might someday occur but seldom expected to live to see. Changes have been introduced that will take years or decades to be completed or to assess fully. The ten-year-old boy to whom the book was first dedicated has grown to become an eminent scholar (in a related field, Byzantine history), and the author is not only older but in some ways gladder, in some ways sadder.

In this edition revisions have been made on almost every page, with many rewritings and substitutions. Dates are given in Old Style—the Julian calendar, up to February 1/14, 1918, when the Bolsheviks adopted the Gregorian calendar—and thereafter in New Style. Transliteration from Cyrillic follows Library of Congress practice except when common usage has altered names, with some resultant inconsistency. Romanization of Chinese names accords with Wade-Giles generally until 1949, pinyin thereafter, except that province names are consistently pinyin and cities bear the name they bore at the time. Some are under the impression that the adoption of pinyin meant renaming, which is quite wrong. I shall not explain the (I trust commonsensical) exceptions I have made. My thanks go to Jane Raese and Peter Kracht at Westview Press and copy editor Jon Taylor Howard for their valued and professional assistance.

Donald W. Treadgold
Seattle, February 7, 1994

PART ONE

New Currents in Old Russia

Introduction:
Into Totalitarianism
and Out of It

The Peoples and the Land

Russia, or the Russian Federation (both names are legal), contains slightly more than half the people who inhabited the Soviet Union (a shortened form of the official designation, Union of Soviet Socialist Republics), and four-fifths of its territory. The Russians are the predominant people of Russia; in contrast, in some of the former Soviet Union's ethnically named subdivisions, the peoples concerned are not even the majority (for example, Kazakhs in Kazakhstan, Abkhazians in Abkhazia; the Latvians keep a sliver-like edge in Latvia).

The Russian language, together with Belarusian and Ukrainian, make up the Eastern Slavic subdivision of the Slavic branch of the Indo-European family.[1] The three peoples who speak them are linked not only by language but by their traditional religion, Eastern Orthodox Christianity. The Russians, however, are by no means Russia's only ethnic group. The Russian republic has thirty-one administrative subdivisions named for what is or was the most numerous non-Russian people of the area concerned. The two politically most active in the early 1990's are the Tatars of Kazan (the Crimean Tatars seem more concerned with reestablishing themselves in their former homeland than with political self-assertion) and the Yakuts or Sakha. Both are Turkic,[2] as are the Chuvash and Bashkirs; the

---

[1] The two other subdivisions are the Western Slavic (mainly Polish, Czech, and Slovak) and Southern Slavic (Serbo-Croatian, Slovene, Bulgarian, and Macedonian).

[2] The Uralic and Altaic language family, totally different from Indo-European tongues, is, according to one classification, composed of the Uralic, in turn divided into Finno-Ugric (first subdivision, Finnic: Finnish, Estonian, Mari, Mordvinian, and Lapp; second subdivision, Ugric: Hungarian, Mansi, and Khanty) and Samoyedic; and Altaic (Turkish, Mongolian, and Manchu or Tungus). Most of the

Udmurts (formerly Votiaks) and Mari are Finnic; the Buriats and Kalmyks are Mongols, and dozens of other small peoples dot the map of Russia from the Gulf of Finland to the Bering Sea. The Chuvash and Udmurts are Orthodox Christians, but most of the other Uralic and Altaic peoples are Muslims or pagans, except for the Kalmyks and roughly half the Buriats, who are Buddhists.

Of the units that formerly made up the USSR, three have gained independence and have distanced themselves from the rest: Estonia, Latvia, and Lithuania; eleven are independent but are currently part of the Commonwealth of Independent States (Sodruzhestvo Nezavisimykh Gosudarstv), or CIS. Declarations of sovereignty and independence have been endemic since August 1991, and what those terms are going to mean in a given instance is still being worked out.

The first Slavic state on what later became Russian soil was organized in the ninth century in the region of Kiev. By 1240, when the Mongols invaded Europe, the Kievan state of "Rus" had disintegrated into small independent principalities. An important effect of the Mongol conquest was the devastation of the vicinity of Kiev and the consequent separation of the Eastern Slavs into two sections, to the west and northeast of the ruined city. The western area fell under the control of the large Lithuanian state, which first accepted dynastic union with Poland (1385) and then full union (1569). The northeast came to be ruled by the Grand Prince of Moscow, who in effect assumed the position of viceroy for the Mongols. About 1450 the Muscovite principate threw off its dependence on the Mongols (by this time Tatarized, so often called simply "Tatars"). In 1721, under Peter the Great, Muscovy was renamed the Russian Empire. During the next two centuries almost all Eastern Slavs were brought under the rule of St. Petersburg (Petrograd 1914–24, Leningrad 1924–91), which Peter built on a marsh by the Gulf of Finland and made his capital.

Many non-Slavs also inhabited the Empire. A small Jewish community had appeared in seventeenth-century Muscovy, and shortly before 1800 Catherine the Great established a Jewish "pale" (area of settlement) in the territories newly annexed from Poland. Finnic peoples lived intermingled with Russians, and Finland proper was taken from Sweden during the Napoleonic Wars. In 1814 the Congress of Vienna awarded a truncated "Congress Poland" to Russia. Both Finland and Poland achieved independence after the Russian Revolution. The Empire also included three other Christian peoples: Romanians ("Moldavians") in Bessarabia, Armenians and Georgians in the Caucasus, and, almost entirely Muslim, the Central Asian Turks (today known as Kazakhs, Kyrgyz, Uzbeks, and Turkmens) and the Persian Tajiks. Central Asia was conquered in the late nineteenth century, Bessarabia and the Caucasus earlier.

---

peoples who speak all the Uralic languages listed (except for most Hungarians) live in the Russian Federation; the same is true of sizable minorities of the three Altaic groups listed.

The Georgians and Armenians had a history of civilization and independence that long antedated the history of the Russians. As the new ideology of nationalism spread through nineteenth-century Europe, at least the intellectuals among peoples who in modern times had never known nationhood, such as the Ukrainians, developed nationalist aspirations. Sometimes nationalism went hand in hand with socialism, and St. Petersburg severely repressed the expression of such ideas.

Only in the late nineteenth century, however, were active measures of Russification carried out. The very name "Russian Empire" may seem to imply an official preference for the Russian language and those who spoke it, but in fact it was a cosmopolitan state, where the imperial family was mostly German through almost two centuries of foreign marriages, and up to the mid-nineteenth century high officialdom was drawn from several European backgrounds. Discrimination was practiced against the Jewish religion but not against Jews who converted to Orthodox Christianity. The name "Ukrainian" was unknown to imperial law, which used the term "Little Russia" (Malorossiia). On the positive side, Finland enjoyed much autonomy until the Revolution, Poland until the Revolution of 1830. There was little effort to interfere with the religion and customs of the Muslim peoples or the Lamaistic Buddhists and pagans of Asiatic Russia. Schismatic (Old Believers, who had broken with the official church in 1667) and sectarian (Dukhobors, Molokane, Khlysty, Skoptsy) Russian Christians suffered more from governmental pressures than non-Christians (except Jews). In the Baltic region a German upper class descended from the Teutonic Knights ruled over Estonian and Latvian peasants and contributed many men to imperial officialdom. Individual foreigners, especially Germans but also Frenchmen, Englishmen, Scots, and others, received privileged treatment and held high positions in the government, universities, and professions. In general the tsars treated a multinational state as if it were a single nation but refrained from pressing such a policy to its logical conclusion.

The land is mostly flat and cold, and much is not tillable. Inadequate transportation has made it difficult to put to use the country's immense store of natural resources. European Russia's vast network of rivers, most of which rise near Moscow and flow to the Caspian, Black, Baltic, and White Seas, is useful when frozen or free from ice, but for much of the year it satisfies neither condition. The rivers of Siberia are wide, long, and of little use for commerce. They run from south to north to empty into the Arctic Ocean, and though Cossacks originally crossed Siberia by boat, using the rivers' tributaries and portages between them, modern commerce does not lend itself to the same methods. Roads are too few and often poor, reduced to mud by the spring thaws. Railroads are extensively used but in 1994 are sadly in need of upgrading; the same is true of the gigantic national airline, Aeroflot.

Mountains are of little benefit. High ranges lie along the borders with China and nowhere else. Through the Ili gap in northern Sinkiang many nomadic conquerors passed en route to the European steppes; the Urals—by American or

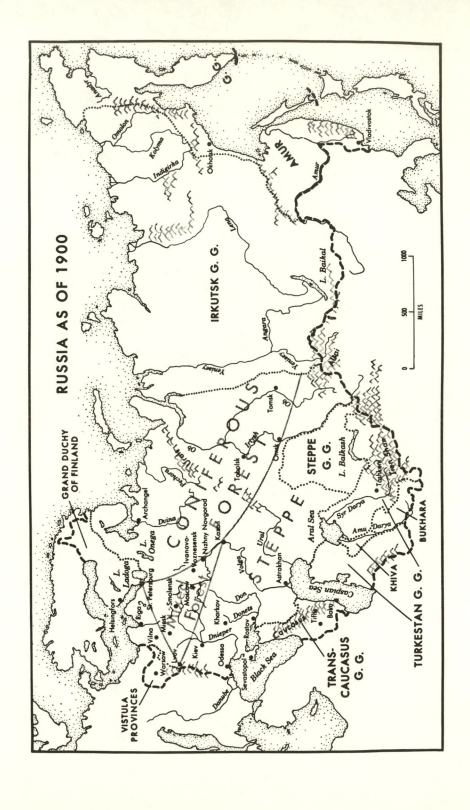

RUSSIA AS OF 1900

GRAND DUCHY
OF FINLAND

VISTULA
PROVINCES

TRANS-
CAUCASUS
G. G.

TURKESTAN G. G.

BUKHARA

KHIVA

STEPPE
G. G.

IRKUTSK G. G.

CONIFEROUS FOREST

STEPPE

Mixed Forest

Helsingfors
Riga
St. Petersburg
L. Ladoga
L. Onega
Archangel
Dvina
Vilna
Minsk
Smolensk
Moscow
Ivanovo-
Voznesensk
Nizhny Novgorod
Kazan
Warsaw
Lvov
Kiev
Dnieper
Kharkov
Donets
Don
Volga
Ural
Astrakhan
Odessa
Sevastopol
Rostov
Danube
Black Sea
Caucasus
Tiflis
Baku
Caspian Sea
Aral Sea
Syr Darya
Amu Darya
Tashkent
Tien Shan
L. Balkash
Omsk
Tobolsk
Irtysh
Tomsk
Yenisey
Ob
Yenisey
Angara
L. Baikal
Altai
Amur
Vladivostok
Okhotsk
Lena
Indigirka
Kolyma
Omolon
Anadyr

60
40

0   500   1000
MILES

Swiss standards scarcely more than rolling hills—give way to flat plain several hundred miles from the Caspian Sea and allowed the nomads to proceed without hindrance to plunder Russia and territories beyond. On the west Russia is completely exposed geographically. From the Teutonic Knights in the thirteenth century to the armies of Napoleon in the nineteenth and those of Hitler in the twentieth, invaders have advanced across open plains. Moreover, mountains do nothing to lessen the rigors of the climate. They are high in the south, cutting off warmth, but there are none in the north of a size to prevent Siberian Arctic winds from sweeping south and westward.

Russia has some very rich soil: the black-earth (*chernozëm*) strip, which runs broadly across the south of European Russia, then narrows and disappears in central Siberia. North of it is the enormous forest known as the taiga, and along the Arctic coast is the treeless tundra. Russia's warm southlands nearly disappeared when Ukraine and the three Caucasian states became independent, though a Mediterranean climate prevails in a strip of eastern Black Sea coast.

The Character of Russian Absolutism

By the nineteenth century Russian state and society had assumed a despotically regulated pattern which had been imprinted on the borderlands to a considerable extent. That pattern, whose chief characteristics were correctly identified by the early revolutionaries as autocracy and serfdom, had not taken shape in Russia until modern times. In the period of the Kievan state and its succession principalities under the Mongol yoke, medieval Russia had enjoyed a more fluid type of political and social organization. Trading city-states in the north, such as Novgorod and Pskov, which maintained close ties with Western Europe, had a large, free farmer class and a turbulent form of self-government in which the urban masses took part. The Kievan and other princes were restrained from arbitrary deeds by the popular assembly (*veche*), and although there were slaves, there was also a very numerous class of agriculturists whose relationship with their landlords was a contractually circumscribed one.

When the Muscovite princes threw off the Mongol yoke, they began to claim despotic prerogatives, partly in conscious or unconscious imitation of their former Mongol overlords and of their Byzantine coreligionists, whose primacy in the Orthodox world they claimed to have inherited when the Turks captured Constantinople in 1453. The tsars (as they now styled themselves) of Muscovy subjugated the northern trading city-states, dispersed the old assemblies, and although they summoned an assembly representative of the estates (*Zemsky Sobor,* or Assembly of the Land), it never acquired any power to limit the will of the monarch. In order to crush the old independent aristocracy (the boyars, who served any given prince at will), the tsars built up a new noble serving class (the *dvoriane* or gentry). In return for the support of the gentry, the state allowed them to reduce to serfdom the peasants who lived on their newly granted lands. The old village institution of peasant self-government, the commune (*mir* or *obshchina,* though the terms mean slightly different things at different times), was partially converted into an organ subservient to both the gentry landlords and the state, and was used to enforce the increasing weight of fiscal and other obligations which the peasants owed to both.

The last tsar and first Emperor, Peter the Great, virtually completed the long process of fixing the population into a small number of social classes with legally defined obligations and rights. Chiefly these were the gentry (into which the remnants of the boyars passed), the merchant groups, the state peasants (who lived on state lands and had no gentry landlords), and the private serfs—the last two groups constituting the great mass of the people of Russia. The remaining few slaves passed into serfdom.

In later Muscovite theory, the task of the peasants was to produce food, pay taxes, and (for a selected number of them) to serve as common soldiers in the army, while their gentry lords were bound to serve the state all their lives as civil officials or military officers. During the eighteenth century the obligations of the gentry were reduced and finally abolished, while their powers over their serfs became virtually those of slave-owners. However, they never attained the prerogatives of the earlier Western feudal lords, or even those of the contemporary nobles of the Germanic countries, and remained excluded from political power.

The imperial authority was vested in the Emperor alone. His will was not limited by law or any regularly constituted political body. The agency of his will was the imperial bureaucracy, whose powers reached far down into local affairs. In practice the Emperors did not press their powers to their theoretical limits. The opinions of their advisers and their judgment of the state of mind of the various social classes (chiefly of the legally favored gentry), the laws (especially after they were codified in the early nineteenth century), and their public allegiance to the precepts of the Christian religion, all had varying but substantial effects in restraining the monarchs from the extremes of arbitrariness. The Emperors did not attempt to exact positive commitments to an official ideology from creative artists and writers. Penalties were applied to revolutionary agitation by the secret police and the courts, but in a form and degree mild and irregular in comparison with twentieth-century totalitarianism.

The old pattern of autocracy and serfdom was greatly modified under Alexander II (1855–1881). Through the Emancipation edict and accompanying legislation serfdom was abolished. Other "Great Reforms" gave the freed peasant a share in a newly-created system of provincial and county self-government (the zemstvo), set up elective city councils for urban administration, and vastly improved the administration of justice and the method of recruitment of soldiers, from both of which the old principle of class preferment was eliminated. Nevertheless, the institution of autocracy remained intact, despite certain measures envisaging its limitation considered by Alexander II in his last days, which were laid aside only after he was assassinated by revolutionaries.

Through the efforts of officials responsive to gentry demands for restoration of their pre-Reform privileges, the Great Reforms were to some degree abridged in letter and spirit during subsequent decades. Mass discontent and the political demands of the intelligentsia combined to produce a ferment which erupted in the Revolution of 1905. As a result an Imperial Duma, or legislative assembly, was established as part of a new semi-constitutional system comparable to that of Prussia. The old absolutism was substantially modified, and in the later years of Nicholas II's reign (1894–1917) showed signs of breakdown. Meanwhile the peasantry was making progress in the direction of economic independence, and the old class lines were crossed ever more frequently. Russian culture was developing new variety, refinement, and also breadth. The growth of industry was very rapid. The final breakdown of tsarist absolutism in the midst of the domestic strains produced by the First World War seemed to foreshadow the establishment of some type of "open society" in Russia.

The Rise and Fall of Totalitarianism

The revolutions of 1905 and 1917 were mass upheavals not planned by anyone and anticipated by few; however, the revolutionary leadership devolved upon the few members of the intelligentsia who had worked out an a priori analysis of events and a program that they wished to put into effect. The revolutionary intelligentsia were unanimous in desiring the end of autocracy and the creation of a democratic government, and most of them supported some kind of plan for a socialist society. The masses generally believed themselves to be fighting for freedom and political rights as well as economic independence—or, as the slogan of the old peasant uprisings and two of the early revolutionary societies had it, "land and liberty."

The shape of the revolution depended, however, not merely on programs but on leadership. A new regime might be formed from the old bureaucracy, or "public men" who had worked in the zemstvos, city councils (or Duma), or from the inexperienced intelligentsia, or a mixture of the three. After Lenin and the Bolsheviks seized power in the October Revolution, that section of the intelligentsia who were Bolshevik or pro-Bolshevik, along with many Bolshevik workers and a very few peasants, undertook to construct a new type of government—even though Lenin for a time used prerevolutionary bureaucrats, army officers, and the like where needed.

When the Communists (as the Bolsheviks renamed themselves in 1918, reverting to Marx's term) had defeated their antagonists in the Civil War, their regime was still in the process of taking shape. Almost immediately after the seizure of power a new secret police and Red Army were organized, under the leadership and control of the expanding Communist Party. In 1921 Lenin made concessions to the peasants and small businessmen and traders through the New Economic Policy, but the Communist Party retained its monopoly of political power. Intra-Party debates about how far the policy of economic concessions should be pursued became intertwined with personal and factional rivalries. From the Party struggles of the 1920's Stalin emerged as dictator over both the Party and the country.

In 1928 Stalin unleashed the apparatus of terror (directed against the mass of ordinary people) and purge (directed against Communist Party members) in order to revolutionize the economy and social system and to consolidate his own power. Great numbers of arrests were carried out by the secret police, thereby intimidating the whole population and filling the concentration camps with a large labor force whose use on public works was economically significant. By the late 1930's Stalin had built up a totalitarian dictatorship resting on three institutional pillars: the Party organization, the secret police, and the army. The purges destroyed a large part of the leadership of all three, and Stalin replaced those removed with people loyal to him.

Totalitarianism was a word that came into general usage as a way of linking the chief features of the Nazi and Soviet systems. Hitler and the Nazis' power lasted only twelve years; the Soviet regime lasted seventy-four. During that period it changed somewhat, to be sure. But as it was formed, it was designed to achieve several ends: to preserve and strengthen Communist (and Stalin's personal) power and to stifle overt political opposition; to plan and operate the entire economic system from the center, rooting out the remnants of individual enterprise; to stamp out local nationalist or autonomist feeling among the ethnic minorities and to subject the borderlands to Moscow's fiat; to prevent or punish any academic or creative work that ran counter to the currently applied ideological line in the arts, social sciences, and even for a period the natural sciences, and to force intellectuals to render overt and active support to that line; to crush organized religion and eradicate religious belief, and, when that proved difficult, for the time being to use the religious hierarchies as instruments of propaganda; to create an all-pervading atmosphere of fear and coercion in which the potential nonconformist hesitated, in full awareness of the penalties that might be visited upon him at any moment, even to speak freely to members of his own family; and, finally, to prepare the way for an extension of Soviet power and the Communist system wherever the opportunity might arise, eventually to cover the entire globe and to transform the lives of mankind. Such a panoply of objectives was new to the earth's surface. Russian tsarism had never attempted anything comparable, and Nazi objectives were never as structured and systematically worked out. Some have compared Islam, at least in the days of its conquering armies; it can only match parts of that vision.

When Hitler invaded the USSR in 1941, the initial shock seemed nearly to topple the whole structure of dictatorship. However, Stalin at length managed to mount a successful counterattack, retain power, and with the help of the Western Allies defeat and overthrow Hitler. After a sustained effort at retrenchment, accompanied by the sharpest ideological repression of any period of Soviet history, Stalin died, yielding power to a group of men who had served him loyally but now tried to distance themselves from his heritage and cope with the problems he bequeathed to them. Khrushchëv and Brezhnev differed in style and substance; however, for almost thirty years they both managed to retain the totalitarian apparatus but exercise it sparingly, assuring a degree of economic stability and sufficiency to the population despite glaring defects in the functioning of the system. Obvious debate and hesitation at the summit of power served as a signal for expressions of individual criticism and a few outbreaks of mass discontent.

Western scholars debated whether the post-1953 Soviet Union should still be called "totalitarian." With Brezhnev's death in 1982 the system moved into deep crisis, first with the short-lived tenures of Andropov and Chernenko, then with the dramatic changes during the secretaryship/presidency of Gorbachëv, which began with tentative reform and ended with the failed coup of August 19, 1991, which inaugurated a new Russian revolution led by Boris Yeltsin. At the time of writing (April 1994) it is still continuing; the foremost political personalities profess commitment to the creation of a stable democracy and a prosperous market economy. However, the difficulties of achieving those objectives are proving enormous. Someone has said that you can make fish soup out of an aquarium, but you cannot make an aquarium out of fish soup; creating totalitarianism is much easier than dismantling it. The history of twentieth-century Russia and the USSR is laden with unspeakable suffering and disappointed hopes, and the student of those events may be led to echo Virgil: *O passi graviora, dabit deus his quoque finem!* (You have suffered worse things; God will put an end to these also.) But how soon that might happen remains in doubt.

1

The Russian People

Moscow and St. Petersburg

If one could revisit Russia as it was in the year 1900, the most profitable way to use a few days might be to concentrate on Moscow and St. Petersburg (which resumed its old name in 1991). One would find signs of the tensions between different cultural currents and epochs that were central to the development of modern Russia. One of the most important tensions was between influences stemming from the Christian East—the Greek and Orthodox Empire and succession states of Byzantium—and those coming from Rome—the Latin and Catholic states to begin with, then Protestant and Germanic nations.

The boundary between the areas in which the two influences were paramount begins at the southern shore of the Barents Sea, follows the eastern borders of Finland, the Baltic states, and Poland, then roughly those between the old Austro-Hungarian Empire and the Balkan countries, ending in the Adriatic Sea. Russia lies entirely east of that line, yet for much of her history Byzantine and Western influences competed for ascendancy in the theory and practice of her government and church and in her secular thought.

About 1450 Russia was emerging from over two centuries of Mongol and Muslim domination, at the same historical moment when the Muslim Turks were conquering the last remnants of the Byzantine Empire and occupying its capital, Constantinople, the chief city of Eastern Orthodoxy. As B. H. Sumner writes, "Byzantium brought to Russia five gifts: her religion, her law, her view of the world, her art and writing."[1] They had been transmitted to the Kievan state beginning in the tenth century, before any real cultural barriers had been erected between Eastern and Western Europe.

The first serious challenge to Byzantine ideas in Russia came in the fifteenth century. Not long after the fall of Constantinople to the Turks, Ivan III (the first

---

[1] *Survey of Russian History,* 2nd rev. ed., London: Duckworth, 1947, p. 178.

Muscovite prince to take the title "Tsar") married Sophia, niece of the last Byzantine emperor. However, Sophia had been reared in Rome, not Constantinople, and she brought a retinue of Italians with her to Moscow. Thus began a flow of Latin and Catholic political and religious influences which grew stronger during the sixteenth and seventeenth centuries, until the head of the Russian church, Patriarch Nikon, formulated a clearly papal theory of ecclesiastical supremacy which was narrowly defeated, not by other clergymen who held fast to the Byzantine tradition of "symphony" between church and state, but by the Tsar Alexis in the name of state authority.

Around 1700 Peter the Great inaugurated a new cultural revolution. Swiftly and often brutally the Catholic influences were pushed aside in favor of ideas and institutions borrowed from the Protestant and Germanic north. Although Latin became the language of the schools of the eighteenth century, the prevailing ideas were not those of Rome. They mirrored the Lutheran and Anglican church establishment, Atlantic mercantilism, and Swedish and German state administration. It has been said that Peter broke through "a window into Europe," but European contacts were far older. The old windows looking south toward Byzantium and then Rome were shuttered up; Peter's new one looked westward toward Stockholm, Amsterdam, and London. Its physical embodiment was the city of St. Petersburg, built on a marsh with the same prodigal brutality which Peter showed in changing the Russian state and church and the manner of life of the nobility.

The mass of the Russian people were little affected by either the Italian attendants of Sophia Paleologus or the German and Dutch advisers of Peter the Great. They remained Orthodox, although not Greek in any direct sense, since from the time of the conversion of Russia to Christianity the liturgy had been in a language (Church Slavonic) akin to their own. Like most simple peoples, they were distrustful of foreign innovations. The center of their world was Moscow, which had been affected by European architectural and other influences but was still a city which had grown spontaneously, without any attempt at planning or reconstruction, and was older than the Mongol conquest.

Moscow was the capital from the time that its Grand Prince declared his independence of the Mongols, shortly after 1450, until just after 1700 when it was officially displaced by St. Petersburg. Even then it remained a sort of second capital, so that the phrase "the two capitals" refers to both cities. Moscow lay at the center of European Russia's magnificent system of rivers, with near access to the Western and Northern Dvinas, the Dnieper, the Don, the Donets, and the Volga. The city took its name from the smaller river Moskva, and grew in the shape of a wheel whose hub was the *Kreml* or Kremlin, a fortified enclosure on the north bank of the river.[2]

---

[2]A fine description of the city in 1917 may be found in Diane Koenker, *Moscow Workers and the 1917 Revolution,* Princeton U. Press, 1981, pp. 12–25.

Moscow is steeped in the oldest Russian traditions and memories. In the center of Moscow's Kremlin are three ancient cathedrals where old Russia's pomp and pageantry had unfolded. In the Cathedral of the Archangel all the tsars before Peter the Great are buried. In the Annunciation, the tsars were baptized and married. In the Assumption, the Emperors were crowned. Close by the cathedrals is the Bell Tower of Ivan the Great (Ivan III, Sophia's husband), from whose height the city of Moscow was viewed at different times by Joseph II of Austria, Napoleon, and the celebrated Madame de Stael. The Kremlin forms a rough triangle along whose hypotenuse to the east lies Red Square, whose name was convenient for, but not conferred by, the Bolsheviks.[3] At the south end of the Square stands the fantastically ornamented Cathedral of St. Basil the Blessed, which was pillaged by the Poles in 1611, used as a stable for French horses in 1812, and long served as an inappropriate background for Communist parades. From the Kremlin, radial streets extend in all directions, including the *Ordynka,* a reminder that Moscow princes once took that route to carry tribute to the Mongols in the southeast, who were known as the Golden Horde (*Orda*).

If Moscow was a part and even the center of the life of old Russia, St. Petersburg was an intrusive symbol of foreign innovation. The Slavophiles used the slogan "back to Moscow," signifying abandonment of St. Petersburg in favor of the pre-Petrine past; the Westernizers regarded the city as a visible sign of the progress which they thought could come and had come only from the West. St. Petersburg was built near the Gulf of Finland on the Neva River, near which Prince Alexander Nevsky earned his sobriquet by virtue of a victory against the Swedes five centuries before Peter the Great.

The heart of St. Petersburg was the south bank within the loop of the Neva, a district cut through by the straight artery called the *Nevsky Prospekt,* which leads from the Moscow Station down to the Admiralty on the edge of the river. Just east of the Admiralty is the Winter Palace, residence of the tsar when he came to the city from the palaces of Tsarskoe Selo (today Pushkin) or Peterhof (today Petrodvorets) a few miles away. The Winter Palace was designed by the Italian architect Rastrelli; an appendage to it was the Hermitage, Russia's finest art museum (which today has taken over the entire Palace), housing collections of Rembrandt and the Spanish and French painters which are among the world's best. Not far from the Palace is the famous equestrian statue of Peter the Great which inspired Pushkin's poem *The Bronze Horseman.* Between St. Isaac's (one of the most richly adorned churches in the world) and Kazan (under Communism an antireligious museum) cathedrals is the Mariinsky Palace, the former seat of the Imperial Council. This body, created by Alexander I in 1809, had the task of preparing and considering legislation for the Emperor's approval. After the Revolution of 1905 it

---

[3] The name originally meant "beautiful"; the etymology is suggested by the relation between the modern Russian *prekrasnyi* (beautiful) and *krasnyi* (red).

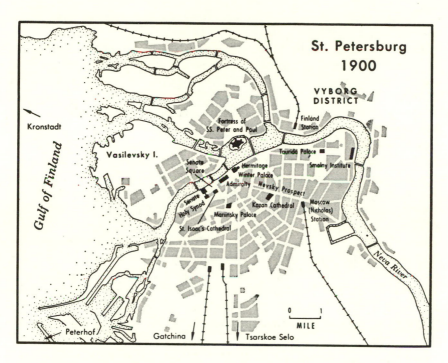

St. Petersburg
1900

VYBORG DISTRICT

Kronstadt

Gulf of Finland

Vasilevsky I.

Fortress of SS. Peter and Paul

Finland Station

Taurida Palace

Senate Square

Hermitage
Winter Palace

Smolny Institute

Admiralty

Nevsky Prospect

Senate
Holy Synod

Mariinsky Palace

Kazan Cathedral

Moscow (Nicholas) Station

St. Isaac's Cathedral

Neva River

0   1
MILE

Peterhof   Gatchina   Tsarskoe Selo

Moscow—1900

SOKOLNIKI

St. Petersburg

Yaroslavl Station

Nicholas Station

Kazan Station

Yauza River

PRESNIA DISTRICT

Bell Tower of Ivan III

Kursk Station

KREMLIN   Red Square

Cathedrals of the Assumption
Archangel
Annunciation

St. Basil's Cathedral

Moskva River

Ordynka

ZAMOSKVORECHE

0   1
MILE

was made partially elective and was transformed into the upper house of Russia's new parliament.

Just west of the Admiralty are the buildings of the Senate and the Holy Synod, now museums. Peter the Great founded the Senate, which ruled in his stead during his journeys, but under his successors became transformed into the country's supreme judicial authority. In the adjoining Senate Square occurred the events of the Decembrist uprising of 1825, Russia's first attempted revolution in the modern style. The Holy Synod was the body created by Peter the Great to provide state control over the Russian Orthodox Church, on the model of the Protestant "established churches" he had seen in England and the German states.

Walking east along the Neva, one would see on the north bank the Fortress of St. Peter and St. Paul, where many distinguished revolutionaries were held for a time. It had been the first building in St. Petersburg and had become the symbolic prison of the old regime. At first, defense against the Swedes had been concentrated here, but it was later moved westward to Kronstadt, the island base whose garrison was to figure prominently in the revolutions of 1905 and 1917. Further east, one would be opposite the Finland Station, the place of Lenin's triumphant arrival in 1917. Beyond is the Taurida Palace, built by Catherine the Great for the most capable of her many favorites, Prince Potëmkin of Taurida (the Crimea). In 1906 this Palace became the seat of the newly created legislative assembly, the Imperial Duma, and in 1917 of the Provisional Government. Around the bend of the Neva is the Smolny Institute, Catherine the Great's school for young ladies, which became Bolshevik headquarters in 1917.

St. Petersburg was the monument not only of its great builder but also of the whole Imperial period, from the time when Peter took the title of "Emperor" until the last ruler, Nicholas II, was induced to abdicate. The Empire was an attempt to remake the nation on the foundation of the West European Reformation and Enlightenment and the Germanic bureaucratic principles of the Hohenzollern and Hapsburg monarchies—whose empires, like that of the Romanovs, perished in World War I. In 1918 the Bolsheviks moved the capital back to Moscow. They did so in part for strategic reasons, but they also had in mind a repudiation of the Empire for which St. Petersburg stood. This repudiation was indeed in certain respects superficial. Since the Bolsheviks based their doctrines on those of Karl Marx, who owed much to the Enlightenment tradition, and in their practice borrowed heavily from German bureaucracy, they could scarcely claim to reject *in toto* Peter's heritage to Russia, and as time went on they in fact emphasized their links with him—even to an unwarranted extent. Still less could the Bolsheviks claim ties with the religious and patriarchal Russia of old Moscow.

In any case, by 1918 the city of Moscow could no longer serve as a valid symbol of the truly "old" in Russia, the Byzantine tradition. The "old" was defended only by a few (and not necessarily influential) clergymen; and, in a way, by the Russian people, although their voice had never directly counted for much in the life of their nation.

The Expansion of Russian Settlement

The Eastern Slavs became agricultural settlers first in the mixed-forest zone within the triangle bounded by the three cities (built later) of St. Petersburg, Kazan, and Lvov (or Ukrainian, Lviv; or Polish, Lwów; or German, Lemberg). It was on the southern edge of that area that the Kievan state of Rus developed. It collapsed in the twelfth century, just before the Mongols rode in to establish overlordship over both the mixed-forest zone and the largely empty steppe to the south. Under Mongol rule the Russians organized a new center of state power farther east in that triangle, around Moscow. At the same time traders and explorers from the city-state of Novgorod penetrated the vast coniferous forests which border on the mixed-forest triangle, and even crossed the Ural Mountains into a tiny corner of what was to be called Siberia.

In the view of Sir John Maynard, the Russian is "a sort of land-sailor."[4] It is a shrewd observation, comparable to the perception by Windwagon Smith, the character in American frontier legend, that if the landlubbers would simply treat the Western prairie like an ocean, many of their problems would diminish. The Russians moved southeast from the mixed-forest into the rich, unforested steppe and east into the forests of Siberia as if they were sailing to new lands, during the same centuries of the early modern era in which West Europeans were experiencing their "Age of Discovery." Sometimes Russians (or Cossacks, as the roving, chiefly Slavic freebooters of the steppe came to be called) moved in the rear of the conquering armies of the Muscovite Tsar, sometimes ahead of them.

Moscow officially threw off the Mongol yoke in 1480, and one hundred years later crushed the succession states of the defunct Mongol Empire which lay along Moscow's southeastern borders from Astrakhan to western Siberia. Only the Crimea, whose Muslim ruler had found a new protector in Ottoman Turkey when the Golden Horde disintegrated, managed to survive until Turkey was sufficiently weakened for the Russians to annex its Crimean dependency just before 1800. When Moscow seized the small Tatar khanate in western Siberia, it found that it had broken through the thin Mongol crust and that all of northeastern Asia lay open. The conquest of this vast area, explored by Cossacks actually traveling in boats (see map, p. 6), took only a little over fifty years. To the south of Siberia the Russians encountered the Chinese Empire, and in 1689 made their peace with it. They then turned northward and penetrated up to the Bering Strait, finally crossing to Alaska, from which they withdrew only in the latter part of the nineteenth century.

Into the territories freed from the Mongols north of the Black and Caspian Seas and opened for settlement in north Asia, there moved a steady stream of Russian peasants, seeking freedom from serfdom and onerous state obligations, and a

---

[4] *Russia in Flux,* Macmillan, 1948, p. 14.

chance to build a new life for themselves. Private landlords did not follow them to Siberia, which never knew serfdom. At first no landlords followed them into the south either, and there grew up free and self-governing Cossack bands whose only bond was Orthodox Christianity and whose only master was themselves.

However, the southern steppes were the target not only of the conquering armies of (or fugitive peasants from) Muscovy, but of Poland-Lithuania and Turkey as well. Until the end of the eighteenth century these two nations, along with Sweden, kept Russian armies fighting continually in the north and west, while on the south the Tatars[5] from the Crimea continued their raids far into Russia. The Tatar danger required yearly mobilization along the line of fortified outposts on Moscow's southern frontier. Poland was neutralized by 1667, Sweden by 1721, Turkey by 1774. Shortly after the western borders had been thereby secured, Russian domination moved to the Black Sea and into the Crimea, and the Tatar raids ceased.

By 1800 the territory inhabited by Eastern Slavs was almost wholly under the control of the Russian Empire. When the south fell under Imperial rule, serfdom soon followed. Imperial decrees of Catherine the Great and others turned over to servitude thousands upon thousands of Ukrainians. By the time of the Emancipation of the serfs in 1861, there remained in the south few free peasants and not much free land. In Siberia the peasants were freer and there were vast expanses of good land to be had for the taking; however, migration was severely restricted by law (which was often evaded) until the latter part of the nineteenth century.

During the Napoleonic Wars the Empire annexed Poland, Finland, Bessarabia, and much of the Caucasus. Though much of this territory was tillable, it was already fully inhabited. The expansion of the Russian peoples thereafter had to take place within the confines of the Russian state. The only later acquisitions of significance, the Far Eastern provinces including Vladivostok (1858–1860) and Central Asia (1868–1885), could not support many immigrants. During the nineteenth and early twentieth centuries, millions of people moved south and east to outlying regions of the Empire, while West and South Europeans were crossing the Atlantic in even greater numbers to the New World.

The colonization of the steppe has been interpreted by several major historians of Russia as the central thread in her whole development. Vasily Kliuchevsky, perhaps the greatest of the Russians who wrote the story, asserted, "Russia's history, throughout, is the history of a country undergoing colonization. ... Migration, colonization constituted the basic factor of our history, to which all other factors were more or less directly related."[6] B. H. Sumner, perhaps the ablest foreigner to

---

[5] Less correctly, "Tartars." Note that while the words "Mongol" and "Tartar" or "Tatar" are often used interchangeably for the Golden Horde in Russia, the Mongols and the Turkic "Tatars" were and are different peoples, speaking different languages. The substantial Turkicization of the Golden Horde that occurred after the Mongol conquest accounts for the confusion of terms.

[6] *Kurs russkoi istorii*, reprint, I. W. Edwards, 1948, I:20–21.

study Russia, declared, "throughout Russian history one dominating theme has been the frontier; the theme of the struggle for the mastering of the natural resources of an untamed country, expanded into a continent by the ever-shifting movement of the Russian people."[7]

Although the Russian might be a natural "land-sailor," he was not necessarily a born nomad. There was much in the political and social institutions of old Russia to provoke men to attempt an escape to freedom. Part of the migration was also prompted by the phenomenal growth of the population during the nineteenth century. In Peter the Great's time there were only 13 million people in the Empire, less than in France. By the end of the Napoleonic Wars a century later, the population had tripled and Russia was the most populous country in Europe. Probably around 1880 the total passed 100 million, and reached 170 million in 1914.

All these people had to live somewhere. In the less fertile mixed-forest zone congestion on the land was growing serious, and in the steppe to the south population density was highest of all. The additional population might choose to leave the land, and throughout the nineteenth century and later many peasants streamed into the cities to find work in new industrial plants, although they frequently kept alive their membership in their old village communes (see p. 20) and other ties with the village. If they wished to remain on the land, they could try to solve their problems either by migrating to areas where there was room to employ the old farming methods, or by changing the ancient and wasteful three-course open-field strip system.

During the last century of tsarism millions of peasants migrated, illegally or legally, to the southern and eastern frontier. At the same time the old farming methods, which were closely linked with the functions of the village commune, began to be gradually replaced by new ones. As migration opened up new opportunities for many in the east, the old system was slowly breaking down in the west. As long as the commune continued to carry out periodical redistribution of land—a function encouraged by the state to assure the payment of taxes and the furnishing of recruits on an equitable and reliable basis—there could be little incentive either to improve the land which a family occupied or to limit the increase of that family. However, despite Alexander III's (1881–1894) efforts to keep the commune alive, redistribution was coming to an end. Moreover, in the northwestern provinces, spontaneous enclosure of the common land into individual peasant farms was taking place in imitation of German and other western neighbors. In Siberia the commune never had much more than a shadowy existence. During the early decades of the twentieth century, in many localities of both west and east the communal system was giving way to individual, intensive, diversified farming coupled with the raising of livestock, the development of craft industry,

---

[7] Sumner, *op. cit.*, p. 9.

the growth of agricultural co-operatives, and altogether the tracing of a new path for much of Russian agriculture to follow.

Logically, migration might have been expected to defer the time of the necessary readjustments in Russian agriculture by draining off population from areas of worst congestion and thus making change less urgent. Certain reactionaries advocated large-scale migration for that very reason, as certain revolutionaries deprecated any such movement in the hope that not readjustment but revolution would result. In fact migration may, by relieving some overcrowding, have smoothed the adoption of new methods here and there; but more important, the migrants themselves were accepting agricultural innovation, and showing by example what could be done by an individual farmer. The commune was the object of a frontal attack by Prime Minister Stolypin's agrarian legislation during the last years of tsarism. Millions of peasants were trying their luck as farmers in the new east, other millions were leaving the communes to enclose new farms in the west. All of them were in search of a better life through economic improvements and a new vision of moral self-sufficiency.

Peasants and Other Russians

In 1900, 80 to 90% of the Russian people were peasants, and an even larger percentage were Christians, as they had been since the time of the Kievan state. The Russian peasants had had a good deal of freedom in the early centuries, but in the early modern period had been pressed into serfdom, just as the serfs of medieval Western Europe were winning freedom. They had been emancipated in 1861, after the Germanic empires had already freed their serfs. At that time the Russian peasants were liberated either from private landlords, to whom about half of them had been in virtual personal bondage, or from the state, which had controlled the other half. However, they did not then become free farmers; they remained bound to the village commune.

The village commune was not peculiar to Russia. There were similar institutions in ancient Germany and modern India, but the Russian commune had been given distinctive shape by action of the state. Before 1861 the needs of the government included taxes and recruits; after 1861 there was added the collection of the redemption payments, which the peasant owed the state as purchase price for the land received at Emancipation. Many officials felt that the commune should also replace the landlord as an agency of authority and a channel of loyalty. Efforts toward that end, however, were not very successful.

The peasants' age-old devotion to the land was expressed in the old Russian proverb, "We are yours [addressing the landlords], but the land is ours." Toward the beginning of the twentieth century it was rapidly becoming theirs by rental or purchase, as the portion left to the landlords at Emancipation passed out of their increasingly inefficient or impoverished hands. Simultaneously the commune was withering in fact and in law, and its lien of ownership on peasant fields was disappearing as its fiscal and other political powers over the peasant came to an end. Their ancient thirst for "land and liberty" was much nearer to being satisfied than ever before; they were legally free men, on the way to becoming owners of their own farms, and although their political rights and privileges were still circumscribed and not always fully understood or even exercised, they had a vote for the Duma and a growing consciousness of the hitherto mysterious realm of politics. They kept their diet of cabbage soup and bread and vodka, their wrapped stockings enclosed in boots, their squatting dances and fur caps, and the rest of their traditions. Yet new staples, clothes, and customs might also find acceptance, as the peasants became free farmers and obtained a range of choices denied them before. Their fundamental aspirations were very old, yet the realization of some of them was new.

A small percentage of Russians had by 1900 become industrial workers. Many retained their ties with the village, and during the economic collapse of the Civil War period Lenin was to be alarmed by what appeared to be the evaporation of the Russian proletariat, as peasant-workers returned to the land in search of food and security. Nevertheless, a few years or decades of city life had left their imprint. The miserable living conditions, so common in the early stages of industrial-ization in other countries, generated a willingness in many factory laborers to lis-ten to revolutionary agitators and to try to puzzle out their "little books" of pro-paganda. Peasant unrest had been chronic in Russia for centuries, but even the great peasant revolts (the last was that of Pugachëv in the 1770's) had had virtually no chance of success because, originating in the borderlands, they were smashed as they approached the centers of state power. However, worker unrest developed in the centers themselves, shook the government in 1905, and toppled it in 1917.

It is difficult to determine how much of the traditional peasant outlook had been altered by the relatively brief sojourn in urban industrial life. Although Le-nin worried about the danger that the workers would "stop" at "trade-union con-sciousness," the reformist trade-union principle never obtained much of a foot-hold among them. "Socialism"—no doubt understood in various senses and often very imperfectly—was offered as a dramatic solution to their widespread and searing miseries and accepted by large numbers of them in that spirit. Even if it was only a small minority which espoused socialism, it was a noisy and active minority. Socialist views tended to go along with militant atheism, as the two were directly linked in Marxist doctrine, although among the Russian workers, as elsewhere, there were religious socialists and nonsocialist atheists. In general the urban workers found themselves in a setting so different from the village that reli-gious practices could not have the same role in their lives as before, but some of them entered urban congregations, and many others retained their faith even if not their habits of church attendance and religious observances.

As a whole the Russian people remained Christian, as they had been for a thou-sand years. For them, as for so many peasant peoples, the church was the fount of their ideology, the reminder and sanction of their morals, the symbolic com-memorator of their birth, baptism, marriage, and death, and the center of their social and community life. The high clergy of the two capitals were often wealthy and influential, but the village priests shared the poverty and even the outlook of the peasants among whom they lived and worked. If the peasant had a grievance against his village clergyman, it was more likely to be personal than institutional.

The official church was the Russian branch of the Eastern Orthodox Church, whose superior dignitary was the Patriarch of Constantinople. The Russian Church had acquired autocephalous status (that is, autonomy under its own pa-triarch) before 1600. Its emancipation from the headship of Constantinople, never more than a shadowy type of final appellate court in ecclesiastical matters, was followed in only a century by the very real subjection to the Russian state, which was effected by Peter the Great and lasted until 1917.

In the late seventeenth century the Russian Orthodox Church experienced its only schism of importance, when the so-called Old Believers rejected the official hierarchy, some maintaining their own clergy and others recognizing no clergy at all. Since then the Old Believers had suffered varying degrees of oppression by the state. They made up tightly-knit, hard-working, puritanical communities, scat-tered over European and Asiatic Russia.

Besides the schismatics, there were several sects composed of Christians who claimed no continuity with the official church (the Old Believers did), such as the *Dukhobors* ("spirit-fighters"), the *Molokane* ("milk-drinkers"), the orgiastic *Khlysty,* and the sexually mutilated *Skoptsy.* Protestantism had made negligible headway among the common people, except in the Lutheran Baltic states where there was an upper class of German origin. Among the Russians, the Baptists were the only Protestant denomination with a sizable following, and even they were few. Roman Catholicism, which was popularly identified with Polish-Lithuanian oppression of the Orthodox Eastern Slavs, had no Great Russian converts worth mentioning. The western Ukrainians, who had been Orthodox before 1596, were forcibly incorporated into the Roman obedience by Poland through the establish-ment in that year of a Slavonic-rite "Uniat" church. For over a century Ukrainian resistance to the Unia continued. However, the Uniat church acquired a hold on many Ukrainians which was not entirely broken when Poland was partitioned in the late eighteenth century and the tsars ordered the reabsorption of its dioceses into Orthodoxy.[8]

Until 1907, when restrictions were relaxed somewhat, the 5 million Jews of the Russian Empire were required to live in certain areas, but they were always per-

---

[8] The last Uniat diocese in the Russian Empire was absorbed only in 1875; however, the church con-tinued to exist among the Ukrainians of the Austrian Empire, who came under the Polish and Czecho-slovak governments in 1919. After the annexation of their lands by the USSR, the Uniat church was suppressed there as well in 1946. It was legalized after Gorbachëv's visit to Pope John Paul II in Decem-ber 1989.

mitted by the state to practice their religion, though they suffered from periodic anti-Jewish pogroms, which certain local authorities did little to prevent or punish. Islam had a larger representation, mainly among the Tatar and Turkic peoples who made up the bulk of the population of Central Asia and were scattered here and there in the east and south of European Russia. Although it was identified with the Golden Horde and the Ottoman Turks, Islam tended to excite condescension in the Russians rather than the fear and hatred felt for the Roman Catholics. The Tatars who practiced Islam were mostly poor and backward. Moreover, some Russians knew that the Mongols had made no attempt to interfere with Christianity once the conquest was over, and that even the Turks permitted Orthodoxy to be practiced freely in the Ottoman Empire. Finally, the Kalmyks near the Caspian and the Buriat Mongols near Lake Baikal practiced Buddhism or shamanism without serious interference from the Russian authorities. Except for the Jews, the Empire was always gentler with its non-Christians than with Christian heretics.

To the peasant of 1900 Christianity did not mean anything very different from what it meant to his ancestors. That was no defect in Christian eyes. Although Christianity may be compatible with a theory of progress, it does not imply one; it seeks to minister to the universal qualities of man regardless of time and place. There were "modernist" movements within the high clergy, whose members were discussing whether Christianity could or should be reconciled with science, socialism, and other innovations in thought. The lower clergy to some extent took part in the new political agitation, and numerous priests appeared in the Imperial Duma after the 1905 Revolution, which had started with a procession of workmen, led by a priest, on which the authorities had fired ("Bloody Sunday"). But baptisms, weddings, and masses were the same as before, and there is no evidence that the religious faith of the Russian people had weakened substantially in the years when the revolutionary movement was growing strong.

The Russian peasant always had ardent admirers, including a host of foreign travelers from Mackenzie Wallace to John Maynard and Bernard Pares. He also had his critics, and often the educated men in Russia and in the West who sympathized with him and pitied him still despised him and justified the whip laid on his back by the Soviets, if not the tsars. In the peasant's make-up could be found many seeming contradictions. He was almost always hospitable to strangers and outsiders, including beggars and criminals, for whom there was traditional and widespread sympathy. At the same time he might be distrustful or hostile to foreigners who were thought to be influential in the central or local government or economy. He was respectful of learning and had often managed to acquire a smattering of it; numerous foreign travelers were dumbfounded at the books they encountered in isolated peasant homes. Yet he was often illiterate and ignorant, and some responded to the shattering events of 1917 by telling one another that there was a new tsar named "*Revoliutsiia.*" The peasant was generally devoted to his family, and yet frequently would drink up the last kopek, insensible to the suffering which resulted. He was an assiduous and often shrewd farmer, yet commonly damaged his own soil by ruinous methods. He was a soldier whose powers of endurance and tenacity and sense of discipline were fabulous; nevertheless, in 1917 peasant soldiers ran away from the front by the thousands. He was humbly law-abiding, yet might cheat the government's agents regularly and on occasion rise up against them in blood. He revered the tsar as his "Little Father," though he seems to have been little moved by the demise of the monarchy in 1917. He was a fervent Christian, who practiced extensively the virtues of forgiveness and brotherly love, but still might keep here and there a pagan remembrance or custom, and at times could be guilty of bestial cruelty. He was a contradictory person indeed, but possibly no more so than any other human being.

The peasant was preoccupied with the fate and fortune of himself and of his own family. He always had, in addition, a strong sense of community; but even in the village he neither held goods nor tilled the soil in common with his neighbors. Generations of intellectuals tried in vain to find socialism in him. The Communists did realize he was no socialist, but they did not learn how fiercely he would resist socialism until they undertook to introduce it in the countryside. His aspirations were modest: he sought security based on the enterprise of his family and the respect and freedom to which a human being is entitled—or, as the old leaders of the serf revolts had put it, "land and liberty."

In the past the Russian peasants had revolted against authority many times. There were four great peasant uprisings in modern Russian history, the first just after 1600, the second in the 1670's, the third just after 1700, the fourth in the 1770's. Each began as a movement among the Cossacks of the southern frontier, rolled up like a cyclone toward Moscow, and was put down by regular army troops. Their unlettered chiefs, Bolotnikov, Razin, Bulavin, and Pugachëv, were possessed of a peasant cleverness, but had no clear idea what they wanted or how to get it. Many peasants followed them; there was no one else to follow. Actually such revolts were mainly aimed at the officialdom, whom the people tended to blame for their miseries. It was thought that if somehow they could get through to the tsar he would listen to their troubles and help them as a father would. The rebel leaders thus appealed to the principles of the traditional monarchy, and Pugachëv even pretended to be the rightful tsar himself.

The same confidence in the "Little Father" permeated the workers of St. Petersburg who marched to his palace on "Bloody Sunday" in 1905, but the bullets fired that day virtually killed that confidence forever. The peasant riots later that year and the next also cast doubt on village loyalty. Nicholas II had more sympathy for the peasants than understanding of their plight. When he stumbled onto ministers who had a program for relieving it, he was still unable to use the success of agrarian reform as a means for reviving peasant trust in the monarchy. The gentry were too preoccupied with their own grave economic problems to be of much help. Communication between the peasants and the upper classes was faint and interrupted. It was as if one tried to shout from St. Petersburg to Moscow.

2
Marxism Comes to Russia

The Revolutionary Movement

It was not from the peasants but from the intelligentsia that the leadership of the revolutionary movement came. There were antecedents, which might be traced as far back as to the eccentric Prince Ivan Khvorostinin, a sharp critic of his own Muscovite surroundings at the court of the First False Dmitry, about 1600, or to the writer Alexander Radishchev, who advocated emancipation of the serfs in the 1780's, and the young veterans of the Napoleonic Wars known as "Decembrists" because they attempted an abortive coup in December 1825, but the intelligentsia took form as a recognizable group in the 1860's. It may be defined as the politically oriented portion of the educated class, whether its members came from the gentry or, as was true especially from the 1860's, from the village clergy or other less-favored strata of society, who were termed *raznochintsy*, literally, men of mixed ranks (later in the century a few women also might be so classified).

Their leaders in the 1860's, such as Nicholas Chernyshevsky, borrowed socialist ideas from the West and tried to relate them to the Russian setting. Pre-Marxist socialism in nineteenth-century Russia is often called "populism" (*narodnichestvo* from *narod,* people), and though its proponents are sometimes wrongly regarded as having ignored industrial or craft workers, their deepest concern was apt to be the peasantry. In 1873–1874 many of the young populist intelligentsia undertook a remarkable movement of "going to the people," taking up residence in villages to preach socialism to the peasants. The almost universal response was indifference or hostility, so that some villagers cooperated with the police when they rounded up the newcomers who brought their puzzling message—socialism sounded like the return of serfdom, said some peasants.

Some revolutionaries concluded that the peasants were hopeless, at least for the time being, and they turned instead to terrorism, that is, political murder, as their only alternative instrument. They succeeded in killing or wounding several officials and finally, in 1881, in assassinating Alexander II himself. A few years earlier, however, George Plekhanov and a few other revolutionaries had decided that terrorism was either unjustified or self-defeating. And so it proved, when the police managed—with widespread public approval—to arrest almost all the terrorists after the murder of the emperor. There is broad agreement among historians of varied political hues that the murder, far from benefiting the people, put political reform in Russia into deep freeze for a generation or more.

Plekhanov and others then sought a more sophisticated guide to the past and a more dependable path to revolution than that given in the theoretically weak and practically ineffectual Russian socialism of their fellows—and they found both in the teaching of Karl Marx.

No man was ever such a failure in his lifetime and such a success afterward as Marx. That he should require substantial treatment in a work devoted to twenti-eth-century Russia is only part of the evidence supporting this contention. Al-though his principles were modified in various ways in theory and practice by his followers, probably no single individual outside the higher religions has ever preached doctrines that have had a greater impact on humanity than his. To be sure, Marx never intended to "preach a doctrine"; he believed he was merely dis-covering the meaning of history. When men understood that meaning, they would be able to act with an understanding and a foresight denied to all previous generations.

Marx's philosophy came to Russia not as a surprise or sudden importation, but after the Western thinkers whom he acknowledged as his predecessors had already become known in Russia in their own right. If British political economy, French Utopian socialism, and German idealist philosophy were the forerunners of Marxism in the West, so were they in Russia. Adam Smith and David Ricardo were read and discussed in the early nineteenth century; St. Simon and Fourier were popular in the Petrashevtsy circle, whose members attempted to erect a Fourieran phalanstery in the 1840's. In the same decade differences of view about Hegel had led to the end of personal friendships within the circle of Herzen and his friends. Russians had been at least as interested in Hegel as Germans had been, as interested in St. Simon as Frenchmen. The men whose thought formed the raw material of Marx's ideas were well known to Russians before he actually put his system on paper.

The Development of Marx's Thought

Karl Marx was born in the German Rhineland in 1818, the son of a Jew who had become a Protestant. By the age of twenty he had entered the University of Berlin and joined a circle of young Hegelians there. What appealed to Marx in Hegel's thought was his conception of the universe as a single whole, in which every bit and piece was related to every other one, in contrast to the older British empiri-cism, which tended to look at the bits and pieces carefully and separately. Hegel saw mankind as one organism, living and evolving, and he glorified man's reason, which would make the world itself reasonable as man came to understand the reason which resided in things. Thus for Hegelians there was no sharp division between the realms of thinking and being; or, as Hegel himself put it, "The real is the rational, and the rational is the real."

However, Hegel was not so naive as to think that gradual and smooth progress had been the law of history. He interpreted history as a series of sharp, sometimes ugly, stabs and jerks forward and backward, as the net result of which a civilization or mankind as a whole moved forward. This type of motion was conceived to resemble the rhythm of an intelligent dialogue, as Socrates had talked to his pupils, and Hegel therefore termed this motion "dialectical." A made an assertion, B denied it, C denied the denial—or "negated the negation"—and in so doing stated the truth more accurately than either A or B had done. The idea of ancient Oriental civilization had been that one (the despot) is free; of classical civilization, that some (the citizens) are free; Germanic civilization affirmed that every man is free. He is, and ought to be free—to Hegel what was desirable was also necessary, and so it remained to Marx.

So far Marx followed Hegel. Leaving Berlin, he returned home and then made his way to Paris. There he read the works of Ludwig Feuerbach, who examined Hegel's views on religion and concluded that his idealism embodied "the deceased spirit of theology." "Idealism" meant not that Hegel was addicted to highflown or impossible standards or aims, but that he believed that the fundamental stuff of reality was "idea" with a capital "I," and that external objects and institutions were important only as representing ideas—as for example the state was seen as the embodiment of divine purpose, "the march of God on earth." Like Feuerbach, Marx could find no place for God in his philosophy. While he was pondering this obstacle, he met Friedrich Engels, who was two years younger than he. Engels was the son of a well-to-do manufacturer; he himself remained an affluent and pleasure-loving bourgeois while he fought, and helped and financed Marx to fight, the capitalist order.

In their attempt to cleanse Hegel of error, Marx and Engels found the thought of Saint-Simon and also Proudhon useful. What was most significant about society, the French thinkers contended, was the play of economic forces and social classes. Marx's account of his solution was that he abruptly realized that Hegel's thought was standing on its head, and what was needed was simply for it to be set upright. That is, the dialectic was the correct method of analyzing reality, but it was not mind, but matter, which constituted reality. Some sympathetic critics of Marx, like G. D. H. Cole, have suggested that what Marx really meant was that not matter but the economic process underlay human history. It is certainly true that Marx's writing dealt not with natural science but with either economic history or political history interpreted as the reflection of economic developments. Engels made a few excursions into the field of science, but they were weak at best. Nevertheless, Marx and Engels called their system dialectical materialism, in order to emphasize its difference from Hegelianism, with its smuggled-in God. One may take them at their word.

By the middle 1840's Marxism was nearing the dimensions of a system. In the *Communist Manifesto* of 1847 Marx and Engels popularized it for the use of the Communist League, a small and unimpressive association of West European radicals. The *Manifesto* was a short pamphlet in which historical materialism (Marxian philosophy applied to human affairs) is expounded as a guide to and a prediction of action. The way goods are produced—the "mode of production"—and the structure of social classes defined in terms of how each fits into the productive process, are made the basis for all history. The classes behave in an antithetical, a dialectical manner; that is, they struggle. The battle for ownership of the means of production and for the political power which such ownership confers is incessant. Thus all history is said to be the history of class struggle between the exploiter and exploited class of the given moment. In the past there were four modes of production, the Asiatic (as found in China or India), slavery (as in Greece and Rome), feudalism (the Western Middle Ages), and capitalism (nineteenth-century England).

Near the end of the *Manifesto* appears the assertion that Germany "is on the eve of a bourgeois revolution that is bound to be carried out under more advanced conditions of European civilization and with a much more developed proletariat than that of England" or France at the time of their "bourgeois revolutions." Russian Marxists hoped their country might benefit from similar circumstances.

Marx and Russia

Unfortunately the *Manifesto,* as E. H. Carr points out, was deficient in two respects which were to cause Lenin difficulty in applying Marxism to Russia.[1] The problems of nationalism and the peasantry were passed over briefly. The proletariat was said to "have no country." Consequently the orthodox Marxists of Russian Poland, for example, taking Marx at his word, refused to consider any plan for a Polish nation; as a result they remained insignificant in strength, while another group which called itself the Polish Socialist Party (PPS), but was openly nationalist, attracted wide support. For the same reason the intellectuals of such borderlands as Armenia, Georgia, and the Baltic states gravitated to populism more often than to Marxism. Lenin's tortuous attempts to solve the "national question," in which efforts he found Stalin useful, were for a long time fruitless if measured by the growth of Bolshevism among the national minorities of the Empire. Marx's treatment of the peasants was an even more serious problem for the Marxists in Russia. He noted the service of capitalism to mankind in rescuing people from the

---

[1] Edward Hallett Carr, *Studies in Revolution,* Macmillan, 1950, pp. 25–37.

"idiocy of rural life" and lumped peasants with small shopkeepers and the like as "petty bourgeoisie." Lenin made heroic efforts to compensate for such cavalier treatment of the group which made up the overwhelming majority of the whole population of the country, but Marx was no help to him.

Of course Marx did not have Russia particularly in mind in writing the *Manifesto*. He did make several later comments, especially in the preface written jointly with Engels to a Russian edition of the *Manifesto,* which they ended with the conditional but optimistic prophecy, "If the Russian Revolution becomes the signal for a proletarian revolution in the West, so that both complement each other, the present Russian common ownership of land may serve as the starting point for a communist development." Here Marx suggested an even more prodigious leap in history than the one he hoped for in Germany: from a mode of production at least partly primitive-communist, over slavery, feudalism, and capitalism to communism.

In fact the Russian Marxists paid little attention to the allusion to primitive communism and often spoke as if Russia were basically "Asiatic" or "feudal," though rapidly developing a capitalist sector in its economy. It was tidier to do so, and also less embarrassing, for their ideological adversaries, the populists, had long said that the Russian peasant commune could develop directly into rural socialism. The fact that Marx himself said the very same thing, and repeated it in a letter to a populist leader, could be forgiven only because Marx died in the same year that Russian Marxism was born.

Marx's Later Years

The *Communist Manifesto* predicted revolution, and revolution actually followed in a matter of weeks. In 1848 almost every great capital of Europe was shaken by turmoil, but within a year the republican or radical forces had been routed. Communism also seemed to be a lost cause, not that its "specter" to which Marx referred in the *Manifesto* had materialized in 1848; among the revolutionaries had appeared certain of the radical groupings which he criticized, but no "Communists" had been visible. Nevertheless for Marx, as for orthodox Marxists ever since, failure was regarded as temporary and hopes were simply deferred.

In 1853 Marx withdrew from overt political activity to spend his days in the British Museum in London reading and writing. For a decade he was occupied with a work on political economy. From Manchester Engels helped him through more than one crisis in the family finances; Marx declared wryly, "I don't suppose anyone has ever written about 'money' and suffered such a lack of it himself." But he managed to publish the first volume of *Capital* in 1867, and for the rest of his life he worked on the remaining two volumes, which were published by Engels after his death. The whole work included both a theoretical exposition of the nature of the "capitalist" economic system and a history of modern capitalism.

During Marx's later years he witnessed the formation of the First International Workingmen's Association in 1864, the war of the Paris Commune in 1871, and the consequent collapse of the International as a result of dashed hopes and government repression. In writing about the Commune, Engels hailed its "shattering of the former State power and its replacement by a new and really democratic State." At the same time he warned against the retention of the state in any form, and traced the "superstitious reverence" for the state to the conception that the state is "the Kingdom of God on earth"; in other words, to Hegel. Lenin was to expand these comments on what the proletariat ought to do with the state in his pamphlet of 1917, *The State and Revolution*.

In the 1870's, in the wake of the failure of the Paris Commune, Marx became fascinated with Russia. In a preface to a Russian edition of the *Manifesto* written jointly with Engels, they declared, "Today Russia forms the vanguard of revolutionary action in Europe." A Russian revolution might occur before a socialist revolution in the West, and it might even be possible for Russia to build communism on the village commune—provided a Western revolution could then show "how it's done" (*wie man's macht*). Marx learned Russian and corresponded with several Russian socialists. He noted that *Capital* was translated into Russian before any other foreign language, in 1872, and that, like some earlier works, it sold well in Russia. He was hopeful that the Russo-Turkish War of 1877–1878 might lead to Russian defeat and thus bring the revolution closer. In 1883 he died.

The Teachings of Marxism

According to Vilfredo Pareto, Marxism is like a bat: some see in it a mouse, others a bird. Our concern here is less with what Marx's followers made of his ideas than with which of them he himself believed to be fundamental. As a matter of fact, Marx was probably understood by posterity as well as any theorist who advocated doctrines of comparable complexity. It is a tribute to his intelligibility that even revisionist Marxists knew quite well which of his teachings they were discarding and which they were accepting. Even if they wanted a mouse, they knew they had to extract it from a bat.

Briefly and simply, Marxism begins with two basic propositions. First, matter exists and nothing else does. Second, matter changes constantly in accordance with the "laws" of the dialectic; that is, it changes by the interpenetration of opposites, through which quantitative change becomes qualitative and the antithesis of a given thesis is itself denied to form a new synthesis, and so on over and over again. The two propositions combine to form the philosophy of dialectical materialism. That aspect of it which undertakes to explain history is known as historical materialism. The body of this doctrine can be stated in Marx's own words:

> In the social production of their means of existence men enter into definite, necessary relations which are independent of their will, productive relationships which

correspond to a definite stage of development of their material productive forces. The aggregate of these productive relationships constitutes the economic structure of society, the real basis on which a juridical and political superstructure arises, and to which definite forms of social consciousness correspond. The mode of production of the material means of existence conditions the whole process of social, political and intellectual life. It is not the consciousness of men that determines their existence, but, on the contrary, it is their social existence that determines their consciousness. At a certain stage of development the material productive forces of society come into contradiction with the existing productive relationships, or, what is but a legal expression for these, with the property relationships within which they had moved before. From forms of development of the productive forces these relationships are transformed into their fetters. Then an epoch of social revolution opens. With the change in the economic foundation the whole vast superstructure is more or less rapidly transformed. In considering such revolutions it is necessary always to distinguish between the material revolution in the economic conditions of production, which can be determined with scientific accuracy, and the juridical, political, religious, aesthetic or philosophic—in a word, ideological forms wherein men become conscious of this conflict and fight it out. Just as we cannot judge an individual on the basis of his own opinion of himself, so such a revolutionary epoch cannot be judged from its own consciousness; but on the contrary this consciousness must be explained from the contradictions of material life, from the existing conflict between social productive forces and productive relationships. A social system never perishes before all the productive forces have developed for which it is wide enough; and new, higher productive relationships never come into being before the material conditions for their existence have been brought to maturity within the womb of the old society itself. Therefore, mankind always sets itself only such problems as it can solve; for when we look closer we will always find that the problem itself only arises when the material conditions for its solution are already present or at least in process of coming into being. In broad outline, the Asiatic, the ancient, the feudal and the modern bourgeois modes of production can be indicated as progressive epochs in the economic system of society. Bourgeois productive relationships are the last antagonistic form of the social process of production—antagonistic in the sense not of individual antagonism, but of an antagonism arising out of the conditions of the social life of individuals; but the productive forces developing within the womb of bourgeois society at the same time create the material conditions for the solution of this antagonism. With this social system, therefore, the prehistory of human society comes to a close. ...[2]

To restate the doctrine of historical materialism, the "material productive forces" determine the "productive relationships" which are the basis of history, the social classes and the interaction between them, which has always had the character of antagonism. In other words, what is crucial to the Marxian theory of history is the concept of class struggle. A class, in Marx's view, is a function of the

---

[2] Karl Marx, Author's Preface to *A Contribution to the Critique of Political Economy,* 1859, in Emile Burns, *A Handbook of Marxism,* International Publishers, 1935, pp. 371–373.

mode of production; it is composed of individuals whose relationship to the productive process is similar, whatever their external or conscious differences. History is the history of class struggles, but when capitalism ends it will enter a new phase. This conviction leads Marx to term all previous history "prehistory" to distinguish it from the epoch ahead, when reason and consciousness will determine mankind's actions and society will no longer be dependent on the organization of production. Until that time ideas will be derived from the economic process, and all questions about human society can be answered, as Lenin put it, by tracing them to "who exploits whom" in a given situation; in other words, who owns the means of production and who does not.

Neither in Hegel nor in Marx was there any clear distinction between the descriptive and the normative. The "is" and "ought" of history merged closely into each other. As Marx put it in his *Theses on Feuerbach,* "The philosophers have only *interpreted* the world in various ways; the point however is to *change* it." Therefore a history implied a politics; theory and practice were inseparable, and right theory and right practice were dependent one upon the other. History showed that the proletariat would win, and the self-destructive tendencies of capitalism would help bring this to pass. However, with the emergence of the "rational" to the level of the "real," the action of individuals or groups of intellectuals could be important or decisive in hastening the ultimately inevitable denouement of "prehistory." Then it would come about that, in Marcuse's phrase, "reason, when determined by rational social conditions, is determined by itself."[3] The role of human intelligence and of intellectuals was thus clearly set forth. It was the task of the scholar to forsake history as a Muse and take it up as a political and military plan of campaign.

The Politics of Marxism

Marx did not consider himself responsible for the way in which Communist political action would have to be worked out. In reference to the Paris Commune, he suggested that the proletariat would have to seize and destroy the old state machinery, substituting simpler forms (but still state machinery) of its own as long as remnants of antagonistic classes remained to be dealt with. The new "dictatorship of the proletariat" would thereupon undertake to build a new type of economic order. In his *Critique of the Gotha Program* (of the newborn German Marxist party), Marx distinguished between two phases through which the new order would develop, "socialism" and "communism." Under both man would work according to his ability; under socialism he would be remunerated according to the amount of his work, under communism according to the extent of his need.

---

[3] Herbert Marcuse, *Reason and Revolution* 2nd ed.; The Humanities Press, 1954, p. 319.

There were a few other hints and suggestions, but no plans for organization of a Communist political party or for the state which that party would establish on the ruins of the old capitalist one. If communism was a specter, Marx did little to make it materialize.

The transformation of Marxism into a political force was the work of others. The First International Workingmen's Association, founded in 1864, was not led by Marx, who like Engels thought congresses and meetings to be of little value. His opposition to the rather disorderly views and activities of the Russian anarchist, Michael Bakunin, led to the disruption of the International—whose members were in any case suffering from the aftermath of the Paris Commune—but he did little to organize or lead it toward positive action. The First International was, in any event, not so much an association of Communist parties as a loose federation of labor groups.

It was only in the later 1870's that Marxist parties began to be formed. In order to escape the onus of the Paris Commune they called themselves "Social Democratic" rather than "Communist." (Lenin was to negate this negation by reviving the label "Communist" during the First World War.) The first Social Democratic party, which remained the senior and strongest until the Bolshevik Revolution, was the German one. It was formed out of a merger of the followers of Ferdinand Lassalle, whose Hegelian devotion to the state had only a superficially Marxian gloss, and the German Marxists led by August Bebel and Wilhelm Liebknecht. The merger, carried through at a congress in Gotha in 1875, provoked objections from Marx which went unheeded. The German party remained an amalgam of narrow-construction Marxists with deviationists and innovators, even after it adopted a more orthodox Marxist program in 1891.

The first prominent Revisionist, Edward Bernstein, approved the development of German Social Democracy along rather empirical and reformist lines. Moreover, he attempted to provide theoretical justification for such moderation by pointing out that current economic changes disproved Marx's prophecies of the progressive impoverishment of the proletariat and the increasing concentration of capital in fewer and fewer hands. Bernstein concluded that there would be and should be no sudden cataclysmic revolution, that the proletariat was in the process of acquiring fatherlands in Western Europe, and that to assist not revolution but evolution was the proper task of the Social Democrat. Meanwhile Georg von Vollmar and other party members from the agricultural south of Germany pointed to Marx's sins of omission and commission on the agrarian problem and rejected the proposed expropriation of peasant property. Vollmar's views impressed the German party less than those of Bernstein. All orthodox Marxists regarded the elimination of peasant smallholding as essential, and in consequence a delegate to the Halle Congress of 1890 noted sadly and correctly, "We have not got as yet a single Social Democratic peasant." However, the German Marxists were sufficiently flexible to acquire a large following of industrial workers, though not enough support to reach the opportunities and dangers of national power.

The parties which were organized in the 1880's in France, Italy, Austria, Holland, Belgium, the Scandinavian countries, and England were either very weak in numbers or very broad in their Marxism. In France the orthodox Marxists under Jules Guesde remained for years a small group, and in England the followers of H. M. Hyndman never did succeed in creating a large orthodox Marxist party. Marx and Engels criticized and squabbled with Social Democratic leaders in several countries. After Marx's death, a Second International was formed in 1889, containing some groups the orthodoxy of whose Marxism was dubious, but purporting to be an association of Marxist political parties.

It was in 1883 that Marx died; Engels lived until 1895. At Marx's graveside Engels declared, "Just as Darwin discovered the law of evolution in organic nature, so Marx discovered the law of evolution in human history. ..." Whatever the merit of this contention, it was true that Marx's contribution to Communism was its history. Its politics remained to be worked out successfully. In the countries where the Second International was represented, the Social Democratic parties seemed to prosper to the extent that they abandoned or ignored Marxist theory. Russia was to prove no exception, but Lenin was to provide an innovation: he would ignore Marxist theory when it suited him, without abandoning belief in or the intention of realizing any fundamental part of Marx's vision.

Marx, Russia, and the "Asiatic Mode of Production"

There has been much misunderstanding of Marx and Engels's interpretation of Russia's past. They came to consider Russia not feudal, as Western Europe had been, but to have had at root a different (that is, "Asiatic") mode of production. They identified "two circumstances" that "had always been the solid foundation of Oriental despotism": state management of public works (especially artificial irrigation by canals and waterworks) and a system of self-contained and dispersed village communities that the public works made possible. Russia lacked large-scale public works (though in fact not as completely as they thought) but had self-contained villages (which needed from outside, in one version, only salt, matches, and alcohol). Marx and Engels termed Russia "semi-Asiatic" and fully an Oriental despotism, relating it to the kind of society they thought characterized China, India, and the whole of mainland Asia (not Japan). Marx traced the social system of modern Russia, which was "but a metamorphosis of Muscovy," in turn to "the bloody mire of Mongolian slavery" (the so-called Tatar yoke, 1240–1450) instead of "the rude glory of the Norman epoch" (opened by the Viking conquest of the ninth century).[4]

---

[4] See Joseph Schiebel, "Marxism and *Aziatchina*," in Charles E. Timberlake, ed., *Religious and Secular Forces in Late Tsarist Russia*, U. of Washington Press, 1992, pp. 145–167, for details.

George Plekhanov, who refined his previous socialism into a commitment to Marxism by 1883, came at that point to reject the notion, dear to Russian socialists of the time, that the village commune could serve as the basis of a socialist order, for it was, as Marx had argued, the foundation of Russian despotism. (He ignored Marx's waffling on the issue during the 1870's.) In any case the commune was disintegrating, and capitalism was coming onto the scene. In 1884 he told socialists gathered in Bern, Switzerland, that "capitalism is bad ... [but] despotism is even worse." (Lenin was to use almost identical language in his last months.) Plekhanov declared, "capitalism lays its filthy hands on literature and science, despotism kills literature and science." The primary task was to fight absolutism; to fight *capitalism* in Russia would simply strengthen "Eastern despotism."

Russian Marxists subsequently showed themselves ambivalent about capitalism; they saw it as progressive, especially in Russian conditions, since it was powerful enough to shatter Russia's "semi-Asiatic" order, and yet they feared and hated it, since it was on behalf of the workers and against their capitalist employers that the force of Marx's writings was first launched.

Other Marxist émigrés began to follow Plekhanov's lead in identifying tsarism as the main enemy. V. N. Alexeev, writing in the London journal *Sotsial-Demokrat* in 1890, wrote, "The foremost of all contemporary Russian social questions is the question of the struggle against our Asiatic despotism, which not only crushes all life inside the country but also menaces the cause of progress in all of Europe." Paul Axelrod informed readers of the German Marxist organ *Die Neue Zeit* that the revolutionary intelligentsia of Russia was "a kind of European oasis in the immeasurable desert of the Russian *Aziatchina*" (apparently thereby coining that word), but saw Europeanization as growing every day, preparing the way for revolutionary change. After Marx died, Engels (who lived until 1895) urged Plekhanov to apply Marxist insights to Russia systematically; the result was his "legal Marxist" book, *The Development of the Monist View of History* (1895).

By that time industrialization and the growth of a proletariat were well under way. Sergei Witte had been named minister of finance (1892) and undertook to promote rapid industrial development as meeting Russia's chief needs. As factory workers multiplied, Vladimir Lenin came to St. Petersburg to join others trying to influence them in a Marxist direction, and a new phase began in the history of the Russian revolutionary movement.

Marx might or might not have the key to history—to many Russian youth of the 1890's onward he seemed to, and they contemptuously turned their back on the theoretically loose and unsystematic varieties of socialism that had prevailed among the revolutionaries thus far. But he did not make it easy for Marxist propagandists in Russia by his treatment, or failure to treat, two problems: nationalism and the peasantry. The proletariat was said to "have no country." Consequently the orthodox Marxists of Russian Poland, for example, taking Marx at his word, refused to consider plans for a Polish nation. As a result they remained insignificant in strength, while another group that called itself the Polish Socialist Party

(PPS), but was openly nationalist, attracted wide support. For the same reason many intellectuals of such borderlands as Armenia, Georgia, and the Baltic gravitated to populism rather than Marxism. Lenin's tortuous attempts to solve "the national question," in which efforts he found Stalin useful, were for a long time fruitless if measured by the growth of Bolshevism among the national minorities of the Empire. Marx's treatment of the peasants was a serious problem for Marxists in Russia as well as several of the borderlands. He noted the service of capitalism to mankind in rescuing people from the "idiocy of rural life" and lumped peasants with small shopkeepers and the like as "petty bourgeoisie." It was left to Lenin to try to fit both ethnicity and the peasantry into a Marxian program for Russia.

Bolsheviks and Mensheviks

Plekhanov and his friends were émigrés. Among the intelligentsia in Russia, Marxism acquired immense prestige, especially in the 1890's. There were many socialists who acknowledged Marx's importance but refused to accept Marxian teachings on agriculture and the peasantry, including those who wished to revive the terrorism of the 1870's. They formed a loosely organized Socialist Revolutionary party in 1900–1902; its chief theorist was Victor Chernov, a man from Tambov whose talents lay more in journalism than leadership. The party had an autonomous, secret subdivision called the "Combat Organization," which was to conduct terrorist activity while the rest of the SR's propagandized for revolution.

Russian socialists who described themselves as Marxists attempted to found a Russian Social Democratic Labor Party at an abortive meeting held in Minsk in 1898. The meeting was dispersed by the police; it was considered, however, to be the I Congress of the party—in a series that continued into the 1980's. Lasting organization, however, came only from the II Congress held in 1903 in Brussels and London—which promptly split into two factions, Bolsheviks and Mensheviks. The names mean "majority men" and "minority men," respectively, in reference to the two sides of the vote taken in the Congress on who was to belong to the editorial board of the Social Democratic newspaper, *The Spark (Iskra)*. The name alluded to Pushkin's remark about the Decembrists, "From the spark will come the flame." The newspaper had been the organ of those "orthodox" Marxists, including Vladimir Lenin and Julius Martov, who wished to combat the real or alleged tendency of some Social Democrats to neglect political action for the economic benefits that were the objective of Russia's first great round of industrial strikes in the 1890's. (These Social Democrats were dubbed "Economists.") Prior to this vote Lenin's faction was outnumbered, and he acquired a scant majority only after a good deal of complicated maneuvering took place. He then promptly labeled his faction the "Majority," which proved him as shrewd as Martov, and others were fatuous to accept the permanent designation of the "Minority."

At the Congress, the issue between Bolsheviks and Mensheviks seemed to be whether a rigid or a broad criterion was to be used for selection of a party member. In *What Is to Be Done?* (1902), Lenin had argued that the party leadership should consist of a small group of "professional revolutionaries" since "the Russian proletariat will have to fight a monster beside which an anti-socialist law in a constitutional country [that is, Germany] is but a dwarf." Moreover, it was essential to prevent liberals from taking over the workers' movement and introducing "mere trade-unionist" ideas in place of revolutionary objectives, to head off an effort to "convert Social Democracy into a democratic reformist party ... to introduce bourgeois ideas and bourgeois elements into socialism." Party members must be chosen with the utmost care.[5] Lenin believed that the Economist camp was already infiltrated with bourgeois ideas and that the Mensheviks were willing to open the way to such infiltration. However, the Mensheviks agreed with their fellows in the Spark group (indeed a majority of *Spark* writers became Mensheviks) that political work was the first priority.

In what was arguably his best book, *The Development of Capitalism in Russia* (1899), Lenin wrote—echoing Marx on the "Asiatic" system—that before capitalism came Russia was characterized by a system of "tiny groups of small producers, severed from each other by their separate farms, by the innumerable medieval barriers between them, and by the remains of medieval dependence." Capitalism might have the merit of breaking down these barriers, and lead to a political revolution against the autocracy that would have as an important participant the peasantry as a class. In several articles he argued that tsarism had both furthered and held back the growth of capitalism, in which "Asiatic forms of labor, with their infinitely developed bondage and diverse expressions of personal dependence, [were being converted] into European forms of labor." He also stressed "the Asiatic nature even of those of our institutions which most resemble European institutions."

Building on the work of J. A. Hobson and others, Lenin was later to explain that capitalism had been able to prolong its life in Europe by exploiting overseas areas and thus had become even more international in character. Therefore a decisive blow at one part of the capitalist system would certainly involve the whole of the system. In Lenin's theory of "imperialism, the highest stage of capitalism" (the title of his book of 1916) Russia's relation to the system of imperialism was a dual one. It was part of the exploiting network, since it had its own capitalist class and exploited its own "backward" eastern areas, and at the same time was partly a victim of the machinations of French, German, and other West European capitalists through large investments and loans. Lenin hoped that the Western proletariat, especially through the strong German Social Democratic party, would be able to contribute mightily to the general overthrow of capitalism, but he intended

---

[5] *The Essentials of Lenin*, 2 vols.; London: Lawrence & Wishart, 1947, I:154.

that the Russian party should also take a prominent role and perhaps even initiate the whole upheaval.

At this point the divergencies between Bolsheviks and Mensheviks emerge. The Mensheviks believed that, while it was true that a proletarian revolution might break out all over Europe in a crisis, the Russian Marxists could not speculate on such an event. Their task was first to help bring about a bourgeois revolution in Russia which could involve the vigorous and even leading participation of the proletariat, although it was bound to promote the interests of the bourgeoisie. The Marxists might push the bourgeois liberals into a degree of radicalism not native or congenial to them, but the Marxists could not take the government into their hands themselves without setting themselves socialist tasks—tasks which at that historical stage they could not possibly fulfill. Therefore there was no other way for Marxists to take part in the political events they believed imminent without allying themselves with liberal elements. As Plekhanov wrote, "a significant interval" must separate bourgeois and proletarian revolutions, and any attempt by Marxists to seize and hold power during that interval would inevitably discredit Russian Social Democracy, since the proletariat would demand socialist measures which were not in the power of the socialists to give at that time.

Lenin and the Bolsheviks repudiated this view. They agreed that at the outset the revolution must be "bourgeois." However, the bourgeois liberals were contemptible beyond any hope of redemption and useless as political allies. Therefore the correct method of participating in the bourgeois revolution was through alliance with the most numerous of that element in Russia, namely the peasantry. Since the peasantry as a whole was being drawn more and more into agricultural capitalist relations and strove to free its property from precapitalist fetters, the peasant masses could bring about the bourgeois revolution under proper leadership—that is, under the guidance of the proletariat and its Marxist spokesmen. When the revolution was victorious, there would be set up a "revolutionary democratic dictatorship of proletariat and peasantry," without the participation of any bourgeois liberals. The unfolding of the revolution in the West might open the way to the second stage, that of proletarian revolution; or, if this did not occur immediately, the Russian proletariat, no longer together with all the peasantry, but still with the poorest, semiproletarian peasant elements, could pass on to socialist revolution and the construction of a socialist order.

The Mensheviks counted on what could be done by a loosely organized, mass party of workers. They had little fear of bourgeois liberal infiltration; they had little trust in or hope for what the peasantry might do. The Bolsheviks feared the liberals would successfully subvert a loose party, and so favored a tightly-knit and exclusive one; they expected a great peasant revolt which, lacking any conscious leadership of its own, would follow the lead of the Social Democrats. These were the clashing views of the two wings of Russian Marxism as expressed in analysis and tactics. The emotional roots of the clash can be traced to Lenin's deep-seated fear and hatred of the liberals and of everything "bourgeois," which disrupted the

united front of the editors of *The Spark* at the II Congress and from then on provoked taunts and suspicions of "Jacobinism," "Blanquism," "dictatorial tendencies," and the like.

One gifted Marxist who was present at the II Congress never became an adherent of either the Menshevik or the Bolshevik view as just outlined, nor did he become a wholehearted and loyal member of either faction, although he was a Menshevik for a time and later on joined the Bolsheviks. He was Leon Trotsky, born
Bronstein, son of a Jewish farmer of Ukraine. Trotsky was troubled by the split in
the party mainly because he thought it had occurred over the wrong issue. Like
the Mensheviks, he placed no hope in the peasantry; like the Bolsheviks, he hated
the bourgeois liberals. Precisely because he found no trustworthy allies for the
proletariat within Russia, he emphasized most strongly the need to find them
outside, in the industrial workers of Western Europe. Russia would pass directly
from the bourgeois to the proletarian stage—through what he called "uninterrupted" or "permanent" revolution—with the help of the workers of Germany
and other nations of the West. Trotsky was to devote his best efforts to patching
up party differences—in vain—from 1903 to 1917, when he became convinced that
Lenin had adopted the views he had long espoused, and he was then belatedly received into Bolshevik ranks.

Following the II Congress, Russian Social Democrats found themselves divided
in two. The Bolsheviks had the party Central Committee, but no newspaper, for
the Mensheviks gained control of *The Spark* and then, a few months later, the
Central Committee as well. Lenin was not daunted. Both Marxist factions organized workers' groups and party committees in widely scattered areas of Russia; at
the local level the differences between Bolsheviks and Mensheviks were seldom as
clearly stated or understood, or produced such antagonisms, as among the top
leaders. When big strikes erupted in the south of Russia in 1903 and the war with
Japan began in 1904, there was ample opportunity for revolutionary agitation,
and for the time being factional differences yielded the spotlight to the exigencies
of mass action and street fighting.

For ten years prior to the Revolution of 1905 and during the decade which followed, the intelligentsia devoted much of their energies to propaganda, agitation,
and debates over the future of the revolutionary movement. In part the devouring
passions of the revolutionaries can be explained by their lack of opportunity for
free expression and free participation in politics and government under the
Tsarist regime. Such liberals as Miliukov, who understood this, expected that once
free institutions and representative government came to Russia, their hotheaded
socialist and revolutionary friends would calm down and acquire the qualities of
moderation and reasonableness which characterized many Western Social Democrats. Miliukov did not foresee that Lenin's variety of socialism would cause any
special problems, for the good reason that during the early years of the century
the groups which would be called "moderate" socialists in 1917 were still behaving
much like the Bolsheviks. The outlines of "Leninism" were still blurred.

Lenin and Leninism

Vladimir Ilich Ulianov, better known as Lenin, was born in Simbirsk in 1870. He was the son of the provincial school inspector, who had been raised to the ranks of nobility through promotion in government service, hence the legend that Lenin was a "nobleman." Probably his first contact with the events of the revolutionary movement was the arrest and execution of his eldest brother, Alexander, in 1887, for leading an unsuccessful attempt to assassinate Alexander III under the auspices of *The People's Will.*

Young Vladimir went from the Simbirsk secondary school to the University of Kazan, but was expelled after a few months for taking part in a student demonstration. It was then that he began to read Marx, and he organized a Marxist circle in Samara, where his family had moved. In 1891 he took and passed the law examinations of St. Petersburg University as an extern (that is, he never attended classes there). Returning to Samara, he neglected law practice for his Marxist circle, and in 1893 he moved on to St. Petersburg and full-time revolutionary activity for good. At the age of twenty-three he earned himself the nickname of "The Old Man" for his ability and intensity; he laughed, not at jokes, but when he solved a knotty theoretical problem.

After his arrest in 1895 he was soon exiled to Siberia, where he was joined by Nadezhda Krupskaia, who became his wife and lifelong coworker. Under the lenient conditions imposed on exiles in tsarist Russia (and generally the same leniency was enjoyed by Soviet exiles during the 1920's, after which all privileges were removed), Lenin was able to have books and paper, and wrote his first major work, *The Development of Capitalism in Russia,* while he was in Siberia. The book's very title as well as its substance, was directed against the populists. Like virtually every other book or article he ever wrote, it coupled immediate polemical purpose with exposition of general principles. Most of his later important books and pamphlets were aimed, not at adversary or competitor groups or parties, nor at the tsarist government, whose turpitude and historical obsolescence he took for granted, but rather at other Social Democrats and even Bolsheviks His sole philosophical work, *Materialism and Empirio-Criticism* (written in 1908), was largely an attack on fellow Bolsheviks; his two most important interpretations and extension of Marxist historical and political theory, *Imperialism, the Highest Stage of Capitalism* (1916) (see p. 83), and *The State and Revolution* (1917), assailed foreign and other Russian Social Democrats. In the sense that for him thinking and acting (indeed, fighting) could never be separated, he was a better Marxist than most. His personal life was always subordinated to his political objectives. He refused to listen to Beethoven because it made him feel weak. The story is told that he decided against pursuing one liaison because, as he told the lady, she was "not a Social Democrat," to which she amicably but accurately replied that he was "only a Social Democrat." However, being a Social Democrat, or rather a Bolshevik, meant to him, in all aspects of life, obligations of which he never lost sight during his waking hours and scarcely in his dreams.

Lenin nowhere attempts to set forth an integrated doctrine of "Leninism," partly because he was too busy with the polemical or practical needs of the moment, partly because he regarded himself as a Marxist and not the author of some new doctrine. That estimate of himself is defensible on both empirical and logical grounds: many Marxists became Leninists without consciously changing their position, and ground for Lenin's central contentions may be found in Marx. It is likewise clear that Leninism is not the only possible or existing latter-day variety of Marxism, although it is true that persons who accept Marxism fully but reject Leninism seem neither numerous nor prominent. The Trotskyites, who reject Stalin's doctrines and practices, regard themselves as both good Marxists and good Leninists. It is at any rate true that Marx did not pretend to be the author of an analysis valid for the future, but regarded future change, whose nature he did not claim to be able to predict, as certain. Lenin undertook to analyze developments subsequent to Marx's time, an undertaking of which Marx would no doubt have approved, but more important, one which the terms of Marxism itself suggested.

In extending Marxist historical analysis, Lenin sought to explain why European capitalism had prolonged its life and disappointed Marx's hope of imminent proletarian revolution (see p. 29). The Leninist analysis of imperialism was widely accepted, and is influential today in Asia and Africa even among those who are not consciously or fully Marxists or Leninists. The aspects of Lenin's doctrine which have troubled many admirers of Marx and which seem most at variance with the emphasis of Marx's chief works constitute Lenin's politics. To be sure, his argument that "professional revolutionaries" were needed to lead the proletarian party was conditioned by his view of tsarism and his belief that bourgeois infiltration was more dangerous in the Russia of his time than elsewhere. However, he himself undertook to establish a Communist International composed of parties modeled on that of Russia, and sanctioned a tradition which has formed all Communist parties in the partly illegal and underground mold he set for the Russian party, even though its leaders may not be barred from part-time practice of another profession than revolutionism.

Lenin's prescriptions for party organization were closely linked with his strong revolutionary activism. As Alfred G. Meyer points out, "in the long range of historical perspective [Lenin] looked at the world through the eyes of Marx and subscribed to everything the latter had said about the inevitable breakdown of capitalism and the dawn of socialism. In that sense Lenin was an orthodox Marxist, and he joined other orthodox believers within the Second International in their fight against revisionism. At the same time Lenin's short-range analysis . . . tended to yield different results. In place of the fighting optimism typical of Marx, he substituted a fighting pessimism, based on the realization that things were not developing in as smooth and rapid a fashion as the Marxist algebra of revolution had foretold."[6] Out of fear that he might, at least for the time being, fail, and the perspective of revolution might fade, Lenin advocated and practiced a type of active leadership which was governed not by morality but merely by expediency, and he claimed that such leadership was not only capable of directing the cause of the whole proletariat, but moreover was indispensable to the success of that cause. Without the proper leadership of the intellectuals, proletarian class-consciousness could not develop beyond what he scornfully termed "trade-union consciousness," that is, reformist demands, and the revolution would not occur soon. Strictly speaking, it is hard to see how Lenin could ever expect it to occur at all.

In his insistence on the role of a revolutionary elite, Lenin was sharply criticized by the Mensheviks and other Social Democrats in Russia and abroad for being a follower of the Jacobins, or Blanqui, or their Russian admirers such as Tkachëv, or other populists who emphasized the importance of the "critically thinking individual" in history. Lenin's elitist activism perhaps owed inspiration to all these sources and more, but he saw himself as involved with the problem as Marx posed it: against the background of the historical inevitability of socialism, to change the world which philosophers had so far only interpreted.

However, Lenin's teachings on party organization led him into the further problem of how the party should behave when it had attained power. There is no doubt that he took Marx's slogan, "dictatorship of the proletariat," seriously and literally. However, if the party shall lead the proletariat to power, it must certainly secure and maintain that power, and it must be ruthlessly employed against all who would undermine or weaken it, intentionally or otherwise, regardless of the class origin of the individuals concerned. Trotsky correctly foresaw that Leninism implied a situation wherein "the organization of the Party takes the place of the Party itself; the Central Committee takes the place of the organization; and finally the dictator takes the place of the Central Committee. ..." The fact that he himself, over a decade later, shared in the dictatorship when it already lay in fewer hands than those of the Central Committee, only bears out the accuracy of his prophecy. Lenin wrote many times of the genuine democracy which would come after the revolution, but it could only be realized if the masses understood the truth of history, which was in the custody of the party elite. Lenin assumed that they would or could come to understand and failed to ask himself what would have to be done if they did not. The unsolved practical problem he left as a legacy to his successors, including Stalin.

On the eve of the Revolution of 1905, however, such perspectives were not being weighed seriously, even by Trotsky. For a decade the Marxists, liberals, and SR's

---

[6] Reprinted by permission of the publishers from Alfred G. Meyer, *Leninism,* Harvard U. Press, Copyright 1957, by The President and Fellows of Harvard College, p. 84.

had discussed and quarreled over their views of history, their expectations, their programs, within their own ranks and with rival groups. However, they were apparently united in having faith that a Russian revolution was imminent and would first bring conditions of "bourgeois" freedom and a freely chosen government. After that, it was tacitly agreed, some would confine themselves to social reform and some would go on to fight for socialism. But the "old regime" would have been destroyed root and branch: the tsar would be stripped of his powers or his position, the Orthodox Church would be disestablished or destroyed, the peasantry would be fully enfranchised and freed from any economic or political influence of their former landlords, and Russia would become a "modern" state. None of them doubted that absolutism would soon lie behind, and democracy lie ahead. Few of them suspected what Lenin understood by "democracy," but still fewer thought that Lenin would hold in his hands the future of Russia.

3

The Last Tsar: Reaction and the Revolution of 1905

The Regime of Nicholas II

In 1900 central and eastern Europe were governed by empires, but there were constitutional limitations on the power of the German emperor, of the Hohenzollern dynasty, and the person who was both emperor of Austria and king of Hungary, of the Habsburgs. The Ottoman sultan and Russian emperor were autocrats. Autocracy and serfdom were the chief evils of tsarism, as far as the opponents of the regime were concerned; Alexander II, the Tsar-Liberator (1855–1881), had swept away serfdom (see p. 20). Though he hesitated to abridge the powers of autocracy, on the morning of his assassination he approved a law providing for consultation with elected representatives that some termed the "Loris-Melikov constitution." It was an exaggerated description, but nonetheless the measure moved in a constitutional direction. After the tsar's murder, however, his stern and strong-willed son Alexander III (1881–1894) was determined not to encourage forces seeking to end autocracy. He bequeathed unlimited power to his successor and son, Nicholas II (1894–1917). Unfortunately he could give him neither the strength of character or breadth of understanding required to deal with the endless crises of his reign that finally brought down the dynasty and the monarchy itself.

Nicholas lived an exemplary and tender family life. His chief moral defect lay in the duplicity he repeatedly exhibited toward those who served him. He was often gruff and curt with those in favor, expansive and warm toward those he was about to dismiss. Less than a month after his accession he married the former Princess Alix of Hesse-Darmstadt—a German, like every Russian consort since the time of Peter the Great, with the single exception of Nicholas's own Danish mother. It was a marriage of love, and Nicholas's affections extended to no one else but his children, four daughters and the boy Alexis, born in 1904, the joy of his parents' life.

It was soon learned that Alexis suffered from hemophilia, inherited from his mother. The disease was then not well understood. The desperate family's efforts to keep the boy alive later led to the incredible episode of Rasputin. The deeper cause of Rasputin's influence—grossly exaggerated though it was by the media of the day—lay in the tsar's refusal to concern himself with political questions and his narrow interpretation of his duty as simply maintaining the power his father had passed on to him.

From the beginning of his reign he made this unmistakably clear. Soon after his accession he rejected constitutionalist hints of a zemstvo delegation with the words, "Let everyone know that I ... shall safeguard the principles of autocracy as firmly and unwaveringly as did my ... father." The liberals were divided between those who, saddened by such intransigence, continued to hope for the tsar's willingness to accept moderate political reform, and those who expected and even welcomed the immovable stance he had assumed. If it was to be all or nothing, revolution was the only answer. The socialists had long been of this opinion and remained so.

The tsar held the reins of central government in his own hands. There were ministries, but their heads reported individually to the tsar and met only for discussion. The most important was Minister of the Interior because he controlled the police—the civil police, who regulated many aspects of life, collected taxes and received bribes (without which they would seldom take action), the quite distinct political police (called gendarmerie), and the secret police (Okhrana). An appointed State Council of roughly fifty persons was supposed to advise the tsar on lawmaking; a smaller Senate, also appointed, acted as the highest court of appeal for both civil and criminal cases and could also judge the propriety of new legislation. Both bodies had more power in fact than in law, simply because Nicholas II often felt unable to decide matters unaided. An unwieldy, inefficient central government often mattered less to a given locale or citizen than the local government, headed by governors of the provinces (*guberniia*), many of whose affairs were run or influenced by the elected zemstvos that existed at the province and county (*uezd*) levels but not at the lowest level, the village, or the highest, the nation. There was also a structure of elective urban government, the municipal dumas. The powers of the police and bureaucracy clashed with the elected bodies, and any kind of governmental action was slow, often costly, and sometimes absurd (Gogol's play *The Inspector General* was a fair sample). The bureaucracy was organized into fourteen ranks, each with a civil and military form, in a hierarchy established by Peter the Great. One could rise to ennoblement through these ranks, which were intended to produce an officialdom (and officer corps) selected by merit but instead produced one that was stultified, rigid, and servile.

It may be argued that three ingredients must be at hand if one is to make a revolution: a regime that has lost its ability to govern and its nerve; mass discontent that is capable of being channeled toward political goals; and a counterelite credible in its claim to be able to govern. The reign was first to show promise in its statesmen: Sergei Witte, who was instrumental in sponsoring industrial growth, and Peter Stolypin, who understood that the core of the Russian people, the peasantry, had to be transformed if the country were to move forward. But the promise was dashed by what happened afterward. Sparks of discontent appeared in the villages from 1902 on, but jacqueries have never achieved political change. However, the industrial workers' movement, from the strikes of the 1890's on, sporadically showed the way to revolution, together with student bodies permeated with radical ideas. The tinder could perhaps be set afire by the leftist parties beginning to form. But the failures of the government to meet the crises that developed during the Russo-Japanese War and then during World War I were decisive in encompassing its own downfall.

Reaction and Oppression

Nicholas II carried on his father's curtailment of the rights of minority nationalities and discrimination against non-Orthodox religious groups. The monarch applied to Finland measures that Alexander III designed to limit Finnish autonomy, respected by Russian emperors since 1809. By a manifesto of February 1899 he in effect abrogated the Finnish constitution and gave the function of making laws for Finland to the State Council. Both the Finns and the Russian opposition groups reacted with sharp protests. In such borderlands as the Baltic and the Caucasus, political organizations demanding cultural autonomy or more made their appearance, especially among the Latvians, Georgians, and Armenians. Ukrainian intellectuals, who were permitted a degree of cultural freedom in neighboring Austrian Galicia, demanded similar or wider privileges from the Russian tsar.

Although certain of Alexander III's advisers, such as Count Pahlen (who chaired a committee which recommended removal of all disabilities on the Jews), tried to restrain him, he pursued a strongly anti-Semitic policy. Jews could enroll in higher schools only under quota limits and were excluded from law practice and the zemstvos and city councils. The most influential bureaucrats feared the prominence of Jews in both the revolutionary movement and in business. St. Petersburg was sensitive to Western condemnation of anti-Semitism, however, and the government managed to keep down pogroms to a large extent up to the time of the 1903 outbreak in Kishinëv, which received world-wide publicity. By then Jewish political organizations had been formed, motivated less by any new anti-Semitic measures of Nicholas II than by his inconsistency of policy toward the Jews. In 1897 Zionism appeared with its contention that Jews must build their own exclusive nation, since everyone else insisted on building his own. A Jewish (but not Zionist) Marxist Bund was organized among the Polish and Belorussian industrial workers.

Partly inspired by the zeal of Pobedonostsev, Christian dissenters also were persecuted. In 1894 the Stundists, a Russian variant of the Baptists, were prohibited from holding services. The pacifist Dukhobors, who had been made subject to military service like everyone else by the army reform of 1874, had migrated to Cyprus and in 1899 moved on to Canada. Their arrival there served to deepen foreign hostility to tsarism. The fifteen per cent of the Empire's population who in 1897 were dissenters from Russian Orthodoxy had no love for the regime of Nicholas II.

Among the Orthodox Russian population, the mass movement which most encouraged the revolutionaries was the mounting wave of strikes. The industrial boom of the early 1890's led to Russia's first significant strike movement in 1895–1897. The chief official supporter of industrialization, Minister of Finance Sergei Witte, asserted bluntly that the strikes had been provoked by mismanagement, and in 1897 the government passed a law limiting working hours to eleven and a half per day, but still rounded up and punished those strike leaders whom it could find.

Certain officials, recognizing the justice of the workers' economic grievances, thought it advisable to lend them support, also hoping thereby to steal the thunder of the revolutionary agitators. S. V. Zubatov, an ex-revolutionary who had become an agent of the security police, was allowed to form workers' associations whose members were encouraged to read the books of the German Revisionist, Bernstein, and demand improvements in working conditions. This remarkable movement, which has been called "police socialism," spread rapidly in 1901–1902. In 1903, after widespread strikes had occurred in the south, the government became alarmed and tried to bring the risky experiment to an end. However, it was to be a police socialist leader, Father George Gapon, who was to organize the revolutionary demonstration of "Bloody Sunday," inaugurating the Revolution of 1905.

The university students had also begun to organize demonstrations and strikes. In 1899 a clash with the authorities of St. Petersburg University led to what was in effect a general strike in Russian higher education, and a number of student strikers were drafted into the army as punishment. In 1901 a former student (he was a Socialist Revolutionary, but was not a member of the party's Combat Organization) assassinated the minister of education, Bogolepov. In vain Nicholas II tried both leniency and harshness as ways of quieting student unrest.

The SR Combat Organization unleashed its terrorist campaign with a series of political murders or attempted murders of provincial governors and other officials, climaxed by the killing of two successive ministers of interior, Sipiagin and Plehve, in 1902 and 1904. The zemstvo organizations, while not countenancing violence, began in 1901, after a period of inactivity, to meet for political discussion and publish liberal demands which contributed to the growth of public opposition to the regime. Finally the most dangerous form of mass action, in the view of many officials, reappeared with the peasant riots of 1902 in Ukraine.

If Plehve, minister of interior when the Russo-Japanese War broke out, did not (as alleged) hope that a "small, victorious war" would drown the flames of unrest in a wave of patriotic fervor, he might well have done so. The revolutionary movement was growing swiftly. The rebellious intelligentsia were reaching ever-widening circles of the politically unsophisticated and providing slogans and leaders for the expression of their grievances. The government had neither the monarch, the ministers, nor the policy required to deal with the situation.

Imperialism in the Far East

In form, the foreign policy of Nicholas II was comparable to and patterned after that of the other East European monarchies, Germany and Austria-Hungary, and was not so different from that of the West European democracies, France and Great Britain. The main effort of all the great powers was not so much to win control over new territories as to preserve the European status quo. However, mutual distrust and the suspicion of a given power that another sought to change the status quo at its expense often provoked crises. Since in the last quarter of the nineteenth century most of the great powers of Europe were extending their influence and possessions in Asia and Africa, there was much friction in the latter areas and also concern as to whether imperialist gains, losses, or transfers abroad might upset the balance of interests in Europe itself.

While the Western powers operated in overseas areas, Russian imperialism was concerned with contiguous territory. Along Russia's southern borders, there lay a politically spongy and malleable band of states extending thousands of miles, from Ottoman Turkey to Manchu China, from which the Russians were excluded by British power. On the far eastern end of that band of states, however, Britain was a less important contestant than Japan, a newcomer to imperialist competition. A number of Russian officials thought Japan might safely be challenged and bested in Manchuria and Korea. Japan's military mettle had been tested only once since her emergence from seclusion and her dramatic Westernization. In the war of 1894–1895 with the weak and crumbling Chinese Empire, Japan had won the victory. However, Russia had promptly organized diplomatic intervention of the great powers to bring about modification of the peace terms in China's favor. Russia's reward was a concession to build a railway across northern Manchuria from Chita to Vladivostok. This Chinese Eastern Railway connected with the unfinished Trans-Siberian route, which would otherwise have had to follow a much longer and more difficult course on Russian soil to the north to reach Vladivostok.

In 1898, following a renewed imperialist scramble for Chinese concessions, Russia obtained the further right to build a railway spur from Harbin on the new Chinese Eastern to Port Arthur on the Liaotung Peninsula, and a lease of the peninsula itself. There was some debate within the Russian government as to how much risk it was wise to court in pressing a forward policy in the Far East. The chief advocate of a cautious line, Minister of Finance Witte, was overruled by the enthusiastic imperialists, one of whom was Foreign Minister Muraviëv. Even when Muraviëv died and was replaced by the cautious Lamsdorf in 1900, the imperialists kept the ear of the Emperor. During the Boxer Rebellion rebels attacked the Chinese Eastern, and Russia retaliated by military occupation of the whole of Manchuria. An adventurer named Bezobrazov persuaded Nicholas II to finance a timber concession on the Yalu River on the northern border of Korea, in which country Russian influence had become decisive. Plehve, who became interior minister in 1902, was identified with the more aggressive policy, and when the following year Witte was dismissed from the finance ministry, advocates of restraint were virtually silenced.

Anticipating trouble, the Japanese attempted overtures to St. Petersburg. When a viceroy was appointed by the tsar to administer both the Liaotung Peninsula and the Amur region, thus closing a political vise on Manchuria from north and south, Tokyo concluded that the Bezobrazov clique had won out. In January 1904 the Japanese attacked the Russian fleet at Port Arthur without bothering to declare war.

The War with Japan

The course of the Russo-Japanese War was marked by an uninterrupted series of Russian defeats on land and sea. Russia suffered from severe handicaps from the outset. The Trans-Siberian Railway remained an inadequate supply route, since it was not yet finished in the area of Lake Baikal; from the beginning Russian land forces in the Far East were outnumbered; the British and American governments and public opinion tended to support the Japanese out of both financial interest and sentiment. However, the war was lost by mismanagement in the field. Japanese troops proceeded to assault Russian positions in two directions, north toward Mukden and south toward Port Arthur. Port Arthur was besieged almost at once and surrendered in December 1904. In August and September the Russians lost two battles, at Liaoyang and the Sha River, and in February 1905 the battle of Mukden ended in another defeat which narrowly missed becoming a rout. Nevertheless the Russian armies remained in being, and the *coup de grâce* was administered not by land but by sea.

The capable Admiral Makarov took over the damaged Port Arthur squadron in February 1904, but in April he went down with his ship when it was struck by a mine. In August the fleet tried to break out of besieged Port Arthur to reach Vladivostok, but it was intercepted and destroyed. There ensued a fantastic episode in which the Russians tried to replace their Far Eastern fleet with their Baltic squadron. In October 1904 Admiral Rozhdestvensky sailed from the Gulf of Finland, shooting at several English fishing smacks on the way in the belief that they were Japanese torpedo boats. In May 1905 he finally reached the Tsushima Strait off Korea, where he was met by the Japanese and his fleet promptly sunk.

There was now virtually no alternative for the Russians except to make peace. Witte was retrieved from the bureaucratic discard and sent to Portsmouth, New Hampshire, where he negotiated the peace treaty on September 5, 1905. Russia conceded Japanese hegemony in Korea, the annexation of southern Sakhalin, and the lease of the Liaotung Peninsula and the South Manchurian Railway, but the Empire was extricated from the war, and the cost seemed not excessive in view of the grave crisis which the government was then facing at home.

The Revolution of 1905

The tsar and his officials expected the outbreak of war to rally patriotic support to the side of the regime, but the effect was mainly the opposite. The vocal segment of public opinion was mainly liberal and revolutionary. The advanced liberals had recently formed a Union of Liberation (*Soiuz Osvobozhdeniia*) whose chief figure was Paul Miliukov, a first-rate historian and publicist. They had great influence on the intelligentsia to the right of orthodox Marxism, including professional men of all sorts. Prodded by the Liberationists, a wide variety of semipublic bodies seized the occasion of the war to meet to discuss the "crisis," denounce the government, and demand reform. The government encountered very little public support for the war, but instead a mounting wave of domestic criticism arose with which it seemed to wrestle in vain.

Only a few months after the war broke out, the SR's assassinated Minister of Interior Plehve. He was replaced by Prince Peter Sviatopolk-Mirsky, who announced a "new course" in which he would endeavor to inspire the trust of enlightened public opinion. In November 1904 the zemstvo men met in national congress, demanded that the tsar grant a legislative assembly, and summoned local bodies to discuss their demands. The resulting "banquet campaign" (as it was labeled with France's 1848 Revolution in mind) drew in a variety of urban groups, including the municipal councils. The Mensheviks advocated efforts to include worker participation in these discussions, but very little of the plan was realized. Mirsky persuaded Nicholas II to promise to adopt some of the zemstvo men's demands in the hope of calming the gathering revolutionary storm. However, the tsar balked at a legislative assembly, and in consequence Mirsky resigned and was replaced by A. G. Bulygin.

The first violence came on the heels of the fall of Port Arthur. A puzzling quasi-political priest, George Gapon, leader of a workers' group which had arisen as a "police socialist" union, was the instigator. He persuaded himself that it was his duty to lead a procession to the Winter Palace in order to claim redress of grievances from the Emperor personally and used revolutionary language in his appeals. The procession was fired upon by order of one of the grand dukes (Nicholas II was absent from the Palace). The event was termed "Bloody Sunday" and may be considered the beginning of the Revolution of 1905.

In 1905, for the first time in the history of modern Russia, millions of people in the cities as well as villages took part in a genuine mass movement, although they were far from unanimous in their goals. The political slogan of the hour was that of the opposition parties, whose platforms were substantially in harmony on immediate objectives; it demanded a "Four-Tail Constituent Assembly," that is, a body to be elected on the basis of universal, secret, equal, and direct suffrage to decide the future form of government. Other widespread demands were for enactment of full civil liberties, especially freedom of speech, press, and assembly, and prescription of an eight-hour maximum working day. For the socialist parties, the demands amounted to realization of a bourgeois regime, under which they could fight for the final goal of socialism; for the liberals, they would inaugurate democracy, under which all other political and social problems could be dealt with in time. Any public attempt to express some more modest demand was usually shouted down.

The evidence does not suggest that either the industrial workers or the peasants were chiefly interested in political changes, although the spokesmen of their organizations formed during 1905 repeated the demands which had been voiced by the zemstvos and municipal councils. The officials would not and the uneducated masses could not think up any slogans which could compete successfully with those of the intelligentsia. After Bloody Sunday, Mirsky could only wring his hands and, reportedly, lament, "Everything has failed. Let us build jails." The initiative seemed to lie in the hands of the revolutionaries. Strikes, demonstrations, and public meetings grew in number and boldness, and in February the SR's killed the Grand Duke Sergei.

The tsar issued a series of contradictory edicts, coupling threats with promises. Two weeks after the assassination of Sergei, Nicholas hurled an imperial anathema at the opposition but simultaneously signed a rescript to Minister of Interior Bulygin promising a consultative assembly and a ukase to the Senate confirming the right of every subject "to be heard directly by the monarch." The promise of a "Bulygin Duma" was ignored by the opposition, and such a body never met. However, the ukase to the Senate was interpreted by many as blanket permission to carry on political agitation—not that the revolutionary leaders were waiting for permission. In May the Union of Unions, including in its make-up fourteen "professional unions," was founded under strong Liberationist influence. In July a Peasant Union came into being, under the urging of SR's and other revolutionaries. The zemstvo representatives were holding frequent sessions. At length they sent a deputation to the Emperor which had no visible effect on his actions, but the July zemstvo congress, angry at being snubbed, reacted by open demands for a Constituent Assembly. The radical Petrunkevich declared, "Now we must go to the people, and not to the tsar."

On August 19 the government issued the promised law for a "Bulygin" or consultative Duma, but it made no impression on the opposition leaders. The conclusion of peace with Japan in the same month earned no plaudits; the opposition denounced the treaty terms and declared they revealed the incompetence of the government. The strike movement, which had been mounting almost from month to month, now became the spearhead of political action. Real trade-unions were practically nonexistent, and during the autumn the strikers seldom presented employers with any demands for better working conditions or wages. In fact, many employers, sympathizing with the political movement, continued to pay their workers while on strike.

In late September and early October the movement swelled toward a dramatic climax. A railway strike on October 20 spread rapidly throughout all communications, and then to most industries. The first successful general strike in modern history became a reality without any overall planning. On October 26 there was organized in St. Petersburg a Council (*sovet* or Soviet) of Workers' Deputies, beginning with thirty or forty delegates from a single district of the city and rapidly rising above the five hundred mark, theoretically on the basis of a deputy for every five hundred workers in the factories.

The St. Petersburg Soviet was later evaluated by one of its leaders, Leon Trotsky, as a "general staff of the revolution." It might be more accurate to describe it as the device by which the revolutionary intellectuals rallied the urban workers to the support of the political program they advocated. In the Soviet the Mensheviks, Socialist Revolutionaries, and Bolsheviks worked together, maintaining harmony not through the orders of a leader, but rather through a common analysis of the "historical tasks" in prospect. There was no room for the views of those who regarded strikes as a method of improving living and working conditions for industrial laborers, or in any event those who considered any major improvement possible aside from a successful revolution. In October 1905 the striking workers followed the lead of the revolutionary intellectuals in the political struggle which the Marxists had long advocated and predicted; few of them were Marxists, but that too had been expected. The result of the struggle was paralysis throughout the economy and panic among the leaders of the government.

The October Manifesto

A few weeks earlier Witte had returned from making peace at Portsmouth to find the country rent by strikes, demonstrations, and even mutinies in the armed forces. When the general strike of October occurred, Witte advised the Emperor to decide between a constitutional regime and a military dictatorship, but declared he would take part only in the former. Nicholas II finally yielded. On October 30 the Emperor issued the "October Manifesto," drafted by Witte, and simultaneously appointed him Russia's first prime minister.

After declaring that the revolutionary disturbances filled his "heart with great and deep grief," Nicholas declared that he had "found it neccssary to unite the activities of the Supreme Government, so as to insure the successful carrying out of the general measures laid down by US for the peaceful life of the state." He continued, "We lay upon the Government the execution of OUR unchangeable will:

"1. To grant to the population the inviolable right of free citizenship, based on the principles of the freedom of person, conscience, speech, assembly, and union.

"2. Without postponing the intended elections for the State Duma and in so far as possible, in view of the short time that remains before the assembling of that body, to include in the participation of the work of the Duma those classes of the population that have been until now entirely deprived of the right to vote, and to extend in the future, by the newly created legislative way, the principles of the general right of election.

"3. To establish as an unbreakable rule that no law shall go into force without its confirmation by the State Duma and that the persons elected by the people shall have the opportunity for actual participation in supervising the legality of the acts of authorities appointed by US." The tsar ended with an appeal to "all the true sons of Russia" to help reestablish order in the country.[1]

The Manifesto was too much for the conservatives, much too little for the opposition. Only the Union of October 17 or "Octobrist" party, which took its name from the date of the Manifesto and organized in its defense against both Left and Right, professed satisfaction. There was widespread rejoicing among ordinary people who, although unable to subject the document to legal exegesis, understood that Russia was freer than before. The ranks of the opposition, led by the St. Petersburg Soviet, were thrown into confusion. The country hung poised in a new but uneasy balance, and the Soviet, faced by impending collapse of its strike, called it off hastily. The public watched to see "whether Khrustalëv[2] would arrest Witte, or Witte would arrest Khrustalëv." The government waited for its opportunity, which came with an unsuccessful attempt at a second general strike in November. Witte arrested Khrustalëv, and a few days later his successor as chairman, Trotsky, and the whole Soviet.

By this time the Soviet form of organization had spread far beyond St. Petersburg; in fact, the first Soviet had been organized as early as June in the textile center of Ivanovo-Voznesensk. With the collapse of the Soviet in the capital, the initiative passed to Moscow. The Moscow Soviet launched a third general strike in December which soon became an armed uprising in the Presnia district of the city. However, Moscow's population did not rise as hoped, and government troops from the capital crushed the revolt.

The repression of the Moscow uprising marked the virtual end of the Revolution of 1905 in the cities, but a revolt of a different sort, beginning later but lasting longer, took place in the countryside. Especially in the overcrowded provinces ly-

---

[1] Quoted portions of trans. in Frank A. Golder, ed., *Documents of Russian History, 1914–1917*, The Century Co., 1927, pp. 627–628.

[2] The shadowy, nonparty figure who was the first chairman of the St. Petersburg Soviet.

ing near the fiftieth parallel and in the Baltic, village riots mounted in the autumn and continued into the spring of 1906. In ten provinces alone almost 30 million rubles' worth of damage was done. The intelligentsia endeavored to mobilize peasant opinion and action behind their political program through the Peasant Union and other organizations, but the attempt was a failure. Neither the intelligentsia nor the government seemed to understand very clearly what had happened in the countryside. The first returns from the elections for the new assembly, held in March, led Witte to exclaim, "Thank God, the Duma will be peasant." Indeed the First Duma was to a large extent peasant in its composition, but the deputies came neither to profess their loyalty to the regime nor to follow the revolutionaries' lead, but for purposes of their own most easily summed up in the old phrase, "land and liberty."

The First Duma

Russia emerged from the Revolution of 1905 with several important reforms, some of them promulgated during the period of struggle and almost ignored at the time. In April religious toleration had been granted, in August university autonomy restored, in October Finnish autonomy partly restored, in November the redemption payments for Emancipation lands canceled. The October Manifesto had granted civil liberties—which were subsequently abridged at times in law or in fact, but never abolished—and a legislative assembly.

What the new assembly would be like remained to be seen. In February the new Duma was declared to be merely the lower house of a two-chambered legislative body. The old Imperial Council became the new upper house, half of its members (instead of all, as before) being appointees of the crown, half being elected by the zemstvos, nobles, commerce and industry, the clergy, the universities, and the Finnish diet. Laws were to require the approval of both houses and the Emperor, and though the Duma had control over much of the budget, it could not question military and certain other types of expenditure. Since the ministry was to remain appointive and, like that of Germany, responsible only to the Emperor, the Duma's powers were far short of those of the British House of Commons, which was the standard of much liberal judgment. These and other constitutional changes were codified by the Fundamental Laws issued on May 6, 1906, on the eve of the opening of the Duma.

The franchise for election of deputies to the Duma was unequal and indirect, but it was close to universal, partly because the government still believed in the loyalty of the peasantry when the law was issued, on December 24, 1905. At first all the revolutionary parties decided to boycott the election. Only when they realized that the country took it seriously did they try to repair the consequences of their blunder. The Mensheviks entered the lists in the Caucasus and emerged with several seats in the Duma; the SR's set to work to try to influence the large number of nonparty peasant deputies; only the Bolsheviks found themselves uneasy by-standers, deprived of influence over the Duma.

The Kadets (the party just formed by Miliukov's liberals) went into the elections at full tilt. They emerged with the largest number of deputies, and with their plurality were able to lead the Duma. Such a stance in the assembly was not a sign of reconciliation with the regime; on the contrary, they intended to utilize it for revolutionary purposes, as the French States General had been used in 1789. The second largest group of deputies was to begin with not a party fraction at all; it was a caucus of men calling themselves the *Trudoviki* (Toilers), who were the closest thing to direct spokesmen the peasantry had. The real conservatives were entirely absent, and the Octobrists, the only group which supported the institutions in which they undertook to participate, were but a handful.

The course of the First Duma was short and stormy. The tsar's speech from the throne was immediately answered by a unanimous manifesto demanding a full-fledged representative democracy and land expropriation on behalf of the peasants immediately. An appearance by Prime Minister Goremykin, a lazy but wily bureaucrat who had been substituted for Witte just before the Duma opened, provoked a prompt vote of censure. A land bill which had no chance of Imperial acceptance was moved along parliamentary channels toward passage, but the First Duma was dissolved before a vote could be taken, after a turbulent existence of only two months. The Kadet leaders made for Finland, where in the "Vyborg Manifesto" they called for passive resistance from the public as a protest against the Duma's dissolution, but response was negligible. Neither the socialists' tactics in the strikes nor the liberals' tactics in the Duma had succeeded in bringing about "bourgeois" democracy. The major figures in the struggle were left to try to decide what had happened.

The government had ridden out the urban storm in some alarm, but with a deep conviction that the countryside was "healthy." However, as peasant riots grew serious, and especially after the *Trudoviki* followed the Kadet lead in legislating land expropriation, the bureaucrats were compelled to recognize that the "loyalty" of the peasantry was a mirage. Having confidently felt that victory was near during the general strikes, the revolutionary leadership had counted on the support of the peasantry, but this calculation also proved unwarranted. If the peasantry had gone anywhere, it had gone to the parliamentary institutions which the revolutionaries scorned and assumed to be a matter of indifference to the peasants. Nevertheless, they had failed to obtain from the Duma what was apparently their first concern, a land reform. Plainly the peasantry remained a powerful potential which the right leadership could presumably exploit. The eleven years from 1906 to 1917 were marked by redoubled efforts by both government and revolutionaries to win over rural Russia.

4

The "Silver Age" of the Arts

Censorship from Left and Right

Under the oppressive regime of Nicholas I (1825–1855) and the milder reign of Alexander II (1855–1881), Russia experienced a "Golden Age" of literature. Under the intermittently severe censorship and repression of Nicholas II (1894–1917), Russia enjoyed a "Silver Age" in literature as well as in other arts. Artists and writers were plagued by officials who scented radicalism; they were also subjected to strong pressures of a quite different kind from the revolutionary-minded intelligentsia. Under neither Nicholas did the regime exact positive conformity to a set of governmentally prescribed ideological principles. The official censorship confined itself to suppressing or threatening to suppress offensive material, chiefly in the field of journalism. The unofficial "censorship of the Left," however, demanded positive conformity in several of the arts. It asked that creative artists serve revolutionary political ends and applied a variety of sanctions against artists who balked. This kind of censor could not seize a newspaper or book, nor exile an artist, but it could make it difficult for him to get a public hearing and could even sometimes hound him into bewildered silence. Despite these very different kinds of pressures, the artists and writers of the reign of Nicholas II managed to attain high creative levels and to spread appreciation of the arts among a broader public than ever before in Russia.

The "temporary" censorship rules of 1882 remained in force up to the Revolution of 1905. By their provisions newspapers and magazines which had been officially warned three times could be subjected to preliminary censorship. There were other laws which were intended chiefly for use as a political counter-weapon against the revolutionary intelligentsia. In 1905–1906 preliminary censorship of periodicals and books was abolished, but published material alleged to violate the law still could be and was seized from time to time as long as tsarism lasted.

The "censorship of the Left" operated in a subtler but not necessarily less effective manner. Since the time of the capable but rather singleminded critic Vissarion Belinsky (1811–1848), the intelligentsia had deemed any theory or practice of the independence of the arts, such as use of the slogan, "art for art's sake," to be treasonable to the revolutionary cause. The so-called "social command" of the radical critics was that art should serve as an instrument of social improvement. Since most of the radicals thought that no effective reforms could be enacted without a complete overturn of the existing system, the "social command" tended to insist that art should exist only for the sake of the coming revolution. Works of art and literature which did not portray the wickedness of the government, the miseries of the common people, or the virtues of the revolutionary intelligentsia, were often ignored, scorned, or savagely attacked, as Belinsky had macerated Gogol's *Correspondence with Friends*. Nonpolitical activity by the younger generation might be equated with reactionary politics or be subject to invasion by revolutionary youth who considered their own aims more important than any others. For example, at the University of Moscow in the 1890's the students were left with only one extracurricular organization which enjoyed official recognition, the student orchestra and choir. Certain young radicals, including the future SR leader Victor Chernov, systematically set about to capture this organization for purposes of revolutionary propaganda. They succeeded, and the result was that the government disbanded the orchestra and choir.

Against such pressure from two directions, the nonpolitically-minded were placed in a difficult position indeed. The government seldom directly interfered with them. The chief obstacle to their charting their own course was the power of the "social command," for the radicals maintained ascendancy over the literary and to some extent the whole intellectual world throughout the reign of Alexander III. The radical domination was successfully challenged, however, in the 1890's, and the "Silver Age" followed. Although the "social command" remained influential, the defenders of the independence of the artist won a hearing. When, a quarter-century later in 1915, Maxim Gorky protested against the staging of Dostoevsky's *The Possessed* (a novel critical of the revolutionaries) at the Moscow Art Theater, the protest was widely regarded as a last gasp of the "censorship of the Left" (a censorship by no means limited to those who, like Gorky, were Bolsheviks).

At that time artists and critics of many different persuasions were indeed able to reach the public. It was not a reversal of trend in the world of the arts but the political events of the Revolution and Civil War which changed the picture drastically. Those events raised Gorky himself to the position of dean of Communist letters and led to the artistic and personal ruin of his opponents—many of whom, it should be said to his personal credit, he tried to help and save. In the end Gorky himself fell victim to the "censorship of the Left," which had become transmuted into a weapon of the Soviet power and was applied with a rigor unmatched by any of the pre-totalitarian censorships.[1]

---

[1] The fate of Gorky is the subject of an interesting novel partly based on what is known of the facts: Igor Gouzenko, *The Fall of a Titan*, Cassell, 1954.

New Currents in Literature

It was in the field of literature that the Russian arts had first attained world re-
nown by producing works of genius in European genres. In the 1820's and 1830's
Alexander Pushkin and Michael Lermontov had written great poetry, and
Nicholas Gogol great prose. During the 1860's and 1870's Fëdor Dostoevsky, Leo
Tolstoy, and Ivan Turgenev had produced first-rate fiction. However,
Dostoevsky's *The Brothers Karamazov* (which, along with Tolstoy's *War and Peace*,
marks the high point of genius in Russian prose), written in 1880, was the last of
the great novels. During the Silver Age, as Wladimir Weidlé writes, "Russian liter-
ature produced no genius comparable to Tolstoy or Dostoevski or Pushkin or
Gogol, but in all branches of letters the number of talented writers had never been
so great, their public so large or the general level of its culture so high."[2]

Since Belinsky's time poetry as a genre had been rather unpopular, except for
the "civic poetry" of such writers as Nicholas Nekrasov (author of *Who Can be
Happy and Free in Russia?*). Novels had been approved by the radical critics if they
had an intentional "social emphasis." If such emphasis was lacking, the critics often provided it for the puzzled author. The radicals reigned supreme in the field of
literary criticism, and from that stronghold they exerted great influence on the
arts in general. In the words of D. S. Mirsky, "only a small minority of thinking
people—but among them perhaps the most independent, original, and sincere
minds of the day—showed a critical attitude towards the dogma of agnosticism
and democracy, and strove towards a creative revival of Christian and national
ideals."[3] The minority did not by any means consist entirely of Christians or Russian nationalists. Its diversity of outlook was considerable, but it was united in its
resentment of the "censorship of the Left."

The challenge to the ascendancy of the radical critics began in the early years of
the reign of Alexander III. In 1884 two articles appeared in a Kiev newspaper
questioning the validity of the "social command." A few years later A. L. Volynsky
(pseudonym of Flekser) began to do the same in the pages of the St. Petersburg
magazine *Northern Messenger.* The journal's circulation rose from a few hundred
to several thousand before it was wrecked by the censor, for personal rather than
ideological reasons. In 1892 Dmitry Merezhkovsky produced a book called *Sym-
bols,* which showed the influence of the poetic conceptions of Baudelaire and Edgar Allan Poe. The following year he wrote *On the Present Condition of Russian
Literature and the Causes of Its Decline.* The work served as a sort of manifesto on
behalf of the younger artists in search of new directions who were beginning to
appear.

In 1894 Valery Briusov, a twenty-year-old student at Moscow University, published three short books whose intent was clearly *épater les bourgeois.* His poem of

---

[2] Wladimir Weidlé, *Russia: Absent and Present,* trans. John Day, 1952, p. 88.
[3] D. S. Mirsky, *A History of Russian Literature,* ed. Francis J. Whitfield, Knopf, 1949, pp. 324–325.

a single line: "O cover thy pale legs!" produced a sensation. But he was more than an *enfant terrible,* and soon he and his friends became recognized as a new school of poets, the "symbolists." Sometimes they were bitterly attacked, sometimes gently satirized, as by the philosopher Vladimir Soloviëv (which flattered and delighted Briusov). Briusov was joined first by the exuberant Constantine Balmont: "Who is equal to me in the power of song? No one!" A few years later there appeared the troubled but original Andrew Bely, and finally perhaps the most gifted of the symbolists, Alexander Blok. A number of other talented poets, as well as literary critics and hangers-on, grouped themselves around either Briusov's *Scorpio* publishing house in Moscow or the circle which met Wednesday evenings (usually until early morning) at the St. Petersburg apartment, known as "the Tower," of Viacheslav Ivanov. The name "symbolism" was taken from the French contemporary school which included Rimbaud and Mallarmé, but the Russians were far from simple imitators. They combined a crusading spirit of innovation with an effort at re-evaluation of the whole Russian literary past. The symbolists shared with certain of their rival and successor schools the aims of rejecting the "social command" for art and of developing appropriate techniques and forms for expressing their own individuality, philosophical convictions and mystical insights, and anticipations of the future.

By 1911 Nicholas Gumilëv, Anna Akhmatova, and Osip Mandelshtam were rebelling against symbolism, and they adopted the title "Acmeists." They declared, "We want to admire a rose because it is beautiful, not because it is a symbol of mystical purity." The Acmeists wanted to deepen the poetic sense of immediacy, but they were in accord with the symbolists in seeking to refine the craft of poetry. Gumilëv's *A Prayer* is illustrative:

> Fearful sun, menacing sun,
> Like the mad face
> Of God going through space,
>
> Burn the present, oh! sun,
> That the future may last,
> But protect the past.[4]

At the same time that the Acmeists were starting to work, the Futurists (taking their name at least from Italian futurism) were experimenting in rowdy and startling fashion with the uses of the sounds of words rather than or aside from their meaning. One of them, Vladimir Mayakovsky, became the declamatory poet of the Bolshevik Revolution but later proclaimed by his suicide his failure to adapt himself to the Soviet order.

---

[4] Trans. reprinted by permission of the publishers from Leonid Strakhovsky, *Craftsmen of the Word,* Harvard U. Press, 1949, p. 5.

Poetry rose from a position of neglect to impose "its own laws on fiction and drama," and on other prose as well. The distinctive work of Basil Rozanov, with its partly Christian, partly naturalistic religion of the family and procreation, and the searchings of Leo Shestov for God beyond logic and reason, are permeated with poetic feeling. The stories and plays of Anton Chekhov, which became so well known in the West, the novellas of Ivan Bunin, such as *The Gentleman from San Francisco,* much of the work of Leonid Andreyev, who seemed to be an old-style "realist," and particularly the writing of the prose symbolist Alexis Remizov, reflect the impact of the new poetic currents of the time. The new aesthetic and individualist ideas were debated and discussed in such places as Ivanov's "Tower" apartment. There were many other such gathering points; some of the futurists preferred the cafes. For the leading lights of the Silver Age, it was a period of passionate though often transitory love affairs and marriages, stormy and broken friendships, and slightly aberrant ideological quests, but it was an exciting time to be alive.

A type of writing very different in spirit from the modernists was developed by Maxim Gorky, to some extent by Leonid Andreyev, and several others. Gorky rose rapidly from a provincial proletarian background to national renown; by 1900 he became the most popular writer in Russia. He was a Social Democrat and, when the party split, became a Bolshevik. In a few years, however, as Mirsky indicates, Gorky sank to the level of Bolshevik "party pet." Before the Revolution of 1905 Andreyev displaced him in public favor, but his vogue was transitory. If any single fad succeeded that of Andreyev, it was the brief cult of Artsybashev, whose artistically crude, straightforwardly sexual novel, *Sanin,* experienced a *succès fou* and was read for a time by all the students, waitresses, and clerks, no doubt often with undesirable moral consequences. *Sanin* was, however, only a somewhat unpleasant bubble on the surface of the great churning and boiling pot of the Russian literary renaissance. The politically single-minded and artistically unimaginative atmosphere of the 1880's had yielded to a whole spectrum of diverse creative currents, developing side by side.

Music and Painting

The death of Dostoevsky in 1881 and that of Turgenev in 1883 mark the passing of the great age of the Russian novel;[5] in somewhat similar fashion the passing of Mussorgsky in 1881 and that of Tchaikovsky in 1893 bring to an end the age of solitary giants and inaugurate a period of gifted individual diversity in music. Serious professional training in music had begun in Russia only in the 1860's owing

---

[5] Tolstoy lived until 1910, but the religious experience he underwent in 1880 separated his later works somewhat from those of the other great novelists.

largely to the schools established in the two capitals by the brothers Anton and Nicholas Rubinstein.

The influence of the rather conventional and Westernized schools was challenged in the same decade by a group of talented amateurs, led by Mily Balakirev, who became known as the "Mighty Band" (*Moguchaia Kuchka*). The group aggressively espoused "Russian" music, reflecting the same nationalism which was expressed, although rather less attractively, in the policy of Alexander III. Modest Mussorgsky represented, especially with his two great operas *Boris Godunov* and *Khovanshchina,* the highest achievements of this circle. A survivor of the Mighty Band, Nicholas Rimsky-Korsakov, arranged both of Mussorgsky's masterpieces and also Alexander Borodin's *Prince Igor,* unfinished at his death in 1887. Rimsky-Korsakov lived until 1908, writing distinguished music, but by the time of his death new currents had invaded the musical scene. Sergei Rachmaninov attempted to continue the lyric tradition of Tchaikovsky, but the change in fashions left him more popular abroad than in Russia.

In the 1890's, as Miliukov puts it, "we approach the moment when, like painting, Russian music became cosmopolitan without, however, losing its national character."[6] The pioneer of the new movement was Alexander Skriabin, fragile, iconoclastic, and addicted to such odd ideas as that of a "Mystery," wherein all would join the performance and there would be no audience. He spent much time in the West. Western composers like Debussy and Ravel were beginning to discover Russian music and were considerably influenced by Mussorgsky fifteen years after his death. Western acclaim and the changing public mood in Russia combined to revive Mussorgsky's operas, with leading roles sung by the glorious voice of Fëdor Chaliapin. Following the Revolution of 1905 *Boris Godunov* and *Khovanshchina* were triumphantly performed both in Russia and the West.

The new currents in music were linked with innovations in literature and the visual arts in the *World of Art (Mir Iskusstva)* group, formed in 1898 by Sergei Diagilev and others, which published a magazine of the same name until 1902. They included the impressionism of Vladimir Rebikov, who set poems of the symbolists Balmont and Briusov to music, and the expressionism of Igor Stravinsky, as shown in *The Fire Bird,* which he composed for the Ballet Russe in 1910, and his subsequent *Petrushka* and *The Rite of Spring.* In this period Stravinsky was justifiably compared with the German Schoenberg. Stravinsky's music contained exotic and also "Russian" elements, but the music and the composer himself were soon to be absorbed into Europe, and later America. Sergei Prokofiev, in such early works as his *Classical Symphony,* returned to more conventional forms but with a far from antiquarian spirit. Stravinsky soon did much the same thing, but the two differed both as musicians and men; Prokofiev be-

---

[6] Paul Miliukov, *Outlines of Russian Culture: Part III: Architecture, Painting, and Music,* ed. Michael Karpovich, trans. U. of Pennsylvania Press, 1943, p. 121.

came a Soviet composer, whereas Stravinsky in an important sense ceased to be Russian at all. Especially after Diagilev's Festival of Russian Music in Paris in 1907, the last years of the tsarist period witnessed a fruitful and congenial interchange and appreciation between musicians and publics of Russia and the West.

In painting as in music a change of line occurred in the 1890's. Academic training in painting was older than in music, dating back to the organization of the Academy of Arts in St. Petersburg under Catherine II (its founding date was even earlier, 1758). In the 1850's a rebellion against the academism of St. Petersburg was organized by Moscow painters at about the same time that a new art school was founded there. The rebels, who called themselves the Itinerants, were strongly civic-minded, realist, and nationalist in a way which invites comparison with the Mighty Band in music. Their outstanding painter, Ilia Repin, produced works of social message such as the famed "Volga Boatmen," as well as of historical realism, like the hair-raising "Ivan the Terrible Embracing the Body of His Son," at which knots of people gaze in horror in Moscow's Tretiakov Gallery to this day.

As Alexander Benois wrote in 1902, "in the seventies and even in the eighties there was no connection between [the Russian painters] and the truly creative art in the West. … But during the last ten years conditions have changed very rapidly. Thanks to frequent exhibitions of the works of Western artists in St. Petersburg and Moscow, the greater accessibility of foreign travel, and wide circulation of illustrated art publications, we were brought nearer to the West. … We saw our own art from a different point of view."[7] The young artistic revolutionaries, banding together in *The World of Art* group, repudiated both traditional academism and Itinerant realism. However, Repin, who was by that time both dean of the Academy and the foremost Itinerant, belonged to their group for a time, which illustrates their lack of insistence on a single artistic line.

The young men of *The World of Art* sought inspiration in the modern West and in the Orient. They also looked to Russia's own artistic heritage, especially its medieval iconography. Igor Grabar and other members of the group were instrumental in rediscovering these forgotten masterpieces and in establishing the study and restoration of them on a scientific footing. Victor Surikov, who painted a memorable canvas of Yermak's successful assault on the Tatar khanate of Sibir and a striking picture of the *"Boyarynia Morozova,"* was known for his historical subjects but praised by *The World of Art* group for his artistic sense. The French impressionist influence was displayed by Arkhip Kuindzhi, the colors of whose paintings have unfortunately darkened, and the less derivative Isaac Levitan and Valentine Serov. Michael Vrubel used subjects drawn from folklore but applied to them an inner vision, comparable to that of William Blake, shown in such paintings as "The Demon." The outstanding painters of *The World of Art* group itself,

---

[7] Quoted in Miliukov, *op. cit.,* p. 63.

as distinguished from those influenced by or admired by it, include Alexander Benois and Nicholas Roerich.

The Cultural Scene

The formation of *The World of Art* group, whose influence owed most to Sergei Diagilev, a young man who was an artist but even more an impresario, and the foundation a little later of the Moscow Art Theater by Stanislavsky and Nemirovich-Danchenko, gave great impetus to the new movements in the arts. Diagilev was instrumental in the rapid development of a superb ballet which, fusing the arts of scenery painting, choreography, and music, assumed first place in the world and kept it. The Ballet Russe, founded in 1900, developed such peerless dancers as Nijinsky and Pavlova. The first puzzling, then popular, plays of Chekhov, wherein characters were made "equal" in prominence for purposes of portrayal by the Art Theater company, also illustrated the new threads which were linking the individual arts to each other. The Russian cultural scene became known in the West. In 1900 the paintings of Russian artists were shown at the Paris Exposition; in 1906 an Exhibition of Russian Art was held in Paris; in 1906 the Ballet Russe began its Western seasons. *The World of Art* group's rediscovery of the Russian artistic past, especially the icon, was shared with Europe and America.

Simultaneously the Russian public gained increased familiarity with the great historic figures and productions of West European culture. Merezhkovsky began the work of popularization with such books as *The Romance of Leonardo da Vinci*, and it was continued by others with the result that many more Russians read *Faust* and the *Divine Comedy,* Molière and Shakespeare, Balzac and Dickens, than ever before. The literate public was more than ever conscious of the distinction which Russia had attained within European culture without sacrificing Russian individuality. After Dostoevsky and Tolstoy, Russia no longer needed to prove that she could produce artistic geniuses of the first magnitude. For the moment there were no more giants in Russia, nor in the West either. The difference between the cultural level of Eastern and Western Europe was no longer such as to make Slavophiles glorify it or Westernizers deprecate it. The cultural base of the Silver Age was solider and broader by far than that of the Golden Age.

The artistic renaissance was accompanied by new philosophical searchings of diverse kinds. In the 1890's, Mirsky suggests, "between atheism and progress, on the one hand, and religion and political reaction, on the other, the alliance was complete. To dissolve these alliances, and to *undermine the supremacy of political over cultural and individual values,* was the task of the generation of intellectuals who came of age in the last decade of the nineteenth century" (italics mine).[8]

---

[8] Mirsky, *op. cit.,* p. 407.

To assert the independence of cultural and individual values meant different things to different people. To Chekhov, it meant explaining to "those who read between the lines trying to find a definite trend of thought" that "I am neither liberal nor conservative, nor gradualist, nor ascetic, nor indifferentist. I should like to be an independent artist—and that is all. ... Any trade mark or label to me means a prejudice." Chekhov had no religious faith nor any interest in philosophy pursued as an independent discipline; his outlook was profoundly influenced by his medical and scientific training. To Ivanov-Razumnik and Alexander Blok, independence meant not avoiding politics but viewing political developments from the standpoint of a transcendent socialist messianism, and they later welcomed the Bolshevik Revolution as a means of realizing the mission of the "Scythians" (Blok wrote a poem with that title) to change the world. To such men as Nicholas Berdiaev, Sergei Bulgakov, Paul Novgorodtsev, and others who wrote a symposium called *Signposts (Vekhi)* in 1909, independence meant efforts to apply the insights of Christianity and idealistic liberalism to the post-1905 situation. From 1901 Merezhkovsky, his wife Zinaida Gippius, and others joined with Orthodox clergy to try to cross the long-existing gulf between secular intellectuals and Christians, both clerical and lay, in the Religio-Philosophical Meetings and Societies that existed in St. Petersburg, Moscow, and Kiev.[9]

The old civic morality of the radical, socialist, and atheist intelligentsia was being undermined by the new civic morality of the Christian liberals of *Signposts,* by the scientific individualism of Chekhov, and by other philosophical currents. The result was a creative and fruitful colloquy among diverse viewpoints, which gave the artist and thinker the opportunity to choose the concept of obligation he preferred, to join a group or not, to subordinate his art to his politics (if he had any) or not, to adopt his own view of his or Russia's place in the world and the future.

Art Appreciation and Education

The overall effect of the Silver Age was simultaneously to extend the base and raise the level of cultural activity. According to Weidlé,

> Even during the war, on the very outbreak of the revolution, the reading of a new poem by Alexander Blok or Anna Akhmatova was for many an important personal event, a joy or an anguish, an intimate communion with reality. When Scriabin was at the piano, his music evoked an emotion that was very much more than mere aesthetic pleasure. To hear Shaliapin or Sobinov, to see a Meyerhold production or one at the Art Theatre, to be transported once more by that strange voice of the great Komissarjevskaia, young students of both sexes would queue at the box-offices in

---

[9] George F. Putnam, *Russian Alternatives to Marxism: Christian Socialism and Idealistic Liberalism in Twentieth-Century Russia,* U. of Tennessee Press, 1977.

their hundreds all night. New writers and artists seemed to be born every day; universities and picture-galleries, every institution devoted to the arts or sciences or letters, were being transformed or modernised under one's very eyes; the country's past was being studied with more love than ever, and with more objectivity. Ikons, the most beautiful painting that Russia had ever produced, were being discovered once more after being forgotten for centuries. Privately, too, there were fine collections being made of pictures and drawings, books, engravings and all works of art; exhibitions, both of ancient and modern art, could always be sure of attracting crowds. Ancient churches throughout the country, ancient towns and dwelling-houses, were now for the first time being gazed on with wonder not only by artists but by ordinary travellers.[10]

What Weidlé is pointing out is that the art of the Silver Age evoked a wide public response—in fact, one wider than ever before. Only a relatively few people could be invited to Ivanov's apartment on Wednesday evenings, but multitudes could be induced to look again at the monuments of their country's rich past with the "shock of recognition." Even the rural folk could be persuaded to keep alive their traditional or even half-forgotten arts, such as the lacquer-painting of Palekh or the singing of ancient poems in the Lake Onega district, their dances and costume-making, when the educated urbanites showed interest through visits and questions or even a merely financial demand for such things.

Mass education may not necessarily produce mass interest in the fine arts, but it is essential if public awareness of creative effort is to be extensive. And education was moving in the direction of mass instruction. In 1887 Minister of Education Delianov had ordered the schools to get rid of the children of "coachmen, valets, cooks, washerwomen, small shop-keepers and other people whose children it would be wrong to draw away from the environment to which they belong." Delianov correctly observed the influx of lower-class children into Russian schools, but he was unable to check it.

In 1908 the Third Duma passed a bill providing for free and compulsory public instruction for all children aged eight to eleven. The plan, which required a great expansion of school building and teacher training, was scheduled for realization in 1922. In 1911 a much more ambitious bill was passed by the Duma but was rejected by the Imperial Council. Count P. N. Ignatiev, who was appointed minister of education in 1915, had still more sweeping plans for expansion and reorganization of public education, but there was no time for their consideration before the Revolution.

The intellectuals who produced the Silver Age and the enlarged audience for the arts which popular education was building provide impressive evidence of the fact that in the early twentieth century Russia was finding a new cultural footing for herself. Diagilev and Stanislavsky, Nijinsky and Pavlova, Rimsky-Korsakov

---

[10] Weidlé, *op. cit.*, pp. 90–91.

and Stravinsky, Tolstoy and Chekhov, Gorky and Blok became European and world figures in their lifetime, and there were many innovators of real merit who deserved wider recognition outside Russia than could be gained before the Revolution. In the realm of culture, Russia was more nearly at one with Europe than she had been at any time since the days of the Kievan state.

5

Growth of the Russian Economy

Prerevolutionary Agriculture

Before the Revolution the Eastern Slavic peasant is often thought to have two characteristics that impeded any kind of development as an independent farmer in American or West European fashion and provided ample raw material for a revolution. They were thought to be his strongly rooted instincts for collective rather than family farming and his utter misery, stemming from his poverty. Both impressions need correction. He and his family never farmed their scattered strips collectively; they tilled, planted, and harvested their own fields, and their attitude toward collective farming was demonstrated about as clearly as to be found in the social history of any country, at least in historic times, by their fierce resistance to collectivization under the Communists. Their economic situation was far from hopeless and in a number of ways it was improving on the eve of the Revolution.

To be sure, there were serious problems, as regards both land tenure and land use. The peasants lived in communes of two types: chiefly, redistributory in Great Russia, hereditary-tenure in Belarus and Ukraine; after Emancipation, the commune was the owner of the land. Before Emancipation their personal status was also of two types: they were either serfs, in effect the private property of private landowners or gentry, or state peasants, who lived and worked on land owned by the state. A small number were also *udel* (sometimes called "appanage") peasants, whose landowners were members of the imperial family, or had the Orthodox church for landlord. Under serfdom the peasants said, "We are yours, but the land is ours." In 1861 serfholding was abolished and the peasant was no longer "yours," though the process took decades to work out, and in 1866 the state peasant was given comparable benefits. A small part of the land the peasant had previously farmed for himself was "cut off" and retained in the manorial land he had farmed for the lord; and he received less pasture and forest than he had been able to use before.

However, the chief defect of Emancipation was probably financial: the redemption payments the peasant had to pay to the government (which in turn paid the landlord in interest-bearing certificates) were too high, based on capitalizing money dues (*obrok,* common in the north) and converting labor dues (*barshchina,* common in the richer land of the south) into money dues. But re-demption dues were abolished and most arrears written off effective in 1907. The peasant may have been dealt with in niggardly fashion at Emancipation, but in succeeding decades he corrected part of the problem. From 1861 to 1914, in forty-seven out of fifty provinces of European Russia, the landholding of the lord de-creased from 85 million desiatinas to 39 million and the peasant got most of it.[1] Nevertheless the peasant tended to believe that his main problem was lack of land, which ought to be corrected by acquiring (through legislation, or if not perhaps seizure) the land of the lord (often, in 1917, he seized the land of his ancestor's lord and no other). For the most part the intelligentsia believed as the peasant did, de-spite the fact that there was, in the view of some scholars, "a significantly more ra-tional distribution of landholding than in the most developed countries." More-over, in contrast to most countries of the third world, the trend was for the small peasant to gain more land.[2] There remained in any case little land in the lords' hands to be taken, and the way to improve the peasants' situation lay in changing the pattern of land use, rather than in simply increasing the amount to be tilled in the old way. But the peasant, and the *intelligent,* did not think so, and misconceptions may be politically more important than realities.

There is a question about how serious the peasant was about private property as against mere occupation of land. In the communes where redistribution was practiced it tended to discourage improvement, though there is evidence that some improved land was excluded from the process.[3] Redistribution is thought to date from Peter the Great's soul (or poll, that is, head) tax in 1724; the idea was to make the payment of the tax equitable by making the amount and quality of land held reflect the size of family taxed. That reason disappeared with the tax itself in 1886, and private holdings grew apace.

The situation as regards land use was one of moderate improvement. The zemstvo-employed agronomists were doing their best to advise and assist the peasant. Whatever the peasant's type of commune or status, he farmed according to the so-called three-field system. A given field was sown in successive years with a winter grain, then with a spring grain, then left fallow; thus one out of three fields lay fallow in any given year. One obvious need, easy to meet, was to plant nitrogen-fixing grasses in the "fallow" field, thereby increasing the supply of fod-der and improving livestock, and in the later nineteenth century many peasants

---

[1] Arcadius Kahan, *Russian Economic History: The Nineteenth Century,* U. of Chicago Press, 1989, pp. 8–9.

[2] Heinz-Dietrich Löwe, *Die Lage der Bauern in Russland, 1880–1905,* St. Katharinen, Scripta Mercaturae Verlag, 1987, p. 377.

[3] Peter Gatrell, *The Tsarist Economy 1850–1917,* B. T. Batsford, Ltd., London, 1986, p. 123.

were doing so.[4] Iron plows were also replacing the ancient wooden variety in some areas.

Transport remained difficult. Roads were not very passable in either spring or fall, and maintenance was poor if it existed at all. For many months rivers were frozen but not dependably so; often they were not navigable or traversable by vehicle. It was therefore of first importance to have a good network of railways, and in the nineteenth century they were built rapidly, especially in the decades 1865 to 1875 and 1890 to 1900, mainly by the state. Nevertheless imperial Russia became a great grain exporter, as contrasted with the Soviet period, through Odessa. In addition to grain, quantities of Siberian butter (much of it produced by cooperatives) and forest products were sent out through Riga and elsewhere to western Europe. Minister of Finance I. A. Vyshnegradsky (1887–1892) was reported to have said, "We may go hungry but we must export grain," but in fact, after the famine of 1891–1892, the country seldom went hungry though it exported in quantity.

Russia's Industrial Revolution

As a result of both state and private enterprise before and during the reign of Peter the Great, Russia came to produce substantial quantities of pig iron; between 1750 and 1800, half of the output of the Ural factories went to Europe, three-quarters of that to Great Britain. It also produced many textiles, to make uniforms for the army but also to supply civilian demand, especially woolens to begin with; linen and cotton came later.

The beginning of Russia's industrial revolution may be dated to the 1840's and 1850's.[5] "Congress Poland" (the part given to Russia by the Congress of Vienna) led the way; its industrialization in the 1870's became rapid, especially in metal and textiles. As demand increased for iron in the nineteenth century, the Ural factories could not keep up, and foreign capital was called in to develop the south, where coal and iron were close to each other. The pioneer was an Englishman, J. Hughes, who gave his name to Yuzovka (today Donetsk). By 1900 the south forged ahead of Poland in metals, while St. Petersburg and Moscow surpassed her in textiles.

As in England, the Industrial Revolution in Russia owed much to the growth of cotton manufacturing, beginning in Ivanovo-Voznesensk and spreading into the Vladimir and Moscow provinces. A German named Knoop, who had been a clerk in England, equipped and built a number of factories in the middle of the century. A popular couplet of the 1840's ran: "No church without a *pop* [priest], No mill without a Knoop." By that time the new cotton industry's employees con-

---

[4] Ibid., p. 125.
[5] Kahan, *op cit.*, p. 13.

sisted almost entirely of hired rather than serf laborers. Whereas Russia up till 1800 produced more pig iron than England, it fell far behind in the subsequent decades, partly because of the lower output of the serf workers used in the Ural plants.

The inferior productivity of serf labor in industry was one factor in bringing about the freeing of the serfs, but probably more important was the mounting number of peasant revolts during the reign of Nicholas I. The precipitating factor for all the Great Reforms of Alexander II, including Emancipation, was the Crimean War, which exposed the economic and other weaknesses of Russian society in glaring fashion. Emancipation was favored by many revolutionaries who thought chiefly in terms of the eventual coming of socialism, and by officials, including Alexander II himself, who thought in terms of order and justice. Probably few gentry or merchants clearly anticipated the profits which agriculture or industry based on free labor might bring, and in fact many were unable to make the transition to capitalism and were ultimately ruined by the Emancipation.

Others managed to become agricultural or industrial entrepreneurs. To do so they required not only free labor, but also capital. Already there were sizable private fortunes in Russia, derived originally from such diverse sources as war booty, military contracts, gifts of the ruling house, private banking, leases, monopolies, and the like. In addition former serf-owners received government bonds (for whose value the ex-serfs had to reimburse the state) in payment of the land taken from them and given the peasants at Emancipation. In the post-Great Reform era, the entrepreneurs were drawn partly from the previously wealthy class, but also it was easier for men from the lower ranks of society to rise in status and to accumulate capital. By the end of the nineteenth century a new industrialist class, including such families as the Morozovs and the Guchkovs, was becoming both powerful and socially acceptable. Meanwhile there emerged a new proletariat, recruited from the former household serfs (who were freed without land) and also from former state and private serfs who sought a livelihood in the growing industries.

Within a generation after Emancipation the Industrial Revolution had begun to make its mark upon Russia, but old habits lingered. The Western, or at least British, traditions of enterprise, risk, and self-help did not thrive in Russia, partly because state control had been so extensive for so long. Western technology began to be borrowed early but was extended slowly. Not until the 1890's did mechanical weaving take over the cotton industry, open-hearth methods the steel industry; rotary and turbine methods of oil-drilling were not tested until 1911. Railway construction began in 1836 but an extensive network built and run by Russians did not make headway until the 1890's. As a result of the technical lag in Russia, sometimes remarkable inventions appeared, such as Lodygin's incandescent lamp and Popov's wireless telegraph, which never became widely known because there was no place to use them under the technological conditions prevailing in Russia.

The gentry who continued to try to live on their land by using the hired labor of their former serfs or other peasants did less well than the new industrialists. There was ample demand in the West for Russian agricultural products, especially bread grains, and much was shipped out through Odessa and other ports. During the early seventies it was profitable to export, but after 1875 world grain prices began to turn downward, and by 1894 Russian wheat and rye export prices had declined by approximately a third. The crop failure and subsequent famine of 1891–1892, coming on the heels of the fall in prices, brought disaster to many producers. Few of the gentry had had reason to develop habits of thrift and financial foresight, and their burden of debts, in many cases already heavy before Emancipation, now became almost insupportable. Neither the efforts of Alexander III's ministers nor their own exertions were able to arrest the decline of the gentry, which continued generally down to the Revolution.

During the seventies and eighties the growth of industry was steady but not yet spectacular. Foreigners continued to play a prominent role, witness the Swedish Nobel brothers' oil operations in Baku. Nevertheless, Russians furnished most of the capital for the more than three hundred joint-stock companies which were founded in the sixties and seventies. Most of these were banks, railroads, and steamship companies, but some capital also went into factory enterprise. The new private banks were supplemented by a reorganized State Bank.

Industrial and commercial expansion was checked somewhat by a depression in 1873–1875 and another in 1881–1882. The plight of the workers, who toiled fourteen hours a day or more for low wages and under inadequate conditions of sanitation and safety, became still worse. The new enterprises did not recover immediately from the slump, and it was only around 1890 that a pronounced upturn in business activity occurred.

The Prosperity of the 1890's

The upturn, however, soon became a boom. During the 1890's the number of enterprises increased by over a quarter, the number of workers by almost 60% and the value of production more than doubled. Such data indicate that industry was becoming increasingly concentrated in plants with a large labor force. Concentration tended to be geographical as well, rapid growth taking place in a small number of industrial regions. The coal industry almost tripled its output in the 1890's, the Donets Basin coming to produce almost 70% of the total in 1900. The oil industry also increased its production by nearly three times; in 1900 Baku furnished 95% of it. Iron ore output was more than tripled; over half in 1900 came from Krivoi Rog and the surrounding region of Ukraine, while the old Ural iron industry faded into insignificance. Cotton and other industries also underwent increasing concentration. It has been computed that almost half of all industrial workers in Russia in 1902 were employed by plants with a labor force numbering one thousand or more.

One of the most striking aspects of the boom of the 1890's was railway construction. Russia's vast land area still suffered severely from poor communications. In the first half of the seventies 5,000 miles of rail lines were laid, but thereafter progress lagged for fifteen years. This figure was nearly reached again in the first half of the nineties, and in the second half over 10,000 miles of line were built. This was the period of greatest construction before the Revolution, but Russia was still left with a far less adequate rail network than the advanced industrial powers of Western Europe. About half of the capital used for the building of railways came from the central government, which also guaranteed a portion of the private loans employed. A large share of these state funds came from indirect taxation, especially from the vodka monopoly. One is tempted to say that even if Russia's communications were landbound, they had an extensive liquid foundation.

Of the capital invested in Russia's railroads in 1900, some 70% came from the government, which had expended nearly half of its share during the 1890's alone. Only about 7% came from foreign investment. Nevertheless the outside funds which had gone into railways were significant, for they formed the first sizable Western investment in the Russian economy. Once foreign capital invaded the Russian rail network, it spread rapidly into Russian industries as well. Sergei Witte, minister of finance from 1892 to 1903 who did his best to stimulate industrial development generally, worked hard to attract Western capital in order to hasten the process. Whereas investment from other countries accounted for over a third of all corporation capital in 1890, it approached one-half of the total in 1900. In mining, for example, its share reached 70%, though it was only 42% in metallurgy, and in textiles it was negligible.

In 1900 the nation holding the largest share of foreign investment was Belgium, with almost 300 million rubles; next came France and Germany with around 220 million rubles each; Britain's share was about 135 million, and America's only 8 million. France had been first in 1890, and by 1914 she was first again, with about one-third of all nongovernmental foreign investments, while next in order came Britain, Germany, and Belgium. The French investors went heavily into mining and metallurgy, the British into mining, especially in the Urals and eastward, the Germans into a number of industries particularly in the western regions, the Belgians into the metallurgy of Ukraine.

Witte was also instrumental in the floating of large government loans, much of the proceeds of which were expended by the Russian government in railway and industrial development. In 1914 nearly half of the national debt was held abroad, and of this figure France held a preponderant 80%. Although it was German loans that helped carry through the Russo-Japanese War, both public and private French money had a greater influence on Russian foreign policy and was one important consideration in Russia's alignment with the Entente powers. It also enabled the government to ride out the Revolution of 1905 and the uncertain period of the First Duma. Witte supported the protectionist tariff which had been enacted in 1891, following a policy then fashionable in the West. However, it led to two tariff wars with Germany over grain prices, at the beginning and end of his ministry, which embittered Russo-German relations and further tightened the connection with the French.

Toward the middle of the nineties, the growing industrial proletariat had begun to voice protests at the abominable working conditions prevailing in the new factories. There was a swiftly increasing demand for labor, which was partly met by a new outpouring of peasants into industry on the heels of the disastrous famine of 1891–1892. However, the demand remained unsatisfied, and the workers felt themselves in a strong position to insist that they benefit from the boom of the nineties. Beginning in 1894 a wave of strikes gained momentum in and near St. Petersburg up to the time of the textile strike in the summer of 1896 and spread into the Moscow region. The government responded by enacting the first important piece of tsarist labor legislation, in June 1897. The law limited the workday to eleven and a half hours and prohibited labor on Sundays and holidays in plants employing more than twenty workers; it also provided for inspection and enforcement. Actually inspection was unevenly carried out, but the fact remained that strikes had brought about significant government intervention on the workers' side. It is a paradox that by stepping in, the government strengthened the hand of those revolutionaries who told the workers that strikes should be political rather than economic. There were no large labor unions before 1905, and up to 1917 they remained weak; in both revolutionary years the intelligentsia assumed leadership of the workers virtually by default.

Witte's policy of industrialization continued to bear fruit after his effort to solve the labor crisis through the 1897 law. In the field of government finance he achieved his greatest success by introducing the gold standard in 1897. Russia had nominally possessed silver convertibility for a few years following 1840, but that system had collapsed before it was officially abandoned in 1858. Although the landowners profited from the existence of an unstable paper currency, which produced in effect a financial premium for exporters, Witte was not greatly concerned about them. His introduction of a gold currency was designed to increase the industrialists' ability to attract foreign capital, as well as to stabilize the financial side of domestic trade. A painful effort to build up gold reserves succeeded in raising them above the value of the notes in circulation by 1897, at which time the new system was enacted into law.

Russian industry grew rapidly in the nineties; in fact, more rapidly than the industry of the other major powers. From 1880 to 1900 Russia moved from seventh to fourth place in the smelting of pig iron, and the percentage increase in output of iron, coal, and cotton textiles was greater than in any other country including the United States. Such rapid industrial growth incidentally settled the argument which raged between the populists and the Marxists during the 1890's as to whether Russia could somehow escape "capitalism."

In the Empire's borderlands there was considerable industrial development. Poland's industry, especially in textiles, grew rapidly and spawned a more literate and impatient proletariat than that of Russia. Baku in Transcaucasia was Russia's greatest oil center, and Georgia produced important quantities of manganese, coal, etc. Tashkent and other cities of Turkestan developed cotton-ginning and other mills. Although during this period the chief feature of the Siberian economy was the development of peasant agriculture by millions of new immigrants, Siberia also came to produce butter, forest products, and other goods which were sold in quantity west of the Urals and abroad.

Bust and Boom

As the decade of the 1890's ended, Russia's prosperity faltered and halted. By 1899 a business crisis common to all of Europe was being felt in Russia. Prices of finished goods began to fall rapidly, and industrial output slackened. Although a number of workers were discharged, and the bargaining position of labor was weakened, a new strike movement made its appearance in 1902–1903. This time the Marxist agitators had a puzzling competitor for the leadership of organized workers, the government itself. The experiment in "police socialism," authored by Zubatov, chief of the Moscow secret police, was somewhat too successful, and after the strikes of the summer of 1903 it was largely abandoned. The workers had genuine grievances and were determined to air them, but only the revolutionary leaders were prepared to furnish direction.

An industrial revival began in 1903 but the strike movement continued. The labor scene remained turbulent until the great political strikes which occurred during the Revolution of 1905. The year 1904 saw a new peak in industrial production, but partly owing to the disturbance in the economy which accompanied the revolutionary events, there followed four years of leveling off or slight decrease in output.

In 1909 a new upsurge began. The major trends continued much as before. Industrial production became even further concentrated in plants which had a large labor force. The newer regions, for example the Donets Basin, improved their position vis-à-vis the older ones, such as the Urals. In general Russian capitalism went on expanding rapidly, although the rate of growth seems to have leveled off somewhat. According to Molotov, per capita production in Russia was one-eighth of that of the United States in 1900, but dropped to one-eleventh in 1913; it was one-sixth of Germany's in 1900, one-eighth in 1913.[6] However, Russia had permanently become one of the world's major industrial producer nations.

An important feature of the two decades following 1900 was the formation of syndicates and concentration of ownership in Russia's industrial structure. In 1902 a great metallurgical syndicate (*Prodamet*) was formed to sell the metal produced by plants whose output was almost three-quarters of all metal sales, and an agreement was soon reached to regulate and apportion production, prices, and

---

[6] Cited by Peter I. Lyashchenko, *History of the National Economy of Russia to the 1917 Revolution*, trans., Macmillan, 1949, p. 674.

market territory. However, the plants at Yuzovka in Ukraine and the Polish mills stayed out of this arrangement. Syndicates were also formed for the sale of iron pipes, special-alloy pig iron and mined ore, coming to include the greater part of the mining and metallurgy of the south. The Ural region established other and weaker syndicates. Farm machinery and railway car construction industries followed suit. About three-quarters of all coal production was syndicated in the combination called *Produgol.* Such associations were less conspicuous in light industry; they made some headway in maritime shipping enterprise. In general, the type of amalgamation taking place was not the formation of unified trusts, but syndicates based on sales agreements. No important trusts appeared in tsarist Russia; that remained for the Soviets to bring about under state ownership and control.

By 1909 to 1913 Russia was investing 12% of its national income, about one-fifth of that abroad.[7] The foreign investment was greater, but domestic contribution to capital formation was impressive. On the eve of the war Germany led in Russian foreign trade; she took one-third of Russia's exports and supplied 47% of her imports, England 19% and 12%. Domestic production was climbing rapidly. Pig iron output rose from 175 to 283 million poods; iron and steel, from 163 to 246; coal, from 1,591 to 2,214.[8] Oil lagged, and did not reach the 1905 level again before the Revolution, largely because of the damage done to the Baku oilfields during the Revolution of 1905. Farm machinery, cotton and linen output increased, and sugar production mounted swiftly. Under the conditions of economic prosperity and greater political freedom (resulting from the October Manifesto) in the final years of tsarism, labor unions made some progress, although not enough to produce a leadership capable of competing effectively with the revolutionaries. One union complained that "the membership ... resembles rather a crowd of wandering gypsies than a properly organized body." It is true that stable organization and solidarity among members tended to be only gradually realized in other industrial countries, but Russia's union movement did not exist long enough to permit any estimate of how it might have developed.

In the period between revolutions agriculture underwent some of the most dramatic changes in the whole Russian economy. Certain of these changes, such as the attempted destruction of the ancient village commune and the enclosure of individual land under the Stolypin laws, had social and political as well as economic causes and results. The appearance of large numbers of peasants who had full legal title to the land they worked, and the spread of enclosed farms (of one contiguous plot as contrasted with the scattered-strip system characteristic of the communal farms), placed small independent agriculture on a much more solid

---

[7] Gatrell, *Tsarist Economy,* pp. 228–229, but see F. V. Carstensen's cautions cited by Gatrell regarding the figures.

[8] A pood equals 36 pounds.

footing than before. Although the large landowners continued to decline and even disappear from the economic scene, it appears that the peasantry was able not only to fill the gap thereby created in the export market but also to increase the volume of agricultural products sent abroad. The value of cereal products exported increased 133% between 1901–1905 and 1911–1913; the value of animal products 241%. Much of the produce of the independent peasant farms was for home consumption; it improved diet and health without appearing in trade statistics.

At the outbreak of the war, the economic structure of Russia presented a mixed picture of strength and weakness, rapid and slow development, foreign and domestic control, profit and loss, governmental fiat and private initiative. During World War I Russia failed to utilize its wealth and resources to the maximum. In part the failure must be laid to the economy: the backwardness of technique, the inefficiency of business methods, the inadequate transportation system, and other structural weaknesses. However, even more important, and probably decisive, was the misdirection or lack of direction of industrial effort on the part of the government, which in 1914 lay in the hands of the least capable officials on the scene for a generation, perhaps for a century or more.

6

The Last Years
of Tsarism

Stolypin and the Political Parties

When the First Duma was dissolved in 1906, the tsar appointed Peter Stolypin prime minister. He was the ablest and most clearsighted official to serve Nicholas II and the best government servant since Michael Speransky, a century earlier. His policy was twofold: to restore order and institute reform. That is, he attempted to break up the revolutionary groups and also to undermine their popular support by carrying through necessary social and political changes. He was a monarchist, but he was also a constitutionalist, and he wished to work harmoniously with the new Duma in the passage of reform legislation.

He staked almost everything on turning the peasant into a small proprietor. Knowing the government had lost the loyalty of the village, he sought to regain it by improving the peasant's economic position and setting him on the road to prosperity. Born in Dresden, Stolypin was a landowner in Kovno. As governor of Grodno (both western provinces) he had observed something striking. By force of example from their German neighbors, who farmed on small plots, peasants were beginning to dissolve their communes and consolidate the scattered strips into farmsteads. Stolypin concluded—as Witte before him had finally done—that the remedy for Russia's agrarian ills should begin with abolishing the commune and transforming the peasant into a Western-style farmer who owned his land. There-fore, beginning in late 1906, the prime minister introduced laws that enabled him to do so in two stages: first he could obtain title as full owner of the scattered strips currently allotted for his use, then he could enclose them (a process prop-erly termed "commassation") in a single plot through transfer within the village. The first step was easy, consisting in simply drawing up legal papers; the second entailed an immensely complex surveying operation, overshadowing in difficulty the Emancipation itself.

The results were soon to confound the skeptics—of whom there were many, including all of the opposition parties. As the movement gained momentum, Stolypin exulted, "You cannot stop it with cannon." The scorn of the revolutionaries changed to alarm, and Lenin grumbled, "The homesteads are helping out a handful of the rich. But the masses continue to starve as heretofore." Nevertheless he clearly recognized that if Stolypin's program continued it would make revolution immeasurably more difficult to bring about. By 1917 some two-thirds of peasant households had completed the first step, that of obtaining title. One tenth had finished the immeasurably more complex step of commassation and had become independent farmers. Whether or not, as Robinson has suggested,[1] the success of the Stolypin program was in large part accounted for by governmental pressure, there is no contesting its remarkable results. In the view of many scholars, the program succeeded because it was compatible with one of the most deepseated aspirations of the Russian peasantry, the desire to own and manage their own land.

Stolypin's relations with the Dumas were less successful than his land program. The "demi-semi-constitutional monarchy," as Richard Charques terms it,[2] provided a political arena very different from the heady atmosphere of 1905 to 1907. The parties were forced to revise their position. In the Second Duma, since the revolutionaries had abandoned their boycott as useless, a sizable extreme-left contingent was elected: 65 Social Democrats (12 of them Bolsheviks), 37 SR's, and over 100 more radicals. Correspondingly greater activity by reactionary forces, who viewed the October Manifesto as a pernicious innovation, produced a large—some 70-odd—rightist delegation as well. In the center, the Constitutional Democrats, or Kadets (from the initial letters in Russian, "K" and "D"), who had been the dominant force in the First Duma, emerged with only 98 deputies. There were 32 Octobrists—who took a stand in defense of the October Manifesto.

It proved impossible to persuade a body so split to legislate constructively. When the Duma defeated a resolution condemning revolutionary terrorism, Stolypin drew the conclusion that it would reject his proposal for land reform. He therefore decided to dissolve the body and revise the franchise. He trumped up evidence purporting to prove that SD deputies were planning armed uprising (they and the SR's were in fact doing so, but the "evidence" was falsified), and before a Duma commission could report on the charges he prevailed on the tsar to dissolve the Duma. At the same time he altered the electoral law—an action that contravened the Fundamental Laws. By what was termed the coup d'état of June 3, 1907, the representation of Poland and the Caucasus was much reduced and that of Central Asia eliminated; it increased the weight of the gentry vote and decreased that of the peasantry, and in other ways made the franchise less direct.

---

[1] Geroid Tanquary Robinson, *Rural Russia Under the Old Regime,* Macmillan, 1949, p. 264.
[2] Richard Charques, *The Twilight of Imperial Russia,* Oxford U. Press, 1974, Ch. 7.

Meanwhile Stolypin was carrying out his program of "pacification," that is, re-pression of revolutionary groups. The Socialist Revolutionaries killed many offi-cials: nearly 1,600 in 1906, over 2,500 in 1907, from generals and governors to sim-ple village policemen.[3] After two of Stolypin's own children were injured in an attack on his summer residence on Aptekarsky Island in St. Petersburg, where thirty-three others were killed and many wounded, emergency legislation created field courts-martial, which, it was claimed, pronounced 683 death sentences. "Stolypin neckties" (hangman's nooses) dispatched at least that many, perhaps more, suspected terrorists and bank robbers—who had carried out so-called "ex-propriations," initially to fill revolutionary party treasuries. SR's and Bolsheviks (not Mensheviks, who denounced the practice at the IV Congress) continued the robberies for some time.

In 1909 the accidental exposure of the amazing case of the double agent Evno Azef, who served both the police and the SR party, apparently with a degree of loyalty to both, nearly wrecked the party. The Social Democrats were also hunted down systematically, and by 1908 the chief leaders were either driven abroad (for example, Lenin and Trotsky) or exiled to Siberia (Stalin).

The theorists of the Social Democratic party struggled through several debates about what to do then and in the future. At the IV ("Unification") Congress of the party held in Stockholm in April through May 1906, Lenin argued with Plekhanov regarding the prospects of revolution. Plekhanov feared that it might end in res-toration of the "Muscovite version of the economic order which lies at the base of all great Oriental despotisms." In order to avoid such a thing, he opposed the "na-tionalization" of land that Lenin supported for the party's agrarian program. Le-nin acknowledged the possibility of such an "Asiatic restoration," but asserted that the only real guarantee against it would be "a socialist revolution in the West." During and after 1917 those debates were remembered by SD's—and others—trying to decide what had gone wrong. At the V Congress "unification" was forgotten; the two chief factions fought—and in 1912 the Bolsheviks declared themselves a separate party.

The Third and Fourth Dumas

The elections held in November 1907 returned a Third Duma of the following composition: the right, 147; Octobrists, 154; KD's, 54; Progressists, 28 (a new party, with a strong industrialist component); SD's, 19; others, 40; the total fell from 513 to 442. The SR's boycotted both the Third and Fourth Dumas. The Octobrists, with a plurality, held the chair of the Third Duma for the five years it lasted. Stolypin and the center—the Octobrists plus a new Nationalist party—now had

---

[3] Michael T. Florinsky, *Russia: A History and an Interpretation,* Macmillan, 1970, II:1195.

an effective alliance, which was able to carry through a legislative program, especially to approve the land reform. Stolypin had originally enacted emergency
measures under Article 87 of the Fundamental Laws, but by the laws of June 14,
1910, and May 29, 1911, the Duma and the tsar approved the program. All those
measures were opposed by the parties of the Left, including the liberal Kadets,
distrustful of private property, as well as by the Right, which feared for the fate of
the gentry.

Stolypin had, however, to yield to rightist pressure—some of it coming from
the court. As a result his policies acquired more than a tinge of Russian nationalism. In 1909 a law was introduced, and finally passed only in 1912, by which Russian administration was imposed on a part of eastern Poland termed the province
of Kholm—a measure some called "the fourth partition of Poland" (the first three
having occurred under Catherine the Great). In 1910 the Duma received power to
legislate for the internal affairs of Finland, though the Finnish Diet could elect a
few members of the two Russian legislative bodies. Although Stolypin tried to enact legislation reducing Jewish disabilities, the tsar refused, though the prime
minister did manage to increase quotas for Jews in secondary schools. Anti-
Semitic nonsense deriving from the minister of justice himself produced the accusation that one Mendel Beilis, a Jew, had committed a ritual murder of a Christian
child, and only after a prolonged trial was Beilis acquitted in October 1913; the affair was compared to France's Dreyfus case.

In 1911 a crisis was precipitated when Stolypin introduced a bill to establish
zemstvos in six western provinces in which the predominance of the Belorussian
and Ukrainian peasantry was secured over the Polish gentry. The left opposed it
as too nationalistic, the right as insufficiently so. As a result the upper house, the
Council of State, rejected it, partly because the right hated the prime minister.
Stolypin chose that moment to force the issue and compel the tsar to prorogue
both houses for three days, during which he enacted the bill into law in accordance with Article 87. Nicholas II did not like ministers who forced his hand—as
Witte had done with the October Manifesto—and probably Stolypin would soon
have been dismissed. However, in September 1911 he was shot between acts of an
opera performance in Kiev; he turned toward the tsar's box, made the sign of the
cross, and fell, dying four days later. His assassin was a double agent of the Azef
stripe whose motives remain cloudy to this day.

During Stolypin's ministry the tsarist government made its last best effort. The
chief officials understood both the nature of peasant aspirations and the magnitude of the revolutionary threat to all they held dear. But the moment passed.
Stolypin's able assistant, A. V. Krivoshein, survived him in life but not for long in
power.

For the next two and one-half years V. N. Kokovtsev, competent but unimaginative, was prime minister. During the period the Duma enacted laws on
workingmen's compensation for illness and injury. Signs of trouble began to appear. In 1912 revolutionary newspapers began to be published again, including the

new Bolshevik organ *Pravda,* repeatedly closed by court order but each time reopening under a slightly altered name. In April 1912 a strike occurred in the Lena gold fields of Siberia; troops fired on strikers and killed two hundred or so men, wounding about the same number; to critics the interior minister replied, "Thus it has always been so and always will be."

In the fall, elections to the Fourth Duma yielded 98 Octobrists, 88 Nationalists, 65 of the Right, 59 Kadets, 48 Progressists, 15 SD's (one of the Bolsheviks was also the police agent Roman Malinovsky), and a scattering of others. Zemstvo employees increased in number; doctors, paramedics (feldshers), teachers, agronomists, and others helped to improve the countryside: medical care spread to a point where, in 1913, there were 6,773 hospitals and 19,000 doctors in 51 provinces of European Russia. In the years after 1900 cooperatives of three types flourished: credit (in which Russia led the world), consumers', and producers'—especially agricultural and dairy. In 1914 over 30,000 cooperatives of all types had almost 12 million members.[4] Literacy for the whole population was estimated to have risen to 44% in 1914, and was found to be 68% among men (largely peasants) drafted for the army in 1913. On the basis of interviews Timasheff writes that just before the war broke out "almost all recruits from Central Russia were literate."[5] The widespread impression that in 1917 Russia was an illiterate country is quite unjustified, and there had been significant advances in other respects as well.

In January 1914 Kokovtsev was replaced by Ivan Goremykin, who described himself as "an old fur coat taken out of mothballs." At the age of seventy-five he managed to appear and act decades older, but he had the approval of Rasputin.

The Ascendancy of Rasputin

Gregory Rasputin (real name: Novykh) was a figure truly unparalleled in history. He was a *starets* or "holy man"— not, as has often been said, a monk or priest— from the Tobolsk region. The crown prince, Alexis, had inherited hemophilia from his mother and stood in constant danger of death from any slight injury. Rasputin gained entrance to the court in 1905 because he was, according to several reputable witnesses, able to stop the bleeding when the doctors could not. The empress regarded him as a "man sent by God" to preserve her son and the dynasty from destruction, and would listen to no criticism of him. When police reported sexual scandals involving Rasputin and ladies of St. Petersburg's highest society to the empress, she replied, "Read the Apostles: they kissed as a sign of greeting."

---

[4] Sergei Pushkarev, *The Emergence of Modern Russia 1801–1917,* Holt, Rinehart & Winston, 1963, esp. Ch. 8.

[5] N. S. Timasheff, "Overcoming Illiteracy: Public Education in Russia, 1880–1940," *Russian Review,* 1942, 2:84.

Until Stolypin's death Rasputin had little influence on government, but afterward his recommendations came to matter, even though popular ideas about his importance were unwarranted.[6] The left found in him a convenient symbol of corruption and decay in the regime, but it was the center and right who attacked him most sharply in the Duma, for they recognized in him a formidable threat to any kind of efficient government. His political views were not a major issue; his influence was exerted not necessarily on behalf of reactionary policies but rather to advance to posts of authority his friends and confidants, many of whom proved incompetent or mentally impaired. This psychopathic tragicomedy was played up to the time when any serious Russian participation in World War I ceased.

On the eve of the war industrial prosperity opened the way to a strike movement mounting in intensity in 1913 and early 1914.[7] Rural reform continued to make progress but could not offset the unstable condition of the cities or paralysis creeping over the central government. Under such circumstances Russia entered World War I.

The Coming of the War

The war was the result of the foreign policy of all major European powers in an age of secret diplomacy and political and economic competition outside Europe. Perhaps the most important underlying cause was nationalism, in particular the unsatisfied nationalist aspirations of the Serbs and the nationalist pride of Austro-Hungarian and Russian public opinion on the most influential levels. The powder keg had been readied for the nationalist spark by the formation of the alliance between Austria-Hungary and Germany (and Italy, which, however, refused later to implement the alliance and eventually fought on the opposite side) on the one hand and the entente between Great Britain, France, and Russia on the other.

Russia found herself in unwonted company. Britain had been her chief diplomatic bugbear of recent times, the power which had frustrated Russian objectives in regard to Turkey, clashed with Russian influence in the Middle East, and supported Japan in restraining Russian expansion in the Pacific. France was Russia's ancient enemy, the ally of her formerly most dangerous neighbors (Turkey and Poland), and since the French Revolution ideological hostility had been added to the historic antagonism between governments. In contrast, Germany had been Russia's closest friend, as she had been England's, too, up to the last decades of the century. Until the middle of the century, Austria had also been friendly toward

---

[6] Martin Kilcoyne shows this in "The Political Influence of Rasputin," his unpublished dissertation, University of Washington, 1961.

[7] Leopold H. Haimson, "The Problem of Social Stability in Urban Russia, 1905–1917," *Slavic Review*, 1964, No. 4, and 1965, No. 1.

Russia. In 1849 Nicholas I had crushed the revolution in Hungary and handed the country back to the Hapsburgs, asking nothing in return; however, Austria adopted a hostile attitude during the Crimean War, and since then relations between the two powers had become increasingly embittered. Bismarck's attempt to mediate foundered on Austro-Russian rivalry for influence over the emerging independent states of the Balkans.

There were many diplomatic crises near the turn of the century, but those which led to the war were in the Balkans. Traditionally the Serbs, even more than other Slavs outside Russia, looked to St. Petersburg for sympathy, which Pan-Slav circles willingly gave, and support, which the government was often reluctant to give if the risk seemed great. In 1908 Austria flouted Serbian nationalism by annexing Bosnia-Hercegovina; in 1913 it succeeded in setting up an independent Albania, barring Serbia from the Adriatic; in June 1914 Serbian nationalists assassinated the heir to the Austrian throne in Sarajevo, and Vienna retaliated by an ultimatum to Serbia, followed by a declaration of war on July 28. Russia had the choice of permitting Austria once again to humiliate and possibly destroy Serbia, or to come to its aid. The first alternative would have been a confession of national weakness and moral abasement in the eyes of public opinion within Russia and abroad. After hesitating between partial mobilization (intended as a threat to Austria but a reassurance to Germany) and general mobilization, on July 30 the Russian government decided on the latter. The result was general war.

Within Russia there were immediate and strong manifestations of patriotism. To an assembly of dignitaries in the Winter Palace the tsar solemnly repeated the oath taken by Alexander I in 1812, vowing not to make peace while a single enemy remained on Russian soil. He then stepped onto the balcony, while the multitude below fell on their knees and sang "God Save the Tsar" as it had not been sung in Russia for many years. The Duma met and voted war credits. The pattern of the West European socialists' behavior in the face of the war waged by their "capitalist" governments was approximated in the Duma, where Alexander Kerensky, leader of the Trudovik party, led the revolutionaries in abstaining from the vote on war credits but in offering help in defending the country.

In Lenin's eyes the war was nothing but an "imperialist" war—that is, a war into which the development of capitalism in its highest stage had unavoidably thrown the governments of the European powers, which were struggling for a new redivision of the world's colonies and spheres of influence. He took for granted that the "capitalist" governments would behave as they did; his chief animus was directed against the parties and men of the Second International who either in theory or in practice supported or condoned to any degree whatsoever the war efforts of their respective governments. In effect the Second International ceased to function at the outbreak of war. The majority of the German, Austrian, French, English, and Belgian socialists accepted a "class truce." However, socialists of Russia, Italy (which declared war on Austria-Hungary in May 1915 but not on Germany until August 1916), the neutral nations, and dissidents from other belligerent powers tried to restore the International on the basis of rejecting the "truce." At Zimmerwald in September 1915 and Kienthal in April 1916 they met for that purpose, but they were themselves divided, since Lenin wished not to go back to the prewar organization but to launch a new Third International devoted to active revolutionary preparations. The meetings failed, but Lenin's leadership of the "Zimmerwald Left" foreshadowed the direction in which he led the Bolsheviks when he returned to Russia in 1917. Before that time, however, few Russians knew or cared who he was or what he thought about the war or anything else.

The War on the Eastern Front

The government of Russia was unprepared for war, but so were the British and, later, the United States governments. What was decisive was that the government was incapable of carrying out preparations and was unable or unwilling to utilize the patriotic enthusiasm of the people and public bodies toward effective prosecution of the war. The gigantic enterprise of mobilization took place successfully, with little effort by recruits to evade service and much evidence of willingness to fight, but many were neither trained nor supplied properly. The Duma set to work to organize Red Cross assistance and the zemstvos and municipalities to improve supply services, but the government received their offers of support coolly and lackadaisically.

The whole economy was greatly strained by the war. Although the mobilization did not severely damage peasant farming (since women and boys could fill the breach, and much produce was consumed rather than sold), it did great harm to the large estates (which depended on hired labor, and produced chiefly for market). The inroads of war in the west, by cutting down the cultivated area available to Russia, further diminished the food supply. The railway network, insufficient even for peacetime needs, was not adequately maintained or furnished with rolling stock, owing to the stringent economies carried out by the communications ministry from 1909 right up to 1915. Instead of taking measures to increase production the government initially told manufacturers to anticipate a decrease in demand because of the shrinkage of international trade, and the warning led many to slash their output.

Civilian rule in areas adjacent to the front was at once replaced by military control. The commander-in-chief was the Grand Duke Nicholas, the Emperor's uncle, who was popular among the soldiers but none too competent in his post. His military government in the western provinces provoked innumerable complaints, which consumed a good deal of the time of the central authorities without leading to any significant result. The army's officer corps ranged from good to indifferent in quality, and the majority of the recruits lacked proper training and equipment. This force was hurled into a battle in which the vastnesses of distance, numbers of

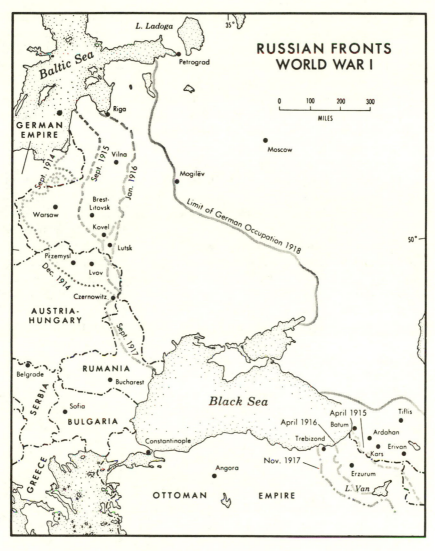

RUSSIAN FRONTS
WORLD WAR I

men, and quantities of supplies were greater than in any previous military campaigns.

The Russian plan was to strike through Austrian Galicia, in order to save Serbia, prevent an attempt to seize Russian Poland from the right flank, and to annex "Russian" (Ukrainian) territory held by Austria-Hungary. However, the crisis which immediately developed on the Western front because of the German dash for Paris led the Russian command to mount a hasty offensive against the Germans in East Prussia. Their armies were shattered by Hindenburg and Ludendorff in battles in which the Russians lost some 300,000 men. Nevertheless the simultaneous Russian offensive in Galicia, using twice the number of troops which were deployed on the German front, hurt the Austrians even more than the Germans had hurt them. Russian troops captured Lvov, and by the middle of September 1914 they were nearing Przemysl. The Germans had diverted troops from the Marne battlefront to meet the danger in East Prussia; the diversion slowed down their offensive and thus helped to bring about the stalemate in the West which continued for almost the whole duration of the war. In the fall campaign the Russian armies had helped to save France, damaged Austria severely, and although defeated in East Prussia had repulsed a German thrust toward Warsaw.

At the beginning of hostilities St. Petersburg had announced as Russian war aims the reunification of Poland as an autonomous state of the Russian Empire and the annexation of the Austro-Hungarian territories inhabited by Ukrainians (although the word "Ukrainian" was not used). A few weeks later Foreign Minister Sergei Sazonov announced a program of "Twelve Points," which Woodrow Wilson's Fourteen were to resemble in many details. They even included affirmation of the "principle of nationalities" as determining future territorial changes. The main objective of "the three allies" was said to be "to strike at German power and its pretensions to military and political domination"; Austria-Hungary was to become a triple monarchy (Bohemia was to take its place beside the two existing divisions), but would not be dismembered.[8] Sazonov's policy of close harmony with Britain and France and genuine autonomy for Poland aroused little enthusiasm on the Rightist side. However, when Turkey was drawn into the war in November 1914 through the guidance of the pro-German war minister, Enver Pasha, and the question of the Straits entered diplomatic and public discussion, the Right warmed to the cause of the war.

Sazonov was not primarily interested in the Straits, but when the British prepared to seize the Dardanelles at the beginning of 1915 he became suspicious that they intended either to annex Constantinople themselves or to turn it over to Greece. Both conservatives and liberals in the Duma supported Sazonov in seeking Allied acceptance of Russian control of the Straits. In March 1915, with certain reservations and accompanying compensation for Britain in Persia and France in Syria, the Western Allies conceded the point in the secret Straits Agreement. The collapse of Turkey was widely anticipated at the time of the British landing at Gallipoli in April; this expectation finally led Italy to enter the war on the conditions outlined in the secret Treaty of London the same month. By the treaty Russia consented to Italian annexation of a part of the South Slav coast; Serbs and other South Slavs protested, but they had only rumors to tell them what had been done.

---

[8] The text of the Twelve Points is given in C. Jay Smith, Jr., *The Russian Struggle for Power, 1914–1917*, Philosophical Library, 1956, pp. 46–48.

The Crisis of 1915

The spring campaign of 1915 opened with the Russian capture of Przemysl in Galicia in March. The Russian armies pressed on toward Hungary, and the very existence of the Dual Monarchy seemed in danger. However, on May 2 the Germans and Austrians began a full-scale offensive, and the tide turned very rapidly, wiping out the Russian gains of the previous fall and early spring. On July 1 a new combined Austro-German offensive began, closing a gigantic pincer on Poland. By early August the Austrians had advanced to Lutsk; the Germans captured Warsaw and continued on to take Brest-Litovsk and, in September, Vilna. By October the Eastern front ran roughly from Riga south to Czernowitz.

It is surprising that the Russian armies were extricated from the disaster at all. It was not that troops could nor would not fight, but because of the faulty replacement system, front-line units were short of manpower, and the deficiency in munitions was grave. There were staggering casualties—2 million in 1915 alone. The civilian population retreated with the armies voluntarily, or, more often, because they were ordered to do so. Well over 3 million refugees were hurled into the interior, despite the protests of the civilian authorities at the policy of the high command responsible for the human flood.

The shock of defeat did produce a temporary improvement in the domestic situation. A new effort at "mobilization of industry" sharply reversed the previous passive economic policy of the government. In the summer of 1915 "special councils" were established for national defense, transportation, fuel, food, and refugees by initiative of the Duma; war industries committees were set up at the urging of business circles; and the Unions of Zemstvos and Towns (*Zemgor*) took an increasingly active role in the supply crisis.

The liberals took heart when four of the most reactionary ministers were removed from the government. The occasion for their fall was the continuing debate about treatment of Poland. In February 1915 the Poles were given a new and sympathetic governor-general, Prince Engalychev, and even the reactionary military governor of Galicia was persuaded to take a more pro-Polish view by Professor Stanislaw Grabski of the University of Lvov. The Emperor was prevailed upon by the Sazonov camp to order an end to restrictions on the Roman Catholics of Poland and to promise the Poles zemstvo institutions. Minister of Interior N. A. Maklakov and others sharply opposed the concessions to Poland but committed political suicide by linking their opposition with support of immediate peace with Germany, and in June the Emperor dismissed them. The majority of the Duma was alarmed by the military debacle and hoped that the Emperor could be persuaded to adopt a political line of national unity. In September the formation was announced of a Progressive Bloc of parties ranging from the Kadets to the Progressive Nationalists, demanding a "united government consisting of persons who enjoy the confidence of the country and are in agreement with the legislative chambers … ," the end of religious and ethnic discrimination, restrictions on trade-unions, extension of the Great Reforms, and an amnesty for religious and political offenders. Many public groups echoed the manifesto, some flatly demanding a ministry responsible to the Duma.

Although the majority of the ministers was willing to accept the program of the Progressive Bloc, Prime Minister Goremykin was not. He ran to the Empress, who was by now nearly all-powerful, and obtained the proroguing of the Duma. Two days later, on September 18, Nicholas II dismissed his uncle and himself assumed the command at the front. The military consequences of this Imperial gesture were fortunately not serious, since his chief of staff, General Alexeev, was capable and had good judgment, and there was also a new and energetic war minister, General Polivanov. However, the effect on the domestic situation was much worse; the direction of government was left in the hands of the Empress and Rasputin. Public opinion was aghast, and in spite of Goremykin's efforts, ten ministers begged the Emperor to reconsider his fateful decision to assume the command—quite in vain. Several were soon dismissed for their courage, and in February 1916 even Goremykin was replaced by Boris Stürmer. Stürmer's mental endowments were still more modest than those of his predecessor; his chief asset was that he was the choice of Rasputin. In the Duma one reactionary deputy, begging consent to his violation of the ban on the use of the "enemy language," German, uttered two words: "Oberhofmeister [the official title of a court post which the man held] Stürmer."

At the beginning of 1916 the military situation looked bleak. In the closing months of 1915 on the heels of the Russian defeat, Bulgaria had been drawn in on the side of the Central Powers, both Serbia and Montenegro had been completely overrun, and the British assault on the Dardanelles had been abandoned. Nevertheless the picture was not wholly dark. Russia had suffered a grievous blow, but the army could still fight, and no one publicly discussed any other aim than victory; moreover, it was realized that the Central Powers were also war-weary. Owing to the initiative taken by private and semipublic bodies, the munitions and supply situation had been considerably improved. On the Caucasian front, Russian troops pushed into Turkish Armenia, reaching Trebizond in April 1916.

On the Eastern front, Russia could still mount an offensive. After several changes of plan, Alexeev decided to concentrate on the Austrians. Under General Brusilov, a large-scale attack began in June and made swift progress. Brusilov's forces recaptured Lutsk, and neared the railway junction of Kovel; the number of Austrian prisoners approached half a million. Romania, which had engaged in hard bargaining with the Allies for many months, finally entered the war in August. The German chief of the general staff, General von Falkenhayn, who had been preoccupied with the West and the siege of Verdun, was promptly relieved by Hindenburg, who had consistently advocated a decision in the East. Austria, caught by surprise, was compelled to ease its pressure on Italy.

However, the Russians had suffered a third of a million casualties even while the offensive was making progress. German forces were rushed from the Western front; Brusilov continued to attack, and the total of Russian casualties for the year approached a million, but nothing was gained, and his forces were nearly demoralized. The entry of the Romanians, though it alarmed the enemy, proved disastrous for the Allies. In a swift campaign the Central Powers crushed Romania, entering the capital, Bucharest, on December 6, 1916.

In the spring of 1916, partly because of French pressure but in line with Sazonov's policy, the Russian government prepared a new declaration about Poland, promising a separate Polish Council of Ministers and a two-house legislature. Especially in view of Brusilov's success on the front in Poland in the summer, Alexeev gave Sazonov strong support. The Emperor was won over to the declaration, but Rasputin opposed it. In July Stürmer and the Empress visited the Tsar at Supreme Headquarters at Mogilëv, and obtained Sazonov's dismissal, even though the decision for Polish autonomy (for the time being secret) was to stand.

The Fall of the Monarchy

The final crisis of the regime began in the fall of 1916. In the capital an atmosphere of intrigue and suspicion poisoned serious efforts to continue the war. In September the appointment as minister of interior of A. D. Protopopov, a Duma deputy and a moderate liberal, had an effect opposite to that intended. It was revealed that he was Rasputin's choice, and at least as serious was the exposure of his mental deterioration to the verge of insanity. In November the Duma reconvened. Poor Stürmer, who understood little of what was happening but was blamed by all shades of public opinion for the military debacle, was scheduled to announce to the Duma both the secret agreement on the Straits and the decision on Polish autonomy. However, he could not bring himself to go through with the plan. The sensational speech of the session was made not by Stürmer but by the Kadet leader, Paul Miliukov. He angrily enumerated the failures of governmental policy, mentioning the Empress and Stürmer by name, and ending each indictment with the question, "Is this stupidity or treason?" In the ensuing uproar Nicholas could either have dismissed Stürmer or have chastised his critics into silence. On Alexeev's urging, he dismissed Stürmer but did nothing further to quell rising dissatisfaction with the government.

The reactionary deputy, Purishkevich, now attacked Rasputin openly in the Duma. Schemes for a palace coup were being bruited around the court with little effort at secrecy. In the last days of December a conspiracy of Purishkevich, the Emperor's nephew, and one of his cousins by marriage planned and executed the murder of Rasputin. This puzzling figure, who combined a personally scandalous and corrupt manner of life with a peasant's naive and ignorant love for his country, had to be poisoned, shot, and drowned before he would die, in an evening of horror and suspense. An episode unprecedented in the modern annals of a great country thus reached an appropriately melodramatic denouement. The Empress was deeply shocked but helpless to suggest anything further. The Emperor could only appoint as prime minister a friend of the Empress's, Prince N. D. Golitsyn, who was utterly unprepared for office. In fact he said that he took the post to have one more memory for his old age, which indeed was already upon him.

In the beginning of February 1917 the country was full of rumors of coming change, peaceful or violent. However, an inter-Allied military conference was held in Petrograd to plan the campaigns for the year, and the Emperor went off to Supreme Headquarters at Mogilëv, leaving behind him a capital in which everything appeared on the surface to be normal and calm. On March 8 demonstrations were held celebrating International Women's Day, which merged with crowds in rioting in protest at the shortage of bread in Petrograd. The garrison commander wired reports to the Emperor at the front, who merely ordered that the disturbance be halted. The day before he had written to the Empress, "I greatly miss my half-hourly game of patience every evening. I shall take up dominoes again in my spare time."

As the riots continued, the Emperor could think of nothing but to prorogue the Duma, which he did on March 11. The next day the Duma met in defiance of the order and elected a provisional committee composed of members of the Progressive Bloc and two representatives of parties to the left of it, Alexander Kerensky (Trudovik) and N. S. Chkheidze (Menshevik). The committee had the vague mission "to restore order and to deal with institutions and individuals." The garrison was still patrolling the streets. "But a junior French diplomat," writes Sir John Maynard, "took note of a trifling incident. He saw a Cossack wink to the rioters."[9] By evening the garrison had broken discipline and was no longer at the disposal of its commander. On the same day, February 27,[10] the Taurida Palace was invaded by men who, entering rooms not occupied by the Duma, founded a Petrograd Soviet of Workers' Deputies, modeling itself on the institutions prominent in the 1905 events. (On March 2, taking note of the attitude of the soldiers in the capital and at the front, it was to rename itself the Soviet of Workers' and Soldiers' Deputies.)

By the night of February 28 most of the old ministry was under arrest. The same night the Emperor tried to reach Petrograd, but his train was halted and sent on to Pskov. There General Alexeev, other high officers, and two Progressive Bloc leaders, V. V. Shulgin (Progressive Nationalist) and Alexander Guchkov (Octobrist), talked with the Emperor, begging him to abdicate. He decided first to turn over the throne to his son but then changed his mind, and on March 2 he abdicated in favor of his brother, Grand Duke Michael. A delegation from the provisional committee of the Duma (by now renamed the Provisional Government)

---

[9] *Russia in Flux,* p. 177.

[10] By the Julian calendar in use in Russia until February 1/14, 1918.

waited on the Grand Duke, who found it prudent to refuse. The monarchy thus perished without a murmur from either the dynasty or its supporters.

What had happened? The leaders of the army played a crucial role. Hasegawa writes that at the start of the revolution they

> supported Nicholas's counterrevolutionary measures, because they believed that the capital had been taken over by radical elements. But as soon as they were assured that power had been transferred to the liberal forces, they fully cooperated with the Duma Committee—some, like Ruzskii and Brusilov, because they agreed with their general goals; others, like Alekseev, because they were outwitted by the Duma Committee's manipulation of information.[11]

They were concerned with continuing the war and preserving the power of the army to fight, and were willing to sacrifice the monarchy to those ends. But they did not foresee what lay ahead.

Although his family had ruled Russia over three centuries, and although he had previously accepted demands for reform only rarely and under great pressure, Nicholas II renounced power calmly. On his train the next day he wrote in his diary, "I had a long and sound sleep. Woke up beyond Dvinsk. Sunshine and frost. … I read much of Julius Caesar." He and the whole imperial family were detained in ambiguous circumstances in the palace at Tsarskoe Selo outside of Petrograd. It was planned that they would be sent to England, but the plans never bore fruit. During the succeeding months Nicholas developed a certain enthusiasm for the man who most nearly became his successor in power, Kerensky. In July he wrote in his diary that Kerensky "was the right man in the right place. The more power he gets, the better." In the summer of 1917 the Romanovs were moved to Siberia, and in July 1918 they were all murdered by the Communists.

Nicholas II was a man who wished the best for his country and his people, and he sometimes recognized and tried to correct the abuses others pointed out to him. But he also made a series of stupid mistakes, and failed to understand the grave problems which Russia faced. Perhaps the least competent of his dynasty for a century, he was weak, and so were many of the high officials he appointed and trusted, but he also found able advisers, such as Stolypin, Witte, and Krivoshein. However, even if they were strong and competent, the officials had to operate within the framework of an oppressive bureaucratic system. Although its nominally all-embracing power had fortunately long been tempered by inefficiency, and some of its former functions had latterly been entrusted to the zemstvos, city councils, and the Duma, nevertheless the structure of tsarism remained strong

---

[11] Tsuyoshi Hasegawa, *The February Revolution*, U. of Washington Press, 1981, pp. 585–586. See also E. N. Burdzhalov, *Russia's Second Revolution: The February 1917 Uprising in Petrograd*, trans., Indiana U. Press, 1987.

enough to discourage or override any political initiative which came from outside it, as shown in the period of Russia's participation in World War I.

Russia's government proved itself unequal to the strain of conducting twentieth-century warfare, in which the front depended heavily on the morale and political and economic vitality of the rear. As the political bankruptcy of the regime became increasingly clear, many expected that it would crumble and in so doing open the way to a continuation and acceleration of the enormous changes in Russian society during the past half-century. In Russia and its borderlands, the years of Nicholas II's reign witnessed a speedy industrial growth; a sweeping transformation of the peasantry into small proprietors; the rapid spread of education; new, diverse, and original cultural developments; the schooling of a generation in political experience through the zemstvos, municipalities, the Duma, and the courts; and an amazing growth of Siberia. Nicholas II and the government favored most of these changes, although they were not originated or even steadily supported by the regime.

When the Communists came to power, however, they either reversed these currents, so full of promise for Russia's future, or (as in the case of education and industrialization) brought them under the control of the Soviet state and used them to serve their own purposes. The old dynastic absolutism left behind it much that was healthy and promising which the new totalitarianism stifled or corrupted. Russia's tragedy lay in the fact that although many of those who led or supported the Revolution did so in the hope of giving free rein to the currents of modernization, nevertheless the new regime which emerged was ultimately committed not to creative economic, social, political, and cultural diversity but to monolithic unity of all aspects of life. While Nicholas II and his government no doubt stunted Russian political growth, they left many other realms of life alone to develop as they might. The men of the February Revolution desired more state control of society, not less, but by making the government responsive to the people's wishes they intended that change should depend on initiative from below. The Communists aimed at total control and initiative from above, and in the generations which followed the extent to which they achieved their aims was impressive indeed.

PART TWO

The Communists Take Power

7

The February Revolution

Prospects for Democracy

According to Alexander Kerensky, the February Revolution "marked the end of a long and painful trail from pure absolutism to absolute democracy. That which only the day before appeared as a distant dream came true so suddenly and so very completely. ... The people themselves were in power, the people themselves were the owners of Russia." In contrast to the earlier English, American, and French revolutions, the Russian Revolution proclaimed the theory of democratic government as a settled principle at the moment the monarch was dethroned. Even the most conservative of the White leaders in the Civil War, General Wrangel, angered his fellow monarchists by declaring that the question of monarchy was one that only the people could decide. On the day after the Romanov dynasty fell there were virtually no defenders of royal absolutism left.

The question was, How was Russia to find the institutions and leaders through which democracy could be realized? Where the power lay was in doubt from the first. On February 27 two authoritative bodies had been organized in the Taurida Palace: the provisional committee of the Duma and the Petrograd Soviet of Workers' Deputies. As he abdicated, Nicholas II appointed Prince George Lvov prime minister, in order that power should be legally transferred to his successor. Led by Wilson's America, the Allies were soon to recognize the Provisional Government as the legitimate one. However, it actually existed only by sufferance of the Soviet.

The Provisional Government consisted of representatives of the major parties of the Duma Left and Center—the parties of the Right very nearly evaporated overnight. The Kadets furnished the prime minister, Lvov, a figure who owed his prominence more to his war work in *Zemgor* than to his party regularity, and the foreign minister, Paul Miliukov, gifted historian and the real party leader, who was also the most influential man in the cabinet. The Octobrists contributed their leader, Alexander Guchkov, as war and navy minister. The prominent Ukrainian businessman, M. I. Tereshchenko, became minister of finance. There was only one representative of the revolutionary parties, Alexander Kerensky, who was minister of justice. The former leader of the Trudoviks, he became a "March SR," as did many others who had belonged to one of the small parties or to no party prior to the Revolution. Both Lvov and Kerensky exhibited an intoxication with history, rather than a clear appraisal or a firm policy. Kerensky repeated over and over, "I am sent by the revolution," and similar phrases; in fact, he seemed an inexhaustible font of speeches, orders, and activities of all sorts, and constantly managed to appear to be in several places at the same time.

Kerensky was the only revolutionary in the cabinet, but even he was not there because his party, or the Soviet in which his party shared control with the Mensheviks, wanted him to be. The Soviet decided to stand aside from the Provisional Government, and he violated the decision, telling the Soviet what he had done and then departing abruptly before it could remonstrate with him. The Petrograd Soviet began with a seemingly spontaneous meeting of revolutionary leaders on the afternoon of February 27. They established an Executive Committee for the Soviet, which did not convene until evening. The Soviet was supposed to represent the workers of the Petrograd factories, but it is difficult to determine how accurately it did so. Almost three weeks elapsed before it was decided to have one deputy for each two thousand workers (or soldiers), and even this rule was not always followed.

The Taurida Palace soon became something like a madhouse, filled with milling deputies, ministers, petitioners, onlookers, etc., and the Soviet moved its headquarters elsewhere. Business was done by a handful of men within the Executive Committee of the Petrograd Soviet, who continued to make the important decisions even after Soviets had spread all over the country and, in June, a national Central Executive Committee had been elected by the I Congress of Soviets. The first act of the Petrograd Executive Committee was to issue the famed Order No. 1, which provided for the setting up in every army unit of elective committees and announced that military orders of the Provisional Government should be obeyed only if they did not conflict with Soviet orders. The actual effect of this order was to initiate election of officers and open the way to a breakdown of the discipline and morale of the army on the widest scale.

Although Order No. 1 was nothing if not a governmental act, it was not followed by any other such acts of significance. The policy of the Petrograd Executive Committee was to abstain from exercising the authority which it in fact possessed, and upon which the Provisional Government depended. The reason for this puzzling behavior must be sought in revolutionary political theory—specifically the view of the Mensheviks, who dominated their partnership with the SR's in controlling the Soviets (until September). In Menshevik eyes, the February Revolution was a "bourgeois revolution"; history determined that power must be held by bourgeois liberals; it was the task of the workers' party to refrain from compromising itself in the workers' eyes by taking power and undertaking historical tasks which were bound to be premature and could only discredit the party (see p. 38). The Menshevik leaders of the Executive Committee, Chairman

Chkheidze, M. I. Skobelev, N. N. Sukhanov, and others, took this theory very seriously. The Socialist Revolutionaries, never as sure of themselves about doctrine as their Marxist colleagues, went along with it despite some grumbling. Sukhanov recounts how he chatted with Miliukov, the Kadet leader and presumably the foremost "bourgeois liberal." Identifying himself ironically as "your worst enemy," Sukhanov proceeded to tempt Miliukov with what he regarded as historically inevitable: "Do you propose, now that we are in an atmosphere of revolution, to take state power into your own hands?" and was much annoyed that he received only an equivocal and puzzled answer.[1]

The theory of obligatory abstention from power was compromised from the start by Kerensky's participation in the Provisional Government, as well as by Order No. 1, and was soon to be stretched still further. Nevertheless, it was not discarded. As a result the Provisional Government limped along, dependent on the Soviet, in a situation which was characterized by Trotsky in the phrase, "dual power." Dual power, wherein one agency would not and the other could not rule, prevented any possibility of effective government.

Frist Crisis of the Provisional Government

On March 3 the Provisional Government, in agreement with the Executive Committee of the Petrograd Soviet, announced its objectives. They included the convening of a Constituent Assembly (for which generations of revolutionaries had waited), immediate granting of unqualified civil liberties, democratization of local government, and an amnesty to political prisoners. The amnesty had largely taken effect already. On March 20 equal rights were granted to all irrespective of race or religion. Democratic self-government was not achieved, although a proliferation of committees and officials occurred which made local authority in fact supreme in large areas of the country, and a little later many of the self-constituted local bodies submitted to free elections. However, the Constituent Assembly was continually postponed. Since the government and the major parties insisted that all major decisions, including the determination of the new constitutional structure, the ending of the war, and the distribution of land, must await the assembly, the delay was of fundamental importance. Everything the government did was bound to be temporary and conditional. The leaders of the Soviets declared that they could not take power; the Provisional Government explained that it could not use its power until the Constituent Assembly was convened. The result was mounting public impatience and a growing breakdown of reliance on law and government.

---

[1] N. N. Sukhanov, *The Russian Revolution, 1917*, ed., abridged, Oxford U. Press, 1955, p. 56.

In March the political spectrum was distributed as follows: the Kadets and Octobrists dominated the Provisional Government, the Mensheviks and Socialist Revolutionaries controlled the Soviets and thereby wielded the actual power in the cities but refused to assume a share of responsibility in the government. The Bolsheviks were only a small minority in the Petrograd Soviet. At the outset they wavered between the old Leninist hostility to the Mensheviks, their new Soviet, and the government it supported on the one hand, and on the other an enthusiasm for whatever was being done in the name of the "revolution," willingness to reconcile themselves with their old Menshevik comrades, and a sense of obligation to maintain "working class" unity.

The Kadets and the Octobrists were the first to go. The occasion was a dispute about whether to continue the war. Addressing the Western Allies, who had just recognized the Provisional Government, Miliukov explained that the Revolution had been a protest against the bungling of the war effort and that Russia would now fight better than ever. In a newspaper interview on March 23 he spelled out the war aims which Guchkov as war minister and he as foreign minister were pursuing; he mentioned among other things the annexation of Constantinople as an "immemorial" national objective. (The Straits Agreement was still unknown to the public.) Miliukov's statement provoked a flurry of denunciation and further explanation between the Soviet leaders and himself. The attitude of the Soviet toward the war was far from clear. On March 14 it had issued a "Manifesto to the Peoples of the World" which tried to harmonize the views of those who favored going on with the war and those who wanted to bring it to an end, without knowing quite how it might safely be done. The formula "peace without annexations and indemnities" was widely used, and the newspaper *Izvestiia* (*News;* the organ of the Soviet) proposed the slogan, "war for freedom." On April 18 another note of Miliukov to the Allies, employing the phrase "war to decisive victory," served as a signal for demonstrations in front of the new seat of government, the Mariinsky Palace. Miliukov could find no effective support for his policy, and as a result, Guchkov resigned on April 30 and Miliukov followed two days later.

Lenin's "April Theses"

By this time the exiled revolutionary leaders were returning to Petrograd: the Menshevik Heracles Tsereteli, and the Socialist Revolutionary Victor Chernov, who assumed the leading role in their parties; the Bolsheviks Joseph Stalin and Leo Kamenev from Siberia; then Trotsky and Lenin from abroad. Lenin arrived at the Finland Station in Petrograd on April 3, after his journey in the famous "sealed train" which the German authorities had allowed to go through in the hope that its cargo would weaken Russia's war effort. For three years Lenin had raged impotently against the Western Social Democrats' "betrayal" of the Marxist cause by their refusal to oppose the war (see p. 83). His first utterances on his return to Russia restated these views and announced a startling program of action on the war and other issues.

He offered his program to a slightly dazed Bolshevik party in the "April Theses." In retrospect what they did not contain appears quite as important as what they did. They did *not* demand "peace and land," which was the Bolshevik slogan in the fall. First of all, said Lenin, it was necessary to understand that the war from the start had been imperialist and would remain so until the bourgeoisie, which ruled all European countries including Russia (after the February Revolution), was overthrown. "The fundamental question is," declared Lenin, "which class is waging the war? ... When the masses declare they want no conquests, I believe them. When Guchkov and Lvov say they want no conquests, they lie." Here he applied the doctrine of *Imperialism, the Highest Stage of Capitalism,* to the current moment, using the rule of thumb which he crudely but effectively phrased, "who exploits whom?"

As he later explained it, the bourgeois revolution was being completed, but not as he had hoped. In 1905 he had envisaged two possible outcomes of the first revolutionary stage, either a simple "bourgeois dictatorship" or his own prescription, a "revolutionary democratic dictatorship of proletariat and peasantry." In 1917, however, *both* alternatives (represented respectively by the Provisional Government and the Soviets) had been realized simultaneously, and the first had spoiled the second; the tail was wagging the dog. Therefore—the logic is Lenin's—the Bolsheviks had to push on to the second stage, that of rule by proletariat and *poor* peasantry, that is, to the socialist revolution. The way to do so was to convert imperialist war into civil war.

Secondly, Lenin demanded that the Bolsheviks oppose the Provisional Government and uphold the slogan, "All Power to the Soviets." The Soviets, even though unfortunately still dominated by the Mensheviks and SR's, must be prodded into taking power and then as soon as possible must be transformed into correctly class-conscious (that is, Bolshevik) bodies. Their next move should be "not the introduction of socialism as an immediate task," but merely the placing of social production under Soviet control. As for the land, all of it should be nationalized in principle, but most important was the conversion of the remaining estates into socialist farms. The Bolsheviks "must make it clear that small peasant farming under a commodity production system *offers no escape* for mankind from the poverty and oppression of the masses" (italics original). Finally, the party should break with the Second International, change its own name from Social Democratic (written with the word Bolshevik in parentheses following) to "Communist," and establish a new International of like-minded parties.

The other Bolshevik leaders reacted to the April Theses with groans and protests and only after a time accepted them, with misgivings. The Mensheviks found confirmation of their suspicion that the Leninists had all along been opportunists cloaking themselves in Marxist doctrines. Trotsky, who had avoided identification with either Social Democratic faction, triumphantly declared that in the April

Theses Lenin had accepted *his* doctrine, and that in approving them the Bolshevik party had "rearmed itself." He himself, along with a number of his followers, was admitted to the party not long afterwards.

The effect of the Theses was to popularize the slogan, "All Power to the Soviets" and to weaken further the prestige of the Provisional Government in the eyes of the politically-minded semi-intellectuals and workers of Petrograd, many other cities, and at the front. It struck directly at the anomaly of the doctrinally based refusal of the Soviet leaders to assume the reins of government as they could have done. For that very reason the Theses had little effect in increasing the support of the Bolsheviks; Lenin did not appear to advance his own party as a claimant to power. The Bolsheviks continued to grow, but for the time being other parties grew as fast or faster.

The First Coalition

With the resignations of Guchkov and Miliukov, the liberal parties lost their last chance to maintain an independent lead in the government. On May 5 a new cabinet was formed in which Lvov remained prime minister and minister of interior, Kerensky succeeded Guchkov as war minister, and Tereshchenko replaced Miliukov as foreign minister. There were ten non-socialist ministers, but there were also six socialists. They entered the cabinet, not in defiance of the Soviet's views as Kerensky had done, but with the approval of their respective party leaderships and acknowledged their responsibility to their party organizations. The two most important new socialist ministers were the effective leaders of the main socialist parties. Victor Chernov, leader and chief theoretician of the SR's from the beginning, became minister of agriculture. Heracles Tsereteli, who was not only the Mensheviks' strongest man but also the most influential single leader of the Petrograd Soviet, became minister of posts and telegraphs.

The cabinet of May 5 became known as the First Coalition and signified a partial reversal of the Menshevik stand against taking power. The socialists still refused to take all power or all responsibility for governing but agreed to accept a minor share of both. The main figure in the First Coalition cabinet was not Lvov but Kerensky. Although Kerensky was nominally an SR, he depended for his undoubted popularity not on the support of his party, but on the adulation of people who were intoxicated with "revolution" in much the same way that Kerensky himself was. The SR leaders, in fact, were more embarrassed than pleased by his prominence, finding the prestige he gave the party insufficient compensation for the indifference he displayed toward party decisions.

Kerensky was conscious that the issue of the war had wrecked the first cabinet, and he was determined to resolve it. He planned an offensive which would place Russia in a position to make an effective peace through proving the army's continuing capacity to fight. As "persuader-in-chief" he ranged up and down the front addressing the soldiers and using flamboyant phrases: "I summon you forward, to the struggle for freedom, not to a feast, but to death. We, revolutionaries, have the right to death." The morale of the army had been severely undermined by the socialist sponsored Order No. 1 and the activities of party agitators among the soldiers. It had been further shaken by the Bolshevik propaganda against the war—the nuances of Lenin's "first revolution then peace" position escaped not only the soldiers but also many Bolshevik propagandists. The Allies urged Kerensky on, and the Soviet grudgingly consented to a large scale operation.

On June 18 an offensive was launched against the Austrians, toward Lvov in Galicia, and initially it made progress. The question of whether further advance was compatible with the concept of a "defensive war" was debated by army committees at the front. The solution was provided by the soldiers themselves; one does not risk his life willingly when his fellows are openly debating the wisdom of doing so. By July 1 the offensive had come to a halt. A few days later the Austrians and Germans struck back and the Russian front sagged, then collapsed. Troops fled in disorder, and some continued in the direction of home. From then on desertion increased from month to month.

Kerensky now had to face popular demonstrations directed against his government. The pent-up impatience of Petrograd workers was spurred by the failure of the Galician offensive. On July 3 and 4, which became known as the July Days, disorder and violence erupted. A mob besieged the Taurida Palace with the demand that the Menshevik-SR leaders of the Soviet take power. The crowd howled against Tsereteli and seized Chernov; a nameless hoodlum waved his fist in Chernov's face and shouted, "Take the power, you son of a bitch, when they offer it to you!"—thereby expressing the puzzlement of radical workers at the intricacies of revolutionary theory. Chernov was freed by Trotsky. After the SR minister of justice, Pereverzev, released evidence that Lenin had received funds from Germany, there was a sharp reaction against the Bolsheviks. Loyal forces raided *Pravda* and Bolshevik headquarters and attempted to arrest the leaders—but caught only Anatole Lunacharsky, the mildest of them, and Trotsky.

Was it an attempted coup by the Bolsheviks? Richard Pipes cites evidence that it was.[2] If it was, Lenin held back at the last moment.

The Second Coalition

Despite the government's tardy show of firmness, it was in the throes of collapse. Prince Lvov resigned on July 8, chiefly in protest at the policy of Minister of Agriculture Chernov. Chernov had refused to enact the SR land program, following the Menshevik lead in observing the presumed laws of history, but he did want to

---

[2] Richard Pipes, *The Russian Revolution 1899–1919*, Collins Harvill, London, 1990, pp. 426–431.

push through the stoppage of all land sales except by official permission and did so four days after Lvov resigned. Kerensky replaced Lvov as prime minister, but over two weeks elapsed before he could put together a new cabinet. Whereas the First Coalition had had a socialist minority, in the Second Coalition there were eleven socialists out of eighteen. Nevertheless, sobered by the July Days, the cabinet was less radical than the previous one.

The Bolsheviks evaluated the effect of the July Days in their VI Congress (the first since that held in London in 1907) which met in Petrograd in August. It was reported that the party membership had risen from 80,000 in April to 200,000, of whom almost half were in and around Petrograd and Moscow. The Congress renounced the slogan "All Power to the Soviets." The July demonstrations had failed, and the charge that Lenin was a German agent had palpably damaged Bolshevik prestige. As a result Lenin declared, "The substance of the matter is that it is already now impossible to take power peacefully. ... " The Menshevik-SR Soviets had proved impervious to Bolshevik manipulation, and the party would therefore concentrate on the factory committees, in which it already had the upper hand. Actually Lenin gave up hope in the Soviets too soon, for only a few weeks later they started to go over to the Bolsheviks.

The new prime minister, Kerensky, was alarmed by the Bolshevik threat to his government, and also was forcefully reminded by the July Days that he ruled by grace of the Soviets, who could take power at any time even if they thus far had refused to do so. Accordingly he attempted to find institutional support and backing elsewhere. The Provisional Committee of the Duma was still functioning, and on April 27 the surviving members of all four Dumas met informally to discuss the situation; however, the socialists watched such bodies suspiciously, scenting in them a danger of "counterrevolution," and Kerensky had little enthusiasm for them anyway. He sought to create his own forums of public opinion. On August 12 he summoned a Moscow State Conference, including all former Duma deputies along with representatives of Soviets, unions, local governments, and many other associations. Chief among the speakers who addressed this unwieldy gathering of nearly 2,500 persons were General Lavr Kornilov and Kerensky himself. On July 18 Kerensky had appointed Kornilov commander-in-chief, replacing General Brusilov (who two months earlier had succeeded General Alexeev, who had taken command when the monarchy fell). Kornilov, the son of a peasant family, had gained renown by successfully escaping from the Austrians after his capture in 1915 and was popular with the troops. In his speech he referred to an anticipated German offensive toward Riga, and he warned that "we must not allow that order in the rear should be the result of the loss of Riga."

The Left interpreted Kornilov's warning as a threat to surrender Riga to the Germans in order to find an excuse for establishing a military dictatorship; others thought that Kornilov might be a suitable person to restore law and order. Of course Kerensky was not in favor of chaos; when the Second Coalition had been formed, he had spoken of the need for "iron rule," but he meant his own, not someone else's. His own speech at the Conference, however, did not suggest firmness: "Let my heart become stone, let all the springs of faith in man perish, let all the flowers and wreaths of man dry up—I shall throw far away the keys of my heart, which loves men, I will think only about the state." (Woman's voice: "You cannot do that, your heart will not permit it.") Flamboyance is a matter of taste, but Kerensky's weakness was that oratory became a substitute for action.

The Kornilov Affair

Kornilov's forcefulness had justified Kerensky's faith in him as a commander. He had done what seemed impossible by stabilizing the front after the collapse of the Galician offensive, and he had restored some measure of discipline in the army. However, he was unable to hold Riga when the expected German offensive materialized, and the city fell on August 21. Certain ministers attempted to implement Kornilov's call for "order in the rear" by restoring the death penalty behind the lines, as it had been restored at the front—by Kerensky's order, before Kornilov had been appointed commander.

On August 23 Boris Savinkov, former terrorist but now acting minister of war, requested Kornilov to send a cavalry corps to Petrograd to be ready if a Bolshevik uprising should occur. However, Kornilov had already decided to send a force to the capital to effect a reconstruction of the cabinet, with Kerensky participating. V. N. Lvov,[3] who had been procurator of the Holy Synod earlier under the Provisional Government, attempted mediation between Kerensky and Kornilov in which, because of his ineptness, each thought Lvov was the representative of the other. On August 26 Lvov thought agreement had been reached for the "legal and peaceful" replacement of Kerensky by Kornilov, although Kerensky was to remain in the cabinet. However, Kerensky, treating its text as an ultimatum, arrested Lvov and dismissed Kornilov. The commander-in-chief refused to acknowledge the order of dismissal and denounced the Provisional Government, asserting that "under the pressure of the Bolshevik majority of the Soviets," it acted "in full agreement with the plans of the German general staff. ... "

Did Kornilov attempt to overthrow the Provisional Government? Early on August 28 Kerensky, under pressure from both his cabinet colleagues and other army officers, tried to stop publication of charges to that effect—too late. The cavalry corps was on its way to Petrograd. Whatever the intentions of its commander, General Krymov, the soldiers were certainly in no mood to carry out a seizure of power. In fact Krymov was arrested before he reached Petrograd and after an interview with Kerensky committed suicide. On September 1 Kornilov surrendered

---

[3] Not to be confused with Prince George Lvov, the former prime minister.

to arrest at Mogilëv. Kerensky himself assumed the title of commander-in-chief, while at length General N. N. Dukhonin became his chief of staff.

It seems plain that Kornilov was seeking to establish a "strong government," and had violated an order of duly constituted authority. However, it was his intention to strengthen the Provisional Government, not to overthrow it or to restore the monarchy, whatever effect his actions had or might have had. As Trotsky wrote, if this was Bonaparte, it was but a pale shadow of him. The only ones to profit from the imbroglio were the Bolsheviks, who wrenched from the Soviet an official authorization to form a Red Guard. The Bolsheviks maintained that they would not fight for Kerensky but would fight against Kornilov. It was their good fortune that no occasion arose in which they were required to translate this dialectical slogan into action.

The Kornilov affair brought about the collapse of the Second Coalition. On September 1 Kerensky, dismissing a number of SR ministers, formed a ministerial "directory" of five. The Executive Committee of the Soviet regarded the Kadets, as well as the whole "bourgeoisie," as compromised by their support of, or ambivalence toward, Kornilov's alleged "counterrevolutionary plot." On September 14 the Executive Committee summoned a Democratic Conference, made up chiefly of the Left membership of the Moscow State Conference, but no firm decisions could be reached. Not until September 25 was Kerensky able to form a Third Coalition cabinet, including ten socialists (a majority, as before) and six non-socialists.

In order to pacify the Left, Kerensky had been trying to free himself from any taint of the Kornilov affair. He proclaimed Russia a republic, punished the officers involved or suspected of involvement with Kornilov's cause, arrested such moderate politicians as Guchkov, and, in the end most important of all, he freed Trotsky and other Bolshevik prisoners. He reiterated orders for the observance of strict discipline in the army, but nevertheless a number of officers were lynched by their troops as suspected supporters of Kornilov.

Revolution from Below

By this time discipline in the ranks had broken down almost completely. The old army had been largely destroyed in 1915. As the junior officers were killed, they had been replaced by lower-class lieutenants, often educated peasants. The enlisted men were, as Lenin said, "peasants in uniform." They had listened to civilian agitators and read revolutionary pamphlets, while "Order No. 1" had done much to substitute talking for fighting. The application of the decree restoring the death penalty, issued in July, had never been seriously attempted. Kornilov proved to be the last commander determined to maintain the army as a fighting force. Especially after his dismissal, deserters streamed eastward from the front. If the government did not want them to be soldiers, they had business awaiting them at home. In mounting numbers, they simply went home to get the land. By October, according to one official report, the army that remained was "a huge crowd of tired, poorly clad, poorly fed, embittered men united by common longing for peace and general disillusionment." During 1917 the Russian units that had been sent to France and Macedonia also disintegrated. That is, despite the existence of soldiers' Soviets, soldiers took no significant part in the revolution. The navy was a different matter. In 1917 there were twenty-five times as many soldiers as sailors, yet sailors were more prominent in revolutionary action—as they had been in 1905.[4]

The peasants were not involved in the February Revolution; the first known cases of agrarian unrest occurred weeks later, sometimes as revenge for brutality in 1905–1907 or as chauvinist attacks on German landowners. There followed a period of calm, then in the spring two or three kinds of peasant committees were formed. Some started to seize idle lands or crops, with partial acquiescence by the Provisional Government. On June 28 the latter suspended the Stolypin reforms and many peasants were forced back into communes.[5]

Successive cabinets had warned that the land question must await the Constituent Assembly; they were ignored. The peasants began to pasture their cattle on gentry meadows, cut gentry wood, refuse to pay rent, cultivate gentry land without asking leave or make off with gentry supplies or belongings, and finally demanded houses and estates. Often there was no violence. The landlords were persuaded to leave for their own good, and often enough of the old patriarchal relationship between lord and serf survived so that partings were amicable or even tearful. Peasants sometimes murdered, but they might also lynch, "apparently with the best of conscience, some army deserter or tramp who had been caught stealing horses. In short the peasants' complete contempt for the property rights of the landlords was accompanied by a keen attachment to their own. ..."[6] But even peasant contempt for gentry rights was limited, for the tendency was to follow the rule that the estates belonged not just to anyone but to those peasants whose families had before 1861 been owned by the landlord in question or worked for him.

The Socialist Revolutionaries had the most influence in the countryside in 1917, but this does not prove that the peasants were SR's at heart any more than the 1906 elections prove they were really KD's (see p. 55). No party stood for what they wanted, namely, increase of their own private holdings through seizure of the land of the gentry, state, and church. In vain did the SR's declare, quite accu-

---

[4] Allan Wildman, *The End of the Russian Imperial Army*, Princeton U. Press, 1980; Evan Mawdsley, "Soldiers and Sailors," in Robert Service, ed., *Society and Politics in the Russian Revolution*, St. Martin's Press, 1992.

[5] Maureen Perrie, "The Peasants," in Service, ed., *Society and Politics*.

[6] W. H. Chamberlin, *The Russian Revolution, 1917–1921*, 2 vols., Macmillan, 1952, I:254–255.

rately, that "socialization [their complicated land program] of the land cannot be confused with arbitrary seizure of it for personal advantage." Not only the peasants, but also many nominal SR's in the "peasant committees" or in local peasant Soviets, were happily guilty of such confusion.

Already in March Soviets of Peasant Deputies had begun to spring up alongside the Soviets of Workers' and Soldiers' Deputies. In May the Peasant Soviets held a national congress that was dominated by the SR's and in which the Bolsheviks had only a handful of deputies. The Congress called for enactment of the SR program of "socialization" of land (which demanded the abolition of private ownership and the establishment of a "labor norm" for land to be occupied without payment—that is, a peasant family was to occupy no more land than it could cultivate itself). However, the Congress reiterated, again in accordance with SR doctrine, that the land problem must await solution by the Constituent Assembly. For the rest the Congress echoed the line of the Menshevik-SR leadership of the Workers' and Soldiers' Soviets: support of the Provisional Government and continuation of a defensive war.

The peasantry as a whole neither knew nor cared about the Menshevik theory of revolution or the SR formulations on the land in question. Neither Lvov, Kerensky, Chernov, nor anyone else succeeded in making any dent in the peasants' determination to divide the land among those deemed to have right over it, and no one seriously tried to prevent them from carrying out their intentions. Exhortation to avoid violence may have sounded paradoxical coming from the SR's, who had assassinated more people before the Revolution than the peasants killed while it was in progress, but the peasant had no interest in paradoxes.

While the 100-million-odd peasants were carrying out a revolution quite independent of party program and government orders, the 4 million or so industrial workers (excluding families) were in a quite different situation. Concentrated in and around a few cities, the workers had suffered from inflation, which by October drove prices up to a level more than fourteen times higher than Prewar,[7] and in particular from shortages of meat in March 1916, sugar in August, and bread in December—which contributed to the February Revolution directly. In Petrograd workers were more concentrated in large factories, especially the metalworkers— among whom 92% of the males were literate in 1918; in Moscow they were more dispersed in smaller-plants and workshops, especially textile—"calico Moscow" was one nickname for the city.

After February workers took part in three kinds of organization: factory committees, Soviets, and trade unions. There was "no clear delineation of functions" among them; trade unions cost money, the Soviets might seem superfluous, but factory committees were taken seriously—and, not surprisingly—political parties less seriously than any of the three. The eight-hour day was granted by Petrograd

---

[7] S. A. Smith, *Red Petrograd: Revolution in the Factories 1917–18*, Cambridge U. Press, 1983, p. 116.

employers at once, elsewhere more slowly. In reaction to the harsh factory discipline of earlier times, the workers sometimes gave managers and foremen rough
handling; a favorite device was to trundle them out of the plant in wheelbarrows.
The factory committees launched the slogan of "workers' control," and in May the
Bolsheviks took it up: Mensheviks and SR's opposed it.[8] It meant different things
depending on time and place; by midsummer it had come to mean actual workers' management in a minority of Petrograd factories. At one point following the
October Revolution Lenin seemed captivated by the idea, but the moment
passed.[9]

At first Mensheviks and SRs dominated the industrial scene. In the June 25 municipal Duma elections the SR's "clearly won the mass support of Moscow's workers" but did not follow up with organizational work.[10] From the time it was set up
in June the Petrograd Central Council of Factory Committees was "a bulwark of
Bolshevism," and by that time the Bolsheviks were the strongest party in the Petrograd Council of Trade Unions also, though they lacked the control they had in
the factory committees.[11] Outside of Petrograd, nationally and in Moscow, the
Bolsheviks were less influential in the trade unions than the Mensheviks. After the
July Days disillusionment spread with the socialist parties that went into the coalitions, insisted on worker abstention from power, and delayed any kind of decisive action.

By fall the position of the workers, especially the less skilled, was growing desperate. Prices climbed higher, the supply of food and consumer goods dwindled.
The Mensheviks and SR's got much of the blame, as the Soviets that they led spent
time debating political questions while the economic crisis drove the workers
close to despair. The peasants could depend on their own resources, but the
workers had to rely on others to keep in operation the factories on which their
livelihood depended. The Soviets apparently would not act to do so, and the employers were no longer able to. It seemed that the Bolsheviks alone promised a
way out of the crisis.

Revolution in the Borderlands

While the Russian-inhabited areas of the Empire were in turmoil, the borderlands
had a chance for autonomist or independence movements to make headway. The
end of the war witnessed a new nationalist upsurge among the peoples of eastern
Europe, Asia, and elsewhere. The submerged national groups of the empires of

---

[8] Ibid., p. 154.

[9] Ibid., pp. 209–210, 240.

[10] Diane Koenker, *Moscow Workers and the 1917 Revolution*, Princeton U. Presss, 1981, pp. 157, 187,
220.

[11] Smith, *Red Petrograd*, p. 112.

Austria-Hungary and Turkey were shortly to tear them into pieces. As Russia virtually ended her part in the war a year and a half earlier than the other powers, the Russian minorities began to assert themselves first.

Out of the multitude of minorities within the Russian Empire, only the Poles and Finns had enjoyed some degree of autonomy during the nineteenth century. The deepest national antagonism within the Empire was probably that between the Russians and the Poles. The Poles were proud of the past achievements of their country and regarded Russians generally as less civilized than they, while the Russians and Ukrainians remembered Polish domination of their lands and invasions of the heart of Russia and hated the Poles' Roman Catholic religion. Nevertheless, the question of Poland offered the least difficulty, for the Polish-inhabited territories were occupied by the Germans and Austrians. On March 16 the Provisional Government promised Poland independence, although the only practical consequence of this act was the formation of some Polish units in the Russian army—units which maintained discipline in the face of the Russian military collapse until disarmed by the Germans.

Finland's status under the Empire was by far the best of any of the national minorities, but the last two Emperors had sought to limit its autonomy. In March the Provisional Government made a number of concessions to the Finns, but the Finnish Social Democrats demanded independence, an issue which the Russians declared was something the Constituent Assembly must decide. In July the Finnish SD's finally prevailed upon the Finnish Diet—a body which had existed under the Empire—to proclaim what amounted to independence. The Provisional Government retorted by dissolving the Diet and calling new elections resulting in a majority for the non-socialists under Pehr Svinhufud. Negotiations were continuing between the new Diet and the Provisional Government when the Bolsheviks seized power.

The tsars had recognized no such entity as Ukraine. During the nineteenth century Ukrainian intellectuals had gathered to work for the cause of their new nationalism in Lemberg (Lvov) in Austro-Hungarian territory, where the Austrians permitted and even encouraged their activities, since they threatened Russia far more than the Dual Monarchy. The movement had adepts also in Kiev and among intellectuals in other parts of Russian Ukraine. Whether or not Ukrainian nationalism was, as Florinsky asserts, "a weak and artificial growth,"[12] the intellectuals who espoused it assumed the direction of political events in Ukraine soon after the February Revolution. The first effort of the Ukrainian leaders, through the self-constituted Central Rada (Council), was to obtain autonomy by agreement with the Provisional Government of Kerensky, who had from Duma days the reputation of sympathy for Ukraine. Meanwhile, however, the Rada endeavored to govern Ukraine as a separate administrative unit.

---

[12] Michael T. Florinsky, *Russia: A History and an Interpretation* 2 vols.; Macmillan, 1953, II:1424.

In June a kind of ministry, known as the General Secretariat, was established by the Rada under the chairmanship of the novelist Volodimir Vinnichenko. He was a member of the Ukrainian Social Democratic party (which, to the chagrin of the Russian SD's in the Ukraine, fellow-traveled with the Ukrainian nationalists). The Provisional Government recognized Ukrainian autonomy *de facto* under the Rada regime. Though not broad enough to satisfy the extreme Ukrainian nationalists, the action conceded more than most of the Kadet ministers of the Provisional Government were willing to accept. They resigned in protest, but the Ukrainian issue was shunted aside by the prolonged crisis provoked by the July Days in Petrograd. There was little further Russian discussion of the Ukrainian issue before the Bolshevik coup.

However, the Rada itself had to face wide discontent within Ukraine. The Ukrainian peasants, like those of Russia, were increasingly impatient with delays on the "land problem." Although Ukrainian army units were formed and the sailors of the Black Sea Fleet ran up a Ukrainian flag, they did not want to continue fighting any more than Russian soldiers and sailors did. The Bolsheviks in Ukraine played a double game; they criticized the Rada, and especially the Ukrainian SD's, for nationalist tendencies, while at the same time they courted popularity in Ukraine by supporting the Rada's side in negotiations with the Provisional Government, thereby also multiplying difficulties for the authorities in Petrograd whom they opposed. As the Bolshevik coup approached, the Ukrainian nationalists virtually made common cause with the Bolsheviks.

In Belorussia there occurred a pale reflection of events in Ukraine. One scholar doubts that in 1917 the Belorussian masses had "any consciousness of ethnic separateness"[13] at all, and certainly Belorussian political parties were almost nonexistent. A Belorussian Rada was established in July, but the Russian Bolsheviks and SR's were the only parties to gain any considerable strength in the region before the October Revolution.

Estonia, Latvia, and Lithuania had developed native nationalist movements, and autonomist aspirations spread rapidly there in 1917. In Transcaucasia the Menshevik- and SR-dominated Soviets of Tiflis and Baku were the focal points of political discussion. Georgia was a stronghold of Menshevism and had given Russia some of its most prominent Menshevik leaders, such as Chkheidze and Tsereteli. In contrast, Azerbaijan and Armenia had produced their own nationalist parties, the Mussavat and Dashnaktsutiun respectively. The Armenian Dashnaktsutiun actively supported the Allied war effort, provoking the Turks to conduct a stupendous massacre of one million Armenians in Turkish territory in 1915. Fear and hatred of the Turks led the Armenians to give fervent support to the Provisional Government. In 1917 Georgia and Armenia thus held the Caucasus to relative tranquillity, and friction with Petrograd was at a minimum.

---

[13] Richard Pipes, *The Formation of the Soviet Union*, Harvard U. Press, 1954, p. 73.

In Central Asia there had also been violence during the World War, although on a much smaller scale than in Armenia. Although the Kazakhs (then called Kirghiz) had enjoyed considerable autonomy and exemption from military service, in 1916 the tsarist government decided to draft some of them for rear-area duty. The order came at a time of increasing friction between Kazakhs and Russian settlers over the steppe lands and was interpreted as an act of further Russian encroachment on native rights. The Kazakhs retaliated by attacking Russian settlers, especially in Semirechensk province, and killing thousands of them. The rebellion was put down, and some 300,000 natives were driven off their lands, many of them into Chinese Sinkiang.

In 1917 Central Asian leaders concerned themselves with both religious and political demands. Kazakh congresses met in Orenburg, seeking to create a "Greater Kirghizia," and founded a nationalist party called the Alash-Orda. On the initiative of the Muslim deputies of the Duma, a nationwide Muslim Congress met in Moscow in May, proclaimed the emancipation of Muslim women, and established a religious administration independent of state control for all Russian Islam, somewhat as the Russian Orthodox Church did in 1917. The Congress also made plans for a federal solution for the problem of autonomy for the Muslim peoples, including the Bashkirs, Crimean Tatars, and others in addition to the Central Asian groups. By the summer of 1917 Kazakhs were trickling back across the Chinese border to their former homes in Russian territory. Russian settlers in the areas from which the natives had been evicted, either to defend their new homes or from motives of revenge, attacked the returning Kazakhs brutally and killed over 80,000. The October coup found the Central Asian steppes in a state of conflict and disorder, with relations between the Russians and natives far more bitter than they had been for generations.

Farther south, in Turkestan, the native leaders formed a Turkestan Central Council, dominated by liberal Muslims, although there was also a weaker conservative faction. However, the chief city of Turkestan, Tashkent, was dominated by the local Soviet, led by Mensheviks and SR's. The Soviet was striving to keep the Russian minority from being swamped by Muslims in the event that universal suffrage and effective regional autonomy were introduced. The Provisional Government failed to harmonize these conflicting interests and to establish its own authority. In September the Tashkent Soviet, swinging in a Bolshevik direction, attempted a coup and arrested the agents of Petrograd, but a military expedition was dispatched and order was temporarily restored.

Thus the control of the Provisional Government over the borderlands was almost universally tenuous and nominal. Everywhere local nationalists demanded autonomy, pro-Menshevik-SR groups temporized, and Bolsheviks exploited the confusion as best they could. Throughout the borderlands the Bolsheviks, although they started 1917 with negligible strength or none at all, built up a following and gained prestige by playing upon whatever grievances and antagonisms existed, never hesitating to push toward intransigence groups or parties which they intended to destroy as soon as they could.

If the Provisional Government had taken measures to establish some kind of federation, it might have held the borderlands. However, the dogmas prevailing in Petrograd blocked decisive action of any kind. Part of the reason for inaction was the Provisional Government's adherence to the principle that no solution was possible prior to the Constituent Assembly. At least as important, however, was the Menshevik-SR insistence that those who had such power as there was should not rule, while those who were trying to rule should not be given real power. If there had been no disciplined and organized force, such as the Bolsheviks, ready to turn the situation to its own advantage, the period of turmoil might well have been lived through somehow. But the Bolsheviks were present and visible to those who, more or less unwittingly, prepared the ground on which Bolshevik tactics could succeed.

The end of the Provisional Government came less than a month after the Third Coalition was formed on September 25. During the Kornilov episode Kerensky had appealed to the Bolshevik party for aid and had released the arrested Bolshevik leaders, who were untroubled by any feelings of gratitude to the man whose overthrow they proceeded to organize. The Central Executive Committee of the Soviets had summoned a Democratic Conference, making plain its dissatisfaction with the Moscow State Conference where some approval of Kornilov had been demonstrated. Kerensky refused to recognize the Democratic Conference as an official body, but he wished to summon a new forum which could provide some semblance of representative support for the government. The statute for the Constituent Assembly was published at last, and elections were fixed for late November.

At length Kerensky and the Soviets reached a compromise whereby a new body recognized by both was summoned. It was called the Provisional Council of the Republic, or "Pre-Parliament," and met on October 7. It was dominated by the socialists, and there were only 150 non-socialists out of a membership of 550. The Bolsheviks walked out of its first meeting, and Kerensky knew very well what they had gone to do, but he declared, "I have more strength than I need. They will be finally smashed."

It was by now plain to the Mensheviks and SR's not only that a Bolshevik coup was in prospect but also that it might have a good chance of success unless the government acted speedily. On the afternoon of October 24, the orthodox leaders of the two parties forced through the Council of the Republic a resolution demanding immediate action on the questions of peace and land. Fëdor Dan, a prominent Menshevik, and Abram Gots, an SR, went to Kerensky and insisted that poster and telegraph immediately carry the word to the country that this was the aim of the Provisional Government. At this ultimatum Kerensky threatened to resign, but the Bolsheviks were already beginning to take over the city of Petrograd.

8

The October Revolution

Bolshevik Gains Before the Coup

By autumn the Bolsheviks had gained markedly both in membership and popular support. On the Russian political scene those were two different things, particularly in the case of the Bolsheviks, whose closely knit and disciplined organization always more nearly approximated a military unit than a political party in the sense hitherto familiar in the West. In strength the party had increased to over 200,000 members. In popularity the gains had been manifold and striking. At the I Congress of Soviets which opened in Petrograd on June 3, the Bolsheviks had 105 deputies, the SR's 285, the Mensheviks 248; Lenin's party was outnumbered more than five to one by the socialist coalition. The Bolsheviks had labored mightily among the soldiers to make their Military Organization influential, but progress was slow. As for the peasantry, even in November the Bolsheviks' "independent power in the countryside was still negligible," writes E. H. Carr, who is by no means inclined to minimize Bolshevik achievements.[1]

However, even at the time of the I Congress of Soviets the balance had begun to shift in favor of the Bolsheviks. On June 1 the Workers' Section of the Petrograd Soviet had voted by a narrow margin to support the Bolshevik slogan, "All Power to the Soviets." The Soldiers' Section at that time was still dominated by the Menshevik-SR coalition. The Kornilov affair, during which the Bolsheviks had been authorized to form Red Guards openly, swung the Soldiers' Section over. On August 31 both sections of the Petrograd Soviet adopted a Bolshevik resolution, and a more decisive vote occurred on September 8. Meanwhile, on September 5, the Moscow Soviet had also passed to the Bolsheviks; in Krasnoiarsk, Ekaterinburg,

---

[1] Edward Hallett Carr, *The Bolshevik Revolution, 1917–1923*, 3 vols.; Macmillan, 1950–1953, II:41.

and many other cities of the south and east the same thing took place. The October elections to the Moscow ward councils, held under universal suffrage, indicated that a major shift of opinion was under way. Comparing the October results with those of elections held in July, one observes a sharp decline in the aggregate vote, but the Bolsheviks increased their percentage from 11% to 51% while the Kadet vote held steady numerically (and thus leaped proportionately, from 17% to 26%), and the SR and Menshevik support disintegrated. The last two parties named polled 70% in July, but only 18% in October. These data may furnish a fair index of what happened in the autumn in the large cities: the Bolsheviks drove home to the active political elements their claim to stand firmly for the broad revolutionary slogans of peace and land and thus won many supporters away from the two moderate socialist parties.

The Bolsheviks were immensely successful in exploiting to their own advantage the failure of the Galician offensive, the Kornilov episode, and other events. The fact that Prime Minister Kerensky was nominally an SR but would not follow the decisions of his own party, although he demanded its loyalty, hampered the socialist leaders in meeting the competition of Lenin, who was able to count on the generally unswerving support of his party. Such opportunities, nevertheless, could not have been utilized as they were if it had not been for the theoretically grounded insistence of Tsereteli and the Mensheviks that history did not permit them to exercise the power which was in fact theirs. The socialist ambivalence about power opened a gap in the ranks of the supporters of the February Revolution through which the Bolsheviks were ultimately able to drive with an ease which surprised even themselves.

The Uprising

Lenin had begun the revolutionary year with the slogan, "All Power to the Soviets." After the July Days he had renounced it in favor of armed uprising. When the Petrograd Soviet passed into Bolshevik hands in the fall, Lenin reverted to "All Power to the Soviets" without, however, abandoning armed uprising. In the Bolshevik party itself there was again, as in April, some reluctance to go along with Lenin's tactics. On October 10 there was a secret meeting of the Bolshevik Central Committee in the apartment of N. N. Sukhanov, a Left Menshevik, though it was his Bolshevik wife who acted as hostess. Lenin declared that the political situation was ripe for action, and that the foremost need was organization of the uprising. He recognized that the Constituent Assembly would not have a Bolshevik majority, and thus to await its meeting would "mean a complication of our problem" (a little later he did stake the success of the coup on the likelihood of the party's obtaining a majority in the II Congress of Soviets, scheduled to meet on October 25). Gregory Zinoviev and Leo Kamenev, two of the most influential leaders, warned of the risks and opposed Lenin on the vote, which was ten to two. The historic meeting not only decided on an uprising, but also chose the party's first Political Bureau of the Central Committee. The first Politburo consisted of Lenin, Trotsky, Stalin, Zinoviev, Kamenev, G. Y. Sokolnikov, and A. S. Bubnov. It seems, however, not to have been active in the events immediately following, and achieved importance only during the Civil War. Zinoviev and Kamenev took their objections to the coup to the party press, thereby revealing its imminence to the public, although in any event it was an ill-kept secret.

Amid the turmoil of October the very decision to convene a II Congress had to be forced on the Soviets' Central Executive Committee. On October 11 a Soviet congress was held for the northern region alone, and the Bolsheviks triumphantly assumed control over it. Two days earlier they had managed to push through the Executive Committee approval of the setting up of a Military Revolutionary Committee to control the Petrograd and nearby garrisons. This body was actually employed as the "general staff of the insurrection." Colonel Polkovnikov, the government's commander of the Petrograd military district, at first hoped to avoid bloodshed by simply ignoring the existence of the Committee. However, on October 23 the Provisional Government made another about-face in its attitude to the Bolsheviks and ordered the rearrest of Bolshevik leaders free on bail as well as the carrying out of other legal steps against the party. Simultaneously loyal troops were to be concentrated in Petrograd.

October 24 brought a showdown. Cadets of the military schools patrolled various key points in the city. The crew of the cruiser *Aurora,* who were pro-Bolshevik, brought their ship into the Neva River to anchor near the Winter Palace, seat of the Provisional Government, and defied orders to put out to sea. In the afternoon the Council of the Republic adopted its resolution for immediate action on the issues of peace and land (see p. 111). Its wording led Kerensky to take offense, and he declared he would resign. However, the events already afoot both led him to change his mind and made his resignation superfluous. Kerensky fled the next morning to seek loyal troops, his automobile accompanied by a casually commandeered embassy car flying the American flag.

On the night of October 24 Bolshevik troops began seizing public buildings and other key points in Petrograd. There was a fight for the Winter Palace, but in the early morning of October 26 it was overrun by soldiers led by Antonov-Ovseenko. The ministers of the Provisional Government, headed after Kerensky's flight by A. I. Konovalov, were removed to cells in the Fortress of St. Peter and St. Paul. Sukhanov, a member of the Soviet Executive Committee, encountered insurrectionary troops on the afternoon of October 25 and chatted with their commander, who declared:

> "Incomprehensible! The order was to march. But why—no one knows. Against one's own people, after all. All rather strange. ..." The Commander smiled with embarrassment, and it was evident that he was indeed rather baffled by everything. There

was no doubt about it: there was no spirit; such troops would never fight; they would never fight; they would scatter and surrender at the first blank shot. But there was no one to do any shooting.[2]

The II Congress of Soviets

On the same afternoon, the II Congress of Soviets convened. Lenin's calculations on obtaining a majority of delegates proved justified. Out of about 650 delegates, 390 were Bolsheviks. The Mensheviks and orthodox Socialist Revolutionaries walked out in protest at the armed insurrection, but the Left SR's, who had by now broken off and formed a separate party, remained. As Sukhanov says, they "had no objection to being the sole representatives of the peasantry."[3] Their usefulness to Lenin was considerable; the Bolsheviks stood for the "proletariat," the Left SR's for the "poor peasantry." This uneasy and unequal partnership lasted only a few months, but upon the participation of the Left SR's for even that short a time hung both Lenin's claim to have realized his slogan of "dictatorship of the proletariat and the poor peasantry" and his contention that there was a Soviet government rather than a purely Bolshevik government in power.

How broad was Lenin's support at the time of the October Revolution? He could not even claim a clear majority in the Soviets. Although the Bolsheviks were the largest faction at the Congress of Soviets of Workers' and Soldiers' Deputies, the Soviets of Peasant Deputies returned an anti-Bolshevik majority at their meeting several weeks later. Any doubt about the attitude of the people as a whole was shortly to be dispelled by the elections to the Constituent Assembly. However, not long before, Lenin had made it clear that majorities were not of primary importance to him. In the pamphlet, *Will the Bolsheviks Retain State Power?* he declared that 130,000 landlords had been able to govern Russia after the Revolution of 1905 and certainly 240,000 Bolsheviks would be able to govern "in the interests of the poor and against the rich ... The state is an organ or instrument of violence of one class against another. While it is an instrument of violence used by the bourgeoisie on the proletariat, the proletarian slogan can only be *destruction* of that state. But when the state becomes proletarian, when it becomes an instrument of violence used by the proletariat on the bourgeoisie, then we will completely and unconditionally stand for strong state power and centralism." In other words, the new government would be a dictatorship, and indeed it was.

The cabinet of the new regime was announced at the II Congress of Soviets on the evening of October 26. It was called a Council of People's Commissars—the word "minister" was rejected as redolent of bourgeois governments. The chairman, or prime minister, was Lenin; Alexis Rykov was commissar of interior;

---

[2] Sukhanov, *The Russian Revolution, 1917*, p. 624.
[3] *Ibid.*, p. 654.

Trotsky foreign commissar; agriculture went to V. P. Miliutin, labor to A. G. Shliapnikov, education to Lunacharsky, nationalities to Stalin.

The main business of the Congress was to pass a Decree on Peace and a Decree on Land. The Decree on Peace simply proposed ending the war "without annexations and indemnities," which had been the formula of the Soviets in the spring. Neither did the Decree on Land enact the Bolshevik program. The measure transferred private and church lands to land committees and the Soviets of Peasant Deputies, declared the abolition of private property in land, and fixed a "toiling" norm for actual peasant holdings—a peasant was to hold only as much land as he could till himself. Certain delegates hastened to point out that this was nothing more or less than the SR land program. Lenin replied, "Life itself is the best teacher, and it will show who is right; let the peasants solve this question from one end and we from the other. It isn't important whether the problem is solved in the spirit of our program or in the spirit of the Socialist Revolutionary program." Chernov, leader of the orthodox SR's, complained bitterly, "Lenin copies out our resolutions and publishes them in the form of 'decrees'," but he could do nothing to stop it. The Left SR's, now in coalition with the Bolsheviks, retained the old land program of the SR party, and they were pleased to see it enacted into law. After passing the two decrees, approving the new government, and electing a new Central Executive Committee composed of 62 Bolsheviks and 29 Left SR's (there were, however, no Left SR commissars in the cabinet at first), the II Congress of Soviets dispersed.

After they walked out from the Congress, the Mensheviks and orthodox SR's organized, with the co-operation of the old Soviet Central Executive Committee, a Committee for the Salvation of the Country and the Revolution. The Committee did little but urge government employees to refuse to co-operate with the newly installed commissars. The Menshevik and SR leaders declared that the II Congress of Soviets was merely a private meeting of Bolshevik deputies. They thought the Bolsheviks were behaving badly but seemed to have no conception of the magnitude of the change that had occurred. They continued to demand that a "broad" (including Bolsheviks) socialist government be formed, and indeed a number of Bolsheviks were willing. They worried, as did the Bolsheviks, about rumors that "counterrevolutionary" troops were en route to Petrograd. Few realized that a new era had opened in Russian history, and that the Bolsheviks were already on the way to the establishment of a single-party dictatorship.

Kerensky had managed to find help from General P. N. Krasnov at Pskov, and with a few hundred Cossacks had advanced to Tsarskoe Selo. However, the troops were routed at a skirmish at Pulkovo, twelve miles from Petrograd, and Kerensky fled, this time abroad. Meanwhile, after a week's fighting, the Bolsheviks took control of Moscow. Within a month or two, local Bolshevik detachments of workers and soldiers seized power in most of the cities of Russia. In the industrial town of Ivanovo-Voznesensk the take-over was easier than in Petrograd; in Kazan there was fighting, as in Moscow. With or without bloodshed, the Bolshevik power spread over most of the urban centers. However, the Cossack atamans kept their authority in the southeast; Kiev remained in the hands of the Ukrainian Rada; and, not very far from Petrograd, General Dukhonin at Supreme Headquarters in Mogilëv refused to recognize the Bolshevik coup.

Peace

There no longer existed any dependable armed force at the disposal of either the Bolsheviks or their opponents. Lenin's government attempted to implement its promises as well as to ward off any possible danger of attack by army units loyal to the Provisional Government, by ordering General Dukhonin to begin negotiations for peace with the enemy high command, but he refused. N. V. Krylenko (who with Antonov-Ovseenko and P. E. Dibenko made up a sort of triple-headed commissariat for military and naval affairs) was sent to replace him, and Dukhonin was lynched by the soldiers. Krylenko ordered subordinate units to make their own cease-fire arrangements, simultaneously offering the Germans general peace negotiations. On November 22 a preliminary armistice agreement was reached at Brest-Litovsk.

Soon after Krylenko assumed command the old army dissolved entirely, many of the officers trying to reach anti-Bolshevik centers, the soldiers streaming homeward. The Bolsheviks were left with no weapons but those of diplomacy in facing the Germans. It was now the turn of Trotsky, as foreign commissar, to achieve "peace." His view of his functions was reflected in the remark attributed to him by friends, "I will issue some revolutionary proclamations to the peoples and then shut up shop." The Soviet Government was not created to make agreements with bourgeois regimes but to overthrow them. However, the first task was to prevent the Imperial German army from advancing; "our final negotiations," Trotsky declared hopefully, "will be with Karl Liebknecht"—the leader of the German Communists.

On December 9 (O.S.) parleys began at Brest-Litovsk between the Soviet Government (the delegation was at first headed by Adolf Joffe, then by Trotsky himself) and the Central Powers (the main figures were German Foreign Minister von Kühlmann and General Max von Hoffmann). Hoffmann made it clear at once that the price of peace was Bolshevik surrender of German-held territory. He introduced representatives of the Ukrainian Rada into the negotiations as an example of the way he interpreted the phrase "no annexations"—that is, he demanded that any borderlands which desired should be permitted to secede from Bolshevik Russia. On January 5 Hoffmann pointed to a line on the map which was both the boundary of opposing forces and, he said, the future boundary of Russia. At this Trotsky decided to return home for discussions.

By now the Bolsheviks were deeply split about how to attain "peace." Nicholas Bukharin and others, especially in the Moscow party organization, advocated rejection of Hoffmann's ultimatum and wanted to proclaim a "revolutionary war." Lenin believed that the need of the Bolshevik regime for a breathing spell overshadowed all else. Although the expected socialist revolution in the West "must and will come," he declared, it might be delayed for a time. Attempts to fight on would not only strengthen the Anglo-French "imperialists," but would also imperil the popular acceptance of the Bolsheviks and of the Soviet power. Zinoviev, Kamenev, and Stalin concurred. Trotsky attempted a dialectical resolution of this disagreement by offering the formula, "no war, no peace," which was no solution at all. On January 8 in Petrograd a Bolshevik conference considered the matter and voted 32 for Bukharin's proposal, 16 for Trotsky's, and 15 for Lenin's. However, three days later the Bolshevik Central Committee canceled out that verdict in favor of Trotsky's formula by a nine-to-seven vote, and a joint Bolshevik-Left SR session assented the next day.

Trotsky returned to Brest-Litovsk hoping to play for more time, trusting that propaganda and agitation among German and Austrian troops might yield results. On January 27 Hoffmann produced a peace treaty with the Ukrainian Rada—at the moment, as it happened, when the Bolsheviks were occupying Kiev.[4] The next day Trotsky invoked his "no war, no peace formula"; he refused to agree to the German demands, announced that the war was at an end, and left Brest. Trotsky's gesture had the sole effect of eliminating his formula from further serious discussion by Bolshevik leaders. Within a week the Germans launched a new offensive which moved forward unopposed. On the day it opened, February 18, Lenin's demand for acceptance of the German terms was narrowly adopted by a seven-to-six vote of the Central Committee. The Germans, however, replied by new and harsher terms. Lenin insisted that they be accepted, threatening to resign if they were not, and the party leaders, realizing there was no alternative, agreed. On March 3, 1918, a Bolshevik delegation signed the Treaty of Brest-Litovsk. Trotsky thereupon yielded the foreign commissariat to Gregory Chicherin and became war commissar.

The Significance of Brest-Litovsk

The Allies had done their best to prevent Russia from signing a separate peace. It was in direct response to an appeal by an American agent in Russia, Edgar Sisson, to "restate anti-imperialistic war aims and democratic peace requisites of America ... in short, almost placard paragraphs" that President Woodrow Wilson delivered his "Fourteen Points" speech on January 8. Wilson's sixth point was a demand for evacuation of all Russian territory and a call to give Russia "a sincere

---

[4] On February 1/14, 1918, the Bolsheviks adopted the Gregorian calendar. Subsequent dates given will be N.S.

welcome into the society of free nations under institutions of her own choosing; and, more than a welcome, assistance also of every kind that she may need and may herself desire."

Such influential though only quasi-official diplomats as Colonel Raymond Robins, head of the U.S. Red Cross Mission, R. H. Bruce Lockhart, British special agent, and Captain Jacques Sadoul of the French Military Mission attempted to sound out Trotsky on the possibility that the Bolsheviks might continue the war with Allied aid. When this question was discussed in the Party Central Committee on February 22, Lenin sent his proxy: "I ask to add my vote in favor of taking potatoes and arms from the bandits of Anglo-French imperialism." Although Trotsky kept up contacts with Robins and Lockhart even after the peace treaty was signed, nothing came of them. The IV Congress of Soviets (which ratified the treaty) replied to a friendly message from Wilson with a statement of "its firm conviction that the happy time is not far away when the working masses of all bourgeois countries will overthrow the yoke of capital and establish the socialist order." In those days the Communists were more direct, as their immediate expectations were greater.

By the Treaty of Brest-Litovsk Lenin's government lost Poland, the Baltic states, much of Belorussia, Ukraine, Finland (which had already been given its independence), and a strip of territory on the Turkish border of Transcaucasia: in total, about 1.3 million square miles and 62 million people. On March 9 another treaty between the Central Powers and defeated Romania also sanctioned the latter's annexation of Bessarabia. Lenin's concessions were certainly necessary. However, the calculations on which he based his surrender to German terms were erroneous. Although he talked of a "Tilsit peace," comparing Brest-Litovsk with the treaty of 1807 between Alexander I and Napoleon, he did not expect renewal of the war (as in 1812) but rather the speedy overthrow of the Imperial German government by a Communist revolution. The treaty was indeed to be torn up very soon, but for a quite different reason: Germany's surrender to the Western Allies.

The Brest peace had immediate consequences for the Bolshevik regime. The new frontier was perilously close to the capital, and the government was promptly transferred from Petrograd, where it had been for over two centuries, to Moscow, where it had been in the days of the Muscovite tsars and where it has remained. The popular response to the peace was mostly apathy, although it is likely that an attempt to pursue any kind of war would have produced a sharply negative reaction. Within the Bolshevik and Left SR ranks there was open opposition to the treaty. The VII Congress of the Bolshevik party (which incidentally renamed the party "Communist" as Lenin had demanded in the April Theses) met March 6–8 and ratified the treaty; the IV Congress of Soviets did so again a few days later. However, Bukharin openly attacked the treaty, particularly for its provision compelling the Communists to renounce propaganda against the Central Powers, and others were at best sullen in their acquiescence.

The Communists' junior partners, the Left SR's, showed no such restraint. In March their representatives resigned from the cabinet and the Central Executive Committee of Soviets in protest at Lenin's peace. By July they had an additional grievance, the activities of the Communist-directed "Committees of Poor Peasants" (see p. 127). Thereupon they resorted to their old and preferred weapons against their former allies. A Left SR named Blumkin, hoping to provoke a renewal of hostilities, assassinated the German ambassador, Count von Mirbach, and there were several attempts at insurrection. On August 30 Left SR's wounded Lenin, inflicting an injury from which he never fully recovered, and killed two other Communist leaders. To this effort to overthrow the Communist power and reopen the war, the now single-party government retaliated swiftly. A Red Terror was launched by the Extraordinary Commission for Struggle with Counterrevolution and Sabotage ("Cheka" from the initial letters of the first two words in Russian) under Felix Dzerzhinsky.

Destroying the Old State

The Cheka had been established in December, replacing the Petrograd Military Revolutionary Committee as the agency of revolutionary force. Its creation was but one of a series of measures by which the Bolsheviks sought to destroy the old state and build a new one—to use the formulation which came out of Marx's analysis of the Paris Commune of 1871 and was restated in Lenin's pamphlet of 1917, *The State and Revolution.*

Much was to be done to achieve such an objective. Even the Provisional Government was not finally disposed of by the October Revolution. The socialist ministers were soon released, and they proceeded to meet as a government, issuing orders which affected state institutions. On November 17 they even proclaimed themselves the "sole legitimate organ of power," spoke of the Bolsheviks as "rebels," and urged support of the Constituent Assembly. Lenin's government promptly deported them to Kronstadt, and the last remnant of the Provisional Government disappeared. The anti-Bolshevik Petrograd and Moscow municipal councils were dissolved. On November 24 the Senate, which had been in effect the Imperial supreme court, placidly pronounced the Bolshevik regime illegal and was thereupon abolished. Not for another month did Lenin get around to dissolving the zemstvo organs of local self-government, including the township zemstvos created by the Provisional Government. The crumbling army was pushed to complete disintegration by decrees ordering election of officers (but now called "commanders") and abolishing all ranks and decorations. What units were left in being were speedily demobilized. Neither Reds nor Whites managed to take over the old army; it simply ceased to exist.

The old marriage and divorce laws were repealed. Only civil marriage was to be officially recognized, illegitimacy was to entail no disabilities, divorce might be had by either partner for the asking. On February 14, 1918 (February 1, Old Style), the Gregorian calendar was adopted, and the Julian calendar was abandoned by all except the ecclesiastical authorities. Even the old Cyrillic alphabet was purged of dispensable letters, although there was no attempt—as in Turkey, for example—to adopt a Latin alphabet.

The Russian Orthodox Church, the official religious institution of the old regime, was attacked, not with the intent of destroying it instantly but rather of penning it into a corner where, it was hoped, it would wither and die. On January 23, 1918, the government proclaimed the "separation of the Church from the state and from the schools." Actually the separation of the Church from the control which the state had exercised, through the Holy Synod, had already been begun under the Provisional Government. The Church itself had taken the initiative in summoning a council and in restoring the Patriarchate which Peter the Great had abolished. However, the Communists had never made any secret of their belief that religion was ideologically pernicious and institutionally an instrument of the exploiting classes. It was not "separation" but destruction which they planned for the Orthodox Church and all other religious institutions and doctrines. Nevertheless Lenin had repeatedly cautioned against a premature frontal attack on the "superstitions" of the masses. The Communists believed that the overturn of the economic foundation would undermine the "superstructural" institutions, including religion, of a bygone time. Time would show that they had grossly underestimated the magnitude of their task in obliterating religious belief.

The Constituent Assembly

One institution which the Provisional Government had promised and had finally prepared to convene still plagued the Bolsheviks. That was the Constituent Assembly. There had never been such a thing, and yet as a slogan it had a history of several generations and widespread popularity. Like all the other opposition parties, the Bolsheviks had always claimed to support it, although as long ago as 1903 Plekhanov (in his fleeting Bolshevik phase) had declared that if a good assembly was elected, it would be kept, if a bad one, it would be dispersed. Even though Kerensky's government had at last fixed the elections to the Constituent Assembly, the Bolsheviks had charged that he intended to subvert it, and immediately after the October Revolution, *Pravda* had declared, "Comrades, by shedding your blood you have assured the convocation ... of the Constituent Assembly."

The elections were held as scheduled on November 12, with the exception of a few districts. It is impossible to give a precise and complete tabulation of results, but the general picture is clear enough. In the large cities the Bolsheviks polled the most votes, with the Kadets a reasonably close second, but in the smaller towns and the countryside the SR's won enough to give them a majority in the election as a whole. Radkey's study yields roughly the following figures: SR's and Ukrainian SR's 17.1 million, Bolsheviks 9.8 million, Kadets 2 million, Mensheviks 1.36 million out of a grand total of 41.7 million (including a number of nationalist or minority groups).[5] Out of 703 deputies, 380 were regular SR's (Russian and Ukrainian), 39 Left SR's, 168 Bolsheviks, 18 Mensheviks, 17 Kadets and Rightists, 4 Popular Socialists, 77 minority group representatives.

The elections were carried out under conditions wherein freedom of campaigning was partially (for the Kadets very severely) curtailed, and the results were undoubtedly clouded by the prevailing political confusion, misinformation, and uncertainty. The Bolsheviks did not try to make a case that the country was really in favor of their party, but they argued that the Left SR's were not adequately represented since they had broken off from the rest of the party after the electoral lists had been drawn up, and thus that the peasants had no opportunity to distinguish between the Bolsheviks' allies (the Left SR's) and their enemies (the orthodox SR's). However, according to Radkey, those who did attend the assembly as Left SR deputies sometimes managed to do so only because the new party had obtained control of certain party organizations and "rigged the lists." In that way their participation in the Soviet Government certainly offset to a considerable extent the handicap to which the Bolsheviks pointed.

In any case Lenin did not much care what the elections proved, as his attitude toward the Constituent Assembly was purely instrumentalist. He had desired to postpone the elections but had been outvoted on that. When the results he feared had come in, he tried in several ways to render the assembly impotent. He arrested a few deputies, dispersed forty-three of them who invaded the Taurida Palace on November 28 (the date set by the shadow Provisional Government) and tried to hold a session. He outlawed the Kadets and arrested two of their leaders who were deputies to the assembly, A. I. Shingarëv and F. F. Kokoshkin, who were murdered in a detention hospital a few weeks later. Uritsky (himself to be assassinated by the Left SR's within a few months) spoke for the Bolsheviks: "Shall we convene the Constituent Assembly? Yes. Shall we disperse it? Perhaps; it depends on circumstances." In *Pravda* Lenin made it clear that the only way the assembly might survive would be to vote confidence in the Soviet Government.

On January 5 the Constituent Assembly met for the first and last time in the Taurida Palace. The session was dominated by the leaders of the SR and Menshevik parties, Chernov and Tsereteli. Chernov was elected president of the assembly over Maria Spiridonova, a Left SR leader fronting for the Bolsheviks, by a vote of 244 to 153. Three measures were adopted: a Land Law, an appeal for peace (which deprecated the separate-peace character of the Soviet-German negotiations then in progress and proposed an international socialist conference to realize a "general democratic peace"), and a decree proclaiming Russia a democratic federative

---

[5] Oliver Henry Radkey, *The Election to the Russian Constituent Assembly of 1917*, Harvard U. Press, 1950, esp. pp. 16–17.

republic. At 5:00 A.M. on January 6 a sailor informed Chernov that the "guard is tired," and requested the deputies to disperse. The assembly adjourned until noon, but the delegates were prevented by force from reassembling. Bolshevik troops fired on street demonstrators in favor of the Constituent Assembly, but there was little popular reaction to the dissolution.

It is difficult to prove from these events that the "people" supported the Bolsheviks, the Constituent Assembly, or anything else. The assembly had the same leadership as the Soviets in early 1917—the Mensheviks and SR's (even though actual Menshevik strength in deputies was negligible, the plurality of their SR friends accounted for the continued partnership). The leaders of the two parties had persistently refused to recognize the problem of power and continued to do so. They had been unwilling to countenance the creation of police or military forces which might have prevented the Bolshevik coup, and as a result no force existed sufficient to defend the Constituent Assembly. It has been argued that the failure of the assembly proved that the Russian people were unready for democracy. More concretely and perhaps more accurately, it showed that the leadership of the assembly had learned little from the success of the Bolshevik coup. The Menshevik and SR leaders, with some exceptions, remained ambivalent about whether democracy is justified in using arms in self-defense, and many of them readily accepted the contention that their own weaknesses were at root the fault of the peoples of Russia.

With the Constituent Assembly there disappeared virtually the last institutional toehold for the political forces opposed to Bolshevism. Thenceforth the only alternative appeared to be an attempt to build a territorial base on the periphery of the country from which to attack the Bolshevik-controlled center.

Building the New State

As Lenin well realized, the creation of new institutions was a much more difficult task than the destruction of old ones. If, as John Reed reports, his first words to the II Congress of Soviets were, "We shall now proceed to construct the Socialist order!"[6] he still recognized that such construction would take some time. It was the Bolshevik view that the building of a new state structure was already well begun at the time of the October Revolution. The Soviets, organized in many divergent and informal ways in different parts of the country, were to be the building blocks of the new edifice.

However, certain of the blocks required some reshaping. Although the Workers' and Soldiers' Soviets fell completely into Lenin's hands at the moment the Mensheviks and SR's walked out of the II Congress, thus saving the Bolsheviks

---

[6] John Reed, *Ten Days that Shook the World,* International Publishers, 1919, p. 126.

much trouble, the Peasant Soviets were a more serious problem. In early December a Congress of Peasant Deputies was summoned in Petrograd; it promptly voted confidence in the orthodox SR leader, Chernov, and no confidence in the Bolshevik-Left SR coalition. Lenin and Maria Spiridonova, who owed her leadership of the terrorist Left SR's to notoriety earned by her own past murder of a tsarist official, thereupon forced a split in the Congress.[7] This time, in effect, the majority walked out. The remaining delegates fused with the Workers' and Soldiers' Soviets and elected several members to the Central Executive Committee. From then on the Peasant Soviets were safely Bolshevik-controlled, by exclusion of opponents. There was never any pretense that "Soviet democracy" was going to mean that any Soviet body could override the will of the Bolshevik party Central Committee. Legislation might or might not be formally ratified by one of the Congresses of Soviets or the Soviet Central Executive Committee between sessions of the Congresses, but it was initiated in the top party echelons.

The recasting of the economic system began slowly. On October 29 the eight-hour working day was universally introduced. Two weeks later "workers' control," the slogan advanced by the Bolshevik-led factory committees earlier in the year, was enacted, and workers' committees were thereby awarded the right to oversee all steps in production. On December 1 a new organ, the Supreme Economic Council, was created to supervise the whole national economy. Shortly afterward banks were nationalized and in February all debts of the tsarist regime were cancelled. Nevertheless, except for a number of arbitrary financial levies on businessmen which were carried out in many cities, there was little effort at this stage to disturb private enterprise as a whole.

In the spring of 1918 the Communists were apparently solidly in power. Enough of the old structure had been wrecked or undermined to make its restoration very difficult, and enough enthusiasm had been aroused among veteran and recently recruited Communists to make it hard for any non-Communist group or coalition to build a corps of comparably dedicated leaders. The Russian people were still mostly peasant and Christian, but the Communists had not as yet made it clear that their real objective was to tear the people away from their own soil and their ancestral religion.

The masses knew that the "Revolution" had become very puzzling indeed, that it was hard to tell who was really in favor of it and who was not, and that the government in Moscow was quite unpredictable, unlike the Tsarist regime which, although often oppressive, was at least familiar. The politics of the Revolution had passed beyond popular comprehension:

---

[7] Evidence has come to light that much of the Spiridonova story was invention. See Ekaterina Breitbart article in *Kontinent* 28 (1981):321–342.

From house to house
A rope is strung,
A sagging placard on it hung:
"All Power to the Constituent Assembly!"

A bent old woman, tearful, trembly,
Stares at the placard in despair.
Her blear eyes see
How many fine foot-clouts could be
Cut from the canvas wasted there,
While the children's feet go bare. ...

The masses shed few tears for the "old" regime, and many of the youth (and by no means only the Communists) ripped into what was left of it with gusto:

Comrades, show spunk, take aim, the lot!
At Holy Russia let's fire a shot,

At hutted Russia,
Fat-rumped and solid,

Russia the stolid![8]

Millions hoped the powerful would be brought low and the wretched would be exalted, but after the miseries of three years of war and another year of revolutionary turmoil, they were confused and weary. What awaited them, however, was not peace and a resumption of their quest for human dignity and security, but three more years of civil war.

---

[8] From Alexander Blok, *The Twelve*, trans., in Avrahm Yarmolinsky, ed., *A Treasury of Russian Verse*, Macmillan, 1949, pp. 155 and 159. Reprinted by permission.

9

The Civil War
1917–1921

"War Communism"

From the start Lenin's efforts to establish a new political and social order in Russia were severely hampered by war and domestic chaos. Both problems were in part legacies from the tsarist regime and the Provisional Government, but they were soon aggravated by developments of the winter of 1917–1918. Even before the Treaty of Brest-Litovsk brought Russia's participation in World War I to an end, anti-Bolshevik forces had been assembled which were to launch a Civil War lasting three more years. The economy was already disorganized by the events of 1917; workers had spent much time on demonstrations and meetings and little at their jobs, their transportation and communication systems were near a breakdown, food shortages were spreading, and sporadic local seizures of property were occurring all over the country. Much war industry was dismantled before the magnitude of the needs of the Civil War was clear, and as a result unemployment spread.

However, it was plain that some kind of army would be needed by the new government, and the old army was passing out of existence. The elected commander of the 2d Army, Kiselev, reported in despair on January 27, 1918: "units in unauthorized fashion discharge soldiers, abandon positions ... seize property, divide it among themselves ... reports even arrive that the sale of horses and other property to the Germans has begun."[1] Soon the process of what was called "self-demobilization" was complete. About that same time a decree provided that any Russian citizen eighteen years of age or over could volunteer for the new Red Army, if vouched for by a trade union or an army committee, for three months at a salary of 150 rubles per month. Thousands of recruits responded, but they remained a

---

[1] M. Frenkin, *Russkaia armiia i revoliutsiia*, Logos, Munich, 1978, p. 738.

rabble, not an army. After Brest-Litovsk Trotsky became war commissar, and in April he began to create a regular army based on conscription, authority, and discipline—of a "new sort," to be sure. Compulsory military training was ordered for all workers and for peasants who did not hire labor. The honor of military service was denied to the "bourgeoisie" (which sometimes meant, in practice, simply those who wore hats or overcoats), but they were conscripted for labor service. The death penalty, for which Kornilov had asked in vain before October, was restored. Deserters were sometimes shot but more often were sent into punishment units. Election of officers was terminated, and army committees were given to understand that their time of decisionmaking was past.

Trotsky not only accepted officer volunteers from the old army but conscripted old officers, warning them that desertion would result in harm to their families, and almost 50,000 officers of the old army were used by the Reds in the Civil War. To reassure worried Communists and unhappy worker-soldiers, Trotsky declared that he was building socialism with bricks left over from the demolished old order. He appointed political commissars to watch the officers and to carry out propaganda among the recruits. Thereby a full-fledged Party hierarchy was built into the army at every level. Long after none but loyal Communists could be found anywhere in the army, the commissar device continued to be used. Perhaps half of the total Party membership served in the Red Army during the Civil War. They fought devotedly for their cause, for they believed that torture and death awaited them if captured by the Whites and thought that their victory would usher in the millennium.

In the summer of 1918 the economic situation deteriorated further. The government responded with several measures which tended, however, to make things still worse. At the start the Reds had perforce virtually to leave the rural areas alone; for the first six months of Soviet rule "the countryside was governed by the peasants themselves."[2] On June 11, 1918, Moscow's policy took a sharp turn. The Committees of Poor Peasants were established; their task was to "carry the class war to the village" by fighting "kulaks" (rich peasants) and at the same time requisition the grain needed to feed the cities. Civilian "supply detachments," under military command, were sent to the villages with a commissar attached to organize the committees. Among a peasantry where there were no recognized class distinctions, such an order provoked chaos. If a peasant did turn informer for a reward, the moment the supply detachment withdrew "he would be chased out of the commune, if not killed."[3] One student concludes that in terms of the numbers involved, "the magnitude of the Bolshevik war with peasants on the internal front eclipsed by far the front-line civil war with the Whites."[4]

---

[2] Orlando Figes, *Peasant Russia, Civil War,* Clarendon Press, 1991, p. 70.

[3] Pipes, *The Russian Revolution,* p. 739.

[4] Vladimir Brovkin, "On the Internal Front: The Bolsheviks and the Greens," cited ibid., p. 735.

Thus the declaration often heard was "I am for the Bolsheviks, but against the Communists." The peasants' confusion was understandable. They knew that the Bolsheviks had sanctioned (not ordered or advocated) land division, and they also saw that the Communists were trying to loot their property and disrupt their villages. The only item of information lacking was that the two groups were identical, since the party had been renamed in the meantime. Peasant risings against the Reds multiplied in July and continued; in 1920–1921 they erupted into mass revolts (see p. 141).

In July 1918, at the V Congress of Soviets, the Left SR's had a large delegation (all orthodox SR's and Mensheviks had been expelled from the Soviets in June). Left SR's at the Congress attacked the Committees of Poor Peasants (*kombedy*) as committees of "village loafers" and protested the requisitioning detachments. Two days later the Left SR's attempted an uprising (see p. 120); their party was promptly expelled from the Soviets. A former SR who had been Kerensky's assistant for military affairs, Boris Savinkov, organized a revolt that seized the city of Yaroslavl and held it almost two weeks. At Moscow's orders the entire imperial family was murdered in Ekaterinburg (all bodies were found in 1992 except Alexei's and one of the girls').

On June 28 the Soviet government nationalized all major industries without compensation and placed them under a Supreme Economic Council. Management, nominally in the hands of *Glavki* or main departments of the Council, was at first actually left to workers' committees. The only difference from the earlier regime of "workers' control" was that now the managers were gone. However, disorganization soon forced the government to appoint new ones. Again "bricks of the old order" had to be used; many new managers were the old ones back again, watched over like the army officers by political appointees.

The measures of the spring and summer of 1918 inaugurated so-called "War Communism." It has sometimes been attributed to the motive of prosecuting the Civil War more effectively, but the result was instead to imperil Communist rule in a fashion requiring drastic corrective action. Lenin and Trotsky wished for the time being to keep the "capitalist" sector intact and simply place it under state supervision; but, in the words of Pipes, the Left Communists, following Valerian Obolensky-Osinsky, "overruled Lenin, plunging Russia headlong into the utopia of instant socialism."[5]

July 19, 1918, marked the promulgation of the first Soviet Constitution, intended to reflect the Marxist-Leninist principles that underlay government policy. The "bourgeoisie" was excluded from voting, and urban residents were given a considerable edge in suffrage over village dwellers. The objective was said to be "the pitiless suppression of exploiters, the socialist organization of society, and

---

[5] Ibid., p. 679.

the victory of socialism in all countries." If one accepts Lenin's definition of "exploiters" and "socialism," this was a very fair description of what the Communists were doing in Russia and what they hoped to do abroad.

The White Challenge

Immediately after the October Revolution, anti-Bolshevik leaders began to organize opposition. They were drawn from three groups: the non-Bolshevik Russian party politicians, the former officers of the army, and nationalists seeking independence or autonomy for the non-Russian peoples. Not all non-Bolsheviks were disposed to resist. The Mensheviks generally held aloof from the struggle; by temperament and outlook they were closer to their former Bolshevik comrades than to the White leaders. Most orthodox SR's felt ambivalent, although many at first took the road of resistance. To a varying degree Kadets leaned toward the Whites. The old opposition shibboleth, "No enemy on the Left," retained some of its power, and many party politicians had been used to countenance armed struggle only when directed against tsarism. The nationalists wanted to fight their own battles, and were seldom ready to carry the struggle beyond their own lands. By default the generals thus became the White leaders. Most declared their aim to be establishment of some kind of republican and representative government; they were not always believed.

An unforeseen event was the Czechoslovak rising. The Czechoslovak brigade that had fought in the war with the Russian army remained in being and after the February Revolution was augmented by volunteer former Austro-Hungarian prisoners of Czechoslovak origin. The Czech leader, Thomas G. Masaryk, wished to send this corps to France to fight for Allied victory and Czechoslovak independence, despite the hopes of General Alexeev and others that it might stay in Russia and fight the Reds. The Czechs had helped Reds resist German advance into Ukraine, and their relations with Moscow were cordial. On March 26, 1918, Soviets, Czechs, and Allied representatives signed an agreement whereby the corps would be transported as "free citizens" to Vladivostok and thence to France, but with French advice some wished to exit via Arkhangelsk and Reds tried to persuade them to join their army. On May 14 an accidental brawl at the railway station at Cheliabinsk led to an open break between Reds and Czechs, and as a result the Czechs soon seized the railway from Penza to Tomsk, and Reds held on only in eastern Siberia. Now the French urged the Czechs to stay where they were and prepare for the Allies to arrive.

The upshot has been much misunderstood. As Mawdsley points out, as far as foreign intervention was concerned, the role of the Central Powers was by far the most important, not that of the Allies. Before and after the Treaty of Brest-Litovsk hundreds of thousands of German, Austrian, and Turkish troops occupied seventeen Russian provinces as well as Poland.[6] A harsh supplementary treaty was imposed on the Bolsheviks by the Germans in August 1918, specifying details of cooperation against the Allies.

Allied intervention was tiny in comparison, was driven by decidedly mixed motives, and had no clear aim. Initially there was hope of restoring an Eastern front or at any rate of preventing Allied-furnished munitions and other supplies from falling into German hands; a few, like Churchill, wanted to "scotch the Bolshevik snake" and eliminate the Red danger, but such an aim was never adopted by the British government or the Allies together. President Wilson "abhorred the very thought of intervention [in a Russian civil war]," Prime Minister Lloyd George was "completely skeptical" regarding the idea; both consented "reluctantly and unhappily" to expeditions on the urging of subordinates who were supposed to be well informed about Russia. In each Allied country there were people who believed that Communists either represented the true wishes of the Russian majority or would at least "listen to reason."

In December 1917 Britain and France agreed that each would have certain areas of operations: the British were assigned to the Cossack areas and the Caucasus; the French, to Ukraine, Crimea, and Bessarabia. There was little result. In March a few British marines landed at Murmansk, in April some Japanese and British marines at Vladivostok. The American part was trivial: a few Americans were under British command in the White Sea coastal area; an American Expeditionary Force was, after much soul-searching on the part of President Woodrow Wilson, sent into Siberia under the command of General Graves. The American contingent never attacked Communist forces; in one minor skirmish against partisans who had fallen under Red influence a few shots were fired in anger. After the end of World War I no allied force took any part at all except for one armored train carrying gunners from H.M.S. *Suffolk* until January 1919.[7]

The Bolsheviks managed by mid-February 1918 to take over most of the former empire, but they then lost control of much of it. By mid-1918 there were seven areas where White governments or forces had been established: in Samara, Victor Chernov headed a "Government of the Constituent Assembly"; in Arkhangelsk a government headed by the old populist Nicholas Chaikovsky; in Estonia an army led by General Yudenich; a group of Czechoslovaks had seized much of the Trans-Siberian Railway and with it, in effect, most of Siberia; in eastern Siberia, Ataman Semënov held power; in Omsk, the West Siberian Commissariat, proclaiming Siberian autonomy under a white and green flag, symbolizing snow and forest; in the south, General Anton Denikin. The Whites had not been fortunate with their leaders: General Kaledin, ataman of the Don Cossacks and head of *the* center of

---

[6] Evan Mawdsley, *The Russian Civil War,* Allen & Unwin, 1987, p. 43.

[7] George Kennan, *Russia and the West Under Lenin and Stalin,* Little, Brown & Co., 1961, pp. 109, 115, 117–118.

THE CIVIL WAR
1918

········· Fronts of Civil War,
August, 1918

opposition for some fifteen weeks, committed suicide in February 1918; General Kornilov, who had escaped from Bolshevik custody, was killed by a lucky hit of Red artillery in April; General Alexeev, former chief of staff to the tsar but a wise old man whose leadership might have made a real difference, was ill for a year before he died in October. Lenin told the Moscow Soviet in April 1918 that "in the main, the civil war has ended." He was quite wrong.

For several months the Whites were able to profit from the Czech rising, capturing Kazan on August 6 and the tsarist gold reserve of over half a billion rubles. However, in late August Trotsky himself managed to rally the Reds to win a skirmish at Sviazhsk, called the "Valmy of the Russian Revolution" (recalling the first check to foreign armies by French Revolutionary troops in 1792, although the Whites were of course not foreigners). The Red Army then went on to recapture Kazan. Under pressure from the Czechs a State Conference was called to harmonize differences among the Whites; it met at Ufa and established a "national" government called the Directory to sit at Omsk. It assumed authority there on October 9, but antagonism among the SR's, KD's, and generals remained strong. A week after the November armistice ending World War I, conservatives carried out a coup in Omsk and persuaded Admiral Alexander Kolchak to become "Supreme Ruler" and commander of all White armed forces. Kolchak set as his goal "victory over Bolshevism and the establishment of law and order, so that the people may choose the form of government which it desires without obstruction and realize the great ideas of liberty which are now proclaimed in the whole world." His intentions seem the best. Baron Budberg, a bitter critic of his, wrote that he was devoid of selfishness and "passionately desires everything good." But as a leader he was a failure. In April 1919 a comparable coup placed General Eugene Miller in power in Arkhangelsk, replacing a local SR regime, and he acknowledged the authority of Kolchak, as did Denikin in June. The Japanese were protecting both Ataman Semënov in Chita and Ataman Kalmykov in Khabarovsk; Semënov nominally acknowledged Kolchak's authority, Kalmykov did not. The SR's detested Kolchak but split on what to do about it: one faction, under Volsky, made their peace with Moscow and obtained a hollow promise to legalize the SR party on Red territory; the other, under Chernov, resolved on a "struggle on two fronts," damning Reds and Whites alike. A party conference in the spring of 1919 decided that SR's ought to fight with all possible weapons against the Whites, but by that time the party had ceased to play any significant role.

In January 1919 the Allies decided to try to settle the conflict by inviting representatives of both sides to a conference on Prinkipo Island in the Straits. The Whites refused; the Reds agreed, but disgusted Wilson by offering to cede territory to the Allies, and the plan was dropped.

Both Whites and Reds were cheered by the armistice. As the Central Powers could no longer distract the Allies, some thought they could be persuaded to help the anti-Red cause, and as they withdrew the Whites hoped to replace them in the west. The Reds hailed the news that the Hohenzollern and Habsburg monarchies had crumbled, that what they hoped would prove "Kerensky-type" socialist regimes had succeeded them, and that Soviets had appeared in Berlin, Munich, Warsaw, and Riga. Lenin could now tear up the Treaty of Brest-Litovsk and hope for the "international proletarian revolution" to break out all over Europe. In March 1919 there was held in Moscow the founding Congress of the Third or Communist International (Comintern), which proclaimed world revolution as its objective. The Comintern included, along with Russian Communists, the newly formed Communist parties of Central and Eastern Europe, the Swedish Left Socialists, the Norwegian Labor Party, and the Italian Socialist Party. During the Congress the Reds were fighting for control of Finland and Latvia; by April the Hungarian Communists under Béla Kun proclaimed a Soviet Republic, and Bavaria followed suit. It looked as if world revolution was finally at hand.

These adventures soon failed, but they spurred the Allies to take action. Premier Clemenceau, on behalf of the Allied Supreme Council, promised recognition to Kolchak if he agreed to reconvene the Constituent Assembly, recognize Poland and Finland and the autonomy of other minority regions, and renounce any intention to restore the old regime. Although he refused to acknowledge Finnish independence in advance of the Constituent Assembly, he had already met the other conditions, and the Allies declared themselves satisfied with his reply to Clemenceau's note.

However, recognition did not follow. On December 25, 1918, the right wing of Kolchak's forces under Czech General Gajda captured Perm. The left wing, whose success might have led to a link-up with Denikin in the south, faltered, so Kolchak decided to head for Arkhangelsk, where Miller and the British were. At the end of April Gajda captured Glazov, halfway from Perm to Viatka. At once Michael Frunze and the Reds launched a counteroffensive. In June they captured Ufa. Lenin thought it best to pursue Kolchak; Trotsky favored shifting troops to meet Denikin, whom he considered the greater danger. The Red Army did as Lenin wished and advanced east of the Urals, where Siberian peasant partisans harassed Kolchak's rear. Kolchak had issued a statement indicating a gingerly acceptance of land division where it had occurred, which was enough to attract much White support west of the Urals where Communist land policy had been applied. However, in Siberia there had been no gentry and no estates to divide. Gajda resigned his command and left Siberia. By late spring 1919 Allied supplies started to reach Kolchak's army in quantity, but it was unable to put them to good use. In the fall General Knox wrote to Kolchak's chief of staff that all seemed to be chaos: "It is my wish to help you, but frankly at present you make help impossible."[8]

The army was forced back until the Czechs seized Kolchak in January 1920 and handed him over to a local authority in Irkutsk that in turn was displaced by a Bolshevik-dominated group, which interrogated Kolchak but shot him on February 6 before finishing that task, despite Lenin's orders not to do so. In early 1920 the Reds set up a puppet Far Eastern Republic; when the Japanese withdrew from Transbaikalia the FER replaced Semënov's regime in Chita, but one of Kolchak's officers, General Diterikhs, held out in Vladivostok until the final exit of the Japanese in October 1922, when the FER was absorbed into the Russian Soviet Federated Socialist Republic. One of Semënov's lieutenants, an unbalanced Baltic nobleman named Ungern-Sternberg, marched into Mongolia and captured Urga in February 1921, but the Reds seized it and executed him in the summer.

In February-April 1918 the Volunteer Army, created by Alexeev after November 1917, undertook in the Kuban a cruelly difficult campaign called the Icy March. After Kornilov was killed Denikin recaptured the Kuban in the summer. By February 1919 Wrangel's cavalry cleared the north Caucasus of Red troops, the biggest Red loss of the Civil War. The Volunteer Army, strongly Russian nationalist, did not get on well with the Don Cossacks, who wanted to use local feelings to build a broader movement. In June the Whites took Kharkov and Tsaritsyn, and Denikin prepared an assault on Moscow. General Mamontov led a spectacular cavalry raid that penetrated as far as Tambov and Voronezh before returning to White lines,

---

[8] Mawdsley, *Russian Civil War*, p. 153.

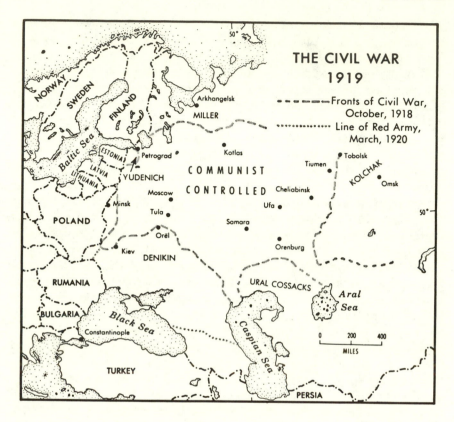

THE CIVIL WAR
1919

▪ ▪ ▪ ▪ ▪ Fronts of Civil War,
October, 1918
••••••••••• Line of Red Army,
March, 1920

COMMUNIST
CONTROLLED

but some looting marred this achievement. Only then did the Reds change their negative attitude toward cavalry and Trotsky called, "Proletarians, to horse!"

The Red Victory

In the fall what was now termed the Armed Forces of South Russia advanced north. On October 14 Denikin took Orël, 120 miles short of Tula, the main armory of the Reds; from there Moscow was only 120 miles further. Meanwhile General N. N. Yudenich was attacking toward Petrograd; on October 21 he entered Pavlovsk and Tsarskoe Selo (later "Pushkin"), twenty miles from the center of the city. After Trotsky reached the front, the White forces, outnumbered five-to-one, were thrown back to the Estonian frontier and fell apart. On October 20 Orël was evacuated in the face of the sudden appearance of the Latvian Rifle Division on the left and Budënny's cavalry on the right. The White retreat continued until the beginning of 1920. Novocherkassk and Rostov fell on January 7; it was said that the Don River froze to let the Whites cross, then thawed to prevent the

Reds from crossing—for ten days. Only then did Denikin raise the slogan, "Land to the peasants and laboring Cossacks."

In the north Miller and entourage escaped; he was murdered by Soviet secret police in Paris in 1937. The Reds entered Arkhangelsk February 21 and Murmansk March 13, 1920.

There remained only one White-controlled area: the Crimea. By early April 1920 the Cossack bases were lost, Denikin driven into exile—but a council persuaded him to appoint Wrangel as his successor before he departed for Constantinople on a British destroyer.

Wrangel, although more conservative than either Kolchak or Denikin, was a man who understood the failings of the White leaders before him. He established iron discipline in the army and ended the pillaging and plundering that had marred Denikin's campaigns. He enlisted the services of such able civilian officials as Stolypin's former assistant, Krivoshein, who became his prime minister, and Peter Struve, former Marxist, as his foreign minister. Wrangel devoted much effort to a land reform program that was applied in 90 out of the 107 counties he occupied during the few short months he was in power, and established zemstvos at the township (*volost*) level, as the Provisional Government had sought to do with scant success. By July his chief of staff told him, "The population is on our side now; they have faith in the new regime, and realize that it is fighting to free Russia and not to punish her." Wrangel claimed, perhaps justifiably, that if the "conditions of harmony between the Army and the wishes of the peasants [that prevailed in 1920] had been achieved at the time when the Russian Army was advancing victoriously on Moscow and nearly half of Russia was freed from the Red yoke, the fate of the White movement would have been quite different."

On April 25 the newly independent Poles under the ex-socialist Joseph Pilsudski opened an offensive that swept into Kiev on May 6. The avowed aim was to recreate the "Poland of 1772" (that is, before the First Partition among the three eastern monarchies), and he was willing to cooperate closely with Petliura, leader of the Ukrainian regime that the Reds had expelled, in the hope that an independent Ukraine could be established in order to weaken his giant Russian neighbor. The Reds sought to mobilize nationalist feelings to resist, and managed to attract to their side such former tsarist generals as Brusilov, who assumed headship of a special military council to advise the Red high command. But they did not forget they were Marxists: they appealed to the Polish "toiling masses" to set up a Polish Communist state, and prepared the nucleus of a Red government they hoped to install in Warsaw.

In May General Tukhachevsky launched a counteroffensive, and the Reds approached Warsaw from two directions. Fearing that this time they might succeed in assisting a Communist victory in Germany, the Allies were alarmed. On July 12 British Foreign Minister Lord Curzon hastily proposed a truce along a roughly ethnic border known ever since as the Curzon Line. Moscow was not interested in a truce, and Red troops continued to advance. But in August Pilsudski and his new French military adviser, General Weygand (later to become French commander-in-chief during the last weeks of resistance in 1940), mounted a counterattack which was successful in virtually routing the Red Army. Moscow accepted an armistice in October, and its provisions, confirmed by the Treaty of Riga in March 1921, left many Belorussians and Ukrainians in Polish territory. In early 1920 Wrangel proposed a Polish-Ukrainian-Russian coalition under a French commander, without result. The British would not help and warned him not to attack; he did so anyway in June. France continued aid and gave him *de facto* recognition in August but made "excessive economic demands and sent very little equipment."[9] Wrangel's troops in one week reached the lower Dnieper, doubled his territory, almost wiped out the Reds' I Cavalry Corps, and kept the initiative until late fall. In October he crossed the Dnieper but was forced back into the southern Crimea, from which 146,000 people were evacuated to Constantinople. Many White supporters were left to face Béla Kun's Crimean RevCom, and tens of thousands may have been executed. The survivors of the White struggle were dispersed to Belgrade, Berlin, Paris, London, New York, Harbin, and Shanghai.

The Civil War in the Western Borderlands

In Ukraine there were seven stages of the complex conflict, which may be summarized: Rada, Reds, Germans, Rada, Reds, Whites, Reds back to stay. On November 6, 1917, the Rada proclaimed Ukraine a People's Republic[10] and a component part of a projected Russian Federation. However, in and near the Donets Basin to the east, where there were more Russians and more industrial workers, the Bolsheviks had greater strengths. They set up a Ukrainian Soviet regime in Kharkov, and for a short time Ukraine was in effect partitioned between west and east. On January 26, 1918, Bolshevik troops took Kiev, but on the same day the Rada's delegation in Brest-Litovsk was signing a separate peace with the Central Powers, and on March 3 (N.S.) the Germans entered Kiev, nominally restoring the Rada to power. In two months they reversed themselves, dispersed the Rada, and replaced it with a puppet regime headed by Hetman Pavlo Skoropadski. For eight months German occupation removed Ukraine from the arena of civil war. Popular discontent with the brutality of the military authorities spread rapidly, so that the Germans were kept too busy in Ukraine to have much influence beyond it. After the armistice forced the Germans to withdraw, the Rada was back.

The Reds did their best to replace the German and Austrian troops in the territory ceded by Brest but now lost to them. Moscow tried to set up a puppet government in Estonia, and failed; they set up a Latvian SSR, but General von der

---

[9] Ibid., p. 267.

[10] Not to be confused with Communist employment of this phrase.

Goltz recaptured Riga in May 1919; this "miracle of the Dvina" was said to be the first check to Moscow's expansion,[11] and the Latvian SSR was no more. In December 1918 a Lithuanian SSR was established in Vilnius and a Belorussian SSR in Minsk; in February 1919 a combined Lithuanian-Belorussian Soviet Republic (*Litbel*) was formed in Vilna. The Poles took Vilnius and then Minsk in August 1919, and *Litbel* ceased to exist.

In the fall of 1918 the Rada under Vinnichenko and Simon Petliura formed a Ukrainian Directory, which took over as Skoropadski fled in December. Ostensibly having recognized its legitimacy, the Reds nevertheless invaded and took Kiev in February 1919. Bulgarian-born Christian Rakovsky replaced Gregory Piatakov as head of a Red regime which promptly alienated the population by collectivizing land and displaying contempt for Ukrainian nationalism. The peasant partisans of Makhno and Hryhoryiv, who had allied themselves briefly with the Reds, now turned on them and launched a campaign against "Communists, Jews, and Russians."

Into this chaotic situation the White army of General Denikin advanced north, took Kharkov and the whole of eastern Ukraine in June—and then was forced to retreat south; the Bolsheviks returned for good although Polish forces briefly occupied western Ukraine in 1920. In the fighting in Ukraine anti-Jewish pogroms (which Denikin neither ordered nor condemned fully) were conducted by White troops—but also by Petliura's forces, bandits, peasants, and sometimes Red forces.[12]

Further south, but north of the Caucasus mountains, from March to August 1918 a regime existed at Vladikavkaz calling itself the Terek People's Soviet Socialist Republic, where Communists accepted a temporary coalition with Mensheviks, SR's, and local parties, since they were as yet too weak to rule alone. Terek Cossacks overthrew it, and the Red leader Ordzhonikidze managed to induce the two mountain Muslim tribes, Chechen and Ingush, to reestablish Communist rule by turning over to them the property of the Terek Cossacks.[13]

The chief nationalities of the Caucasus were the Georgians, Armenians, and Azerbaijanis, who joined to form a Transcaucasian Federative Republic on April 22, 1918, but it lasted only a month. Orthodox Christian Georgia, speaking a language unlike any other anywhere, declared independence. The government was led by the Menshevik Chkhenkeli, accepting German control as an evil lesser than the Turkish conquest that appeared imminent. It was the only place where Mensheviks, who disdained power in Russia for theoretical reasons, led a government. They nationalized most industry and communications, but wisely carried out

---

[11] Ibid., p. 126.

[12] Ibid., p. 210.

[13] This did not save the Chechens and Ingush from mass deportation at the hands of Stalin in World War II.

land reform; they first leased plots to peasants, then in 1919 sold them outright. When the armistice of November 11 came, Chkhenkeli, who had become identified with German occupation, was replaced as prime minister by Gegechkori while Noah Zhordania became president. The arriving British preserved Georgian independence for the moment.

Muslim and Turkic-speaking Azerbaijan and Christian Armenia, speaking an Indo-European language of its own, declared independence two days after Georgia did. Reds had seized the oil city of Baku in March, a coup in which 3,000 Muslims died. For a short time a Bolshevik-Left Menshevik government was in power, but its leader fled and was killed. The SR's, taking over, invited the British General Dunsterville to stop the Turks from taking over. It was too late; they took Baku on September 15, 1918. The nationalist-socialist Mussavat party allied itself with Turkey, but soon quarreled with the occupiers. After the armistice, the British General Thomson landed in Baku, and soon recognized a government headed by Fathali Khan-Khoisky, a former liberal Duma deputy.

In 1918 Armenia was the orphan nation of the Caucasus—Georgia had the Germans and Azerbaijan had the Turks, but the old protectors of Armenia against Turkey, the Russians, were unable to help though Armenia supported the Whites as they had the Provisional Government. The radical Dashnaktsutiun party dominated the government, which as the Whites faltered hoped fleetingly to persuade the U.S. to assume a League of Nations mandate over it. Poor and hungry, Armenians did escape the worst ravages of famine by means of American relief aid.

At the beginning of 1920 the Allies recognized the *de facto* independence of the three Caucasian nations and persuaded the defeated Denikin to do the same, but did nothing more. Moscow prepared to retake the whole Caucasus, first quietly arranging a rapprochement with the Turkish revolutionary regime of Mustafa Kemal. In the spring the military under Tukhachevsky, with the political direction of Ordzhonikidze, moved in. In April Azerbaijan yielded to the Red ultimatum, and in August Baku was the scene of a Congress of the Peoples of the East, evincing the continued Communist interest in Asia. An ultimatum to Armenia, which had become weakened by struggle with Kemal's troops over eastern Anatolia, led to its surrender in December. Georgia was last; the Reds attacked in February 1921 and completed the conquest in March.

The Muslim Borderlands of the East

At the time of the October Revolution Bolsheviks seized power in Tashkent and a few other centers where there were numerous Russians, but their influence among Muslims was minuscule. An All-Russian Muslim Assembly known as the Medzhilis, sitting in Kazan, rejected Red overtures and supported the Constituent Assembly. In February 1918 a Medzhilis attempt to form an autonomous Volga-Ural Muslim state was thwarted by Reds in Kazan.

Moscow attempted to subvert the Muslim autonomist movement from within. Commissar of Nationalities Stalin made a Tatar, Mulla Nur Vakhitov, chairman of a newly established Muslim Commissariat. He was instructed to set up a state with the same territory proposed a few months earlier, which was proclaimed an Autonomous Tatar-Bashkir Republic. The Czech rising put an end to this. In late 1919 Red troops entered the area, and the Turkic peoples were given not one but five administrative areas. The Orthodox Christian Chuvash and Mari were given Autonomous Regions; the Muslim Tatars of Kazan, Votiaks, and Bashkirs got Autonomous Soviet Socialist Republics. The rough treatment given the Bashkirs led to a serious uprising in late 1920, and when formally organized the Bashkir ASSR had no Bashkirs at all in its government. A little earlier a Communist spokesman had told a Bashkir delegation in Moscow, "that whole autonomous republic, which you take so seriously, is only a game to keep you people busy."

Southeast of Bashkiria, the Kazakh-Kirgiz area was dominated by the native party called the Alash-Orda. In 1918 it collaborated with the Whites, before and after Kolchak's coup in Omsk. However, when Red troops penetrated the region and invited members of Alash-Orda to join them, many did so. A few, not as representatives of the party, were taken into the government of the Kyrgyz (Kazakh) Autonomous SSR, proclaimed in October 1920. A severe famine postponed the formation of an effective government and paralyzed native resistance to the Communists.

In Turkestan the Bolshevik stronghold was Tashkent. Red forces from there attacked the city of Kokand, where liberal Muslims had founded an autonomous regime, destroying much of the city and massacring uncounted people. They next attacked Bukhara, which had been a semi-independent emirate under the tsars, but were repulsed. There now appeared partisan bands calling themselves the Basmachi who challenged the authority and resented the brutality of the Tashkent regime. Moscow, alarmed at the spread of resistance, ordered the establishment of a Turkestan Autonomous SSR, announced in April 1918, but it existed mainly on paper.

The armistice brought British troops into central Asia as into the Caucasus, but not enough to achieve much. A weak SR regime in Ashkhabad, Turkmenistan, invited the British General Malleson in to help it resist the Tashkent Reds. He did so, but evacuated his forces in April 1919, and the Communists arrived in Ashkhabad two months later.

The penetration of Red forces into the steppe in mid-1919, in pursuit of Kolchak, enabled Moscow to put a bridle on the uncompromising Tashkent leadership. In February 1920 a Turkestan Commission, including Michael Frunze, commander of the Red Fourth Army, and Valerian Kuibyshev, his political commissar, arrived in Tashkent. They promptly adopted a "soft" policy, by which they hoped to cut the ground out from under the Basmachi. For a time this tactic appeared to yield some results, but the partisan bands remained in existence. The

Red capture of Khiva in February and of Bukhara in August provoked the Basmachi to renewed activity.

In the fall of 1921 Enver Pasha, a formerly influential Turkish minister who had fled his country and gained Red confidence, was sent to Turkestan to put down the revolt. Instead he joined the Basmachi himself and became their leader. In 1922 he captured the town of Diushambe (later for a time Stalinabad), but in October of the same year he was killed by the Reds. Although the Basmachi did not cease resistance until 1926, in 1923–1924 the Communists crushed the backbone of the movement. Khiva became the People's Socialist Republic of Khorezm and Bukhara also was designated a PSR.

By the spring of 1921 the Reds were victorious almost everywhere in the territories of the old Russian Empire. The exceptions were Finland, Estonia, Latvia, Lithuania, and Poland, which had become independent states; Bessarabia, which had been ceded to Romania, and parts of Belorussia and Ukraine, ceded to Poland; the Amur region, where the Far Eastern Republic could not yet be liquidated in the face of Japanese occupation; and Bukhara, where the last organized resistance to the Communists had not yet been stamped out. Moscow retained the core area of Great Russia, most of Ukraine, some of Belorussia, the Caucasus, Siberia, and Central Asia. But although the Civil War was at an end, there was still no revolution in the West, and there was serious trouble inside Russia.

10

Lenin and the
New Economic Policy

"The Peasant Brest"

Just before the X Congress of the Party in early 1921, Lenin declared that socialism could be built in Russia only on one of two conditions: if there was an international socialist revolution, or if there was a compromise with the peasant majority within the country. The essence of the "New Economic Policy" which he adopted soon afterwards was acceptance of a compromise with the peasantry. The Bolshevik theoretician Riazanov labeled the NEP "the peasant Brest"; that is to say, a temporary truce was concluded with the peasant adversary, as with the German Empire at Brest-Litovsk, but its purpose was *reculer pour mieux sauter.*

In reluctantly accepting the terms of Brest-Litovsk, Lenin had not given up hope that a revolutionary situation would still develop in the West. In 1919, when Communist regimes appeared briefly in central Europe, and in 1920, when Red armies were approaching Warsaw and hoping to reach Berlin, such hopes revived. However, even though the Comintern tried twice more to foment a revolution in Germany, by 1921 it was plain enough that the Russian Communists could not count on their foreign brethren to solve their immediate problems.

These problems were domestic. Peasant risings had erupted in the south and east of Russia, for centuries the regions from which *jacqueries* had sprung. In western Siberia, Ukraine, Belorussia, Tambov Province, and much of the Volga Valley from north of Tsaritsyn to the area east of Kazan, there erupted several different kinds of uprising.[1] Several of the leaders—A. S. Antonov in Tambov,

---

[1] Several recent studies have dealt with them, notably Orlando Figes, *Peasant Russia, Civil War: The Volga Countryside in Revolution, 1917–1921,* Clarendon Press, 1991; Oliver H. Radkey, *The Unknown Civil War in Soviet Russia: A Study of the Green Movement in the Tambov Region 1920–1921,* Hoover Institution Press, 1976; and M. Malet, *Nestor Makhno in the Russian Civil War,* Macmillan, 1982. Soviet attempts to explain them away as "kulak revolts" were quite unsuccessful.

Makhno in Ukraine, A. P. Sapozhkov in Samara, and others—were former Soviet officials and Red Army officers. Why had they not coordinated operations with the Whites? Radkey declares, "as long as the Whites had a serious chance of victory the Greens would not lift a finger to help them. ... [They refused to help] the oppressors of the past achieve victory over the oppressors of the present."[2] The remark may be unfair to the Whites; certainly some of them were determined not to be "oppressors" but liberators; we shall never be sure. But the Greens were sure of one thing, that the Reds had betrayed them and the peasants whose interests they strove to defend. They were, of course, defeated by the superior forces of Moscow; but they also achieved a victory, even if good for only a few years. "Having defeated the White Army, backed by eight Western powers [though not very strongly, to be sure], the Bolshevik government surrendered before its own peasantry."[3] So argues Figes; Lenin himself refers to "discontent not only among a considerable part of the peasantry but among the workers as well," and something of the fury of both was shown in the climactic event of Kronstadt in March 1921.

Kronstadt had been a great tsarist naval base, but during 1917 its sailors had become one of the strongest bulwarks of the Bolshevik cause. Its location on an island in sight of Petrograd made the political orientation of its garrison most important. During the Civil War, many of the most active leaders during the 1917 events had gone off to become Red political and military officers in various districts, and in 1921 most of its personnel consisted of new peasant recruits. The uprising in March fleetingly threw off Communist rule and proclaimed the slogan, "Soviets without Communists." Opposition elements of all kinds, in Russia and among the *émigrés,* from Mensheviks to monarchists, pricked up their ears. Red forces moved in, shot down thousands, and quelled the revolt. But Lenin understood well enough that Kronstadt was no isolated or accidental outbreak, but evidence of widespread popular discontent.

He appeared before the X Congress of the Party in March 1921 and proposed a far-reaching measure, that the requisitioning of agricultural surpluses, which had been part of War Communism, be abandoned in favor of a tax in kind set at a fixed percentage of production. Only a year earlier Trotsky had proposed just such a measure, but it had been blocked by his colleagues, including Lenin. However, Lenin now pushed it through, and thereby inaugurated the "New Economic Policy"—although the actual phrase seems to have been first used in May, without capitals or quotation marks, and with them only several months later.

Lenin had evidently decided that a serious and many-sided retreat from Communist objectives (although a conditional and temporary one) was essential if the regime was not to be endangered by revolt from within by the very elements who had adhered to the Red side during the Civil War. His own formulation was that

---

[2] Radkey, *Unknown Civil War*, p. 407.
[3] Figes, *Peasant Russia*, p. 321.

the reason for the NEP was "the maintenance of the alliance of the proletariat with the peasantry, in order that the proletariat may keep the role of leadership and state power." The economy was prostrate, and the food tax could reasonably be expected to revive agricultural production and trade by providing the peasant with an incentive and security hitherto lacking. Nevertheless the economic motive was not the crucial one; as Lenin said, the question of the new tax was "preeminently a political question, since it is essentially a question of the relation of the working class to the peasantry." The peasantry, he declared candidly, "cannot be driven out as we drove out and annihilated the landowners and the capitalists. It must be transformed with great labor and great privations."

Maxim Gorky was blunter and more pessimistic in confiding to a French visitor, that same summer:

> "In the struggle which, since the beginning of the revolution, has been going on between the two classes, the peasants have every chance of coming out victorious. ... The urban proletariat has been declining incessantly for four years. ... The immense peasant tide will end by engulfing everything. ... The peasant will become master of Russia, since he represents numbers. And it will be terrible for our future."[4]

Obviously the real opponents of the peasantry were the Communists, not the proletariat, who were (as Lenin said) discontented with their urban situation—in fact, sufficiently so (as Gorky said) to return to the villages from which many of them originally came.

Lenin had long realized that the peasantry as a whole did not thirst for socialism, but he had counted on the "poor peasantry" to come to the Communists' aid. In 1918 he had tried to use them in the Committees of Poor Peasants, but the device had been a resounding failure (see p. 127). In November 1918 the Committees had been abandoned, and the decision was taken to work temporarily with the "middle peasants" instead.

At that moment Lenin had scarcely finished saying, "Things have turned out just as we said they would. ... *First,* with the 'whole' of the peasantry against the monarchy, against the landlords, against the medieval regime (and to that extent, the revolution remains bourgeois, bourgeois-democratic). *Then,* with the poorest peasants, with the semi-proletarians, with all the exploited, *against capitalism,* including the rural rich, the kulaks, the profiteers, and to that extent the revolution becomes a *socialist* one."[5] As he soon learned, those assertions were premature, to say the least. But they were no empty words; they represented Lenin's basic solution to the dilemma posed by the attempt of the Communists to take power in an agricultural country. If "poor peasants" could not be found to perform their allotted tasks at the proper time, they must be found later. The stubborn refusal of

---

[4] To A. Morizet, quoted in E. H. Carr, *The Bolshevik Revolution, 1917–1923,* II:291, note 1.

[5] V. I. Lenin, *The Proletarian Revolution and the Renegade Kautsky.*

the Russian peasantry to "split" and conduct its own civil war was a great blow to Lenin. However, he was prepared to wait for it, as he awaited the revolution in the West.

For the moment, in any event, the "poor peasants" remained a mirage. As E. H. Carr puts it, instead of a split in the peasantry between rich and poor, there had occurred "a striking equalization of the size of the unit of production ... the smallholding worked by the labor of the peasant and his family ... already typical in 1917, had become by 1920 the predominant unit in Russian agriculture."[6] Therefore the Communists had to compromise with the "middle peasants"—that is, the overwhelming majority of the Russian people. In March 1919 Lenin defended such tactics by declaring that the middle peasantry "does not belong to the exploiters, since it does not draw profits from the labor of others," but it was not exploited either, since it was self-employed. Lenin never came closer to an admission that a Marxian class analysis simply did not apply to the country where he had sought to lead the world's first Marxist revolution.

In fact Lenin did not "compromise with the middle peasant" in 1919; his talk of doing so was translated into action only in 1921 when he inaugurated the NEP. By that time he had largely ceased to talk about the "middle peasant" and simply referred to "the peasantry." NEP, like Brest-Litovsk, was an admission of defeat; however, neither was intended as a surrender, but rather as a tactical maneuver to be pursued only until the inevitable change of conditions which would make victory possible. NEP was like Brest-Litovsk in another respect: the end of the compromise was not that foreseen by Lenin. What enabled him to tear up the treaty was not a Communist revolution in Germany, but Allied victory. What enabled Stalin (Lenin had died in the meantime) to abandon NEP was not a split of the peasantry into rich and poor—to which sanction for a capitalist development in the villages was supposed to lead—but the accumulation of sufficient power in the Communist state to do the job which the "poor peasants" were supposed to do, namely, liquidate the kulaks and establish collective farms.

Limited Freedom in the Economy

In 1921 the economy of Russia lay in ruins. Seven years of war and civil war had produced catastrophe. Industrial production stood at thirteen per cent of prewar volume; the grain harvest had fallen from 74 million tons in 1916 to 30 million tons in 1919 and continued to decline still further. Inflation was rampant, and although the Communists hated and feared it, they saw no alternative but to contribute to it by printing paper money. The immediate economic measures taken to meet the crisis could not be directly financial, nor could they involve any plans

---

[6] Carr, *op. cit.*, II:168.

for extensive change in the structure of the economy. They aimed merely to persuade people to work and produce more, in the city or in the village, so that some kind of regular trade could be resumed, the urban masses fed, and the villagers supplied with the goods for which they would willingly exchange their grain.

Although as indicated the food tax was prompted by basically political motives, it also initiated the revival of the economy. The law provided that the peasant must pay the government a tax in kind consisting of a certain percentage, varying somewhat from region to region, of his produce; he could then dispose of the remainder on the free market. A year later the tax was fixed at a standard 10%. In 1922 also the peasant was permitted to lease land and hire labor, although purchase and sale of land were still prohibited. By the Fundamental Law on the Exploitation of Land by the Workers, enacted in May 1922, the government guaranteed the peasant freedom of choice of land tenure—individual, communal, or other. Thus the villager was permitted, within rather broad limits, to manage his own economic life as he saw fit.

The small businessman was also granted a measure of economic freedom. Although the state retained in its hands the ownership of the so-called "commanding heights"—including the largest enterprises, railways, and banks—private entrepreneurs were permitted to resume management of smaller concerns, to hire labor, and to trade more or less freely with the goods produced. The new class of small urban capitalists, who became known as "Nepmen," suffered from social pressures from which the peasants were exempt. It was difficult for them to obtain credit at the banks, the rentals for their apartments were often higher than their neighbors', their children had to pay higher tuition fees at schools. Many of them expressed their suspicion that their situation was precarious and temporary by free spending and high living.

The new era of "free enterprise" benefited not only the peasants and small businessmen, but also the industrial workers. The trade-unions, organized under the leadership of Michael Tomsky, were permitted to strike against the private capitalists, and accordingly it was thought necessary that they be allowed to strike against state enterprises also, even though they were urged not to do so and reminded that by so doing they were by definition striking against themselves.

Under the new dispensation, the economy began to revive. Lenin addressed himself to the disagreeable topic of gold, and he announced that in the future gold would be used to construct public lavatories in the streets of the great cities of the world, but that for the time being orthodox principles of finance, as well as of trade, must be taken seriously. He handed the slogan, "master trade," to the rank-and-file Communists, who picked it up in a generally uneasy and gingerly fashion. State industries and state farms were now commanded to show profit and to operate on commercial principles generally. Financial stability was slowly recovered. By the end of 1922 a third of the government revenue was coming from the food tax, one-third from a variety of direct money taxes, and one-third from the issuance of bank notes. As a result of the growing tax yield, in 1924 a new currency (the unit was the *chervonets*, which means "red") could be introduced and the old note issue gradually abandoned.

However, by this time a crisis had arisen in urban-rural trade. The new nationalized industry was producing again, but its costs were much higher than prewar levels and thus the prices of manufactured goods were high. As the marketing of agricultural produce was resumed, the greater supply drove grain prices down. The terms of trade thus moved against the countryside. Whereas the peasant had formerly been able to get a shirt for thirty-odd pounds of rye or the equivalent, by 1923 he needed two hundred and fifty pounds. The result was the "scissors crisis," so called from a diagram Trotsky used in a speech, which showed the intersection of a falling rural price curve and a rising urban price curve. The curves intersected, said Trotsky, in September 1922, and the "scissors" was thought to have continued to open until October 1923.

Recent research has cast doubt on whether the dramatic diagram represented what actually happened. It seems that the peasants did not withdraw from the market, although the Bolshevik government feared they would. As a result, Moscow took drastic action, exerting direct pressure on the nationalized trusts and employing credit rationing and the importation of cheap foreign goods, in order to lower industrial prices. Many Party members resented the leaders' firmness with the state enterprises.

By 1923–1924 it was apparent that the regime was managing to stabilize itself, at least for the time being, as the economic revival made headway. The open although limited encouragement given to private enterprise led many in and out of Russia to conclude that "capitalism" had returned for good, and that the Communists had jettisoned their long-proclaimed ideological objectives, which might never have been seriously meant anyhow. The introduction of the NEP was the first in a long series of occasions in Soviet history when foreign observers decided that Communist doctrine was ceasing to be significant in influencing the Soviet leaders.

No doubt many of the peasants expected NEP to be permanent, and although the Nepmen had fewer such illusions, they too hoped the policy would last for some time. Many Communist Party members feared that NEP might be prolonged and fought to end it before it got out of hand. Perhaps indeed it might have lasted somewhat longer than it did, if it had not been for certain developments which restricted political freedom, in and out of the Party, at the very time when the regime was experimenting rather boldly with economic freedom.

The End of Organized Opposition

The first measures to silence opposition were directed against the remaining non-Communist parties. The Left Socialist Revolutionaries were briefly tolerated even after their resignation from the government at the time of Brest-Litovsk, but after

they resorted to violence against the regime in late summer, they were sternly repressed. The Kadet party was declared illegal before the end of 1917. Certain Kadet
leaders were placed on state-appointed committees to deal with problems of the
severe famine of 1921–1922, but already by then the party as such had disappeared
from the Russian scene.

Orthodox Socialist Revolutionaries and Mensheviks were still permitted to at-
tend the VIII Congress of Soviets of Workers', Soldiers', and Peasant Deputies in
December 1920, although there was no pretense that they were present on the
same footing as the Communist deputies. The chief Menshevik leaders still inside
Russia were allowed to emigrate to Berlin in 1921, and Berlin became a sort of
Menshevik capital until the rise of Hitler (thereafter moving to Paris and then
New York). However, the Socialist Revolutionary leaders did not receive the same
courtesies. In 1922 a number of them were put on public trial and charged with
counterrevolutionary crimes. Foreign radicals interested themselves in the case,
and the Belgian Socialist, Emile Vandervelde, was allowed to undertake their defense. Despite findings of guilt, several SR leaders were permitted to go abroad after short prison terms, and they proceeded in stages to Berlin, Paris, and New
York. After 1922 no non-Communist political organization was tolerated on Soviet soil.

Sharp differences of opinion had appeared within the Communist party itself
during the Civil War. In 1918 the "Left" Communist faction, following Bukharin,
had opposed the Brest-Litovsk peace and demanded a revolutionary war. After
the treaty was signed many of Bukharin's followers, who included Radek, Lomov,
Uritsky, V. M. Smirnov, Bubnov, and Piatakov, resigned posts of prominence in
protest, but they remained in the Party. At the VIII Party Congress in March 1919,
a new Party program was adopted, replacing the old one of 1903. It proclaimed
that the "dictatorship of the proletariat" had been brought into being in Russia,
based on the Soviets, and among other things reasserted the right of national self-
determination (see p. 28). Bukharin and the "Left" Communists objected. Lenin
replied, "Scratch certain Communists and you will find a Great-Russian chauvinist." That may well have been true; however, the militant "Lefts" did not defend
Russian preeminence, but the primacy of the international proletariat over any
nation, in tactics as well as doctrine.

At the IX Party Congress in April 1920, many former "Left" Communists appeared as the "Democratic Centralism" group. Led by Osinsky, Sapronov, and V.
M. Smirnov, they criticized the growth in power of Communist bureaucrats and
their use of "bourgeois" specialists. By the time of the VIII Congress of Soviets in
December 1920, the conflicts in the Party came to center on the question of the
dangers of "bureaucracy." Trotsky was quite willing to have strict central control
and quasimilitary discipline; in fact, he was enthusiastic about "labor armies" and
"shock methods," as a result of his experience as war commissar. However, he was
concerned about the power of the bureaucrats, which he proposed to curb by

turning trade-unions into organs of state, while carefully selecting leading personnel through what he called "sandpapering" the unions.

Those who feared state control most deeply were now forming a group known as the "Workers' Opposition," led by Shliapnikov, the colorful Mme. Kollontai, and others, who urged that the existing state organs turn their powers over to the trade-unions. Lenin disagreed with both Trotsky and the Workers' Opposition. He insisted that the trade-unions must remain separate from the state (because the poor peasantry was "represented" in the state but not in the trade-unions, and therefore it had to fall to the unions to defend the class interests of the proletariat alone). He also expressed reservations on the use of military methods. While Lenin disagreed with Trotsky, he did not denounce him but he promptly branded the Workers' Opposition as anarchist or anarcho-syndicalist, which to a state socialist is a very bad name.

At the X Party Congress in 1921 Lenin obtained the adoption of NEP, which both Trotskyites and the Workers' Opposition opposed in whole or part as involving undue concessions to the peasantry. But Lenin led the Party to stigmatize the Workers' Opposition as a "deviation towards syndicalism and anarchism." At the opening of the Congress, he declared, "We are going to put an end to opposition now, to put the lid on it; we have had enough of oppositions!" The Congress proceeded to do just that. All factional groups within the Party were "dissolved" and prohibited. In a secret resolution, the Central Committee was given the power to expel Party members (including members of the Central Committee itself) for engaging in factionalism.

In the summer of 1921 a nation-wide purge of the Party was carried out which resulted in the reduction of Party strength from 730,000 (at the time of the X Congress) to 530,000. Almost one-third of the Party members were thus expelled. Such measures might have been expected to "put the lid" on any opposition beyond doubt; but more was to come. The following year the Cheka was abolished and replaced by the GPU (*Gosudarstvennoe Politicheskoe Upravlenie* or State Political Administration), which was given the right to arrest Party members—a right not possessed by the Cheka. The creation of the GPU was announced at the XI Party Congress in March 1922.

The XI Congress was the last Lenin attended. Addressing it, he forecast decisive battles with foreign capitalism, but these were far ahead, while the one "in the near future" would be with "Russian capitalism ... which grows out of petty peasant economy"—in a word, with the peasants. Lenin defended the necessity of using "bourgeois specialists," declaring that Communists in Russia were only "a drop in the ocean of the people." He discussed the *émigré* Kadets and others who had published a symposium entitled *Change of Signposts* (*Smena Vekh*), in which they declared that the Soviet regime was undergoing an evolution into a new "national" and normal regime meriting the support of all Russians. This current had found support also within the country. Lenin declared himself willing to use such ideological fellow travelers (however mistaken their analysis) for Communist purposes in the same way as the "bourgeois specialists" were being used already.

Taking note of the fact that "former" members of the Workers' Opposition had taken their grievances to the Comintern, charging that the Russian Party leaders had become isolated from the workers and were paying undue attention to the peasantry, the XI Congress cracked down again on dissidents, and meted out further expulsions from Party ranks.

The Emergence of Stalin

Shortly after the Congress ended, Lenin suffered a stroke of arteriosclerotic paralysis. Suddenly the ranks of the highest Party and state leadership were thrown into confusion. As long as Lenin was at the helm, everyone in the Party, even including the members of the opposition, knew where he was, what arguments he might urge with some hope of success, what the consequences might be. With Lenin removed from effective leadership even temporarily, all was uncertainty.

Virtually from the moment of the Bolshevik revolution, the actual governing body of the country had been the Politburo (Political Bureau of the Central Committee of the Party). During the Civil War the Politburo was composed of five men: Lenin, Trotsky, Stalin, Kamenev, and Bukharin. Its functions were to settle policy questions; such decisions were then communicated to the Orgburo (Organization Bureau of the Central Committee) to be translated into action by the assignment of jobs to specific persons. The liaison between the two bureaus was effected by Stalin, who from the first had been given "practical" jobs, often the ones nobody else among the theoretically-minded leaders wanted.

In 1919 Stalin had become commissar of the Workers' and Peasants' Inspectorate (*Rabkrin*), whose job was to combat corruption and inefficiency in all branches of the government. One month before Lenin's stroke, Stalin was also made general secretary of the Central Committee, with his old colleague, Viacheslav Molotov, and Valerian Kuibyshev as his assistants. The functions of the Secretariat included the composition of the agenda for the Politburo, which had now added Zinoviev and Tomsky to the five of the Civil War period. The Secretariat had also to co-ordinate the joint sessions which the Central Committee and the Central Control Commission (a new body created by the XI Congress) began to hold and, in general, smooth the relations between them. The Commission had been proposed, paradoxically enough, by the Workers' Opposition, which envisaged it as a means of keeping the Party pure of careerist and bourgeois infiltration and therefore truly proletarian. However, it was a weapon which was soon turned on its authors and all other dissidents from Politburo policy; Stalin's powers in it were very great.

From the first Stalin had also been commissar of nationalities. As such he was responsible for the Red Army invasion of Georgia and the destruction of its Menshevik-led independent government in the early months of 1921. He seems to have been determined not to allow the right of "self-determination," in the name of which he had countenanced the secession of Finland from Russia, to be invoked in any other case where a country sought to escape Soviet power. Actually he could support his position on Marxist grounds. The Marxian analysis was a class analysis, and the category "nation" had to be reduced to class terms. "Self-determination" for a nation was thus bound to mean self-determination for that nation's proletariat, which would of course be Communist, unless duped or seduced by the bourgeoisie into a misapprehensie of its true interests. The Communist leaders' patience with backward proletarians who failed to grasp their own interests fluctuated, but no principle of Marxism-Leninism excluded the possibility of the Soviets' "coming to the aid" of local Communists anywhere. This was Stalin's justification in the case of Georgia, although the brutality of the conquest of his own native country provoked some puzzlement and criticism among his colleagues.

In mid-1922 Stalin intervened in a dispute over the government of Ukraine, and again there was criticism from within the Party leadership. Soon afterward he attempted to bolster his prestige by coming up with a proposal for a constitutional change fixing the relationship between Russia and the various non-Russian Soviet "republics." Lenin supported the idea and at first defended Stalin against his critics. However, by November Lenin's whole attitude toward Stalin was apparently shifting. In December he suffered another stroke, and this time he was sufficiently convinced that he was near death to dictate a will which dealt not with his private affairs but those of the Party and government.

In this will Lenin emphasized again the necessity of agreement between the peasantry and the working class which he believed indispensable to the survival of Communism in Russia. However, the danger which concerned him was not a class antagonism but a personal one: that between Stalin and Trotsky, whom he called "the two most able leaders of the present Central Committee." Trotsky he declared to be the more able of the two, but he thought he had recently shown "too far-reaching a self-confidence and a disposition to be too much attracted by the purely administrative side of affairs." On the other hand, Stalin had "concentrated an enormous power in his hands; and I am not sure that he always knows how to use that power with sufficient caution." Lenin recalled Zinoviev's and Kamenev's hesitation on the eve of the October Revolution and Trotsky's tardy adherence to Bolshevism, but he said these facts ought not to be used against the men personally. Bukharin he labeled "the greatest and most valuable theoretician," but lamented "something scholastic" in his make-up.

Thus Lenin's will did not point to any single individual as unqualifiedly worthy of his mantle; in fact, he seems to have taken care to emphasize that each one had strengths and weaknesses. However, only ten days later he added a postscript in which he singled out one man as currently causing the most trouble in the Party. Stalin, he wrote, "is too rude, and this fault ... becomes unbearable in the office of General Secretary. Therefore I propose to the comrades to find a way to remove Stalin from that position and appoint to it another man ... more patient, more loyal, more polite and more attentive to comrades, less capricious, etc." This remark was dictated on January 4, 1923.

While Lenin lived the whole document remained known only to his wife, Krupskaia, and his secretaries; but Lenin went on to attack Stalin publicly. In *Pravda* he sharply criticized Stalin's conduct of the Workers' and Peasants' Inspectorate. He followed this up by a promise to the disgruntled Georgian Party leaders to support them against the "arrogance of Ordzhonikidze and the connivance of Stalin and Dzerzhinsky"; finally he wrote Stalin that he "broke off" all personal relations with him. He was preparing to launch an open onslaught at the XII Congress, scheduled for the spring of 1923, for which he had concerted measures with Trotsky, but on March 9 he suffered his third stroke and never recovered from it.

The Constitution of the USSR

Stalin was aware of at least part of his danger, but he also knew that if attacked he was entrenched in a multitude of important and powerful Party posts. However, he did not confine himself to manipulation behind the scenes, but sought to enhance his public prestige. As commissar of nationalities, he was able to take credit for the constitutional "reform," by which in December 1922 a Union of Soviet Socialist Republics was established.

Up to that time the formal Constitution had been the one adopted July 10, 1918, by the V Congress of Soviets for the "Russian Socialist Federated Soviet Republic." It had begun with a Declaration of Rights of Toiling and Exploited People, and had gone on to legalize the "government" (as distinguished from the central organs of the Communist Party, which were actually running the country) which had come into existence at the time of the October Revolution.

The supreme authority was said to be the periodic meeting of the All-Russian Congress of Soviets, elected by a system under which the urban population considerably outweighed the rural in representation; moreover, the rural deputies were elected only indirectly. Between meetings of the Congress, power was wielded by a Central Executive Committee (VTsIK), a very large "committee" of not more than two hundred members elected by the Congress. This committee was supposed to appoint the Council of People's Commissars (*Sovnarkom*), a sort of cabinet. A hierarchy of local and regional soviets was also written into the Constitution. The Constitution of 1918 made no mention of the Communist Party, and in general bore only the vaguest relationship to the actual facts of govern-

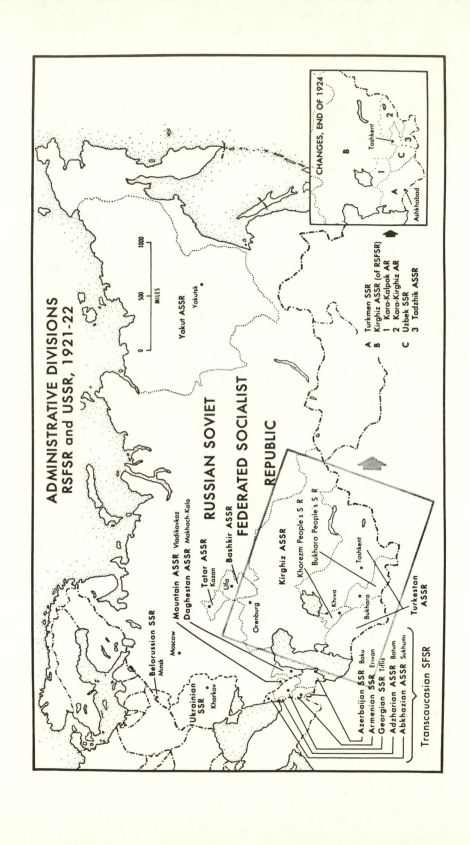

ADMINISTRATIVE DIVISIONS
RSFSR and USSR, 1921-22

RUSSIAN SOVIET
FEDERATED SOCIALIST
REPUBLIC

MILES
0   500   1000

Yakut ASSR
Yakutsk

Belorussian SSR
Minsk

Mountain ASSR Vladikavkaz
Daghestan ASSR Makhach-Kala

Tatar ASSR
Kazan

Ufa
Bashkir ASSR

Moscow

Orenburg

Kirghiz ASSR

Khorezm People's S R

Bukhara People's S R

Khiva

Bukhara

Tashkent

Turkestan
ASSR

Ukrainian
SSR
Kharkov

Azerbaijan SSR Baku
Armenian SSR Erivan
Georgian SSR Tiflis
Adzharian ASSR Batum
Abkhazian ASSR Sukhumi

Transcaucasian SFSR

CHANGES, END OF 1924

Tashkent

B

A
C
1
2
3

Ashkhabad

A   Turkmen SSR
B   Kirghiz ASSR (of RSFSR)
1   Kara-Kalpak AR
2   Kara-Kirghiz AR
C   Uzbek SSR
3   Tadzhik ASSR

mental life at the time. The reality was a highly centralized state—even the provisions of the Constitution made that clear—in which no fundamental questions were to be subjected to popular will, nor were significant decisions to be made by any level of the imposing and intricate "governmental" machinery.

Decision-making rested with the central organs of the Communist Party. In theory "democratic centralism" characterized the process of arriving at decisions. That is to say, free discussion of any particular issue—to be sure, within the limits of the basic Bolshevik viewpoint—was supposed to be permitted at all levels of the Party until the national Congress pronounced upon it. From that moment all Party members were bound to accept the decision and act on it without question. Structurally "democratic centralism" was and is supposed to be assured by election of all "leading Party bodies, from the lowest to the highest," periodic reports of such bodies to their organizations, strict Party discipline and "subordination of the minority to the majority," and "the absolutely binding character of the decisions of higher bodies upon lower bodies." "Democratic centralism" actually did operate in some such fashion in the Party during the early years of the Soviet regime. However, the central organs, headed by the Politburo, soon in fact acquired more power than the Party Congresses, and after the ban imposed on "factions" at the XI Congress, it became increasingly difficult for dissenting opinions of any kind to obtain a hearing. But whether the central organs submitted to guidance from the rest of the Party or not, the Party decisions from the very first determined governmental policies and practices.

Besides the description of governmental machinery, the Constitution included the Declaration of Rights already mentioned. Freedom of speech, press, association, assembly, and access to education was guaranteed, but only to the "working class." Church was said to be separated from state, and school from church (that is, the Russian Orthodox Church, for a thousand years the national religion of the Russians, Belorussians, and Ukrainians), and all citizens were assured freedom to conduct religious and antireligious propaganda. Discrimination against national minorities was forbidden. "Regions with special usages and national characteristics" were authorized to unite in "autonomous" groupings to be admitted to the Russian Soviet Federated Socialist Republic. The duty to bear arms, and the duty to work—"he who does not work shall not eat," a very fair rendition of 2 Thessalonians 3:10—were also specified.

By 1921 there nominally existed six separate Soviet republics: Russia, Belorussia, Ukraine, Azerbaijan, Georgia, and Armenia. In late 1922, at Stalin's behest, the last three were amalgamated into a Transcaucasian Republic, despite stiff opposition from several Georgian Communists. The resulting four were to be formed into a union. In March 1921 the X Party Congress had already set the stage by declaring for a "union of the several Soviet republics." Actually all four already had representation in the All-Russian Congress of Soviets when, in December 1922, that body was superseded by the I Congress of Soviets of the USSR, of similar composition. The December Congress declared a Union of Soviet Socialist Republics to be in existence, and approved a new draft constitution.

However, the national issue, already settled in theory, caused sharp debate within the Party through the early months of 1923. Again Stalin rode down opposition, especially from the Ukrainian Party leaders headed by Rakovsky, and pushed through his own final version of the Constitution. "Nationalist in form, socialist in content," was the accepted formula for uniting several nationalities under Communist rule—and one honest enough when it is remembered that for a Marxist content is everything. Stalin's Constitution, as finally approved by the Central Executive Committee in July 1923 and ratified by the II All-Union Congress of Soviets in January 1924, made no substantial changes in the Constitution of 1918. A provision was inserted ensuring the right of each republic to "secede freely," but it was repeatedly made clear that a request for secession could only arise from class feelings hostile to those of the proletariat, and such a demand has indeed never been expressed.

The remainder of the governmental structure was not revised in any essential particular. The Congress of Soviets, Central Executive Committee, and Council of People's Commissars were now "All-Union" instead of "All-Russian." The Central Executive Committee was divided into a Council of the Union, with numerical representation only, and a Council of Nationalities composed of five delegates from each union republic—which provision, unmodified, would have left the Russian Republic greatly outnumbered—and also five from each autonomous republic and one from each autonomous region. At this stage the Russian Republic had seven autonomous republics—the Turkestan, Bashkir, Tatar, Kirghiz, Daghestan, Mountain, and Yakut republics—and ten autonomous regions, while all the other union republics together had a total of two autonomous republics and two autonomous regions. Not that the make-up of the Council of Nationalities made much practical difference, but psychological factors were at stake.

The Constitution contained lists of the cabinet ministries (that is, the People's Commissariats), in which certain offices, such as Foreign Affairs, and Military and Naval Affairs, were present only at the All-Union level; certain others, such as the Supreme Council of National Economy, at both All-Union and Union-republic levels; and still others at the Union-republic level only, such as Internal Affairs, Justice, and Education. There was a new provision for a Supreme Court and a procurator, but they were in law as well as in fact made subject to the Central Executive Committee, and there was no pretense of any kind of judicial independence. Like the 1918 Constitution, the Constitution of the USSR made no mention of where the real power lay, or in fact referred to the Communist Party at all.

This document was touted by Stalin as an achievement equal in importance to the organization of the Red Army in the Civil War, an implied assertion that he was at least the equal of Trotsky. He praised the constitutional reform as a "decisive step on the road toward uniting the toilers of the whole world into a World Soviet Socialist Republic." Although Lenin had, some time after his first stroke, approved the principles of Stalin's plan for a new constitution, he was pointedly silent about the whole business in December 1922 when the USSR was being formally proclaimed. His break with Stalin remained, however, unknown to the public and to all but a few individuals at the top levels of the Party.

The Triumvirate

The final attack of Lenin's illness forced his colleagues to seek a substitute for the single leader whose word had become, although it had not always been, final. The Politburo did not formally select any successor, but in fact Zinoviev, Kamenev, and Stalin began to act together as such. The bond that seemed to unite them was their "old Bolshevik" status, reaching all the way back to the schism of 1903, against the "ex-Menshevik" and newcomer to the party, Trotsky, whose brilliance, personality, and achievements seemed to match if not surpass Lenin's. Zinoviev was a successful speaker and effective with crowds; he had strong local power in Petrograd as chairman of its renowned Soviet, and as president of the Comintern he had wide prestige. Kamenev probably had the stronger intellect; he had enjoyed a close association with Lenin as his assistant and held considerable power as chairman of the Moscow Soviet. Stalin's many offices have already been cited; it should be added that as commissar of nationalities he had come to have great influence in the outlying areas of the country, where his colleagues had little. Zinoviev and Kamenev still had a tendency to regard Stalin as the junior partner and glorified errand boy, but for the moment they could all together manage the Politburo, and the Politburo could manage the Party.

That did not mean that all of the Party was yet willing to be managed. The XII Congress in April 1923, at which Lenin and Trotsky had planned to attack Stalin (see p. 151), was instead marked by the triumvirate's victory over its opponents, in which Trotsky assisted the triumvirs. On the eve of the Congress the "Workers' Truth" group, following A. A. Bogdanov (whom Lenin had attacked in *Materialism and Empirio-Criticism*), were denouncing NEP as a simple return to capitalism. The "Workers' Group," led by Miasnikov (who had earlier been expelled from the Party for advocating freedom of speech for all "from monarchists to anarchists"), also attacked NEP, declaring it ought to stand for "new exploitation of the proletariat." At the Congress, both Zinoviev and Trotsky anathematized these two groups. Stalin forcefully invoked the shade of the not-yet-dead Lenin, and the Party opposition outside the Politburo was effectively trampled down. For the moment, the antagonism among the leaders seemed to recede into the background.

However, it broke out afresh in connection with the new economic crisis provoked by the Party's attempt to solve the "scissors" problem (see p. 146). In the spring of 1923 industrial enterprises were feeling the pressure exerted to bring prices down; credit was being curtailed, and low wages and unemployment were widespread. Although Trotsky did not raise the economic issue, he chose the moment of crisis to give point to an attack on "bureaucratization" in the Party. Hard upon his heels, forty-six prominent Communists echoed his criticism in a public "platform." Although there was no direct evidence of collusion between Trotsky and the "forty-six," the substance of the criticism was the same. Thus, as Isaac Deutscher points out, Trotsky "had the worst of both worlds"[7]: that is to say, he had not approved of the pressure on state industry, but had remained silent until the opposition groups which had been publicly objecting were crushed; thus it was too late to find allies outside the Politburo, while he was already isolated within it.

The triumvirate nominally bowed to the criticism by announcing a Party discussion on all issues about which members were concerned. Trotsky was thereby provoked into writing an open letter, on December 5, 1923, to the Communists of Red Presnia, the section of Moscow in which the armed uprising of December 1905 had occurred. In the letter he warned against the possible degeneration of the revolutionary "old guard" into bureaucracy. The conflict behind the scenes was thus made public, and there was open hostility between the triumvirs and Trotsky. Zinoviev even urged the arrest of Trotsky, but Stalin was for restraint. For one thing, Trotsky retained immense popularity within the Party. Stalin contented himself with further thunder at the "opposition," choosing to be ambiguous about whether he included Trotsky in it or not, and taunting him with refusing to identify himself clearly with either the Politburo or the opposition. On January 21, 1924, Lenin finally died. Trotsky himself was not well, and perhaps his illness had something to do with the apparent indecision he displayed during the last months of 1923. At the moment of Lenin's death he was absent from the capital. Probably this coincidence was not decisive, although it gave Stalin the chance he needed to identify himself publicly with the heritage of the fallen leader. Five days after Lenin's death, Stalin addressed the II All-Union Congress of Soviets and delivered a remarkable statement:

> We Communists are people of a special mold. We are made of a special stuff. We are those who form the army of the great proletarian strategist, the army of Comrade Lenin. There is nothing higher than the honor of belonging to this army. There is nothing higher than the title of member of the party whose founder and leader is Comrade Lenin. ... Departing from us, Comrade Lenin adjured us to hold high and to guard the purity of the great title of member of the Party. We vow to you, Comrade Lenin, that we will fulfill your bequest with honor! ...
>
> Departing from us, Comrade Lenin adjured us to guard the unity of our Party as the apple of our eye. We vow to you, Comrade Lenin, that this behest, too, we will fulfill with honor! ...
>
> Departing from us, Comrade Lenin adjured us to guard and strengthen the dictatorship of the proletariat. We vow to you, Comrade Lenin, that we will spare no effort to fulfill this bequest, too, with honor! ...

---

[7] I. Deutscher, *Stalin: a Political Biography,* Oxford U. Press, 1949, p. 260.

> Departing from us, Comrade Lenin adjured us to strengthen with all our might the alliance of the workers and the peasants. We vow to you, Comrade Lenin, that this behest, too, we will fulfill with honor! ...

Stalin's oath, cast in the form of a church litany, grated on a number of old Bolsheviks and puzzled a number of others. The triumvirate's decision to place Lenin's body in a mausoleum in Red Square also was repugnant to many. The changing of the name of Petrograd to Leningrad—the first city to be renamed by the Soviets—seemed more in the revolutionary tradition and served as a precedent for similar changes. Ekaterinburg became Sverdlovsk, after Sverdlov, who had died in 1919. Shortly afterward, Elizavetgrad became Zinovievsk, honoring a leader who was still very much alive. Still playing the role of caution and modesty, Stalin waited until one of his fellow triumvirs was so honored before he allowed Tsaritsyn to be renamed Stalingrad, in April 1925.

However, Stalin had made it clear that he aspired to be Lenin's heir as he claimed to have been his true disciple. And although it was true that before he died Lenin had in some sense disowned Stalin, it was also true that Stalin had done Lenin's bidding, had never embroiled himself in a conflict with him on either principle or tactics—unlike Trotsky, Zinoviev, or Kamenev—and in the famed "oath" presented, in however crude a manner, a digest of the essentials of Leninism. On such factors rested his title to succeed Lenin.

The last words of Lenin himself were not spoken until, in May 1924, the will was read aloud in the Central Committee. The scene was one of consternation. Stalin and Trotsky sat silent, wrestling with their emotions, while Zinoviev referred obliquely to the "oath" that had been taken to execute Lenin's wishes, adding, "we are happy to say that in one point Lenin's fears have proved baseless. I have in mind the point about our General Secretary. You have all witnessed our harmonious co-operation in the last few months; and, like myself, you will be happy to say that Lenin's fears have proved baseless." The will was not published, and Stalin was saved. Zinoviev would live to regret his statement, but it was not yet the power of Stalin, only his adroitness, which had led Zinoviev to make it. Not fear of Stalin but assurance that they could make good use of him led the other two triumvirs to preserve the third. The moment was decisive for Stalin's rise to power; for Trotsky, it was virtually the last chance, which went by without an effort to seize it.

In the fall of 1917 power in the former Russian Empire had passed to the Communist Party; by 1922 it had passed into the hands of Lenin and the other leaders of the Central Committee; by 1924 it lay at the disposal of the three men who dominated the Politburo. It was to narrow further. However, much more than personalities was at stake. All the leaders, despite the hostility among them, were committed to the realization of the Communist program at home and abroad, and the struggle for personal power was at the same time a debate on the best and fastest way to realize that program.

11

Stalin, Trotsky, and Bukharin

Dzhugashvili and Bronstein

Joseph Stalin, born Dzhugashvili, and Leon Trotsky, born Bronstein, were the same age, and both had been from early youth members of the Russian Social Democratic party. As dedicated Communists, they had a common basic outlook: they were philosophical materialists, committed to the unity of theory and practice and bent upon spreading communism throughout the whole world. Until 1922, at any rate, both men had a secure place in Lenin's favor and therefore in the party as a whole. Stalin had always adhered closely to Lenin's most cherished principles and practices. Since 1917, at least, Trotsky had supported Lenin on the main issues and seemed to have more of his candor and flexibility than Stalin. However, as Lenin sickened and died, the mutual antagonism between Trotsky and Stalin, who had never been compatible, deepened into a life-and-death struggle.

It is difficult to compare the later lives of the two men, for Stalin achieved sole power and Trotsky was exiled, and since Trotsky thus escaped Stalin's dilemmas, it is uncertain how he would have responded to them, although he detested Stalin's rule. Stalin hated his adversary so deeply that he caused his name to be written simply "Judas Trotsky" in officially commissioned books, but he borrowed many of his ideas and methods. Their earlier lives, however, suggest something of the personal differences which were to be complicated by disagreements over doctrine and practice.

Stalin was the eldest surviving child of the shoemaker Vissarion Dzhugashvili of Gori in Georgia. As a boy he attended a church school in Gori and then the theological seminary in Tiflis. Today the seminary has been converted into a museum of medieval Georgian art. Young Joseph joined a Marxist society known as Mesame-Dasi while a student at the seminary, but it is not clear whether this had anything to do with his expulsion in 1899. During the next two years his Marxism crystallized, and his first Marxist essays appeared in a Georgian newspaper in 1901. At that time he was already an enthusiastic defender of Lenin and the other orthodox Marxist exiles who published the newspaper *Iskra*. His literary style was not then distinguished; in fact, it never got much better.

Stalin was active in the revolutionary movement in Tiflis, Batum, and elsewhere, not as Dzhugashvili, nor yet "Stalin," but as "Koba." This meant something like "courageous" in Turkish, and it was also the name of a fabled Georgian freebooter; it is uncertain which the nickname first signified. Later he was called, indeed, practically dubbed himself, the "Lenin of the Caucasus." However, he was not necessarily the most outstanding leader of the Caucasian Social Democrats, nor even of the Georgian Bolsheviks after the party split in 1903. The great majority of the Marxists in Georgia became and stayed Menshevik; among the Bolsheviks Stalin was prominent, but that did not mean a great deal. Very soon after the news of the London Congress of 1903 reached the Caucasus, he took a firmly pro-Bolshevik stand, and he continued to do so in 1905. It seems that it was at the Tammerfors Party conference at the end of 1905 that Stalin first met Lenin.

After the Revolution of 1905, in defiance of the ban of the then Menshevik-controlled Party, "Koba" led "fighting squads" in raiding banks in order to augment scant Party funds. In one raid in Tiflis a squad seized a quarter of a million rubles. This is the basis of the legend that Stalin was a bank robber; but he did not act as gunman, and he did not pocket the proceeds. He spent much of the period between revolutions in jail or in exile, but made a few important trips abroad in 1912. By this time the Bolshevik organizations in Russia had been gravely weakened, and the Bolsheviks of the Caucasus had assumed an importance quite out of proportion to their numbers. Stalin had become editor of the Party newspaper, *Pravda,* and he was co-opted by Lenin onto the Party Central Committee just after the Prague conference of 1912, at which the Bolsheviks broke permanently with the other Marxist factions. He visited Lenin in exile and spent some time with him. As a result of their talks, he wrote an essay on the "nationalities question" which led Lenin to inform Gorky that a "wonderful Georgian" had done a fine job on the subject. The pseudonym with which the pamphlet was signed was "K. Stalin."

At the outbreak of World War I Stalin was in Siberian exile, sharing a hut with Sverdlov, future Chairman of the Presidium ("president") of the Soviet republic, who, it seems, found Stalin an uncomradely hut partner. Stalin chose not to try to escape during the war. In 1916 he was summoned to Krasnoiarsk to be drafted but was found physically unfit for military service owing to his withered left arm. During the war period he apparently wrote next to nothing.

Liberated by the February Revolution, Stalin hastened to Petrograd and, as the only member of the Central Committee on the spot, assumed temporary leadership of the Bolshevik Party. Like almost all other Bolsheviks, he became identified with the movement for reunification with the Mensheviks. When Lenin arrived and sharply castigated such tendencies to compromise, Stalin took his scolding without protest. He owed his position in the Party to the fact that he worked hard and did not argue with his comrades, especially Lenin.

Trotsky, like Stalin, was born in 1879. His real name was Lev Davidovich Bronstein; his father was a well-to-do Jewish farmer in the Ukrainian province of Kherson. He attended school in Odessa, developing an early brilliance and book-ishness. He reports his observation of the composition of his class: "the tale-bear-ers and envious at one pole, the frank, courageous boys at the other, and the neu-tral, vacillating mass in the middle." He was to apply the same threefold classification to his fellow revolutionaries and fellow citizens of the Empire and the world. In his teens he went to Nikolaev, met a number of populists, became enamored of a girl in the group, and accepted the populist doctrine. Soon, how-ever, he became converted to Marxism, engaged in revolutionary activity, and for it spent his eighteenth birthday in jail. He was exiled to Siberia but soon escaped and arrived in London in 1902 to join Lenin. In Western Europe he met another young lady. The girl from Nikolaev was known as Mrs. Bronstein, the Parisian as Mrs. Trotsky, and neither seemed to complain.

After the II Congress in 1903 Trotsky was for a time associated with the Men-sheviks, but in 1905 he developed an independent doctrinal line (see p. 42) and between revolutions belonged to neither the Bolshevik nor the Menshevik wing. In 1905 he won renown for his brief chairmanship of the St. Petersburg Soviet of Workers' Deputies. During the next few years he tried to reunite the Party and for that reason refrained from trying to build a faction of his own. During the years just before World War I Trotsky's anti-factionalist stand became in effect an anti-Leninist one. After the war began he went to New York, and it was from there that he traveled to Russia in the spring of 1917. During the summer he joined the Bol-shevik Party, although he clearly implied that his only reason for doing so was that the Party had belatedly adopted the analysis and tactical line which he had es-poused all along.

His ability and his logic did not always endear him to his comrades, but his or-atorical and practical gifts did win him broad popularity among the urban work-ers and soldiers in late 1917 and during the Civil War. Having failed as foreign commissar to put into effect his dialectical but quixotic policy of "no war, no peace," he had become war commissar, and his most brilliant success was achieved in organizing the finally victorious Red Army. As war commissar he clashed with Stalin, who ensconced himself at Tsaritsyn with some of his old friends from Caucasus days and flouted Trotsky's authority. However, Stalin was as yet no adversary in the field of theory and policy, which Trotsky considered fundamental.

As the triumvirate took form, Trotsky was plainly the most important figure outside it; but no one regarded Stalin as the most eminent of the three. Zinoviev, especially, had an international prestige which Stalin lacked, while both Kamenev and he were regarded as theorists in a way Stalin was not—and a Communist leader had to be a theorist. As the struggle developed between Trotsky and the tri-umvirs, Stalin counted less on his own influence than on Trotsky's vulnerability. He did not at first try to turn the struggle into a personal contest; an eye witness has told the story of how Zinoviev and Kamenev would snub Trotsky in Politburo meetings, while Stalin would greet him warmly.

Trotsky Against the Triumvirate

On the eve of Lenin's death, the Thirteenth Party Conference published, on Stalin's motion, the decision empowering the Central Committee to expel Party members for factionalism. At the moment the leader died a new sanctity enveloped his every word and deed, including this decision, in which Lenin had taken part. Simultaneously the triumvirs decreed a new recruiting campaign, nominally with a view to strengthening the actual worker element in Party ranks. Actually Stalin, as general secretary, was able to bolster his own influence by guiding the Party machinery in selecting new members. In a few short weeks nearly a quarter of a million men and women were admitted in the new "Lenin enrollment."

At the time of the XIII Party Congress in May 1924, the economic situation was improving sufficiently to enable the triumvirs to call their critics to account. Zinoviev openly attacked Trotsky and demanded that he retract his "errors." As Stalin had only shortly before opposed Zinoviev's demand for Trotsky's arrest, he found it wise to remain in the background. Trotsky replied to Zinoviev with a *cri de coeur* which went to the root of his whole position, morally requiring him to sit passive in the face of doom:

> The party in the last analysis is always right because the party is the single historic instrument given to the proletariat for the solution of its fundamental problems. I have already said that in front of one's own party nothing could be easier than to say: all my criticisms, my statements, my warnings, my protests—the whole thing was a mere mistake. I, however, comrades, cannot say that, because I do not think it. I know that one must not be right against the party. One can be right only with the party, and through the party, for history has created no other road for the realization of what is right.

The Congress was unmoved. It promptly took steps to discipline the Russian Trotskyites, as well as dissidents in the other parties of the Comintern.

After the XIII Congress, as far as could be seen the chief antagonists were Trotsky on the one hand and Zinoviev and Kamenev on the other. In the autumn of 1924 Trotsky published *The Lessons of October*, in which he distinguished between objectively revolutionary situations and subjective failures of revolutionary leaders in such situations. As illustrations of the latter, he cited Zinoviev's and Kamenev's opposition to Lenin's decision to launch an armed uprising in the fall of 1917—thus reopening an extremely ugly wound—and he also implied that Zinoviev was largely responsible for the failure of the German Communist revolt of 1923. Trotsky restated his old theory of "permanent revolution," with its emphasis on the world leadership of the proletariat and its implicit challenge to the

Leninist position on the role of the poor peasantry in building socialism. "October," said Trotsky, was the crucial stage in the history of the Party; "October" meant to him the time when Lenin adopted Trotsky's theory of permanent revolution—at least in the sense of rapid passage from the bourgeois to the socialist stage.

Trotsky had made a tactical error. By his emphasis on "October" he opened the way for Zinoviev and Kamenev to retaliate by reminding the Party again of Trotsky's sharp disagreements with Lenin prior to 1917. Stalin's caution had reaped its reward. Since he was not directly drawn into this controversy, he was in a position to make public statements in November which in effect forgave Zinoviev and Kamenev for their earlier mistakes—he even acknowledged some of his own—but forcefully recalled to his hearers the fact that Trotsky was, after all, a newcomer in Party ranks.

Meanwhile Stalin unleashed a new weapon, which Trotsky probably had not considered him capable of producing. He set forth a theoretical position of his own from which he could challenge Trotsky. In order to do so he had to reverse himself within the space of a few months. In *Foundations of Leninism,* published early in 1924, he had denied that a proletarian dictatorship could establish socialism before the victory of the world revolution. A few months later, in *Problems of Leninism,* he advanced his theory of "socialism in one country."

The theory was an innovation and a repudiation of some things which Lenin had said years earlier; but it was a perfectly logical extension of what Lenin had said and done in 1917 and later. If the Russian Communists were not to be indefinitely bogged down in the NEP stage, they must push on to socialism, even if the world revolution was still further delayed. Like Lenin, Trotsky believed the building of socialism could be begun in Russia alone; but what Stalin did was to assert that it could be completed with success and to furnish reasons for his contention. Russia was an enormous country, rich in natural resources. Provided that "capitalist" intervention was not renewed, the Russian proletariat, drawing on Russia's great potential wealth and protected by its vast spaces, could accomplish the task.

For a time, however, the theory of "socialism in one country" was overshadowed by the acrimonious personal struggle between Trotsky and the two most prominent triumvirs. In January 1925 the Central Committee removed Trotsky from the War Commissariat, even through he remained in uneasy possession of a seat on the Politburo. This was the decisive blow. Although he was still not completely crushed, Trotsky receded to the background. If he had been another kind of man, he might have tried to use the Red Army against his adversaries, but his loyalty to the Party was paramount, and he accepted his deposition without trying to resist.

Although Trotsky was defeated, Zinoviev and Kamenev soon discovered that the victory was not theirs. In March 1925 the Fourteenth Conference of the Party accepted Stalin's theory of "socialism in one country," while Zinoviev and Kamenev paid little attention. Soon afterward Stalin was able to break up the triumvirate quietly. Too late Zinoviev and Kamenev attacked Stalin's new theory. By the middle of 1925 he had found new allies in Bukharin, Rykov, and Tomsky, who accepted "socialism in one country." Far from yet aspiring openly to individual power, Stalin chose to be regarded as a mediator, and he asserted that "after Ilich [Lenin]" collegial—or what would later be called "collective"—leadership was the only conceivable way of running the party.

Stalin Allied with the Right

Rykov, Lenin's successor as prime minister ("chairman of the Council of Peoples Commissars"), was of peasant origin; Tomsky, leader of the trade unions, was the only proletarian on the Politburo; Bukharin, whose parents were both primary school teachers, was the real leader of the Right, which believed the NEP a success and the proper way to approach socialism.

Nicholas Bukharin was short (just over five feet), brilliant (he was to lament the influx of people into the party who didn't know "Bebel from Babel, Gogol from Hegel"), personally charming and popular (Lenin's "testament" called him "the favorite of the whole party"; Zinoviev called him "our Benjamin"). By the age of seventeen, in 1905, Nicholas had become a Marxist and was drawn into the Bolshevik faction. Escaping from Russian exile in 1911, he was in emigration (finally in New York) until April 1917. By 1919 he was on the Politburo, and his *ABC of Communism* (with Preobrazhensky) was out and would become the best-known exposition of the subject before Stalin. In early 1925 he and Stalin formed in effect a duumvirate, which lasted almost three years.[1]

Zinoviev and Kamenev were profoundly uneasy about the continuation of the NEP, but they had been abruptly thrust into the minority. In the autumn of 1925 Zinoviev published his *Leninism,* attacking NEP as a policy of "continuous retreat," and demanded a renewal of the "policy of 1918" directed against the kulak. Zinoviev managed to use his position in Leningrad to rally the powerful Party organization there to his support, in opposition to the new Politburo majority.

Zinoviev and Kamenev tardily recognized Stalin as the man from whom they had most to fear and carefully prepared an attack on him for the XIV Party Congress, to be held in December 1925. However, the plan completely miscarried. Kamenev, who spoke most sharply in criticism of Stalin at the Congress, was punished by demotion from full member to candidate member of the Politburo. As reconstituted just after the Congress, the Politburo had three new full members: Molotov, Voroshilov, and Kalinin, all loyal henchmen of Stalin's. Stalin also added several supporters to the list of candidate members of the Politburo and to the

---

[1] Stephen F. Cohen, *Bukharin and the Bolshevik Revolution: A Political Biography 1888–1938,* Knopf, 1973, Ch. VII.

newly enlarged Central Committee. Shortly before, Voroshilov had replaced Michael Frunze, who had been named Trotsky's successor but had died soon afterward, as war commissar. Stalin had established a formidable position of strength within both Party and government. Leningrad remained the only stronghold of resistance, and Stalin followed up his victory at the XIV Congress by sending Sergei Kirov to replace Zinoviev as Party leader there, ordering him to clean out the opposition.

Only then, in the spring of 1926, when the supporters of all three had been scattered, did Zinoviev and Kamenev make common cause with Trotsky. Stalin's reaction was, "Ah, they have granted themselves a mutual amnesty"—since a few short months earlier they had been bitterly attacking each other. The three were united enough in their opposition to continuance of the NEP and the "alliance with the middle peasantry" on which it was based; but their past personal antagonisms made their alliance an uneasy and incongruous one.

In the meantime the Right wing of the Politburo was championing the NEP and all that it implied. Bukharin advised the peasants, "Enrich yourselves," which was a phrase Guizot had used under the French monarchy of Louis Philippe, whatever Marxist glosses might be given it. At the XIV Congress Bukharin had set forth the basis on which he accepted Stalin's theory of "socialism in one country": "We shall creep at a snail's pace, but ... we are building socialism and ... we shall complete the building of it." This amounted to a frame of mind to which the NEP idea was congenial, rather than something uneasily and temporarily accepted for tactical reasons.

For the time being, however, Stalin was less concerned about policy than with getting rid of his enemies in the Left Opposition led by Zinoviev and Trotsky, which was not hard for him to do. In July 1926 Lashevich, a Zinovievite who was Voroshilov's deputy war commissar, was accused of organizing oppositionist groups within the Red Army and was dismissed. Stalin seized the opportunity to expel Zinoviev from the Politburo. On October 4 all the major opposition leaders replied with a statement admitting violation of Party statutes and pledging disbandment of the opposition, but they could not refrain from repeating their policy criticisms of the Politburo majority. Stalin's reply was to remove Trotsky from the Politburo and Zinoviev from the presidency of the Comintern. However, lesser figures in the opposition leadership were allowed to recant and to obtain well-publicized rewards for their submission. At the end of October 1926 the Fifteenth Party Conference sanctioned all these maneuvers and applauded Stalin's description of the Opposition leaders as "Social Democratic" deviators who were reverting to the line of the Second International.

By the beginning of 1927 the Left Opposition had thus lost any immediate hope of success, but its leaders were not yet silenced. Trotsky and his colleagues attacked the Politburo for "Thermidorism, degeneration, Menshevism, betrayal, treachery, kulak-nepman policy against the workers, against the poor peasants, against the Chinese revolution," as the Stalinist writer Popov sums it up.[2] The opposition leaders were able to blame the Politburo majority for a series of foreign setbacks: Britain's rupture of diplomatic relations with the USSR, the assassination of the Soviet ambassador in Warsaw, and especially the crushing of the Chinese Communists by Chiang Kai-shek.

In an article submitted to *Pravda* Trotsky climaxed opposition criticism by calling on his adherents to follow the example of Clemenceau (who had opened the way to take over as French premier by attacking his predecessor's failures in World War I) in case war engulfed the USSR (a prospect taken seriously by the Communists in 1927) (see page 179). However, advocating a change of government was dangerous in the Soviet Union. If, as all good Communists agreed, the existing regime represented the proletariat, then any move to change it was bound to be anti-proletarian and therefore treasonable. For that reason Stalin promptly engineered the expulsion of Trotsky and Zinoviev from the Central Committee. After the two men led street demonstrations on the tenth anniversary of the October Revolution (November 7, 1927), they were expelled from the Party.

The way was now clear for Stalin to oust the opposition from the Party en masse. The XV Congress, in December 1927, decreed as much. It might have been expected that Stalin's tactics would have drawn his opponents together, but on the contrary, the result was that they were neatly split down the middle. Trotsky refused to accept the Congress decision and was thereupon exiled to Alma Ata in Central Asia. But Zinoviev and Kamenev submitted and renounced their earlier-stated views; they were permitted to crawl back into the Party.

Trotsky Defeated

As far as the Soviet Communist Party and the Comintern were concerned, the controversy between Stalin and Trotsky was now at an end; the followers of Trotsky left what they henceforth called "Stalinist" ranks and attempted to build their own parties and organize them into a Fourth International. The dispute shook and divided the Communist parties throughout the world as no such controversy before or since ever did (the immediately ensuing struggle between Stalin and Bukharin had fewer repercussions abroad, for it seemed to center on the peasant, for whom most Communists had little use). By 1927, however, Trotsky and his sympathizers had given up any immediate hope of overcoming Stalin's ascendancy from within the Russian Party. They declared that a "bureaucracy" had come to power in the USSR, and that it must be eliminated. This assertion was difficult to explain on Marxist grounds, unless it were to be on the basis of Marx's

---

[2] N. Popov, *Outline History of the Communist Party of the Soviet Union* 2 parts; Moscow-Leningrad: Cooperative Publishing Society of Foreign Workers in the USSR, 1934, II:313.

analysis of Oriental society, and the Trotskyites shrank from that. Since Trotsky continued to believe that a distorted socialism still existed in the USSR, it was also difficult to think of any way through which the Stalinist leadership could be displaced without disturbing the economic foundation. As a result the Trotskyites had to retreat into a position comparable to that of the prewar Social Democrats, opposing all existing governments and declaring that there could be no basic improvement unless they took power. They never managed to do so anywhere.

The rank and file of the world's Communists had little chance to observe the personal differences and antagonisms between Stalin and Trotsky, and supported one or the other on the basis of his theoretical position. The differences may be briefly formulated thus: Trotsky declared that it was impossible to build socialism in Russia because the peasants did not want it; that it would only be possible to do so if the workers of the West revolted, and he was right. Stalin declared that it was impossible to wait for the Western workers to revolt before building socialism, because they were not likely to revolt in the immediate future. Therefore socialism could be built in Russia only if the Party used the peasantry, and he was also right. However, that the Western workers were not Communist, Trotsky could never admit; he could only assert that they would be soon. That the Russian peasants were not Communist, Stalin could never admit, but he could try to compel them to be. As a result Trotsky retreated into utopianism, while Stalin proceeded to establish a minority dictatorship built on terror.

Bukharin Defeated

The XV Party Congress heard Stalin declare that since the economy had been essentially restored to the prewar levels of production, the next task was to alter its character. The fundamental objective was to change agriculture, since it still included the great majority of producers. The "way out," said Stalin, was to "amalgamate the small and tiny peasant farms gradually but steadily, not by means of pressure, but by example and persuasion, into large-scale undertakings. ..." At the same time efforts already begun to construct new factories and expand the industrial base were to be redoubled. In retrospect the First Five-Year Plan seems to have been foreshadowed clearly enough in those decisions, but what they would mean in practice was still uncertain.

In early 1928 the Rightist adherents of "snail's pace" construction of socialism tended to think that the victory against Trotsky and Zinoviev had been theirs; indeed, the latter had predicted that it would be. Kamenev had disappeared from the ranks of the Politburo two years earlier, and Trotsky and Zinoviev had been removed shortly before the XV Congress. After the Congress the Politburo received two new recruits, Rudzutak and Kuibyshev. Added to the veterans, Stalin, Bukharin, Rykov, and Tomsky, and the three additions from the XIV Congress, Molotov, Voroshilov, and Kalinin, that made a total of nine. Both the defeated and the presumed victors were wrong. Stalin clearly dominated the new Polit-buro, and the three veterans of the Right were completely isolated.

During 1928 the major economic problem which the Communist leadership faced was, or was said to be, grain collection. Already in January grain purchases were short, and in the spring and summer "emergency measures" were decreed in order to obtain the grain. Stalin blamed the "kulaks," and in July ordered the Party to "strike hard at the kulaks." At this point the Right was seriously alarmed. At the July 1928 plenum Stalin had talked of the Soviets' having no colonies and therefore needing to extract something like tribute from the peasants to finance industrialization; Bukharin now dubbed his course "military-feudal exploitation of the peasantry."[3] Bukharin now approached Kamenev, his erstwhile opponent, with a proposal to make common cause against Stalin, whom he termed the "Genghis Khan" of the General Secretariat. The conversation came to light, and Bukharin was compelled to make a humble apology to the Politburo.

Although not long before Stalin had been hewing to the NEP line and de-nouncing supporters of "super-industrialization" and hasty economic transfor-mation, he now appeared in the role of foe of the independent peasant. His sup-porters tried to turn this *volte-face* to advantage. They approached the adherents of Trotsky and Zinoviev, urging them to come back and help do what they had—only slightly prematurely—wanted to do all along. (Trotsky had predicted that the XV Congress would be followed by a "swing to the right" and the "restoration of capitalism"; he was completely wrong.) Delighted with the prospect of at any rate a theoretical victory, many of the former opposition responded favorably, though not Trotsky. In a party where inconsistency could always be explained away on di-alectical grounds, Stalin's tactics were able to achieve remarkable success.

Although outnumbered in the Politburo and now facing again some of their former opponents on the Left who had recovered their voice (though not their power), the Rightists had what seemed formidable support at their disposal. Bukharin had replaced Zinoviev as president of the Comintern; Tomsky counted on the backing of the trade-unions which he headed; Rykov as prime minister held great prestige in the administrative apparatus. Moreover, the Right had ad-herents in many Party organizations.

In November 1928 Stalin courted a test of strength with the Rightists. Within the Moscow Party organization, once Kamenev's province, a Rightist named Uglanov was chief. Stalin attempted to remove him, and succeeded. In April 1929 Uglanov was stripped of other posts, and Stalin quickly followed up his advan-tage. Bukharin was removed from the Comintern presidency, Tomsky from the trade-union leadership. In November 1929 Bukharin was ejected from the Polit-buro; at the XVI Congress in June 1930 Tomsky was also removed. The last of the Rightists, Rykov, lost his membership on the Politburo in December 1930, and si-

---

[3]Ibid., p. 306.

multaneously was replaced by Molotov as chairman of the Council of People's Commissars. The Politburo was now composed of Stalin, Voroshilov, Kalinin, Kuibyshev, Rudzutak, Kaganovich, Kirov, S. Kosior and Ordzhonikidze. All were Stalin's supporters.

Although Stalin did not finish disposing of his Rightist adversaries until the end of 1930, his victory in both Party and governmental apparatuses was secure over a year earlier. In January 1929 he had won approval from the Politburo for the expulsion of Trotsky from the Soviet Union, Bukharin alone dissenting. Trotsky had proved not only Stalin's most capable opponent, but the only one among the first rank leaders to refuse to submit when he was beaten. He went first to Prinkipo Island, near Constantinople, then to Norway, and finally to Mexico. As Stalin's chief foe, he was punished first, which proved a blessing in disguise, for it was only later that Stalin began to execute his enemies. Trotsky enjoyed more years of freedom and eventually three years more of life than his colleagues who groveled before Stalin and remained in Russia.

From his successive places of exile, Trotsky edited his *Bulletin of the Opposition,* copies of which found their way to Moscow and were carefully scanned by the men he attacked. In somewhat similar fashion Alexander Herzen, tsarist Russia's first internationally renowned exile, during the 1850's had published a newspaper, *The Bell,* which his tsarist adversaries at home had eagerly devoured. There was a world of difference between Alexander II and Stalin; there were also many differences between Trotsky and Herzen, one of which was that Trotsky remained ambivalent about what should be done with Stalin, while Herzen wished to sweep away tsarism root and branch. Trotsky regarded himself as a Communist until his death. He believed that a proletarian revolution had occurred in Russia; that the tender shoots of socialism had only been stunted and not uprooted; and that attempts to overthrow Stalin by force would only contribute to the cause of counterrevolution. However, Trotsky's restraint did not prevent Stalin from eventually murdering him.

In December 1929 the Soviet Party and government led the celebration of Stalin's fiftieth birthday. The slogan, "Stalin is the Lenin of today," was widely and incessantly employed. In some sense, indeed, it was factually correct; in any event, from 1929 to 1956 no one in the Soviet Union was suffered to deny it, or to raise openly any questions about its accuracy.

12

Finding a Soviet
Foreign Policy
1917–1927

Foreign Policy and World Revolution

The phrase, "Soviet foreign policy," was a self-contradictory one. The adoption of the very name, "Union of Soviet Socialist Republics," from which the word "Russia" was absent, was designed for the administrative convenience of the Communists in handling the anticipated world-wide revolutions of coming years. The Russian Bolsheviks thought they were merely doing their part in a universal upheaval whose completion could not be long delayed. Trotsky expressed this early optimism when he declared that as foreign commissar he would simply issue a few revolutionary proclamations and then "shut up shop." While he was negotiating with the Germans at Brest-Litovsk, he was so confident of imminent victory throughout the world that he divulged the Bolshevik anticipations and plans to General Hoffmann. The general regarded the revelations as a curious form of madness and little more. Hoffmann's reaction was a natural one; however, even after the Soviets had spent two generations making their intentions plain, no one seemed to take them seriously.

From 1917 until 1991 the Russian Communists did not visibly change their objectives, but their tactics underwent much transformation. Lenin always denounced the idea of "spontaneity" as used by the Mensheviks and emphasized in contrast the principle of organization, insisting that the Party had to lead the masses to revolutionary victory. Nevertheless, he believed in trying to gauge whether a "revolutionary situation" had developed in which the Communists might usefully act, and warned against adventures in revolution in countries where the proletariat was not yet "politically conscious." Although he was excited by the prospects when the German Communists raised minor rebellions in 1919, 1921, and 1923, the Hungarian and Bavarian Communists effected briefly successful coups in 1919, and the Polish Communists rode toward Warsaw in the baggage of the Red Army in 1920, he did not believe such attempts could succeed unless supported by the mass of the proletariat.

In Communist discussions of a later time, "world revolution" no longer necessarily implied mass uprisings. Lenin's reliance on old-style insurrection was to a large extent replaced by another set of tactics, based on the armed seizure of power from above. To be sure, Lenin (for example, in 1920) did not overlook the utility of military action in bringing Communists to power, while Stalin (for example, in Eastern Europe in 1944–1946) did not neglect to use whatever semblances of mass organization he could find; but the shift in emphasis is considerable.

Means may alter ends, and no doubt the Communist regime in Poland in 1946 had a relationship to the masses very different from that of the Russian regime of 1918. But although Lenin emphasized consent (of the proletariat, not necessarily of the majority of the people), he also and more strongly emphasized Communist power, and the aim of Communist leaders remained Communist power throughout the world. When Lenin declared that the Party spoke for the proletariat, the way was clear doctrinally for the Party to do anything it pleased, the Marxist trappings of analysis being dragged along by simple definition.

When a chorus is announced, and only one singer appears on the stage, he has the choice of calling off the concert or singing alone. The latter is the alternative the Russian Communists chose, temporarily, even though they were forced to wait decades for anyone else to appear. The course of both internal and external policy was determined by the fact that the Communists came to power in Russia and nowhere else for twenty years. Domestically the result was "socialism in one country"; internationally the result was "Soviet foreign policy." In both cases the Communists accepted a tactical compromise whose end was hoped for at any moment; but if it was deferred indefinitely, so must they prolong the compromise, without forgetting the final and unchangeable objective.

The long period of waiting did have one important effect on the picture which Lenin envisaged. He warned the Bolsheviks to be prepared for the time that Communism won elsewhere and Russia again became a relatively "backward" country in the Communist camp. But during the period when Russia alone was ruled by Communists, Russia acquired prestige and seniority and above all became a strong enough industrial and military power to be able to enforce its mandates within the Communist camp—as late as 1968 in Europe, though in Asia it did not try.

Attempts at Communist Revolution in Germany

From the moment the Bolsheviks came to power in Russia, they glued their eyes on developments in Germany. Here were the strongest Marxist party in Europe, the most politically minded working class, and the most prominent leaders outside the Russian Party who sympathized with Communism, the Spartakist chiefs, led by Karl Liebknecht and Rosa Luxemburg.

On November 10, 1918, a Council of People's Commissars was established in Berlin, consisting equally of Social Democrats (led by Friedrich Ebert, who was also chancellor) and Independent Social Democrats (who had broken off from their more conservative fellows in 1916, and among whose ranks the extreme leftist Spartakist Union had been formed). Ebert, however, was far from being a Bolshevik, or even an orthodox Marxist, and called on the army General Staff for support. The Independent Socialists were divided; some leaned more toward Ebert, while others sympathized with Liebknecht. The Liebknecht faction soon withdrew from the government, and at the end of December 1918 the Spartakists entirely severed their connections with the Independent Socialists. Assuming the name "Communists," they led riots in Berlin in January but were gravely weakened by the assassination of both their leaders, Liebknecht and Luxemburg.

There followed the holding of free elections for a national assembly at Weimar, from which Ebert's Majority Social Democrats and the Catholic Center party emerged with the strongest representation. In the spring of 1919, while the new assembly was in session, new Communist outbreaks occurred in several cities. Shortly after the Communists under Béla Kun seized power in Budapest, Munich was the scene of a successful coup by Bavarian Communists led by Eugen Levine. The newly founded Comintern hailed the revolutions in Hungary and Bavaria, but Moscow was unable to send aid, and after a few weeks the Communist regimes in central Europe were overthrown.

The German Communists were still weak, but Moscow was able to provide political, if not military, assistance. In October 1920 the Independent Socialists were debating whether they should try to overthrow the Republic or defend it from the threat from the Right. The Rightist threat seemed serious; a few months earlier the government of the Weimar Republic had managed to suppress the Kapp Putsch only with great difficulty. Zinoviev appeared at the Independent Socialist conference and forced the secession from the party of the pro-Communist elements. Taking the latter into the KAPD (*Kommunistische Arbeiterpartei Deutschlands* or Communist Workers' Party of Germany), he more than doubled its membership, at a stroke converting it into something like a mass party. Moscow hoped that German Communism was now ready for a real revolution, but the first effort of the augmented party miscarried. During the Kronstadt crisis of March 1921, Béla Kun arrived from Moscow with instructions to organize a "diversion." The German Communists struck in the Ruhr with the Mansfeld "March Action," but it was a total failure.

The III Congress of the Comintern, which met in June 1921, thereupon executed a change of front. Lenin declared that the time for hunting out "Centrists" had passed, and that the important thing was now to obtain majority support among the workers. The policy of "united front" with non-Communist workers' groups was proclaimed, and it was to be used many times during the decades to follow. With this slogan Lenin in effect confessed that expectations of "world revolution" had to be deferred for a time. The "united-front" period of Comintern tactics fitted well into the domestic needs of Russia as expressed in the NEP. Many foreign governments, businessmen, and others were ready to interpret both tactical shifts as permanent, and to seek a "business-as-usual" arrangement with the Soviet regime.

Diplomatic Relations with the "Capitalist" World

The Soviets established diplomatic relations with a foreign power for the first time by the Treaty of Brest-Litovsk, but the Imperial German signatory was swept away only a few months later, in November 1918. The first treaty which lasted for some years was signed in February 1920 with the independent government of Estonia—a treaty which, according to Foreign Commissar Chicherin, prepared the way for "the first experiment in peaceful coexistence with bourgeois States." The British watched closely as Lithuania followed suit in July, Latvia in August, Finland in October, and Poland in March 1921. In the latter month they signed an Anglo-Russian trade agreement.

The Communists had not troubled to make it easy for the British. At a Congress of the Peoples of the East, held in Baku in September 1920, Zinoviev had said that the Comintern "turns today to the peoples of the East and says to them, 'Brothers, we summon you to a Holy War first of all against British imperialism!'" At this there were cries of "Jehad, Jehad!" and much brandishing of picturesque Oriental weapons. However, Moscow followed up this colorful beginning in Asian foreign relations not with an Eastern crusade, but instead, in February 1921, with treaties with Afghanistan and Persia, where British interests were considerable. Thereupon the Anglo-Russian trade agreement went forward to signature. Similar commercial treaties were promptly negotiated with a number of other European states. The blockade of the Civil War period was at an end, and economic relations of sorts between Soviet Russia and the "capitalist" world were launched.

In East Asia, as in the Middle East and Europe, the stabilization of the international situation was accompanied by Soviet economic overtures. At that time (and in fact up to 1945) regarding the United States as having been more ambivalent in its participation in intervention than other powers, the Soviet regime counted on America to keep a rein on Japanese ambitions in East Asia. There was discussion with two American businessmen about concessions in the Far East; Vanderlip was to be granted oil, coal, and forest rights in Kamchatka and eastern Siberia, and Sinclair to get oil rights in north Sakhalin. It seems that Lenin regarded such proposed concessions as devices bound to insure United States governmental support for Soviet interests in East Asia, since U.S. capitalists were thought to control their government. Actually American pressure played a decisive part in bringing about Japanese evacuation of the Russian mainland in 1922, but it was not until 1925 that Japan recognized the Soviet regime and evacuated north Sakhalin, for which not Sinclair but Japan received the oil concession. By that time the Soviets had regained the ascendancy which tsarist Russia had enjoyed since 1912 in Outer Mongolia, and in 1924 a Mongolian People's Republic was established under Soviet auspices. However, it was not formally annexed to the USSR.

As for China, by the time of the Russian Revolution its central republican government, established by the anti-Imperial revolt of 1911 led by Sun Yat-sen, had fallen into a state of disintegration. At the time of the Chinese Revolution Lenin had greeted it, along with comparable uprisings in Turkey and Persia, as the beginning of a great movement of "advanced Asia" against the plundering imperialists of "backward Europe." After the October Revolution in Russia, Lenin renounced on behalf of the Soviets the "unequal treaties" which had bound China, and called on it to join "its only allies and brothers in the struggle for liberty"— namely, the Russian Communists. Sun Yat-sen, who by this time had become established in the Canton region in an effort to lead the Chinese Nationalist party (Kuomintang) in overthrowing the warlord regime in Beijing, in turn responded to the October Revolution with enthusiasm. He welcomed the Soviet government as the product of a revolution which marked the breakaway of the Slavs from the "white races" and could make them the chief allies of the Chinese, just as Lenin had contended.

In 1921 the Comintern established a tiny Communist Party in China—as in many other countries of both Asia and Europe, for the Comintern soon became a creator of parties rather than a union of previously existing ones. Soon Stalin was to put the new "united-front" policy into practice in earnest in China. However, as in Germany, the Soviet foreign office sought "friendly relations" with the same government the Comintern was trying to overthrow, to last until it should succeed in doing so. In May 1924 the Soviets and the Beijing government signed an agreement by which the Communists in effect recovered the tsarist rights over the Chinese Eastern Railway through Manchuria, and later in the year the *de facto* dictator of Manchuria, Chang Tso-lin, accepted the arrangement in a supplementary agreement.

Anti-Versailles Diplomacy

The Soviets correctly interpreted their improved relations with the British, resulting from the Anglo-Russian trade agreement, as the beginning of regularization of diplomatic contacts with the other Western powers. When the Allied Supreme Council met at Cannes in January 1922 and planned a European Economic Conference at Genoa later in the year, Lenin accepted with alacrity an invitation to take part. At Cannes the Allies even obligingly endorsed Chicherin's "coexistence" thesis, declaring that "It is for every nation to choose for itself the system (of ownership, internal economy, and government) which it prefers. ..." Although the United States did not take part in either the Cannes meeting or the Genoa conference, Britain dragged a reluctant France into sitting down with the Communists (and with the Germans as well, which was even more repugnant to France's Poincaré).

At Genoa the Russian delegation appeared in top hats and cutaways, which surprised and pleased a number of Western representatives and which they took as further evidence that the Russian Revolution had run its course and that its leaders had settled down to be reasonable and businesslike. Nothing came of the Genoa conference itself, but the Soviet and German delegates went farther up the Italian Riviera to Rapallo and there signed an agreement of considerable significance. By the terms of the Treaty of Rapallo (May 1922) the Soviets canceled their war claims based on destruction caused by the German army, while the Germans canceled tsarist debts to their government on condition that the Soviets paid no other government debts. Thereby Soviet-German diplomatic relations, established officially at Brest-Litovsk, were resumed, and the two outcasts of European power politics found solace in each other.

The kind of friendship the Soviets were seeking with the "bourgeois" German Republic was obviously a limited one; the Communists had already tried repeatedly to overthrow it, and were to try again in a few months. Nevertheless the Treaty of Rapallo did inaugurate a period of relatively extensive commercial and military intercourse between the two countries. From 1922 to 1934 Soviet relations with Germany were closer than with any other power.

However, the significance of the treaty to Soviet foreign policy was broader than any "friendship" with Germany resulting from it. Official Soviet doctrine on international relations emphasized the "two camps"; there was the camp of "capitalism" and the camp of socialism (the USSR only). In the former, it was argued, existed exploitation, misery, and aggressive tendencies; in the latter, the opposite. However, the evil capitalist world was not to be treated as a single unit. The Soviet doctrine of diplomacy always held that when the USSR enters into relations with the capitalist powers, it should behave as they do (although that, to be sure, often meant behaving like a caricature of how capitalist governments were mistakenly thought to behave). As soon as the Soviets accepted the necessity of having a foreign policy, what they tried to do, beginning at Rapallo, was to restore something like a balance of power in Europe.

In 1922 the European diplomatic scene was dominated by France, as one of the victorious powers of World War I and the peace of Versailles. By then the United States had defected from the Allied coalition and Britain was reluctant to accept postwar continental commitments. France had labored to construct an alliance system in which the *cordon sanitaire* of Poland, Czechoslovakia, and Romania was to check Germany—and Soviet Russia as well. Therefore the Soviets attempted to offset that system by agreement with "bourgeois" Germany—hoping it would soon be replaced by a Communist Germany—victim of Versailles. They tried to do something similar in the Middle East, where French influence was newly installed in Syria but where British power continued to be strong, by agreement with the new nationalist regime of Mustafa Kemal which had arisen in defeated Turkey. Similar calculations went into the collaboration with Sun Yat-sen's Kuomintang, which sought power in China, where British interests were also considerable. For more than a decade after 1922 Britain and France, the architects of intervention and the chief capitalist powers, were the chief targets of Soviet diplomacy; the other arm of Moscow in foreign affairs, the Comintern, impartially tried to foster revolution against all bourgeois governments.

The Ruhr Crisis

In 1923 the Communists thought their hour had struck in Germany. Poincaré answered German default on reparations by French military occupation of the Ruhr, the industrial heart of Germany and all Europe. The inhabitants of the Ruhr responded by passive resistance, but the German economy was hard hit, and inflation reached an extent unparalleled in any other industrial country in recent times. The "united-front" policy was invoked by Moscow's German specialist, Karl Radek, in an astonishing manner. The extreme Right in Germany was in the forefront of the outcry against French occupation, and it was in that direction that Radek made overtures. A nationalist, Albert Leo Schlageter, who had been shot by the French for sabotage, was hailed by Radek as a martyr. The new line of "National Bolshevism," in which Germany was depicted as the suffering semi-colony of France, shocked the doctrinaire Communists without evoking much response from the Right. However, there was without doubt deep popular discontent and many strikers were evincing a militant mood. In Moscow there was some dissension about how to act. Zinoviev, Radek, and Trotsky were in different ways inclined to hope for great things from a German uprising, while Stalin believed insurrection foolhardy at the moment.

At length the leader of the German Communists, Heinrich Brandler, was given a set of confused instructions, which were executed in an equally confused manner. In October 1923, when the worst of the crisis had already passed, the Communists attempted, by entering "united-front" governments with Social Democrats in the states of Saxony and Thuringia, to work from the country in toward the capital. They were smashed in the provinces. Adolf Hitler seized the occasion to launch his beer-hall putsch in Munich, invoking the Communist danger and attacking the Republic as well, but his Rightists were suppressed too for the time being. It seemed that the German Republic had weathered the worst and survived. Brandler lost his leadership in the KAPD. In June 1924 the V Congress of the

Comintern decided that the remedy lay in "bolshevization" of all Communist parties—that is, for them to be modeled more closely on the lines of the Russian Party—but the "united-front" line was not changed.

The "United Front" in Britain and China

The two countries where the "united-front" tactic was used with most determination were Britain and China. Britain's first Labor Government, formed in 1924 under Ramsay MacDonald, extended diplomatic recognition to the USSR, despite the King's undimmed memories of how the Bolsheviks had dealt with his late relatives, Nicholas II and his family, not to mention very strong political pressures. The MacDonald government did not last out the year. The Conservatives published a letter which was alleged to be from Zinoviev to the British Communists urging forcible overthrow of the government, and the "Zinoviev letter" hastened MacDonald's fall.[1]

Although elections removed the Labor Government, a section of British workers continued to move leftward, in part as a result of economic depression. In 1925 there was established an Anglo-Russian trade-union committee. Among its wider aims was that of bringing about fusion between the International Federation of Trade Unions, sponsored by the socialist or "Amsterdam" International, and the weak Communist league of unions called the Profintern.[2] The committee's chance for revolution in Britain seemed at hand in May 1926. A general strike erupted, with the Communist-infiltrated coal miners taking a prominent role. However, the strike proved a great disappointment to the Communists. The disciplined Londoners tried to walk to work even though the subway ("underground") had ceased to operate. Worst of all was the sort of social cohesion shown in the famed football game played in Plymouth between the strikers and the police, in which the chief constable's wife kicked off. The strike soon collapsed, and the leaders in Moscow argued over who was to blame. Trotsky ascribed the failure to the tactic of collaboration with the British Laborites, but Stalin denied it and insisted on continuing the alliance until the British unionists themselves abolished the Anglo-Russian committee in 1927.

Many Communists hoped that the chief capitalist stronghold, Britain, could be stormed by way of China. The report of the Sixth Plenum of the Executive Committee of the Comintern (February 1926), published under the title *The Itinerary*

---

[1] It also may have hastened Zinoviev's fall in the USSR. Lewis Chester, Stephen Fay, Hugo Young, *The Zinoviev Letter*, J. B. Lippincott, 1968, concludes that the forged document was probably transmitted to the British government by master spy Captain Sidney Reilly.

[2] The Russian use of the phrase *professionalnyi soiuz* (abbreviated *profsoiuz*) to mean trade-union originated in the period of the Revolution of 1905, when the first large national unions formed were actually unions of professional men rather than of workers.

of Revolution, suggested as much. While prospects of success in Europe had dimmed, much was expected, in Zinoviev's words, from "a new, exceptionally important factor ... *the movement in China,* which is fraught with many surprises." At that stage the Communists were less interested in the repercussions which success in China might have on the rest of Asia than in the effects on Europe. What excited them was the hope that if the tentacles of British imperialism could be cut off in China, the helpless body in the home island could be speared easily.

By 1926 the Russian Communists were already deeply embroiled in Chinese events. Five years earlier one of the Comintern's East Asian specialists, G. Maring, had talked with Sun Yat-sen in the Canton region. Maring was a former Dutch teacher, whose real name was Sneevliet. In Java he had observed the local Communists work with some success within the Javanese nationalist organization, *Sarekat Islam.* He recommended a similar tactic for China: co-operation between the tiny Chinese Communist Party and Sun's Kuomintang. Adolf Joffe was sent by Moscow to continue talks along such lines. In 1923 he concluded an agreement with Sun by which the Chinese Nationalists on the one hand and Moscow and the Chinese Communists on the other were to work together to overthrow the Peking government. That September Michael Borodin was sent from Moscow to China with the mission of putting the agreement into effect. He was supported by ample funds and a host of Russian experts, advisers, and military men.

Sun responded by sending many Chinese, including Chiang Kai-shek, to study in the Soviet Union, and many returned, as did Chiang, to attempt to incorporate their experience in action. "In reorganizing the party," said Sun, "we have Soviet Russia as our model, hoping to achieve a real revolutionary success." To a correspondent who inquired what Borodin's real name was (it was Gruzenberg), Sun replied, "His name is Lafayette." Sun, whose own political conceptions were always vague and eclectic, began to mix Marxism into his philosophy during his last months. However, his real bond with Moscow was an organizational rather than ideological one, and the organizational ties between the Kuomintang and the Communists continued after his death in 1925.

Stalin's ideological program for China was to secure the "hegemony of the proletariat" within the "bloc of four classes" (proletariat, peasantry, petty bourgeoisie, and national bourgeoisie) which the Kuomintang as a whole was deemed to represent in the struggle against imperialism. Stalin argued that China internally was on the threshold of a "bourgeois democratic" revolution, complicated by a common national antagonism to foreign imperialism. Therefore, he contended, the Chinese situation was in important respects parallel to that in Russia on the eve of 1905.

However, Trotsky dissented sharply from this view. He had the same scorn for any possible allies of the Communists within China that he had had for any within Russia. He argued that capitalism was already strong in China, that it was necessary to strike for Communist power and a socialist economy, and that to collaborate with the Chinese bourgeoisie was "Menshevism"—which, in a way, it was. Thus the prerevolutionary polemics of the Russian Marxists were revived in a context where they bore an even dimmer relation to reality than they had in Russia. The important difference was that in 1925–1927 Stalin and Trotsky were engaged in a struggle for power in an existing Communist government, and theoretical successes or failures in China might have immediate power implications in Russia as well as China.

In 1925 the revolutionary tide seemed to be rising in Chinese cities, and the preparations of the Nationalist-Communist alliance were beginning to bear fruit. As Sun had demanded, the Kuomintang had been reorganized on the lines of the Soviet Communist Party. The Nationalist army had been revamped with a new officer corps trained at the military academy established at Whampoa near Canton under Chiang Kai-shek, assisted (and sometimes resisted) by the Soviet General Bliukher (called Galen in China). The allies were ready to advance north to take over the entire country.

However, there were signs that Sun's successor as Kuomintang leader, Chiang Kai-shek, lacked enthusiasm for the alliance with Moscow. In March 1926 he purged a number of Chinese Communists from high political and military posts and even arrested some Russians. Borodin tried to patch up the rift by going along with what Chiang had done, and surface harmony was restored. Since only a month earlier the Kuomintang had actually been admitted to the Comintern as a "sympathizer-member," Moscow chose to believe that all was well.

In the summer of 1926 the Nationalists marched north. One column, headed by the more leftist Kuomintang leaders, Borodin and the Russians, and some Chinese Communists, moved inland through Wuhan. Chiang led another column to Nanchang, and then headed for the coast. The evidence suggests that he was hoping to rid himself of the Soviet connection and obtain Western aid. He paused in his march to take over Shanghai and in so doing crushed the Communists there in April 1927. The conflict between Chiang and the Wuhan group now came into the open, and as Chiang established his capital in Nanking the break was complete.

Amid a confused series of negotiations and struggles, the Wuhan government broke up, and in July 1927 Borodin returned home. By 1928 Chiang completed the unification of China under his own leadership. Whatever Trotsky's plan for China might have achieved, Stalin's efforts had failed completely. Moscow now repudiated the Kuomintang, and ordered the Chinese Communists to conduct an insurrection against Chiang. This was the affair of the "Canton Commune" in December 1927, resulting in a final and bloody defeat for the Communists. The fiasco to which Stalin's tactics had brought Communism in China—and which Trotsky had virtually predicted—was an important factor behind Trotsky's fall from power; Stalin could not permit him to claim events had proved him right.

Trotsky had hastened his own political ruin by his "Clemenceau statement," issued during the synthetic "war crisis" of 1927 (see p. 165). As the Soviets had admitted their intention to use China as a means of weakening Britain, the British grew restive. After conducting a raid for documents on the Arcos trading company in May 1927, Britain's government broke diplomatic relations with the USSR. Paris followed suit by a *de facto* break. The assassination in June of Voikov, the Soviet minister in Warsaw, was the climax to a series of diplomatic disasters.

In July Stalin spoke of a "real and actual threat" of an anti-Soviet war by the capitalist powers led by England. The "war scare" of 1927 had no substance whatsoever in fact, although it may have assisted Stalin in disposing of the opposition within the Party and diverted attention from the failures of Soviet foreign policy. In 1927 the only bright spot abroad was Central Asia, where a series of interlocking pacts among the USSR, Turkey, Persia, and Afghanistan were signed from late 1925 to late 1927. Otherwise the record of both the Soviet foreign office and the Comintern seemed to be one of general catastrophe. At the beginning of the period of his personal rule, Stalin found the slogan, "socialism in one country" especially useful, for it did not look as if Communists were going to succeed in taking over any other country in the near future.

13

The Revolution, the Arts, and the Church 1917–1927

The Revolution and the Arts

In Lenin's view, art and nothing else could serve as a substitute for religion. Since he believed religion ought to be and would be destroyed in the future, he considered the role of the arts to be of great importance. Amid the heated debates and revolutionary intoxication of the first years of the Soviet regime, he told Clara Zetkin, "Every artist, and every one who regards himself as such, claims as his proper right the liberty to work freely according to his ideal, whether it is any good or not. There you have the ferment, the experiment, the chaos. Nevertheless, we are Communists, and must not quietly fold our hands and let chaos bubble as it will. We must also try to guide this development consciously, clearly, and to shape and determine its results."

Lenin recognized the fact that the artist claimed creative liberty, but he declared that the regime, not the artist, should and would determine the outcome in the arts. He himself was far from being a cultural revolutionary in the sense of wishing to break all the artistic images of the tsarist period and build *de novo*. Of the cultural "isms" which churned around him, he said, "I do not understand them. I take no joy in them." He preferred Pushkin, who wrote a century earlier, to his contemporary Mayakovsky, even though the latter became a sort of quasi-official bard of the Bolshevik Revolution. Lenin's personal esthetic preferences ran to a kind of Russian Victorianism, as did Stalin's; the difference was that Lenin did not try to enforce his preferences. He looked for new and exciting developments in the arts, but he did not pretend to know exactly what they would be like, and while he lived he attacked what he regarded as "unhealthy" schools of the arts without prohibiting other artists from working.

During World War I, many writers and artists had been swept into uniform or war work and added patriotism to their other attitudes with which Bolshevism was incompatible. On the morrow of the October Revolution, few of them adhered to the Bolshevik regime. During the five years following many of the most outstanding emigrated, including the prose writers Bunin, Andreyev, Kuprin, Merezhkovsky, Remizov, Gorky, and Alexis Tolstoy, the poets Balmont and Ilia Ehrenburg, and the artists Repin, Benois, Somov, and Korovin. Others, including the Acmeists Akhmatova and Mandelshtam, fell silent but remained in Russia. Several prominent symbolists, especially Blok, Bely, and Briusov, and the young "peasant poets," Sergei Esenin and Nicholas Kliuev, made peace with the regime, "accepting" the Revolution as a merited catastrophe for the social order they had known, and an event which brought Russia a new hope to which they ascribed a mystical or religious character. The Futurists, led by Mayakovsky, threw themselves boldly into the Bolshevik camp. However, genuine Bolshevik artists were rare indeed. Even Gorky, who had been a friend of Lenin's and a Bolshevik sympathizer for years, went back to Italy, maintaining an ambiguous kind of link with the regime. The only prominent Old Bolshevik artist to remain in Russia was Demian Bedny (pseudonym of E. A. Pridvorov), a poet of peasant origin and strong atheist convictions.

The ideological *mariages de convenance* entered into by the non-Bolshevik poets were ill-fated from the start. In his remarkable poem of 1918, *The Twelve,* Blok celebrated the Revolution in a non-Marxian vein. The same year, in *The Scythians,* he sang of Russian self-sufficiency and greatness as well as his own scorn for the West. In 1921 he commemorated Pushkin's birth in a public address, charging that freedom—not "the freedom of being a liberal," but "the freedom of creation, the secret freedom"—was being taken away in Russia; he continued, "And the poet dies because he can no longer breathe: life has lost its meaning." A few months later Blok died. Briusov died in 1924; Bely lived until 1934, although he ceased to write poetry and turned to novels and memoirs. In 1925 Esenin committed suicide, writing in his own blood his last poem:

> My poems are no longer needed here.
> And I too—by your leave—I am no longer needed. ...

The individualistic poets of the Silver Age stifled under the Soviet regime and disappeared. Only Boris Pasternak, who was writing avant-garde verse before the Revolution, and Anna Akhmatova, whose work lay in the great tradition of love poetry, survived to publish again in the post-Stalin period.

The Civil War Period: The Proletkult

Not merely the coming of the Bolsheviks, but also the hunger, cold, and misery of the Civil War transformed the conditions under which artists had to work. What it meant for the artist—or any man—to survive the winters of 1918–1919 and 1919–

1920 in the great cities is well shown in Eugene Zamiatin's short story, "The Cave." Although during these grim years little creative work could be done, the lines were drawn for the ideological struggle over what sort of art was proper to a Communist system. In 1919 and 1920 the writers gathered at their preferred cafes in Petrograd and Moscow to declaim their works, debate the shape of the art to come, and revel in what many regarded as new-found freedom. Mayakovsky in his "Left March" produced a revolutionary ode characteristic of this dissonant period, which fairly begs to be shouted:

> Deploy in marching ranks!
> There is no room for verbal tricks.
> Silence, you orators!
> Your turn to speak,
> Comrade Rifle.
> Enough of living by the law
> Given by Adam and Eve.
> We will ride the mare of history 'till she drops.
> Left!
> Left!
> Left! ...

However, the creative artists, exhilarated with revolution and drunk with history, were not to be the ones to decide what a Communist esthetic should be like; that was already being debated by the ideologists. The group around the magazine *Proletarskaia Kul'tura,* or *Proletkult,* led by A. A. Bogdanov, laid claim to express proletarian interests in the sphere of culture as the Party did in social and political matters and the trade-unions (so Bogdanov said) in the realm of the economy. This amounted to a demand that *Proletkult,* free from Party control, should itself be allowed to act as collective dictator over the arts. *Proletkult* labored assiduously at organizing writing schools for workers in many Russian towns, and in these schools Bely and Briusov, Zamiatin, Gumilëv (who was to be shot in 1921 for alleged counterrevolutionary activity), and other prominent writers served as instructors. Lunacharsky, the people's commissar for education, took the organization under his protection, although he had a milder attitude toward the great art of the past than some of the spokesmen of *Proletkult.* At this point Lenin saw a danger of revival of the old currents of 1909, then supported by the same Bogdanov and Lunacharsky, against which he had inveighed in *Materialism and Empirio-Criticism.* In December 1920 the Central Committee attacked *Proletkult* as a cover for the philosophical deviation of "Machism" and subordinated the group to state control.

Proletkult was composed of theoreticians rather than artists and did not include the extreme radical wing of the writers, who talked of uprooting all the culture of the past. Such men belonged to the Smithy-Cosmist (*Kuznitsa-Kosmist*) group, so called from their organizations in Moscow and Petrograd respectively. One of their number, Vladimir Kirilov, in a poem entitled *We,* called for the proletariat to destroy museums "in the name of our Tomorrow." The same title, *We,* was given by Eugene Zamiatin to a novel he wrote during the Civil War period, but it was a humanist attack on Soviet Utopianism, which Zamiatin already foresaw would lead to a dehumanized monster state and what would later be called totalitarianism.[1]

The NEP: The Fellow Travelers

The coming of the NEP marked a sharp turn in cultural as well as political and economic policy. In February 1921 there was formed a group of young men, for the most part writers of prose, called the Serapion Brothers. When asked whether they were for or against the Revolution, they replied that they were "for the Hermit Serapion"—a character in a story by the German writer E.T.A. Hoffmann. However, the Formalist critic and extreme Westernizer, Leo Lunts, added that this did not mean indifference to politics: "Each of us has his own ideology, each paints his hut in his own color." Indeed the more prominent members of the group, Michael Zoshchenko, Constantine Fedin (at thirty their oldest adherent), Vsevolod Ivanov (who pioneered the literary treatment of Asiatic Russia), and others, were of such diverse persuasions that, as one scholar puts it, the Brothers constituted "a defensive alliance rather than a literary school."[2]

To such writers who were willing to go along with the regime but eschewed ideological battle either for or against it, Trotsky sympathetically applied the word, "*poputchiki*" (fellow travelers)—a term which was to find a much wider usage abroad. Many of the fellow travelers found haven in the pages of a new "fat monthly" (*tolstyi zhurnal*), *Red Virgin Soil* (*Krasnaia Nov'*), edited by A. A. Voronsky. Voronsky was a Marxist critic who agreed with Trotsky's opinion that art had its own "peculiar laws," in opposition to the militant ideologists who argued that art should merely reflect life mechanically. Both *Red Virgin Soil* and the large publishing enterprise named *International Literature,* under pressure from Gorky and supported by Trotsky, gave the nonpolitical writers both protection and subsistence.

The "literary NEP" produced a modest quantity of good, rather than great, writing. Boris Pilniak, in his novel of 1922 called *The Naked Year* (*Golyi God*), employed the artifices and stylistic idiosyncrasies of prerevolutionary times and interpreted the Revolution in a neo-populist manner as a resurgence of the native

---

[1] Aldous Huxley's *Brave New World* and George Orwell's *Nineteen Eighty-Four* later followed the pattern of Zamiatin's *We* very closely.

[2] Victor Erlich, *Russian Formalism: History-Doctrine,* The Hague: Mouton, 1955, p. 127.

tradition. Eugene Zamiatin, in *We* (which he read aloud in public but which remained unpublished in Russian until an *émigré* edition of 1952) and other satirical novels and stories, combined experimental craftsmanship with the ideology of the non-Communist Left. Other satirists, such as Valentine Katayev and the team of Ilia Ilf and Katayev's brother, "Eugene Petrov," produced amusing and biting works which were officially approved in the NEP atmosphere, where both survivals of a "presocialist" past and unavoidable present concessions to "capitalism" were recognized to exist and to merit the writer's scourge.

From 1923 to 1925 the debate over literary ideology reached its height. In March 1923 the so-called LEF ("Left Front of Literature") movement, composed largely of Futurists following the lead of Mayakovsky, founded a journal called *LEF.* It was backed not only by writers but also by men from the theater, especially the two wayward pupils of the great producer Stanislavsky, Meyerhold, who wanted to introduce "the October Revolution into the theater," and Vakhtangov. LEF came under fire from two directions. It was too authoritarian to suit the fellow travelers in its ideological demand for "integration of literature into life"; while the militant proletarian writers attacked it for its "decadent" roots and "intellectual-bourgeois" membership.

The proletarian writers launched their attack on LEF in a magazine called *On Guard (Na postu)*, which began to appear in the summer of 1923. The *Napostovtsy* proclaimed the "primacy of content" over artistic form, and proceeded to bait not only the avant-garde Futurists and nonpolitical fellow travelers, but also ideologically-minded critics who disagreed with them. LEF was torn apart, and its magazine disappeared in 1925; Mayakovsky attempted to revive it in 1927 as the *New LEF,* but in vain.

The militants of *Na postu* were finally bridled, as the *Proletkult* had been, by the regime itself. In January 1925 the I All-Union Congress of Proletarian Writers was held; it passed a resolution denouncing the line of Trotsky and Voronsky, who defended the fellow travelers. However, the militants were soon chastised. In July the Party Central Committee issued a warning against a "frivolous and disdainful attitude toward the old cultural heritage and toward literary specialists"—that is, toward the fellow travelers. The resolution was drafted by Bukharin, who believed that "snail's pace" progress toward socialism left ample time for the development of a "proletarian culture" and thus, like Trotsky, wanted to refrain from cultural controls.

For the next three years the fellow travelers—not, it should be made clear, anti-Communist writers—were relatively free to write what they liked. Publishing houses multiplied, newspaper circulation mounted rapidly, and the normal academic life of the universities was resumed. Already in 1923 relations with *émigré* writers in Berlin, Paris, and Prague had become possible, and in that year Ilia Ehrenburg and Alexis Tolstoy returned to the USSR. Many artists took advantage of the opportunity of visiting the West and of entertaining Western visitors in Russia. Along with economic recovery seemed to come a hope of a newer, brighter future, purged of the old evils and entailing a better life and broader cultural interests for the masses.

Under the new atmosphere the great tradition of the Russian novel seemed to stir again in Isaac Babel's *Red Cavalry* (1926), which depicted the savagery of the Civil War along with the nobler emotions, and Leonid Leonov's *The Thief* (1927), which appeared to owe part of its inspiration to Dostoevsky. Despite the thrusts of Communist critics, Pasternak continued to write fine poetry and some prose, and the poet Nicholas Tikhonov passed through a period of exoticism and experimentalism before 1930, when he turned to convert his talent into a weapon on the "ideological front."

The later NEP was a time of innovations and ferment in the other arts as well. The greatest Soviet film-maker, Sergei Eisenstein, produced *Potëmkin,* praise of which sounded around the world. In the theater Meyerhold and Vakhtangov attempted to develop new types of play production, and while Stanislavsky was aging, his old collaborator Nemirovich-Danchenko, continued to work to preserve his techniques and achievements. In the field of music, an early Group of Revolutionary Composers, comparable to *Proletkult* in literature, was followed in 1925 by a Group of Young Professional Composers, led by A. A. Davidenko. The young militants criticized the composer Dmitry Shostakovich (also young, but not then militant) for his kinship to the modern musicians of the bourgeois West, but he continued to work, and in 1927 one of the greatest living Russian composers, Sergei Prokofiev, returned from exile. In the realm of the arts all was ferment, as Lenin expected. Much of the diversity and talent of the Silver Age had been lost, but some of it remained or had been restored, and the spread of theaters and schools throughout the country and the appearance of new writers and artists even from the backward eastern borderlands argued that culture was more widely diffused than before. So far the state had intervened chiefly to prevent rather than to enforce cultural dictatorship, even though the noisy ideologists who had governmental connections could still make it difficult for real artists to do their work. Under Stalin, however, the state was shortly to assume quite a different role in the arts.

The Revolution and the Church

In an article written in 1905, Lenin restated succinctly the Marxist view of religion:

> Religion teaches those who toil in poverty all their lives to be resigned and patient in this world, and consoles them with the hope of reward in heaven. As for those who live upon the labor of others, religion teaches them to be charitable in earthly life, thus providing a cheap justification for their whole exploiting existence and selling them at a reasonable price tickets to heavenly bliss. Religion is the opium of the peo-

ple. Religion is a kind of spiritual intoxicant, in which the slaves of capital drown their humanity and their desires for some sort of decent human existence.[3]

Lenin not only criticized the social effects of religion as he saw them, but as a philosophical materialist he objected to any kind of religious belief in principle. However, in the same article he warned that "the religious question must [not] be pushed into the foreground where it does not belong. We must not allow the forces waging a genuinely revolutionary economic and political struggle to be broken up for the sake of opinions and dreams that are of third-rate importance ... and which are being steadily relegated to the rubbish heap by the normal course of economic development."

After taking power, Lenin applied the same caution in approaching problems affecting religion and the churches. He preferred to let the churches "wither away" along with the state as the economic "foundation" of society was transformed. However, he did so not because he minimized the importance of religious belief as an obstacle to Communism but because he was wary of its surviving strength among the Russian masses and preferred to avoid direct combat with it.

While the Russian peasants and many of the urban groups held fast to Orthodox Christianity, the intelligentsia had in large part defected from religion before the Revolution, accepting philosophical materialism and socialism in one form or another. Even some of the advanced clergy had embraced variations of a "social gospel" and even socialism. There had been countercurrents; some former radicals such as Nicholas Berdiaev and Sergei Bulgakov had embraced Christianity, and there were elements among the clergy striving for a genuine theological revival which would restore to the church some of the vigor it had lost during the two centuries it had lain under state domination. However, the leadership of the Russian Orthodox Church in general remained weak, and in 1917 it appeared divided between a dominant group which resisted any kind of change and a party of dissidents who were willing to compound with the Communists.

The overthrow of the monarchy hurled the clergy into a situation for which they were ill prepared. The Provisional Government was largely composed of men who were hostile or indifferent to religion, but outside of proclaiming freedom of religion in July (including that of altering one's denomination or professing no religion at all), it left the Orthodox Church for the most part to its own devices. In the first few months after the February Revolution several clergymen who had been compromised by association with Rasputin resigned or were eased out of posts of influence. The clerical leaders then set about to convene an All-Russian Church Council (*Sobor*), the first since 1681. It met in Moscow in August 1917.

---

[3] From the article "Socialism and Religion," written for *Novaia Zhizn'*, No. 28, December 16, 1905. The phrase, "Religion is the opium of the people," was earlier used by Marx.

At the council a new dissident current was in evidence. There had arisen around the Theological Academy in Petrograd a League of Democratic Clergy and Laymen, led by Dean Alexander Vvedensky and others. It was linked with the socialist clerical groups of the prerevolutionary period, and certain members of the Provisional Government worked closely with it. Some of its representatives spoke publicly and to soldiers at the front, favoring continuation of the war and attempting to counter Bolshevik agitation.

However, the Petrograd liberals were outnumbered at the council by traditionally minded conservative clerics. Although there was no official expression of the council's view, the dominant conservatives there voiced open sympathy for General Kornilov before and after his attempted march on Petrograd. Over the objections of the Petrograd liberals, the council proceeded to elect (again for the first time since Peter the Great) a Patriarch, who, unlike the early patriarchs, was to be merely *primus inter pares* in relation to the other bishops and responsible to periodic church councils. Three candidates were chosen by vote of the delegates; the name of one of the three was then drawn by lot. Metropolitan Tikhon of Moscow was proclaimed Patriarch, and he was invested in November—in accordance with the procedure followed in Acts 1:26. Tikhon was personally popular after he was chosen, and indications are that his popularity increased thereafter.

In the meantime the Bolsheviks had come to power. Lenin's policy toward the Orthodox Church at first was as cautious as his earlier pronouncements on religion. In January 1918 the Soviet government decreed the separation of "church from state, and school from church," and for the time being did not attack the church directly, although there was some official seizure of church properties. Patriarch Tikhon anathematized the Bolsheviks and condemned the peace of Brest-Litovsk, and he was echoed by other members of the church council. In August the council dissolved itself; Tikhon was left in control, assisted by the Holy Synod and the Higher Church Administration also chosen by the council.

In October 1918 Tikhon boldly denounced Communist rule: "Where is freedom of speech and of the press? Where is freedom of religion?" The government retaliated by placing him under house arrest. During the Civil War Lenin stepped up the seizure of church properties, which netted the regime over 7 billion rubles, and dissolved the monasteries, at the same time exposing a variety of "relic frauds" in which purportedly miraculously preserved saints' corpses were revealed to be wax images and the like.[4] During the same period the Communist Party sometimes had to prescribe expulsion for young male members who yielded to their brides on the question of church weddings and other religious observances (such measures had to be invoked for many decades thereafter to re-

---

[4] Such exposures seem to have had only limited effect on the faithful, for many decades later the Soviets were still prominently displaying "relic frauds" in the museums attached to the few surviving monasteries, suggesting that simple piety still retained an attachment to such relics.

strain the weak from ideological compromise). Many priests sympathized with White forces, and some even fought in their ranks. However, in September 1919 the Patriarch called for submission to the temporal power and dissociated the church from the White cause. Plainly the Soviet regime was going to last longer than the church council had anticipated.

During the famine of 1921 which followed the Civil War, the high clergy undertook to organize relief for the starving. However, the state itself took over the relief organization and began to requisition church treasures for the purpose. The Patriarch acquiesced but insisted that consecrated articles be exempt from requisition. *Pravda* admitted that the Soviets' main interest was not in obtaining the consecrated articles themselves but in making their confiscation "serve to sunder the crumbling body of the former state church." Charged with withholding the sacred vessels, collusion with the monarchist ecclesiastical council held in Sremski Karlovtsy in Yugoslavia in November 1921, and other anti-Soviet activities, Patriarch Tikhon was arrested in May 1922.

At the same moment a group of Petrograd liberals, including Dean Vvedensky but now headed by Father Krasnitsky, organized a movement called the "Living Church." They established an irregular Temporary Higher Church Administration, which received Communist recognition. The personalities of the leaders were shadowed in various ways. Bishop Antonin had twice been under psychiatric treatment; Krasnitsky, Vvedensky, and Archpriest Kalinovsky had belonged to the Black Hundreds, and Kalinovsky had been excommunicated. All four had served willingly as witnesses for the prosecution in the trial of the Roman Catholic clerics Cieplak and Budkiewicz in early 1923. One scholar concludes that, in the popular view, "these leaders were all cowards, adventurers, or Soviet agents."[5] No doubt among the religious radicals were honest and decent men who thought the Gospel of Jesus Christ required them to support the destruction of capitalism, the advent of socialism, and the smashing of the old church fabric. From such people the Bolshevik leaders could count on approval when they said things like, "We are attempting to construct socialism in Russia. Christ Himself was a socialist"; the only difference is, continued the official, we use compulsion.[6]

The emergence of the Living Church also reflected, in part, a desire among the parish priests to curb the power of the monks and the bishops (who were drawn from the ranks of the monks), and in part a genuine wish among the clergy for liberalization of church regulations and practices. However, the movement was utilized by the regime, in particular the secret police, for political purposes. As a Soviet official declared, the regime intended to "profit by the discord existing

---

[5]William C. Fletcher, *A Study in Survival: The Church in Russia, 1927–1943*, Macmillan, 1965, p. 21.

[6]Quoted in John S. Curtiss, *The Russian Church and the Soviet State, 1917–1950*, Little, Brown & Co., 1953, p. 58.

among the clergy with the sole purpose of drawing the people away from all and every religion."

At first the Living Church was allowed to convene a council, in April 1923, which declared Tikhon unfrocked and abolished the Patriarchate. The Soviet regime accepted these decisions; nevertheless, immediately after the council met, it released Tikhon from arrest in return for his confession of error and a promise not to oppose Soviet rule. Apparently with the approval of the authorities, Tikhon promptly embarked on a struggle with the Living Church, which was by this time also beset from within by its own dissident and splinter movements. The reformist groups, nevertheless, continued to believe that they had governmental support, and they managed to take over control of about one-third of the Orthodox churches in the whole country.

In April 1925 Tikhon died.[7] A gathering of bishops named Metropolitan Peter head of the "Patriarchal" Church, but he was arrested in December and in the summer of 1926 exiled to Siberia. Peter was replaced by his own choice as deputy, Metropolitan Sergii of Nizhny Novgorod. Sergii was also arrested in early 1926 but was soon released. In June he appealed to the government for recognition of the Patriarchal Church. Shortly afterwards a group of bishops who were in exile at the Solovetsky Monastery in the White Sea issued a remarkable statement on church-state relations. The bishops of Solovki attacked the reformists for making "pitiful attempts to instill into the consciences of the faithful the idea that Christianity in its essence did not differ from Communism," but they warned that reconciliation between the Patriarchal Church and the regime was necessary to prevent the schismatic reformists from becoming a "state church" and called on the clergy and faithful to render allegiance to the Soviet power while retaining their doctrinally orthodox belief.

In May 1927 Sergii was recognized by the regime, and the Living Church was allowed to die unregretted. A large number of the clergy went along with the conditional reconciliation, although many abroad accused Sergii of having surrendered the church to the secret police, whose influence on clerical appointments mounted rapidly. It seems that two different types of "conciliators" were to be found among the clergy: one, following the reasoning of the Solovki bishops, accepted what they considered the lesser evil out of repugnant practical necessity but disdained theoretical compromise; the other, of which Sergii was an example, soon grew hazy to where compromise stopped and integrity began, and ended by serving as pliant tools of the Communists.

Although the Soviet regime recognized Sergii, it was far from surrendering to religion. The government's manipulations of the various church groups had gone along simultaneously with a campaign of antireligious propaganda and agitation. In 1922 there began to be published a newspaper called *The Godless (Bezbozhnik)*,

---

[7] In 1989 the Gorbachëv regime permitted the Orthodox Church to canonize him.

and such books as Sir James Frazer's *The Golden Bough* and the works of the French materialists of the Enlightenment were issued in Russian editions for anti-religious purposes. In 1925 a group around the newspaper *The Godless* organized itself as the League of the Militant Godless, and by 1929 it claimed close to half a million members. Emelian Yaroslavsky, Demian Bedny, and other leaders of the league wrote treatises and satires attacking religion, which were widely distributed.

A decade after the Bolsheviks took power, the Russian Orthodox Church was functioning on a scale not much smaller than that of 1917, and Islam and other religions retained much of their former following. However, the evidence suggests that antireligious propaganda had made a good deal of headway among the youth of the cities, and the organized religious bodies had been shrewdly weakened and divided. Believing that religion had already been undermined by being deprived of its influence on the young people and by suffering disruption of its institutional leadership, Stalin prepared to launch the kind of direct attack on the churches against which Lenin had warned.

PART THREE

Stalin's Rule Through World War II

14

Stalin and the
First Five-Year Plan
1928–1932

The End of the Breathing Space

Under the New Economic Policy the ordinary citizen of the USSR had obtained a partial respite from state interference in his life, and the economy had undergone substantial recovery from the collapse brought on by World War I and the Civil War. By 1928 the indices of production were generally back to what they had been in 1914. Although a severe struggle was still raging at the top levels of Party leadership over who and what policy would determine the fate of the people, for seven years they had been for the most part left alone to lead their own lives.

The results were examined under peculiar circumstances by an old monarchist, V. V. Shulgin. In 1926 he was approached by the purported representatives of monarchist groups inside Russia with an invitation to return clandestinely and visit the country and his political confreres. He accepted, talked with circles in Russia which appeared to be monarchist, and returned to Western Europe, only to find that he had throughout been the guest of the secret police. In any case he saw something of Russia and reported that the country "is just the same, only shabbier." During NEP an American, Calvin Hoover, asked peasants if they had more freedom or less under the Communist regime and frequently received in essence the same answer: that the peasant after the Revolution had more freedom, since he obtained land. This was not necessarily a stupid reply, for although land was not the same as freedom—and the old peasant revolutionary tradition had always distinguished between the two in its slogan "land and liberty"—the peasant in fact had considerable freedom as well as the land under NEP conditions.

The ordinary man was free even to indulge in political criticism. Men and women who retained openly anti-Soviet views were barred from holding certain jobs but otherwise were not sharply penalized. An aphorism was current that there were any number of political parties in the USSR, but one was in power while the others were in jail. Not only many supporters of non-Communist parties, but some Communist dissidents, were in prison—but by no means all of either, and some prisoners might look for release in the near future. Moreover, although many were in jail, they were not in the cemetery, which was a decade later to be the destination of not only dissidents, but multitudes who were not opponents of the regime at all.

Undoubtedly many of the common people responded favorably to what appeared to be the Communist program as enunciated by Bukharin. The peasants should "enrich themselves," the country would "creep at a snail's pace" to socialism, and whatever exactly socialism would be like, no doubt it would be very fine. Some enthusiasm for the Soviet regime was reflected in the names given newborn babies, such as Vladlen (from Lenin's first and last names), Barrikada, Antikhrist, Elektrifikatsiia (Lenin had declared that "Soviet power plus electrification equals socialism"), and Diamata (from *dialekticheskii materializm*). In a country where babies' names had always come exclusively from saints' names, this was a remarkable development.

It is difficult to find a parallel for a regime or a party which held power for ten years, biding its time until it felt strong enough to fulfill its original program. It had been observed that West European Marxism had been tamed when its representatives obtained governmental posts, and Western commentators were inclined to discount any possibility that the original Communist program could somehow be kept in cold storage for some time in Russia, to be defrosted and served up again in the future. Thus the coming of the *velikii perelom* ("the great change"), "Russia's Iron Age" (W. H. Chamberlin), or the "Second Revolution" (B. H. Sumner) startled foreign observers and produced a mass of admirers of the gigantic "Soviet experiment." The "Second Revolution" began with the First Five-Year Plan (1928–1932) in both industry and agriculture, which was attended by political and cultural changes as well.

When the economic offensive began in earnest, the political struggle had already been decided. Stalin and his supporters had rendered impossible any serious challenge from the Right Opposition led by Bukharin, while the members of the former Left Opposition of Zinovievites and Trotskyites were at least initially persuaded that Stalin had simply adopted their earlier demands as his own policy—although they too were powerless to impede Stalin's policies if they had wished to do so. This was something of a paradox, for the Stalinists interpreted the new offensive as the practical embodiment of the theory of "socialism in one country," which had served Stalin as a weapon in the fight with Trotsky. In any event, it was clear that the NEP line of compromise with the peasantry, which the Right had wished to extend and prolong, was being discarded.

The decision was taken to industrialize rapidly and to industrialize the countryside as well as the city, by converting the peasantry into a landless agricultural proletariat. This program was to be carried out by employing all the power of the Communist state, in such a way as to strengthen state control over all branches of economic, social, and cultural life. Technically the First Five-Year Plan was a purely economic scheme; in actual fact it inaugurated a new phase in Russian history, in which governmental fiat invaded every area of life in a manner unparalleled in the history not only of Russia but of any other country up to that time. The First Five-Year Plan marked the real beginning of Soviet totalitarianism.

Before launching an effort of the magnitude of the First Plan, Stalin had taken pains to prepare to meet all foreseeable opposition inside and outside the Party by silencing all open criticism of himself among the Party leaders as well as among the rank and file, and by constructing an apparatus by which he could enforce his orders on the masses.

The Secret Police

The necessary apparatus, outside of the Party organization itself, consisted mainly of the secret police and the army. The first secret police organization had been the Cheka, which had earned for itself a fearsome reputation. Especially after the Cheka order of February 1918 to local Soviets to shoot on sight all "counterrevolutionaries" or those who aided and abetted them, such a reign of terror developed that even local Communist authorities complained. In February 1922 the Cheka was abolished and replaced by a GPU, renamed OGPU (*Ob"edinënnoe Gosudarstvennoe Politicheskoe Upravlenie*), or Unified State Political Administration, at the time the RSFSR was reorganized as the USSR.

Unlike the Cheka, which was completely independent, the GPU was subordinated to the Commissariat of Interior, at that time under Rykov. It was entrusted with the tasks of suppressing "open counterrevolutionary outbreaks" (rather than indiscriminate shooting of all individual "counterrevolutionaries," as informally and arbitrarily defined) and of administering international border control, along with some vaguer functions. Moreover, the GPU was compelled either to release prisoners after two months or remand them for trial to courts under the jurisdiction of the Commissariat of Justice. It seemed as if the wings of the secret police had been clipped somewhat; however, the GPU obtained the power of arresting Party members, which the Cheka never had.

During the NEP period the operations of the secret police were on a fairly limited scale. Most often arrests fell into one of two categories: first, the so-called "KR's," or "counterrevolutionaries," including former members of the Kadet party and all parties to the right of the Kadets as well as non-party supporters of the pre-Communist regimes, prominent churchmen, and the children of "exploiters"; second, the so-called "politicals," comprising members of the non-Communist Left—Mensheviks, SR's, and anarchists. Generally the "politicals" received better treatment than the "KR's," including that *sine qua non* of the political exile, the privilege of having access to books and writing materials, which the tsarist regime also had granted its political prisoners.

During the intra-Party battles of the 1920's the successive chiefs of the OGPU, Felix Dzerzhinsky and (after Dzerzhinsky died in 1926) V. R. Menzhinsky, put the agency increasingly at Stalin's disposal. The OGPU arrested or cowed dissident Party members and kept a watch on industrial performance and suspected opposition in the armed forces. It spied on all foreigners in the Soviet Union, and its Foreign Section organized espionage abroad and carried out surveillance of Soviet diplomatic agents as well as Russian *émigré* groups.

The secret police acquired special troops of its own, some of which were used to operate the concentration camps for "KR's" and "politicals" and for the most dangerous (nonpolitical) criminals. Among the most important OGPU camps were those on or near the island of the former Solovetsky Monastery in the White Sea. Many prisons and camps remained outside OGPU jurisdiction, and under the NEP, the secret police was used much more to keep an eye on the economic and political leadership than to terrorize the mass of the people directly. However, its apparatus had been built up to considerable dimensions and lay safely in the hands of Stalin's men, ready for the larger-scale operations which began with the First Five-Year Plan.

From 1928 on the OGPU was called upon to arrest Nepmen (private entrepreneurs), "kulaks," and members of the old intelligentsia. The police had little interest in the Nepmen; the purpose of seizing their persons was to lay hands on their wealth, especially gold and foreign currency needed for purchases abroad. The specialists who came from the old intelligentsia, however, were often brought before "show trials," a device which Stalin used for the first time during the First Five-Year Plan. Persons known to be innocent of the charges against them were tried and sentenced in order to intimidate critics of the regime and to evoke greater efforts from those who feared similar treatment. During the First Plan there were three especially publicized "show trials." These were the 1928 trial of engineers from Shakhty, in the Donets coal basin, who were accused of "wrecking" for Germany; the trial in 1930 of the so-called "Industrial Party," including Professor Ramzin and other engineers, accused of working for France; and in 1931 the trial of a number of ex-Mensheviks headed by Professor Groman of the State Planning Commission, who were said to have acted for *émigré* Mensheviks.

The accused were intimidated, but not liquidated. Stalin was merely trying to frighten the specialists trained in prerevolutionary days into doing what he demanded of them. In June 1931 he was ready to call off Menzhinsky and the OGPU. In his "Six Points" speech, Stalin declared that the period when "wrecking" had been in fashion and had necessitated stern measures had passed, and that a section of the old intelligentsia had shown itself ready to work loyally for the regime. He therefore called for a new attitude toward the intelligentsia. In part the speech signified that he thought the managers and technicians could now be controlled more effectively with cajolery than with intimidation; in part he was thrusting at poor labor discipline among the trade-unionists, who in the early years of the Soviet regime had thought that since they were in control, it was their prerogative to treat the "bourgeois" managers or engineers as they pleased.

The Unions and the Army

The trade-unions for a decade had enjoyed considerable power of their own. They were supposed to represent the proletariat, and some of their defenders had even suggested that since this was so, they ought to run the government. Although they achieved no such power, they had a good deal of weight in the state industries and, paradoxically, the reemergence of some private industry under the NEP had strengthened the independence of the unions. Since they had the right to organize and strike against Nepmen employers, and it was regarded as unwise to try to prevent them from acting also to protect workers in state enterprises, the disappearance of the Nepmen would therefore mean circumscription of the rights of unions.

As Tomsky saw that headlong, state-controlled industrialization would threaten union prerogatives, he resisted such proposals along with the rest of the Right Opposition. In 1929 he was removed from the leadership of the unions; his nominal successor was Nicholas Shvernik, but the reins actually passed to one of Stalin's trusted men, Lazar Kaganovich. For two years longer Stalin was willing to encourage the workers to bully the old technicians. When Stalin thought he had the old intelligentsia intimidated, in his "Six Points" speech he called off the workers, and his control over the union apparatus was sufficient to enforce his demand. He was telling the workers to get back to work and stop interfering with decisions of an engineering or management character; moreover, that all decisions affecting industry were to be made neither by the unionist rank and file nor by the "bourgeois" technicians but by the state apparatus. By the end of the First Plan, the trade-unions had been converted into an organ of state control over the industrial workers.

Under the NEP the Red Army also remained partly outside direct control by the Party leadership. The Political Administration of the army, which since 1919 had been charged with safeguarding its ideological purity and either making or transmitting major policy decisions on its organization, was far from subservient to the triumvirs of the Politburo. The political commissars were in no one's pocket, but for the most part they supported Trotsky, who was war commissar from 1918 to 1924, in his struggle with the triumvirs. Only when Voroshilov took over the commissariat in 1925 did Bubnov become chief of the Political Administration and proceed to replace the political commissars, where necessary, with reliable Stalin men.

The Political Administration of the army worked energetically to indoctrinate new recruits, especially those taken in at the close of the Civil War, who were mostly peasant boys who neither knew nor cared what "ideology" was. Still more intensive efforts went into rebuilding the officer corps; the political commissars managed to remove over 90% of the ex-tsarist officers who had been coaxed or blackmailed into serving during the Civil War. It was easier to rid the army of the old officers than to find reliable new ones. Political indoctrination of the officer corps and the enlisted men was a long-term job, but the main thing was that the Political Administration, by the beginning of the First Plan, was rapidly becoming Stalinized, and thus the whole army was being brought under closer control of the Party leadership.

By 1928–1929 Stalin had substantially completed taking over the secret police, the trade-unions, and the army, through adroit use of the Party apparatus. Some of his critics within the Party he had won over; others he had not, but he was able to keep watch on what they were saying and doing. He counted—rightly—on winning over many by the magnitude of the effort to carry through the "Second Revolution." He also calculated accurately that resistance would be met from the masses, and that the apparatus would be powerful enough to overcome it.

Aims of the First Five-Year Plan

Why did the "Second Revolution" occur? Partly because Stalin found it expedient to launch it, but the deeper reason was, as one well-known economist says, that without such an effort it would have been "impossible to solve those ideological problems for the sake of which the Revolution had been made."[1] An attempt was to be made to transform the economy and to increase the production of capital goods and other items. But that was not the chief purpose of the First Five-Year Plan. The essential point was to convert the entire labor force, rural as well as urban, into employees of state-controlled enterprise.

The assumption was that once the economic "foundation" was changed, the noneconomic "superstructure" would change correspondingly. Once the economy was put into a state socialist mold, men's minds would come to accept that mold. No longer would the regime be troubled by the attachment of the peasantry to its land, the ambivalence on the part of the workers as to what their "real" interests were, the persistence of religious belief, the survival of prerevolutionary values in the family, and in general mass indifference or hostility to the aims of the materialist and socialist Soviet state. Stalin and the Russian Communists ex-

---

[1] Alexander Baykov, *The Development of the Soviet Economic System*, Cambridge U. Press, 1946, p. 158.

pected some resistance and were ready for it, repeating to each other that "one cannot make an omelet without breaking eggs." Nevertheless, it is doubtful that anyone realized in 1928 quite what the human cost would be, since the human factor was left out of the oversimplified ideological equation.

The First Five-Year Plan was not an inflexible blueprint prepared in advance and inaugurated at a given moment. Soviet economic planning—though the planning was never exclusively economic—was always characterized by a periodic revision of goals. Such revision might have scaled down targets as unforeseen obstacles were encountered; instead, more often the targets were revised upward. It has been argued that in the strict sense the USSR never employed "planning" at all: overfulfillment of goals was always praised, underfulfillment criticized or punished, yet the former was no more reconcilable with the original "plan" than the latter and sometimes led to serious distortion in resource allocation. In this light Soviet "planning" appears not as a rationalized method of the satisfaction of human wants, or even of the demands of the regime (which intentionally subordinated the welfare of the consumer to the task of strengthening its own military strength and potential), but as a means of universal and permanent intimidation of the labor force.

In 1926 the State Planning Commission, headed by Professor Strumilin, was first entrusted with the task of preparing an over-all plan. The plan as actually instituted is known as the "August version," presented in August 1928 and covering the period through August 1933. It was predicated on four assumptions: that there would be no serious crop failure, that world trade would increase (since the USSR could, it was hoped, export more and obtain more foreign loans), that "qualitative indices" (cost of production and individual laborer productivity) would show improvement, and that the proportion of expenditure for national defense would fall.

These expectations were all disappointed, in part because of the Soviets' own mistakes. The Great Depression, beginning in 1929, which brought on a catastrophic decline in world trade, was not the Soviets' fault, nor was the Japanese invasion of Manchuria in 1931, which occasioned an increase in Soviet military spending. But the savagery of the assault on the village was the result of Communist action, and the failure of costs to decline and of productivity to rise as expected was the consequence of a combination of the managers' inexperience and ignorance with the regime's disregard of human welfare and the incentives for which men may be induced to work. It was planned that productivity would rise twice as fast as wages; instead the wage rise was over twice the rise in productivity. In consequence many more workers were taken on than intended and the urban demand vastly increased, pushing up prices and forcing the regime to introduce rationing once more, as in the time of the Civil War. The real miscalculation was not in any of these specific respects. It lay in the attempt to use political fanaticism as a substitute for rational principles of management, and in the failure to grasp the limits of what brute force could achieve when inspiration and persuasion failed.

The Plan in Industry

The First Five-Year Plan was formally adopted in April 1929 by the Sixteenth Party Conference. The XV Congress had merely considered a draft plan, and one generally much more modest in its goals than the "August version" finally instituted. The objectives were stunning: total industrial output was to increase by 250%, that of heavy industry by 330%; output of pig iron was to be nearly tripled, that of coal more than doubled, that of electric power to increase more than four times. Agricultural production was scheduled to increase 150%, and 20% of the peasant farms were to be collectivized.

Bukharin and the Right were at that time still resisting such targets. Stalin repeatedly accused Bukharin of wanting to "put the brake on the revolution ... surrender the position to the capitalist elements." There was a grain of truth in what he said. Of course Bukharin was a Communist and not a defender of "capitalism" at all; but his voice was the last raised in Stalin's time in open defense of at least the economic freedom of the Russian people, against which large-scale violence was about to be used. When he called for "normalized" conditions of trade, when he cited Lenin as urging caution in regard to the peasantry, when he spoke of "military-feudal" exploitation of the villagers, he was to be sure not speaking for the "kulak," as Stalin charged, but he was expressing doubts about the advisability of crushing the independent peasantry which still made up the bulk of the Russian population.

Far from paying any attention to Bukharin's insistence that the targets of the "August version" were too high, the Party Central Committee in the summer of 1929 raised them still higher. In November Bukharin was removed from the Politburo and was no longer in a position to protest; in fact, he joined the other Rightist leaders in a public recantation of error. No one was left to urge putting on the "brakes." By the end of the year the pace of industrial construction and especially of collectivization had reached breakneck speed. In November 1929 Stalin declared, "We are advancing full steam ahead along the path of industrialization to socialism, leaving behind the age-long 'Russian' backwardness ... when we have put the USSR in a motor car and the muzhik upon a tractor ... we shall see which countries may then be classified as backward and which as advanced."

Optimism surpassed all limits. The XVI Party Congress, held in June and July 1930, adopted the slogan, "the Five-Year Plan in four years"—although five years had seemed a short enough time for the realization of Stalin's announced objectives. The Congress also approved a revision of the plan for agriculture so as to bring about wholesale collectivization of peasant farms within the next few years.

A further decision was taken to create a "Ural-Kuznetsk Combine," based on the exchange of Ural iron for Kuznetsk Basin coal, which would place an especially heavy strain on the whole transportation system.

In 1930 signs of trouble were beginning to appear. Factories were erected for which no machines were available; machines were delivered to plants unable to house them; hastily recruited and untrained workers ruined shiny new machines in one place, while skilled workers elsewhere sat idle for want of equipment. In the last quarter of 1930 there was an attempt to overcome all difficulties at once in connection with a statistical change-over from the agricultural (autumn to autumn) to the calendar year: October, November, and December were proclaimed a special "shock quarter." (This was one of many cases in which Stalin borrowed Trotsky's device of using military terminology in nonmilitary situations for propaganda purposes.)

The "shock quarter," Stalin's efforts to wheedle and frighten workers and technicians into greater exertions, and all other expedients were not enough. In 1931 something went wrong, and from that year onward the USSR ceased to publish price indices. At the end of 1932, when four and a quarter years had elapsed, the First Five-Year Plan was declared to have been fulfilled, but the claim had a hollow ring. Stalin contended that production of machinery and electrical equipment had risen 157%, but it was admitted that output in heavy metallurgy (iron and steel) had increased only 67%, coal output 89%, and consumer goods 73%, and even these figures are questionable.

No doubt in the First Plan great industrial expansion occurred, and in subsequent plans continued to occur, whether or not goals were precisely fulfilled. But the aim was not primarily to increase industrial output, but rather to achieve a transformation of society in which industrial growth is only one aspect, related to a much broader and more fundamental set of changes in men's way of life, attitudes, and allegiances.

By 1931 the headlong rush of the "Second Revolution" had evoked alarm among the technicians who were accustomed to operate on the basis of costs and rational calculations in general. Addressing a group of industrial managers in February of that year, Stalin admitted, "It is sometimes asked whether it is not possible to slow down a bit ... ," but he declared that on the contrary a still swifter pace was dictated by the Party's "obligations to the workers and peasants" of the USSR and its "still higher" obligations to the world proletariat. He continued, "We are fifty to a hundred years behind the advanced countries. We must cover this distance in ten years. Either we do this or they will crush us."[2]

---

[2] This statement has been interpreted as a prophecy of Hitler's invasion in 1941. However, it should be noted that in 1931 Soviet relations with the Germans were better than with either the British or French. As far as Hitler was concerned, moreover, Moscow and the German Communists were for their own purposes co-operating with his Nazis against the forces supporting the Weimar Republic.

Thus Stalin stated the doctrine of no respite which thereafter was not only to govern the effort to increase industrial production, but was to become the keynote of all sides of life under Soviet totalitarianism.

The Plan in Agriculture

The aspect of the "Second Revolution" which was the most dramatic and sweeping—indeed it was laden with sheer horror—was the collectivization of agriculture. The problem of the "alliance between the proletariat and the peasantry," which Lenin considered so crucial to the Russian Communists, was to be solved by the elimination of the peasantry in its hitherto familiar form. The class struggle which Lenin had in 1918–1919 tried in vain to foment within the village was to be carried into the village, if necessary, from without. The kulaks or rich peasants would be destroyed; the "poor peasants," carrying with them a portion of the "middle peasants," would emerge victors from the struggle. They would then establish collective farms in token of their achievement of the attitude proper to a proletariat.

Who were the kulaks? By the 1927 census estimates, the peasantry was divided into "proletarian" peasants (without land or livestock), who made up about 4% of the total, and "independent" peasant smallholders, who constituted the remaining 96%. Of the "independent" group, about 5% were classified as "kulaks"—defined as those who owned property worth roughly $800 and who hired labor for fifty days out of the year. By the Marxist definition, exploiters are those who own the means of production but do not work it themselves; Stalin's census-takers had used criteria bearing only the feeblest and most distant relationship to those of Marxism. Stalin could not be entirely blamed, however, for such ideological dubiousness. Long ago Lenin had also used a distinction resting on wealth rather than on economic function in trying to discover classes within the peasantry when he calculated "rich" and "poor" peasants on the basis of number of horses owned. As for Marx and Engels, they were fortunate enough not to be writing about countries in which the peasants made up the majority of the people. Although they did not embarrass themselves with attempts to divide the rural masses into "exploiters" and "exploited," they provided justification for collectivization by holding that the peasantry as a whole represented a survival of feudalism and would disappear in the modern world. Engels had indeed advised giving the small peasant plenty of time to ponder whether he was ready to enter a cooperative farm, but the assumption was that he ought to and would be ready sooner or later.

In December 1929 Stalin quoted those very lines of Engels but asserted that they were inapplicable in the situation existing in the Soviet Union. Although in May 1928 he had declared that the "expropriation of the kulaks would be folly," in the summer of 1929 he had ordered Party workers to "liquidate the kulaks as a class."

One Soviet analyst writes that the decrees of June-July 1929 ended the NEP in the village; a decree of 1930 demanded that one-third of the kulaks be sent to concentration camps and their families deported to remote regions, one-third deported merely from the region of their residence, one third not deported but given the worst land.[3] The details of such legislation should not be taken too seriously. What ensued was not any precise execution of directives; it was rather chaos, pillage—the slogan of the brigades in Smolensk was "drink, eat, it's all ours"—and murder.

When traveling with Rykov in the Volga region in the mid-1920's, William Reswick, a foreign correspondent, heard the peasants question Rykov anxiously: "What is a kulak? Can it be a muzhik who owns a horse, a cow, and some poultry?" Rykov replied that a kulak was simply a village usurer—which was indeed the original meaning of the word, but was not the meaning employed by Lenin and the Communist Party. The Communists meant by "kulak" a peasant who had more property than his neighbors and therefore might exploit them in some way. It is doubtful that the criteria of the 1927 census were ever taken very seriously in determining who a kulak was, and in many cases no economic criteria were applied at all. It is reported, for example, that Uzbek peasants were catechized: "What is socialism?" and "When was Darwin born?" If a recalcitrant peasant failed to give a satisfactory answer, he might be branded a kulak.

It remained for Tito, many years later, to confess that Communists defined a kulak to mean any peasant opposed to "socialism," but Soviet collectivization had already put that definition into practice. Peasants who resisted inclusion in collective farms were uprooted and transported away from their homes, often to the far north in unheated freight cars. Many times whole villages were simply surrounded and attacked. During this period an OGPU colonel confided to a foreign journalist, "I am an old Bolshevik. I worked in the underground against the Tsar and then I fought in the Civil War. Did I do all that in order that I should now surround villages with machine-guns and order my men to fire indiscriminately into crowds of peasants? Oh, no, no!"[4] The peasants who could not fight openly resorted to passive resistance by killing their own livestock and burning their own crops. They were able to do grave economic damage to the regime as well as to themselves, but they could not halt the pursuit of the political objective of creating collectives.

On January 20, 1930, there were slightly over 4 million peasant families in collective farms, most of them having been taken in during the previous year or two. By March 1 of the same year the number had risen to over 14 million—55% of all peasant families. There were supposed to be over 110,000 collective farms, but it would be more accurate to say that 14 million peasants had surrendered and were

---

[3] Alec Nove, *An Economic History of the USSR*, Penguin, 1980, pp. 161–168.

[4] Deutscher, *Stalin*, p. 325, n. 1.

waiting the orders of the terrible and incomprehensible invaders of their country-side. Then, abruptly, on March 2 Stalin published an article in *Pravda* entitled "Dizziness from Success." In it he contended that "the fundamental turn of the village toward socialism may be already considered secured," but he warned, "It is impossible to establish collective farms by force. To do so would be stupid and re-actionary."

The peasants who were heard later saying that things improved when Stalin got over *his* dizziness from success were quite right. Stalin in the *Pravda* article tried to blame the chaos in the village on Party underlings, but for the most part they had merely tried to obey his orders. At any rate the Communists who were carrying on the virtual civil war in the countryside responded at once. By May 1, 1930, it was reported that the number of peasant families on collective farms had fallen below 6 million. However, Stalin had made it clear that the objective was unaltered. By the end of 1932, 60% of peasant families were reported collectivized. Infinite brutality, suffering, and bewilderment lay behind the fantastic fluctuation in these statistics.

The political victory was substantially won, but the economic consequences were disastrous. In 1933 the number of horses in the Soviet Union was less than half the 1928 figure; during the period from 1929 to 1931 alone, the number of cattle fell by one-third, the number of sheep and goats by one-half. It was intended that the horses, which had been used as draft animals, should be replaced by tractors, but they could not be supplied in anything like the quantity needed. Nothing could replace the other animals. Tractors do not give milk, furnish meat, or produce manure. Politically, however, the introduction of tractors had great significance. They and other agricultural machines were pooled in Machine-Tractor Stations (MTS's), each of which served several collective farms. The MTS became the political headquarters of the victorious Communists in the defeated countryside, where records were kept and orders were received from above and transmitted to the collectives.

The new collective enterprises were of two basic types: the state farm (*sovkhoz,* short for *sovetskoe khoziaistvo*) and the collective farm (*kolkhoz,* short for *kollektivnoe khoziaistvo*). The state farm was the full property of the Soviet government; its manager operated it with hired labor, in accordance with the directives of the Ministry of State Farms or any other ministry to which the farm in question was allotted. The state farm, as a "factory in the field," was the Communist objective for agriculture; there the peasant was truly a proletarian with no property of his own.

In contrast, the collective farm was supposed to be a self-governing co-operative made up of peasants who voluntarily pooled their means of production and divided the proceeds. The first collectives were of various kinds of which three were the best known. The "commune" (not to be confused with the prerevolutionary village commune) was the closest to the state farm; all implements and livestock were owned in common by the members, who lived in communal buildings. The *toz* (or "society for joint land cultivation") was the loosest type of collective; it was a production co-operative, in which each peasant family kept title to its own plot of land, livestock, and implements, and joined with others to work the land and buy machinery. Intermediate between the "commune" and the *toz* was the *artel* (not to be confused with the prerevolutionary craft association). Under the *artel* the peasant retained possession of his own livestock and a small garden plot, on which he might raise crops either for his own use or for sale on the market.[5]

The resistance of the peasants to collectivization was not entirely in vain, for it forced the Communists to accept the *artel* as the prevalent, in fact, almost universal, type of collective. At the beginning of the plan Stalin, although he did not expect *state* farms to be set up everywhere immediately, continually referred to "state and collective farms" as the goal of the collectivization campaign. After the disastrous first quarter of 1930, however, he reversed the order of priority, and began to speak of the goal as "collective and state farms." A considerable number of state farms were actually dissolved and their holdings turned over to collective farms. The type of collective farm to which Stalin gave his support in the "Dizziness from Success" article and which the XVI Congress approved two months later was the *artel*.

The Communists viewed the *artel* as a temporary compromise. The XVI Congress's resolution declared that the *artel "does not complete, but is only the beginning* of the creation of a new social discipline, of the task of teaching the peasants socialist construction." Most of the land was held by the *artel,* and that "collective sector" of the land was tilled in common. The *artel* was clearly dependent on the state: the state agency, the MTS, dealt with the *artel,* not the individual peasant, furnishing the machinery required to sow and harvest. In the apportionment of the proceeds, the compulsory grain deliveries had first to be made to the state—this was called the collective farm's "First Commandment." Next the MTS had to be paid for the machinery the farm had used, and only then was the residual share divided among the individual households. However, the peasant retained his own tiny garden plot and his livestock, and thus every day he was able, even compelled, to compare the advantages of individual and collective farming, since he engaged in both. The *artel,* wholly satisfying the aims of neither the Communists nor the peasants, thus contained a built-in contradiction. Since by 1933 over 96% of all collective farms were of the *artel* type, and the state farms included only a very small proportion of the tilled land, the contradiction within the *artel* affected most of Soviet agriculture.

---

[5] It should be noted that none of these types of collective resembled the prerevolutionary commune, wherein each peasant family had its own house and land, which it worked by its own labor even when the land lay in widely scattered strips.

The Five-Year Plan in agriculture had two crowning moments of incredible horror. Dekulakization, collectivization, and famine were three different things. In early 1930 the village was dekulakized and collectivized; in 1932–1933 the mostly collectivized peasantry was afflicted with man-made famine, especially but not only in Ukraine. The results were disastrous: Stalin himself admitted to Churchill 10 million (presumably meaning "dead") kulaks and had the gall to report that "the majority of them were very unpopular and were wiped out by their laborers"—though he himself was the real author of the deed. Robert Conquest's sober estimate is 14.5 million dead (6.5 million in dekulakization, 1 million in "the Kazakh catastrophe," and 7 million in the 1932–1933 famine—5 million of them in Ukraine alone).[6]

By 1937 it is believed that the overall pre-1928 per capita level of all agricultural production was barely regained; food production did not do that well. Half the cattle in the country were killed in a few months, so that only in Khrushchëv's time was the numerical level of 1916 equaled. What Stalin admitted to be a "revolution from above," though he insisted that it was supported "from below" by the "poor peasants," would be more accurate to call a war of urban Communists against the village. The regime obtained much capital for industrialization by selling compulsory grain deliveries at high prices. Above all, collectivization was the decisive step in the building of Soviet totalitarianism; for it imposed upon the majority of the people a subjection that only force could maintain. In the 1990's the effects of the calamity were still felt in the USSR's successor republics.

Other Aspects of the Plan

During the First Five-Year Plan rationing was introduced, not as a means of keeping the cities from starvation as during the Civil War, but as a system of differential privilege which provided extra-monetary income for technicians, skilled workers, and other groups essential to the fulfillment of the plan. Rationing was again abolished in 1935, when the Stakhanovite movement (see p. 222) was launched to achieve some of the same objectives.

Pressure was exerted in a variety of ways to obtain a stable labor force. In October 1930 it was announced that unemployment had ceased to exist, and unemployment relief was cut off. Excessive demands for manpower or failure to enforce discipline on the part of managers were defined as criminal offenses. In August 1932 the death penalty was introduced for theft of state property. In November 1932 workers guilty of one day's unauthorized absence from the job were ordered to be dismissed and deprived of their housing, which, the regime openly admitted, might mean starvation. In 1930 and 1931 legislation provided that a worker must

---

[6] Robert Conquest, *The Harvest of Sorrow: Soviet Collectivization and the Terror-Famine*, Oxford U. Press, 1986, p. 306.

go where he was sent by the authorities. In December 1932 the passport system, which had been adopted by the tsars as a means of catching runaway serfs, was restored, and thereafter individuals could move only with police consent. All such measures served to reduce absenteeism and labor turnover but did not eliminate them.

Even if all workers currently employed in industry could have been made to stay on the job, they would have been too few to satisfy the plan's needs for labor. Other workers had to be found, and from 1928 on the system of "organized intake" of labor was introduced. By this system industrial managers might conclude "agreements" with collective farm chairmen under which the latter undertook to furnish "redundant" collective farmers as new urban laborers. In the following decade millions of peasants were conscripted into industry by way of this system.

Open compulsion might prevent workers from leaving the job and obtain additional workers, but to raise productivity other methods were necessary. In 1929 the Soviet regime resorted, at first cautiously, to the device of competition. To begin with, groups of laborers were authorized to engage in what was called "socialist emulation," which was ordered "not to impinge upon the solidarity" of the proletariat. By 1931 the regime decided to sanction competition between individuals. Wage differentials and payment of piece work were gradually introduced, and comprehensive wage statistics ceased to be published.

In these changes the trade-unions had no voice at all. Working conditions and wages were fixed by the regime, either in the Five-Year Plan or in supplementary legislation. In 1933, when a law abolished the signing of collective bargaining agreements between unions and managers, the unions had already lost most of the substantive rights they had possessed.

The First Five-Year Plan witnessed a transformation of the Soviet financial structure. At the end of 1930 a new tax, called the "turnover tax," was introduced, and it soon became the cornerstone of all state receipts, providing the largest part of the Soviet budget. The turnover tax was levied as part of the wholesale price on all goods—thus the wholesale price consisted of cost price plus planned profit plus turnover tax. For years foreign travelers in the USSR reported that many Soviet citizens were unaware of the existence of any such tax. An income tax was also levied, and the Soviet citizen knew he paid it, but it was not a major source of state income.

Russia's "Second Revolution" was thus infinitely more far-reaching in its scope than the Revolution of 1917. Certain scholars, such as Isaac Deutscher, although acknowledging the human sacrifices and brutality which accompanied the First Plan, have mustered some sympathy for "the rulers' determination to overcome at any cost the prodigious difficulties involved in the mobilization, training, and education of many millions of raw, undisciplined peasants."[7] All industrial revolu-

---

[7] *Soviet Trade Unions: Their Place in Soviet Labour Policy,* London: Royal Institute of International Affairs, 1950, p. 138.

tions it is said, have their casualties. In Russia under the First Five-Year Plan there were certainly casualties, and there was an industrial revolution; but even more important, Stalin achieved an unparalleled degree of state control over the peoples of the USSR, and individual freedom, political, economic, and other, fell near the vanishing point. There was one unique achievement: in the words of Alec Nove, "1933 was the culmination of the most precipitous peacetime decline in living standards known in recorded history."[8] In 1929 the average city dweller ate 47.5 kilograms of meat, poultry, and fat; in 1932, less than 17 kilograms. The concentration camps were filling up, and a large sector of the economy was run by the secret police directly. Under such circumstances the widespread official use of the slogan, "Life has become better, life has become happier," can scarcely have been very persuasive.

---

[8] Nove, *Economic History*, p. 207.

15

The Consolidation
of Totalitarianism
1933–1941

The Dilemma of the Old Bolsheviks

Stalin and his colleagues were somewhat shaken by the upheavals which their own policy had produced. In November 1932 Stalin's own wife, the former Nadezhda Allilueva,[1] spoke up bluntly in a small gathering about the misery the country was suffering; Stalin retorted with abuse, and the same night she died, apparently by suicide. Victor Serge tells a widely accepted story that about this time Stalin offered his resignation to the Polituro. Two of his formerly trusted henchmen, Syrtsov and Lominadze, had shortly before been jailed for suggesting that the Central Committee depose Stalin as general secretary, and no Politburo member would risk urging that the offer of resignation should be taken seriously. After a strained silence, Serge reports, Molotov said, "Come, come! You have got the party's confidence. ..."[2]

The members of the former Left and Right oppositions watched with mixed feelings the travails which the country was undergoing. Some of the Left had demanded that a "Second Revolution" be launched earlier, but none had clearly envisaged the extent of the violence, waste, and suffering which actually took place. In any case neither the Left nor the Right could very well deny that the cause of socialism—defined as the extension of control over the economy by the alleged "proletarian" state—had been advanced, whether or not they lamented the cost. Even Trotsky, writing from Prinkipo in his *Bulletin of the Opposition*, said in the

---

[1] His second wife. The first, Ekaterina Svanidze, died during the Revolution of 1905, leaving one son who was raised in the Caucasus by her parents. Stalin married Allilueva in 1918.

[2] *Portrait de Staline*, Paris, 1940, p. 95.

fall of 1932 that the overthrow of Stalin "would almost certainly benefit the forces of counterrevolution."

In 1932 Zinoviev, Kamenev, and others were exiled to Siberia, but in the spring of 1933 they recanted once more and were allowed to return, shortly after Rykov, Tomsky, and Bukharin had added recantations to their own records. The opposition could not bring itself to do any more than grumble and hope for the best. Its members could bring themselves neither to admit nor to deny fully that the regime of Stalin and the casualties of the "Second Revolution" were logical consequences of the single-party oligarchy—one which they themselves had labored with great pains to create—which was attempting to create state socialism in a deeply anti-socialist country. As Marxists, they could not admit that the person of Stalin, or any other individual, could be decisive in history. Although Trotsky abroad and others inside Russia might talk of "bureaucratic deformation," Marxism itself could not explain how a proletarian dictatorship could be converted into something else without a change in the ownership of the means of production.

Nevertheless there were a few who were willing to criticize Stalin. The most important case was that of Martimian Ryutin. In 1930 he composed a lengthy "Platform" calling Stalin "the evil genius of the Russian Revolution" and demanding retreat from the Second Revolution. He was arrested, but then released. In June 1932 he and others composed an "Appeal" for the removal of Stalin by force. In the Politburo Stalin demanded Ryutin's execution; the majority refused. Four years later almost to the day, Stalin told the OGPU that it was "four years behind"; the reference was almost certainly to Ryutin and his colleagues. (They were shot in 1937 and 1938—and praised in the Soviet press only fifty years later).[3]

"Cadres Decide Everything!"

At the end of 1932 the First Five-Year Plan was declared to have been fulfilled. Immediately the Second Plan, covering the years 1933–1937, went into effect, although it was not formally adopted until January 1934 when the XVII Party Congress met. By that time, it was reported, 99% of all Soviet industry was controlled by the state, while the *kolkhozes* and *sovkhozes* included 90% of the total crop area. Private business and trade had virtually come to an end in the USSR, with the exception of the legal peasant markets for garden-plot produce and the illegal (but more or less tolerated) black market.

The aim of the Second Plan was purportedly "to eliminate completely the capitalist elements" in the USSR. The implication was that they were substantially gone already. If the First Plan had been an era of "shock" methods, the second was

---

[3] Robert Conquest, *The Great Terror: A Reassessment,* Oxford U. Press, 1990, pp. 25–26.

to be a time of consolidation. The previous emphasis on quantity was to be replaced by stress on quality. "Gigantomania" became an epithet applied to the fascination for the big and the dramatic which had characterized the First Plan. The approved new slogans were "consolidate the gains already won" and "master the technical base." In his characteristically spare and elementary style, Stalin declared,

> Formerly we used to say that "technique [that is, machinery and capital goods] decides everything." This slogan helped us to put an end to the dearth in technique and to create a vast technical base. ... That is very good. But it is not enough, it is not enough by far. ... In order to set technique going and to utilize it to the full, we need people who have mastered technique, we need cadres capable of mastering and utilizing this technique according to all the rules of the art. ... [The old slogan] must now be replaced by a new slogan, the slogan "cadres decide everything." That is the main thing now.

Cadres meant simply people able to do their jobs. The feverish efforts of the First Five-Year Plan had produced a broader "technical base"; they had also done much to develop a system of central economic controls and, above all, political controls based on the Party machinery and supplemented by the secret police, army, trade-union and other apparatuses. The systems of control depended on the individuals who operated them. For the apparatus of totalitarianism to function, *apparatchiki* were indispensable. In the early 1930's such a group did not need to be created; it already existed. What it needed was to be expanded, rewarded, prodded, intimidated, and terrorized. Only then would it become a completely reliable instrument.

The Great Purges

In 1934 the XVII Party Congress was held. It was called the "Congress of Victors," in ostensible reference to the achievements of the Five-Year Plans. The "victors" in fact were those who, following Stalin's lead, had beaten into silence the party dissidents. At the Congress, Stalin announced complacently, "There is nothing more to prove and, it seems, no one to fight," and he appeared to be right. The terror directed against the enemies of the Party or simply those outside it, that is, the mass of the people, was not at an end, but its objective had evidently been achieved. The peasants and workers had been starved, killed, or frightened into submission.

During the 1930's the target of the ruling faction changed somewhat. The mass terror, of which the clearest example was collectivization, yielded to the mass purge of the Party itself. The purge actually began before 1934 and the terror continued afterward, but the shift in emphasis was noteworthy. Having silenced its opponents, the apparatus turned on itself.

By the early 1930's, the Politburo consisted of Stalin, Molotov, Voroshilov, Kalinin, Rudzutak, Kuibyshev, Kaganovich, Kirov, Kosior, Ordzhonikidze, and Andreyev. None had belonged to either the Left or the Right Opposition; all were Stalin's trusted henchmen. Despite the punishment the Ryutin group had received, dissent remained. At the Congress, anywhere from 150 to 300 delegates voted against Stalin for membership in the Central Committee; the official count reduced the number to three. It is now known that some delegates proposed to replace Stalin as General Secretary with Sergei Kirov, who had been sent to Leningrad to "clean up" Zinoviev's supporters there and was rumored to be Stalin's chosen heir. He declined to cooperate. Stalin found out about the conversation; Kirov told him he himself was to blame because of his "drastic" ways. His own murder may have been the result.[4]

On December 1, 1934, Kirov was assassinated in Leningrad. The assassin was a young man named Nikolaev who had earlier had connections with Zinoviev. "Objectively," therefore, Zinoviev was said to be responsible. By the logic he himself used in his later confession, "The former activity of the former opposition could not, by the force of objective circumstances, but stimulate the degeneration of those criminals." A rising young star in the Party apparatus, Andrei Zhdanov, was promptly sent to replace Kirov, and in the early months of 1935 whole trainloads of "Kirov's murderers" were deported from Leningrad to Siberia.

The official story was thus that the old Left Opposition had struck at Stalin through Kirov. It now seems clear that Stalin himself instigated Kirov's murder.[5] The episode was only the curtain raiser for the epic drama to follow. From the middle of 1935 to the middle of 1936, arrests of real or alleged supporters of Zinoviev and Trotsky continued, but on a relatively limited scale. It seemed during those months as if an era of relative relaxation was indeed at hand. In 1935 a new constitution was called for, and much publicity attended its preparation under the guiding hands of Bukharin and Radek. Stalin made many public appearances, smiling at little children and bestowing awards.

Then in August 1936 came the public trial of sixteen Old Bolsheviks, of whom the most prominent were Zinoviev and Kamenev. Although the target still appeared to be the former Left Opposition, the fabricated "confessions" of the accused tarnished the old Right as well. In September Henry Yagoda was removed as head of the NKVD (*Narodnyi Kommissariat Vnutrennykh Del* or People's Commissariat of Internal Affairs, into which the OGPU was changed in July 1934), along with some of his closest assistants. He was replaced by N. I. Yezhov. According to one account, Yezhov thereupon reported to the Party Central Committee

---

[4] Ibid., p. 33.

[5] Robert Conquest wrote in *Stalin and the Kirov Murder*, Oxford U. press, 1989. p. 138: "the open accusation of Stalin's guilt has trembled on the lips of Soviet official spokesmen, and has even been spoken of in scattered references."

that the executed defendants in the "trial of the sixteen" had implicated Bukharin, Rykov, and Tomsky—that is, the leaders of the former Right Opposition; however, Bukharin replied sharply, and the report was rejected by a majority which included five full or candidate members of the Politburo. It is at least certain that the five believed to have acted thus—Kosior, Rudzutak, Chubar, Postyshev, and Eikhe—were all purged in the blood bath which followed, and that they all were rehabilitated in Khrushchëv's "secret speech." (In fact, those five, all trusted Stalinists throughout the fight with the opposition, were the only top leaders killed during the purges whom Khrushchëv did rehabilitate.)

In January 1937 came the trial of the so-called "Anti-Soviet Trotskyite Center," consisting of seventeen lesser-ranking but still prominent opposition leaders, including Piatakov and Radek. It appears that in the February–March 1937 Plenum of the Central Committee Stalin overrode opposition to the broadening of the purges, and the real *Yezhovshchina*[6] rolled into high gear. On the eve of the plenum, Ordzhonikidze was said to have died of "heart disease"; we know that this was false, but it is still uncertain whether he was hounded into committing suicide or was murdered. In either case Stalin was responsible for his death.

Although only a year earlier the army had been reorganized in a fashion presumably more acceptable to the military leadership (ranks and discipline were restored and five marshals were appointed), in June 1937 the chief army generals, headed by the chief of the general staff, Marshal Tukhachevsky, were secretly tried and executed. In March 1938 came the turn of the Right Opposition leaders (and some others) in the trial of the so-called "Anti-Soviet Bloc of Rights and Trotskyites." Tomsky killed himself before the trial; Bukharin, Rykov, Rakovsky, Yagoda, and others were tried and executed.

Altogether the accused included all members of Lenin's Politburo except Stalin himself (even Trotsky was tried *in absentia*), one ex-premier (Rykov), two former chiefs of the Comintern (Zinoviev and Bukharin), an ex-chief of the trade-unions (Tomsky), an ex-chief of the general staff (Tukhachevsky), and two ex-chiefs of the secret policy (Yagoda and Yezhov—the latter was not tried publicly). However, the Great Purges by no means stopped with the elimination of the Bolshevik old guard and many of the newer Stalinite henchmen. The victims included 70% of the members (and candidates) of the Party Central Committee elected in 1934, the great majority of the highest officers of the army, over 90% of the central trade-union committees, and many mangers, intellectuals, and Party and Comintern functionaries. In addition a multitude of ordinary citizens were accused; orders went out to the secret police to arrest a certain percentage of the whole population, varying slightly from district to district. The best recent estimate is that 8

---

[6] In Russian the suffix *-shchina* means roughly, "the wicked deeds of" the person whose name precedes it. By this token *Stalinshchina* would be more accurate for the bloodiest phase of the purges, especially since Yezhov himself became one of the victims, but it is too late to change the terms.

million people were arrested in 1937–1938, of which 1 million were executed; 2 million died in camps. (Perhaps 7 million were in camps at the end of 1938, 12 million in camps in 1952.)[7]

In July 1938 Yezhov himself was shunted aside by the appointment of Lavrenty Beria as his deputy, and in December Beria replaced him outright (Yezhov was later arrested and shot). This was the signal for the end of the mass purges. The mass purge and the show trial feel into disuse, but individuals—sometimes large numbers of them—continued to be arrested, shot, or sent to concentration camps. Those liquidated were dealt with secretly, though sometimes their fate was publicized. During the 1930's Stalin used another device for getting rid of inconvenient persons in high places: murder coupled with public eulogy and grief. Among those who fell in this way may be counted Kirov, Kuibyshev, and Ordzhonikidze, all Politburo members, and Maxim Gorky, dean of Soviet writers.

The show trials themselves, conducted under the direction of Procurator General Andrei Vyshinsky, amazed and puzzled the world. In only one case, that of Krestinsky in the trial of March 1938, did a defendant repudiate a confession in open court, and a night with the NKVD sufficed to change his mind once again. The defendants uniformly confessed to the crimes with which they were charged, which included plotting with the secret services of foreign powers to overthrow Stalin and the Communist Party, "restore capitalism" in the USSR, and cede territory to Germany and Japan. A number of specific acts which the defendants admitted were shown by independent investigation—much of it undertaken by a private commission established under the chairmanship of John Dewey to probe the truth behind the trials—to have been physically impossible: meetings at hotels long since dismantled, landings at airports where no such planes had landed, and so forth.

Why Stalin conducted the blood bath, and why the defendants confessed to lies are questions which have been widely debated. Isaac Deutscher, while acknowledging the falsity of the charges, has argued that they "were based on a perverted 'psychological truth.' ... [Stalin's] reasoning probably developed along the following lines: they may want to overthrow me in a crisis—I shall charge them with having already made the attempt ... if they succeed, they may be compelled to ... agree to a cession of territory. ... I shall accuse them of having entered already into a treacherous alliance with Germany (and Japan). ... No milder pretext for the slaughter of the old guard would have sufficed. ... It is not necessary to assume that he acted from sheer cruelty or lust for power. He may be given the dubious credit of the sincere conviction that what he did served the interests of the revolution and that he alone interpreted those interests aright."[8]

---

[7] Conquest, *Reassessment,* pp. 485–486.

[8] *Stalin,* pp. 377–378.

The sort of diabolical rationality which Deutscher imputes to Stalin may well account for the "slaughter of the old guard." But how then are we to account for the murders of the hitherto devoted Stalinists and the hounding of millions of puzzled little people, some of whom begged their fellow prisoners to tell them enough about the ideological sins with which they were charged (Zionism, for instance), but of which they had scarcely heard before, so that they could make their confessions plausible? What of those who were innocent—as far as one could humanly judge—of even any oppositional thoughts, let alone acts? The only hypotheses so far advanced which account for such facts as the order to arrest a fixed percentage of the population are two: that Stalin was utterly mad, or that he realized that under totalitarianism anyone at all is potentially disloyal, and that therefore the regime would be secure only if everyone was sufficiently terrorized to become incapable of acting independently. Perhaps Stalin was deranged, but he was certainly attempting to secure the totalitarian regime.

Why did the defendants confess? Many succumbed to physical torture and the psychological pressure of the "conveyor"—endless interrogation of the victims while they were in a physically weakened condition. A more complex suggestion was offered by novelists—Charles Plisnier in *Faux passeports* (1938) and Arthur Koestler in *Darkness at Noon* (1941). The best of the accused, Koestler contended, signed confessions "in order to do a last service to the Party. ... They were too deeply entangled in their own past, caught in the web they had spun themselves, according to the laws of their own twisted ethics and twisted logic; they were all guilty, although not of those deeds of which they accused themselves." Some certainly confessed without torture, hoping to save themselves or their families. After Khrushchëv's "secret speech" and the liberation of Cardinal Mindszenty, we can be certain that torture indeed was used on the chief defendants, some of whom went to their deaths with their bodies shattered but their minds intact. No doubt the perverted use of psychiatry to make minds sick instead of well, a technique further perfected by the Chinese Communists later, was first worked out in its fundamentals by the NKVD in the course of the Great Purges. Probably all these techniques were used, in varying combination.[9]

The result was that a very substantial proportion of the entire leadership of the Soviet system was eliminated, and the whole population of the USSR was more or less successfully intimidated into acquiescence. Although Stalin announced at the XVIII Party Congress in March 1939, "undoubtedly we shall have no further need of resorting to the method of mass purges," it was not forgotten that son had informed against father, father had been executed simply because he was the son of grandfather, and that whether there were "mass purges" again soon or ever, there was no such thing as a safe statement on public affairs, whether made to family or

---

[9] See Conquest, *Reassessment*, Ch. 5. "The Problem of Confession."

friends or fellow workers—indeed, in the USSR there was no safety for the individual at all.

The chief state institutions had been gravely weakened. The high command of the army had been decimated through the use of forged documents turned over to Stalin's secretariat by the Nazis. Although it is not certain that Stalin accepted them as genuine, he found that they served his purpose well. The Party, the trade-unions, the factory managements, and even the secret police itself had suffered from arrests of their leaders. All of the basic institutions of the totalitarian system had been shaken; however, by the same token they were less capable of independent stands, more reliable instruments of the remaining elite, and therefore more totalitarian, than before. Whether or not Stalin had sought more power for himself as his sole or chief end, his personal power was infinitely greater, and his apparatus was supreme. From 1933 to 1938 around 1 million technicians, administrators, and professional men had been graduated from the secondary schools, and they were used to replace the victims of the purges—thus, in *Darkness at Noon,* does Gletkin, the "Neanderthal" Stalinite, replace Ivanov, the cultured Old Bolshevik.

The last death sentence of the Great Purges was not carried out in 1938, but two years later. Trotsky, who had fled from Prinkipo to Norway to Mexico, trying to create a Fourth International, writing furiously, inveighing against Stalin but refusing to advocate his overthrow, was the last victim. He was murdered in Mexico in August 1940. The assassin, a shadowy figure who used several pseudonyms, spent twenty years in a Mexican jail, was released in 1960, and died in Cuba in 1978.

The "Stalin Constitution" of 1936

At the moment when the Great Purges were swelling to their full fury in November 1936, Stalin appeared before the VIII All-Union Congress of Soviets to present for formal approval the new "Stalin Constitution." Already in June the Constitution had been published in draft form and a public discussion of its contents was invited. It is reported that 154,000 amendments were proposed, of which only 43 were adopted. The form of the document was obviously influenced by, and intended to be interpreted by those familiar with, the constitutions of "bourgeois democracies." However, it neither purported to be nor was in fact the fundamental law of the USSR. The official ideology of the Soviet state, "Marxism-Leninism," was nowhere mentioned. At one point, in Article 126, the locus of power was indeed clearly indicated: "the most active and politically conscious citizens in the ranks of the working class and other sections of the working people [that is to say, the workers were still distinguished from the peasants] unite in the Communist Party of the Soviet Union, which is the vanguard of the working people in their struggle to strengthen and develop the socialist system and is the leading core of *all* organizations of the working people, both public and state" (italics added). But this was the only mention of the Party.

The stated reason for the new Constitution was to give legal expression to the new stage of development which, it was contended, the USSR had reached by 1936, namely the completion of the building of "socialism" as distinguished from "communism," a distinction first set forth in Marx's *Critique of the Gotha Program.* Under "socialism," it was argued, exploitation had come to an end, and the principle "from each according to his ability, to each according to his work" was to be applied. Class antagonism had disappeared, but not classes *per se.* There were now two "friendly" classes, workers and peasants, with a stratum (not a class) known as "intelligentsia" overlying both. The state, which, it had been supposed, would "wither away" under socialism, was obviously and admittedly no weaker than before (actually it was immensely stronger than it had ever been). This was explained by the persistence of "capitalist encirclement," the continuing external danger which had its counterpart in the efforts of foreign governments to subvert the regime by utilizing domestic malcontents, who were by definition themselves "bourgeois survivals." As long as the Communists had not come to dominate the whole world, the Soviet state would accordingly persist.

The Constitution of 1924 had provided for an indirect suffrage, weighted in favor of the proletariat. The new Constitution provided for a suffrage which was equal for citizens of both sexes eighteen years of age or over, universal except for insane persons and convicts, direct in electing deputies to the new USSR Supreme Soviet, and secret. Thereby it seemed that the old revolutionary demand for "Four-Tail" (universal, equal, secret, and direct) suffrage—then projected for a constituent assembly—had been realized. However, the use of the secret ballot, which was made optional (booths being provided for those who desired to exercise their constitutional right), was taken as evidence that the voter had something to hide and remained a dead letter. The citizen voted for deputies to the Supreme Soviet, which had no power, and he or she had no alternative to voting for the Party nominees except that of crossing out their names, an empty gesture risked by an utterly negligible percentage of voters.

The Constitution declared the Supreme Soviet to be the "highest organ of state power in the USSR," and it was entrusted with all governmental functions which do not "come within the jurisdiction of organs of the USSR that are accountable to the Supreme Soviet of the USSR." Such organs were the Presidium of the Supreme Soviet,[10] the Council of Ministers,[11] and the ministries themselves. The Supreme Soviet had two chambers, the Soviet of the Union (1 deputy for every 300,000 voters) and the Soviet of Nationalities (deputies represented administra-

---

[10] Not to be confused with the Presidium of the Central Committee of the Communist Party, by which name the Politburo was known from 1952 to 1966.

[11] Until 1946 known as the Council of People's Commissars.

tive units; there were 25 from each union republic, 11 from each autonomous republic, and so forth). In actual fact there was never any other vote on a substantive question than a unanimous one in either chamber. What was of even more fundamental importance is that the Supreme Soviet was as a rule presented with *faits accomplis* for approval; even if the proposal in question had not actually gone into effect, "debate" on the floor was confined to laudatory remarks about what the leaders had handed in, and there was no pretense of consulting the deputies in drawing up any proposals nominally submitted for their vote. The Supreme Soviet was often called the "world's dullest parliament."

The Supreme Soviet elected its own Presidium, headed by a chairman, often referred to as "President" of the USSR, who was technically chief of state and carried out such duties as conferring honors and receiving ambassadors. The Supreme Soviet "appointed" the Council of Ministers of the USSR, the ministries being enumerated in the Constitution. Therefore whenever they were changed, as happened many times, the Constitution must be amended. Sometimes such amendments came years after the changes were in fact made.

The Supreme Soviet "elected" the Supreme Court and Special Courts of the USSR and "appointed" the procurator general of the USSR. No powers were listed in the Constitution for the Supreme Court, and there was no procedure for finding any law "unconstitutional." The procurator general was given "supreme supervisory power to ensure the strict observance of the law by all Ministries and institutions subordinated to them, as well as by officials and citizens of the USSR generally." Article 112 stated that "judges are independent and subject only to the law"; a Soviet jurist declared that this article "expressed the subordination of the judges to the policy of the Soviet regime, which finds its expression in the law."[12]

Much was made of Soviet "federalism" in the new Constitution, and Stalin pretended to insist to the VIII Congress of Soviets that the union republics be given the right to secede from the USSR. In 1929 the original four republics (Russian, Ukrainian, Belorussian, and Transcaucasian) had acquired three new sister republics: the Uzbek, Turkmen, and Tadzhik SSR's. At the time of the adoption of the Stalin Constitution, the number was raised to eleven as the Transcaucasian republic was dissolved into its Georgian, Armenian, and Azerbaijani components, and the Kazakh and Kirgiz Autonomous Soviet Socialist Republics were raised to union-republic status. Each of these union republics was given the right of "secession," although it was plainly stated that any attempt to exercise this right would be evidence of bourgeois nationalism directed against international proletarian solidarity.

The Constitution enumerated a number of "fundamental rights and duties of citizens" including the right to work, to rest and leisure, to maintenance in old

---

[12] N. N. Poliansky, in *Vestnik Moskovskogo Universiteta*, November 1950, as quoted by Merle Fainsod, *How Russia Is Ruled*, p. 317.

age or in case of sickness or disability, and to education; and equality of rights for women and all nationalities or races was specified. Freedom of "religious worship and antireligious propaganda," speech, press, assembly, and of "street processions and demonstrations" was guaranteed. As the Constitution stated, these freedoms were granted only "in order to strengthen the socialist system," and did not exist for anyone who, in the view of the regime, wanted to weaken it.

Stalin and his henchmen employed a good deal of frankness in glosses which they publicly gave the document. In his speech to the VIII Congress of Soviets Stalin declared, "I must admit that the draft of the new Constitution ... preserves unchanged the present leading position of the Communist Party of the USSR. ... In the USSR only one party can exist, the Communist Party, which courageously defends the interests of the workers and peasants to the very end."

Why then was the Constitution so phrased as to slur over such important points, which Stalin was willing to mention in public? For one thing, it was realized that many more people would read the Constitution than would hear or read the commentaries. The phrasing of the Constitution was thus designed to appeal to Russians and minority peoples who had fought and hoped for democracy in the past, and it was intended to be misconstrued by statesmen, scholars, and ordinary citizens in Western countries which Soviet foreign policy, by way of the Popular Front, was at that time attempting to influence. The latter aim, to be sure, was widely achieved.

The Position of the Communist Party

During the early years of Communist rule, there was a good deal of open discussion in the lower Party units and in the Party congresses. Although already in Lenin's time "factions" were prohibited, they did in fact exist during the period of the NEP. While they could not count on a fair hearing, their spokesmen could obtain the floor (despite frequent heckling) and they could record their votes. By the time of the XV Congress in 1927, even these possibilities existed no longer. Subsequent congresses became fully subservient sounding boards for Stalin's clique, which summoned them with ever-decreasing frequency.

The original notion of "democratic centralism" was that decisions made by congress majorities must bind the Central Committee, other central organs, and all the rank and file. Stalin simply transferred the process of decision-making to himself and his own picked Politburo. The Party structure was not formally changed, but the views of no Party organ but the Politburo counted, and during the Great Purges several members of the Politburo itself were liquidated. The only security from execution, imprisonment, or dismissal was Stalin's unpredictable personal favor.

Having destroyed so many of the leaders of the Party, Stalin was naturally at pains to try to produce a leadership more amenable to his desires. The militant, even military, character of the Communist Party became fully developed during the thirties. Stalin tried to create a reliable new generation of Party members by emphasizing indoctrination in the principles of *partiinost'* ("party" converted into a generic noun; literally, "party-ness"), discipline, and self-criticism (*samokritika*). An attempt was made to create an atmosphere of unceasing combat, whether against "enemies of the state" or foreign "capitalists," or for the fulfillment of the goals of the Five-Year Plans or achievement of the objectives of Party propaganda and agitation (*agitprop*). A proliferation of "feeder" organizations was developed and expanded. The Little Octobrists for children eight to eleven years of age, the Pioneers for those ten to sixteen, and the Komsomol (Communist Union of Youth) for persons aged fifteen to twenty-six were together designed to produce adults who accepted the fundamental ideological commitments and values of the Party proper and were habituated to its standards of unquestioning discipline.

The cessation of the purges at the end of 1938 was a signal that two processes were nearly complete: members of a suspected older generation had been wiped out or terrorized, and also a younger and presumably more reliable generation had assumed the posts vacated by those purged or new posts established to perfect the control of Stalin's apparatus over all branches of Soviet life.

In that apparatus the Party was both in theory and practice the paramount and central mechanism, and the Constitution was quite accurate in stating that it was the "leading core of all organizations" including the "organs of government." But the Party itself had been converted into an instrument of Stalin and his clique. The Party members as a group were more privileged and more powerful than any other. Within its hierarchy there was a series of gradations of prestige and authority, but even the top functionaries were subject to Stalin's supreme power, and the word *Vozhd* (Leader) came to be used openly to acknowledge and proclaim that fact. In George Orwell's *Animal Farm* all of the animals were equal, but some were more equal than others; in those terms, Stalin was the most equal of all. By 1939 (and there were no further changes until 1946) the Politburo had come to consist of Stalin, Molotov, Voroshilov, Kalinin, Kaganovich, Andreyev, Mikoyan, Zhdanov, and Khrushchëv, while candidate members Malenkov and Beria also wielded considerable power. At the time of Hitler's invasion, probably Zhdanov was closest to being a Number Two man in Stalin's Politburo.

Economic Growth in the Thirties

It was during the thirties that the NKVD became the largest single employer in the Soviet Union. The 1941 economic plan for the Soviet Union, captured by the Nazi armies and later released by the U.S. Government, showed that about one-sixth of all new construction in that year was entrusted to the NKVD. Since the document did not include material on armament production, gold output, or

NKVD labor subcontracting to other enterprises, it is a safe conclusion that the share of the NKVD in the entire Soviet economy was much greater than the over-all figure of one-sixth. In certain industries for which detailed figures were given, the proportion was considerably higher: for example, the NKVD share in chrome-ore production was 40%. Even if the figures were complete, they would not convey adequately even the economic (let alone the political or moral) signifi-cance of the NKVD's gigantic prison labor force.

From 1928 to 1952 the industrial expansion of the USSR was very considerable. The funds in the hands of the state grew eight times, industrial output six times, appropriations for the armed forces twenty-six times. Every time the state relaxed, observes Naum Jasny, improvement occurred; every time the state intervened it caused damage. The year 1927 was a good one; in 1927–1929 there was "warming up," a slight decline in major indices; during 1930–1933, the "all-out drive," they fell fast; in 1934–1936 came "three good years"; during 1937–1941, the "purge era," the indices fell and stayed low; in 1946–1952 "Stalin has everything his way," and there came some decline. Real incomes of the peasantry in 1952 were about 60% of 1928's; the real non-farm wage (that is, of the urban worker) may have been 70% of 1928 in 1952. Jasny concludes: "The most striking event of all was that industrialization was accomplished without its normal concomitant—the im-provement of the living standards of the population." The Bolsheviks wished to fight exploitation, he acknowledged, and improve the lot of everyone; what was achieved was a great increase in the rate of exploitation, "reducing the people's share of the national income to an extent nobody had believed possible."[13]

Taking 1913 as the base year, in 1940 national income was officially claimed to be 611%, gross industrial output 854.9%, and gross farm output 184.1% of the pre-World War I tsarist figures. From a total of 170 million in 1913 the population de-clined sharply to 147 million in 1926, owing to World War I and Civil War losses, famine, and collectivization, and did not reach 170 million again until 1939 (actu-ally this amounted to a slight increase, since the 1939 borders were inside those of 1913 at certain points). Thus no considerable rise in population accounts for the percentage increases in the indices mentioned. Soviet sources claim that coal pro-duction (in millions of metric tons) rose from 29.1 in 1913 to 166 in 1940, oil pro-duction from 9.2 to 31, steel production from 4.2 to 18.3, and electric-power pro-duction went from 1.9 to 48.3 billion kilowatt-hours.

The capital which made this increase possible was amassed by intensive exploi-tation of the ordinary Soviet citizenry, especially the peasantry. The regime made the deliberate decision to hold down the production of the necessities of life, not to speak of luxuries. According to Soviet sources, in 1928 "means of production," or capital goods, accounted for about 46% of all industrial production, consumer goods about 54%. This was at the very beginning of the Five-Year Plans. The plan

---

[13] Naum Jasny, *Soviet Industrialization*, U. of Chicago Press, 1961, p. 1, Ch. 17.

for 1953, as announced by Malenkov (who was at that moment endeavoring to increase consumer-goods production somewhat), was for about 70% means of production, 30% consumer goods; thus during the 1930's the figures were doubtless even more lopsided.

Industrial Labor

To achieve the priority goals of Soviet heavy industry, the regime adopted a series of measures to elicit the maximum effort from the workers. During the First Five-Year Plan limited competition was tried, and official attacks were made on the concept of "equalitarianism." Certainly if, under socialism, pay was to be scaled "according to work," there was no reason why differences in quantity and quality of work done should not be reflected in differences in income.

On August 31, 1935, a new expedient was launched. It was reported that one Alexei Stakhanov, a coal hewer in the Donets Basin, had hewed 102 tons of coal in one shift and thus had overfulfilled his quota by 1,400%. This news was soon followed by other astounding reports of overexertion, and the word "Stakhanovite" came to be applied to all workers who achieved such staggering records of output. These workers were paid very highly and rewarded with various honors and decorations. Such records could not be and were not actually achieved by a single unaided man, and his fellow workers had to set up tools and conditions by means of which he could chalk up vast overfulfillments of quota. This circumstance led to natural resentment among non-Stakhanovites, and intentional frustrations, attacks, and even slayings of Stakhanovites by their fellows occurred. Nevertheless, a considerable part of the new record was the result of the Stakhanovite's own labor, and the life expectancy of many of them was shortened by their glories.

The regime did not trust simply to the inspiration produced by the new records. Usually after a Stakhanovite demonstration the old "norm" was raised, not, to be sure, to the level of the new record, for all workers could not furnish set-ups for each other, but to a point midway between the old norm and the new record. In other countries the device is known simply as the "speed-up." The opposition to Stakhanovism was, though unorganized, widespread. It is probable that the purge of the overwhelming majority of the members of the trade-union central committees in 1937–1938 was particularly intended to crush such opposition. Simultaneously the regime began to give strong emphasis to piecework, so that by 1938 only 16% of the workers received ordinary wages, the remainder of the wages being some combination of simple-piece, progressive-piece, and bonus.

However, incentives of this kind were not sufficient to produce the results the regime demanded. From 1938 to 1940 the most stringent compulsion was applied to the labor force. In December 1938 one law provided that every worker must have a labor book in which his whole employment history was recorded, to be presented to the authorities whenever required. Another defined "absenteeism" as constituting any unauthorized absence from the job, be it as little as arriving twenty minutes late for work, and four cases of such "absenteeism" in two months entailed dismissal of the offending worker. In June 1940 the worker was prohibited from leaving his job without permission. Any attempt to obtain dismissal through intentional "absenteeism" was forestalled by a provision that the latter offense should henceforth be penalized by compulsory work in the same enterprise, at three-quarters of the usual wages. By a law of October 1940 the regime could transfer skilled workers anywhere at will. Legally all labor thus became compulsory in the sense that no worker could select or change his own job, although in fact many violations of labor legislation did occur owing to the feverish efforts of Soviet managers to fulfill their quotas under conditions of labor shortage, and their willingness to countenance infractions to that end.

By the end of the 1930's the system of "organized intake" of "redundant" rural labor (see p. 207) was proving unsatisfactory, often because the laborers drafted not only lacked the requisite skills but might be too old to acquire them easily. Therefore in October 1940 a new system known as the State Labor Reserves program was inaugurated. Close to a million boys aged fourteen to seventeen were drafted annually for skilled training in special schools, and girls aged sixteen to eighteen were added during World War II. The training was to be followed by four years of obligatory work on assigned jobs, after which military service had to be discharged.

At every stage the Soviet worker was closely subjected to state control. The trade-union structure gave him no protection. In 1933 collective agreements between trade-unions and managements were abolished, strikes were at an end, and the trade-unions had no say whatsoever regarding wages or hours, as they were fixed by law or the central planning machinery. The unions' functions were reduced to such things as deciding which workers were to go to which sanatoriums—the nearest equivalent to a Western "vacation"—for short periods, conducting propaganda among the workers in a given enterprise, and watching the towel supply in the washrooms.

The Peasantry

By the end of the First Five-Year Plan the basic structure of Soviet agriculture had been largely decided upon, but efforts were needed to bring all the farms into that structure and to enforce its regulations. By 1938, 93.5% of all peasant households had been collectivized. Most of these were on collective farms (*kolkhozy*); state farms (*sovkhozy*) remained small in proportion (10%) to the total sown area and grain output. Individual farming was still practiced by 6.5% of all households under sharply discriminatory conditions, and was soon to disappear.

The Communists had compromised on the *artel* form of *kolkhoz* (see p. 205). By the new Model Statutes of the Agricultural Artel of 1935, the regime confirmed the *kolkhoznik's* ownership of garden plot and livestock. The collective farms were now permitted to readmit "kulaks" who gave evidence of "reform," and the farms settled down to an uneasy calm. The collective farmer and his wife and children worked as long and hard as they could on their garden plot and as little as they were able to manage on the "collective sector" of the *kolkhoz* land. As a result, in 1937 the tiny plots accounted for an amazing one-fourth of the gross farm output of the USSR. At the XVIII Party Congress in 1939 it was openly admitted that in many places private farming was the peasant's chief concern. In order to combat this, two measures were enacted. First, the regime abandoned all pretense that the farmer worked willingly on the collective sector and established a legal minimum of eighty "workdays" (*trudodni*, often more than chronological days, but variously defined) per year; if the *kolkhoznik* did not fulfill that requirement, he could be expelled from the collective farm, which the regime openly admitted would mean starvation. Second, a new survey was ordered to confiscate any land in each garden plot in excess of a prescribed maximum, usually about one acre. As in urban industry, however, the laws and regulations were by no means always observed. One example is provided by Fedor Belov in a revealing appendix, headed "Bribes to Raion [Regional] Officials in 1948," to a useful sketch of life on a collective farm during these years and later.[14]

Long before, in 1920, Trotsky had declared that Soviet methods "are not less varied than those used by the bourgeoisie, but they are more honest, more direct and frank, uncorrupted by mendacity and fraud. The bourgeoisie had to pretend that its systems of labor was free. … We know that every labor is socially compulsory labor. Man must work in order not to die. He does not want to work. But the social organization compels and whips him into that direction." No doubt the Stalinist regulations for the workers and peasants were not what Trotsky had in mind, but the statement is a suggestive forecast of what actually happened in the USSR by 1941.

The Intelligentsia

According to Stalin, over the worker and peasant classes in the new socialist society there existed a stratum which he called intelligentsia.[15] "No ruling class," Stalin declared, "has ever managed without its own intelligentsia, and there are no grounds for believing that the working class of the USSR can do so." In 1939 Molotov reported that just under 10 million Soviet citizens should be classified as members of this "stratum"; he included in it administrators, industrial managers,

---

[14] *A History of a Soviet Collective Farm,* Praeger, 1955.

[15] Soviet usage of this term should not be confused with its meaning which refers to the pre-1917 oppositionists; see p. 25.

collective-farm chairmen, engineers, doctors, teachers, accountants, army offi-cers, and technicians of all kinds.

Many of these persons were members of the Communist Party, but the major-ity were not. Party membership (both full members and candidates) fell from 3.5 million in January 1933 to 1.92 million in January 1938, in the midst of the Great Purges; even though the purges continued through 1938, during that year the membership began to increase once more. By January 1939 the total was 2.306 million; by January 1949 it was 3.4 million, of whom 40% had been recruited in the previous two years. It is impossible to establish exactly how many Party mem-bers came from the "intelligentsia," but certainly it was a large proportion. In gen-eral the intelligentsia, overlapping with the membership of the ruling Party, formed the peak of the pyramid of Soviet society.

As in other Soviet social groups, there were gradations within the intelligentsia. David J. Dallin provides an example in reference to medical care: each of the highest officials had his own physician who had no other patients; for the second rank of Kremlin employees there was a doctor to each five or six families; in the third rank, one per fifteen to twenty families. For the ordinary population of Moscow there was a "dispensary" (usually one doctor) for every two thousand to three thousand people.[16] A Spanish former Communist who was employed by the Comintern in the USSR during this period writes, "In the Comintern there were three categories, A, B, C. In the Lux Hotel [for the most privileged foreign Com-munists] there were three categories: A, B, C. In the hospitals also there are three categories: A, B, C. Why do they call it a classless society?"[17]

Why indeed? The Stalinist argument ran as follows. The means of production were in the hands of the regime which was assumed to "represent" the "proletar-iat," or, as was sometimes said, the "toilers" (including the peasantry). Since there was no private ownership, and no class antagonism arising from such a basis re-mained, there could be no exploitation. Each was paid "according to his work"— as determined by the regime. Therefore Soviet society was both classless and so-cialist. Any manifestation hostile or unacceptable to the regime was explained on the basis of "capitalist survivals," or the machinations of foreign capitalists. It was all a matter of simple logic, and indeed, given the assumptions, the conclusions followed. All that was necessary was to ignore the evidence.

Stalin's objective was not merely economic transformation or concentration of political power or dictation over thought and the arts. It was all of those things, but it was also much more. It was the alteration of human nature, or, as the offi-cial phraseology had it, the creation of the "new Soviet man." The needs of society (or the state, since for Stalin they were the same thing) were to be placed first, ahead of self, friends, and family. A striking instance was the official story that in

---

[16] *The New Soviet Empire* (New Haven: Yale University Press, 1951), pp. 140–143.

[17] Enrique Castro Delgado, *J'ai perdu la foi à Moscou,* 3rd ed.; Paris: Gallimard, 1950, pp. 115 and 177.

a village near Sverdlovsk a boy named Pavlik Morozov, age fourteen, informed police that his father, the kolkhoz chairman, had kept back some wheat and illegally distributed ration forms; the father disappeared into the gulag forever and Pavlik and his brother were then killed by relatives, who were in turn executed. For years Pavlik was hailed and venerated as hero and martyr.[18] In 1941 Stalin, his Politburo, and the upper echelons of the Communist Party—even some of those who regretted the casualties and feared or even hated Stalin—appeared convinced that the "new Soviet man" was in sight. Stalin and his ideologists cited Marxism to prove that the goal would inevitably be achieved, because the economic foundation of society had been transformed. However, the totalitarian dictatorship had been sufficiently consolidated to ensure that all the power at its disposal would be utilized to hasten the inevitable.

---

[18] Walter Laqueur, *Stalin: The Glasnost Revelations*, Charles Scribner's Sons, 1990, pp. 186–187. In 1989 the magazine *Yunost'* published an article alleging that the story was invented from beginning to end.

16

Lenin, Stalin, and the Non-Russians

The Minority Nationalities

Marx and Engels treated "the national question as peripheral and ethnic divisions as purely contingent to social and economic development. ..."[1] Lenin worked out an idea of national self-determination in stages. First he advocated the right of secession (from Russia), hoping the minorities would not secede; after 1917 he decided that a federation was the best policy for the near future though "on the road to complete unity." Stalin, who had been made Commissar of Nationalities on the basis of his early commission by Lenin to write a pamphlet called *Marxism and the National and Colonial Question,* came to favor "proletarian self-determination" only, but Lenin was worried about less developed peoples who had either a tiny or not clearly differentiated proletariat.

The outcome was the Union Treaty of December 1922 by which the larger non-Russian groups were given "union republic" status within a federation called the Union of Soviet Socialist Republics. (The original name had been simply "Russian.") Each of the 180 or so nationalities within the 1921 borders required study in order to discover which traits had to be suppressed and which encouraged to square with party policy. In more than one case Moscow's ethnic specialists rediscovered virtually forgotten figures and events of a nationality's past to which they could attach some merit for propaganda purposes, only to castigate admiration for them as ideologically harmful a few years later. However, during the NEP the regime followed Lenin's policy of restraint toward the minorities and his belief that Communism could thrive in the borderlands if local traditions could be converted to its needs. In 1923 a policy of indigenization (*korenizatsiia*) was adopted that strove to promote local leaders and develop the local language.

---

[1] Graham Smith, Ch. 1, in *The Nationalities Question in the Soviet Union,* ed. by Graham Smith, Longman, 1990, p. 2.

Stalin's chief objectives in relation to the borderlands were four: 1. to eliminate any threat of centrifugal pressures by stifling local nationalism and substituting as an object of allegiance "Soviet patriotism," or, when that failed, enforcing as a dogma belief in the eternal brotherhood of the nationality in question with the Great Russians; 2. to influence and attract the USSR's neighbors by open and concealed subversion carried out by members of a given local nationality, as well as by propaganda about the alleged economic, political, and cultural gains of that nationality under Soviet rule; 3. economic and social transformation designed to destroy the previous native society and to substitute a social system susceptible of control by Moscow; 4. outright economic exploitation of the borderlands.

Stalin's theoretical position in relation to the nationalities was restated at the XVI Party Congress in 1930 and reiterated at the XVII Congress of 1934 and subsequently. He declared that "survivals of capitalism in men's consciousness are much more tenacious in the sphere of the national problem than in any other sphere." On the national question, he contended, there were twin dangers: "Great Russian chauvinism" and local nationalism. Either one might at a given moment or place be the more threatening to the foundations of the "fraternal" union of nationalities in the USSR.

Actually, "Great Russian chauvinism" never threatened Stalin's domination (though he sometimes pretended that it was the offense for which he removed or punished maladroit functionaries in the borderlands). He was able to decide how and when he would use this or that old Russian hero or writer for his own purposes. There was never any possibility that any genuine Russian nationalist could achieve any power in the Russian republic, or that the Great Russians could somehow break off from the Communist center—they were in it for as long as the regime should hold together. What threatened totalitarian control was local nationalism, which might be found intertwined with devotion to Communism in the border regions and in that form was regarded as especially dangerous.

Ukraine and Belorussia

Ukraine was the most difficult region for Stalin to deal with simply because it was the biggest. In his "secret speech" of 1956, Khrushchëv drew nervous laughter from his audience by declaring that the Ukrainians avoided the fate of small peoples liquidated during World War II "only because there were too many of them and there was no place to which to deport them. Otherwise, he [Stalin] would have deported them also." This sally might have been more effective if Khrushchëv himself had not been one of the key men in Stalin's repressions of Ukraine during the 1930's, but the words doubtless had some truth in them.

Ukraine was also the most important of the border regions. It was not only the most populous republic (next to the Russian), but its rich store of raw materials and heavy industry and its strategic location *vis-à-vis* the Black Sea and eastern Central Europe gave it a decisive significance for the whole USSR.

In 1923 came a "Ukrainization"; it meant expanding the use of the Ukrainian language in the schools and government and placing Ukrainians in positions of authority (in a republic set up by a Bulgarian, Rakovsky, with all too prominent Russian participation). For a time "Ukrainization" flourished, and indeed if such a policy ever had a chance it was in Ukraine, where the national religion was the same as that of the Russians and the language was closely related to Russian, and where, in contrast to such ancient nations as Georgia, Ukrainian national or even cultural self-consciousness was only recently and incompletely developed.

However, reflecting both the popular discontent with the Soviet system and their own nationalist aspirations, the Ukrainian intellectuals took advantage of the "Ukrainization" policy to speak out. In 1925 Mykola Khvylovy began to publish a weekly in which he attacked what he termed the rebirth of Muscovite messianism in Communist guise, styled Moscow the center of "all-Union Philistinism," and, declaring that "The ideas of the proletariat we all know without the guidance of Moscow," called on Communist Ukraine to turn away from the East and to draw nearer to the "progressive" West of Newton, Darwin, and Marx. Khvylovy's "Away from Moscow" slogan was sharply denounced and in 1926–1927 he was silenced. In 1928 Mykhailo Volobuev, a writer on economics, criticized what he already recognized to be Moscow's exploitation of the border regions, Ukraine in particular, for the benefit of the center. He also was at once attacked, and he recanted.

The Ukrainian republic's commissar for education, Alexander Shumski, a former Borotbist (Ukrainian Left SR), was a prime mover in the campaign for "Ukrainization," and complained to Stalin in a personal interview that the policy was being implemented too slowly, adding other grievances. This smacked of a political deviation, and Shumski was attacked. Although he recanted partly several times and fully in 1930, he was arrested in 1933 and disappeared.

Shumski was succeeded as commissar of education by Mykola Skrypnyk, a staunch Communist but likewise a supporter of Ukrainian cultural nationalism. Skrypnyk led the Ukrainian Communist party during the period of collectivization, which was perhaps more brutal and more sharply resisted in Ukraine than anywhere else in the whole USSR. Several alleged (and very possibly real) anti-Soviet conspiracies were uncovered and the participants tried, especially forty-five members of the Union for the Liberation of Ukraine (*Spilka Vyzvolennia Ukrainy* or S.V.U.) in 1930. Other such trials followed, and in June 1933 the Russian Paul Postyshev and the Pole Stanislaw Kosior attacked Skrypnyk in a meeting of the Ukrainian party Central Committee for coddling Ukrainian nationalist deviation. A few weeks later he killed himself. Khvylovy's suicide had preceded Skrypnyk's by two months.

Postyshev and Kosior now launched a campaign against "over-Ukrainization" and repressed the Ukrainian intellectuals. In 1937 Stalin, evidently still dissatisfied, liquidated virtually the entire leadership of Ukraine. Within a year a galaxy of prominent Communists, including three successive Ukrainian prime ministers, the entire Ukrainian Politburo, and Postyshev and Kosior themselves, were eliminated. Apparently only one of the top leaders survived, Gregory Petrovski, president of the Ukrainian republic, who was released from a concentration camp in 1953. In 1938 Nikita Khrushchëv was given charge of the Ukrainian party. He promptly began to enforce the compulsory teaching of the Russian language in the schools, and there was no more talk about "Ukrainization."

Belorussia was a smaller, poorer, and less strategically located republic. This was fortunate for Stalin, since the Belorussian intelligentsia was even less enthusiastic than the Ukrainian about Soviet control. In the 1920's there was a move among the intellectuals to abolish even the name "Belorussia" because it had the word "Russia" in it, and to replace it by "Krivia," taken from a tribe which had inhabited roughly the same area at the dawn of Eastern Slavic history. During the First Five-Year Plan alleged Belorussian nationalist conspiracies were discovered, but only after 1933 did the persecution of the Belorussian intellectuals become intense. In 1937 the chief of the purgers, N. F. Gikalo, was himself purged along with the prime minister, Nicholas Goloded, the president of the Belorussian republic, and many others.

The Caucasus

The region north of the Caucasus Mountains constituted a mosaic of peoples who had practically nothing in common except a detestation of Communism. They clung stubbornly to their own traditions: during collectivization the Ossetians, for example, converted the task of determining who was a "kulak" into a weapon of clan warfare. A clan which managed to win Communist favor would find no kulaks in its midst, while a neighboring clan might be discovered to consist entirely of kulaks.

The problem of Dagestan, the eastern part of that region, was one to make any administrator despair; its population of 1 million comprised thirty-two nationalities living in an area about the size of the state of Maryland. These peoples shared an attachment to Islam, the use of Arabic as a literary language, and veneration of the memory of Shamil, fighter against tsarist armies of conquest. Arabic, as the literary vehicle of the Muslim religion, was to be wiped out; to this end the Soviets tried first to substitute Turkish, then eight selected Dagestani languages, and finally Russian. N. Samursky, head of the Dagestan party committee, tried his best to fight Islam and Arabic against fantastic odds, but in 1937 he was himself executed as a "bourgeois nationalist."

South of the Caucasus Mountains lay the three union republics. Although Stalin himself came from Georgia, the country had not only fought Soviet invasion in 1921 but was also the scene of a mass uprising against Moscow in 1924. The Georgian Communist party leaders, chief of whom was Budu Mdivani, the vice-premier of the republic, did not get on well with Stalin and were purged in 1937. Apparently Ordzhonikidze, though he had been Stalin's trusted lieutenant and seemed no more squeamish about the sensibilities of his fellow Georgians than Stalin, opposed the liquidation of Mdivani and his colleagues, and so perished at the same time (see p. 213).

In Georgia deep resentment was felt against Moscow's insistence on the expansion of tea and citrus farms, when what the country needed was more food. Similar unrest was created in Azerbaijan by central compulsion to grow more cotton, as a result of which the grain acreage substantially decreased. In Azerbaijan "national deviation" was punished repeatedly, by Kirov in the mid-1920's and by Beria in the period of the Great Purges just before he became chief of the NKVD.

Despite troubles with Azerbaijan, Moscow used it with some success as a magnet for interesting the youth among Turkic peoples everywhere in Communism. Armenia, although not Turkic like Azerbaijan, was also a thorn in Turkey's side because Turkey still had a small Armenian minority, but even more because it had a large area in which Armenians had once lived and which they might claim (including Mount Ararat, which is ambiguously shown on the coat of arms of the Armenian SSR). The Armenians were useful to the Soviets especially for their long-developed talents as traders and travelers, and Armenians rose to the Politburo (Anastas Mikoyan) and to the top level of army generals (Ivan Bagramian). However, their ancient nationalism and their Christian religion—although the hierarchy of the Armenian Church was, like that of the Georgian and Russian Orthodox churches, finally forced to serve the ends of the Soviet regime—continued to obstruct the attainment of Moscow's objectives.

The Muslims

Except for the Azerbaijanis and the Crimean Tatars, most of the Muslim peoples in the USSR lived in Central Asia and a contiguous wedge of territory bending northwest from it to Kazan. For the most part the Muslims were ethnically Turkic, and the Turkic peoples were Muslim, although there were a few exceptions: the Tajiks were Muslim but Iranian, the Chuvash (just west of Kazan) were Turkic but Christian. Some, such as the Kazakhs, were nomads, while others, like the Uzbeks, were settled peoples; some had rich and ancient traditions, such as the Tajiks, linked with the culture of Persia, while others had scarcely any written literature of their own. According to a recent scholarly appraisal, although some differentiation among the Turkic peoples could be discerned as early as the fifteenth century, individuals had next to no consciousness of being Kazakhs, Uzbeks, or whatever until the twentieth century; they identified themselves with clans or regions or simply as Muslim.[2] Most were united only in their devotion to Islam and use of Arabic script.

The assault on the old societies therefore started with an "alphabetic revolution," which was begun in Azerbaijan in 1925 and gained momentum after the Turkological Congress in Baku in 1926. It consisted of the replacement of Arabic script, sometimes overnight, by the Latin alphabet. The object was simultaneously to isolate the Muslims from their co-religionists south of Soviet borders and to undermine Islam, whose sacred and legal texts were all in Arabic script. In 1928 Mustafa Kemal also adopted Latin letters for Turkey, thereby undercutting the Soviet desire to prevent cultural intercourse. However, too much effort and expense had gone into the change-over for it to be replaced immediately by some other system, and the vital aim of secularization (which was also Kemal's) was still served by it.

After 1928 Islam was assaulted frontally, along with pan-Islamism, pan-Turkism, and local nationalisms. The Kazan Tatars resisted the new script especially strongly, and Mirza Sultan-Galiev, first prime minister of the Tatar ASSR, who had been arrested six years earlier, was tried for "nationalism" in 1929. About the same time the prime minister of the Crimean ASSR, several prominent Bashkirs, and other Turkic leaders were prosecuted for national deviation.

Simultaneously Stalin advanced to assault the basis of the old societies outright. Elsewhere in the USSR collectivization created great misery and starvation; in Central Asia it threatened to wipe out whole peoples. Until 1928 the old, in some places still tribal, life had scarcely been touched; now it was broken up. Clan leaders were wiped out, nomads were forcibly settled, and an effort was made to uproot Islam and all its institutions. According to Soviet admission, the Kazakh population decreased by almost a million and came for years to be outnumbered by Russians (as occurred in a number of other "national" units, usually more gradually) in the Kazakh SSR. The republic's livestock losses amounted to 73% of the cattle, 87% of the sheep, and 83% of the horses. In the settled area of Uzbekistan, Moscow demanded, as in Azerbaijan, that more cotton be grown, and the food supply accordingly fell off. The Soviet regime built a number of railways and canals (although they announced with much fanfare far more of both than they actually completed), and created much new industry. But the whole economy of Central Asia was disrupted, and the people were terrorized and bewildered.

Stalin had won a victory of sorts, but he rightly reckoned it as far from complete. In 1937 he conducted a thorough purge of national "deviationists" in Central Asia as elsewhere. Already at the end of the First Five-Year Plan, in Kazakhstan and Tajikistan, the chief Communists had been eliminated for failing to

---

[2] Cyril E. Black *et al.*, *The Modernization of Inner Asia*, M.E. Sharpe, Inc., 1991, p. 71.

execute the plan's directives successfully. Nevertheless their replacements were among those who were branded as "traitors" in 1937–1938. They included the Armenian leader of the Kazakh party C. I. Mirzoyan, Tajik prime minister Abdullah Rakhimbayev, Uzbek prime minister Faisulla Khodzhaev and party leader Akmal Ikramov, Turkmen president Nederby Aitakov, Kirgiz State Planning Commission member Abdukerim Sydykov and prime minister Yusup Abdurrakhmanov, and many others.

The Great Purges drove home the necessity of obeying Moscow's political and economic policies; now Stalin attempted once again to enforce his cultural policy through a second "alphabetic revolution." Only three years earlier it had been triumphantly announced that sixty-nine new alphabets had been constructed in Latin letters. However, in March 1938 Moscow issued a decree requiring that the Russian language be taught in all non-Russian schools. In order to make it more accessible by making Russian letters familiar, the regime threw out the new Latin alphabets for the indigenous languages (although the Balts and Finns were left their Latin letters, which they had always used) and replaced them by still newer alphabets in Cyrillic letters. The newest change was immensely costly, difficult, and repugnant to most of the peoples concerned. The Chuvash, Ossetians, and a few other small groups had used the Cyrillic alphabet before 1917, but even they must have regarded its restoration after a decade of Latinization as a mixed blessing. In some cases the second "alphabetic revolution" was not completed until after World War II. Its ultimate purpose, to isolate the borderlands from foreign influences (Central Asia being the chief area affected) and to draw them closer to the center, was not new. However, the behavior of Central Asian soldiers during the war and other developments made it clear that neither that nor the other objectives of Sovietization had been fully achieved.

The Jews and Other Minorities

There were somewhat fewer than 3 million Jews in the Soviet Union. The Russian Empire had generally restricted them to a Pale of Settlement in Ukraine and adjacent areas (large numbers also lived in Russian Poland), but by 1921 much of the old Pale was west of the Soviet border. Around 40% of the Jews who remained in the USSR left the former Pale area before 1939, many to enter the cities, some to take up agriculture.

Both Lenin and Stalin denied that there was a Jewish "nation," Stalin emphasizing that the reason for this was the absence of a large Jewish agricultural population. Nevertheless, at the time of the October Revolution the Jews received all the rights accorded other minorities, and indeed the Revolution was welcomed as an act of liberation by many Russian Jews, perhaps more enthusiastically than by any other national group. Jewish schools which taught Yiddish (the language of most Russian Jews) spread rapidly; a Jewish press sprang into existence, and by 1918, 81

Yiddish and 10 Hebrew newspapers were being published; a Jewish theater backed by the state flourished and produced such great figures as the actor Solomon Mikhoels; and Jewish Sections were organized in the Communist Party. To be sure all of the cultural growth had to be Communist in orientation, and the Judaic religion was attacked in the schools, but often by Jews themselves. Moreover, although popular anti-Semitism, strong in Russia as in other East European countries, persisted even among some non-Jewish Communists, during the 1920's the Soviet government combated it with vigor.

Jewish agricultural settlement was encouraged by Kalinin and others. In scattered areas of Ukraine and Belorussia Jewish farmers through their hard work gained acceptance by their peasant neighbors, who often were at first suspicious. In 1927 the distant and forbidding Far Eastern region of Birobidzhan was reconnoitered for possible Jewish colonization. Soon afterward immigrants began to move, and in 1934 a Jewish Autonomous Province was created there. However, it proved a failure; Jews remained in the minority in the province, and those who came stayed chiefly in the towns. However, Jewish Communist leaders expressed little concern about how well Jewish autonomism was faring. In 1926 one clearly placed "socialist reconstruction" ahead of "national self-preservation" and embraced the prospect of assimilation.[3]

During the middle 1930's the campaign against "national deviation" manifested itself in the beginnings of official anti-Semitism, cloaked in the concepts of Marxism-Leninism. The Judaic religion had always been anathematized along with all other religious faiths, but in addition ties with foreign Jews and Jewish culture, and Zionism in particular, were condemned as consorting with the "capitalist" enemy. The Jewish press collapsed, cultural life withered, and Birobidzhan virtually disappeared from official propaganda. In 1926 the Jewish Sections of the Communist Party had ceased to meet, and not long afterward they were disbanded. In 1937 Semën Dimanshtein, the party secretary of Birobidzhan, who had been Stalin's own assistant in the Nationalities Commissariat, and other prominent Jews fell in the purges.

Moscow's public policy of anti-Nazism, which attracted and misled many Jews abroad, was perhaps for a time some consolation to Soviet Jews. However, after the Nazi-Soviet Pact Stalin assumed a position of official neutrality toward Nazi ideology and prohibited attacks upon it. Thereby, as a prominent authority says, the regime "blinded Soviet Jews to the mortal danger threatening them"[4]; and in the early stages of Hitler's invasion the Nazis overran multitudes of Jews who were quite unprepared for their swift and gruesome fate.

There were other small national groups which Soviet nationality policy was able to turn to account. The Volga German ASSR, set up in 1924, boasting such towns as Marx and Engels, for years served as a show window for the Germans at

---

[3] Salo W. Baron, *The Russian Jew Under Tsars and Soviets*, 2d ed., Schocken Books, 1987, p. 179.

[4] Solomon M. Schwarz, *The Jews in the Soviet Union*, Syracuse U. Press, 1951, p. 310.

home. Although it met strong opposition here as elsewhere, collectivization in the ASSR was almost completed by 1931, ahead of any other district in the whole country. In 1937 "national deviation" brought about the purge of the prime minister, A. Welsch, and the president of the ASSR, but Soviet propaganda continued to sing the republic's praises. No one would have thought that the Volga Germans were fated for genocide a few years later.

Although before 1939 there were few Poles in the USSR, the Soviets found thirty Polish villages in a Volhynian marsh which they proclaimed a "Polish National District" in 1925 to attract support from across the western borders. Although the Baltic states were annexed only in 1940, Communists from there had risen high in the Soviet system, especially the Latvians Janis Rudzutak and Robert Eikhe, who reached the Politburo, and Robert Eideman, president of *Osoaviakhim*, the civil defense organization; all three were purged in 1937–1938. Whether a particular minority was large or small in number, whether it had many or few kinsmen beyond Soviet borders, whether it was organized in a republic or lesser administrative unit, its leaders met the same fate.

Stalin's policy toward the borderlands had its successes and failures. The destruction of the existing societies among the minorities, as among the Russians, was largely achieved. The prevailing institutional patterns were broken up and the religions and traditional cultures were wrecked or perverted to Soviet use. While formal acknowledgment of "statehood" for many minorities was made and proclaimed abroad, any kind of regional combination was broken up or prohibited (as in Transcaucasia and Central Asia), and while usually the minorities' own nationals were made figureheads in the republics, Moscow's trusted men, usually Russians, stood at their elbows in a totalitarian version of old-style colonialism. Local nationalisms were not wiped out, but they were silenced at great human sacrifice. Representatives of minority peoples were used as foreign agents abroad and authors of propaganda for foreign consumption with varying yet considerable success. Economic transformation was carried out with the utmost thoroughness (even reindeer hunting, as among the Samoyeds or Nentsy, was forcibly collectivized). The borderlands were exploited ruthlessly, if not efficiently, for the benefit of the center (Russian Communists turned the Pechora region, inhabited by the Komis, into a coal basin supplying Leningrad, and converted much of Bashkiria into an oil center which was called the "Second Baku").

The result was not the "new Soviet man" in the borderlands any more than in the Russian areas. Many of the minority peoples, faced with the dictation and brutality of Russian Communists, concluded that prerevolutionary Russian colonialism was back, only increased a hundredfold in severity. They failed to give much thought to what Stalin and his cohorts had done to Russian national traditions, institutions, and religion, and what they were doing to the Russian people. It was natural, for the minorities had seen horror to equal the worst that Oriental empires had been able to mete out for thousands of years past to the inhabitants of the vast area now known as the USSR.

17

Stalin's Diplomacy and World Communism 1927–1935

Stalin and the Rise of Hitler

At the end of 1927 ten years of Soviet foreign policy had seemed to produce a general fiasco. At that juncture Stalin's assumption of supreme power in the Soviet Union led to two significant developments in the USSR's international position: he secured Soviet (and at the same time his own) domination of the Comintern, and he reversed the previous "united front" line in attempting to spread Communist power.

Until 1927–1929, opposition was tolerated within the Comintern as within the Soviet Communist Party, although it was increasingly outnumbered and treated more and more roughly as the twenties wore on. In the Comintern, as in the Soviet Party, the Right Opposition was given two more years of grace than the Left Opposition. The chief Rightist, Bukharin, still appeared at the VI Congress of the Comintern in the summer of 1928 as Comintern president, and although he was already a helpless hostage of Stalin's, he was not removed from the post until 1929. At that time no new president was officially selected; Molotov formally took over the functions for a time, but Dmitry Manuilsky actually assumed the direction of Comintern affairs.

At the VI Congress the Comintern, under Stalin's direction, adopted the most uncompromising public position of the entire period of its existence under that name. The congress's resolution repeated the fantasy that the capitalists were preparing to attack the USSR, but interpreted this alleged fact as an effect of growing contradictions—that is, weakness—within the "imperialist" camp. The slogan "class against class" was proclaimed; in other words, an attack was to be launched on all forms of bourgeois political activity. Such forms were said to include social democracy and fascism, the former seeking to subvert the proletariat from within, the latter to destroy it from without. However, as suggested by the fact that Communist use of the phrase "Social Fascist" now was standard, the Social Democrats became the chief enemy.

By 1928 a declaration of war on all socialists could have little effect except in Germany. Most of the Communist parties of all other countries were still little larger than the tiny groups which had joined the Comintern at the time it was founded or had later been formed by Moscow agents (these were chiefly outside Europe). Only the German party was strong enough to have any independent influence on the course of events, and the abandonment of the "united front" policy left Germany as the only country outside the USSR in which Communist acts, as distinguished from words, could be expected to achieve anything without direct Soviet assistance.

In Germany the effects of the Great Depression were more serious than in any other industrial country. The ruin of much of the middle class, begun during the inflation of 1923, seemed on the verge of completion. For a younger generation looking for jobs and recognition, the prospects were bleak. As Bertolt Brecht, a gifted and embittered poet who became the Communists' chief artistic conquest in Germany, put it in the popular *Die Dreigroschenoper* (*The Threepenny Opera*) of the period, "Erst kommt das Fressen und dann die Moral" ("First a man must feed his face; right and wrong come later"). Profound cynicism and disillusionment were widespread.

The Weimar Republic was defended by the Social Democrats, the Catholic Center party, and the Liberals; it was attacked by the Communists and the Nazis. In May 1928 Reichstag elections had given the Nazis 13 seats, the Communists 54. The Social Democrats, the strongest single party, had many prominent members who wanted to make common cause with the Communists against any further gains by the Nazis, and they repeatedly made overtures to this end during the next few years.

However, the Communists were instead pursuing the anti-S.D. tactic of the VI Congress of the Comintern. In 1929–30 they joined the Nazis and other extreme Rightist groups in public attacks on the Young Plan for a reparations settlement, and on the S.D.'s for attempting better relations with the Western powers. In the September 1930 elections the Nazis obtained 105 seats in the Reichstag, while Communist strength increased only slightly, to 77. The Eleventh Plenum of the Comintern, in March–April 1931, labeled the Social Democrats as the most active party in Germany in preparing war on the USSR. When the Nazis and Nationalists demanded a referendum for removal of the Prussian government, which was a bulwark of the Republic's strength, the Communist leaders supported the campaign. The referendum took place, although the proposal failed. In July 1932 another Reichstag election was held, bringing the Nazis to 230 seats and the Communists to 89. A few months later the two parties co-operated in a big transport strike in Berlin. In November elections were held once more. This time Nazi strength fell to 196 seats, while the Communists won 100. The Communists redoubled their efforts to bring down the Republic.

In February 1933 the Social Democrats made a final effort to win over the Communists to an agreement to stop the Nazis. The German party leadership replied, "The Nazis must take power. Then in four weeks the whole working class will be united under the leadership of the Communist Party." Actually Hitler was appointed Chancellor on January 30, but he remained a minority prime minister. Not until another election in March 1933 gave the Nazis and Nationalists together a bare majority—in an election marked by widespread intimidation and fraud— did Hitler manage, after excluding the Communist deputies from voting, to get the Reichstag to abdicate its powers "for four years." He thereupon proceeded to construct the Nazi totalitarian state. The German Communists were among the first to feel the full force of Nazi terror, and the party was soon destroyed.

The Social Democrats, Trotsky, and others have blamed the Communists for the rise of Hitler, citing their refusal to ally with the Social Democrats as well as their open co-operation with the Nazis. A noted scholar writes that the Nazis and Communists "worked together in common cause against the republic." But more was involved; "the collapse of the Weimar Republic and the rise of National Socialism were two distinct but also related processes. The elite classes despaired of a republic they had never cared for and aligned themselves more and more with National Socialism on its triumphal march."[1] Whether or not the German Communists could have done something different, Moscow refused to urge or permit them to try. The two totalitarian parties recognized their own kinship in detesting liberal government and scorning the "bourgeois law" which sustained it—that is to say, the anti-S.D. tactic of the VI Congress found some solid basis on which to operate. However, the Communists failed to see that after the Republic was brought down, one of the two totalitarian parties would certainly try to destroy the other, and that if the Nazis took power, as the Communists explicitly predicted would happen, the Nazis might succeed in destroying them.

As late as April 1933 Eugene Varga, an authoritative Soviet spokesman, declared that the victory of Hitler was a hopeful sign, to be explained away as a result of the terror of the bourgeoisie at the rise of German Communism. The theme of the first Soviet reactions was that Hitler would be swept aside by "history." It was reminiscent of Radek's similar expectations for Pilsudski, who had seized power in Poland in 1926 with Communist support. Pilsudski was not Hitler, but the Communists' refusal to reckon with the possibility that Hitler could, as Pilsudski had done, remain in power and do what he wanted to do, was in both instances a combination of stupidity and a compulsion to justify the Comintern policy. Even as late as December 31, 1933, *Bolshevik,* the Russian Party's theoretical organ, de-

---

[1] Fritz Stern, *Dreams and Delusions: The Drama of German History,* Knopf, 1987, p. 159.

clared, "In Germany the proletarian revolution is nearer to realization than in any other country. ..."

To be sure, there were influential individuals in Germany (such as the geopolitician Haushofer and the philosopher-historian Spengler) who had no use for Communist ideology, but still thought in terms of a national German-Russian collaboration. However, the specious nature of Hitler's "nationalism" soon became as clear as that of Stalin's. The Nazis did—while destroying the German Communists—protest their desire for good relations with the Soviet Union as well as with all other countries, and in May 1933 they actually ratified a renewal (pending since 1931) of the 1926 neutrality treaty with the USSR. However, by the end of the year Moscow's spokesmen were compelled to refer publicly to the Nazis' continued use of the unequivocally anti-Soviet propaganda line of Hitler's *Mein Kampf,* and it seemed that they had at least perceived, without admitting, their mistake.

Litvinov and Soviet Diplomacy

In the late 1920's Foreign Minister Chicherin was ill, and his assistant, Maxim Litvinov, took over more and more of his duties, officially becoming foreign commissar in 1930. At the end of 1927 Litvinov had appeared at the deliberations regarding disarmament being conducted by the League of Nations (which the I Congress of the Comintern had termed a "Holy Alliance of the bourgeoisie for the suppression of the proletarian revolution," and there was no indication of an official change of view since 1919). Litvinov presented to the League a draft convention for immediate disarmament, making clear as he did so that the objective was not to limit weapons. Certain statesmen had argued that disarmament could not be risked because the USSR would refuse to take part. Litvinov wished, by undermining this excuse, to prove that the "bourgeois" powers did not take disarmament seriously. Two years later the Soviet Union offered to take part in pan-Europe discussions, again not out of any interest in the ostensible aims of the European Commission, but, as Moscow declared, "By taking part ... the Soviet Union will wreck the plans of the leaders of the Commission, plans for the secret elaboration of anti-Soviet projects."

When the Kellogg-Briand Pact for the renunciation of war as an instrument of national policy was proposed by the American and French foreign secretaries, the Soviet Union undertook to utilize it for its own purposes by means of the Litvinov Protocol, signed in Moscow in February 1929. The effect of the protocol was to bring the pact into operation on a regional basis without awaiting all the ratifications to the pact itself. The USSR signed along with Poland, Romania, Latvia, and Estonia, and within a few months Lithuania, Turkey, Persia, and the Free City of Danzig had added their signatures. The protocol continued the pattern established by the 1926 treaty with Germany and the Middle Eastern pacts of the same period. Another wave of comparable agreements came with the signature of non-aggression treaties with Poland, the Baltic states, Finland, and France in 1932. Only with Romania did negotiations founder, as they had repeatedly done before, on the question of Bessarabia, whose annexation by Romania the Soviets refused to recognize.

However, none of this apparently peace-loving activity was intended to alter the basic lines of Soviet foreign policy. Under Stalin as well as Lenin it remained based on the effort to mobilize the anti-Versailles powers against Britain and France in the European balance, without assuming either that eternal friendship was possible with the one group of powers or that armed hostilities were inevitable with the other. (Thus there was even a rationale for agreement with Hitler, who was in any case regarded as merely another "bourgeois" leader.) The public trials of the First Five-Year Plan period, which involved accusations of complicity with Britain and France in anti-Soviet activity, served to underline this policy. In October 1929 the USSR resumed relations with Britain as a result of MacDonald's and Labor's return to power, but no dramatic change in Anglo-Soviet relations ensued.

At the end of 1933 there occurred a diplomatic development which in itself brought no shift in Soviet policy, but which was both dramatic and, once the Soviet about-face of 1934–1935 had taken place, significant in its results. This was United States recognition of the Soviet Union. Among the obstacles to the establishment of relations had been American resentment at Soviet debt repudiation and confiscation, but the chief deterrent to recognition, in the view of Secretaries of State Hughes, Kellogg, and Stimson, was Communist propaganda inside America. American commercial and other contacts—the American Relief Administration effort under Herbert Hoover during the famine of 1921–1922 being the most important—proceeded despite the absence of diplomatic relations (a precedent not always remembered during later discussions about the advisability of recognizing Communist China). None of the other American states except Mexico and Uruguay had recognized the USSR, and Mexico had broken relations in 1930, but it was plain that many Latin American governments would follow the U.S. lead if Washington decided on recognition.

It was during the World Economic Conference, held in London in the summer of 1933, which otherwise had negligible results, that contacts were made between Soviet and American representatives which led to recognition. William C. Bullitt, Wilson's envoy of 1919, talked to Litvinov in London and visited the Soviet Union a few weeks later. Finally in November Litvinov himself came to Washington in response to President Roosevelt's invitation to the Soviet Government. In the same month diplomatic relations were established between the U.S. and the Soviet Union, each nation pledging to abstain from hostile propaganda against the other. The USSR acknowledged the religious and legal rights of Americans in the country and waived all claims originating with U.S. intervention in Siberia, thus underlining the factor which they indicated as their chief motive for seeking U.S.

recognition, namely, fear of Japan in the Pacific. Bullitt went to Moscow as ambassador. However, although a trade agreement was concluded in 1935, debt negotiations foundered, and soon Bullitt himself became soured on his post as well as on the Soviet Union in general, for which he had felt a good deal of sympathy.

East Asian Weakness

In East Asia there was real ground for Soviet concern. Before the Japanese attack on Manchuria in 1931, Britain was regarded, there as elsewhere, as the chief enemy. Stalin even suggested that the Japanese might fight alongside Britain in a possible conflict with the United States. It does not seem that the Soviet leaders felt any serious concern about a British "threat" to them in East Asia, although they had counted (in vain) on doing the British harm through their partnership with the Kuomintang in China.

The weakness of the Soviet position in East Asia was partly the result of the failure in China in 1927. The chief asset Moscow retained was the Chinese Eastern Railway through Manchuria. In May 1929, however, Marshal Chang Hsüeh-liang, the *de facto* ruler of Manchuria under nominal Nationalist suzerainty, seized the railway and expelled the Soviet personnel. In July Soviet-Chinese diplomatic relations were officially severed. In November General Bliukher, lately Soviet adviser to the Kuomintang armies, led a military expedition against Chang and repossessed the railway.

However, in September 1931 the situation was completely upset again by the Japanese invasion of Manchuria. The Japanese soon overran the area of the railway as well as the whole province, establishing a puppet regime calling itself the "Government of Manchukuo." The League of Nations debated the question of Japanese aggression at length, but did nothing. The Soviets could not hope to succeed with the tactic of outright attack used on Chang Hsüeh-liang, at least not without courting full-scale war with Japan. Therefore Moscow blustered a good deal but accepted negotiations for sale of the railway to the Japanese. By an agreement finally reached in March 1935 it was sold, and cheaply at that. The Soviets did not discount the Japanese danger, however, and in December 1932, not long after the invasion of Manchuria, they reestablished relations with China.

Of course, neither Moscow nor the Chinese Communists gave up their hostility toward the government of Chiang Kai-shek, who had broken the alliance with the Soviets, nor did Chiang give up his war on the Chinese Communists. Beginning in November 1930 he launched a series of "extermination campaigns" against them, the fourth and last coming to an end in October 1933. After the debacle of 1927, the first Chinese Communist leader, Ch'en Tu-hsiu, was made the scapegoat and replaced by Li Li-san, who was himself purged and recalled to Moscow in 1930.

In the meantime a new leader, Mao Zedong, a former librarian who came from a Hunan peasant family, made his appearance. Sent in 1927 to investigate a peasant revolt in his home province, he returned to Peiping placing much stock in the peasants' role for the future. They were to serve as a mass army for what he called the "national" revolution—that combination of "anti-imperialist" and "anti-feudal" insurrections which would, in Marxist terms, bring about the completion of the "bourgeois" phase and make possible a transition to the "proletarian" one. This was a thoroughly Leninist and Stalinist position, presented with generous invocations of Communist scripture. Mao's reaction to the Hunan riots is reminiscent of Lenin's reaction to the Ukrainian peasant disturbances of 1902.

What was new in the Chinese Communist movement after 1927 was neither some kind of organizational split from Moscow nor any sudden theoretical discovery of the peasantry; it was the disappearance of the urban movement with which the Communists had made a good deal of headway in the mid-1920's. However, the doctrine that the immediate goal was a "democratic dictatorship of proletariat and peasantry" (in Lenin's phrase)[2] or a "people's democratic dictatorship" (Mao's term) remained unchanged even when the Chinese proletariat—in any case small in number—vanished from Communist reach, as it had remained in force when, to facilitate the tactic of co-operation with the Kuomintang, Communist leaders publicly disavowed the utility of peasant uprising.

In the autumn of 1927, following the break with Chiang, Mao was commissioned to organize peasant risings in Hunan. However, he failed to do so and was penalized by dismissal from the Politburo of the Chinese Communist Party. He retreated eastward toward Jiangxi province and in the spring of 1928 was joined there by Zhu De, along with a group of Communist officers who had been trained at the Whampoa academy. Mao assumed political and Zhu De military leadership, and in November 1931 the two together proclaimed a "Chinese Soviet Republic" in Jiangxi. By that time Moscow had purged Li Li-san and replaced him with Mao as party leader. It was this southern nest of Communists which Chiang from 1930 to 1933 tried in vain to dig out, foiled by the guerrilla warfare so skillfully carried on by Zhu De's troops.

Although the Jiangxi regime "declared war" on the Japanese in 1932 in order to exploit national feeling against the invasion of Manchuria, Mao and Zhu De continued to follow the current Comintern policy of refusing to co-operate with "bourgeois" groups. In November 1933 a group of dissident Nationalists seized parts of Fujian province and called for a common front with Mao's Communists, but Mao did not respond and allowed Chiang to suppress the revolt without trying to interfere.

Chiang's pressure was not enough to crush the Chinese Communists, but by 1934 it led them to evacuate their Jiangxi base. In October of that year Mao and Zhu De led over ninety thousand men on the well-known "Long March," a six-thousand-mile movement west and north to Yenan in Shenxi province. In Octo-

---

[2] The phrase was also used in the 1931 Constitution of the Chinese Soviet Republic, headed by Mao.

ber 1935 a remnant of twenty thousand arrived there and established a new base. Here the Communists found themselves close to their Soviet mentors, with their backs to Soviet-controlled Mongolia, west of which lay the nominally Chinese but strongly Soviet-infiltrated province of Xinjiang.

It appears that Chiang Kai-shek regarded Mao's new location as an advantage to his own government. He hoped that the force could be driven to cross over into Soviet territory and thus that his troops might be spared further efforts to cope with the Communist guerrilla tactics used in Jiangxi. But neither Mao nor Stalin was inclined to oblige Chiang by abolishing the Chinese Communist army, government, or party. They had important and immediate tasks to perform. While the Long March was under way, the Comintern line had shifted sharply. In the summer of 1935 the Chinese Communists had halted en route northward to hold a conference in Sichuan in order to repeat the changed policy for Chinese consumption, and to call for a united national effort against the Japanese. In Europe the new tactic was called the "Popular Front."

The Policy Shift in France

Since the Communists declared that Nazism was merely an alternative type of capitalist regime, and since Soviet preference for close relations with Germany had been based on opposition to Britain and France, not fondness for the Weimar Republic, its fall was unlamented in Moscow. The destruction of the German Communist party was a blow; Litvinov declared, "We of course sympathize with the sufferings of our German comrades, but," he added, "we Marxists are the last who can be reproached with allowing our feelings to dictate our policy."

Certain early Nazi statements indicated that they were willing not to hold the German Communists, whom they were busy executing, against the Soviet regime. Actually a certain amount of the co-operation that was begun during the Weimar period carried over for a time into the Nazi era. In 1934 Germany took a considerably larger slice of Soviet exports than in 1933, and her imports from the USSR did not fall sharply until 1936, while Soviet imports from Germany were still considerable in 1937. The collaboration between the German and Red armies continued into 1935.

However, in December 1933 Litvinov publicly distinguished between capitalist states on the basis of their foreign policy. There were, said he, "actively aggressive," "passively indifferent," and "actively co-operative" bourgeois powers. He left no doubt that the Soviet regime had become concerned about the likelihood of Nazi aggression eastward. Finally, in February 1934 came an abrupt about-face by the French Communist party which was the harbinger of a worldwide shift in Soviet policy.

On February 6, in the wake of the Stavisky financial scandal, the Communists in Paris co-operated openly with the French extreme Right—as the German

Communists had done with the Nazis—in a successful riot before the Chamber of Deputies designed to overthrow Daladier's Socialist-Radical[3] government. However, only six days later the Communists threw in their lot with the socialist trade-unions to lead a big strike directed against the Right. Lest the wrong conclusions be drawn, the French Communist chieftain, Maurice Thorez, warned in the party organ, *Humanité,* in April, that "all gossip about a marriage between Communists and Socialists is fundamentally alien to the spirit of Bolshevism." However, before the end of the month he was summoned to Moscow, and he returned with new instructions. Without any apparent embarrassment he now called for the very "marriage" he had scorned a few weeks earlier. The French Socialists, who had just lost much of their right wing in an interparty battle, accepted with alacrity. In July a pact, providing among other things for mutual abjuration of criticism, was signed between the two parties. This was the first "Popular Front" agreement. In November Thorez proposed the formation of a Popular Front government; this offer the Socialists received with some wariness. However, parallel diplomatic developments forced their hand.

In May 1934 Litvinov and J. L. Barthou of France met in Geneva. Already proposals for a Franco-Soviet mutual assistance pact were being considered, and at the May meeting Barthou suggested that the USSR also enter the League of Nations. At first the two diplomats tried to construct a broad security-treaty network which would include most of the East European countries. However, Poland and other nations were reluctant, and so a simple Franco-Soviet Pact was decided upon. Signed in May 1935, it provided for mutual "aid and assistance" in case of unprovoked attack by a third power. In the same month a Czechoslovak-Soviet Pact was concluded, providing for mutual assistance only in the event that France aided the country attacked. It is uncertain which country was responsible for inserting this provision, but it had uses for both sides.

On May 16, 1935, the French press published a declaration by Stalin giving unreserved support to "the policy of national defense followed by France so as to maintain her armed forces on the level necessary to maintain security." In late May and June, on the heels of the agreement with the Socialists and the Communist defensive stand taken with Moscow's express sanction, the French Communists scored heavy gains in local elections.

By now Thorez was extending the hand of co-operation not only to the Socialists, but also to the Socialist-Radicals, puzzling and alarming many Socialists whose ideology remained genuinely leftist. On Bastille Day (July 14), 1935, Thorez, Leon Blum (the Socialist leader), and Edouard Daladier (Socialist-Radical) marched side by side at the head of the parade in Paris—the first time since 1889

---

[3] This party is often called "Radical Socialist" in English, but since in French the modifier follows the substantive, this is a mistranslation; even the accurate rendition misrepresents the real character of the party, but not as grossly.

that the French Socialists had celebrated the bourgeois national holiday; but the presence of the Communists seemed even more astounding. It appeared to many that the French (and therefore all other) Communists had abandoned revolutionism in favor of the defense of the USSR against the threat of Hitler and the support of any other government which was disposed to resist the Nazis.

The VII Congress of the Comintern

The French united-front agreement, by now an obvious success, may be considered the test run for the policy newly adopted by the VII (and last) Congress of the Comintern, held in Moscow in July and August 1935. There was proclaimed the policy of the Popular Front, wherein the Communists expressed willingness to co-operate, not merely with the "masses" in spite of and against the "reformist" leaders whom they might be following, as in the 1920's, but also with the leaders of any group, socialist or rightist, which took a line of resistance to the Nazis or to the Japanese militarists who had taken control in Tokyo.

The Popular Front tactic was linked to the Bulgarian George Dimitrov, who had attracted worldwide attention by his outspoken conduct in the Reichstag fire trial of 1933; he became general secretary of the Comintern at the congress. However, there was no pretense that personalities or factions were at odds in the change of policy; the VII Congress was, as Max Beloff points out, "the first Congress at which a complete display of unanimity was achieved"[4]—put another way, complete subservience to Stalin. Stalin had reversed himself; he had simultaneously recognized the bankruptcy of the "go-it-alone" tactic of 1928–1934, the danger from the new factor introduced into German and European politics by Nazism (whose "newness" Moscow had previously denied), and the gains which might be made by a call to resist "war and Fascism."

It remains obscure whether Stalin ever had any serious intention of collaborating with Britain and France against Hitler, or whether he ever gave up hope (before 1939) that collaboration with Hitler could be arranged. The defected Soviet intelligence chief for Western Europe, General Krivitsky, declared that Stalin never took the Popular Front seriously nor used it as anything but a bargaining counter in the game with Hitler. In any case it is clear that as the anti-Versailles diplomacy of the pre-1934 period reflected no fondness for the Weimar Republic, so the pro-Versailles policy adopted in 1934 was not based on any love for bourgeois France or Britain. The Soviet chose between groups of "capitalist" powers not on the basis of ideological compatibility—none were compatible—but from considerations of power.

---

[4] *The Foreign Policy of Soviet Russia, 1929–1941*, 2 vols.; London: Oxford U. Press, 1947–1949, I:190.

However, it appears that Stalin miscalculated the relative strengths of Hitler on the one hand and the British and French on the other, and that he did not fully grasp Hitler's inflexible hostility to the USSR and his designs on Soviet territory. During the period of the Popular Front, there were indications that Stalin expected nothing from a tie with the English and French; however, there were also moves apparently inexplicable on any other ground but Stalin's desire to create or strengthen such alliances. Probably the truth is that the Popular Front offered an opportunity to the Soviets to gain much foreign popularity and influence at slight cost, whatever the progress of a diplomatic alignment with the West, while Moscow's public pronouncements during the period had the effect of leading many to justify Stalin's domestic brutalities as made necessary by the Nazi danger. Thus although few actual Popular Front agreements or governments came into existence, and none provided a direct bridge to Communist power, the psychological effects of the policy were far-reaching, and Stalin may well have reckoned it an over-all success. Perhaps even he did not look for the effects to be so immediate; in fact, the virulent anti-socialist and anti-liberal campaigns led by Moscow during the previous six years were rapidly forgotten by many of the persons and groups Stalin sought to influence most.

At the VII Congress, the then obscure Wilhelm Pieck (later president of the East German Communist state) gave the opening report, castigating foreign Communists for a "mechanical" interpretation of the 1928 resolutions which led them to scent fascism where it was not and fail to recognize it where it was. Pieck also denounced the "sectarian" views of those who did not defend the "remnants of bourgeois democracy" against war and fascism. Dimitrov discussed the new Popular Front tactic, making clear that the aim of the Communists remained to assure their own pre-eminent leadership over the "masses," but calling for more agreements with non-Communist parties along French lines.

Thorez explained the success the Popular Front had already gained in France, and spoke in reverent terms of the French Encyclopedists and the *Marseillaise*, as did Earl Browder of the American Revolution and the Civil War. Dimitrov concluded that "*national forms* of the proletarian class struggle" furnished the proper means through which the "*international interests* of the proletariat can be successfully defended." However, Palmiro Togliatti, leader of the Italian Communists, explained that even capitalist powers which had signed pacts with the USSR had not come to terms with their own working class; thereby he made it plain that neither bourgeois France nor any other non-Soviet power could enjoy more than conditional support from the Communists. However, the fine print largely escaped the serious attention of the reformist leaders with whom the Communists proclaimed a desire for alliance, and Communism was launched into the period of its greatest international popularity.

18

Stalin's Diplomacy
and World Communism
1936–1941

The Popular Front Government in France

Following the VII Congress of the Comintern, the French Communists, exploiting their earlier successes, managed to create the first Popular Front government. In the May 1936 elections the Communist vote almost doubled and for the first time passed the million mark. Although the Socialists made virtually no gains, their leader, Léon Blum, was designated premier in June. The Communists supported his ministry, on the condition that he carry out the Popular Front program, but they refused to enter it. At the moment Blum was taking office a wave of "sitdown strikes" (then a novel weapon) under genuinely revolutionary leadership broke out, and the Communists aided his government by helping to force the end of the strikes.

The course of the French Popular Front government was stormy. Unending squabbles raged between Communists and Socialists, full of accusation and recrimination. They fought over domestic issues, over French policy toward the Spanish Civil War just beginning, over the Great Purges in the USSR, which the Socialists denounced. Although the Communists had helped Blum into power, they embarrassed his government by leading successive waves of strikes and contributing to a series of financial crises which brought about his fall in June 1937.

The heritage of the first Popular Front government was a forty-hour week (which under existing conditions barred any effective French rearmament), industrial chaos, and political bitterness. A coalition of Socialists and Socialist-Radicals continued in power with the Socialist Radical Camille Chautemps as premier. Thorez repeated the same sort of pledge of support he had given Blum; however, in December the Communists led further strikes, while another financial crisis was impending. Chautemps's cabinet fell in March 1938. Next came the brief tenure of a second Blum government, more Communist-led strikes, and again the fall of the cabinet, followed by a Socialist-Radical ministry under Edouard Daladier. After helping him into power, the Communists soon attacked him as they had his predecessors. By the summer of 1938 the Popular Front in France was at an end.

At the time of the Munich Agreement in the fall the French Communists were again paralyzing rearmament efforts through strikes. However, in November Daladier finally used the army to recapture seized plants. The united *Confédération Générale du Travail,* formed two years earlier by amalgamation of the Socialist and Communist trade unions, suffered a great loss of membership. Once again the French Communist party was deprived of any important influence in the country, but it was France as a whole which suffered most from the turmoil of these years.

Popular Front and Civil War in Spain

Two Popular Front governments were formed outside France: in Spain and Chile (in a few other cases, Communist support was of marginal significance). In both France and Spain, international issues vital to the USSR were at stake, but in Spain these issues became entangled in the large-scale fighting of the Civil War, the European dress rehearsal for World War II.

In 1930 Spain was a country in many ways socially more backward than Russia in 1917. The Roman Catholic Church had a cultural monopoly and economic power greater than the Russian Orthodox Church had had; the peasantry was much more downtrodden; the economic stagnation of the whole country contrasted with the growth of the economy under Nicholas II. The Spanish monarchy had collapsed not long after the seven-year dictatorship of Primo de Rivera, and a republic had been proclaimed in 1931, but national unity was lacking. There was strong autonomist feeling in the Basque northwest and the Catalan northeast; there were large and fanatical groups of anarchists, especially in Catalonia, socialists with much strength among the Madrid workers, a tiny Trotskyite group called P.O.U.M. (*Partido Obrero de Unificacíon Marxista*), and an even tinier Spanish Communist party (in March 1936 its strength was estimated at only three thousand).

Elections in November 1933 had installed a Rightist regime, against which bloody but unsuccessful revolts were raised in October 1934 by the Asturias miners and the Barcelona workers. Shortly afterward the forces of the political Left reached a Popular Front agreement, intended to avert a Spanish fascism. The participants were two Republican groups, the Catalan Left (*Esquerra*), Socialists, and Communists. Even the anarchists supported the Popular Front list, which in the February 1936 elections won a big majority of deputies in the Cortes, though by a narrow margin of the popular vote. The Republican regime which thereupon took power was faced in July by an army revolt started in Spanish Morocco by General Francisco Franco and others. The Republican leaders wavered as to how to meet it, but some army units remained loyal, others were hastily assembled by various Leftist parties, and in Catalonia and eastern Spain the revolt was crushed. However, the rebels captured most of the west.

Stalin thereupon faced a grave dilemma. Soviet military intervention in Spain might frighten the British and French into making a compact with the Nazis, thus confronting the USSR with a formidable bloc of "capitalist" powers, or, if one is to credit such assertions as Krivitsky's, that Stalin's unchanging aim throughout this period was to reach agreement with Hitler, Soviet intervention might imperil the possibility of doing so. On the other hand, if the Spanish Republic were to be quickly crushed, Soviet prestige would be damaged and the infant Popular Front policy might be wrecked.

According to General Krivitsky, the Soviet Politburo decided on August 28, 1936, in favor of intervention in Spain. The USSR would send arms aid; it would also support the Spanish Communists in assuming a more prominent role in the government (indeed, the Russians soon took over a large share of that task themselves). The Communists declared that resistance to Franco should not be confused with social revolution, and called for order and defense of the Republic, thus attracting the favorable notice of the more conservative Republicans. In Catalonia the Communists had increased their strength slightly by amalgamating with local socialists in the P.S.U.C. (*Partido socialista unificado Catalan*), which they controlled, and the unified party entered the autonomous Catalan government. In September the Socialist, Francisco Largo Caballero, formed a national Popular Front government into which went two Communists, Uribe and Hernandez. This was not enough for Moscow; in the same month the NKVD set up a Spanish section, entrusted by the Politburo with control over all Communist activity in Spain. Within a few months the NKVD was carrying out its own arrests and executions on Spanish soil—not of Franco's agents, but of the Trotskyites of the P.O.U.M., anarchists, and socialists, especially in the army.

The Spanish Republic had hoped for Western, particularly French, aid. Stalin also hoped such aid would be forthcoming, as it would spare the Soviets the embarrassment of acting alone and would also commit Britain and France against the Axis. The French Communists from the start demanded Western intervention. However, Britain and France invoked a policy of "nonintervention" to secure peace in Europe and clung to it although Germany and Italy, which also belonged to the nonintervention committee, almost at once sent air and ground forces into action on Franco's side. The Spanish Republic had to accept Soviet aid or go under, and it chose to accept. Some of its leaders recognized the attendant dangers, but were powerless to counter them, while others discounted them altogether.

Once Communist power obtained a foothold in Spain, Soviet armed aid was forthcoming. By November 1936 the International Brigade, recruited first from foreign Communist refugees in Russia and supplemented by genuine volunteers from Western Europe and the U.S., was sent into the line just in time to save Madrid. The same month much of the Spanish gold reserve was sent to the USSR to clinch the bargain. Largo Caballero's war minister, Julio Alvarez del Vayo, accepted the introduction throughout the army of political commissars, who were Communists almost to a man.

By the beginning of 1937 the Communists were ready to provoke a crisis to enforce their demands for centralization, discipline, and no quarter for revolutionism. They chose Catalonia to make a stand, since it was least threatened by the rebel advance and also was the stronghold of anarchism and revolutionary extremism in Spain. The Communists armed the P.S.U.C., and their demands were supported by Indalecio Prieto and Juan Negrín (two Socialist ministers), other Right Socialists, and the Republicans. However, Prime Minister Largo Caballero and his Left Socialists supported the opposing Catalan anarchist union, the C.N.T. (*Confederación Nacional del Trabajo*). When street fighting between the P.S.U.C. and the C.N.T. broke out in Barcelona in May 1937, Largo Caballero hesitated, but finally suppressed the Trotskyite P.O.U.M. as a concession to the Communists and their more conservative allies. Nevertheless he was still forced out of office.

The Communists had gained a good deal. Juan Negrín, a Right Socialist, took office, and Prieto became war minister. While Prieto believed in the necessity of discipline and postponement of social changes, he tried to resist Communist efforts to establish themselves in the decisive organs of control, especially in the army; he was forced out of the war ministry in April 1938. That spring Franco's army reached the eastern coast south of Barcelona and cut off Catalonia from the rest of republican Spain. By this time many of the chief Soviet agents in Spain, including Antonov-Ovseenko (the hero of the storming of the Winter Palace in the October Revolution), General Kléber (Stern) of the International Brigade, and others, had been recalled to Moscow and purged. Nevertheless it was after Prieto's resignation, under the clique of Negrín, del Vayo, and Uribe, that the Communists reached the highest point of their influence. They controlled almost the entire army through the commissars, they ran the government propaganda department and the new Spanish political police (although the NKVD was much more powerful, more active, and more efficient in exterminating the Communists' enemies of the Left). For a time after Prieto resigned, President Manuel Azaña resisted the Communists, but he was silenced by Negrín.

For a few months the Communists were in firm control of the remnant of republican Spain. However, Stalin had plainly decided to end Soviet intervention, and in November 1938 he withdrew the International Brigades and ended arms shipments. In February 1939 Franco took Barcelona. During the last months of the Civil War the military command in Madrid and the Right Socialists joined to send the Communists packing and attempted in vain a negotiated peace with Franco. In March 1939 Madrid surrendered, and Franco mercilessly punished the former defenders of the Republic. The Spanish Communist leaders escaped to Moscow, where Stalin promptly decimated them. The foremost figures were executed or sent to concentration camps, with the connivance of the renowned "La Pasionaria" (Dolores Ibarruri). She emerged as the new Spanish Communist leader, but she had virtually no followers left, either in Spain or the USSR.

It is difficult to say whether Stalin achieved his aims in Spain or not. Certainly Soviet intervention against Franco did not prevent Hitler, who made Franco's victory possible, from signing a pact with Stalin. The Soviets' conduct in Spain, above all their ruthlessness against their fellow defenders of the Republic, alarmed many in the West, but Stalin must have counted that a loss only if he still (or ever) hoped for a real agreement with Britain and France. Stalin had delayed Franco's victory until the uses of the Popular Front were near an end, and his agents had gained experience in warfare and in successful political infiltration which was to be useful in the future.

As Borkenau points out, a number of foreign Communist parties emerged from the Spanish events with a sort of double leadership, one set having had experience in Spain and another having spent much time in Moscow.[1] He might also have pointed out that in each case the Moscow-trained man won out over his rival—Ulbricht over Dahlem in Germany, Togliatti over Longo in Italy, Tito over Gorkič in Yugoslavia, Rákosi over Rajk in Hungary. Although the foremost Soviet agents in Spain were purged, it is not clear that the reason lay in the course of events there; most of the victims of the Great Purges had no connection with Spain, including many prominent foreign Communists living in the USSR. (Among them were Hungary's Béla Kun, Germany's Heinz Neumann and Hugo Eberlein, and virtually the whole leadership of the Polish Communist party, which was soon afterwards formally dissolved. It is ironic that many Communists from democratic countries escaped because the Soviets were then concerned not to provoke their governments, which might well have intervened to protect their citizens despite the latter's commitment to overthrow them.)

Outside of France and Spain, no Popular Front governments were formed in Europe. However, Popular Front party agreements won the Communists increased influence in Yugoslavia, Czechoslovakia, and elsewhere. Even more significant, Soviet prestige and Communist popularity reached a peak in the United States, Britain, Scandinavia, Poland, and other countries, embracing many people unaffiliated with the Communist or even any other political party.

Popular Front in China and War with Japan

The Popular Front policy was formulated in opposition to both German Nazism and Japanese militarism. Accordingly its effects were also important in Asia, perhaps as important as those in Europe. It restored Chinese Communism to a level of strength it seemed to have lost permanently and set Mao Zedong on the road to

---

[1] Franz Borkenau, *European Communism*, Harper, 1953, p. 173.

power, and it gave Communism increased influence among the intellectuals of other Asian countries, especially India, Japan, and Indonesia.

The new policy had been proclaimed in Moscow while the Chinese Communists were engaged in the Long March northward. Their call while still en route in the summer of 1935 for "all classes" to fight Japan evoked no immediate response. However, shortly after Mao's columns reached Yanan, there were demonstrations by the Peiping students under patriotic and anti-Japanese slogans, and the spread of militant nationalist feeling was utilized by the Communists in their agitation for a Popular Front.

Developments in Japan warranted the concern which was felt by growing numbers of Chinese. After a period of party government in the 1920's, during which business interests and the bureaucracy helped restrain the armed forces, the army had launched a bid for power. The conquest of Manchuria in 1931 in effect gave the army a province to rule as its own and greatly strengthened its domestic prestige. During 1935 the Japanese military entered into closer contacts with the Nazis, who shared their scorn for politicians and businessmen. In February 1936 the army carried out a *coup d'état* in Tokyo which led to a cabinet which was virtually controlled by the new war minister, General Terauchi. Although the cabinet lasted less than a year, the military dominance remained through World War II, and the political parties were deprived of any important influence. The tiny Japanese Communist party under Sanzo Nozaka was repressed more severely than ever; its nucleus found refuge with Mao in Yanan by 1943, as did the leading Korean Communists.

In August 1936 the Chinese Communists repeated their offer to Chiang Kai-shek of a united-front agreement. The signing of the Anti-Comintern Pact between Japan and Germany in November, in which Communism was named as the ostensible enemy at a time when Japanese forces were actually attacking non-Communist Chinese areas, helped to suggest that all Chinese must resist Japan together. By this time the Japanese had marched south from Manchuria to occupy much of North China. However, while Chiang was ordering Marshal Chang Hsüeh-liang to attack the Communists at Yanan, he was still engaged in negotiations with the Japanese. In December Chiang flew to Xian to try to enforce his orders to Chang. Instead a curious incident occurred; he was "kidnapped" (that is, detained) by Chang's forces, who were already affected by Popular Front agitation. The Communists were instrumental in arranging for Chiang's release at the price of his accepting co-operation with them and agreeing to lead a united struggle against Japan. Chiang flew back to Nanking amid public rejoicing. In February 1937 the Chinese Communist party and the Nationalist government exchanged messages indicating a general line of agreement.

In July the Japanese attack on the Marco Polo bridge near Peiping launched the eight-year undeclared Sino-Japanese war. A month later, the USSR signed a non-aggression pact with Chiang Kai-shek's government. The Soviets promptly began to send in arms aid through Sinkiang which continued until Hitler invaded the USSR in 1941, meanwhile using the opportunity to strengthen their control over that nominally Chinese province. The League of Nations again discussed Japanese aggression with no result, but in June 1938 Litvinov spoke publicly of the Japanese as aggressors with designs on the USSR. Chiang dismissed the German advisers whom he had been using, and again Soviet advisers came to China. Soviet-Chinese co-operation was also marked by a trade treaty, signed in June 1939.

The Japanese were watching Soviet-Chinese relations closely. In June 1937 there was a skirmish with Soviet forces on the Amur River, which separated the Japanese puppet state of Manchukuo and the USSR. In July 1938 the hill of Changkufeng, near the Soviet-Manchurian-Korean border, was the scene of fighting, and in May 1939 at Nomonhan, near the border between Outer Mongolia and Manchuria, the most serious of such incidents occurred. Each side seemed to be testing the other's determination and military efficiency. While plainly neither was at that time disposed to engage in all out war, there was a sort of mutual notice of preparedness should a real conflict break out later.

Nationalists and Communists

Two months after the Japanese war began, the Chinese Communist party announced the formal abolition of the Chinese Soviet Government and the Chinese Red Army, and the acceptance of Sun Yat-sen's Three People's Principles (nationalism, democracy, and livelihood) as China's most important current need. After 1937 the party ceased land confiscation and other revolutionary actions. The Communists began to enforce the moribund Nationalist 37 1/2% maximum rent law in the rural areas which they controlled, especially in such border regions as that of Hebei-Chahar-Shanxi, in the vicinity of Peiping and nominally controlled by the Japanese, and thereby won the support of many peasants. The tactic was reminiscent of Lenin's adoption after the October Revolution of the land program of the Russian SR's, who had shared power for months previously without enacting it themselves. However, its employment no more converted the Chinese Communists into Nationalists (or "agrarian reformers") than Lenin's action had made him an SR.

The theoretical implications of the Communist policy were explained by Mao in his work, written in 1939 and published the following year, entitled *On the New Democracy*. Using the conceptual framework of the Russian Communists, Mao declared that China had been a feudal society[2] which had become a semi-colony

---

[2] This was not the view held by Marx or many early Russian Communists, but it was Stalin's. Marx spoke of China as possessing an "Asiatic mode of production," characterized by an all-powerful centralized despotism in which a bureaucracy ruled over a mass of scattered peasant producers. In his *Short Course* in the history of the Soviet Communist Party in 1939, Stalin omitted any reference to this Marxist category from his discussion of historical materialism. The concept remained a *malum prohibitum* in the USSR; it might all too easily be converted into a weapon against the Soviet bureaucracy itself. See page 34.

of the Western imperialist powers. The first stage of revolution must then combine the overthrow of the power of "feudal" landlords with destruction of the Western imperialist influence and those Chinese elements associated with it. In this "bourgeois-democratic" stage, the peasantry would furnish the main force, but the leadership would come from the "proletariat" (that is, the Communist party). This stage would merge directly into the "socialist revolution," but until that time leadership would be assumed by a "joint dictatorship of all revolutionary classes" (the proletariat, peasantry, "petty bourgeoisie," and "national bourgeoisie"). Thus Mao appealed to these groups to support the Communists instead of (and against) Chiang Kai-shek.

The Japanese had rapidly conquered the Chinese cities. By the end of 1937 Peiping, Shanghai, and Nanking had fallen, and Hankow and Canton were taken in October 1938. The Chinese government moved inland to Chungking, taking with it considerable industrial machinery and many of the faculty and student bodies of the chief universities. Chiang was now far from the businessmen of the treaty ports and was thrown into the midst of the powerful landlords of Sichuan province. Seeking to combat Communist popularity as it grew as a result of the united-front policy, he had outlawed Communist-front organizations in August 1938, and became increasingly unwilling to tolerate any kind of criticism of his government. Those intellectuals from the universities who retreated with him to the interior reacted with rising hostility. Gloom and defeatism settled over Chungking.

Despite the Nazi-Soviet Pact of August 1939, the USSR continued arms shipments to China, and the Chinese Communists refrained from dismissing the Sino-Japanese War, as they did the war between Hitler and the West, as an "imperialist war," nor did they break openly with Chiang. However, even before the pact Mao's policy as stated in a secret document was "70% expansion, 20% dealing with the Kuomintang, and 10% resisting Japan." The Communists were making special efforts to establish themselves in the crucial area between Nanking and Shanghai, and in January 1941 the Nationalists attacked their forces in an attempt to drive them to the north. After the Soviet-Japanese neutrality pact of April 1941 the Communists made even less effort than before to resist Japan. As the impact of the Hitler-Stalin Pact was less dramatic in Asia than in Europe, so was the effect of the Hitler-Stalin war beginning in June, and Communist-Nationalist relations remained near the Level of armed truce.

Popular Fronts in South Asia

In two cases of note Popular Front agreements were made in South Asian countries, and elsewhere local Communists gained in strength during the period. In 1917 a Marxist group had been organized in Paris among Indochinese students by Ho Chi Minh (pseudonym of Nguyen Ai Quoc), but an Indochinese Communist party was founded only in 1930, after the collapse of the first Nationalist-Communist alliance in China, during which Ho Chi Minh had served as assistant to the Soviet adviser Borodin.[3] In 1936 the Vietnamese Communists, whom the French treated more leniently than the nationalists, set up a Communist-controlled "Democratic Front." In May 1941, at a meeting in the Chinese province of Guangxi, the front was converted into the Vietnamese Independence League or Vietminh. After the fall of France in 1940, the Vichyite governor of Indochina had accepted Japanese protection. At first occupying only a few key points, the Japanese forces by July 1941 occupied the whole of Indochina, and thenceforth the local resistance to the Japanese and to the still formally sovereign French were one and the same.

In the Philippines the government ended the previous illegal status of the Communist party in 1938. It managed not only to merge the Socialist party into its ranks, but also ran many successful candidates on a Popular Front ticket in local elections in 1940. The Popular Front became a fighting force when, after the Japanese invasion in December 1941, the Communists created the Hukbalahap ("People's Anti-Japanese Army") movement. A Communist-led party in Burma, the "Our Burma National League," placed three deputies in the parliament elected in 1937. In Indonesia the Communist party, after a period of some success, had been banned by the Dutch authorities in 1926, and although during and after the war it revived rapidly, in the thirties its action was much less important than the growth of Marxism and admiration for the USSR among Indonesian intellectuals. In India, during the twenties M. N. Roy had attained considerable prominence in the Comintern, but his expulsion in 1929 as a Bukharinist was a severe blow to the Indian party, and, as in Indonesia, the popularity of Communism among Indian intellectuals during the thirties could not be credited to the local party.

In none of these countries was the Communist party strong enough to seize power unaided, but in each it was ready, as a trained and disciplined organization, to exploit the turmoil which resulted when Japanese armies overran Southeast Asia. On the eve of World War II the Communists were in a similar position in many of the Middle Eastern, African, and Latin American countries, but during the war they were rarely able to increase their strength substantially outside of areas occupied by Axis or Japanese troops.

Soviet Diplomacy and Collective Security

While Communist parties everywhere were endeavoring to put Moscow's Popular Front policy into effect, Soviet diplomacy was attempting to exploit the shifts in the European balance of power which resulted from Axis gains.

---

[3] Douglas Pike, *Vietnam and the Soviet Union: Anatomy of an Alliance,* Westview, 1987, p. 19.

In 1933 Hitler had inaugurated a Nazi foreign policy by withdrawing from the League of Nations, and he began his attempts at expansion with a *Putsch* in Austria in 1934. Although Britain and France had bound Austria by the peace treaties never to join Germany, they took no action, and Hitler was forestalled only by Mussolini's mobilization on the Brenner Pass. In 1935 Hitler repudiated the disarmament clauses of the Treaty of Versailles; instead of trying to enforce them, the British signed a naval agreement with Germany. The same year Hitler obtained the Saar, not by conquest but by League of Nations plebiscite. In 1936 he flouted the Versailles treaty again by sending troops into the demilitarized Rhineland. Simultaneously he denounced the Locarno treaties of 1925, by which Germany had accepted her Weimar borders, on the grounds of France's "military alliance" with the USSR, which he described as "exclusively directed against Germany." Although Hitler had ordered his troops to withdraw if resistance was encountered, neither the French nor the British tried to stop them.

In October 1935 Mussolini had embarked on his own adventure of conquest by invading Ethiopia. This time the League of Nations, which sat generally bemused before the spectacle of Japanese and Nazi aggression throughout the 1930's, invoked sanctions on the aggressor, but they were not pressed, and after an embarrassingly long bout against troops often armed only with spears, Mussolini won his war by May 1936. In June Count Ciano, Mussolini's son-in-law, became Italian foreign minister and helped to effect a Nazi-Fascist partnership, which grew closer when both powers intervened in the Spanish Civil War which broke out in July. In November 1937 Italy adhered to the Anti-Comintern Pact which Germany and Japan had signed in November 1936. Mussolini had become Hitler's junior partner, and within three years Hitler had come to overshadow him completely.

Litvinov expressed the Soviet reaction to these events by repeated calls in the League of Nations for "collective security," denunciations of the so-called "nonintervention" policy toward the Spanish War, and, especially in 1937, approaches to France and Czechoslovakia which were designed to build the Soviet-French-Czechoslovak pacts into the military alliance which Hitler had wrongly asserted them to be. It is difficult to determine how seriously any of these diplomatic maneuvers was intended. Plainly the "appeasement" policy of Neville Chamberlain (who became British prime minister in May 1937), pointing toward an understanding with Hitler and Mussolini, was not designed to facilitate Soviet-British collaboration; nevertheless Anthony Eden (foreign secretary from September 1936 to February 1938) was known as a defender of the policy of "collective security," which was Litvinov's public doctrine. The evidence suggests that Soviet policy was not determined by the relative "friendliness" which the various powers displayed toward the USSR. When Stalin finally did sign a definite agreement, it was with Hitler, whose soldiers had fought against the Soviet-supported side in Spain and whose public statements had all along been unswervingly anti-Soviet, although at that moment Stalin had the option of signing a pact proffered by Britain and France, where much public and official sentiment had approved—even demanded—such an alliance.

Whether or not the Soviets could have been brought into an alliance to resist Nazi aggression, Chamberlain and the French premier, Daladier, failed to understand that "appeasement" of Hitler was impossible. The French had been too seriously weakened by internal dissension to do more than follow London's lead. Although France was the power which had signed a pact with the Soviets, the link remained fragile, as shown in December 1937, when Foreign Minister Yvon Delbos toured the East European capitals of Warsaw, Bucharest, Belgrade, and Prague without visiting Moscow. The effect which the Western powers judged the 1937 purges had had on the Red Army made it less likely than ever that anything would be done to give real substance to the Franco-Soviet agreement.

In January 1938 both Zhdanov and Molotov, obviously men more powerful than Litvinov in the Soviet hierarchy and clearly acting with the approval of Stalin, publicly criticized the Foreign Commissariat for failing to take France to task for the "anti-Soviet activity" of "criminals of Russian or non-Russian bourgeois origin" in France. The reference was to a French police investigation into the NKVD abduction of a former White leader, General Miller, in Paris, so it might seem that the USSR was the real offender in the incident, but the important thing was that Stalin had called into question the whole public policy of current Soviet diplomacy. However, there was no suggestion of a response from Hitler in his speech of February 20, 1938, the most openly anti-Soviet thus far: "There is only one State with which we have not sought to establish relations, nor do we wish to establish relations with it: Soviet Russia. More than ever do we see in Bolshevism the incarnation of the human destructive instinct. ..."

By 1938 the USSR thus appeared thoroughly isolated. On the day after Hitler's speech (which was also the day after Eden's resignation), Chamberlain declared that peace would depend on "the four major powers of Europe: Germany, Italy, France and ourselves." It seemed a forecast of the Munich Agreement. In March came Hitler's annexation of Austria, now blessed by Mussolini. Britain and France did nothing, but as Hitler began to threaten Czechoslovakia there was a flurry of diplomatic activity. Austria was made up of German-speaking people; so were the western marches of Czechoslovakia, called the Sudetenland. Hitler talked as if it were merely a problem of applying a Wilsonian right of self-determination until all Germans lived within a single border, when all would be well, and Chamberlain appeared to believe him. Yet on May 28 Hitler ordered that by October 2 preparations to attack Czechoslovakia should be completed.

The summer and fall were a diplomatic nightmare. The Soviets claimed that they were ready to honor the Czechoslovak commitment, provided the French did. Perhaps they felt sure that contingency could be ruled out, for there was no evidence of unusual Soviet military preparations in 1938. Refusing to abandon the hope of "appeasement," Chamberlain personally flew to confer with Hitler in September, first to Berchtesgaden, then to Bad Godesberg, and at the end of the month to Munich, where it was decided that a conference of what Chamberlain had called "the four great powers" was to assemble.

At Munich Chamberlain and Daladier consented to the partition of Czechoslovakia and Hitler's annexation of the Sudetenland, and gave the Czechoslovaks nothing but a solemn guarantee of the integrity of the remnant. Prague felt obliged to acquiesce; the Czechs feared that accepting only Soviet aid would convert their country into another Spain (always assuming it would have been forthcoming, which the Soviets never promised unless France also helped), and they dared not fight alone if the British and French washed their hands of them. Chamberlain arrived home with the unfortunate phrase, "peace in our time," and the conviction that appeasement had succeeded. Whatever his conviction, it was sadly true that Britain and France were in no military position either to fight or to bargain effectively. Many in the West were ashamed of Munich; many Czechoslovaks never forgot the experience of being sacrificed to their enemies by their friends. Hitler, who had received as a gift what he had been prepared to fight for, was jubilant.

Soviet Negotiations with Both Sides

The deception of Munich was soon exposed. In October and November the helpless Prague government had to cede Teschen as the result of a Polish ultimatum, yield a strip of territory holding a million people to Hungary, and grant full autonomy to Slovakia and Ruthenia (now renamed "Carpatho-Ukraine"). For a time Ruthenia was the scene of much real or alleged pan-Ukrainian agitation under Berlin sponsorship, which seemed to portend grave Nazi-Soviet tension. Nevertheless Stalin, in his report to the XVIII Party Congress on March 10, 1939, brushed aside Western forecasts of trouble over Ukraine as designed "to provoke a conflict with Germany without any visible grounds." Declaring that the "nonaggressive" states were "unquestionably stronger than the Fascist states," he argued that their failure to resist Hitler was motivated not by weakness but by desire to embroil the Nazis with the Soviets. He warned against "war-mongers who are accustomed to have others pull the chestnuts out of the fire for them," and proclaimed the Soviet intention to stay out of a "new imperialist war" which was "already in its second year." The Soviet *Political Dictionary* of 1940 described Stalin's report as raising "the question of the good neighborly relations between the USSR and Germany. This declaration of Comrade Stalin," the article added, "was properly understood in Germany."

It is now known not only that this assertion was true but also that Stalin's declaration fell on already receptive Nazi ears. Until the end of 1938 Hitler hoped for a compact with Poland at Soviet expense, in which he would receive Danzig and the Corridor in exchange for supporting Polish gains in Ukraine. When Poland did not respond, he was turning to the idea of a partition of Poland in concert with the USSR.

On March 15 Hitler sent German troops to occupy Bohemia and Moravia, set up Slovakia as an "independent" state, but sacrificed his tiny Ukrainian "Piedmont" by giving it to Hungary. Thus he simultaneously made clear to the West that his ambitions exceeded the boundaries of German-speaking lands and to the USSR that his much-bruited "designs on Ukraine" might at least temporarily be laid aside for purposes of diplomatic discussion.

Much British opinion was now clamoring for an end to "appeasement" as well as an approach to the USSR. After the occupation of the core of Czechoslovakia, even Chamberlain lost his illusions about Hitler. He asked the Soviets what their attitude would be if Romania were attacked and thus launched a series of Anglo-Soviet exchanges which continued into the summer. On March 31 he guaranteed Poland against attack and, after Mussolini seized Albania, on April 13 he guaranteed both Greece and Romania. Meanwhile Hitler had extorted Memel from Lithuania by simple ultimatum, and he now began to demand Danzig and the Polish Corridor from Poland openly.

In September 1938 the USSR had been isolated and ignored. Beginning in March 1939 she was ardently courted as a likely ally by both the Western powers and the Nazis. On May 3 Stalin replaced Litvinov with Molotov as foreign commissar; thus departed the man publicly identified with the policy of "collective security." Nevertheless the British and French pushed on with negotiations for a pact to halt further Nazi aggression. In the meantime discussions about a Nazi-Soviet trade pact were proceeding. On June 15 the Soviet chargé d'affaires in Berlin passed on a message to the Nazis that the USSR was trying to decide whether to conclude the pact with the British and French, drag out negotiations further, or undertake a rapprochement with Germany, adding that "this last possibility, with which ideological considerations would not have to become involved, was closest to [Soviet] desires."

Thenceforth the USSR was negotiating secretly with the Nazis and openly with the British and French at the same time. If it had chosen to take it, the West had ample warning of what was in store. Molotov continually raised the Soviet price for a pact, but the plainest danger signal was an article by Zhdanov in *Pravda* on June 29, in which he said he could not agree with his friends who thought Britain and France were sincere in the negotiations which were taking place. The British and French did not exhibit any hastiness, at any rate; when they sent a military mission to Moscow in August, it went by leisurely boat.

However, Hitler was in a great hurry. An attack on Poland was scheduled for late August, and by the end of July the Nazis realized that they must reach agreement with the Soviets very soon if these plans were to be safely implemented. It seems fairly clear that on the night of August 3 Hitler agreed to pay the Soviet price for a pact. Mussolini was left in the dark about his plans. The Italians learned only on August 11 that Hitler was bent on war, and the news threw them into a panic. On the night of the nineteenth the Nazi-Soviet trade treaty was signed. The next day Hitler telegraphed Stalin with a request that he see Ribbentrop on August 22 or 23. When he received Stalin's assent, Hitler pounded on the wall with his fists and shouted, "I have the world in my pocket!" On the night of August 23, 1939, the pact was concluded; it contained the provision which only totalitarians could insert, that it was to take effect as soon as it was signed.

The Nazi-Soviet Pact and the Outbreak of World War II

The public text of the Nazi-Soviet Pact was simply an agreement of nonaggression and neutrality, referring as a precedent to the German-Soviet neutrality pact of 1926. The real agreement was in a secret protocol which in effect partitioned not only Poland (along the line of the Vistula) but much of Eastern Europe. To the Soviets were allotted Finland, Estonia, Latvia, and Bessarabia; to the Nazis, everything to the west of those regions, including Lithuania; and each was to ask the other no questions about the disposition of its own "sphere of interest." The pact, coupled with the trade treaty and arrangements for large-scale exchange of raw materials and armaments, amounted to an alliance.

When confronted with the public text of the pact, the Western emissaries could only creep home quietly. For the moment the Soviet obtained immunity from attack by Hitler, the opportunity for considerable expansion, and noninvolvement in the war which opened with Hitler's blitzkrieg against Poland on September 1, and which Britain and France entered on September 3. On September 17 the Soviets announced they were entering eastern Poland. Actually the line of the secret protocol was now shifted by mutual consent. The Nazi-Soviet boundary in Poland became the Bug instead of the Vistula; in exchange the Soviets were allotted Lithuania. The Polish state disappeared. The USSR handed Vilna to Lithuania and acquired an area whose western boundaries were roughly the same as the Russian frontier of 1795, plus eastern Galicia. For the moment World War II had no front, except for what was derisively called the *sitzkrieg* or "phoney war" in the West, where neither the French nor the Germans attempted any serious offensive. In September and October the USSR forced the three Baltic states to sign mutual assistance pacts, but for the moment left them independent.

The foreign reaction to the Nazi-Soviet Pact and the annihilation of Poland was one of shock and rage. The Communist parties abroad, which had no official warning of the Soviet switch, reacted with confusion. On September 6 Thorez and other French Communists joined their regiments, calling for aid to Poland, only to desert at Moscow's behest a few days later. Harry Pollitt, the British Communist leader, wrote a pamphlet unfortunately titled *How to Win the War,* and after two weeks both he and his pamphlet had to drop from public gaze. The German Communists in exile made strange noises suggesting that the Allies were worse than Hitler. The general line was that already stated by Stalin in March, that the war was an "imperialist" one for the redivision of the world. The Communists said much more about Allied than about Nazi "culpability," and demanded "peace."

The Soviets brought pressure on Finland for a pact comparable to those signed by the Baltic states, but Finland refused and on November 29 was invaded by the Red Army. Otto Kuusinen, a Finnish Communist in Moscow's reserve for such emergencies (he was to be elevated to the Soviet Party Presidium in July 1957), was brought out and made head of a puppet government which conceded all Soviet demands. The Soviets thereupon declared that they were not at war with Finland at all. Western sympathy for the Finns mounted as they successfully resisted the Reds. In 1939 the USSR was expelled from the League of Nations. Britain and France, observing the apparent weakness of the Red Army, debated sending troops to aid the Finns, and actually decided to do so a few days before a Soviet-Finnish peace was concluded in March 1940. The Nazis also took note of Soviet military weakness and filed it for future reference.[4] The peace was an important factor in Daladier's replacement by Paul Reynaud as French premier, just in time to be faced with a new Nazi offensive in the West.

On April 9 Hitler occupied Denmark and invaded Norway, where British forces landed and tried to resist. When they had been defeated and withdrawn from southern Norway (although troops remained in Narvik a month longer), public opinion forced Chamberlain from office and on May 10 Winston Churchill became British prime minister, heading a coalition government including Labor. The same day Hitler attacked the Netherlands, Belgium, Luxembourg, and France. A break-through at Sedan was followed by a Nazi advance which reached the Channel on May 21, splitting Allied armies and compelling the British evacuation of Dunkirk. The Dutch had already been overrun, and the Belgian king surrendered on May 28. On June 10 Italy belatedly declared war on Britain and France. The French army was already shattered, and on June 16 Reynaud yielded the premiership to Marshal Pétain, who sued for peace at once. Churchill's Britain was left alone.

Nazi-Soviet Tensions

The Soviets reacted sharply to the fall of France even before the signing of an armistice. Stalin ordered military occupation of Estonia, Latvia, and Lithuania, and

---

[4] On December 28, 1992 Voenizdat reported the number of Soviet military personnel killed in the war with Finland as 126,875. The Finns lost about 20,000 dead.

all three were "admitted" into the USSR as constituent republics in July. In late June the Soviets also annexed Bessarabia and northern Bukovina (the latter going beyond the line of the secret protocol of the pact with Hitler) by way of ultimatum to Romania, and most of the annexed territory became a new Moldavian SSR.[5]

The Nazis as well seemed to be closing up to their side of the protocol line. In August and September they began to occupy the rest of Romania, partitioned its Transylvanian province and gave much of it to Hungary, and forced the Romanians to cede the southern Dobrudja to Bulgaria. In July 1940 Hitler had secretly decided to prepare to attack the USSR. In September a German-Italian-Japanese Tripartite Pact was signed, and although it stipulated that it would not affect the relations of any of the three powers with the Soviets, a certain deterioration in Berlin-Moscow amity had become apparent. In November 1940 Molotov visited Berlin for further discussions of a vague and grandiose kind, but Hitler did not cancel his plans for attack. On December 18, 1940, he issued the directive for Operation Barbarossa, the code name for the invasion of the USSR, to be launched in the middle of May 1941.

Beginning in August the Nazis were launching large-scale air attacks on Britain; they were also consolidating their influence in the Balkans. The line of the secret protocol ended where Bessarabia touched the Black Sea, and south of that point neither Nazis nor Soviets could formally object to what their partners did. Hitler now extended the Tripartite Pact (often called the Rome-Berlin-Tokyo Axis) by obtaining the adhesion of Hungary, Romania, and Slovakia in November, and after some tension with Moscow over Bulgaria, the latter too signed in March. German troops went where the pact did.

In late March 1941 Yugoslavia added its signature, but the government was promptly overthrown by a pro-Western coup. Immediately Hitler attacked and overran Yugoslavia, and Greece as well (thereby incidentally extricating Mussolini from a gravely embarrassing position; after his declaration of war in June he had attacked Greece from Albania, but had been forced to retreat under successful Greek counterattack). The brief Balkan campaign compelled Hitler to postpone Operation Barbarossa for a month, but its success left him in control of the whole continent up to the Soviet border, either directly or by way of his allies Mussolini and Franco, except for neutral Portugal, Sweden, and Switzerland. Even in Finland the government had accepted his aid in joint preparations for attacking the USSR.

---

[5] In 1924 a Moldavian Autonomous SSR had been created within the Ukrainian SSR on the left bank of the Dniester to put pressure on Romania. In August 1940 the Moldavian ASSR was transformed into the new SSR, but with mostly different territory; over half of the former ASSR was transferred to the Ukrainian SSR, which also received the southern strip of Bessarabia, the rest of which made up most of the area of the new SSR.

Western sources warned the Soviets that Nazi attack was imminent. It is still uncertain whether Stalin and his colleagues expected the attack. Evidently the Soviets were still thinking in terms of better relations with the Nazis, deliveries to whom were maintained with scrupulous fidelity throughout the period of the pact, as well as with Hitler's Japanese allies. In the spring Foreign Minister Matsuoka came to Europe, and in April a Soviet-Japanese neutrality pact was signed, acclaimed by *Izvestiia* as an "historic reversal in the relations between Russia and Japan." Stalin conducted a remarkable public demonstration of affection for all Germans and Japanese who were in sight as he was bidding farewell to Matsuoka at the railway station. At that moment the Nazi attack was two months away. The Soviets, of course, did not know that; for that matter, neither did the Japanese.

The night before the attack, Molotov summoned Count Schulenburg, Nazi ambassador in Moscow, told him that there were indications that the Germans were dissatisfied with the Soviets, and begged him to explain what had brought about the existing state of affairs. Schulenburg professed himself unable to say, and departed. A few hours later, however, he was back with a declaration of war on the USSR. The Nazi invasion occurred, with Finnish, Romanian, and other aid, all along the front from the Arctic Ocean to the Black Sea, on June 22, 1941.

19

Stalin's Cultural Policy
1927–1945

The Arts and the First Five-Year Plan

During the "Second Revolution" the arts were hurled into an atmosphere of combat. In April 1928 a second All-Union Congress of Proletarian Writers (the first had attacked the fellow travelers in 1925) was convened. The Russian Association of Proletarian Writers (*Russkaia Assotsiatsiia Proletarskikh Pisatelei*, or RAPP), the new name of the former All-Russian Association (VAPP), now emerged alongside a number of other regional writers' groups in one all-embracing All-Union Organization of Associations of Proletarian Writers (VOAPP). However, it was RAPP which became, for the four years following, the arbiter of Soviet literature. Its real chief was Leopold Averbakh, whose brother-in-law was Yagoda, chief of the secret police. Calling for the creation of a "literary front" in the struggle to fulfill the First Five-Year Plan, Averbakh inaugurated what soon became a literary dictatorship. Mayakovsky, declaring that he had "stepped on the throat of his own song," left a poem ending, "No need itemizing mutual griefs, woes, offenses. Good luck and goodbye"; and shot himself. There was no room for anything but "realism," the "social command," and "shock workers" of "artistic brigades."

In 1929 warning was given errant writers by quasi-official condemnation of the "mistakes" of two prominent novelists. Boris Pilniak was chastised, nominally for publishing a novel abroad and for other failings. He attempted to set things right by a larger work glorifying the Five-Year Plan called *The Volga Falls to the Caspian Sea*. However, the death of his hero, "a Communist of the year 1919," in the waters of a newly completed dam, left no doubt that Pilniak thought the "new" was indeed destroying the old—but that he considered it a catastrophe for Russia. Eugene Zamiatin was attacked for the publication of a shortened Russian version of *We* in a Prague journal, but although he declared he was not responsible for the publication, he refused to grovel. In 1931, probably through the intercession of Gorky, he was allowed to emigrate and died in France six years later.

Thus the disappearance from the Soviet scene of Trotsky and Bukharin was followed by notice to the fellow travelers whom they had, for different reasons, defended, that the period of relative freedom was at an end. The writers who wanted to go on publishing hastened to write "Five-Year Plan novels": Fëdor Gladkov produced *Cement* and *Energy;* Valentine Katayev wrote *Time, Forward!* The process of collectivization was depicted in Fëdor Panfërov's *Bruski,* but it remained for Michael Sholokhov to perform the same task with honesty in *Virgin Soil Upturned (Podniataia tselina),*[1] a matchless social document filled with a horror which the author does not try to conceal.

As the First Five-Year Plan neared its end, in April 1932 the Party Central Committee again intervened on the literary scene. RAPP (along with VOAPP and the others) was abolished and replaced by a single Union of Soviet Writers "with a Communist fraction therein." The policy of Averbakh as leader of RAPP was condemned by Paul Yudin (who had been elevated to Party spokesman in the field of philosophy a year earlier, at the time of the attack on Deborin and the other editors of the philosophical journal, *Under the Banner of Marxism,* for their alleged overvaluation of Plekhanov and imputed leanings toward idealism and Menshevism). Yudin particularly attacked the Averbakh slogan of "the living man," his emphasis on individual psychology, and his brand of realism. He also criticized RAPP's strictures on fellow travelers. All this harmonized with Stalin's expressed willingness to "forget" the past errors of the old intelligentsia and utilize them for "socialist construction." Moreover, it conformed with his not yet fully stated line that when socialism was built (as it was declared to have been in 1936) and class struggle disappeared, there was to be no room for "proletarian" particularism; all "socialist" and "Soviet" intellectuals should serve the interests of the system and think in terms of the interests of the USSR rather than any segment of its population. However, although the new policy appeared in the guise of softening the cultural dictatorship, it was immediately to be made plain that the dictatorship was only being taken away from RAPP and placed in the hands of the Party, which would apply it to all artists with an unprecedented rigor.

At the same time the "proletarian" music association was dissolved and replaced by a Union of Soviet Composers. In 1936 the musicians, together with theater artists, painters, and sculptors, came under one Central Art Committee which arranged all contracts for their work. All writers and artists had come under state control, and the period of warring factions ended. No matter how ardently one or another group might support the regime, all intellectuals were to be told what was required of them. Even those artists who were willing to compromise or corrupt themselves by servility to the Party in order to be allowed to work—and, if they were, to be rewarded by increasing privileges—were far from

---

[1] The British edition bears the correct translation as given; the American translation is entitled *Seeds of Tomorrow.*

immune to the risk of denunciation, but only the Party was to decide when to denounce and how to punish. However firm the artist's feelings of loyalty to Stalin might be, he spoke his mind at his peril.

The Party Takes Over: "Socialist Realism"

By the end of 1932 the slogan of "socialist realism," a phrase attributed to Stalin himself, was *de rigueur* in literature and increasingly in the other Soviet arts as well. According to Radek, "Socialist realism means not only knowing reality as it is, but knowing whither it is moving. ..." In other words, authentic "realism" was suspect because its test was truthfulness. What was demanded of the Soviet artists was didacticism, the portrayal less of what was than of what ought to be. They had to become, as Stalin put it, "engineers of human minds."

In August 1934 at the first Congress of the new Union of Soviet Writers, Zhdanov declared, "Soviet literature must know how to portray our heroes, it must be able to look into our tomorrow." The speech was followed by "confessions" of error by Vsevolod Ivanov, Olesha, and other fellow travelers, but in their statements they still endeavored to preserve dignity. Radek indicated the relationship of the new literary doctrine to the Popular Front policy abroad by declaring, "Foreign literature which is still hostile to the revolution but is already hostile to Fascism is of great importance to us." However, he made clear the official attitude to *nonpolitical* foreign literature by calling the work of James Joyce "a heap of dung" and by denouncing the "morbid interest" of certain Soviet writers in Joyce, as well as in John Dos Passos and Marcel Proust.

The use of literature as a "weapon" took a new turn with the 1934 campaign against the historical views of the chief Soviet historian, Michael Pokrovsky, who had died two years earlier. The campaign was launched by Stalin, Kirov, and Zhdanov. Pokrovsky, who had been highly praised by Lenin, had gone to extreme lengths in denigrating the personal lives and reigns of past tsars and in condemning tsarist annexation of territory and rule over minority peoples, in a manner indeed not necessarily Marxist. The new policy demanded that the contributions of certain tsars who were "progressive for their time" be studied, and that the tsarist annexations be regarded as the "lesser evil" confronting small nationalities placed between larger powers. The first demand was in principle quite compatible with Marxism; the second was in itself not Marxist, although authority might be found in Marx's works for asserting the beneficial influence of conquest in introducing higher modes of production (for example, by the British in India).

Many foreign observers erroneously concluded from the new policy that Russian nationalism was replacing Marxism as the basis of Soviet ideology. The important feature of the change, however, had little to do with whether Pokrovsky or Stalin should be regarded as the better Marxist, or even whether Marxism should be used as a political weapon (Pokrovsky so held, and Stalin, although he was shameless enough to attack Pokrovsky for that very view, obviously used it as one). The difference between the periods before and after 1934 in the writing of Soviet history was between an individual's use of Marxism (albeit Pokrovsky was an individual with great academic influence) as an instrument of interpretation on the one hand, and on the other a despotic state's use of Marxism as an instrument of the current needs of policy and severe punishment of those who did not co-operate in such use to the state's full satisfaction. As a result independent Marxists were entitled to claim that the doctrine had been perverted, but not that it had been abandoned. In fact, Stalin's own contribution to the perversion of history, the *Short Course* in the history of the Soviet Communist Party (1939), insisted as strongly as ever on the necessity of interpreting all phenomena in the light of "Marxism-Leninism."

The selective use of Russian nationalist themes was permitted and even demanded, but they had to be themes which served the ends of Stalin and the Soviet state at the moment: defense of the fatherland, ruthlessness against domestic enemies, and the benefits of Moscow's rule for the borderlands. Party policy in literature (as well as history and other branches of writing) used such themes to justify Stalin's cruelties and stimulate "Soviet patriotism" by ostensibly expatiating on the heroic deeds of Ivan the Terrible, Peter the Great, and other early practitioners of social transformation by force. Alexis Tolstoy's unfinished novel, *Peter the Great,* was begun with no such intention in evidence in the late 1920's, but the later portions clearly show the effects of the new policy. During World War II Tolstoy wrote two plays about Ivan the Terrible, in which the elements of apologia for Stalin show clearly through the guise of the sixteenth-century setting. During the 1930's a number of novels of the same kind were written, which attempted to meet the requirement of a "positive" attitude toward the Soviet state, and dealt with either the past or the present in terms of what the regime wished had been the case or wanted it to be in the future.

Despite the growing output of politically motivated trash, a chosen list of West European classics, such as Shakespeare and Molière, and later works of some "social" significance, such as Dickens, Balzac, and Mark Twain, continued to circulate by the millions. The same was true of certain great Russian authors such as Pushkin and Leo Tolstoy (though much less so, or during certain periods not at all, such writers as Tiutchev or Dostoevsky). The works of Michael Sholokhov, a Communist, but one who maintained artistic integrity up to a point, were published in quantity, and his four-volume work *The Quiet Don (Tikhii Don)* became perhaps the most popular single work of Soviet literature. It was a genuinely realistic novel about the Civil War, especially successful in its treatment of the Cossacks, and its characters, both Red and White, have human strengths and weaknesses. However, rumors arose and persisted that little or none of it was Sholokhov's own work.

After 1932 the ideological night closed in rapidly over the Soviet literary scene. In Alexis Tolstoy's *The Road to Calvary (Khozhdenie po mukam),* begun in the

1920's and completed on the day Hitler invaded Russia, one can trace by stages the gradual replacement of creativeness by political hack work, the sort of decline which overtook Soviet literature in general. After Tolstoy's death in 1945, Eugene Lyons repeated what Tolstoy had told him in the privacy of his room years before: "When I enter this room I shake off the Soviet nightmare, I shut out its stink and horror. ... Some day, believe me, all Russia will send *them* to hell. ..."[2] While he lived, however, Tolstoy, like many of his colleagues, publicly prostituted himself in return for a luxurious life and the opportunity to write.

In 1936 the artists felt the first tremors of the coming Great Purges. In January *Pravda* attacked Shostakovich's opera based on Leskov's story, *Lady Macbeth of Mtsensk,* for its "purposely harsh and discordant stream of sounds," and condemned such musical "Leftism" as comparable to that of Meyerhold (who had already fallen from favor) in the theater. Demian Bedny was denounced for his libretto to the opera *The Bogatyrs* for failing to evaluate positively the contribution Christianity made to Russia in the tenth century. Marx was quoted—and aptly—in the denunciation, but what worried the genuine artists was not whether Bedny was a good Marxist, but whether the state should determine what art might be allowed to reach an audience.

In 1937 some of the foremost writers of the NEP period, such as Isaac Babel and Boris Pilniak, disappeared, as did D. S. Mirsky, the foremost historian of Russian literature, a former prince who had been converted to Communism while in Britain and had thereupon returned to his homeland. Artists who fell from favor were accused of "Formalism"—and indeed the school of Formalist criticism had been influential even into the early thirties. Although certain of its prominent adherents, such as the late Roman Jakobson (longtime professor at Harvard) emigrated, others, such as Victor Shklovsky, Boris Eikhenbaum, and Victor Zhirmunsky, remained, compromised, and still influenced the study of language and literature for a time. However, the word "Formalism" as used by the Soviet cultural dictators became only an epithet to justify punishment of artistic offenders of quite diverse kinds, to crush any kind of experimentalism (which was suspect of kinship with the "decadent" West), and to drive home the regime's demands for esthetic didacticism.

The Breathing Space of World War II

The coming of World War II abruptly inaugurated a period of relative freedom for the writer. The regime encouraged the literary use of nationalism, religion, love, anything which might sway the emotions of the reading public into identifying themselves with the struggle against Hitler, with scant effort to apply ideological

---

[2] *Our Secret Allies: The Peoples of Russia,* Duell, Sloan and Pearce, 1953, p. 371.

criteria. At the writers' congress of April 1942, the poet Nicholas Tikhonov declared that Soviet literature "is understanding of and sympathetic to suffering because it has an intense interest in man's inner world and in changes brought about by the war. ..." This sounded a new key, indeed. A multitude of novels, plays, and poems which dealt with the war either with honesty or, if with bombast, then of a nationalist rather than Communist kind, poured forth in edition after edition.

Among such works were those of Constantine Simonov, who wrote, in *Days and Nights* (1944), a popular tale of the inferno through which the defenders of Stalingrad lived, and also produced simple lyrics of "man's inner world" such as "Wait for Me and I'll Return":

> Wait for me and I'll return.
> Only just you wait ...
> Wait, when melancholy brings
> Saffron-colored rain,
> Wait, when snows have fallen,
> Wait, when the season's warm,
> Wait, when others do not wait,
> Forgetting bygone days.
> Wait, when letters fail to come
> From distant, far-off lands,
> Wait, when others waiting too
> Have ceased at last to hope.

Ilia Ehrenburg, like Alexis Tolstoy a man personally fond of the Bohemia of the West but willing to pay the price for privilege in the USSR, was able to produce a novel called *The Fall of Paris,* which was completed before the invasion of Russia and was doctrinally orthodox, yet in its setting managed to escape some of the strictures courted by novels of Soviet life. Alexander Fadeyev's *The Young Guard* (1945) dealt with life under German occupation in such a fashion that later the book was attacked for minimizing the Party's role in the events described, and Fadeyev was forced to "revise" the novel accordingly. During the war the first-rank poets Pasternak and Akhmatova published a few pieces, but Akhmatova's poems ignored the war, as did the novel of Michael Zoshchenko, *Before Sunrise (Pered voskhodom solntsa).*

In 1946 Akhmatova and Zoshchenko were attacked by Zhdanov (see p. 350); at the same time Tikhonov was removed as leader of the Union of Soviet Writers. He was replaced by Fadeyev, who had undertaken to correct his "mistakes" and had not been caught talking publicly about "man's inner world." The brief wartime interlude of relaxed controls was over. It had revealed that when controls were loosened and artists were allowed to choose their own subject and manner of treatment within much wider limits than before, few artists of stature remained to exercise a choice.

Soviet Educational Policy

Stalin's cultural policy aimed at forcing into the service of the state not only the talent and training of professional writers and artists, but of teachers and scholars, and the entire educational system. In a country where mass education was only in the planning stage on the eve of the Revolution, one of the major aims of the Communists was to bring about a physical expansion of the school system to include all the people. Illiteracy of those over ten years of age was reported to have dropped from 49% in 1926 to 19% in 1939, and since then has declined to perhaps 5–10%. Education through the seventh grade has remained free; higher education was also free until 1940, when tuition was introduced on the secondary and college levels. At that time the system of state subsidies for living costs was restricted to those "students of higher schools who excel in their studies." Actually such subsidies were part of a contractual obligation into which students entered which obliged them to pursue certain specified work, often in particular enterprises, for a period of years after graduation. Also in 1940, the system of State Labor Reserves schools was established, providing for the conscription of one million students per year into these vocational training centers.

In consequence of such measures as these, most children in the USSR who combined ability with demonstrated political reliability could obtain both advanced education and a privileged position in the Soviet state. Moreover, there was available in certain fields, among them many of the pure sciences and many branches of technology, training of high quality, little hampered by ideological interference. On the other hand, in all fields Soviet scholars, scientists, and teachers were subject to direct personal surveillance by the Party and the secret police. Beginning in the 1930's, but especially since World War II, the Party repeatedly intervened not only to formulate an obligatory policy on academic issues, but also to silence all views other than its own. Furthermore, the Party line changed several times without warning, so that even those willing to accept the Party as the arbiter of all truth could not protect themselves from the shifting winds of doctrine or from consequences which included academic discrimination or dismissal, confinement in a concentration camp, or execution, for ideological deviation.

The education policy of the Soviet regime evolved through stages comparable to its policy toward the arts. During the 1920's a good deal of experimentalism was permitted. In part the Soviets were employing trial and error to find the kind of education which suited their needs; but at the same time the scholastic innovations served the useful purpose of destroying the old habits of discipline and hierarchy and the type of curriculum which had prevailed in tsarist times. This is not to say that the old education system had been chiefly intended to further the ends of the regime; the tsarist government did not regard education as a means of political indoctrination, and while it tried various ways to combat the phenomenon, the student bodies of higher schools and universities had become open strongholds of political opposition.

In the first decade Soviet educational theorists drew heavily on the ideas of John Dewey and other Americans who espoused "progressive education." Such influential men as S. T. Shatsky and Paul Blonsky emphasized "freedom for the child" and dropped such traditional subjects as Latin from the school curriculum. However, in the middle thirties the Party intervened to restore a differential grading system, classroom discipline, and some of the traditional subjects— taught in a far from traditional way with emphasis on ideological goals. In 1936 Blonsky was attacked by the Party Central Committee and promptly vanished. The notion of group "socialistic competition" in education, popular under the First Five-Year Plan, was dropped. As in all other respects, in his education the individual was to be at the mercy of the state, with as few intermediary agencies as practicable. His position in the school was to be such that his reliability could be constantly tested and rewarded or punished, without reference to a group with which he might be working. Stalin made no secret of his view of education (which Lenin had shared): to H. G. Wells he declared, "Education is a weapon, whose effect depends on who holds it in his hands and who is struck with it."

The Soviet state made no attempt to claim credit for the advancement of truth, knowledge, and art for their own sakes. Any effort to interpret those values as of inherent worth or of some significance independent of the needs of the Soviet state was branded as "bourgeois objectivism" or even, in certain cases, treason. The intent of the Soviet regime was not to educate, but to indoctrinate through a culturally totalitarian system of controls producing, in the words of Stalin, a group of intellectuals who were "engineers of human minds," and for the rest, minds capable of being engineered. In this manner it was intended to create the "new Soviet man."

Nevertheless the proliferation of schools, books, newspapers, theaters, art galleries, concert halls, and the like did not always have the effect the Soviet state desired. In 1956, according to Soviet statistics, 54,000 book titles were published in over a billion copies, 9,000 titles of newspapers and journals were being issued, and over 35 million young people were studying in various levels of the Soviet educational system. By comparison, in 1914–15, 28,000 book titles were issued in something over 100 million copies, 2,000 titles of newspapers and journals were published, and less than 9 million people were studying in the schools of the Russian Empire. Those were no mean educational achievements, but under the Soviets information, skills, and cultural opportunities were made available to much greater numbers of people. Despite formidable efforts to use broader education for its own purposes, the Soviet regime unleashed forces which were not completely susceptible to the controls at its disposal. Even the older generation of artists and scholars had not entirely forgotten the meaning of art and knowledge, as shown by the intensity of the campaign of ideological repression which the regime felt it necessary to carry out after World War II, while the younger generations of intellectuals and students came to attract the attention of the whole world by their search for answers more plausible than those given them by the regime.

Stalin's Policy Toward Religion: Frontal Attack and Compromise

When Stalin became unchallenged master of the Soviet Union, the regime was still pursuing the dual policy of attempting to spread militant atheism on the one hand and pursuing a *divide et impera* line toward the Orthodox Church. With the coming of the First Five-Year Plan, the situation changed abruptly, and a large-scale offensive against religion was launched. In May 1929 the Constitution was amended to omit the previous guarantee of the right of religious propaganda, leaving "the right of professing a religion and of antireligious propaganda." Great numbers of churches were closed, church bells were seized (ostensibly to provide tin and copper for industrial use), and many of the remaining monasteries and nunneries were dissolved. The antireligious significance of the introduction of the "continuous" work week (ending the regular Sunday work holiday) was heavily emphasized in the official press.

By January 1930 the League of Militant Godless claimed 2 million members. Yaroslavsky, its leader, was accused by certain of his enthusiastic followers of unwarranted moderation because he hung back from abolishing all religion by fiat. Early in 1930 the Party criticized overly impatient "Left deviationists" in the antireligious campaign, and Yaroslavsky kept his authority. However, the Party action did not mean the abandonment of the campaign, any more than Stalin's "Dizziness from Success" article had meant abandonment of collectivization. In 1931 it was reported that there were 3,200 "Godless shock brigades" operating among the industrial workers. By 1932 the League claimed a membership exceeding 5 million. In the same year much fanfare attended the conversion of the Kazan Cathedral in Leningrad into an antireligious museum, and several dozen other such institutions were created.

The leadership of the Russian Orthodox Church indicated by its reaction to the antireligious campaign how far it had already gone in subservience to the Communist Party. In 1930 Metropolitan Sergii asserted that the church retained 30,000 parishes (as compared with almost 50,000 which had been functioning in 1914), and he not only refused to criticize the regime for its offensive against religion, but even attacked Christians abroad who had voiced alarm. The campaign continued for some time after Sergii's declaration, but it lost momentum and plainly fell short of success. Yaroslavsky lamented the decline in antireligious activities among League members, and in the middle thirties he admitted that approximately half of the population remained "believers." In 1934 the newspaper *The Godless* discontinued publication, and the decline in militant atheism was plain.

Nevertheless the regime refused to admit defeat. Early in 1936 the Party Central Committee surveyed the situation and demanded a renewal of antireligious efforts. In 1938 *The Godless* was revived. A number of high clergy fell during the Great Purges. Just before 1941 the membership of the League of Militant Godless, having slumped to below 2 million, rose above 3 million again. The prewar situation may be summed up in the episode of the census of 1937, which included a question about religious belief. The entire census results were branded as faulty, and they were not published. Part of the reason for their suppression was certainly the population deficiency they recorded, which resulted from collectivization and the early stages of the purges. However, persistent rumors suggested that another important reason was that 40% of the population had declared their religious belief. That some such embarrassing figure had been obtained was suggested by the omission of the question from the census of 1939.

Until the war the Orthodox Church continued, in obviously difficult circumstances, under the leadership of Metropolitan Sergii. After talks with Stalin, he was elected Patriarch in September 1943, in a dramatic reversal of Soviet policy toward religion. It is uncertain whether by that time he remained in any sense a free agent; certainly the concordat between church and regime was the product of Stalin's and not Sergii's decision. Along with Soviet resumption of relations with the Orthodox Church went strict governmental controls over its clergy and the properties allotted for its use, controls which, it appears, were actually exercised by the secret police. In May 1944 Sergii died and was succeeded by Metropolitan Alexii of Leningrad, who was elected Patriarch early in 1945. Patriarch Alexii took a prominent part in Soviet "peace" campaigns, though for years the more powerful cleric was Metropolitan Nicholas of Krutitsy, who attacked American Christians for countenancing "germ warfare in Korea." Such yeoman service to the regime on the part of the Orthodox hierarchy was not, however, rewarded by the termination of antireligious activity.

When the imprisoned bishops of Solovki recommended reconciliation with the state power (see p. 189), they insisted on the retention of the Orthodox faith and on the understanding of its incompatibility with Communism. For many decades the leadership of the church failed to follow their injunctions. The high clerics of Russian Orthodoxy were willing to serve as instruments of Soviet state policy in both domestic and foreign affairs as the price of being permitted to resume for the time being their functions as the leaders of an officially tolerated religious institution. During the war the leadership of the Orthodox Church of Georgia, the Armenian Church, the (Protestant) Baptists and Evangelical Christians, and the Muslims accepted a similar status (the Roman Catholics did not do so, while the Jews suffered more than any other religious group).

The success of such arrangements, from the Soviet viewpoint, was illustrated by the adherence of other Eastern Orthodox Patriarchs to a number of pronouncements by the Patriarch of Moscow, political benefits of the resumption of pilgrimages to Mecca by Soviet Muslims in November 1944, and the favorable reports about the state of religion in the USSR rendered by poorly informed clergymen visiting from the Western countries for several decades. There were men of integrity, deeply devoted to their professed beliefs, among the officially approved clergy, as there were clearly others who, like many Soviet intellectuals, submitted completely to the state. Some clergymen may have done so to preserve their own privileges; others may have hoped merely to keep the faith of the people alive through the holding of religious services, even though the teachings of their religion had to be mutilated or suppressed.

20

The USSR in World War II: The Military Crisis 1941–1943

A Diplomatic Revolution

On the day before the Nazis invaded the Soviet Union, Stalin was still acting as if he considered Hitler to be his partner. The USSR had protested the British blockade of Germany, exerted pressure on Turkey to reject a pact with Britain and France, and bitterly attacked the United States program of Lend-Lease to Britain. Foreign Communists, although damning both sides in the "imperialist war," reserved their sharpest denunciations for Britain and (before her defeat) France. On Moscow's orders, the Communists in Norway, Denmark, and the Netherlands had at first been willing to accept the ambiguous status of being tolerated by the Nazi occupation forces, and in Belgium they were clearly favored, all other parties having been banned. Although by the autumn of 1940 the Nazi-Communist honeymoon was over in Western Europe, even after the Nazis overran Yugoslavia and Greece in the spring of 1941 Moscow was unwilling to give the Balkan Communists the signal to resist. The British, still smarting from the humiliating circumstances in which they had learned of the Nazi-Soviet Pact and well aware of Stalin's aid to Hitler, along with their supporters in America and elsewhere, regarded the Soviets with bitter hatred.

However, within twenty-four hours of the invasion, Churchill declared that although "no one has been a more consistent opponent of Communism than I have been for the last twenty-five years," nevertheless "any man or state who fights on against Nazidom will have our aid." The United States, still a neutral, extended Lend-Lease to the USSR. Communists abroad abruptly announced that the conflict had become a "people's" war, and gave verbal support to the British war effort and American Lend-Lease policy. Nevertheless even in that hour of the USSR's greatest peril, the Communist doctrine of old did not disappear. British

Communists called on Labor for a common front against "Toryism"—to which Laborites Harold Laski and Emanuel Shinwell responded by advocating a merger between the Socialist International and the Comintern—but still directed their sharpest attacks at the Labor party. The apparently contradictory policy was reminiscent of the Popular Front period, and indeed the professed aims of the Popular Front seemed at last to have been achieved—an alliance was formed between Communists and all anti-Fascist political groups, and between the USSR and all anti-Nazi governments. To be sure, the Popular Front's slogan was "against war and Fascism"; but no Communist (any more than any British Tory) professed to be anything but a fervent supporter of the war until Hitler should be completely crushed. In his first speech to the Soviet people, Stalin referred "with gratitude" to the "historic utterance of the British Prime Minister, Mr. Churchill, regarding aid to the Soviet Union and the declaration of the United States government" regarding Lend-Lease. It seemed that the diplomatic revolution was complete, and, many Westerners thought or hoped, permanent.

The Campaign of 1941

Hitler's objective, as stated in the directive for Operation Barbarossa, was "to crush Soviet Russia in a quick campaign before the end of the war against England." As the invasion opened, he announced that the Soviet Union was dissolved, and the first few days of fighting suggested that he would achieve his aims in 1941. The Nazis achieved virtually complete tactical surprise, destroyed much of the Red air force on the ground by bombing, and their initial onslaught crashed clear through Soviet lines.

Whether strategic surprise was achieved remains uncertain. In his speech of July 3, 1941, Stalin implied that it was when he said that the Nazis attacked "suddenly and treacherously," which meant, if true, that he had ignored the warnings of the British that attack was imminent, and Khrushchëv accused him of precisely such blindness in his "secret speech" of 1956. However, Stalin had mobilized a hundred and seventy divisions and placed most of them near the frontier, which argues against the "surprise attack" explanation. In any event, he acted swiftly after the invasion. The Third Five-Year Plan, begun in 1938, was shelved. A State Defense Committee, consisting of Stalin, Molotov for diplomacy, Beria for the secret police, Malenkov for Party matters, and Voroshilov for the army, was established. In addition Voroshilov commanded the northern front, while Timoshenko and Budënny were the field commanders in the center and south.

Hitler's plan of attack was predicated upon the rapid collapse of both the Red Army and the Soviet regime. He had rejected the more cautious proposal of General Marcks to hold the main Soviet armies north of the upper Dniester while a single great southern offensive struck east to Rostov and then north to Moscow and Leningrad, saving the main Nazi armies for annihilation blows once this of-

RUSSIA IN WORLD WAR II
Period of Nazi Advance, 1941-2

Front line, December 1941

Front line, November, 1942

fensive was well under way. Instead Hitler ordered an all-out frontal assault by three army groups, the northern under Field Marshal von Leeb toward Pskov (headed for Leningrad), the central under Field Marshal von Bock toward Minsk and Smolensk (headed for Moscow), and the southern under Field Marshal von Rundstedt in two wings converging on Kiev.

Within two weeks, owing largely to the speed of Guderian's tank forces, Army Group Center had surrounded and captured almost 300,000 Soviet troops near Minsk, and Guderian's columns had reached the Dnieper. Ten days more, and he was through Belorussia into the territory of the RSFSR at Smolensk. Bock and Guderian were eager to strike on to Moscow at once. However, on July 19 Hitler ignored their pleas and made the fateful decision to disperse his tank forces to keep both flanks moving forward. Guderian was ordered to turn south to assist Rundstedt in Ukraine, while another large armored group was to aid Leeb's advance in the north. It is possible that the outcome of the Nazi-Soviet war was decided then and there. Besides being of immense psychological importance, Moscow was the center of a highly centralized regime, the hub of all Russian railways, and the transshipment point for the supplies which would soon be flowing in quantity from the U.S. and Britain by way of the White Sea and Vladivostok. The capture of Moscow within the first two or three months of the campaign, Guderian was sure, would have had such an effect that the risks attending a single massive armored thrust toward the capital were well worth taking.

At any rate, Guderian's southward movement soon resulted in another great victory. On September 14 his tanks met those of Army Group South east of Kiev and surrounded 600,000 Soviet soldiers. Budënny's army was virtually dispersed, and he was replaced by Timoshenko (Zhukov took over Timoshenko's post on the central front). Rundstedt continued his advance to Kharkov and Taganrog on the Sea of Azov. Nearly the whole of Ukraine had been conquered in four months.

Leeb had succeeded in reaching Leningrad in the middle of September, and in conjunction with Field Marshal Mannerheim and the Finns, invested the city from north and south, but was unable to capture it. Hitler had consented to return Guderian's tanks to Army Group Center when the Kiev operation was complete, but Bock was not ready to resume his advance until October 2. Almost at once another gigantic encirclement was achieved near Viazma, and another mass of 600,000 prisoners was taken. On October 15 Bock's armor reached Mozhaisk, sixty-five miles from Moscow. But now winter was descending, earlier than usual, as in 1812—a precedent German officers had increasingly on their minds. On November 15 another attempt was made; the Nazis floundered through snowy mud for two more weeks, but they remained twenty miles from the city. A last effort began on December 2, and German advance guards actually penetrated the suburbs of Moscow, but the main force made little headway. On December 8 the German army announced suspension of operations on account of winter. Hitler's generals begged him to consent to a retreat, since the troops had no winter clothing or equipment and their positions were unsuitable for defense against the counteroffensive the Soviets were now launching all along the line, but he refused. Thereupon Rundstedt, Bock, Leeb, and the army commander-in-chief, Brauchitsch, resigned. Hitler himself assumed the command and dismissed Guderian. Thus a clean sweep of the field leadership was made.

The Nazi military victory had been great, but Hitler's plan to crush the USSR "quickly" had failed. Guderian's scheme of a massive thrust to Moscow might have achieved the victory on which Hitler counted. Instead he had used the tactic of an in-line advance. Such a scheme was bound to require more time, and yet, in the months of October and November, three things happened for which he had not prepared. Winter came, and the troops, already fatigued, had insufficient clothing to protect them from the cold. The roads became impassable for wheeled vehicles, although if tracked transport had been available, the advance might have continued. The Soviets had time to bring up reserves, whose size the Nazi command had discounted, and the combination of factors spelled failure. The military mistakes were Hitler's; however, he may well have been right in refusing to retreat once the failure was plain. The news that blitzkrieg had miscarried for the first time, coupled with the realization of what United States entrance into the war (December 7, 1941) might mean, had already deeply damaged domestic morale. The psychological and political effects of a withdrawal to the Polish borders might have had further serious consequences.

For the winter German troops were withdrawn into "hedgehogs" (*Igels*), fortified centers with defenses all around their perimeters, in order to prevent surprise attack from the rear by infiltrating forces. The Germans were unable to keep the Soviets from regaining contact with besieged Leningrad through the construction of a road across the ice of Lake Ladoga in January (nevertheless, more than half a million Leningraders starved to death during that winter). On the central front they lost Mozhaisk to Soviet counterattacks, while in the south the Red Army made some gains in the Crimea, but failed in an effort to retake Kharkov. From February to May 1942 the front was fairly quiet.

Hitler and the Soviet Peoples

Just before the invasion, Hitler had written, "We do not want to convert the Russians to National Socialism, but to make them into our tools." In the "Commissar Decree" of May 1941 he ordered that all "political officials" and army political commissars were to be killed on capture. Heinrich Himmler, one of the chief Nazis and master of both the dreaded SS formations and the Gestapo, wrote contemptuously of the *Untermensch*, the subhuman Slav whose fate was to serve Germany or die. The Nazi doctrine on the Soviet minorities was somewhat less savage in tone, and Hitler even regarded the Muslims with some favor, but there was to be no nonsense about "equality" of any of the peoples with the Germans.

In practice, competition and conflict among Nazi agencies—Hermann Goering's economic staffs, Joseph Goebbels's propaganda ministry, Alfred Rosenberg's Ministry for the Eastern Territories, Himmler's empire of picked savages, and the army—prevented a policy of extermination, or any other policy, from being consistently carried out. The main difference in emphasis lay between the SS (until 1944) and political officials who were ideologically committed to the notions of "master race" (*Herrenvolk*) and *Untermensch*, and the army, whose officers judged alternative policies in terms of their effects on the tasks of mounting military operations and administering rear areas, and thus leaned toward less brutality and more "realism." In the army and in the Foreign Office there was even a handful of men who combined sympathy for the Soviet peoples with opposition to Hitler's rule in Germany, although they couched their pleas in "realistic" terms. However, although the army was able to circumvent or thwart certain of Hitler's directives, Hitler never was willing to countenance any real recognition that the peoples of Russia were human beings, and thus the foundations of Nazi policy were never altered. This policy was, from the Nazi standpoint, suicidal, but it is difficult to see how it could have been changed substantially unless Hitler had been overthrown in the course of the war, or the Nazis had ceased to be what they were.

More often than not, the peoples of the Soviet Union at first received the Nazi invaders as liberators. The peasants of Belorussia, Ukraine, and Great Russia met the Germans with the traditional token of welcome, bread and salt. Many collective farms in areas overrun by the *Wehrmacht* were instantly and spontaneously abolished by the farmers themselves. Many churches were reopened by the Russians, and although the German army was not authorized either to abolish collectives or reopen churches, at first they did not try to prevent the local inhabitants from doing so. As Rosenberg wrote, the Germans found in the USSR, "in contrast to the West, a people who went through all the terror of Bolshevism, and who now, happy about their liberation, put themselves willingly at the disposal of Germany ..."[1] yet they were treated far worse than the people of Western Europe.

Rosenberg was referring chiefly to the Ukrainians. He hated Great Russia (he was of Baltic German origin himself) but attempted to foster separatist movements and anticipated the organization of "Greater Finland," "Baltica," Ukraine, and the Caucasus as German satellites. Ukraine seemed the most promising region in which to employ local separatists, and the Nazis had shown Ukrainian nationalist leaders some favor after they conquered western Poland in 1939. At that time Stephen Bandera and others were released from Polish prisons. Bandera criticized the older nationalists, led by Colonel Andrew Melnyk, and the factions that crystallized around the two leaders remained at odds during the war with the USSR.[2]

At first the Ukrainian nationalists hoped for real Nazi support. When the Germans occupied Lvov on June 30, 1941, the Banderists promptly moved in and proclaimed a Ukrainian state, but the SS immediately arrested them. When Kiev was captured in September, the followers of Melnyk attempted to take in hand the organization of Ukrainian public life, but they in turn were shunted aside by the Nazis. A third group, connected with more moderate Ukrainian *émigrés,* and led by Taras Borovets (he took the *nom de guerre* "Taras Bulba" after a Gogol hero), was permitted to organize a partisan force to fight Soviet stragglers. However, af-

---

[1] Quoted in George Fischer, *Soviet Opposition to Stalin,* Harvard U. Press, 1952, p. 9.

[2] The OUN (*Organizatsiia Ukrainskykh Natsionalistiv* or Organization of Ukrainian Nationalists) split into the OUN-B and the OUN-M, the letters after the hyphens standing for the names of the two leaders.

ter German repressions in Ukraine in the winter of 1941–1942, Borovets began to fight the Nazis. The Ukrainians also fought among themselves. The two extreme nationalist groups formed partisan units of their own and squabbled instead of co-operating; in the summer of 1943 the Banderists used force to take away the followers of both Melnyk and Borovets and came to dominate the Ukrainian nationalist movement. By this time, as a partisan congress in August 1943 indicated, the Ukrainian leaders had decided on all-out resistance to both Nazis and Soviets.

The Ukrainian nationalists broke with the Nazis less because they had been personally ill-treated than because the occupation policy had revealed its full savagery. A brute named Erich Koch, who scorned even the plans for a Ukrainian satellite of his nominal chief, Rosenberg, was named *Reichskommissar* of Ukraine. A crucial question in occupation policy was recognized to be that of the collective farms, and plans for their dissolution by Nazi decree had been discussed for months. In October 1941 Hitler had disapproved of the idea, but in February 1942 Rosenberg managed to get his sanction for issuance of a Law for Restoration of Private Land (*Reprivatisierungsgesetz*). However, the law envisaged only "gradual and orderly transition" to co-operative farms, and in the few places where it was implemented the peasant was scarcely able to tell the difference from the Soviet collectives. In any case Koch and others sabotaged any serious effort to put even this weak measure into effect. The reopening of churches, although sometimes permitted by the army, was not made part of occupation policy, and Hitler's fear of nationalism as well as the Nazi hostility to Christianity prevented any propagandistic exploitation of the actual partial revival of religious worship which took place here and there behind Nazi lines. Hitler also decreed that only the most fragmentary education was to be given the occupied peoples.

The Russians, Belorussians, and Ukrainians in occupied areas hoped for real restoration of individual farming and the Christian religion. The Nazis not only failed to restore them, but earned the hatred of the people by the shooting of non-Communist hostages beginning in October 1941, mass deportation of civilians as a penalty for terrorism or sabotage, and mass recruitment of forced labor which began in March 1942 under the direction of the infamous Fritz Sauckel, former *Gauleiter* of Thuringia. After generally unsuccessful efforts to incite the local inhabitants to conduct pogroms, the Nazis simply exterminated the Soviet Jews by the tens of thousands. The civilians also observed the inhuman treatment of prisoners of war. Many were shot before their eyes for lagging behind, and yet it was forbidden to give them food, even to save the starving. When the prisoners reached camps in the rear their treatment defied description. In 1941 over 3.33 million Soviet prisoners had been captured (the total captured during the war was close to 6 million). During the last four months of 1941 alone, half a million prisoners died of hunger and cold in Nazi camps, and of those who remained alive only a small fraction were able to work. The SS was responsible for much of this slaughter and suffering, but the army bore its share of responsibility also. However, a number of high officers soon came to advocate milder treatment, realizing that the immense group of prisoners could provide a great reservoir of trained troops many of whom were eager, despite the treatment they had received at Nazi hands, to fight the Soviet regime alongside the Nazis.

In early 1942 Nazi brutality had already begun to turn the civilians in the occupied areas against the regime, and Soviet partisan activity, at first negligible, had increased markedly. The Germans estimated that in August 1941, 10% of the forests behind their lines were infested with partisans; by October 1942, 75%. By the autumn of 1943, 10% of all German field divisions in Russia were fighting partisans. Partisan units could grow only if a sizable proportion of the civilians would join or support them in some manner. Although Moscow tried its best to obtain and keep control over the partisan units and many of them (not the Ukrainian nationalist ones) were nominally pro-Soviet in allegiance or leadership, others were opposed to both totalitarianisms, and there is evidence that there were many partisan units behind Soviet lines which gave Moscow much trouble. At any rate, it was clear that the occupied areas were becoming actively hostile to the German armies.

Yet during the first weeks of the fighting it had been revealed that millions ruled by Stalin hated the regime, and as popular feeling began to turn against the Nazis, a number of voices were raised to persuade Hitler to alter his policy at least verbally, or to allow the army to turn to account the willingness to co-operate with the Nazis which remained among many war prisoners. In Rosenberg's *Ostministerium* Otto Bräutigam called for a "Russian de Gaulle." A memorandum by a certain Captain Strik-Strikfeldt in the army propaganda office calling for a Russian "army of liberation" and government-in-exile was actually approved by Brauchitsch, shortly before he was removed in December 1941. The commander of the largest army rear area declared he could not fight partisans successfully unless the Nazis promised a future Russian state and put into effect a policy of decollectivization and religious restoration. The quotation from Schiller's *Demetrius,* "Russia can be defeated only by Russians," was frequently employed by the "realists." However, none of these proposals had any result.

Without authorization, the army had begun to use some of the thousands of Soviet prisoners who begged to be allowed to fight Stalin as *Hilfswillige* or "Hiwis" ("Volunteer Helpers"), chiefly for noncombat duties behind the lines. Beginning in November 1941 battalion-size combat units of *Osttruppen* were also being formed, and even Hitler went back on his own order that none but Germans should be armed in order to sanction the organization of Turkic and other non-Slavic "legions." But Slavic *Osttruppen,* some of them called "Cossack" to avoid the use of the word "Russian," also were formed in considerable numbers. By 1943 perhaps half a million to a million "Hiwis" and a quarter of a million *Osttruppen* were being used by the Nazis. Since Soviet citizens were also used widely as individual replacements, it is very difficult to determine the total of such auxiliaries.

In July 1942 the Nazis had captured Lieutenant General Andrei Vlasov while he was commanding an army trying to relieve Leningrad. He was generally recognized as the most suitable candidate available to lead an anti-Soviet Russian army, if one were to be organized. For two years, however, Hitler forbade the creation of any such force. Even the national committees of the minorities which Rosenberg had assembled in his *Ostministerium* were vouchsafed no official notice. Until it was too late, there was no Nazi policy toward the peoples of the USSR but one of terror and exploitation. Scarcely knowing which was the frying pan and which the fire, the Soviet citizenry wrestled with the dilemma posed by the discovery that the Nazis came as anything but liberators. Hitler's political errors were perhaps no less decisive in the long run than his military miscalculations.

Stalin's Response

From June 22 until July 3, 1941, Stalin did not utter a word in public. He then admitted the "grave danger" to the Soviet Union, and although he falsely asserted that the best of the Nazi armed forces had been already destroyed, he called for a "scorched-earth" policy during the continuing retreat and summoned the people to conduct guerrilla warfare in Nazi-occupied areas. Invoking the precedent of 1812, he declared that now as then Russia was waging a "national patriotic war," and the official Soviet name for the war became the "Second War of the Fatherland" (not World War II; that was something being fought elsewhere).

Conceding that it might be wondered how the Soviet government could have "consented" to sign a pact with "such perfidious people, such fiends as Hitler and Ribbentrop," he gave his answer: "We secured to our country peace for a year and a half and the opportunity of preparing our forces." A little later Stalin himself hinted the truth, that Hitler had used the time to much greater advantage in "preparing forces" than the Soviets had. He charged that Hitler wished to turn the Soviet peoples "into the slaves of German princes and barons"; and here, the noble titles aside, was the bald truth. In Stalin's speech lay in germ the propaganda tactic of nationalism which he was to unfold in the coming months.

Stalin doubtless knew that multitudes had defected to Hitler and that many more were awaiting the opportunity to do so. In his speech he warned that "there must be no room in our ranks for whimperers and cowards, for panic-mongers and deserters." Thousands of prominent political prisoners, who might conceivably emerge as popular leaders if the regime cracked, were hastily executed, and local draft commissions were guided by the NKVD to select for front-line service in especially dangerous sectors those who were suspected of potential disloyalty. To prevent the population from hearing German propaganda, radio receivers were gathered in wholesale. Soviet citizens of German descent were rounded up. The entire population—almost half a million—of the Volga German ASSR, which had been vaunted as a showpiece of nationality policy, was uprooted and "deported" by methods which few survived; other ethnic groups would follow later. Stalin's fear was plain. It was reflected in his offer to Harry Hopkins, the special envoy of President Roosevelt, in late July 1941, to "welcome" American troops under their own command anywhere on the front, and his similar invitation to Lord Beaverbrook four months later for British troops to take over part of the Ukrainian sector. When Stalin had recovered a little of his confidence, he would not even allow foreign observers near the front.

Nevertheless, from the time of the invasion Stalin attempted to maintain the appearance of loyalty and solidarity with Britain (on the eve of June 22 the only state at war with Hitler) and the United States (still technically a neutral but deeply committed to aid Britain in her fight). Churchill's blunt remark, "I unsay no word that I have spoken" about Communism, had been coupled with a firm resolve not to say any further words on the subject which would embarrass the Soviets and interfere with the prime objective of defeating Hitler. None of the Allied representatives attempted to disturb Stalin with questions about his past role and future aims.

By tacit common consent, it was assumed in London and Washington that as a result of the grave crisis into which Stalin had blundered, he would shelve all the tiresome nonsense of Marxism-Leninism and assume the role of genuine leader of the Russian nation. As some of the less cautious critics of the Soviets had damned both tsarist and Soviet "expansionism" as part of the same phenomenon, so other careless commentators began to find heroism and humaneness equally in the Russian past and the Soviet present. It was assumed that Communist power and Stalin's dictatorship were at worst a passing phase in Russian history, and that the Soviet leaders were Russian nationalists in a cumbersome and now happily outmoded ideological guise. As not only British and American leaders but Allied public opinion took up this view, Stalin reciprocated by playing the role to the hilt, appearing as "old Joe," the man with the smile and the pipe. The Allied leaders were not shocked, but were even relieved, when he made demands or promises on behalf of the government without pretending—except on the rare occasions when it suited him—that he had to ask someone else's consent. What they asked of him was not that he be a democrat, but only a *nationalist.*

In a speech delivered on November 7 in Red Square to troops marching directly to the front outside the city of Moscow, Stalin invoked the shades of medieval saints and tsarist generals in an unequivocal appeal to Russian nationalism: "Let the manly images of our great ancestors—Alexander Nevsky, Dmitry Donskoi, Kuzma Minin, Dmitry Pozharsky, Alexander Suvorov, and Michael Kutuzov—inspire you in this war!" In effect he begged his soldiers to fight for Mother Russia, not for Communism. Stalin thus assumed the pose which he recognized as his best hope of salvation in the effort to persuade the people to fight for the regime; it was also the attitude which promised to be most useful to him in relations with the Allies. Soviet propaganda actively employed, in its appeals to the peoples behind Nazi lines, the fact that democratic Britain and America supported the USSR. By seeming to behave like a Russian tsar, he might secure for himself the maximum Allied aid for the conduct of the war and the fullest hearing at the peace tables if the war could be won.

On July 12, 1941, Ambassador Cripps, who had talked to Churchill just before his famous speech offering Stalin aid, was instrumental in the conclusion of an Anglo-Soviet mutual assistance pact renouncing any separate peace with Hitler. The former United States ambassador, Joseph E. Davies, expressed sufficient optimism about Soviet capacity to resist so that President Roosevelt thought it important to obtain a direct report. For that purpose Harry Hopkins was sent on a special mission in the last days of July, and he conducted amiable talks with Stalin. Before he went, however, orders had already been given to prepare Lend-Lease shipments to the USSR.

In September W. Averell Harriman was sent to report on Soviet needs, accompanied by the Briton Lord Beaverbrook. During this mission, agreement was reached for America to supply over a billion dollars' worth of goods in 1942. Stalin also presented the Allies with his first demand for a "second front," and was to repeat it many times during the next two and a half years. As far as is known, no Allied representative ever suggested that the Russian front itself was the second of the war (leaving aside the Polish and Balkan campaigns), and that the first, in Western Europe, had been overrun by the Nazis while the Soviets were their allies. It would have been not only tactless but pointless to mention that, but the Allied negotiators' patience and abstention from recriminations against the Soviets, throughout the war and afterward, were nevertheless remarkable.

As a result of the Harriman-Beaverbrook mission, in March 1942 Roosevelt ordered that the matériel promised to Stalin was to be delivered ahead of all other commitments including the requirements of American armed forces. In the course of the war 16.5 million tons of goods were sent to the USSR from America, of which more than 15 million tons were delivered safely. The items sent included railway cars especially built for the Russian broad gauge, trucks, oil, food, medical supplies, and many other goods, to the value of $11 billion.

The Soviets claimed to have moved more than a thousand war plants to the Urals and Siberia from Ukraine alone from September to December 1941, and during the war the growth of new industrial production in the Soviet East was great enough to affect the geographical pattern of industry permanently. Nevertheless, by the end of 1941 the USSR had lost to Nazi occupation for the time being more than half of its previous coal and steel production, virtually all of its ball-bearing production, and almost half of its railways—not to mention 40% of its total population. For this reason Allied shipments were of crucial importance, especially in 1942–1943. They were sent, moreover, at a time when it was far from clear whether the Soviets could stave off complete military defeat, in which case the supplies would have fallen into the hands of Hitler, who became America's enemy along with Japan and Italy after December 7, 1941.

The Campaign of 1942

In 1942 Nazi capabilities no longer included the power to mount a full-scale offensive all along the front, as in 1941; German losses had been too great. There were several alternatives: a war of attrition, which promised to make World War I look swift and painless by comparison, and was ruled out; another effort to take Moscow; or a campaign to seize the Caucasian oilfields with Baku as the final objective. Hitler decided on the last, and issued his order on April 5, 1942. As a preliminary, in May the Germans attacked and cleared the whole Crimea except for Sevastopol, which was not occupied until July 1. On May 12 Timoshenko unleashed another fierce attempt to retake Kharkov,[3] which probably delayed the main Nazi offensive for almost a month, but it resulted in severe losses and the capture of many of his troops by encirclement.

The main blow fell on June 28 near Kursk, where the Nazis broke through Soviet lines. On July 6–7 staunch Red resistance at Voronezh stopped the advance eastward toward Saratov on the middle Volga, but the southern armies moved forward rapidly, on July 27 taking Rostov and crossing the Don River there. Hitler decided to exploit the southern breakthrough with Field Marshal von Kleist's tank forces. In so doing he left intact the railway network supplying Stalingrad and the south, thereby handing the Soviet high command a freedom of movement which may have been the decisive factor in the whole campaign.

In accordance with Hitler's new orders, one force crossed the Don at the bend near Stalingrad in August and on September 9 reached a railway just north of the city. At the same time Kleist's armor fanned out in the north Caucasus. On August 8 the Soviets destroyed and abandoned the Maikop oilfields, and by the end of the month the pursuing Germans were nearing the oil of Grozny. On September 10 they took the Black Sea naval base of Novorossiisk, but Kleist made no further progress in the Caucasus, partly because he ran out of gasoline, but chiefly because Hitler weakened his forces in order to reinforce the armies attacking Stalingrad.

Located on the Volga's right bank, Stalingrad was open to direct assault without a river crossing. The less costly tactic would have been to cross the Volga, cut off river traffic supplying the city, and force its surrender. Hitler chose not to cross the river but to storm the city directly. The attack began on September 15. The oil of Grozny and Baku remained in Soviet hands, and Hitler seemed to have forgotten his objective. Stalingrad possessed nothing of importance to Hitler except its name; the "city of Stalin" had to be taken at all costs. Two weeks earlier General Halder, chief of the General Staff, had tried to persuade Hitler to abandon the as-

---

[3] Evidently it was this unsuccessful attack from which Khrushchëv, in his "secret speech" of 1956, claimed he tried in vain to dissuade Stalin.

sault on Stalingrad and to retreat to the line Kiev-Riga, but he failed to do so and was dismissed in the bargain.

All available forces were hurled into the attempt to storm the city, which continued day after day for a whole month. The new chief of the Soviet General Staff, Vasilevsky, General Zhukov, and Malenkov were all sent to the Stalingrad front, and the Soviet armies under General Chuikov were ordered to defend the city to the last man. Stalingrad was shelled and bombed into a heap of rubble, in which the Soviet garrison hid and inflicted disastrous losses on the attacking enemy. The whole war seemed, to millions of people in various countries, to hang in the balance. Constantine Simonov's *Days and Nights* and Theodore Plievier's *Stalingrad* are two novels which have given the world something of the feeling of what it was like for the Nazi soldier to attack senselessly and endlessly and for the Soviet soldier to hold out in a hell of fire, deprived of reinforcements and supplies, while the situation of both the besiegers and the defenders seemed to grow more and more desperate.

On November 19, 1942, a Soviet force counterattacked heavily on both flanks of the narrow Nazi salient whose apex was Stalingrad. The flanks were held by Romanians and Italians, and both were pierced deeply with little difficulty. General Rokossovsky (who had been imprisoned in the Great Purges and released just before the war) cut off any possible retreat by General Paulus (now named field marshal by Hitler as a reward for his impending sacrifice). Field Marshal von Manstein assembled a relief force and attacked eastward, but by December 27 he was brought to a standstill. Kleist, by a military miracle, extricated his armies from the Caucasus through Rostov, although the Soviets threatened to capture the city and cut him off. The plight of Paulus's surrounded army, again without winter clothes and short of food and ammunition, was hopeless, yet Hitler ordered the troops to fight on. Finally, on January 31, 1943, Paulus was captured, and the last of the pocket was mopped up two days later. Hitler sacrificed the surrounded army in the belief that annihilation was preferable to retreat for psychological reasons. The Soviet high command had not dreamed that the sacrifice would be made and expected their double flank attack to force Paulus's withdrawal immediately.

The Soviet forces continued the attack westward. On February 7 the Kursk "hedgehog" fell; on February 14, Rostov; on February 16, the "superhedgehog" of Kharkov. Hitler then temporarily yielded the command to Manstein, who mounted a counterattack on February 21, and, retaking Kharkov on March 15, was halted only by the coming of the spring thaw. But the Nazi defeat at Stalingrad could not so easily, or in fact ever, be undone.

There has been some dispute about how decisive the battle of Stalingrad was in the whole Russo-German war. Experts have contended that the war was really lost before Moscow in the fall of 1941; that the crucial moment was Stalingrad; or, as

Liddell Hart argues, that it was post-Stalingrad events which made Nazi defeat certain.[4] It seems likely that at Moscow the best Nazi chance to win was missed, and perhaps any chance of *victory* became slim; furthermore, that wiser strategy even after the loss of Paulus's army might have staved off complete Nazi *defeat*, at least for some time, but that nevertheless, both militarily and psychologically Stalingrad was the beginning of the end for Hitler, just as it seemed to the ordinary newspaper reader of the time.

In other theaters of war Stalin's allies were experiencing varying degrees of success. In the Pacific, the United States was just beginning to win victories. Japan's crippling of the United States fleet at Pearl Harbor had inaugurated a period of months of disaster for the West. The Japanese had conquered Malaya and Singapore, the Philippines, the Netherlands East Indies, and Burma; invaded New Guinea and the Aleutian Islands; and threatened Australia and India. Under the slogan of a "Greater East Asia Co-Prosperity Sphere," the Japanese invited and obtained collaboration of substantial elements of the population in occupied areas, directing their animus against white imperialism and ostensibly treating the other Asians as equals—an occupation policy whose apparent success excited Nazi envy as they contemplated the growing resistance of the Soviet peoples.[5] Not until the middle of 1942 was the Japanese advance finally halted with American naval victories in the battles of the Coral Sea and Midway Island and the landing of an expeditionary force on Guadalcanal in August. However, Japan controlled most of the south and east Asian mainland and most of the Pacific islands, and all that could be said by the end of the year was that the farthest tip of the Japanese thrust had been blunted.

In Africa, however, the picture had brightened enormously. From the time when Italy invaded Egypt from Libya in the fall of 1940, the desert battle had seesawed back and forth. Early in 1941 the British counterattacked; in the spring the Nazis rescued the Italians in Libya (as in Albania) and after more skirmishing the Axis troops under General Rommel were approaching the Suez Canal in the autumn of 1942, while the Nazis were thrusting toward Stalingrad and the Caucasus. This was the most dangerous moment of the entire war for the anti-Hitler coalition, when there appeared to be a serious possibility that Rommel from Egypt, the German armies in the Caucasus, and the Japanese from India would make contact somewhere in the Middle East and thereby effect the subjugation of the whole Eastern Hemisphere.

However, the tide turned dramatically in North Africa at almost the same moment that the Germans were defeated at Stalingrad. In October 1942 General Montgomery counterattacked and drove Rommel out of Egypt. On November 8 an Allied force under General Eisenhower invaded Morocco and Algeria, and the

---

[4] B. H. Liddell Hart, ed., *The Soviet Army* London, Weidenfeld and Nicolson, 1956, pp. 114–116.

[5] See, for example, *The Goebbels Diaries, 1942–1943*, Doubleday, 1948, p. 348.

two forces met in Tunisia, clearing Africa of Axis troops by May 1943. The diplomatic repercussions were great. Franco's Spain began to cultivate a sedulous neutrality, Turkey showed increasingly open sympathy toward the Allies, Hitler's occupation of Vichy France merely strengthened the French will to resist, and Mussolini had all too plainly lost his nerve.

By the first months of 1943 it was clear to Hitler that military victory was virtually impossible. Thereupon he tried to stave off compete defeat by seeking to split the coalition facing him and playing on European fears of Soviet Communism. As early as December 1942 it appears that a German approach to Soviet agents was made in Stockholm, proposing a separate peace, and there were further talks in the summer and fall of 1943. It is uncertain how seriously either party took these overtures, which both may have hoped to use as a means of putting pressure on the Western Allies in discussions thereafter.

Stalin's Propaganda Offensive

During the last months of 1941 Stalin's regime had tottered on the brink of collapse and yet survived. But survival was one thing and victory quite another. While the Soviets bent every effort to train larger armies, produce more war matériel, and carry out military preparations for any eventuality, Stalin was also mounting a political offensive—and this was a type of fighting at which he was far more adept than Hitler. His propaganda was directed toward three audiences. To begin with he sought to persuade the Soviet citizens behind Nazi lines to resist Hitler; he did so by spreading word of German atrocities and the desperate economic situation in the occupied areas (which by 1942 the people needed no persuasion to believe), by reminding them that the Allies were on his side, by repeatedly promising that the Soviets would return (which played an important part in determining the people's actions, whether out of fear or hope), and by portraying his regime in new and attractive colors, implying that things would be different after the war was won. To the populace which remained in Soviet territory, he addressed exhortations to fight, using Allied aid and the hints of a changed policy as support. For the benefit of the Allies, as for the ears of the Soviet peoples, he suggested that Communist ideology was being replaced by the cause of the nation. He intended his propaganda to contrast sharply with Hitler's occupation policy and Nazi propaganda, and it did. If the reverse had been true—if Hitler had adopted different propaganda, and Stalin had not changed his line—it is possible that Soviet Communism might not have survived. But fortunately for him, Stalin knew better than most men the uses of political warfare.

In a speech of 1941 he had already asked himself, "Can the Hitlerites be regarded as *nationalists?*" He replied, "No, they cannot. Actually, the Hitlerites are now not nationalists but *imperialists.*" His implication was clearly that to be a nationalist was a good thing—contrary to all Communist teaching of the evil character of "bourgeois" nationalism—and that the nationalism of Russia, at least, was an admirable phenomenon. The openly nationalist slogan, "Death to the German invader!" came to be widely used, and even replaced "Workers of the world, unite!" on the masthead of *Pravda*.

Especially after the battle of Stalingrad, Stalin developed the nationalist doctrine more fully. The Communist Party slogans for the commemoration of the October Revolution (November 7) in 1942 omitted any reference to world revolution. Stalin especially tried to use the army and the church, the two institutions with the strongest links to the nation's past, in his propaganda tactics. In October 1942 the political commissars with the armed forces were formally abolished (even though they survived as "Deputy Commanders for Political Affairs"). The next month *Pravda* declared flatly that the soldier had no socialist obligations, only the duty to defend his fatherland as his ancestors had done. In March 1943 Stalin himself assumed the title of marshal—as if to lend the rank honor—and gave both promotion and publicity to his top officers by the hundred. Epaulettes and saluting were restored; a sense of hierarchy and discipline was widely emphasized. The army, and in particular its high officers, were singled out as the defenders of the native soil and for the moment the most honored institution in the country.

Stalin even pretended to restore the Russian Orthodox Church to favor. During the first days of the invasion, the highest clerics had called for national defense. Evidently the public enthusiasm at being permitted to reopen churches behind Nazi lines spurred the regime to its first gestures in religious policy; it also had Allied opinion in mind. In September 1941 the League of Militant Godless was disbanded—Harriman thought this was because he had transmitted Roosevelt's suggestion to that effect—and the League's printing shop was used to publish a lavish volume inaccurately entitled *The Truth About Religion in Russia*, which was sold for export only.

Nevertheless, a public reconciliation was delayed for some time. In connection with the celebration of the Revolution in November 1942, for the first time Metropolitan Sergii and Stalin exchanged telegrams of felicitation. Only in September 1943, however, did Stalin receive Sergii and other clerics for a talk. As a result a meeting which claimed to be a church council was hastily summoned; it elected Sergii Patriarch—an office vacant since the death of Tikhon in 1925. While the "reconciliation" led to the conversion of the church into a tool to regain the loyalty of the Orthodox laity in the USSR and, later, to assist in the Sovietization of the Balkan Orthodox countries, it did permit limited scope for worship and prayer.

What seemed to the Western Allies conclusive proof of Stalin's change of heart was the dissolution of the Comintern in May 1943. "Dissolution," to be sure, did not even lead to the dispersal of the Comintern staff in the USSR, let alone disturb Soviet control of its foreign apparatus or weaken the loyalties of foreign Communists to the USSR. By that time the alleged conversion of Stalin into a "nationalist" leader was a widespread article of faith in the West. Those who knew little of the USSR—except perhaps, as some had learned in school, that "Trotsky wanted world revolution, while Stalin only wanted socialism in one country"—found it easy to believe or did not dare to doubt that Stalin was a tsar in commissar's clothing.

It would be most difficult to generalize on what the Russian people thought of the purported about-face of the government. It appears however, that some thought Stalin had perceived the error of his ways, and all would be well; others welcomed the concessions of the present while realistically reserving judgment about the future; still others doubted that the leopard had changed his spots, but worked to defeat Hitler, assuring themselves that they could "pull up the weeds ... afterwards"[6]—that is, drive out the Communists. The Soviet peoples had ample experience with the meaning of temporary Communist shifts in tactics. They perceived that although for the moment Stalin was glorifying the army and showing the church public respect in the name of the nation, winking at all sorts of violations of regulations by workers and collective farmers and deviations from Party orthodoxy by intellectuals, and saying little about Communism, still he had not promised to abolish the single most hated economic institution, the collective farm, or to end the totalitarian system of controls. Stalin was not about to grant his peoples freedom.

The Campaign of 1943

In the spring of 1943 Hitler, having resumed command in the East, was still determined on an offensive, partly because he retained confidence in his own power to do the impossible, partly because he had been unwarrantably cheered by Manstein's brief post-Stalingrad counterattack. However, he faced a bigger Red Army and a more experienced group of generals, while Nazi reserves were nearing exhaustion. The Reds shrewdly waited until Hitler had committed most of his remaining armor in an effort, beginning on July 5, to reduce the Kursk salient by double envelopment. After the Nazis suffered heavy tank losses, the Soviets launched an offensive of their own on July 12. By the first week of August they recaptured Orël and Belgorod and began to move forward on a front extending all the way south to the Black Sea. On August 23 Kharkov was retaken, this time permanently; by mid-September Novorossiisk and the Taman Peninsula were occupied. By the end of September Poltava and Smolensk had fallen and the Nazi "Winter Line" at the Dnieper River had been reached.

---

[6] The phrase comes from Michael Soloviëv's novel, *When the Gods Are Silent*. See the discussion by Eugene Lyons in *Our Secret Allies*, pp. 228–235.

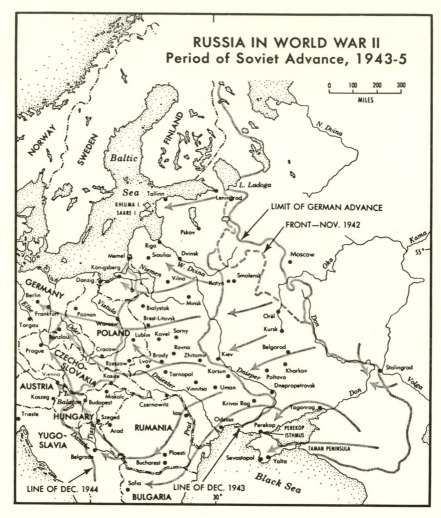

RUSSIA IN WORLD WAR II
Period of Soviet Advance, 1943-5

The Soviets crossed the Dnieper almost without a pause. Rokossovsky, Vatutin, and Konev led their army groups across on October 5–6 both north and south of Kiev. To the southeast, Malinovsky's and Tolbukhin's groups reached the bend of the river at Dnepropetrovsk and neared the Isthmus of Perekop, thereby threatening both the German forces to the north in the Dnieper bend and those to the south in the Crimea. At the beginning of November Manstein delayed the Soviet advance by a strong counterattack south from the bend position. Although the Germans lost Kiev on November 4 and were pushed back to Zhitomir a week later, they mounted another counterattack on November 19 which halted the Soviet westward thrust, recaptured Zhitomir, and made some further progress before being stopped by mud. Farther north the Soviets tried to advance along the

Moscow-Minsk road, but they were repulsed time after time by the German defenders, despite the fact that the latter were outnumbered more than five to one.

At the close of the 1943 campaign the Germans continued to hold the greater part of Ukraine, although the line from Zhitomir to the Dnieper bend ran east and west for roughly three hundred miles, and south of it was an exposed salient which clearly would be difficult for the Nazis to hold. Hitler's armies were still capable of fierce and clever defense, but their losses in manpower could no longer be made up, and they were outnumbered more decisively every month. In contrast, Stalin had managed to patch up domestic controls and morale somewhat, and as for the people in the occupied areas, although they might hate the Communists as much as ever, they were faced with the likelihood that Stalin would, as he had promised, soon be back. Now that the flood of American supplies was continuous, and the output of men from the recruit training centers and matériel from the war plants in the Soviet East was steadily rising, Stalin correctly began to scent victory.

The Diplomacy of the "Second Front"

Evidently taking seriously the possibility that the Western Allies might make a compromise peace with the Nazis, or even join them in an attack on the USSR, Stalin from 1941 on called for a "second front" by way of guarantee against such eventualities. Of course, an Allied landing in Europe would also have great military significance, but the political factor seems to have been uppermost in Stalin's mind throughout. Until the end of 1943 Stalin held aloof from any top-level meeting with Western leaders, plainly awaiting developments.

In the meantime, however, the Soviets endeavored to stay in the picture of Allied plans for the peace. Stalin authorized Litvinov, now his ambassador in Washington, to sign the United Nations Declaration (a sort of expanded Atlantic Charter) on January 1, 1942, along with twenty-five other nations. In May 1942 Molotov visited London and signed an Anglo-Soviet Alliance, valid for twenty years. At that time the ambiguous public announcement was made that the two powers had reached agreement on the "urgent tasks of opening a Second Front in Europe during 1942." Therefore Churchill, when he visited Moscow in August, had the unpleasant task of explaining that an invasion which had been publicly described as likely, and privately (to Molotov) said to be possible, would not take place. Stalin expressed resentment and a general lack of confidence in Allied promises.

When the Allied invasion of North Africa occurred in November 1942, the West made some effort to label it a "second front," but the Soviets refused to acknowledge it as such. Roosevelt and Churchill, when they met at Casablanca in January 1943, had the problem in the forefront of their minds. The chief Casablanca decisions were military: for the time being the war in Europe was to be pressed at the expense of the war in the Pacific, and preparations were ordered for an invasion of northern France in the summer of 1944. However, political questions were also seriously considered. The two Western leaders proclaimed "unconditional surrender"—a phrase which General Grant had used at Fort Donelson in the Civil War—to be the objective of the war in Germany, Italy, and Japan.

As far as the countries subjugated by the Axis were concerned, the goals of peace had already been set forth in the Atlantic Charter, drawn up by Roosevelt and Churchill at a meeting off Newfoundland in August 1941, which promised to all nations self-determination, equality of economic opportunity, and the like—in effect restating the principles of Wilson's Fourteen Points of 1917. "Unconditional surrender," however, implied a very different fate for the peoples of the enemy countries. It clearly suggested to them that they had no alternative but to fight to the bitter end without hope of quarter or compromise, and that any effort to change their rulers in order to bring about peace was useless. But the slogan was not aimed at the enemy peoples; it was intended to strengthen the determination of all Allied nations, and "above all," as Chester Wilmot writes, "as an assurance to Stalin that the inability to open a Second Front in 1943 did not indicate any weakening in the resolution of the Western Allies."[7]

Stalin welcomed the verbal commitment of the Casablanca conference, and must also have felt satisfaction that the Western Allies seemed to have renounced any attempt at political warfare at the very moment that Field Marshal Paulus, whom he was to make the chief of a "Free German Committee," had fallen into his hands.[8] However, the "unconditional surrender" slogan was not enough to eliminate Western-Soviet tensions, which grew more serious in 1943. Rumors of Nazi-Soviet peace feelers aroused suspicions. Stalin rejected an American offer to mediate in bringing about peace between the USSR and Finland.

The most severe strains up to that time followed the Nazi announcement of the discovery of the graves of a large number of Polish officers at Katyn, near Smolensk. As early as July 1941 the USSR and the Polish (and also the Czech) government-in-exile in London had signed an agreement providing for the formation of national troop units on Soviet territory and dealing with other matters. From the first Soviet-Polish relations had been fragile because of the Soviet part in the destruction of Poland, Soviet refusal to confirm Polish borders as of 1939, and, most urgent of all, Moscow's professed inability to solve the mystery of what had happened to almost 15,000 Poles interned by the Soviets in 1939. Repeated Polish inquiries about the men failed to elicit any information. After the Nazis discovered the bodies at Katyn, a German-appointed commission, including some neutral experts, investigated and concluded that the men had been executed in 1940—therefore by the Soviets.

---

[7] *The Struggle for Europe*, Harper, 1952, p. 123.

[8] Actually the committee never came to much, but it was only the beginning of Stalin's political efforts in Germany.

On April 17, 1943, Prime Minister General Sikorski of the Polish regime in London publicly requested the International Red Cross to investigate, whereupon the USSR immediately broke relations with the Poles. Whatever the suspicions of Churchill, who regarded Britain as having special obligations to Poland, he regarded the matter as secondary to the war effort and tried to smooth things over—but quite in vain. After the Soviets recaptured the Smolensk region, they announced that a commission of their own had decided that the murders were committed by the Nazis. At the Nuremberg war crimes trials the Soviets did not repeat this contention. Only in 1990, however, did Moscow admit that it was Stalin's crime.[9]

Shortly after the Katyn revelations, an angry exchange between Stalin and Churchill led to the recall of Ambassadors Maisky and Litvinov from London and Washington. This caused the abandonment of a plan, which had been the result of a mission by former Ambassador Joseph E. Davies, for a meeting between Roosevelt and Stalin in July. Instead Churchill and Roosevelt together proposed a meeting of the three foreign ministers, Eden, Hull, and Molotov. Stalin's assent arrived during the Anglo-American conference at Quebec in August 1943. At the meeting the news was also received that General Eisenhower, whose troops had vaulted from North Africa to Sicily and thereby precipitated the resignation of Mussolini and his replacement by Marshal Badoglio, had been informed by Badoglio that the imminent landing on the Italian mainland would bring about Italy's surrender.[10]

The diplomatic picture had brightened somewhat. The foreign ministers met in Moscow in October, and Eden and Hull were able to notify the Soviets that the cross-Channel invasion was being planned for the summer of 1944. It was agreed that on the conclusion of peace Germany was to be completely disarmed and was to be compelled to pay reparations for the physical damage inflicted upon all Allied nations. The question of the military and political partitioning of Germany and Europe was raised without being settled. The chief result of the foreign ministers' conference was that a meeting of the "Big Three"—Roosevelt, Churchill, and Stalin—was arranged to take place at Teheran one month later. Although the war was far from over, the prerequisites of victory—at least in Europe—were already visible, and the Teheran conference inaugurated the period in which the considerations of postwar politics came rapidly to the foreground of Stalin's relations with the Western Allies.

---

[9] Conquest, *Stalin: Breaker of Nations,* Viking, 1991, p. 229.

[10] This was hardly the whole story. During the weeks that Badoglio and Eisenhower had been fencing verbally about what "unconditional surrender" meant, the Nazis had poured troops into Italy and met the Allied invasion force with a rude surprise which set the stage for a long, tortuous, and indecisive Italian campaign.

21

The USSR in World War II: Political Successes 1943–1945

The Teheran Conference

Three of the dominant personalities of the twentieth century confronted one another for the first time at the Teheran conference of November–December 1943. No wonder the reports of every smirk and toast were eagerly devoured by the public in Allied countries, weary of war and defeat, but now scenting victory. Not long before the conference Roosevelt told former Ambassador Bullitt, "I have just a hunch that Stalin doesn't want anything but security for his country, and I think that if I give him everything I possibly can and ask nothing from him in return, *noblesse oblige,* he won't try to annex anything and will work for a world of democracy and peace." The illusions, by no means confined to Roosevelt, of the Allied leadership at this point could scarcely be more succinctly phrased. A document of alleged "military" authorship which Harry Hopkins had brought to the Quebec conference said, "Since Russia is the decisive factor in the war, she must be given every assistance and every effort must be made to obtain her friendship. Likewise, since without question she will dominate Europe on the defeat of the Axis, it is even more essential to develop and maintain the most friendly relations with Russia." This sounded a more hardheaded note; nevertheless the estimate shared Roosevelt's basic assumption that Stalin was a nationalist speaking for a nationalist regime, and was chiefly concerned with the national security of Russia. Stalin had labored long to achieve Allied acceptance of this image, and he played the role throughout the "Big Three" conferences with success.

In accordance with his hopes, Roosevelt tried his best at Teheran to establish close personal ties with Stalin. He even used Churchill as a foil for this purpose, deliberately evoking Churchill's frowns as a spur to Stalin's grins. Stalin appeared to respond to these overtures, persuading Roosevelt to move to the Soviet Embassy as security against a "German plot." The conferences discussed military questions first. On Roosevelt's invitation, Stalin voiced the opinion that Italy and the Balkans promised little advantage to the Allies, linked a promise to join the war against Japan (after Hitler's defeat) with a demand for a strong cross-Channel invasion of France, and hinted that the one might depend on the other. Churchill had in mind objectives in northern Italy and the Balkans; Stalin bluntly insisted that if anything further was to be done in the Mediterranean, it should be an invasion of southern France in addition to the Channel crossing.

The political implications of this exchange, hinging on the distance which the Allied armies would be kept from Eastern Europe, were plain at least to Churchill and Stalin. The decision was for a southern France landing, more or less coinciding with Operation Overlord, which was to be launched against northern France in May 1944. One agreement of chiefly political character was reached: the British and Americans accepted the Curzon Line (see p. 135) as the future Soviet-Polish border. The London Polish regime, it was virtually certain, would not accept this frontier, and only a month after Teheran, Stalin established a Polish Communist junta in Moscow which would.

After the period of heated debates had passed, the conference closed in a spirit of camaraderie. Churchill presented Stalin with a gem-encrusted sword sent by George VI for the city of Stalingrad, and Stalin bowed to kiss it. Stalin toasted Churchill's birthday with a reference to his "great friend." The conference communiqué affirmed, "We came here with hope and determination. We leave here friends in fact, in spirit and in purpose." Immediately afterward, Roosevelt confided to Frances Perkins at some length how he thought he had won Stalin's friendship.

Soviet Armies Advance Beyond Soviet Borders

The coming of winter in December 1943 did not halt the fighting on the Eastern front. Hitler's troops now not only faced a numerically stronger Red Army, but also were subjected to formidable harassment from partisan units, which in January 1944, on the central sector alone, were estimated to number close to 150,000 men. In several areas partisan sabotage created serious difficulties in moving up reinforcements and supplies. Hitler was no longer capable of mounting a major offensive, and the most he could do was to break the tips of the Soviet spearheads. The vast exposed southern salient which the Nazis still held was especially difficult to defend.

At the end of December Vatutin enveloped Zhitomir, at the base of the salient, from both sides and thrust northwestward to Sarny, just south of the Pripet Marshes. Simultaneously he struck south to Vinnitsa, threatening the Odessa railway and making the salient less tenable than ever. In January 1944 the northern armies relieved Leningrad and advanced almost to Pskov. In February Konev encircled most of a German army on the flank of the salient near Korsun, while Vatutin drove westward close to Kovel, and Malinovsky cut off the eastern tip of the salient at Krivoi Rog.

All these blows were preliminary to the main offensive of 1944. In March it was launched by Zhukov, who had replaced Vatutin as army group commander, with an advance toward Tarnopol. At the same time Konev overran an important Nazi base at Uman and cut the Odessa railway. The salient was now collapsing everywhere. By the end of March Zhukov had crossed the Dniester on a broad front and taken Czernowitz, and both Konev and he reached the Prut River, the border between Romania and Soviet-annexed Bessarabia. Malinovsky mopped up the remnants of the salient. The Nazis in the Crimea were ordered to make a stand but were overrun in April and May.

As the summer began, the Soviets enjoyed a three to one over-all superiority in manpower, and—thanks to American supplies—an estimated five to one advantage in equipment. The Nazi reserves were exhausted. The 1939 borders had been reached or crossed on most of the front, and the Soviets had the military capability of capturing virtually any objectives in Eastern and Central Europe which they chose. Four days after Operation Overlord struck Normandy, in June, a sector-by-sector Soviet advance was begun. First the Mannerheim line was breached and Finland effectively knocked out of the war, although fighting continued until September. On June 23 four army groups with one hundred divisions struck westward on the central front. Minsk fell on July 3, Vilna on July 13, and the Niemen River was bridged three days later. At that moment another large-scale offensive in the north was launched, which swung north to Pskov before bearing down on Dvinsk and sweeping westward to Siauliai in central Lithuania on July 27. Soon afterward the Germans began to withdraw from Estonia and Latvia.

Further south Marshal Konev enveloped Lvov and captured it on July 25, continuing on to Rzeszow. Soviet thrusts from several directions passed through Bialystok and Brest-Litovsk and by July 31 reached points only a few miles northeast and southeast of Warsaw. At this moment the Polish resistance army under General Tadeusz Bor-Komorowski, expecting the Soviet forces to continue into Warsaw, attacked the Germans inside the city. Marshal Rokossovsky, himself a Pole by birth, led his Soviet troops close to the scene, but was halted temporarily by counterattacks. On August 15 he occupied Praga, Warsaw's suburb east of the Vistula, but he made no attempt to cross.

With Soviet forces in plain sight, the insurgents fought on without aid until October 5, when the Nazis completed mopping up and in revenge systematically destroyed the city of Warsaw block by block. Out of a population of a million, some 10,000 remained huddling in the ruins at the end of the war. It has been suggested that if Polish Communists had led the rising, Stalin would have ordered a crossing to assist them; the point is rather that Polish Communists would not have acted at all in the absence of orders from Stalin. It is clear, at any event, that

Stalin shed no tears for the destruction of the non-Communist Polish fighters in Warsaw, since he refused even to allow British or American planes which were attempting to drop supplies to the insurgents to land on Soviet airfields.

The Soviet forces made no effort to cross the Vistula during the rest of 1944. The next offensive was directed at Romania. On August 20 Tolbukhin struck out of his small Dniester bridgeheads, while Malinovsky drove beyond the Prut to Iasi. On August 23 King Michael of Romania arrested his Nazi-collaborator prime minister, Marshal Antonescu, and pledged co-operation with the United Nations on condition that the portion of Transylvania which Hitler had given Hungary be returned to Romania. No one raised any quibbles about "unconditional surrender," and the Soviets officially declared that they aimed neither at annexation of Romanian territory (except for Bessarabia and northern Bukovina, which they considered Soviet soil) nor at "altering the social structure of Romania as it exists at present." Soon afterward King Michael declared war on Germany. The German armies in Romania collapsed swiftly. By the end of August the oil city of Ploesti and Bucharest, the capital, had been occupied. On August 26 Bulgaria withdrew from the war, and on September 16 Soviet forces occupied Sofia. At this point the Nazis were frantically trying to extricate themselves from Greece.

By the time that Soviet armies reached the Balkans, the USSR and the Western powers seemed to have reached full agreement about their fate. Continuing to play the role of a ruler primarily concerned with national security, Stalin had made gestures in regard to Western Europe which appeared to lend striking confirmation to the virtually settled Western interpretation of his motives. In March 1944 the Soviets had recognized the Italian regime of Marshal Badoglio and had compelled the Italian Communists to cease demanding the removal of both Badoglio and King Victor Emmanuel III. Similarly in France, where, as in Italy, the Communists were emerging as the strongest single party, they were told to hold their hand and not to insist on control of the police and the justice ministry.

In June 1944 there was some amicable discussion regarding the division of Europe into spheres of influence, and when Churchill visited Moscow in October he proposed (and Stalin appeared to accept) an oddly arithmetical formula: in Romania the Soviets would have a "90–10" preponderance, in Bulgaria "75–25," in Yugoslavia and Hungary influence would be shared "50–50" with Britain, while in Greece the British would have a "90–10" voice.

Churchill also raised the question of Poland. When Soviet troops had crossed into Polish territory, the Polish Communist junta had been installed in Lublin, and soon afterward Stalin officially recognized it as the legitimate government of Poland. In July Stanislaw Mikołajczyk, the leader of the Peasant party, who had become premier of the London Polish regime after the death of General Sikorski, was persuaded by the British to visit Stalin. On his arrival he was informed of Soviet recognition of the Lublin junta, with which he was amicably advised to conduct his own talks. At this very moment the Warsaw uprising broke out, and Mikołajczyk appealed to Stalin to assist it. At length Stalin promised aid, but he gave none. In October, when Churchill tried to put the case for Mikołajczyk's regime, Stalin would not budge an inch.

However, as far as Churchill could see, Poland was an arena where British and Russian national interests clashed, and little more. Stalin raised no ideological questions; he might appear blunt, peevish, or stubborn, but thus far he had not discarded the pose of hardheaded bourgeois-nationalist statesmanship. In April 1944 he even descended to the level of comedy by receiving personally a bewildered but well-intentioned Roman Catholic priest, Father Orlemanski of Springfield, Massachusetts, and entrusting him with a message of reconciliation with the Vatican (which had no results except to get Orlemanski into trouble with his superiors). It seemed that Stalin had no ideological enemy left on earth.

Vlasov and the Nazis

By 1944 defeat stared Germany in the face. Goebbels's propaganda machine did its best to counter the deterioration of morale, especially emphasizing the bleak prospects with which the "unconditional surrender" slogan confronted the German people. On July 20 a few army officers and government officials attempted to kill Hitler and overthrow the Nazi regime, but the plot miscarried and merely resulted in the liquidation of the chief non-Nazis anywhere near the summit of power.

Opportunely for Goebbels came Allied publication of lists of "war criminals," the mass proscription of the German General Staff, and the approval of the "Morgenthau Plan," which envisaged the destruction of German industry and the conversion of all Germany into "a country primarily agricultural and pastoral in character," at the second Quebec conference in September 1944. Goebbels declared, "It hardly matters whether the Bolshevists want to destroy the Reich in one fashion and the Anglo-Saxons propose to do it in another." Doubtless the Morgenthau Plan did much to confuse those Germans who might be thinking of surrendering to the West while holding out against Stalin, and thus Stalin could only profit by its dissemination by the U.S. and Britain.

At virtually the same moment that the Allies were endorsing the Morgenthau Plan at Quebec, the Nazi regime turned in desperation to a weapon which, if used earlier, might indeed have had great effect on the outcome of the war, but what the Nazis did with it in 1944 was too little and much too late. General Vlasov, who had been captured two years earlier, was to be transformed from a pawn of Nazi propaganda into the leader of a real Soviet anti-Stalinite army and government.

Vlasov, who was born in 1900, the son of a peasant family of Nizhnii Novgorod, had risen in Red Army ranks. A Party member since 1930, he had been Soviet military adviser to Chiang Kai-shek in 1938–1939, decorated in 1940, and in the autumn of 1941 one of the chief army commanders in the defense of Moscow. Apparently he possessed great personal magnetism, integrity, and ability. Not at all the opportunist and Nazi hireling he was accused of being, Vlasov "stressed his nationalism and strove to preserve the independence of the Movement," writes the most recent investigator.[1] Of the most influential men who joined his cause, probably the ablest was the brilliant but mysterious Milenty Zykov, who said he had been on the staff of *Izvestiia* under Bukharin and for a time had been exiled by Stalin. When captured he claimed to be serving as a battalion commissar, but it was suspected that he was much more.

By the end of 1942 Captain Wilfried Strik-Strikfeldt of the German army propaganda section was planning to establish a Russian National Committee led by Vlasov at Smolensk. The plan was vetoed from above, but in December the formation of the committee was proclaimed on German soil instead. Vlasov published a statement of his aims, and he was allowed to tour occupied Soviet areas, meeting a considerable popular response. In April 1943 an anti-Bolshevik conference of Soviet prisoners opposed to Stalin's regime was held in Brest-Litovsk. After Vlasov declared that if successful he would grant Ukraine and the Caucasus self-determination, Rosenberg was persuaded to support the committee. However, in June 1943 Hitler ordered that Vlasov was to be kept out of the occupation zone, and that the movement was to be confined to propaganda—that is, promises which Hitler could ignore later—across the lines to Soviet-held territory.

During 1943 Vlasov's circle, under the protection of Strik-Strikfeldt's section at Dabendorf just outside Berlin, was allowed to carry on remarkably free discussions about a future non-Communist government for Russia and to publish two newspapers in Russian, one for Soviet war prisoners and another for the *Osttruppen*. The political center of gravity at Dabendorf fluctuated between the more socialist-inclined entourage of Zykov and the more authoritarian-minded group close to the *émigré* anti-Soviet organization, N.T.S. (*Natsionalno-Trudovoi Soiuz* or National Toilers' Union). Of course political arguments among Soviet *émigrés* were nothing new; what was new was the hope of imminent action, utilizing the five million Soviet nationals in Germany, to overthrow Stalin—either with Hitler's support or, if he should fall, perhaps in conjunction with the Western Allies. Despite arguments, a fair degree of harmony was maintained among the Russians at Dabendorf. Especially noteworthy was the extent to which Vlasov and his followers succeeded in preventing themselves from being compromised by Nazi ideology and in maintaining the integrity of their own effort to win Russian freedom.

Until 1944, however, the Vlasov circle was confined to discussion and publication. Although the phrase, "Russian Liberation Army," and its Russian abbreviation, ROA (for *Russkaia Osvoboditel'naia Armiia*), were much used in propaganda—with Hitler's approval—there was in fact no such army. "ROA" was only a

---

[1] Catherine Andreyev, *Vlasov and the Russian Liberation Movement*, Cambridge U. Press, 1987, p. 202.

shoulder patch which the *Osttruppen,* scattered in small units throughout the Nazi army, were permitted to wear. In the summer of 1944 the ablest intellectual of the Vlasov group, Zykov, was abducted and almost certainly murdered forthwith by the SS.

Nevertheless it was Himmler, chief of the SS, who not long afterward achieved the reversal of Nazi policy toward Vlasov. In a meeting with Vlasov in mid-September 1944, Himmler agreed to the formation of a Committee for the Liberation of the Peoples of Russia (*Komitet Osvobozhdeniia Narodov Rossii* or K.O.N.R.), which would have the potentiality of a government, and an actual army. It appears that Hitler consented to Himmler's new policy chiefly because his suspicion of other Nazi officials who opposed it was by 1944 greater than his fear of arming enemy nationals—a fear which, it must be said, was justified from the Nazi standpoint. The concrete results of Himmler's decision were meager, largely because the Russians could not, amid the disintegration which overtook the Nazi system during the last months of the war, obtain the material aid they needed to implement their plans.

However, in November 1944 in Prague the K.O.N.R. was officially established at a meeting which issued the so-called "Prague Manifesto." This document, declaring that the irruption of the Red armies into Eastern Europe revealed more clearly than ever the Soviet "aim to strengthen still more the mastery of Stalin's tyranny over the peoples of the USSR, and to establish it all over the world," stated the goals of the K.O.N.R. to be the overthrow of the Communist regime and the "creation of a new free People's political system without Bolsheviks and exploiters." It proclaimed recognition of the "equality of all peoples of Russia" and their right of self-determination as well as the intention of ending forced labor and the collective farms and of achieving real civil liberties and social justice. If such a document had been widely disseminated two or three years earlier and given some substance in Nazi occupation policy, the results might have been important or even decisive; coming in 1944, it had no observable effect on the Soviet peoples.

The Prague meeting did stimulate certain Nazi officials to make efforts to put the minorities into the picture with political committees and armies. A year earlier the Nazis had finally organized a Ukrainian SS division which bore the name "Galicia," but although it fought hard and well at the battle of Brody, on the Rovno-Lvov road, in July 1944, when it was finally overrun there, it dispersed to join Ukrainian partisan forces behind Red lines. In October an SS official, Dr. Fritz Arlt, attempted to secure the consent of the Ukrainian nationalist leaders to the formation of a Ukrainian national committee. To avoid being overshadowed by Vlasov, Bandera and Melnyk agreed to the setting up of such a committee, nominally headed by General Paul Shandruk. Melnyk protested the Prague Manifesto, but many Ukrainians nevertheless joined the Vlasov movement, along with representatives of other minorities.

In January 1945 the formation of the Armed Forces of the K.O.N.R. was announced; however, only two divisions were actually activated and mobilized. The

First Division, under the command of a Ukrainian, General S. K. Buniachenko, was committed in April on the front near Frankfurt on the Oder, but the unit refused to fight under existing circumstances, and amid the Nazi military collapse moved south toward Czechoslovakia. At the call of the Czech resistance leaders in Prague, the division moved into the city and on May 7, with Czech aid, captured it from the Nazis.

However, in the Europe of the spring of 1945 there was no place for an anti-Soviet Russian army. The generals, including Vlasov, were turned over to the Soviet command by American and British forces, with or without authorization to do so. In February 1946 the remainder of the army was handed over by U.S. authorities without warning to Soviet repatriation officers at Plattling, Bavaria. In August Pravda announced the execution of Vlasov and his fellow officers, describing them as "agents of German intelligence" and failing to inform the Russian people that they had organized a movement to overthrow Stalin.

The Defeat of Nazi Germany

In the summer of 1944 the Allies had landed in Normandy and on the Riviera and rapidly cleared most of France and Belgium of Nazi forces. By September the American troops had crossed the German frontier. The British and Americans tried and failed to cross the Rhine at Arnhem. Farther south the advance halted when they ran out of gasoline. Ground transport was powerless to keep the front supplied, and there was not enough air transport to make good the difference. A Western front thereupon came into existence and lasted until spring.

Meanwhile the Soviet armies, having conquered Romania, plunged into Central Europe. The strategic result of the "unconditional surrender" policy, in the view of General Fuller, was that "the Soviet war aim was rapidly expanded from the defeat of Germany into the conquest of Eastern Europe, the strategic key of which is Vienna and not Berlin."[2] There was no need for the Soviets to hurry to Berlin, since "unconditional surrender" precluded the possibility that Hitler or any other Germans could capitulate to the Western Allies alone, and, moreover, Stalin had been promised, by the time of the Yalta conference in February 1945, that Berlin was to be well inside his zone of occupation. He could then proceed to strengthen his political position to the south by moving Red troops there as rapidly as possible. Hitler could still mount counterattacks but in general lacked the power to stop him.

In September 1944 Marshal Malinovsky's forces struck westward, from a line running from the Iron Gate of the Danube to Czernowitz, toward Hungary. Romania, in the hope of regaining the lost portion of Transylvania, had also declared

---

[2] Major-General J. F. C. Fuller, *The Second World War, 1939–45*, Duell, Sloan and Pearce, 1949, p. 281.

war on Hungary. On October 5 Malinovsky crossed the Hungarian border near Arad, while Marshal Tolbukhin advanced from Bulgaria across the Danube into Yugoslavia, made contact with Tito's partisan forces, and on October 19 captured Belgrade. On October 11 Malinovsky crossed the Tisza River at Szeged and turned north toward Budapest, which he was approaching in early November. By the beginning of December he had linked up with General Petrov on a line from Miskolc to Košice in Slovakia but then halted, as the Germans concentrated strong forces for a last-ditch stand northeast of Budapest.

Simultaneously Soviet forces in the Baltic states launched an offensive. On September 21 they captured the Estonian capital, Tallinn, and occupied Oesel (Estonian, Saare) and the other Estonian islands. Other troops neared Riga from the northeast and east. At this point the Nazis decided to withdraw toward East Prussia. On October 10 the Soviets succeeded, by reaching the Baltic coast north of Memel, in cutting off any retreat by land. Three days later Riga fell. However, many of the isolated German troops were withdrawn by sea. Not stopping to clean up the pocket, the Soviets attacked into East Prussia. They moved up to the Angerapp River before fierce Nazi resistance halted them on October 25.

Between the Danubian and the Baltic fronts, the Soviet armies in Poland remained stationary from August 1944, when Rokossovsky reached the Vistula opposite Warsaw, until January 1945. At the end of November 1944 the Danubian campaign was resumed with twin offensives by Tolbukhin and Malinovsky toward Budapest from the southwest and east. Moving up the west side of the Danube, Tolbukhin met Malinovsky north of Budapest and surrounded the city. Despite a strong German counterattack, they continued onward to occupy the Hungarian capital by February 13, 1945.

Meanwhile, in mid-January, four Soviet army groups attacked all the way from the Baltic to the Carpathians. In southern Poland Konev and Zhukov struck together across the upper Vistula. Zhukov moved north toward Warsaw from the rear, forced the Nazis to evacuate, and occupied the city on January 17. Two days later Konev took Cracow. Cherniakhovsky and Rokossovsky attacked through East Prussia and, by reaching the Baltic near Elbing on January 26, created another pocket of Germans. Konev reached the border of German Silesia, crossed the upper Oder, and took Bunslau on February 15, while Zhukov surrounded Posen (Poznań) and on February 10 reached the Oder River north of Frankfurt. Farther north, Rokossovsky stormed Danzig on March 30. The Germans in East Prussia continued to fight fiercely. On February 17 Cherniakhovsky was killed and replaced by Marshal Vasilevsky, who pushed on to capture Königsberg on April 9.

In Western Hungary, on March 3, 1945, the Germans opened a great counterattack comparable to the Ardennes offensive of Marshal von Rundstedt in December 1944. The blow was actually spearheaded by the German Sixth SS Panzer Army, which had led the thrust into the Ardennes. The Germans broke through the Soviet front between lakes Balaton and Velence toward the southeast and came near to reaching the Danube. However, as in the Ardennes offensive, the tanks ran out of gasoline, and by the middle of March the Nazi salient was eliminated. Counterattacking almost at once, Tolbukhin and Malinovsky advanced together, and their opponents began to retreat in disorder. On March 29 the Austrian frontier was crossed at Köszeg, and Tolbukhin from the south and Malinovsky from the east attacked Vienna, using much the same tactics that they had used against Budapest. However, Vienna was easier prey, and by April 13 it was completely occupied. Central and Eastern Europe was in Soviet hands.

In February and March Allied forces, continuing to advance in a cautious and even line, closed up to the Rhine and crossed it. By the first week in April the front had collapsed. The Ruhr was the object of a gigantic and successful double envelopment, and on April 18 the trapped German forces surrendered. At that moment there were sharp verbal exchanges between the British, who wanted to occupy Berlin for political reasons, and the Americans, who believed it militarily necessary to halt the advance at the Elbe while swiftly thrusting into the so-called "National Redoubt" in the Alps, where the Germans were supposed to be preparing a do-or-die defense—but they were by this time quite incapable of doing so. Eisenhower, supported by Roosevelt, pursued the latter strategy. Both Berlin and Prague were left to the Soviets.

On April 17 the final Soviet offensive began. Eight days later Zhukov and Konev encircled Berlin and Konev's patrols linked up with the U.S. First Army at Torgau on the Elbe. On April 30 Hitler committed suicide in his bunker, and two days later the remainder of the troops in Berlin surrendered. As the Allied forces in Italy advanced toward Austria, Mussolini was caught by Italian partisans and executed on April 28. Eisenhower halted his troops on the Elbe and at a line a few miles inside Czechoslovakia. The Soviet forces closed up to the Elbe and entered Prague, already freed by Vlasov's troops. On May 7 a document of "unconditional surrender" was signed, and the war in Europe came to an end at midnight of the next day, but by that time there was virtually nothing left to surrender. The war was ended by complete Allied occupation of German territory before the termination of the armistice formalities.

The Beginning of Peacemaking

For a time after the Teheran conference, the course of Soviet relations with the Western Allies was smooth. The Soviets hailed the Normandy invasion as the "Second Front" for which they had been waiting, and they followed its progress with great interest. However, when the Allied advance was halted on the German frontier in the fall of 1944 Stalin showed no great concern. It is doubtful that he would have welcomed an Anglo-American thrust into the heart of Germany before the Soviets were ready to move in from the east. By that time the outcome of the war was certain, and Stalin, like Churchill—but unlike Roosevelt—was thinking more in terms of the postwar political situation than of the remaining battles which had to be fought.

The Allies began long-range planning for the peace at the conferences held at Bretton Woods in July 1944, where the delegates discussed the establishment of an International Monetary Fund and an International Bank for Reconstruction and Development as means of solving postwar economic problems, and at Dumbarton Oaks in August and September, where the shape of the proposed United Nations organization was debated. However, agreement could not be reached on whether a great power should be entitled to exercise its veto on the Security Council in disputes to which it was a party (none of the Big Three would consider giving up a veto entirely). This question remained to be solved at the highest levels.

At the end of 1944 the most vexing diplomatic problem remained that of Poland, which had been left out of the informal Anglo-Soviet agreement on zones of influence in postwar Europe. After the Soviet refusal to help the Warsaw insurgents, there was little hope of reconciliation between the London regime of Prime Minister Mikołajczyk and Stalin, who had his own men established in authority on Polish soil. In October 1944 Churchill did manage to arrange a meeting with Stalin and Mikołajczyk in Moscow. There Mikołajczyk finally agreed to accept the Curzon Line as Poland's eastern frontier, provided it was modified in the south to leave Poland the oilfields of Galicia and the city of Lwów (Lvov). However, he could not obtain the backing of his London colleagues for this concession and thereupon resigned. Reporting these events to the House of Commons, Churchill argued the "reasonable and just" character of the Curzon Line as a frontier. He did not report that during the October meeting, Stalin had for the first time urged an Allied descent on Yugoslavia and an offensive northward toward Austria. The reason for this unexpected plea may have been the hope that German forces would thereby be drawn away from the Russian front. Stalin may have felt that such a move would force the unruly Tito into a closer dependence on Moscow, or it is even possible that, feeling certain no such proposal would be acted upon at that stage, he hoped by making it to disarm Churchill's suspicions of Soviet designs in Central Europe.

For some time discussions regarding arrangements for a second Big Three meeting had been in progress. During the Ardennes offensive, Stalin proposed to meet Roosevelt and Churchill in the Crimea in a month or two, and both agreed. A few days later, in January 1945, the USSR extended diplomatic recognition to the Lublin (Communist-led) committee as the legitimate government of Poland. In the same month the Soviets occupied most of the country within pre-1939 borders, and by early February they had reached the Oder. In any talks about Poland, Stalin was certain to be negotiating from strength.

At a conference at Malta, Roosevelt and Churchill discussed tactics for the Big Three meeting at Yalta to which they were proceeding. Churchill was eager for a closely concerted plan of action, but Roosevelt was cool. He wished to play the mediator between the British and the Soviets. His conduct was deeply influenced by his constantly expressed belief that while British imperialism remained a serious problem for the postwar world, that of the Soviets did not. As he told Mikołajczyk, "of one thing I am certain, Stalin is not an Imperialist." Roosevelt's close confidant Harry Hopkins was expressing views held also by his chief when he wrote that "Russia's interests, so far as we can anticipate them, do not afford an opportunity for a major difference with us in foreign affairs," that the United States and the USSR were economically "mutually dependent," and that "above all, they—the Russians—want to maintain friendly relations with us. ..."[3] The conviction that British imperialism was wicked, while Soviet imperialism did not exist, had already led to severe Anglo-American friction over internal developments in Italy and Greece but protected Roosevelt from any deep concern over Poland.

The Yalta Conference

As at Teheran, Stalin at Yalta appeared to respond to Roosevelt's efforts to achieve "man-to-man" understanding with him, and again Stalin opened the conference by proposing that the President act as chairman. After an exchange of military reports, the Big Three discussed the problem of the veto in the U.N. Security Council and decided that it should not apply to procedural matters. Stalin advanced and then withdrew a proposal to seat all sixteen Soviet republics in the General Assembly, replacing it by one to seat "the three republics that had suffered the most": Lithuania, Ukraine, and Belorussia. The United States continued to refuse to recognize annexation of the Baltic states, so Lithuania was ruled out, but Roosevelt agreed to "support" at the forthcoming United Nations conference a Soviet demand for separate seats for the Ukrainian and Belorussian SSR's only.

The conferees turned next to German problems. Churchill pressed hard for a French seat on the proposed Allied Control Commission for Germany and a French zone of occupation in order to strengthen the position of the West vis-à-vis Stalin. He succeeded in obtaining the one at Yalta and the other later. Proposals for the dismemberment of Germany into small states and the levy of heavy reparations were discussed; Stalin favored both, Churchill neither, while Roosevelt as on other disputed points suggested a compromise. The proposals were not adopted, but Stalin did not allow Roosevelt to forget his acceptance of Stalin's suggested figure of twenty billion dollars for German reparations, even though it

---

[3] Robert E. Sherwood, *Roosevelt and Hopkins: an Intimate History* Harper, 1948, pp. 922–923. Although the memorandum cited was written after Roosevelt's death, it reflects rather opinions held at Yalta and earlier, about which Roosevelt felt increasing doubts in the last weeks of his life.

was only as "a basis for discussion." It was agreed that all citizens of the Allied powers found on enemy-occupied soil would be repatriated to their homelands—by implication, through the use of force if necessary.

At Yalta the question of Poland occupied more time than any other. It was agreed that the Curzon Line would be the basis for the new Polish frontier. However, Roosevelt said he was "suggesting" but not "insisting" that the line be modified so that Poland could keep Lwów (Lvov) and Galician oil (this had been Mikołajczyk's last line of diplomatic defense, for which his colleagues had repudiated him). Churchill was already publicly committed to the Curzon Line, so he could not openly support this suggestion, but he made his sympathy for it plain. However, he concentrated his demands on an issue even more fundamental for Poland, the guarantee of a "fully representative Polish government" which would hold free elections. Stalin declared that if he conceded modifications of the Curzon Line, his peoples would say he was a "less reliable" defender of Russia than the Briton, Lord Curzon. He rejected Roosevelt's "suggestion," but he urged that Poland be compensated with German territory up to the line of the Oder and Neisse rivers. Churchill disagreed, asserting that "it would be a pity to stuff the Polish goose so full of German food that he will die of indigestion." There was no final agreement on the frontier, but the phrase in the protocol, "substantial accessions of territory in the North and West," left the way open for Stalin to assign the territory east of the Oder-Neisse line to "Polish administration."

On the question of a Polish government, the agreement ran: "The provisional government which is now functioning in Poland [the Communist junta formerly at Lublin] should ... be reorganized on a broader democratic basis with the inclusion of democratic leaders from Poland itself and from Poles abroad"; after reorganization, the government should hold "free and unfettered elections" on the basis of universal suffrage and secret ballot as soon as possible. Roosevelt declared, "I want the election in Poland to be beyond question, like Caesar's wife. I did not know Caesar's wife, but she was believed to have been pure." To this Stalin replied with a smile, "It was said so about Caesar's wife, but, in fact, she had certain sins." A declaration on policy toward liberated European areas, phrased in general terms, was also adopted.

In the agreements on Poland and Eastern Europe, the Western leaders felt they had achieved all they could. The alternative would have been to withhold recognition, to which the Soviets obviously attached much importance (since it would suggest to the Poles and others that the Allies were not going to help them, and many were still hoping for Western aid), unless governments were established which were willing to submit to popular decision. Yalta did not provide in advance for *de jure* recognition of the satellite regimes. However, the agreements reached committed the United States and Britain to support the Communist junta as soon as it included a cabinet minister from London, and this commitment was in fact to be honored.

The last issue discussed at Yalta concerned the conditions under which the Soviets would take part in the Pacific war. As early as October 1943 Stalin had volunteered to Secretary of State Hull a promise to join the fight against Japan after Germany was defeated. At Teheran Stalin had linked such a promise with his expectations for a cross-Channel invasion of France and American aid to the USSR. At that time Roosevelt had on his own initiative mentioned Dairen and free access to warm waters as possible compensation for Soviet participation in the war with Japan. At Yalta, in bilateral Soviet-American discussions, it was agreed that the USSR would enter the war within "two or three months" after the surrender of Germany, provided that: 1. "the status quo" (*i.e.,* Soviet control) be preserved in Outer Mongolia. 2. the Kurile Islands be "handed over" to the USSR. 3. "the former rights of Russia violated by the treacherous attack of Japan in 1904 shall be restored": these were itemized as the restoration of southern Sakhalin, internationalization of the port of Dairen, lease of Port Arthur as a Soviet naval base, and joint Sino-Soviet operation of the Manchurian railways in such a manner as to safeguard "the pre-eminent interests of the Soviet Union," although China was to "retain full sovereignty in Manchuria." It was agreed that "these claims of the Soviet Union shall be unquestionably fulfilled after Japan has been defeated," and although it was stipulated that "the President will take measures in order to obtain … concurrence" of Chiang Kai-shek in respect to Outer Mongolia and the "ports and railroads" concerned, it was crystal clear that neither Roosevelt nor Chiang would have any alternative but to confirm the concessions listed.

All this was contained in a "top secret" protocol, which Eden tried to dissuade Churchill from signing. However, Churchill believed that the security of "the whole British Empire in the Far East" compelled Britain to share in the agreement. Churchill signed, although he had taken no part in the discussion except to listen to a remarkable exchange in which Stalin declared, "I only want to have returned to Russia what the Japanese have taken from my country," and Roosevelt responded, "That seems like a very reasonable suggestion from our ally. They only want to get back that which has been taken from them."[4] Roosevelt recognized Stalin, not as the chief of the world Communist movement, but as the legitimate heir of Nicholas II, who had lost the possessions and rights itemized under 3. above.

Subsequently the secret promises to Stalin of Far Eastern gains were the most sharply criticized provisions of the Yalta agreement. The fact that they were kept secret is not surprising: their publication would have invited Japanese attack on the USSR before troops could be transferred eastward, and in any case would have destroyed any Soviet chance to attack Japanese forces with the benefit of surprise. Their substance is another matter. The "realists" have argued in their favor that

---

[4] Stalin actually got more than had been taken from the Russian Empire, as the Kurile Islands had never formally been Russian territory.

they granted the Soviets nothing more than they could have taken anyway. This argument begs the moral question; it is difficult to justify giving away things which belong to other people, at Munich, Yalta, or elsewhere. But the "realists" also overlook the erroneous analysis on which the promises were based. The American government assumed that the USSR desired only to regain the position of power and security in the Far East which Imperial Russia had lost. This assumption could be supported not by the record of Soviet statements and actions (at least prior to 1941) or by the conclusions of the best expert opinion, but only by trust that Stalin and his regime had undergone some kind of inner transformation—a trust that proved unwarranted. Moreover, the military leadership, including the Joint Chiefs of Staff and General Douglas MacArthur, United States commander in the Pacific, overestimating both the Japanese strength and morale which remained, anticipated a bitter and bloody struggle for capture of the home islands of Japan and believed Soviet aid of great importance in reducing possible American losses. They did not suggest that any particular price should be paid for such assistance, but they indicated that it needed to be bought. This also proved an erroneous estimate of the situation. However, since Roosevelt and Churchill had volunteered consent to Soviet acquisitions in the Far East as far back as the Teheran conference, the military estimate presented at Yalta cannot be regarded as decisive. The ultimate responsibility at the conference was that of the American and British governments, whose leaders there made agreements which, whatever their moral or political justification, were certainly based on a mistaken appraisal of Soviet intentions.

Post-Yalta Tensions

Although in order to win the European war first, the Allied governments had kept their Pacific forces in short supply of men and matériel, a series of hard-won successes had been achieved. Beginning with the invasion of Guadalcanal in August 1942, the "island-hopping" operations led by General MacArthur had moved westward along two axes of advance. One was from Guadalcanal to New Guinea to the Philippines, recaptured from October 1944 to July 1945; the other was to the north, from the Marshall Islands to the Marianas to Iwo Jima, taken in February and March 1945, and Okinawa, in April to June. Meanwhile, the British under Admiral Mountbatten reconquered Burma from August 1944 to May 1945 and reopened land communications with China. By the summer of 1945 Japan was rapidly losing the outer reaches of her war-acquired empire and falling back on her home islands, even though her troops were still scattered over vast areas of Asia and the Pacific. However, the battles of Iwo Jima and Okinawa (where 110,000 Japanese had fought to the death and only 8,000 were captured) misled the Allied leaders into thinking that it would be necessary to overcome similar resistance on the soil of Japan proper before victory could be won. The problem of how to shorten the Japanese war without verbal abandonment of the "unconditional sur-render" slogan was therefore raised at the Big Three conference at Potsdam in July 1945.

There were also political problems pertaining to Europe for the Potsdam conferees to consider; they were, in fact, inherited from Yalta. On February 27 Churchill told the House of Commons, "The impression I brought back from the Crimea … is that Marshal Stalin and the Soviet leaders wish to live in honourable friendship and equality with the Western democracies. … I decline absolutely to embark here on a discussion about Russian good faith." On March 3 Roosevelt told a joint session of the two Houses of Congress, "I am sure that—under the agreement reached at Yalta—there will be a more stable political Europe than ever before."

Nevertheless by March three developments had shaken Roosevelt's confidence in Stalin's intentions. On February 27 Deputy Foreign Minister Vyshinsky arrived in Bucharest and shortly thereafter delivered King Michael a face-to-face ultimatum to dismiss his prime minister, General Radescu, within two hours. Radescu was dismissed; another ultimatum then demanded the appointment of Petru Groza, a Communist tool, and he was sworn in on March 6. In vain the Western Allies referred the Soviets to the terms of the Yalta Declaration on Liberated Europe. Second, the reports of Ambassador Harriman from Moscow made it clear that Stalin was refusing to consider any genuine transformation of the Communist regime in Warsaw. Worse still, fourteen Polish leaders, given safe-conduct assurances by Stalin for the holding of talks, were arrested and held in Moscow despite Allied protests. In an exchange of messages among the Big Three, Stalin remained obdurate. The third incident concerned the arrangements under way for surrender of the German forces under General Kesselring in Italy to Field Marshal Alexander, the Allied commander-in-chief there. Stalin, charging that the British and Americans had promised Kesselring to undertake to soften the peace terms, in effect accused Roosevelt of falsification and bad faith. Roosevelt replied by expressing resentment of the "vile misrepresentations" of those who presumably had given Stalin reports on the Italian arrangements, and Stalin's next message was milder in tone. But Roosevelt's view of Stalin had been deeply shaken. He died on April 12, 1945; a few days before, he had said in private, "We can't do business with Stalin. He has broken every one of the promises he made at Yalta."[5]

One of President Truman's first acts was to send Harry Hopkins (although he was seriously ill) to Moscow, requesting him to approach Stalin personally on the Polish issue and the question of waiving the power of procedural veto in the U.N. Security Council. On the latter point agreement was thought to have been reached at Yalta, but the Soviets had brought the San Francisco conference, then

---

[5] Conquest, *Stalin: Breaker of Nations*, p. 265.

in session, to an impasse by refusing to yield on it as expected. However, when Hopkins appealed to Stalin, he gave way on the veto question, ostensibly after learning for the first time from Molotov on the spot how the matter stood. Hopkins also secured from Stalin a commitment to admit four non-Communist ministers into the Warsaw regime. Actually, Mikołajczyk, the leader of the Peasant party, was the only non-Communist of importance to be taken into the government. Nevertheless this was enough to obtain British and American diplomatic recognition for the "Polish Provisional Government," even though from the first Mikołajczyk found himself a helpless hostage of the Communists.

The Potsdam Conference

The strains among the Big Three, seemingly arrested by expressions of sentiment made on the occasion of President Roosevelt's death, appeared afresh at the Potsdam conference in July and August 1945. By the end of the conference two of the Big Three of Yalta were missing. President Truman represented the United States throughout. Midway in the talks, Churchill and Eden were thrown out of office by general elections. The new prime minister, Clement Attlee, and foreign minister, Ernest Bevin, took over the British delegation, on which they had been included from the start. The only thing new about Stalin was a title he had just conferred upon himself, that of "Generalissimo."

The conferees addressed themselves to the problems of a postwar settlement in Europe and the achievement of military victory over Japan. It was agreed to create a Council of Foreign Ministers which would draw up the peace treaties, deferring action on Germany until treaties were signed with Italy and Hitler's former Balkan allies. Western criticism of Soviet conduct in Eastern Europe and the character of the regimes which the USSR recognized there provoked sharp Soviet countercharges regarding Greece and Italy, followed by an agreement to drop complaints all around.

It was decided that Germany should be administered as a unit by the Allied Control Council, sitting in Berlin, and representing the U.S., Britain, the USSR, and France. Germany was to be decentralized, deNazified, and demilitarized. Beyond that the ACC's mission was vague. There was no final agreement on the extent of reparations; for the time being each power was authorized to satisfy its own demands from its zone of occupation, except that the USSR and Poland were to receive 10% of the war-industrial equipment from the three Western zones and an additional 15% in exchange for food and raw material shipments.

These agreements on Germany were only carried out for a short time, but the boundary arrangements—which were supposed to be temporary—proved to be more lasting. It was decided that the USSR would receive Königsberg and part of East Prussia. Stalin had already turned the region east of the Oder-Neisse line over to Polish administration, and it was agreed that that area and the part of East

Prussia not annexed by the USSR should remain under Polish control until the "final" peace conference (which never took place). The powers agreed to the mass deportation of Germans—in a "humane" manner—by Poland, Czechoslovakia, and Hungary, and the ACC was ordered to distribute those expelled "equitably" among the four zones of Germany. This was as far as the Big Three powers ever got in making "peace" with Germany.

During the Potsdam conference the Japanese secretly requested Stalin to mediate in concluding peace in the Far Eastern war, but he rejected the overture before informing the Western leaders. Stalin was plainly not interested in concluding the war before Soviet troops went into action in the Far East. Truman now knew, on the basis of the New Mexico test, that the United States possessed an operational atomic bomb, and at Potsdam he informed Stalin of the fact, to which Stalin displayed only a casual reaction, having learned it earlier from Soviet spies. Truman realized both the military effect which the bomb might have and the moral and psychological problems its use would create. It was agreed that before using it, the United States would join Britain and China in issuing a declaration to Japan which called for surrender with terms (although without relinquishing the phrase, "unconditional surrender"), and that the USSR might subsequently subscribe to it.

The Potsdam Declaration to Japan incorporated the principles of the Cairo Declaration, which had been issued by Churchill, Roosevelt, and Chiang Kai-shek after a brief meeting in November 1943 on the eve of the Teheran conference. The Cairo Declaration had stated that the three signatory powers "covet no gain for themselves," but would strip Japan of all Pacific islands acquired since 1914; that Manchuria, Formosa, and the Pescadores would be restored to "the Republic of China"; that Japan would be expelled from "all other territories which she has taken by violence and greed" (a phrase on which a justification of the secret concessions to the Soviets at Yalta might rest); and that Korea would become "free and independent." The Potsdam Declaration added the following peace conditions: as penalties, the limitation of sovereignty to the four main Japanese islands, the end of the military ascendancy over the government, the disarming and return to Japan of its armies abroad, the trial of war criminals, and the destruction of war industries, all to be achieved by a military occupation. However, the Japanese people were promised democratic institutions, no enslavement or destruction as a nation, and an eventual return to world trade and access to raw materials.

The Defeat of Japan

The Japanese overtures to Stalin were made both before and after the receipt of the Potsdam Declaration in Tokyo. The Emperor and the Supreme War Council, except for the two army and navy representatives, wished to accept it, but conceded to the army and navy a delay until word had been received from Stalin. None was. On August 6 the United States air force dropped the first atomic bomb on Hiroshima. The Soviets, who had already informed the Japanese in April that the neutrality pact of 1941 would not be renewed on its lapse in 1946, declared war on Japan on August 8. Under the direction of Marshal Vasilevsky, three army groups entered Manchuria from Mongolia, Vladivostok, and Khabarovsk and rapidly enveloped and defeated the Japanese forces there.

On August 9 the second atomic bomb was dropped on Nagasaki. Even the Japanese military now gave way but desired to add a number of conditions. Later in the day, however, an official communication announced Japanese willingness to surrender on the understanding that the Potsdam Declaration did not include any item which "prejudiced" the Emperor's prerogatives. The American reply, on behalf of the Allies, was sufficiently ambiguous so that the Japanese, including the Emperor himself, chose to interpret it as an indication that the Allies would not themselves depose Hirohito. A surrender note was dispatched on August 15 and General MacArthur accepted the signature of the surrender document on September 2 on the battleship *Missouri,* lying off Tokyo.

In his war proclamation Stalin had spoken of the "blemish on the tradition of our country" left by the Japanese victory in 1905 and had declared, "For forty years we, the men of the older generation, have waited for this day. Now it has finally come." In fact not only the Bolsheviks but the entire Russian opposition movement, including liberals, had openly espoused defeatism in the Russo-Japanese War, which had provoked the domestic crisis leading to the Revolution of 1905.

No top-level international conference ever dealt with the problem of how defeated Japan should be treated. From start to finish the United States had borne the brunt of the Pacific war. The subsequent Soviet claim to have effected the defeat of Japan was perhaps the most grotesque case of falsification to which official history descended in the USSR, but in 1945 Stalin did not press any such claims. Although he desired to have a double command in Japan, one of the commanders to be Russian, and a Soviet occupation zone in Hokkaido, those demands were refused, and Stalin had no alternative but to acknowledge General MacArthur as Supreme Commander, Allied Powers. However, after a moment of confusion, it became clear that MacArthur's jurisdiction would not run to Manchuria, where Marshal Vasilevsky's authority was supreme. Soviet representatives sat on an Allied Council for Japan, established in Tokyo, and a Far Eastern Commission set up in Washington, D.C., but the Soviets had no important influence over Japanese occupation policy.

The armistice with Japan, ending World War II, was signed on September 2, 1945, although in fact the fighting had been over for three weeks and in law the war would end only when peace treaties were signed. Stalin, who had faced utter ruin in the autumn of 1941, had managed to regain control of the situation, mobilize nationalist sentiment in Russia against Hitler, hurl Nazi forces back to Berlin and beyond, win the apparent confidence of the United States and obtain major diplomatic and territorial concessions from his wartime allies, and end the war with his control extending from central Germany to the middle of Korea. The Soviet armies and peoples ended the war believing that they had secured international peace, as well as the prospect of at least a degree of domestic freedom and the possibility of regular association with the individual citizens and governments of the Western countries. During the last two months of the war, the shadow of tension had fallen across British and American relations with the USSR, troubling many of the Western leaders, but even they continued to cling to the hope that with patience and firmness, all would be well in the postwar world.

PART FOUR

The Postwar Period

22

Communist Expansion in Europe 1945–1953

Communist Partisans in Eastern Europe

As Stalin's alliance with the Western powers produced important Soviet gains by way of international diplomacy, so it gave the Communist parties throughout most of Europe (except Germany and Spain) an unprecedented opportunity to build up their strength and influence. During World War II they created their own armed forces and political agencies, which were ready for use in 1945 or earlier in establishing regimes subservient to Stalin. Although during the war the Communists devoted much effort to undermining or destroying their organized political opponents, in their public propaganda they employed the slogans of national unity and anti-Fascism in most European countries, achieving particular success with such methods in Greece and France.

In Greece, Yugoslavia, and Albania the Communists created strong underground regimes supported by partisan forces, while in France and Italy they mounted sizable resistance movements. Elsewhere in Europe they did what they could pending the time that Soviet diplomacy or the Red Army (renamed "Soviet Army" in 1946) might come to their aid in establishing Communist control.

In Greece, in September 1941 the Communists had set up the first of the underground regimes, based on an attempt to revive the Popular Front of the mid-1930's—a tactic which was in fact to achieve its greatest successes during the 1940's. The regime was named EAM (*Ellenikon apelevtherikon metopon* or Greek Liberation Front); although it prominently featured non-Communist members, it was fully controlled by Communists. Its army was called ELAS (*Ellenikon laikon apelevtherikon straton* or Greek People's Liberation Army). It carried out a few guerrilla thrusts against the Germans, but it fought harder against non-Communist resistance forces. In October 1944 the British landed in Greece on the heels of the withdrawing Nazi armies and found most of the country in the hands of EAM-ELAS.

Stalin evidently told the Greek Communists to make a try for power on their own. Owing to the mass support they had obtained, their chances of success seemed bright. However, the Communists held their hand for several weeks, apparently underestimating their Greek adversaries as well as the British. Fighting broke out in December. Although the British had to bring in two divisions of reinforcements, they were successful enough so that by February the Communists signed an agreement whereby ELAS would be disarmed but democratic liberties would be guaranteed to all parties including Communists. Though Greece remained in turmoil and rightist vigilantes, ignoring the democratic government in Athens, took over much of the countryside for a time, power had been denied to what was then perhaps the strongest Communist party in Europe.

In Yugoslavia Josip Broz (Tito), the Communist leader who had carried out a Moscow-approved purge of the party in 1937, had also achieved a formidable position. After the Nazis attacked the USSR, he had organized partisans in Serbia, competing with the Chetnik (in peacetime, a sort of National Guard) units of General Draža Mihailović. The general had been fighting the Germans since they invaded the country in the spring and had been made war minister by the Yugoslav government-in-exile of King Peter II. Driven from Serbia into Bosnia, Tito's partisans in November 1942 formed a Popular Front regime called AVNOJ (Yugoslav Anti-Fascist Council of National Liberation), which was a year later converted into a provisional government. Though it included a few genuine democrats, it was under firm Communist control. For a time the British had sent supplies to both Tito and Mihailović, but by the spring of 1943 they had abandoned Mihailović. By then he had ceased to fight Germans and was even willing to collaborate with them on the mistaken assumption that the British shared his view that the postwar danger of Communist take-over was paramount. Tito benefited from popular misgivings with Mihailović's narrow Serbian nationalism and horror at the atrocities of the Italians' Croatian Fascist puppets, since he himself strove for amity among Serbs, Croats, and the other Yugoslav peoples—or at any rate among their lower classes.

Tito embarrassed Moscow by his intransigent anti-Western line and calculated rudeness to his British benefactors, and Stalin urged greater adroitness and caution. However, Tito's unruliness convinced the British that, though Tito was a Communist, he would be apt to take an independent line in the future, and they therefore saved him from the disaster produced by the German parachute raid on his headquarters of 1944. By the time Soviet forces entered Yugoslavia in September 1944, Tito had managed to take over much of the country. He prevailed on the Red Army to stay out of the western portion and to withdraw from the whole of Yugoslavia by March 1945. In the last weeks of the war he kept his reputation for unruliness by clashing with New Zealander and British troops in Trieste and Austria, backing down only under threat of force.

In March 1945 a Yugoslav government, nominally implementing the December 1944 agreement between Tito and the government-in-exile's prime minister, Dr. Ivan Šubašić, was formed in Belgrade. Though Tito had yielded to Western pressure to sign the agreement and Šubašić nominally became foreign minister, Tito shared none of his power with non-Communists, and the agreement merely served to legitimize his regime. Moreover, Albania, where a Communist government headed by Enver Hoxha had taken over following Nazi evacuation in October 1944, was for the time being administered as a kind of satrapy of Tito's.

Communists in the Axis Satellites

In the rest of Eastern Europe local Communists came to power with the aid of Soviet armies. In Romania, Bulgaria, and Hungary the regimes were headed by men who, though they had collaborated with the Axis during the war, had no love for either Hitler or Stalin and since 1943 had vainly tried to surrender to the Western Allies. Stalin decided their fate, replacing them with juntas in which Communists either had from the start or soon acquired control. In Romania the "National Democratic Front" included no important non-Communist groups, since the chief democratic leader, Iuliu Maniu of the National Peasant party, declined to join in protest at the Communists' willingness to cede Bessarabia to the USSR. In March 1945 Petru Groza, the head of a tiny non-Communist peasant group who had permitted the Communists to take it over, was installed as a result of Soviet ultimatum (p. 311) as prime minister of a government in which all vital posts were held by Communists.

In Bulgaria the "Fatherland Front" did include the powerful Agrarian Union, led by Dr. G. M. Dimitrov and Nikola Petkov, the quasi-socialist "Zveno" party, led by Kimon Georgiev, and some Left Social Democrats. In September 1944 the Front seized power in the presence of the Red Army. Kimon Georgiev, like Groza a pliant Soviet tool, became prime minister. A few months later Dr. Dimitrov was forced out of the leadership of the Agrarian Union, and in August 1945 Petkov and the Social Democrats, unwilling to take orders from the Communists, resigned from the government, leaving it entirely in Communist hands.

In Hungary a genuine coalition government was set up in December 1944 and reached Budapest in April 1945. Along with Communists were included the Social Democratic party, delivered into Communist hands by a new leader, Arpád Szakasits; a small National Peasant party; and a strong Small Farmers' party under Zoltán Tildy and Ferenc Nagy. In the fall of 1945 the Communists, presenting a joint list with the Social Democrats, agreed to hold free elections in the city of Budapest. They grossly miscalculated; the Small Farmers won an absolute majority. Marshal Voroshilov, chairman of the Allied Control Commission and in effect Soviet viceroy for Hungary, felt compelled to permit free national elections as well; again the Small Farmers won, with 57% of the vote as against 7% for the

Communists. Tildy and Nagy became the leaders of the newly-proclaimed Hungarian Republic, but the Communists merely awaited their next opportunity.

Communists in Poland and Czechoslovakia

Since Poland and Czechoslovakia were Allies and also were much better known in the West, it was more difficult to subject them to Soviet power than the former Axis satellites. After Harry Hopkins had managed to get Mikołajcyk, leader of the People's (Peasant) party, included in the Communist-controlled Polish regime, Western recognition had been extended in July 1945. Popular hostility to the Soviets was strong, founded on old anti-Russian feelings and resentment of Soviet refusal to help the Warsaw rising and of the usual misconduct of Red Army men while Poland was being cleared of the Nazis. The old Polish Communist party had been destroyed by Stalin himself, and a new "Polish Workers' Party" had had to be organized in 1942. Its weakness had to be compensated for by the direct transfer of many Soviet officers into the Polish forces and other measures that made Communists in Poland more dependent on Soviet bayonets than in any other East European country. Because of public hostility and Western concern, the Warsaw regime at first moved cautiously. It attempted to trade on nationwide satisfaction with annexation of all lands east of the Oder and Neisse, but at the same time set up a virtually separate administration for the "Regained Territories" under the Communist Władysław Gomułka, which undertook to establish there the kind of totalitarian control that could later be extended to the whole country. Underground resistance to the Soviets was a problem, and Mikołajczyk was accused of connections both with anti-Soviet guerrillas inside Poland and with General Anders's Polish forces in exile, who had fought with the British and refused in large numbers to return home.

In Czechoslovakia President Eduard Beneš had long sympathized with "Russia" (which he generally equated with the USSR) and hoped for the best from cooperation with Stalin. He acquiesced in the establishment of a People's Front government at Košice in March 1945 and agreed to distinguish Czechs from Slovaks, so that the new regime included "Czech parties" (the Communists, Social Democrats, National Socialists,[1] and the People's [Catholic] parties) and "Slovak parties" (Communists and Democrats). Thus the Communists alone enjoyed the advantage of being a "national" party through being included in both lists, and from the first held control of the crucial ministries. A Communist enclave, similar to that in the Polish Regained Territories, was created in the Sudetenland, from which the Germans were expelled. Like the Bulgarians and Serbs, the Czechs had

---

[1] Not to be confused with German National Socialists or Nazis.

a tradition of pro-Russian feeling which the regime exploited with some success, and little was said in public about the USSR's annexation of Ukrainian-speaking Carpatho-Ruthenia in June 1945. In December both Soviet and American forces (the latter had occupied a strip west of Plzeň) withdrew from the country. The Communists in Czechoslovakia for the time being behaved with great restraint, despite their great power.

Communists in France and Italy

In Western Europe Communists had a real chance of taking power in only two countries, France and Italy. The French Communists had recognized as their one serious rival General Charles de Gaulle, who had begun organizing French resistance from Britain in 1940. When President Roosevelt sought to build up General Giraud as a counterweight to de Gaulle, the Communists were even willing to play the strange game of supporting Giraud. In close cooperation with him they seized the island of Corsica in September 1943 just in advance of commando landings and unleashed a wave of executions there against "collaborators" (including many of their enemies who had in fact not collaborated with the Nazis). When the Allies liberated mainland France, they carried out similar killings. Having maintained their own partisan forces independent of the Gaullist underground army, they managed to increase their popularity to the point where they emerged as the strongest party in France in the elections of October 1945. De Gaulle, now chief of the government, took in five Communist ministers, although he resolutely refused to let them have charge of foreign affairs, the police, or the army. The Socialists, for a time willing to try once again the Popular-Front experiment of the thirties, soon fell out with the Communists. Finally, on the heels of the Truman Doctrine, in the spring of 1947, the Socialist premier, Paul Ramadier, dismissed the Communist ministers. The Communists' opportunity had passed.

The Italian Communist leader, Palmiro Togliatti, was more capable than Thorez in France and had the advantage of a solid alliance with Pietro Nenni's Socialists. By assuming a pseudo-monarchist position in 1943–1944, Togliatti had managed to convince many Italians that the party was really made up of good patriots. However, by switching to republicanism for the May 1946 referendum, he assured the defeat of the monarchy. The simultaneous parliamentary elections gave the Communists and Socialists together 219 seats to 207 for Premier Alcide de Gasperi's Christian Democrats. However, Giuseppe Saragat led a defection of 50 deputies out of the Socialist party which weakened the Communist position, and early in 1947 de Gasperi removed Nenni as foreign minister and the Socialist Romita as interior minister. After the Truman Doctrine was announced, de Gasperi provoked the remaining Communists and Socialists to resign in May 1947. The postwar Popular Front came to an end in Western Europe. Until 1957 the Communists controlled the minuscule statelet of San Marino, but with that picturesquely irrelevant exception, the Communist bid for power west of the Iron Curtain had failed.

Peace with the Defeated Nations

The failure of the Communists in Western Europe coincided with and was partly caused by the break-up of the wartime alliance between the USSR and the Western powers. It was contemplated, at least by the West, that the alliance would continue to operate in two forms: as the military and diplomatic machinery for the occupation of Germany and Austria and for the making of peace with those two countries, Italy, Finland, and the former Axis satellites; and informally as a harmonious nucleus of the new United Nations organization.

Peace treaties were actually signed with Italy, Romania, Hungary, Bulgaria, and Finland in Paris in February 1947. Italy lost her colonies, the hinterland of Trieste to Yugoslavia, and minor bits of territory to France and Greece (the Dodecanese Islands). Romania lost Bessarabia and northern Bukovina to the USSR and southern Dobrudja to Bulgaria, but regained northern Transylvania from Hungary. Finland lost the northern district of Petsamo (giving the USSR a common frontier with Norway) and the territory west of Lake Ladoga including Viipuri, and yielded the Soviets a fifty-year lease of the base of Porkkala on the Gulf of Finland (which they were to give up in 1956). All except Italy were to pay considerable sums in reparations to the USSR. The treaties reflected the power realities of the moment, wherein the Soviets were in a position to do more or less as they liked with the three former Axis satellites, but were barred from doing so in Italy, while they were prepared to agree to Finland's continued independence at a high price, which the Finns were willing to pay.

The Council of Foreign Ministers, which had drawn up these treaties, turned to the problems of Germany and Austria in March 1947. It was the moment of the issuance of the Truman Doctrine, and discussions made no further progress; but the fate of Germany for some decades had already been decided. The Allied Control Council for Germany had never functioned as intended, and the only fruit of four-power (including France) action was the trial of the major "war criminals" at Nuremberg. The Soviets had governed their zone of Germany without reference to their allies. They had forced the large Socialist party to merge with the tiny Communist one, creating a Socialist Unity party (*Sozialistische Einheitspartei Deutschlands* or S.E.D.) and used it as their tool. By May 1946 Soviet stripping of the Eastern zone had alarmed the Western powers sufficiently so that they ceased delivery of additional equipment from their zones to the USSR, as provided by Yalta.

By this time reports of Soviet ruthlessness, restriction on Western representatives, and repression of freedom in Eastern Europe were overwhelming. In

March 1946 Winston Churchill, in a speech at Fulton, Missouri, said publicly what had been plain to the informed for many months: "From Stettin in the Baltic to Trieste in the Adriatic, an iron curtain has descended across the continent." He recommended closer Anglo-American cooperation as a safeguard against any "temptation to ambition or adventure"—on whose part he did not say, but his meaning was clear.

Not long afterward George F. Kennan, the chief United States State Department expert on the USSR, wrote, under the pseudonym "X," an article in *Foreign Affairs* which set forth a basic element of United States foreign policy from that time forward: "a long-term, patient but firm and vigilant containment of Russian expansive tendencies. ..." In a speech in Stuttgart in September, Secretary of State James F. Byrnes renounced the Morgenthau Plan for the economic pauperization of Germany, which the Soviet press in the Eastern zone was using extensively in its anti-American propaganda, and he unequivocally promised U.S. support for West German reconstruction and defense.

In December 1946 the British and Americans merged their occupation zones to produce "Bizonia," but Stalin apparently expected the French to refuse the inclusion of their zone in a new West German state. In June 1948, when it became clear that the French were wavering, Stalin cut off all overland contact between the Western zones and Berlin, which was under quadripartite administration, in an effort to block the Western plan. It was only by dint of great exertions, no doubt unexpected by the Soviets, that the West managed to supply Berlin by air and frustrate the purpose of the blockade, which was lifted in May 1949. At that point the Council of Foreign Ministers was reconvened for the first time since December 1947 to consider a German treaty, but still no progress was made. In the fall a new Federal Republic of Germany was proclaimed. The Soviets proceeded to convert their zone into a German Democratic Republic, whose fortunes followed those of the other East European satellites.

In the United Nations organization the Big Three coalition soon weakened and broke up. In January 1946 the first complaint that the U.N. had to handle was that of Iran against the USSR for its refusal to evacuate the northern region, occupied in wartime in order to protect the supply line from the Persian Gulf, and for its attempt to establish a local Communist-front government there. Under pressure the Soviets finally did evacuate Iranian Azerbaijan.

In few instances did the Soviet and American delegates in the Security Council or General Assembly ever vote on the same side. Paradoxically, in view of later events, one such instance was the approval of the partition of Palestine and the founding of the state of Israel in May 1948. If the Soviet motive was not to support Israel (as the treatment of the new Israeli envoy in Moscow and the Soviet press campaign against Israel suggested) but rather to provide a permanent focus of Arab nationalist discontent which the Communists might exploit, then the paradox may not be unfathomable.

The Coming of the Cold War in Europe

Although the Communist opportunity in France and Italy was already passing, in Greece the Party made another try for power, coupled with Soviet diplomatic pressure on Turkey (where internal Communist strength was virtually nil). The Communists boycotted the Greek elections of May 1946, and the Soviets refused to join the Western Allies in sending observers. The Allied Mission reported that although about 40% of the voters did not cast ballots, less than half of those abstained as a gesture of support for the Communists. In the summer the Communists reopened the Greek Civil War from bases in Macedonia, where they could use Yugoslav, Albanian, and Bulgarian territory to train, rest, and obtain arms.

Events in Germany and the rest of the continent had already led to a growing American realization that whether or not the problem of Communism in Europe was to be conceived solely in terms of Russian power (as Kennan implied), effective opposition to its expansion could come only from the United States. In March 1947 the President proclaimed the Truman Doctrine of support to free countries threatened by "armed minorities or by outside pressures," and secured Congressional approval for immediate aid to Greece and Turkey. Americans assumed the former British commitments in Greece, and American advisers entered the country to help defeat the Communist insurgents and to bring some political and economic order into the scene. The Truman Doctrine had an important indirect effect in influencing the Tito-Stalin conflict by securing Tito's rear and enabling him to defy Stalin's wrath with greater confidence. Moreover, the break between Belgrade and Moscow confused the Greek Communists. After Tito closed the Yugoslav-Greek frontier in July 1949, the Greek government forces were able to mop up the rebel centers, and elections were held in March 1950 in which Greek moderates overshadowed the Right. Meanwhile Turkey, strengthened by American aid, rejected Soviet diplomatic demands. The Truman Doctrine had succeeded in its immediate aims.

In June 1947 the new American Secretary of State, General George C. Marshall, announced the "Marshall Plan" for common efforts at the economic stabilization of Europe. The West European response was enthusiastic and even Poland and Czechoslovakia at first replied favorably (then reversed themselves under Soviet pressure). Plans for defense followed. The early Franco-British alliance of Dunkirk, signed in March 1947, was supplemented by the adherence of Belgium, the Netherlands, and Luxembourg in the Treaty of Brussels of March 1948 and further broadened by the North Atlantic Treaty of April 1949, in which Italy, Portugal, Denmark, Iceland, Norway, Canada, and the United States also joined.[2] The signatories established a common defense command, whose first chief was General Eisenhower.

---

[2] Greece and Turkey joined NATO in 1951; the Federal Republic of Germany, in 1955.

In September 1947 the Soviets countered by announcing the formation of a Communist Information Bureau (Cominform), with headquarters in Belgrade, replacing the "dissolved" Comintern. In January 1949 they established a Council for Mutual Economic Assistance (COMECON) for the satellites, and in May 1955 they set up a Communist counterpart to NATO in the Warsaw Treaty, placing all satellite forces under Marshal Konev. Although the planning of the East European economy and the organization of the European Communist armed forces did not then depend on any treaty, such measures suggested that the Soviets had been thrown on the diplomatic defensive in Europe.

The Sovietization of Eastern Europe

According to Hugh Seton-Watson, the Sovietization of Eastern Europe generally proceeded in three stages: first, genuine coalition, in which measures were taken against Axis collaborators and in favor of social reform, and freedom was limited only to the extent of forbidding criticism of the USSR, but in which Communists came to control the police, army, and propaganda machine; second, "bogus coalition," in which the non-Communist parties no longer chose the men who held the ministries assigned to them in the "coalition" cabinets, but Communists instead handpicked nominal members of the other parties for such posts, and freedom of opposition was attended by great risks but was not suppressed; third, the "monolithic" regime, in which opposition was eradicated and Communists controlled the shells of the non-Communist parties that remained.[3]

There was little to correspond to the first two stages in Yugoslavia and Albania, and Poland missed the first one. The third stage, complete Soviet control, was reached throughout Eastern Europe during the year following establishment of the Cominform in September 1947 (though by the end of that period, in Tito's Yugoslavia there was a monolithic regime but not one subject to Moscow). The Western Allies vainly tried through diplomacy to create or broaden genuine coalitions and protested continually over the progress of Sovietization (which violated the Yalta Declaration on Liberated Europe), not to mention specific undertakings on Poland, Romania, and other countries. It was apparent, however, that the Allies were not prepared to do anything more than protest.

In each of the East European countries (except Albania), the opposition that the Communists had to crush centered in the peasant parties and the Christian churches—especially the Roman Catholic, since the Romanian, Bulgarian, and Serbian Orthodox churches succumbed to the sort of infiltration tactics earlier employed on the Russian Orthodox Church, whose clergy were in fact used in bringing the Balkan churches to heel.

---

[3] *From Lenin to Khrushchev*, Praeger, 1960, pp. 248–249.

In Poland elections were to be held, according to the agreement at Potsdam, within a year of that conference, but the Communists postponed them until January 1947. Varied techniques were used to prevent the People's party from showing its real strength in the voting, and its leader, Mikołajczyk, was a few months later just able to escape abroad before he was to be subjected to a faked trial. By December 1948 the last remaining separate party, the P.P.S. (Polish Socialist party) was compelled to fuse with the Polish Workers' party, and the regime became "monolithic."

In Czechoslovakia genuinely free elections were held in May 1946 and yielded the Communists 38% of the popular vote. Part of their support came from peasant gratitude for the postwar land reform (carried out under Communist auspices as in all other East European countries) and a widespread nonideological overoptimism about the prospects of relations with the USSR, colored by memories of the West's betrayal of Czechoslovakia at Munich. Prague's withdrawal of its acceptance of the invitation to confer on the Marshall Plan threw the regime into prolonged crisis. The Communist premier, Gottwald, now doffed the kid gloves with which forms of legality had been generally handled. In February 1948 all non-Communist ministers except the Social Democrats (whose party was already seriously infiltrated) resigned in protest at the packing of the police with Communists, but they had prepared no further steps. After four agonizing days, President Beneš yielded to the Communists' demand for a new government in which they should choose the non-Communist ministers. The only remaining minister who was a genuine non-Communist was Jan Masaryk, son of the founder of the republic; but two weeks later he died in dubious circumstances officially described as suicide. Beneš resigned in June and died in September, when Gottwald became president.[4] The events of February 1948 have been interpreted as Communist "seizure" of Czechoslovakia. This is misleading to the extent that Communists had for three years held crucial ministries and had been gradually introducing measures of Sovietization.

Through the lucky accident of the Budapest and subsequent national elections, Hungary seemed to have a chance to retain its independence. However, the Small Farmers' party lacked any single dominant leader who had been in exile, such as Mikołajczyk in Poland, and it was beset by false charges and invented conspiracies. In May 1947 Prime Minister Ferenc Nagy was compelled to resign while in Switzerland on holiday and was replaced by a Soviet tool. In the partly rigged elections of August 1947 the remaining opposition to the Communists still polled

---

[4] In March 1953 Gottwald was said to have died of pneumonia contracted which attending Stalin's funeral. It is remarkable how dangerous Moscow visits became for satellite Communist leaders. The reported circumstances of the death of President Bierut of Poland, just after attending the XX Congress of the Soviet party in 1956, were almost identical. The Bulgarian satrap George Dimitrov had also died in Moscow in 1949.

35%, but the end was not far away. In 1948 the last independent party, the Social Democrats, was forced into fusion with the Communists (after certain party leaders resisting fusion had been expelled, including Anna Kéthly, whom the Hungarian revolutionary government of 1956 was to send in vain to the U.N. as its representative). Communist domination of Hungary was complete.

In Romania the first elections, in November 1946, were already rigged. In June 1947 the National Peasant party was suppressed and its leader, Iuliu Maniu, sentenced to solitary confinement for life. The other parties were also banned, except for the Social Democrats who in November 1947 merged with the Communists to form a United Workers' party. King Michael, the last monarch remaining behind the Iron Curtain, was compelled to abdicate. Probably he lasted that long only because Stalin had publicly decorated him for his services in surrendering Romania and thereby opening Central Europe to Soviet armies. By early 1948 Ana Pauker and Gheorghe Gheorghiu-Dej headed a monolithic regime.

Two rigged elections were held in Bulgaria. After the second in October 1946, George Dimitrov, the Communist leader, became prime minister. The leader of the Agrarian Union, Nikola Petkov, was arrested and executed in September 1947. The last non-Communist party, the Socialist, was taken over in August 1948 and the monolithic stage was reached.

The Yugoslav Communists made shorter work of their non-Communists than any other East European regime except perhaps that of Albania, which was closely tied to Tito (up to his break with Stalin). Šubašić, the only non-Communist minister of consequence, resigned as early as September 1945. In July 1946 General Mihailović was executed. In September 1947 the Serbian Agrarian leader Jovanović, after offering mild objections to the regime, was arrested and imprisoned. However, he had been elected deputy on the Communist-front list and neither held a ministry nor had any party still in existence to support him. Tito's monolith was quickly hewn.

Eastern Europe's "Second Revolution"

The task of crushing political opposition having been achieved, the new Communist regimes could proceed to the stage of social transformation on the lines of the "Second Revolution" in the USSR. All agriculture was to be collectivized, all industry was to be taken over by the state, and heavy industry especially was to be expanded. Nationalization of industry had already begun, but collectivization would have to reverse the previously pursued program of land division.

Immediately after the war the Communists had sponsored land reform throughout Eastern Europe. The break-up of the estates of the East German Junkers, the Hungarian magnates, and the Polish landlords may have been warranted in its economic and social aspects, but in Yugoslavia and Bulgaria the farms had long consisted predominantly of small-scale peasant holdings, and much land reform had already been carried out by the interwar regimes of Czechoslovakia and Romania. The Communists were not interested in land reform or the peasant agriculture it created or extended as objectives; their aim was temporary good will or at least neutralization of opposition from the peasantry while they destroyed the peasant parties. Land reform actually made collectivization harder, since the peasants tried to defend the land they had just been given as their own. But Stalin's policy in the satellites reflected the lesson that Lenin had learned in Russia in 1917–1918: it is much easier to take control of a peasant country if land division is sanctioned at the start, and once control is firmly established, collectivization can be carried out even in the face of overwhelming opposition.

Nationalization of industry had proceeded at varying speeds, beginning with the seizure of all Axis-controlled property, then that of (elastically defined) "collaborators," and finally all other industries. Only in Czechoslovakia and to a lesser extent in Poland was there enough industry in existence to make this operation very extensive or difficult. The great industrial effort was focused on new construction. Short-term recovery plans were launched in 1947–1948, except for Yugoslavia, which undertook a regular Five-Year Plan as early as 1947. In other countries Five-Year Plans (in the case of Poland, a Six-Year Plan) were adopted soon afterward: in Czechoslovakia and Bulgaria, 1949; Hungary and Poland, 1950; Romania, 1951.

The Communists devoted much effort to constructing heavy industry in Eastern Europe, ignoring most of the effects of pollution of air and water, and slighting needs for consumer goods. Collectivization was carried out at an irregular pace from 1947 on, with several retreats and much talk about "voluntary" collectivization intermingled with the use of physical pressure and force; as in the USSR it was economically unsound. But there was no bloodbath comparable to that of the early 1930's in the Soviet Union; that was one lesson Stalin seemed to have learned. Much of Polish agriculture was left in private hands, but for the rest, family farming was usually replaced by collectives.

Stalin and Titoism

Tito's Yugoslavia advanced into its "Second Revolution" ahead of any other Soviet satellite, but the tempo was reduced after the break with Stalin in 1948. Although the split between Stalin and Tito was to affect the whole Communist movement, neither party desired the outcome that resulted. Tito and the Yugoslav party leaders were Stalin's picked men; they loved the USSR and took their Communism with the utmost seriousness, and they did not want to be cut adrift from their comrades. Stalin certainly did not want Yugoslavia removed from his control; his intention was to bring it into line with the other satellites. He hoped that the Yugoslav Communists would quickly depose Tito and his close associates, once the voice of Moscow (through the Cominform) had spoken. But Stalin made a serious miscalculation. He failed to perceive that the Yugoslav party was as firmly in Tito's hands in 1948 as the Russian party had been in his own hands twenty years earlier.

The Cominform's denunciation of Tito in June 1948 climaxed a series of tensions arising from the fact that Tito and his partisans won substantial control of Yugoslavia for themselves during the war, unlike any other European Communist party. Tito had proposed a Balkan Communist federation, on which he had negotiated with Dimitrov and the Bulgarians as early as November 1944 without objection from Stalin. However, when Tito began to be touchy about Soviet agents in Yugoslavia and gave signs of a successful building up of his own machine, *Pravda* denounced the federation scheme as "problematical and artificial" in January 1948.

In March the Soviet party complained in a letter that the Yugoslavs refused to furnish the Soviets all the information they had asked for. At this point Tito arrested Andrija Hebrang, chief of the State Planning Commission and perhaps Moscow's most influential supporter in the Yugoslav party. In May the Soviets complained that collectivization was proceeding too slowly in Yugoslavia. In June came the Cominform's public denunciation, repeating the earlier charges and adding that the Yugoslav party was run dictatorially. The last charge was, of course, quite true—the V Congress of the Party, which met in July, was the first in twenty years—but Stalin was scarcely in a position to criticize another for such an offense.

However, Tito did not deserve the Cominform's charge that his policy toward the peasantry was milder than that of the other satellites. Before 1948 he had pushed collectivization more vigorously than any other East European regime had done. There was no significant disagreement between Tito and Stalin over ideology or tactics; at root the conflict was one of power. Tito, having his own secret police and system of controls, was in a position to prevent Soviet personnel in Yugoslavia from running the country as they did the other satellites, but he himself was pursuing the Communist program with a vigor unsurpassed by any of Moscow's men in Eastern Europe. However, Stalin demanded not only that the Soviet pattern be followed but also that it be imposed and checked by Soviet agents. Since Tito refused to acquiesce, Stalin decided that he must be removed. Apparently he believed that the Cominform blast would be enough to bring Tito down. Aside from Hebrang and one or two other leaders, the Yugoslav party rallied around Tito. The Yugoslav people, oppressed by Communists of their own nationality, undoubtedly preferred not to have Soviet commissars added to their burdens. As a result, Tito survived.

What has been called "Titoism" was an effect, not a cause, of Stalin's excommunication of Tito. As Adam Ulam points out, only after the break did the Yugoslav regime "begin to exhibit some of the characteristics of which it was wrongly accused in 1948. ..."[5] In 1950 Tito slackened the pace of collectivization and in 1951 called off the drive for the time being. He applied the carrot rather than the stick through economic (not party) "decentralization" and "workers' control." He accepted aid from the West, but avoided any political commitments to it. Milovan Djilas, one of the two party secretaries at the time of the break and also minister of propaganda, criticized the USSR for bureaucratism, state capitalism, and imperialism, and helped forge a "Titoist" ideology of sorts, claiming for it the quality of being "truly Leninist." All this sounded a good deal like Trotskyism, but Tito, attempting to appeal to other Communists who had fought with Stalin against Trotsky, avoided any identification with his name. As for Djilas, he went on from attacking Stalin to attacking Tito and Communism in general and landed in a Yugoslav prison as a result. However, Tito held on to "Titoism," claiming that Stalin, not he, was the one who had ceased to be a good Communist. He managed to survive Moscow's wrath and the peril of invasion, induce the West to help him, and meanwhile maintain firm control over Yugoslavia until Stalin died and the situation changed.

Purges in Eastern Europe

Tito's successful defiance of Stalin's ban had a great impact on the other satellites. Recognizing in Tito a great danger to his entire system, Stalin redoubled his efforts to perfect totalitarian controls that would prevent any successful imitation of Tito in the other countries of Eastern Europe. A number of people were accused of "Titoism," but there is no clear evidence that any of them had a particular attachment to Tito except perhaps in Albania. Certainly some of the leaders were guilty, if not of the crimes with which they were charged, then of the modest wish that they could obtain a degree of independence of Moscow, even if no more than Tito enjoyed before 1948. But none of them had the kind of apparatus loyal to him personally that Tito had had, and it therefore would have been foolhardy indeed for any to provoke Stalin's wrath as Tito had done. In any case, during 1949 the Albanian Koci Xoxe, the Bulgarian Traicho Kostov, and the Hungarian László Rajk were executed for "nationalist deviations," that is, "Titoism." The Pole Władyslaw Gomulka escaped with imprisonment and lived to fight another day. The Bulgarian Dimitrov, who died in Moscow in 1949, earlier had had good relations with Tito, and it is possible that he owed his demise to that fact. The Czechoslovaks Novy, Clementis, and others were purged from the party.

After 1947 the most publicized and most important victims of the Communist regimes in Eastern Europe were Communists themselves. However, high clergy of

---

[5] *Titoism and the Cominform*, Harvard U. Press, 1952, p. 137.

the Roman Catholic Church were also prominent among those attacked. Tito placed the Croatian Archbishop Stepinac under house arrest as early as 1941 and after the war sentenced him to prison, although he was released in December 1951. The Czechoslovak Archbishop Beran was interned in March 1951, and the Polish Cardinal Wyszynski was arrested in September 1953 (after Stalin's death). But the most publicized case of a clergyman was that of Cardinal Mindszenty of Hungary, arrested in December 1948 and forced through torture to "confess" to a series of crimes.[6] The next highest-ranking Roman Catholic cleric of Hungary, Archbishop Groesz, was arrested and "confessed" in June 1951. Many lesser priests were dealt with more harshly and less publicly. The Communists made strenuous efforts to create "national Catholic" movements by using collaborating priests, but such attempts came to little. The Roman Catholic Church remained an unsolved problem, even more intractable than that of peasant smallholding, for the satellite satraps.

During the last years of Stalin's life the only slightly veiled anti-Semitism shown in Soviet policy counted victims in the satellite countries. Leading Communists who were Jewish, such as Ana Pauker in Romania and Bedrich Geminder in Czechoslovakia, disappeared. The most publicized case was that of the general secretary of the Czechoslovak party, Rudolf Slánský. By this time the alleged failings of the purged satellite leaders had become a little mixed. In November 1952 not only Slánský, who had the reputation of being a "Muscovite" (that is, a docile instrument of Stalin) and who was Jewish, but also Clementis, who was accused of "Slovak nationalism" and who was not Jewish, were tried in Prague and hanged. Clementis was apparently left over from the earlier purge of "Titoists," while Slánský was accused of "cosmopolitanism," "Zionism," and other offenses which were being attributed to persons being purged in the USSR during the same period.

The satellites had advanced far enough along the road to "socialism" to enjoy the blessings of Five-Year Plans, collectivization, and purges. Such was Stalin's contribution to Eastern Europe.

---

[6] He was released during the Hungarian Revolution, and after the uprising was put down, he obtained asylum in the American Embassy in Budapest, where he remained until 1971. He died in Vienna in 1975.

23

Communist Expansion in Asia 1945–1956

Communist Resistance Movements

During the war in Asia, as in Europe, the Communists achieved a prominent place in the resistance movements against Axis occupation. However, in Europe the Communists were unable to use their prestige in the resistance to obtain power, except in Yugoslavia; in all the other satellites Communist regimes were installed by Soviet troops. In Asia the Chinese and Vietnamese Communists were able to move on from positions of strength in the resistance movements to take power; in North Korea the Communist regime was installed by Soviet troops; elsewhere the Communist bid for power failed, at least for the time being, as in Europe.

Nevertheless the West reacted to the rise of Asian Communism in a rather different manner than it did to European Communist successes. Debate raged at length over whether Mao Zedong and Ho Chi Minh were really Communists at all and even if so, whether they might refuse to be friendly or subservient to Moscow. Kim Il Sung's North Korean regime was recognized to be similar to the puppet juntas of Eastern Europe, but the other Asian Communists were often regarded as somehow more "reformist" or "nationalist" than European Communists. Many Asian intellectuals and members of other social groups were similarly confused. They often knew less about the USSR than Europeans did, and in particular the Communist use of anti-imperialist slogans appealed to them strongly and made them more willing to accept the party's claims to represent the real interests of Asian peoples. Both Western and Asian confusion about Communist aims and techniques in Asia facilitated the party's task. But the effect on the peoples over whom control was obtained was substantially the same in Asia as in Europe, and Moscow's prestige and power were even more greatly enhanced by the immediate Asian results.

China and Indochina were the chief countries in which Communists built up solid strength for themselves in the resistance period; to a lesser extent they succeeded in doing so in the Philippines, Burma, and Indonesia. By far the most important were the Chinese Communists. During the war they managed to set up, behind Japanese lines in north China (insofar as there were any lines), authorities similar to Popular Front regimes in which the openly Communist membership was restricted to one-third and the other representatives were selected by Communists from smallholder peasants and landlords. In the realm of agriculture, the chief economic activity, the Communists confined themselves to a rent-limitation program (see p. 253) and temporarily muted the ideological note in their public statements and actions. Nevertheless a Party Reform (*Cheng-feng*) movement, directed against both Left and Right "deviationists," was carried out by Mao within Communist ranks during 1942–1943, while the war was in progress.

Despite Nationalist-Communist clashes, Chiang Kai-shek went on record with the view that the Chinese Communists were a "political" problem, and in May 1944 talks began on the relationship of the Communist army and regime with the Chungking government. In September General Patrick Hurley was sent to Chungking as special American ambassador to assist in these discussions, in order to try to foster a consolidated anti-Japanese war effort. General Hurley, who expressed the belief that the Chinese Communists were something like "Oklahoma Republicans," had little effect on the negotiations. In November the Communists declared that they desired a new coalition government, not entrance into the single-party Nationalist regime. Chiang's representatives proposed to convene a "Political Consultative Conference" to discuss the formation of a genuinely unified and constitutional government as well as other matters.

In August 1945 a treaty was concluded between the USSR and the Chinese Nationalist government in which Chiang, bowing to the inevitable, honored those Yalta commitments of President Roosevelt that had been made at Chinese expense. However, the treaty also bound the Soviets to continue to recognize Chiang as the leader of China's only legal government. The Chinese Communists thereupon agreed to the Nationalist proposal for a Political Consultative Conference.

The Aftermath of Japanese Surrender

At this point the surrender of Japan changed the whole situation. It was agreed that Chinese troops would accept Japanese surrender in China (except for Manchuria) and northern Indochina; Soviet troops would do so in Manchuria and Korea north of the thirty-eighth parallel; American troops, in Japan, south Korea, the Philippines, and other areas; British troops, in southern Indochina and Indonesia, and so forth.

In Indochina, where only as recently as March 1945 the Japanese had taken over the country entirely from the French, Ho Chi Minh proclaimed the "Democratic

Republic of Vietnam" in September. Chiang's forces in northern Indochina were so reluctant to permit the French to restore their control that they were willing to cooperate with Ho Chi Minh's regime. The British turned the south over to the French, but not until February 1946 did the Chinese allow the French to regain the north. Having already agreed to concede the kingdoms of Cambodia and Laos a measure of autonomy, the French, finding Ho in control of much of Vietnam and remaining in doubt about his real aims, decided to negotiate with him as well. In May Ho signed an agreement for the inclusion of an independent Vietnam within the French Union. However, when the French attempted to present Ho with the *fait accompli* of a government for Cochin China (the most solid French stronghold in all Indochina) separate from Vietnam, armed clashes resulted. By December 1946 Ho Chi Minh's Vietnamese regime and the French were engaged in a full-scale war which was to continue for eight years.

In the Philippines the Communists under Luis Taruc had taken over the largest resistance group on Luzon island, called the Hukbalahaps (abbreviation of a Tagalog name meaning "Anti-Japanese Resistance Society"), and the "Huks" continued sporadic, small-scale rebellion against the newly independent (1946) Philippine Republic. Similarly, in Burma the anti-Japanese resistance movement gave the Communists their opportunity. They were influential in the federation of resistance organizations, the A.F.P.F.L. (Anti-Fascists People's Freedom League), which immediately after the war demanded independence for Burma from the British. As negotiations on this demand encountered obstacles, the Burman Communists split in two; first one faction, then the other began armed resistance to the British, and Burma entered a period of prolonged chaos. In Indonesia the Communists had taken part in the resistance movement and kept a common front of sorts with the real nationalists in the struggle for independence from the Dutch, to whom the British attempted to turn over control after accepting the Japanese surrender. Immediately after the surrender, in August 1945, an Indonesian Republic was proclaimed, and after a period of sporadic fighting the Dutch granted the Republic a grudging kind of recognition in March 1947. For the time being the Communists held their hand and waited.

In Korea and Manchuria the Soviets accepted the Japanese surrender without incident, but they promptly became involved in the effort to spread Communist control in those areas. North China became the scene of a feverish race for territory between the Nationalist government and the Communists, the Japanese frequently managing only with difficulty to surrender to the former as they were ordered. U.S. air forces aided in transporting Chiang's troops to the Shanghai and Peiping regions.

In December the Moscow conference of the Council of Foreign Ministers considered the problem of Chinese and Korean internal affairs. For Korea a Joint Soviet-American Commission was established to form a provisional government and to prepare a plan for a four-power trusteeship for a period up to five years. The Commission accomplished literally nothing and even failed to agree to submit two contradictory reports with a covering joint letter reporting failure to agree. The Soviets, permitting no Westerner to enter North Korea, proceeded to establish Popular Front organizations and a puppet provisional government, which in February 1946 was renamed the "Provisional People's Committee of North Korea." It was headed by Kim Il Sung, a veteran Communist who, like other prominent members of the Committee, had been trained in Moscow. The North Korean regime proceeded to institute land distribution and nationalization of industry, establish state-controlled "trade unions," hold fraudulent elections, and introduce a constitution modeled on that of the USSR.

The foreign ministers also discussed China. The Soviets, who were watching the United States' assistance to Chiang with alarm, demanded American withdrawal from China. The United States and the USSR thereupon agreed that the troops of both powers should be evacuated as soon as possible and that neither power should interfere in Chinese affairs. However, they jointly expressed the expectation that Chiang would introduce "democratic elements" into his government. The Soviets, and indeed also the Americans for the next few months, interpreted this phrase to mean inclusion of Communists. In order to implement these decisions and to prevent the civil war that seemed likely to break out as a result of the scramble for north China, President Truman sent General George C. Marshall to Chungking in January 1946. Truman simultaneously declared that it was the United States' wish to see in existence a strong Nationalist government; Secretary of State Byrnes added that the government should be broadened to include the "so-called Communists."

The Chinese Civil War

As General Marshall was arriving in Chungking, the previously decided-upon Political Consultative Conference was meeting. With Marshall's help, it reached agreement on a military truce and the maintenance of the political status quo. A genuinely constitutional and parliamentary regime was to be set up in stages, and if that was done, the Communist armies were to be integrated into the national army.

However, a few months later the status quo was shattered when the Soviet troops began to withdraw from Manchuria. This rich province, on which Chiang was counting heavily to restore his grave financial and economic position, was systematically looted by the Soviet army. Midway through the looting operation the Soviet command offered Chiang joint Sino-Soviet management of the remaining industry, but he refused, and the Soviets completed the inflicting of damage amounting to an estimated $2 billion. Manchuria was not included in the truce agreement secured through the mediation of General Marshall. As the Soviet forces withdrew, the all-important character of that omission became clear. The USSR technically adhered to an agreement with Chiang covering terms of withdrawal, even postponing for three months its evacuation of Mukden and Changchun when the Nationalists, blocked by the Chinese Communists, were unable to keep to the schedule that had been arranged. However, the Soviets also rendered vital aid to the Chinese Communists, turning over to them vast stores of surrendered Japanese arms and permitting them to move at will into areas under their control. As the armies of Chiang forced their way into the chief cities, they found themselves virtually besieged by the Chinese Communists, compelled to rely for supplies on uncertain rail traffic, and thus no better off than the Japanese had been in many Chinese centers they had "occupied." The military mistake (pointed out by American advisers at the time) involved in Chiang's unsuccessful effort to regain Manchuria soon became plain, especially since he committed his best troops to the task and meanwhile left the Communists still in control of much territory between Manchuria and south China, where his power was more solidly based.

By the summer of 1946 the situation was rapidly deteriorating. The Soviets were publicly attacking both U.S. Far Eastern policy and the "Kuomintang" regime, even though they still recognized it as the only legal government in China; and they were supporting the Chinese Communist cause with increasing frankness. General Marshall's efforts to patch up violations of the truce earned him little thanks from either side. In November a National Convention, though boycotted by the Communists and certain other parties, adopted a new constitution in the spirit of the PCC agreements, thanks largely to the efforts of the Social Democratic leader Carsun Chang. The Social Democrats and the Youth party joined the government established by the constitution, but the "Democratic League" of other smaller parties defected to the Communists. The new National Assembly elected Chiang president, but chose as vice-president the anti-Kuomintang candidate, General Li Tsung-jen.

At the start of the Marshall mission the Nationalist government had been warned that U.S. aid would be contingent on a settlement with the Communists and the introduction of reforms. Since these conditions had not been met, in August 1946 the U.S. embargoed all arms assistance to Chiang,[1] just at the moment that the Chinese Communists had received from the Soviets substantial quantities of the arms taken from the Japanese in Manchuria. Chiang was also experiencing grave political difficulties, stemming from criticism of corruption, maladministration, and intellectual repression. General Marshall decided that his mission could not be achieved. Shortly after he was recalled in January 1947 to become secretary of state, full-scale civil war broke out.

In the Chinese Civil War the Nationalist government suffered a virtually unbroken series of defeats as the victorious Communist armies marched southward. The Nationalist strategy, which was generally to capture cities rather than to de-

---

[1] The embargo was formally lifted in May 1947, but still no substantial U.S. aid was forthcoming.

stroy enemy forces, proved disastrous. Chiang's best armies were bottled up in Manchuria, where by the summer of 1948 they had to be supplied by air. By the autumn they had been forced to surrender, and Peiping capitulated soon afterward. Although still faced by superior Nationalist equipment, the Communists skillfully maneuvered and routed an army of over a million men at Tungshan, just south of the Grand Canal, in December 1948. As a result Chiang retired and General Li became acting president, but he had neither the prestige nor the resources to succeed. In April 1949 the Communists regrouped and crossed the Yangtze River. The Nationalist government fled to Sichuan province, but it was forced to move again in December. General Li escaped to the United States, while Chiang, who had already withdrawn to Taiwan with many troops, resumed the presidency in March 1950.

On October 1, 1949, the Chinese People's Republic was proclaimed with Beijing (formerly Peiping) as its capital. Maintaining the Popular Front facade, the Communists called representatives of the Democratic League and a few defected Nationalists together with their own delegates to a People's Political Consultative Conference. This body legitimized the new regime, in which Mao Zedong was chairman of the government and military council; he was also chairman of the party. Other important figures were Zhu De, Zhou Enlai, and Liu Shaoqi.

In February 1950, after a lengthy visit by Mao to Moscow, a Sino-Soviet treaty was signed covering political, military, economic, and cultural matters. It provided for an alliance against any possible further aggression from Japan or by any state joining Japan "directly or indirectly" in such aggression. The Soviets promised to supply important industrial equipment to China and to return the rights obtained at Yalta over the Manchurian railways, Port Arthur, and Dairen either at the time a Japanese peace treaty was signed or in 1952, whichever came first. Four Sino-Soviet companies were to be set up in Sinkiang and Manchuria. But even before the treaty was signed, the USSR had gained in China—the most populous nation on earth, with the potentiality of becoming a great power—at least for the time being, something less than a satellite, something more than ally.

The Communist Offensive of 1948

The launching of an all-out Chinese Communist advance in 1947 was immediately followed by a coordinated Soviet offensive in much of south and east Asia. Evidently important directing functions were assigned to the Cominform, which, though nominally an association confined to European Communist parties, issued material for Asia and elsewhere as well. In February 1948 a Cominform-sponsored Youth Conference in Calcutta apparently served to plan the beginning or intensification of armed Communist rebellions in India, Burma, Malaya, the Philippines, Indonesia, and Indochina that occurred within the next few months. The East Asian offensive was climaxed by the direct armed aggression in Korea, which was from all indications intended to have a powerful effect on Japan and also to maintain the tremendous psychological momentum that had resulted from Communist capture of the entire Chinese mainland.

In India the Communist provincial organization in Andhra was entrusted with the task of converting endemic peasant unrest in Hyderabad into an armed uprising. By July 1948 the Communists claimed to have "liberated" 2,500 villages, and they seemed to be on the way toward establishing an enclave of control similar to Mao's earlier domains in northwest China. However, in September Nehru's government occupied the state of Hyderabad and crushed the uprising by force.

In Burma the AFPFL leader, U Nu, secured British consent to independence for the Union of Burma, proclaimed January 1948. The "Red Flag" Communists, already in the field, were now joined in open warfare against the new government by Than Thun's Moscow-oriented "White Flag" Communists. Revolt also flared among certain of the non-Burmese minority peoples. In March 1949 U Nu banned the Communist party and launched a concerted effort to suppress the rebels. The government began to gain ground in 1950, and in two more years had pacified most of the country.

In Malaya the British had taken a step toward self-government in February 1948 by creating a Malay Federation that excluded the British crown colony of Singapore, which was mainly Chinese in population. Soon afterward the Communists of Malaya (who were mostly Chinese) attacked the British and the new government, combining guerrilla warfare with individual murders. In February 1949 the Communists proclaimed formation of a "Malayan National Liberation Army" with the aim of establishing a Communist state of Malaya. The British tried several tactics, finally using a device similar to that used in the Philippines of resettling Chinese squatter-farmers in the guerrilla-held areas. By 1954 they had managed to reduce the Communist threat to a minimum.

In the Philippines it appears that Moscow's orders to Luis Taruc and the "Huks" to launch a full-scale revolt arrived just at the moment when the government was attempting a peaceful settlement with them. Taruc broke off the talks abruptly, admitted he was a Communist, and proceeded to exploit agrarian discontent in order to spread his rebellion. The government had little success in combating it until the spring of 1950 when the new defense minister, Ramon Magsaysay, embarked on a policy of resettling the peasant guerrillas and protecting the loyal villages. After his election as president in 1953 he succeeded in capturing Taruc and breaking up most of the remaining "Huk" forces.

In Indonesia the March 1947 agreement between the Dutch and the new Republic broke down four months later when the Dutch launched a "police action" to restore control of the archipelago. The United Nations arranged a truce in January 1948. In September the Communists, led by Muso (who had just returned from Moscow) revolted against the Republic, but the nationalists swiftly suppressed the uprising, and the Communist leaders, including Muso, were either killed in the fighting or executed. Profiting by the confusion, in December 1948 the Dutch conducted a surprise parachutist attack that captured all the chief nationalist leaders. However, American and other foreign pressure brought about their release and induced the Dutch finally to recognize Indonesian independence in 1949.[2]

In Indochina Ho Chi Minh's war on the French was intensified. Recognizing that Ho had managed to mobilize much of the force of Vietnamese nationalism on his side, the French attempted to counter with the establishment of an Empire of Vietnam under Bao Dai, with little effect. Chinese Communist victory led to Peking's recognition of Ho's regime in January 1950 and Moscow's shortly afterward, and Ho was emboldened to declare his Communist aims more forcefully as result of Communist Chinese and Soviet psychological and material support. The French fought on until 1954 (see p. 365) before acknowledging failure.

In Korea was launched the adventure that marked the high point of the offensive. After the Joint Soviet-American Commission failed, the case of Korea was taken to the United Nations, which in November 1947 passed a resolution calling for free elections for an all-Korean government—in vain. In October 1948 the USSR recognized North Korea, and in January 1949 the United States recognized the Republic of Korea in the south. A few months earlier the Soviets had withdrawn their troops from North Korea as a means of forcing the Americans to do likewise in the south, and U.S. evacuation was completed by June 1949.

In March 1950 Kim Il Sung visited Moscow in preparation for the planned invasion of South Korea; Stalin allowed him to attend a Politburo meeting and "gave him the green light."[3] On June 25 the large North Korean army, trained and equipped by the Soviets, crossed the border, advancing the palpably absurd claim that the South had attacked first. To Stalin's surprise, President Truman ordered U.S. forces to aid the Republic of Korea. The U.N. Security Council condemned the North Korean attack; because the Soviet delegate had walked out in January 1950 in protest at the failure to seat Communist China, no Soviet veto could be cast. As a result the forces resisting could be led by General MacArthur under the U.N. flag. Simultaneously Truman announced an accelerated program of aid to Taiwan and other Asian nations.

The North Koreans speedily overran the whole peninsula except for the southern port of Pusan. However, in September MacArthur counterattacked from Pusan while launching a seaborne invasion near Seoul, and soon ejected the Communists from South Korea. With implicit sanction from a resolution of the Gen-

---

[2] The Communists later regained their strength with the help of President Sukarno, but after the unsuccessful coup and successful counter-coup of September 1965, the party was decimated and Sukarno's power ended.

[3] Conquest, *Stalin: Breaker of Nations*, p. 302. Materials from Russian archives enable Kathryn Weathersby to conclude that the North Korean claim that the invasion of June 25 was a defensive response to provocation by the South "is simply false." Cold War International History Project *Bulletin*, Issue 3, Fall 1993, p. 14.

eral Assembly, U.N. forces advanced into the north, nearing the Chinese and Soviet borders. Abruptly in November Chinese Communist "volunteers" crossed the frontier and sent MacArthur's soldiers retreating hastily southward. MacArthur was replaced by General Matthew Ridgway, who by June 1951 had advanced his lines once more so that they were slightly north of the thirty-eighth parallel over most of the front. The Soviet delegate to the United Nations suggested truce negotiations, and the proposal was accepted. In July 1951 truce talks began at Panmunjom, while fighting continued on a reduced scale. The talks dragged on for two years; the single point finally remaining at issue was exchange of prisoners. Remembering the moral and psychological effect of the forced repatriation of Soviet citizens after World War II (see p. 346), the U.S. government insisted that prisoners on both sides should be free to decide whether or not they wished to be returned to their former command. On this point the Communist negotiators refused to give way, and the talks made no further progress during the last year of Stalin's life.

The North Korean attack had apparently been coordinated with an effort by the Japanese Communists, under Cominform instructions of January 1950, to disrupt the domestic political scene and prepare for the seizure of power in Japan. Their tactics were successful enough so that Washington accelerated its preparations for making peace with Japan. In September 1951 a peace treaty was concluded, although the USSR, the Communist and Nationalist Chinese governments, India, and Burma did not sign (Nationalist China and India signed separate treaties in 1952 and the USSR did so in 1957). In April 1952 Japanese sovereignty was restored. The Japanese Communists made little further headway.

By 1951 the Communist East Asian offensive was checked (except for Indochina). Nevertheless the balance of postwar developments in east Asia had been heavily in the Communists' favor. The fall of China to Communism was the greatest success the movement had achieved since the Bolshevik Revolution in Russia. It enormously increased Communist (both Chinese Communist and Soviet, at least for several years) prestige and contributed to the spread of Communist doctrines among the intellectuals, whose political importance in most Asian countries was great. If United States' success in defeating the North Koreans discouraged speculation on Communist success, the subsequent spectacle of Communist Chinese forces' hurling back Americans had a great psychological effect throughout Asia.

First Steps of the Chinese Communist Regime

Beginning in 1949, the more than half a billion people of China experienced a rapid transformation closely patterned after that imposed upon the peoples of the USSR. Mao wrote, in his pamphlet *On People's Democratic Dictatorship*, published in July 1949, "the Communist party of the USSR is our very best teacher, and we must learn from it." The result, according to Richard L. Walker, was an effort "to capsule over two decades of Soviet history into a few years."[4]

A series of mass "drives" was undertaken, designed both to remove inconvenient social groups and to develop patterns of behavior that would be useful later on in programs of forced industrialization and social transformation. All such measures were accelerated during the Korean War and justified with reference to it, so that the war served some of the same purposes of the regime in inducing patriotic effort that the Allied intervention of 1918–1920 had served in Russia.

In China a civil war preceded the Communists' assumption of control of the national government, in contrast to Russia where it came afterward. As in the European satellites, in China it can scarcely be said that there was any period comparable to that of War Communism (1918–1921). In China, as in Eastern Europe, land division was carried out by the Communist authorities themselves and not reversed for several years.

The Chinese land problem was a serious one, but it rested largely on pressure from a vast population on an insufficient tillable area, rather than from concentration of ownership in a few hands; Mao's assertion that a few landlords owned most of the land was sheer propagandistic invention. Nevertheless what could be done by way of liquidating landlord holdings was done, and landlords were killed under conditions designed to implicate as many villagers as possible in their murders and thus bind them to the regime. One feature of the period was propaganda attacks on "American imperialism," falsified public trials of white foreigners, especially missionaries, and palpably untrue charges of "germ warfare" by U.S. forces. Simultaneously campaigns were launched to destroy private enterprise and "remold" the thought of intellectuals, in a fashion going beyond anything attempted in the USSR. "Thought-struggle" or "brainwashing" was the aim of group "discussions" designed to produce confessions of errors and promises of repentance. American estimates were that all these campaigns resulted in 15 million deaths and the dispatch of even more to concentration camps.

In October 1950 Beijing announced the invasion of the last piece of territory accessible without large-scale warfare, Tibet. By September 1951 Mao's troops were able to enter Lhasa, the capital. Sporadic resistance by the Tibetans continued. Although India at first reacted sharply to the conquest of Tibet, in April 1954 a pact between Beijing and New Delhi was signed by which Prime Minister Nehru accepted the *fait accompli*. The agreement on Tibet was based on "five principles" of international cooperation, which were stated to be nonaggression, noninterference, mutual respect, equality and mutual benefit, and peaceful coexistence. The same principles were proclaimed, in a joint declaration of Zhou Enlai and Nehru in June, to be a proper basis for a "peace area" in Asia. The USSR announced that the "five principles" also expressed the essence of Soviet policy. The "principles"

---

[4] *China Under Communism*, Yale U. Press, 1955, p. 3.

were legitimized among Asians by the use of the term *pañchaçīla* to refer to them; the term means the five commandments of Buddhism (and also Taoism). Thereby the Communists hoped to implant their "peace" campaign in the soil of Asian cultures.

"Second Revolution" in China

By 1953 the Chinese Communists were in a position to begin the kind of gigantic socioeconomic offensive that Stalin had undertaken in 1928 in the USSR. In that year a Five-Year Plan, prepared by the State Planning Commission under Gao Gang, went into effect. Collectivization and a program of constructing heavy industry were launched simultaneously. First the Plan was to put half the peasantry into "producers' cooperatives" (less rigid than collectives), but in 1955 Mao declared that all peasants were to be collectivized by the end of the Plan in 1957.

A constitution adopted in September 1954 opened with a preamble declaring, "China has already built an indestructible friendship with the great Union of Soviet Socialist Republics and the People's Democracies." It provided for a National People's Congress comparable to the USSR's Supreme Soviet, with a standing committee analogous to the Presidium to operate between sessions. Mao was reelected chairman of the Republic. A cabinet, like the Soviet Council of Ministers, was chaired by Zhou Enlai. The Constitution contained a "bill of rights" much like that of the Soviet Constitution, making clear that "traitors and counterrevolutionaries" had no rights whatsoever. In March 1955 Gao Gang was purged, and it was announced that he had committed suicide.

As Stalin had done in the 1930's, Mao entered literary discussions to demand that historians point out the "positive" contributions of early figures and movements in Chinese history, such as Confucius and Taoism. A writer named Hu Feng, despite the fact that he was a pupil of the regime's favorite author, Lu Hsün (sometimes called the "Chinese Gorky"), was made the butt of a nationwide attack designed to frighten intellectuals into submitting to the new doctrine.

Though unable to "liberate" Taiwan, where the Nationalists had found refuge, Mao sought to win the support of non-Communist groups for Chinese Communist foreign policy by espousing antiimperialist and anticolonialist slogans, notably at the Asian-African Conference held in April 1955 at Bandung, Indonesia.

Under the Sino-Soviet Treaty of February 1950, the Soviets had bound themselves to return their Manchurian rights and holdings by 1952 or the time of conclusion of a peace treaty. Since neither party had signed the 1951 Japanese treaty, the Soviets' obligation was to return them in 1952. They did return the railways, but on Beijing's "invitation" they retained the Port Arthur naval base for the time being.

The establishment of Communist power in China was regarded by the Soviets and other Communists as a great victory (and acknowledged as such by most non-Communists). Nevertheless it brought the Soviets problems as well as advantages. China was unlike any other country that fell into Communist hands at the close of the war (except Yugoslavia) in that virtually all the fighting in the conquest of power was done by the forces of the national party. Mao, like Tito, built up a reliable party machine of his own. In size and population, China was unique; China had more than twice as many people as the USSR. If the Soviets should try to force some issue, as they did with Tito, and Mao should resist, Moscow could not count on a quick military decision, of the sort that Stalin may have considered seeking in Yugoslavia and that the Soviet Army easily gained in Hungary in 1956.

The evidence is that the Chinese party before the conquest of the mainland in 1949 had a leadership quite as doctrinally and organizationally subservient to Moscow as that of the other "fraternal" parties, and that Mao did not deserve to be regarded as a heretic in the camp of Marxist-Leninist orthodoxy. In many ways the links between Moscow and Beijing were drawn tighter after 1949, as Mao's regime consolidated its power. From 1949 to 1956 the Soviets maintained a powerful hold on the Chinese Communists based on their acknowledged primacy in the international Communist movement and the fact that they had formed the first Communist state, reinforced by the dependence of Mao on Soviet financial, technical, and military aid in domestic change and on the alliance with the USSR in foreign affairs. Sino-Soviet unity survived Stalin's death in 1953. However, when Stalin's successors showed signs of changing their policy, especially in Khrushchëv's secret speech of 1956, the Moscow-Beijing relationship began to change as well.

24
Stalin's Retrenchment 1945–1953

Forced Repatriation

One of Stalin's most notable achievements was his success in concealing from the West the depth of disaffection which the Soviet peoples demonstrated in 1941 and later. At the end of the war in Europe, his first concern seemed to be to cover the traces of mass hostility to the Soviet regime. This required speedy repatriation of Soviet citizens still outside the zone of Red Army authority. Other domestic objectives could be deferred for a time.

There were 8.35 millions displaced Soviet nationals in World War II; 5.6 million survived at the end of the war. The Red Army overran 3 million. By November 1945 the Western commands had repatriated over 2 million, a rough estimate is that 500,000 evaded return.[1] These people had been either prisoners of war, forced laborers, or simply civilians retreating from the front. Many had deliberately fled or surrendered to the Germans. A great many others, although captured in battle or sent to forced labor by the Nazis, were glad to have escaped the clutches of the Soviet regime. For some, the attractions of home prevailed over hostility to the Soviet regime, at least at the start, but many such people redefected, either en route or after they reached the USSR, when they found that Soviet authorities looked on them all with suspicion and regarded them as possible traitors. They had to be repatriated twice. Others were determined not to return home and to stay in the West at any cost.

At Yalta the Big Three had agreed that all citizens of Allied countries should be repatriated at the end of the war, and there was no provision for any alternative. The agreement chiefly affected the citizens of the USSR and countries newly occu-

---

[1] Mark R. Elliott, *Pawns of Yalta: Soviet Refugees and America's Role in Their Repatriation*, U. of Illinois Press, 1982, pp. 2 and 83.

pied by Soviet troops where Communist regimes were being set up, since there were few Western nationals behind Red lines. There was no special discrimination against Soviet citizens. The Western commanders, like the Western statesmen at Yalta, took it for granted that everyone wanted to go home. If someone did not, it was often thought that he must have been a traitor who feared justice. Most American soldiers took this view readily, since they were thinking above all of home and how soon they could get back. Therefore the orders for repatriation of all Allied nationals were at first widely thought by Westerners to be self-evidently reasonable.

The Soviet citizens were herded into camps for "displaced persons" (DP's). Many successfully pretended to come from the Ukrainian areas of pre-1939 Poland, which exempted them from the repatriation to the USSR, or the Baltic states, whose annexation by the Soviets had not been legally recognized by the United States, although no effort had been made at the Big Three conferences to secure their actual freedom. Other Soviet DP's said they were Poles, Czechoslovaks, or Yugoslavs. (Similarly, many Russians who had fallen into Hitler's hands had claimed to be Ukrainians or Cossacks to obtain the relatively preferential treatment accorded to the minorities.) Many others simply vanished into the local population. However, large numbers of Soviet citizens were so classified and placed in DP camps by United States army authorities for transportation to the USSR.

The camps were managed by the United Nations Relief and Rehabilitation Administration (UNRRA), under the direction of Fiorello LaGuardia, former mayor of New York. UNRRA employees were ordered to "try to persuade the DP's to agree voluntarily to proceed to Russia." Anti-Soviet propaganda in the camps was prohibited, although ample Soviet propaganda was made available, and mass meetings in the camps were discouraged lest they "provide an opportunity for dissidents, hecklers, and anti-repatriation organizers and ... result in emotional mob action" against Soviet liaison officers. Mixed Soviet-Allied teams undertook to question those labeled as Soviet citizens and persuade them to accept repatriation. For the most part Western officers simply undertook to assist the Soviet officers in inducing the DP's to return, and if persuasion failed, used force.

Truly horrible scenes ensued. Men and women killed themselves in large numbers rather than be sent back. They fought soldiers who were trying to load them on trucks, threw themselves from moving trains, even burned themselves to death. One by no means unique incident occurred at Kempten, Bavaria, in August 1945. According to a report based on eyewitness accounts, "American troops drove up to the camp and ordered the inmates, who were mostly in church, to board the trucks for transportation to the nearest Soviet assembly point. When the Russians unanimously refused, the troops broke into the church, overturned the altar, manhandled the priest, dragged out men, women and children, clubbing them with rifle butts and throwing them into the trucks. Some of the women, to save their children, tossed them into a neighboring camp for Baltic refugees"[2]—where they were safe from forcible repatriation, at least.

At first U.S. troops adhered strictly to the Yalta agreement, but General Eisenhower wrote that "quickly" they saw that rigid application would violate humanitarian principles and thereafter gave anyone objecting "the benefit of the doubt." But it was not true; although American soldiers were increasingly puzzled and appalled by what was happening, it was eleven months after Yalta before the United States—after long debate within the government—officially did so for civilians, much less soldiers, and forced repatriation was halted only in early 1947. U.S. officials repeatedly lied about what had happened.[3]

There remained in the West, now apparently secure from being sent back to the USSR, but with uncertain futures, something like half a million "non-returners" (*nevozvrashchentsy*). After talking to many of them, Louis Fischer wrote, "They love Russia and yearn for Russia. They are political fugitives ... [they] demonstrate that when Soviet Russians had a choice they voted against the Bolshevik dictatorship. This is the most revealing fact I know about Soviet Russia."[4]

The Vlasov forces received the most publicity, but Red Army men captured in Wehrmacht ranks were only 17% (900,000 out of 5,236,130 repatriates); among military repatriated, they were less than one-third (29% out of 3.1 million).[5] But military defections did not cease with the fighting. It has been estimated that 20,000 Soviet soldiers deserted from 1945 to 1948; in early 1948 two American journalists, the Alsop brothers, reported that over 13,000 (including 4,000 officers and two generals) had fled during the year just past. However, American and British forces were under orders to turn deserters over to their Soviet allies. Such action was usually followed by immediate execution of the men before the eyes of their own units, as a warning to anyone else who thought of flight. Therefore many who escaped avoided Western headquarters and vanished into civilian life as many DP's had done. At the time of the Berlin blockade in 1948, the West generally ceased to return deserters.

While the Soviet army obtained Western co-operation in retrieving defectors, the secret police could not count on that. Nevertheless, under the cover of "Soviet military missions" to Paris and other cities, the Soviet secret police was permitted to operate for a time without serious interference, and in its efforts at "military repatriation" received from Western governments the same facilities given the Soviet army command. MGB[6] abductions from homes in the heart of Paris were frequent until the French press publicized some of the more notorious cases. From

---

[2] W. H. Chamberlin in the *New Leader,* as quoted by Eugene Lyons, *Our Secret Allies,* p. 264.

[3] Elliot, *Pawns of Yalta,* pp. 102 and 120–121.

[4] Quoted by Eugene Lyons, *op. cit.,* p. 257.

[5] Elliott, *Pawns of Yalta,* p. 97.

[6] In 1943 the NKVD had been divided into two commissariats, a new NKGB, which assumed secret police functions, and the NKVD, which was given the rest. When in 1946 all commissariats were re-

then on the MGB had to use greater caution, but still continued its work. As late as the spring of 1956 such a kidnapping occurred in New York, under the very eyes of U.S. officials. Of course the Soviets did not manage to kidnap or murder all defectors or avert all defection, but there was no doubt about their determination to be thorough and not to overlook any individual, especially if he had been prominent.

The Zhdanovshchina

For the most part Stalin achieved his objective of reclaiming the masses of people who had been removed from Soviet soil and control during the war, getting them out from under Western observation, and then executing, punishing, or reindoctrinating them—in general an operation of "reconversion" beside which the restoration of Western soldiers to civilian life was a very minor one indeed. Returning Soviet soldiers, who had seen something of Central Europe while they were still under the regime's control, also required a great deal of reindoctrination. Soviet annexation of territory taken from Germany, Poland, and Czechoslovakia yielded additional millions among whom anti-Soviet attitudes were prevalent. Still vaster was the problem of some 65 million who without moving at all had been for varying lengths of time under Nazi occupation, and there was finally to be considered the attitude of the remainder of the Soviet citizenry, who hoped for the gratitude of the regime which they had saved and expected it to take the form of concessions to freedom and democracy. Stalin had no such acts in mind.

Instead, he and his cohorts began a series of repressive domestic measures, coupled with the invention of a foreign danger which inaugurated the "Cold War." According to Soviet escapees, as early as 1944 the more reliable Party members were informed in closed meetings of the new slogan, "The war on fascism ends, the war on capitalism begins."

In April 1945 Stalin told the Yugoslavs that the war would soon be over, "we shall recover in fifteen or twenty years, and then we'll have another go at it." In June 1946 Maxim Litvinov, then deputy foreign minister, told a U.S. correspondent that the cause of the increasing tension was "the ideological conception prevailing here that conflict between the Communist and capitalist world is inevitable." What if, asked the journalist, the West should give Stalin everything he wanted? The reply: "It would lead to the West being faced, after a more or less short time, with the next series of demands."

---

named ministries they became MGB (*Ministerstvo Gosudarstvennoi Bezopasnosti* or Ministry of State Security) and MVD.

At the end of the war Malenkov had been Stalin's chief henchman for several years. Early in 1946 Stalin decided to replace him, and brought from Leningrad Andrei Zhdanov, who had, in the words of one scholar, been a "worthless figurehead" there who had not been able to handle leadership during the long siege.[7] He was entrusted with the task of conducting a full-scale ideological attack on those who had expressed admiration for the West and by implication dissatisfaction with the regime. He thundered, "Does it suit us, the representatives of the advanced Soviet culture, to bow before bourgeois culture or play the role of its disciples? Our job is to scourge boldly and to attack bourgeois culture, which is in a state of miasma and corruption!"

At the start Zhdanov's fire was directed at literature; in particular he chose as scapegoats two writers who had gained renown already before the Revolution, the introspective poetess Anna Akhmatova, whom Zhdanov called "a harlot and nun who mixes harlotry and prayer," and Michael Zoshchenko, perhaps the most popular Soviet humorist, whom he labeled "a literary swindler." In August the Party Central Committee passed a resolution declaring that "Soviet literature neither has nor can have any other interests except those of the people and of the State." Neglect of ideology and subservience to Western influence were charged to men prominent in the other arts, including the composers Sergei Prokofiev and Dmitry Shostakovich, and the great film director Sergei Eisenstein, who confessed, "Like a bad sentry, we gaped at the unessential and the secondary, thus forgetting the main thing and abandoning our post." Soon he died, plainly never having recovered from the shock of condemnation.

From the arts the campaign soon spread into other areas of creative and scholarly endeavor. The philosopher G. F. Alexandrov, himself a member of the Orgburo, was denounced for his *History of West European Philosophy.* The foremost Soviet economist, Eugene Varga, was attacked for questioning the certainty of an imminent depression in the United States. The lash of official spokesmen, following the lead of *Culture and Life,* the organ of the Propaganda and Agitation Section of the Party Central Committee, fell on historians, geographers, architects, and even circus managers. The government called for "full unmasking of the cosmopolite-theoreticians and formalistic directors who have planted in the arenas of Soviet circuses alien bourgeois tendencies. ...." From a host of different fields flowed a torrent of accusations, confessions, and promises to do better in the future.

In August 1948 Zhdanov carried his attack into natural science. At a congress of the All-Union Academy of Agricultural Science, a poorly educated plant breeder named Trofim D. Lysenko attacked accepted doctrines of genetics, labeling them as "metaphysical-idealistic," and declaring that the inheritance of acquired char-

---

[7] Conquest, *Stalin: Breaker of Nations,* p. 273.

acteristics was possible.[8] Lysenko's contentions were imposed upon the assembled Soviet biologists by his unequivocal announcement that the Party Central Committee had "examined and approved" his address. The chief "Mendel-Morganist" geneticists were liquidated. After crowning his work with this ideological coup, Zhdanov died suddenly on the last of August 1948.

Stalin's Pseudo-Nationalism

However, Zhdanov's death by no means terminated the cultural purges which he had begun. In 1949 a gifted critic, Stein, announced in a writers' meeting that he had read twenty plays about collective farms, and that they all followed the same pattern:

> First Act. A *kolkhoz* which has suffered under the Nazi occupation: (a) there are no seeds; (b) there is no fuel; (c) the tractor station has been destroyed; (d) the chairman of the *kolkhoz* is either away or on a drinking bout, or he has lost faith, or he is simply a dolt. ... Curtain of the First Act: (a) the district party secretary arrives on the scene; (b) also the assistant chief of the Political Department; (c) a war veteran is made chairman of the *kolkhoz*. ... Second Act. The new chairman tells all the *kolkhoz* members "the earth is given us for our eternal use; we must gather in the harvest; comrades, let us work!"[9]

Stein had well summarized the havoc wreaked on the Soviet arts by the *Zhdanovshchina;* but he was savagely attacked for his remarks. He had implied that the "new Soviet man" was a fantasy; moreover, Stein was a Jew.

In the early months of 1949 the target of the campaign of ideological repression had been redefined as "bourgeois cosmopolitanism," a phrase to which the adjective "homeless" was often prefixed—and when it was, it referred to Jews. Penalties against Jews were not new in the Soviet Union. Large numbers had been disenfranchised during the 1920's and 1930's as "bourgeois," but at least the ostensible reason for penalties had been occupational rather than racial. During the period of the Nazi-Soviet pact, dismissals of Jews and restrictions on them had been increased, but they could be rationalized by reference to diplomatic necessity. However, in 1949 a quite unequivocal anti-Semitic campaign was launched.

The timing of the campaign is explained by the establishment of the state of Israel and the evident wish of many Soviet Jews to emigrate there, but in its aims it appeared to be an extension of the anti-Western propaganda policy laid down by Zhdanov three years earlier. Emphasis was placed on the Jewish names of many who, like Trotsky and Zinoviev, had adopted Russian aliases, and cartoons were

---

[8] These assertions were not, however, applied to human genetics. See Loren R. Graham, *Science in Russia and the Soviet Union: A Short History,* Cambridge U. Press, 1993, pp. 123–124

[9] Quoted by Edward Crankshaw, *Russia Without Stalin,* Viking, 1956, p. 125.

published employing the grotesque features which anti-Semites have long labored to make recognizable as caricatures of their chosen enemies. It was hinted that Jews had some kind of inherent tendency to worship the West and should be "hounded out of Soviet life." The anti-Semitic campaign was to continue to mount in intensity until Stalin's death. However, there remained for the use of foreign apologists Kaganovich in the Politburo and Ilia Ehrenburg in the writers' organizations, proving that the Soviets were not anti-Semitic. After all, some of Stalin's best friends were Jews.

In the summer of 1950 Stalin himself showed his hand in the campaign of repression, when he intervened in a "discussion" organized by *Pravda* on questions of linguistics. The hitherto officially favored linguistic theorist, Nicholas Marr, who had died in 1934, interpreted language as part of the Marxian superstructure of society, and in effect forecast that when the socio-economic foundation was everywhere transformed, there would then emerge some kind of new "language of socialism." Stalin now denounced Marr, arguing that language was independent of social development, and that not a merger of languages but the triumph of a single (and by implication superior) language was to be expected in the future. It was not very obscurely hinted that that language would be Russian. Stalin thereupon came to occupy a paradoxical position in which not only did Soviet linguists hail his doctrine as one of "genius," but also Western linguists, who had long regarded Marr as more or less a charlatan, found themselves in agreement with much of what Stalin said about language—though not, to be sure, with his forecast of "victory" for the Russian language. Part of his pronouncements on this occasion, however, had nothing to do with linguistics (as indeed much of what he said about linguistics had no necessary connection with Marxism): he declared that the state would not wither away under the last stage, "communism," and that the superstructure, especially the state which forms a part of it, might act powerfully on the base which "produces" it. Thus the attack on Marr was accompanied by a new theoretical defense of the universal significance of the Soviet state. Moreover, the statement seemed to contain overtones of Russian nationalism.

Indeed, as the attack on the West mounted, the Party ideologists were apparently trying to pretend that all the important discoveries, inventions, and innovations of the past had been the work of Russians. It was quite true, and well known to Russians educated before the Revolution, that A. N. Lodygin had produced an electric light in 1874, four years before the news of Edison's lamp was published, that Alexander Popov in 1895 had demonstrated radio transmission independently of Marconi's work, and that a number of other discoveries had occurred very early in Russia, but had been virtually forgotten, partly because the technological basis for applying the inventions was still lacking in Russia at the time they were produced. However, the ideologists distorted these and other facts and apparently fabricated still other contentions out of whole cloth.

On the surface the whole campaign appeared to be similar to Stalin's invocations of Russian nationalism during World War II. However, there was in reality a

significant difference. During the war Stalin did not need to create popular veneration for Alexander Nevsky and other national heroes; such an attitude already
existed. What he did was to try to identify the regime with the traditions of pride
in and defense of the motherland, and thus to make such traditions serve his own
purposes. In contrast, the dubious existence of obscure eighteenth-century "in-
ventors," for example, meant little or nothing to the people or to the scholars of
integrity who remained. Interest in the great minds of the Western past could
serve as a cover for interest in and admiration for the contemporary West, and as
a substitute (however inadequate) for the contact with the outside world for
which the Soviet intellectuals in particular had ardently hoped, and which had
been temporarily and partially realized for a few months at the end of the war.
This type of "cosmopolitanism" actually developed alongside the surge of genuine Russian national feeling among the people during the war and conflicted not
with real nationalism but with the ethos of the Soviet regime. Stalin pretended to
invoke forgotten or bogus Russian discoveries in order to try to stifle admiration
of the West, suppress the nationalist aspirations of the minority peoples,[10] and
rally Russians to his support, while never verbally abandoning the Marxist doctrine of "two nations": "the Russian people, the Russian workers, peasants and the
progressive elements of the Russian intelligentsia on one side and the tsars, the
Russian squires, the capitalists and the tsarist colonial bureaucracy on the other."

Changes in the Party and the Government

At the end of the war no time was lost in restoring the prewar structure of Party
and government. The jurisdiction of the military—in the USSR often less severe
than civil courts—was ended in all districts except the western frontier regions. In
February 1946 the first elections to the Supreme Soviet since 1937 were held. As before they yielded a virtually unanimous vote to the single list of candidates
printed on the ballots. In March the Council of People's Commissars was renamed "Council of Ministers." Again the creation of new ministries and the abolition of old ones became frequent, and it was as difficult as ever to ascertain
whether such changes involved real alteration of function or of the personal
power of the ministers in question.

The Communist Party, which in 1940 had had 3.4 million members and candidates, had undergone an enormous wartime expansion, ordered by the regime
with a view to broadening its base of support. In January 1945 the total was 5.76
million; by September 1947, 6.3 million—approximately half of whom had been

---

[10] The Volga Germans, Crimean Tatars, Chechen-Ingush, Karachai, Kalmyks, and Balkarians were
nearly exterminated as ethnic units during the war. Khrushchëv, in his "secret speech" of 1956, criticized Stalin for the extermination of four of these groups; he was silent about the two largest, the Volga
Germans and the Crimean Tatars, but both were subsequently rehabilitated.

admitted since Hitler's invasion. The Party was summoned to what was admittedly a herculean task, that of reindoctrinating the whole population in Communist ideology. In an article in *Pravda* in October 1944 it was contended, "It is the duty of party organizations to stimulate tirelessly the political activity of the workers. ... Particular attention must be paid to the question of implanting in the population a socialist attitude ... overcoming the private-property, anticollective farm, and antistate tendencies planted by the German occupants."

The swollen Party itself needed much political reindoctrination. Since the Party was highly centralized and dependent on orders from above, the Soviet leaders evidently concluded that it was wiser to keep the politically shaky newcomers in Party ranks and try to "train" them, than to expel them into the ranks of a populace evidently suffering from the ill effects both of Western "bourgeois" culture and "anticollective farm and antistate" attitudes (which, by the way, could scarcely have been legacies of the Nazis, who had refused to abolish the collective farms and were far from sympathetic to anarchist ideas). One indication that much work remained to be done within the Party ranks is that no Party Congress was summoned until 1952 (the first since 1939).

Just after the war the Politburo itself was reshuffled. The membership of 1939, consisting of Stalin, Molotov, Voroshilov, Kaganovich, Mikoyan, Andreyev, Khrushchëv, Zhdanov, and Kalinin, lost two by death, Kalinin in 1946 and Zhdanov in 1948 (apparently Kalinin died naturally, but the circumstances of Zhdanov's death were suspicious).

In 1946 Lavrenty Beria and Georgy Malenkov were raised to full membership. Beria, who had risen within the Party and secret police of his native Georgia and had been chief of the All-Union NKVD since 1938, was the biographer of his fellow Georgian, Stalin. During the war years Malenkov had been closely associated with Beria, while there were strong indications of rivalry between him and Zhdanov. Zhdanov was superseded for a time by Malenkov. After the former died Malenkov came into increasing public prominence, and in January 1952 his fiftieth birthday was given a degree of attention thus far reserved for Stalin alone.

In Stalin's lifetime three more members were added to the Politburo: Nicholas Voznesensky in 1947, Nicholas Bulganin in 1948, and A. N. Kosygin in 1949. All three were identified with work in state administration. Voznesensky, whose rise to prominence had occurred under Zhdanov's auspices in Leningrad, had become chairman of the State Planning Commission (*Gosplan*) in 1938. In a book published in 1947 on the Soviet economy during the war, he had emphasized the primacy of state planning in the construction of communism, which seemed in harmony with Stalin's assertions in his attack on Marr's linguistics. Nevertheless, in July 1949 the Party Central Committee condemned his views as implying that the state could arbitrarily override economic laws. Voznesensky was removed from the Politburo and executed. At the same time certain other supporters of Zhdanov were liquidated in what has been referred to by Soviet leaders as the "Leningrad case," and thus the Zhdanovite clique followed their patron into the discard within an interval of a few months.[11]

Bulganin had followed the career of an administrator of industry during the 1920's. For his work as political commissar on the Moscow front during the campaign of 1941 he was rewarded with the military rank of lieutenant-general. In 1944 he had replaced Voroshilov on the vital State Defense Committee; in 1946 he had become head of the newly amalgamated Ministry of the Armed Forces and while in that post was promoted to the rank of marshal. Kosygin had been associated with the administration in light industry and during the war was prime minister of the Russian republic.

All the men on the Politburo during the period were, at least at the time they were appointed, trusted henchmen of Stalin's. It is quite clear that no one on the Politburo opposed Stalin openly; the assertion of Khrushchëv in his "secret speech" that the Politburo numbered many who opposed some of Stalin's measures privately but not publicly—either for fear of this wrath or out of concern that the "people" would not understand such opposition—rested on his completely unsupported testimony, uttered in circumstances which rendered its credibility profoundly suspect.

Economic Reconstruction

The Soviet Union suffered wartime losses which elude description. Much of the south and west of the USSR had undergone utter devastation, industry had been wrecked, and half of the total prewar railway network had been destroyed. The population losses were staggering; there were perhaps 7 million civilian dead, an even larger number killed in the fighting, and taking into account the deficiency in births which might have been expected except for the war, the total loss ran between 20 and 30 million.

The purpose of the Fourth Five-Year Plan, to run from 1946 to 1950, was to make good the whole of the economic damage and raise the output of the economy higher than that of 1940 by a substantial extent. The Fifth Plan, which ran from 1951 to 1955, projected a continued sharp rise in the indices of production. In 1948 the inauguration of the "Stalin Plan for the Transformation of Nature" was announced, envisaging the creation of gigantic forest belts in the southern steppes, the construction of great hydroelectric stations on the Volga and the

---

[11] Victor Abakumov, minister of State Security at the time, was executed in December 1954 for his alleged responsibility for the "Leningrad case." It seems plain that Malenkov was influential in these executions.

Dnieper, and long canals, in particular a Great Turkmen Canal in Central Asia. Much of this was before long quietly forgotten, although a Volga-Don canal was completed.

The volume of construction and the rise in industrial output during the period were indeed tremendous. The Soviet state, allocating its resources in a manner which only a totalitarian state can carry out, without regard to the needs of its people, achieved a level of industrial production approaching that of Western Europe, and in the output of aircraft and certain kinds of nuclear weapons and missiles matched or exceeded the United States. In all important sectors of the economy production in 1945 was well below that of 1940. However, steel production, which had been 18.3 million metric tons in 1940, rose to 38 million in 1953; coal production, 166 million metric tons in 1940, attained 318 million in 1953; oil output, which had been 31 million metric tons, reached 52.6; electric power production rose from 48.3 billion kilowatt-hours in 1940 to 133 billion in 1953. Although the official statistics may incorporate substantial inaccuracies as usual, other evidence confirms that heavy industry, including potential or actual war production, underwent a breathtaking rate of growth. However, light industry and the output of consumers' goods continued as ever since 1928 to lag sharply behind, and in the largest cities housing, shoes, furniture, and many types of food were harder to come by than during the 1920's.

In 1947 the regime introduced a currency "reform," requiring exchange on the basis of ten old rubles for one new one, which had a double effect. It supported the value of current income and thus encouraged persons who were idle or had been dislocated by the war to enter the labor force with vigor, and at the same time virtually wiped out the wartime savings of workers and peasants alike. The urban workers were as always directly at the mercy of the regime. In the summer of 1946 Stalin took severe measures to combat the wartime laxity in the use of the labor books, which were a principal control over labor turnover, and proceeded with a new sternness to punish absenteeism and similar offenses. As the regime recognized, the peasants presented a more difficult problem, both because of the war experiences and because of the loopholes remaining for their private endeavor in both agricultural production and trade.

Farm Policy

In 1946 the implementation of Soviet agricultural policy was entrusted to A. A. Andreyev as chief of the Council on Collective Farm Affairs. He led the postwar crackdown on the common practice (dating from the thirties, but winked at by the officials during the war years) of "illegal land seizure"—that is, gradual and surreptitious enlargement of the private plots at the expense of the collective sector for the *kolkhozy*. At the same time Andreyev understood the strict enforcement of the compulsory labor requirements on the collective farms. By a law of

1942 the minimum number of annual "work-days" (*trudodni*—units measuring work done which were quite independent of the chronological day) which a peasant had to perform on the *kolkhoz* was raised to between 100 and 150, depending on the region, for adults, 50 for boys twelve to sixteen years of age, and the minimum was spaced throughout all four seasons of the year. If the farmer failed to meet the minimum, he was to be forced to work six months for the collective, for that period losing twenty-five per cent of his earnings. The requirements of the law were not always closely observed during the war period, but beginning in 1946 determined efforts at enforcement were made.

The regime waited three years before carrying out mass collectivization in the newly annexed Western regions. The largest part of this task was carried out in late 1948 and 1949. Although Andreyev apparently worked hard enough at all his politically defined tasks, he seems to have been guided also by a desire to restore production even at the cost of temporary neglect of political objectives. In early 1947 he criticized the state farms (*sovkhozy*) for overspecialization and other faults, and his report resulted in the allotment of about an acre of garden plot to each *sovkhoz* worker for private cultivation—a radical innovation in the state farm structure. For collective farm work, he sanctioned the employment of small "link" (*zveno*) work teams.

In February 1950 a *Pravda* editorial criticized Andreyev for the use of the "link" system on the collective farms and called for the reinstatement of the "brigade" (*brigada*), a team of from fifty to a hundred or more workers, as the basic work unit. Nikita Khrushchëv followed up with criticism of the size of collective farms, demanding their amalgamation into still larger enterprises. The amalgamation, carried out along with the break-up of "links" in favor of "brigades," proceeded very rapidly. At the beginning of 1950 there were 254,000 collective farms in the USSR; by the end of 1951 the total was a little over 100,000; in 1952 it fell below 100,000. Roughly speaking, the typical operation involved combining three farms into a single one—an administrative rather than a physical change, since there was no effort to move the farm installations. As a result, each Machine-Tractor Station came to serve about ten collective farms instead of thirty as formerly. The whole campaign for amalgamation and "brigades" was aimed at strengthening the Party's control over agriculture and bringing the peasant's perennial aspirations toward economic independence still further under the regime's surveillance.

One aspect of Khrushchëv's proposals for agriculture proved premature. He had suggested that the objective ought to be the eventual formation of "agricultural cities" (*agrogoroda*), in which the peasants would live in central apartment buildings, with their private plots no longer in their back yards but together in a large common area (where it would be impossible to work unobserved). At the start *Pravda* took the unusual step of disassociating itself from this suggestion. At the XIX Party Congress in October 1952 Malenkov attacked Khrushchëv (though not by name) for proposing "forcing the pace" of amalgamation and thereby putting "consumer" tasks ahead of "production" objectives. The reference to "consumer" tasks was presumably meant to imply that the urban amenities of the "agricultural cities" were intended to result in excessive benefits to the peasants themselves. It is extremely doubtful that this was either the truth or the peasants' interpretation of the proposal, but it is indeed probable that the operation would have brought about a decrease in production, as collectivization had done, and that either actual peasant resistance or anticipation of such resistance led the regime to postpone the attempt.

The XIX Party Congress

In October 1952 the first Party Congress since 1939 was convened in Moscow. It was noteworthy by the indications of the rise of Malenkov to the clearly recognized position of Stalin's heir and by the announcement of a broad reshuffling of the Party machinery. During the four years since Zhdanov's death, henchmen of Malenkov had been placed in a series of high Party and government posts. At the Congress Malenkov was entrusted with the delivery of the main report, the first time since Stalin's power had been consolidated that anyone but he had given it.

The Congress announced the replacement of both the Politburo and the Orgburo by a Presidium of the Party Central Committee. Against eleven in the old Politburo, there were twenty-five full members of the new Presidium. Kosygin was dropped from full membership, and those added included M. A. Suslov, who was to emerge as the regime's chief ideologist, and O. V. Kuusinen, president of the Karelo-Finnish Republic. Eighteen out of the twenty-five had joined the Party in 1924 or later and of those eighteen, eight had not even been prominent enough to be named as delegates to the last previous Congress in 1939.[12]

The new and larger Presidium was notable for its inclusion of a number of the highest governmental functionaries in the highest *Party* body. This stratum of administrators was reputed to be especially close to Malenkov—somewhat paradoxically, since his rise had taken place within the Party rather than the administrative hierarchy. At the same time the number of Party secretaries, which had been five (Stalin, Malenkov, Khrushchëv, Suslov, and Ponomarenko), was increased to ten, among them L. I. Brezhnev.

On the eve of the Congress Stalin had published an article entitled "Economic Problems of Socialism in the USSR," which set the doctrinal tone for the Congress. Therein he discussed problems of the "transition from socialism [deemed to have arrived in the USSR by 1936] to communism," although he gave no date for the completion of that process. He seemed to change his emphasis somewhat; he talked less about the role of the state, on which he had said so much in his article on Marr's linguistics, and more about "objective" economic laws "which take

---

[12] Merle Fainsod, *How Russia is Ruled*, p. 279.

their course independently of our will." This was consistent with the condemnation of Voznesensky in 1949, and it harmonized with an apparently less intransigent line in foreign policy, emphasizing the likelihood of conflict between different capitalist countries above that of "contradictions between the camp of socialism and the camp of capitalism." It was further implied that the revolutionary flood of the past few years might be followed by an "ebb." Anticipation of a slight *détente* with the chief Western powers, as well as a slight relaxation of the current Soviet posture of aggressiveness, were suggested also by the Congress's dropping of the name "Politburo," associated in Western minds with recent Soviet conquests, and the final discarding of the word "Bolsheviks" in parentheses from the official Party name, "Communist Party of the Soviet Union (Bolsheviks)."

At the Congress the slogan of "peace" was widely featured, not for the first time. In 1949 the Soviets had organized an international front group known as the "Partisans of Peace" (later renamed the "World Peace Council"). This group, meeting in March 1950, drew up the "Stockholm peace petition," which obtained, according to Communist claims, almost half a billion signatures in the five years following. The "peace offensive" was an attempt to blame the Western powers for the so-called Cold War and to foster pro-Soviet sympathies among genuinely antimilitarist and pacifist groups and circles as well as among those who combined a fear of nuclear war with a low level of political sophistication. Such aims were broadly hinted by Stalin in "Economic Problems of Socialism in the USSR" when he wrote, "Under a certain confluence of circumstances, the struggle for peace may possibly develop in one place or another into a struggle for socialism"—that is, Soviet power.

The XIX Congress was not designed as the beginning of a period of retreat from the Party's objectives. That was evident from the adoption of a Fifth Five-Year Plan (for the period 1951–1955) which was replete with plans for gigantic hydroelectric and other projects whose implications for the Soviet nuclear program were plain, and which as before strongly emphasized heavy industry. Apparently the Congress was intended to begin a period of concentration on the assimilation of foreign conquests and consolidation of political and economic controls within the USSR.

Stalin's Last Months

During the winter of 1952–1953, there occurred puzzling developments which plainly threatened to affect the chief aides of Stalin. In January *Pravda* announced that nine doctors, six of them Jewish, had been charged with assassinating, through medical mistreatment, a number of prominent Soviet figures including Andrei Zhdanov. The epithets "cosmopolitanism and Zionism" were again employed in discussion of the case, while similar phrases were used in the simultaneous trial in Prague of the Czechoslovak party's general secretary, Rudolph

Slánský (see p. 333). At the same time the MVD, whose chief was Beria, was accused of insufficient vigilance in failing to detect the "doctors' plot." During the month of February the Soviet press sharply decreased the amount of attention paid to Malenkov, whose ties with Beria were thought to be close. There has been speculation that Alexander Poskrebyshëv, the chief of Stalin's personal secretariat, was instrumental in these moves directed against Beria and possibly against Malenkov as well.

At this juncture, March 4, 1953, it was abruptly announced that Stalin had suffered a stroke two days earlier, and then that he had died on the evening of March 5. The circumstances surrounding his death remain obscure. Since so many prominent persons in the Soviet hierarchy had previously been murdered, it is not surprising that the possibility was discussed that Stalin himself died by violence, or that his end was hastened in some way. Certainly Beria and apparently Malenkov benefited by Stalin's death at the time it came, and the instant disappearance of Poskrebyshëv and other persons known to have been personally close to Stalin was out of harmony with the official version of the time, that the beloved leader had died a natural death. Evidence has since appeared that Beria and Malenkov delayed medical care for Stalin for several crucial hours, but no charges of murder seem to have any basis.

At his funeral on March 9, when he was buried in the Lenin (from 1953–1961 Lenin-Stalin) Mausoleum in Red Square, many people were crushed to death. At the ceremony, only Molotov of the three orators exhibited any grief, while Malenkov and Beria delivered impassive statements. The three warned the populace against "confusion and panic." Many who later regretted it did lament his passing; Andrei Sakharov admitted that he wrote, "I am under the influence of a great man's death." Since Stalin had symbolized both Soviet power and Communist aspirations to rule the world, among Communists at home and abroad both sorrow and confusion were indeed widespread.

25

The Rise and Ascendancy of Khrushchëv 1953–1964

The Era of Malenkov

On the death of Stalin in March 1953, many expected some one person would succeed to the full range of powers the dead dictator had possessed. By implication Malenkov had been designated heir at the XIX Congress, and whether or not he had fallen into Stalin's disfavor during the ensuing months, after Stalin's death he was featured in the Soviet press ahead of all other leaders. For ten days he held both of the crucial posts, senior Party secretary and chairman of the Council of Ministers; it was then announced that he had yielded the former (and historically decisive) job to Nikita Khrushchëv. Nevertheless, the triumvirate of Malenkov, Beria, and Molotov continued to be treated in the press as the chief personalities of the Party and government.

In the Presidium as reconstituted after Stalin's death, the new roster of full members (reduced from twenty-five to ten) included, in addition to the triumvirate, Bulganin, Kaganovich, Voroshilov, Mikoyan, Khrushchëv, M. Z. Saburov, and M. G. Pervukhin. The Party secretariat was reduced from ten to five. Voroshilov replaced Shvernik as chairman of the Presidium of the Supreme Soviet ("president" of the USSR). The slogan of "collective leadership" was widely used to describe the new dispensation, but the fact that the same slogan had been used in Lenin's last days and for a time after his death suggested that the arrangements of March 1953 might be no more permanent than those of 1924.

During the following months Stalin's name was mentioned in print with sharply fluctuating frequency. Often the phrase, "the cult of personality," was used, calling into question at least the overt conventions of the Stalin period. Several policy statements by Malenkov and Beria implied at least an awareness that his policies had deepened popular discontent with the regime and a belief that a "new course" might evoke a different reaction from the Soviet peoples. Malenkov identified himself with promises of a higher level of production of consumer goods in "two or three years." Beria took an even more startling tack by suggesting that mild legal reforms were in order. On April 3 he announced that the "doctors' plot" that had been "exposed" during Stalin's last days was a hoax. Fabrication of the "plot" was ascribed to M. D. Riumin, who had been deputy minister of the MGB,[1] and he was arrested, while S. D. Ignatiev, his chief, was sharply criticized. Beria further reported that "inadmissible" methods had been used by the police in handling suspects, called for revision of the criminal code to reduce the severity of penalties for minor crimes, and even spoke of the need for protecting the rights of citizens guaranteed under the Constitution.

These developments found echoes in Eastern Europe. The precedent of Soviet division of Party and governmental leadership between Khrushchëv and Malenkov was followed in several satellites. The death of President Gottwald of Czechoslovakia shortly after he attended Stalin's funeral led to his replacement as president by Zápotocky and as party chief by Antonín Novotný. In July 1953 Mátyás Rákosi yielded the premiership of Hungary to Imre Nagy, who inaugurated a "new course" patterned after Malenkov's policy of increasing consumer goods production. He also permitted peasants to leave collective farms and released a number of political prisoners, including the socialist Anna Kéthly. In the early months of 1954 in other East European countries a separation of offices occurred, though unaccompanied by any such substantial shift of policy as in Hungary. The Bulgarian Vlko Chervenkov and the Romanian Gheorghiu-Dej kept their premierships and gave up their party secretaryships, while the Pole Bolesław Bierut and the Albanian Enver Hoxha kept their party secretaryships (now everywhere the title became "First Secretary" instead of the one Stalin had used, "General Secretary") and gave up their premierships.

Already by June 1953 the post-Stalin changes in leadership and policy had created a public impression of indecision and weakness at the top. In the satellites as well as in the USSR several demonstrations of unrest occurred within a few weeks of each other. On June 1 there were strikes in several Czechoslovak cities, occasioned by a financial "reform" that had wrought much hardship on the industrial workers. In Plzeň the strikers held a political demonstration, seized the city hall, and demanded free elections, before secret police troops intervened. On June 16 an increase of labor "norms" in East Germany provoked a protest that rapidly turned into a revolutionary general strike in Berlin and other East German cities. Soviet troops had to be brought in to crush the strike.

---

[1] After Stalin's death the MGB was again absorbed by the MVD under Beria, but in 1954 a new KGB was separated from it, controlling security police and troops as well as border guards. In 1960 the USSR MVD was abolished and its functions transferred to Union Republic MVD's, but the change made little difference.

On July 10 it was announced that Beria, who had identified himself most clearly with the new measures, had been arrested. His appointee as East German police chief, Wilhelm Zaisser, and many of his Soviet supporters were also purged. In December the regime reported that Beria and six henchmen had been executed without public trial—possibly because he had refused to "confess." Beria was charged with having attempted to seize power, acting as a "capitalist agent," and so forth. What his plans actually were is not known, but the sequence of events suggests that he was made the scapegoat for the East Berlin uprising.

In any event, little more was said in the USSR about legal or political changes, although Malenkov continued his policy of promising economic concessions; the "new course" was proclaimed in Hungary and a few similar measures were announced in other satellites *after* the Berlin rising. Perhaps the most astonishing of the first series of post-Stalin disorders occurred in the USSR itself a few days after Beria's arrest. In the concentration camp complex at Vorkuta, in the Pechora basin, there developed a mass strike of prisoners who voiced political demands. After initial hesitation, the strike was put down and mass executions were carried out.

The Rise of Khrushchëv

Nikita Khrushchëv was born in Kalinovka, just northeast of the Ukrainian border, in 1894. When he joined the Party in 1918 he was a completely uneducated coal miner, but after attending a special workers' school (*Rabfak*) he soon was able to demonstrate high aptitude for Party management. In 1934 he became Kaganovich's assistant in running the Moscow Party organization and the next year succeeded him as its secretary. In 1938 he was placed in charge of the Ukrainian party (see p. 230), and except for 1946–1947 when Kaganovich replaced him briefly, he remained in that position until 1949. In 1939 he became a full member of the Politburo. In 1949 he returned to Moscow to take over the Party organization there once again and became a secretary of the Central Committee. In 1951 he had authored the *agrogorod* proposal (see p. 357) and had in general gained some reputation in the field of agricultural policy. Such are the outlines of what is known about him before he became party leader in 1953.

In September Khrushchëv made an important statement on agriculture that indicated an increase in his power (ten days later he was formally elected "First Secretary") and at the same time admitted more bluntly than ever had been done before the horrifying state of the collective farms. Among other things, he reported that the total number of cattle in the country was lower than it had been in 1916 under Nicholas II. The point of Khrushchëv's report was of course not to indict the *kolkhoz* system, but to evoke the greater efforts on the "agricultural front." As a result, state-paid prices for compulsory deliveries were raised and taxes on private plots were lowered.

In February 1954 Khrushchëv inaugurated as dramatic and sweeping a measure as the *agrogorod* idea would have been: in order to increase grain output it was directed that a vast area of "virgin and idle lands," most of it in the fertile but arid regions of Asiatic Russia, be plowed up and sown. First the plan embraced just over 30 million acres; the goal was soon raised to over 70 million; the increase in cultivated area from 1953 to 1956 (most of it in the "virgin lands") was in fact nearly 90 million acres. Thousands of young people and Party workers were dispatched as labor and supervisory personnel to do the job. In January 1955 Khrushchëv demanded that 60 million acres be added to the very small area then under corn (maize) in order to produce fodder for increased livestock production. The resulting cornfields, on flat and hilly country, in cold and warm regions, earned him the nickname of *kukuruzchik* ("the corn enthusiast").

Khrushchëv's takeover of agricultural policy and the increase in his power in the Party were the prelude to a number of important personnel changes that strengthened his position. The fall of Beria was followed by a purge of the Georgian and Azerbaijani organizations, in which Beria's influence had been strong, and in November V. M. Andrianov, the Leningrad party secretary, was removed and changes made in other regions as well. Few if any of these men were executed, hitherto the usual fate of disposed Party leaders. However, in 1954 two were shot: M. D. Riumin, who died in July, though his accuser, Beria, had already fallen, and in December Victor Abakumov, former head of the MGB, who was charged with framing the defendants in the so-called "Leningrad case" (see p. 355). Since this case involved the purging of Zhdanov's supporters and thus presumably had the approval of Zhdanov's rival Malenkov, Abakumov's execution suggested that Malenkov's position had been seriously undermined.

Signs of Khrushchëv's ascendancy multiplied. In November and December his signature appeared alone on certain decrees, and he made speeches and granted interviews on a variety of subjects. In December 1954 and January 1955 the Malenkov-Khrushchëv conflict came into the open in a fashion unfamiliar in the USSR for a quarter of a century. Whereas *Izvestiia,* the government organ and thus presumably controlled by Malenkov, emphasized the need for consumer goods, *Pravda,* the organ of the Party and thus, it seemed, the voice of Khrushchëv, attacked unnamed persons who wanted to encourage light industry as guilty of "a belching of the Rightist deviation ... views with which Rykov, Bukharin, and their ilk once preached." This was an unmistakable declaration of war on Malenkov.

Foreign Policy and Cultural Affairs, 1953–1955

The first notable act of the Malenkov-Beria regime in international affairs had been to approve the signature, by the North Korean and Chinese Communist "volunteer" representatives, of an armistice in the Korean War, on July 27, 1953.

This was made possible by Communist acceptance of the United States' demand that the repatriation of prisoners be entirely voluntary; on this point negotiations had been stalled for a whole year. A neutral commission under an Indian chairman supervised prisoner exchange. Three-quarters of the Chinese prisoners, despite considerable pressure, decided not to go home and went to Taiwan instead. By the truce the Soviets and the Chinese Communists thus accepted a remarkable public humiliation, though world opinion took less note of the prisoners' preferences than American policy-makers had expected.

In January 1954 the Council of Foreign Ministers, moribund for years, was convened again in Berlin to discuss peace treaties for Germany and Austria, on which it accomplished nothing, but it did decide on another conference on Indochina and Korea, in which the People's Republic of China would join. No progress was made on Korea, but France had now determined to end the war in Vietnam, and the conference agreed to the partitioning of the country near the seventeenth parallel. Ho Chi Minh's Communist regime took over the north; Communist guerrillas were to be withdrawn from the south, where Bao Dai's Empire of Vietnam was to be independent, remaining along with Cambodia and Laos in the French Union. (In fact Bao Dai was expelled by the new prime minister, Ngo Dinh Diem, after elections in late 1955, and Vietnam became a republic.) The United States did not formally participate in the Geneva agreement, but separately declared assent to its provisions. At Geneva Molotov supported Zhou Enlai and treated with deference the Chinese, who appeared quite pleased with the outcome.

Secretary of State Dulles reacted to the Geneva conference with efforts that led to conclusion of a pact in Manila in September 1954 establishing a Southeast Asia Treaty Organization (SEATO) on the model of NATO. The United States, Australia, New Zealand, the Philippines, Great Britain, France, Pakistan, and Thailand there made a compact for common defense against Communist aggression and also "internal subversion," which NATO was not bound to consider.

China's new eminence within the Communist orbit was reflected in the fact that in September 1954 Khrushchëv led a delegation to Beijing, where a second Sino-Soviet treaty (see p. 344) was concluded. This pact yielded to Mao all Soviet rights in Manchuria including Port Arthur, which was returned in May 1955. The scale of Soviet assistance to China was expanded, but the Chinese were to pay for what they received.

The developments after Stalin's death had a notable impact on Soviet cultural policy. In the fall of 1953 Ilia Ehrenburg and Vladimir Pomerantsev published articles questioning the propriety of Party dictation to the creative artist. Pomerantsev frankly advised Soviet writers: "Don't think about prosecution [*sic*]. ... Be independent." Soon afterwards the outstanding Soviet composers Aram Khachaturian and Dmitry Shostakovich[2] spoke in similar terms, emphasizing the

---

[2] The most gifted of them all, Sergei Prokofiev, died within a few hours of Stalin.

right of the artist to "independence, boldness, and originality." In February 1954 a Party ideologist, P. K. Ponomarenko, who had been named minister of culture after Stalin's death, was replaced by G. F. Alexandrov, whose *History of West European Philosophy* had been condemned in the Zhdanov period for undue favor toward its subject. In mid-1954 Ehrenburg's novel *The Thaw* (*Ottepel'*), by its unusual realism and its very title, summed up the intellectuals' hopes of that period, though its importance was greater as a symbol than as a literary work.

However, the II All-Union Congress of Soviet Writers (the first in twenty years), which met in September 1954, showed that a few icicles remained. The regime's favorite writer, Michael Sholokhov, repeated the standard formula that there could be "no contradiction" between what the Party and the individual (in this case the writer) wanted, because "our hearts belong to the party. ..." There was to be no sharp change in cultural policy. There were, however, signs of both thaw and freeze. In March 1955 Alexandrov was dismissed from the culture ministry, though ostensibly for undervaluing Western culture in his work during Stalin's last years—the exact opposite of the failings earlier attributed to him. In the spring the grossest perversion of science perpetrated by Stalin was challenged by the official *Botanical Journal*, which labeled Lysenko's genetics as "factually unsound and theoretically and methodologically erroneous and ... not of practical value. ..."

The Khrushchëv-Bulganin Regime

On February 8, 1955, Malenkov resigned as chairman of the Council of Ministers, making an unprecedented statement in which he referred to his "inexperience," assumed the "guilt" for what was admitted to be "the unsatisfactory state of affairs in agriculture" (even though for a year and a half Khrushchëv, not he, had evidently had the major responsibility therefor) and acknowledged that the policy of basing the economy on heavy industry was the "only correct" one. On Khrushchëv's motion, the Supreme Soviet promptly elected N. A. Bulganin as the new prime minister. Marshal Zhukov replaced Bulganin as minister of defense.

At that time the Party Presidium underwent no change, but at a Central Committee plenum in July 1955 two new full members were added: A. I. Kirichenko, first secretary of the Ukrainian party, and M. A. Suslov, one of the Party secretaries, who had been a full member during Stalin's last months. The total was now eleven, all full members of the Presidium of March 1953 having remained except the dead Beria. As a result of the February and July shifts in personnel, the single most important figure in the regime was Khrushchëv, with Bulganin second.

Their position, however, was not as yet secure. Malenkov remained on the Presidium; the East European satellites had been restless, some of whose leaders had followed Malenkov's lead closely; the two new leaders were little known outside the Communist orbit. They first turned to East European affairs. Imre Nagy, who presided over a "new course" regime in Hungary, was forced out of office in April

1955 and replaced once again by Rákosi. In May the Soviet hold on Eastern Europe was strengthened by the signing of the Warsaw Treaty for the placing of satellite armies under Soviet command. Khrushchëv and Bulganin next made an astonishing visit to Belgrade. Khrushchëv first tried to blame the dead Beria for the sad state of Soviet-Yugoslav relations. After he found that Tito would not swallow this tale, he tried a different tack. On June 2, 1955, a joint declaration by the two governments stated that "differences in the concrete forms of socialist development are exclusively the concern of the peoples of the respective countries." Molotov, though still foreign minister, was conspicuously absent from the Soviet delegation. In September he was publicly criticized for an erroneous formulation about socialism in the USSR—suggesting that Tito's old enemy was about to fall from power.

The "Spirit of Geneva"

Next came the establishment of international prestige. Already in June 1954 Winston Churchill had called for the West to make "a real good try" for "peaceful co-existence" with the USSR. President Eisenhower summoned the Soviet leaders to show their "good faith" by signing an Austrian peace treaty and taking certain other steps before any "summit" meeting of heads of government took place. In April 1955 the Soviets unexpectedly declared their willingness to conclude an Austrian treaty, which was signed the following month. Since the government of Vienna was already recognized as the legitimate government of all Austria (although its writ did not actually run in the Soviet occupation zone), no Soviet puppet regime had to be sacrificed. Soviet and Western troops evacuated the country, leaving an independent Austria committed to neutrality. Eisenhower's bluff had been called, and a "summit" meeting ensued at Geneva in July. Present at the first such meeting since Potsdam, a Big Three meeting, whereas Geneva had also France and therefore the Big Four, were Eisenhower, Bulganin (as well as Khrushchëv), Prime Minister Eden, and Premier Faure. The questions of the reunification of Germany, European security, disarmament, and improvement in East-West relations were discussed without result. However, the "spirit of Geneva," as the atmosphere surrounding the resumption of summit talks was styled in popular parlance, netted Khrushchëv and Bulganin significant benefits. If the Soviet and Western leaders were on such good terms as apparently shown by photographs taken at Geneva, the East Europeans could not well think of "liberation" (a word frequently used in the Republican campaign of 1952, although not to mean the armed action that many hoped or feared it meant) from Soviet control or influence, and the Soviet peoples were duly reminded of the international standing their new leaders had acquired.

The summit meeting had only a few ripples of impact in world affairs. Two months later the Soviet announced return of the Porkkala base to Finland; it was a means of putting pressure on the U.S. to give up or reduce its bases in Western

Europe. In September Chancellor Adenauer visited Moscow and secured Soviet recognition of the Federal Republic of Germany, but was unable to obtain release of all war prisoners still held by the USSR. In October-November the Council of Foreign Ministers met again at Geneva, but fruitless rancor indicated that the "spirit" was not very powerful. Nevertheless, Khrushchëv seemed to believe that a relative stabilization had come to the international scene, one that would support further "co-existence" initiatives on the Soviet part.

Mid-1955 was also the moment when the USSR took the first steps in penetrating a vital new area, the Middle East. In April *Izvestiia* called for a revival in Soviet expertise on that area, and Soviet publications began to devote increasing space to it. Trouble had been smoldering in the eastern Mediterranean since the uneasy Arab-Israeli armistice of 1949, and the emergence in 1954 of Colonel Gamal Abdel Nasser as ruler of Egypt added a new factor of considerable potential on the Arab side. In the summer of 1955 D. T. Shepilov, who had accompanied Khrushchëv on his pilgrimage to Belgrade, visited Cairo and arranged the purchase of considerable armament by Nasser from Czechoslovakia. However, the West seemed to pay little attention to the developing Middle Eastern danger. "K. and B." next made a triumphant tour of India, Burma, and Afghanistan. The year 1955 closed with a Soviet diplomatic victory: the admission into the U.N. of East European satellites still outside it—Albania, Bulgaria, Hungary, and Romania.

The XX Party Congress

At the XX Party Congress, held in February 1956 in Moscow, Khrushchëv dominated the proceedings. The roster of full members of the Presidium remained unchanged; among the additions made to the alternate membership one was especially noteworthy: L. I. Brezhnev, then first secretary of the Kazakh party. The inauguration of the Sixth Five-Year Plan (for 1956–1960) was announced. In his public report, Khrushchëv made a gesture to Tito by referring to different "forms of transition of various countries to socialism" and citing Yugoslavia as an example of one such "form," but he made few other surprising statements.

The sensational development of the Congress was not made public at all, and if it had not been for the U.S. State Department's publication (in June) of Khrushchëv's "secret speech" at a closed session, the outside world might have waited much longer for the news. In this speech, delivered the night of February 24, Khrushchëv itemized a good many of Stalin's crimes, chief among them being the murder of Party leaders loyal to him, and leveled other accusations against Stalin, such as responsibility for the break with Tito. Certain of Khrushchëv's charges were palpably absurd, such as the assertion that Stalin could not read a map and planned military operations on a globe; and many of his most serious crimes were not mentioned at all.

There was much speculation on the reason for what Khrushchëv said and the way he chose to say it. In his public report to the Congress, Khrushchëv had called for a new history of the Communist Party of the Soviet Union to replace Stalin's *Short Course*. However, it was Mikoyan who during the Congress criticized Stalin most sharply, and in doing so had announced rehabilitation of Kosior, whom Khrushchëv had helped purge in Ukraine (see p. 230). Some concluded that Mikoyan had forced Khrushchëv to outbid him in the secret speech; others, that Tito had successfully demanded the attack; still others, that the Mikoyan speech was a trial balloon planned by Khrushchëv to test the reaction before going further.

In general, however, Khrushchëv's motives seem not very mysterious. He was trying to exorcise the incubus of his dead master, whom he had loyally served so long, because of the massive unpopularity of all Stalin stood for among the Soviet peoples, yet he wished to avoid calling into question the structure of the whole regime or opening the way to public queries about the role of the leaders of 1956 during the commission of the crimes that he detailed. Despite the sharpness of his attack, Khrushchëv declared at the end of the "secret speech" that the "whole tragedy" lay in the fact that Stalin's errors were not "the deeds of a giddy despot," but that he "doubtlessly performed great services to the party, to the working class, and to the international workers' movement." Under the slogan of "Leninism," Khrushchëv summoned the Party to eradicate "the cult of personality," strengthen "collective leadership," and restore "the Leninist principles of Soviet socialist democracy" as expressed in the Constitution.

Following the Congress there were several public rehabilitations of Party leaders long dead, and even of a few, such as G. I. Petrovski, a member of the Politburo in the 1930's, who had somehow survived the purges. As word sifted down to the masses in the USSR and leaked out abroad that Stalin had been attacked at the Congress, there were two sorts of responses. One came from foreign Communist leaders, who reacted with a mixture of shock and unwonted frankness. Palmiro Togliatti, the Italian party leader, hinted that he considered Khrushchëv's evaluation of Stalin unduly harsh, but that if it *had* been warranted, then the current leaders were also implicated. Other foreign comrades spelled out these hints. On June 30 the Soviet Party Central Committee felt obliged to speak. Certain comrades, it admitted, were "not completely clear on the question of the personality cult. ...." By noting that the needs of Stalin's day included "iron discipline ... vigilance ... strictest centralization of leadership," the Central Committee clearly implied that criticism had gotten out of hand and should be curbed.

Revolutionary Stirrings Within the Soviet Orbit

By this time a different response to Khrushchëv's speech had become manifest in the Soviet empire. Only weeks after the Congress, over a hundred were killed in riots in Tbilisi, the Georgian capital. Stalin's harsh treatment of his own native land provided scant reason for Georgians to venerate him, but apparently a combination of feelings that "though a bastard, he was our bastard" and opposition to the regime underlay the disturbance.

In Eastern Europe, there had been some hope that reconciliation between Tito and Khrushchëv would bring about a relaxation in Moscow's controls. When nothing of the sort was forthcoming, Poland led the way in open expressions of dissatisfaction. In August 1955 Adam Ważyk published a remarkable *Poem for Adults,* a part of which read:

> We make demands on this earth,
> for the people who are overworked,
> for keys to open doors,
> for rooms with windows,
> for walls which do not rot,
>> for hatred of little documents,
>> for holy human time ...[3]

Public discussion grew increasingly frank, and in May 1956, not long after the "secret speech," the chief diehard among the Polish leaders, Jakub Berman, was forced out of power. On June 28, while an international fair was under way at Poznań, factory workers organized a demonstration that developed into armed clashes with the police, resulting in perhaps a hundred deaths. Some rioters were brought to public trial, but they received unexpectedly mild sentences, and criticism continued.

A little earlier Khrushchëv had taken further steps to improve relations with Tito. Having in the "secret speech" finally ascribed the break of 1948 to Stalin himself, Khrushchëv dissolved the agency used to condemn Tito, the Cominform, in April 1956. Two months later Tito returned Khrushchëv's visit by going to Moscow, just after his old adversary Molotov was replaced by Shepilov as foreign minister. Possibly in consequence of Tito's visit, in July the Hungarian satrap Rákosi was replaced by Ernö Gerö as first secretary.

For some months public criticism had been growing sharper in Hungary, especially in the "Petöfi circle" of writers. Gerö criticized the circle, but took no action against it. On October 6 the reburial of László Rajk (executed in 1949 as a Titoist) turned into a silent mass demonstration. The writers' discussions now broadened to include university students, who successfully demanded the end of compulsory Russian language instruction.

A few days later the Polish events reached a climax. Wladysław Gomułka, who had been Poland's chief alleged Titoist, had been reinstated in August. On October 19 a party plenum chose him first secretary and called for internal reforms. Later the same day Khrushchëv and a Soviet delegation reached Warsaw. Appar-

---

[3] Adam Ważyk, "Poem for Adults," trans., *The Twentieth Century,* London, December 1955, p. 510.

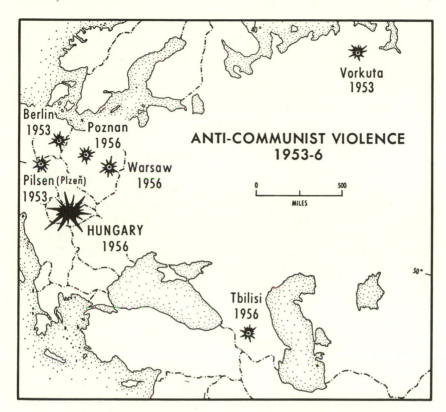

Berlin
1953

Poznan
1956

Warsaw
1956

Pilsen(Plzeň)
1953

**ANTI-COMMUNIST VIOLENCE
1953-6**

Vorkuta
1953

HUNGARY
1956

Tbilisi
1956

0   500
MILES

ently Khrushchëv and Gomułka had a stormy interview replete with threats, by the former to use the Soviet troops stationed in Poland, by the latter to use Polish workers to impede communications. However, publicly it was stated simply that agreement was reached on problems of mutual interest. For the moment the USSR held its hand, while on appeal from Gomułka—and from Cardinal Wyszynski, just released from arrest—the Polish people refrained from pressing what seemed a revolutionary situation into armed uprising.

The Hungarian Uprising

In Hungary the crisis exploded into a revolution of the classic nineteenth-century type, which many historians had believed a thing of the past. It opened on October 23, 1956, with a demonstration organized by university students in support of the Poles, whose war of nerves with the Soviets was being followed with intense interest in Hungary. The next day the students approached the Radio Building seeking to have broadcast the demands they had adopted the day before, including immediate withdrawal of Soviet troops from the country, the reconstitution

of the government under Imre Nagy, free elections, free speech, and sweeping social changes. The students were fired on by the Hungarian secret police (AVH),
and large-scale fighting broke out against AVH troops and Soviet forces that were
sent into Budapest that night. The Hungarian army disintegrated; most of its men
actively joined the rebels; the fighting spread all over the country.

The same night, October 24, the Hungarian Politburo named Nagy premier,
and the government (possibly without Nagy's approval), under the terms of the
Warsaw Treaty, requested Soviet military assistance—which had in any case appeared before the appeal was sent. On October 25 Gerö was removed as first secretary and replaced by Janos Kadar, who had himself earlier been imprisoned. The
following day revolutionary workers' councils—the first genuine Soviets to exist
in the "Soviet" orbit for almost forty years, but like the Kronstadt Soviet of 1921,
opposed to Communist dictatorship—began to be formed all over Hungary. On
October 27 the government was reorganized to include such genuine non-Communists and Béla Kovacs, former leader of the Smallholders' party, and a little
later the Social Democrat Anna Kéthly. The next day a cease-fire was announced,
and Soviet troops withdrew from Budapest. Imre Nagy declared that Hungary
would no longer be a one-party state or a member of the Warsaw Pact but would
be neutral. For a few days the exhilaration of apparent victory and peace reigned
in the country.

Then, in the early hours of November 4, Soviet troops suddenly swept back
into Budapest. As the later U.N. report puts it, "the whole population of Budapest
took part in the resistance," and many civilians as well as soldiers were killed.
Kadar was installed by Soviet troops as prime minister of a new regime, while
Nagy fled to the Yugoslav Embassy.[4] Anna Kéthly escaped to protest in vain to the
U.N. that she should be recognized as Hungary's U.N. delegate; tens of thousands
fled across the border into Austria. The U.N. report accurately concludes that the
uprising "collapsed because of the Soviet armed intervention and because no support was forthcoming for them [the revolutionists] from abroad."

The U.N. did not take up the Hungarian affair, as Nagy had urgently requested
it to do, until the uprising was already crushed. The United States was distracted
by the last days of a presidential campaign; nevertheless, its delegation found it
possible to be active in the U.N. deliberations during those very days on the Suez
crisis. On October 29 Israeli troops had suddenly attacked Egypt and rapidly
neared the Suez Canal. Almost at once Britain and France, still smarting over
Nasser's seizure of the canal in July, in abrogation of an agreement that would
have given him control by 1968, bombarded Egyptian bases and landed troops
near the canal. The USSR immediately demanded international action to stop the
Israeli and Western invasion of Egypt. The Suez crisis was a godsend for the USSR

---

[4] Nagy and a few associates left their asylum under a Kadar pledge of safe conduct, were promptly
seized by the Soviets, imprisoned, and executed in 1958.

in diverting world attention from Hungary, but their concern for Egypt was genuine enough, since overthrow of Nasser would have gravely threatened the Soviets' growing influence in the Arab countries. The United States took an equally sharp line with the invading powers, and a momentary U.S.-USSR partnership brought about a speedy termination of the invasion. Israeli, British, and French forces withdrew from Egypt, and the U.N. installed an international police force near the canal to keep peace. When it was already too late to affect the outcome of the Hungarian uprising, the U.N. turned to denounce, despite angry Soviet opposition, the USSR's actions in Hungary.

Shock and rage at the suppression of the Hungarian revolt swept the outside world. Such prominent Communists as Jean-Paul Sartre in France and Howard Fast in the United States tore up their party cards, and many lesser comrades did likewise. Even in the USSR angry questions were asked at public meetings and the official answers scornfully rejected. Tito did not wholly abandon his new relationship with Khrushchëv, declaring that if the Soviet action "saves socialism in Hungary," then he had to say that "although we are against interference, Soviet intervention was necessary"; nevertheless, Soviet-Yugoslav relations cooled for several years. As for the rest of world opinion, Khrushchëv counted on it to forget, as time passed, what the Soviets had done in Hungary.

The Defeat of the "Anti-Party Group"

Evidently Khrushchëv was blamed, in the secret councils of the Kremlin, for the way he had managed "de-Stalinization," which had engendered the crisis in Poland and Hungary, or for the way he handled the Hungarian uprising, or both. Speaking to a closed meeting of Party leaders, writers, and artists in May 1957 he used the accents of "thunder and lightning," as he said later, and is believed to have threatened that if Soviet writers should follow the path of the Hungarian writers, "my hand will not tremble." Nevertheless, at that moment his own control over the Soviet Party was in danger.

The signs were that Khrushchëv's fortunes declined sharply after the Hungarian uprising, whether or not because of it. In December 1956 the Central Committee assigned the responsibility for supervising all economic ministries to the State Economic Commission with Pervukhin as chairman: the plan was clearly authored by Khrushchëv's critics. However, in February 1957 Khrushchëv proposed a complete reversal: most non-military enterprises were to be taken away from the central ministries and placed under 105 new regional Economic Councils (*sovnarkhozy*), and the State Economic Commission was to be abolished. In May these proposals were adopted by the Supreme Soviet. The result was to enhance the power of local Party secretaries at the expense of the Moscow ministerial bureaucracy, and thus the power of Khrushchëv as against that of his opponents.

Malenkov, Molotov, and Kaganovich evidently then decided to strike back before it was too late. In June a seven-to-four majority of the Presidium, consisting of the three named and Bulganin, Voroshilov, Saburov, and Pervukhin, informed Khrushchëv of his dismissal. In an unprecedented fashion, the First Secretary announced that only the Central Committee could so decide, and hastily convening that body from all over the country with the help of army planes, he won from it a vote of confidence. All seven of his opponents except for Bulganin were promptly dropped from full membership in the Presidium, and of those six only Pervukhin retained even candidate membership. Four candidates were raised to become full members: Brezhnev, Furtseva, Shvernik, and Zhukov. Five other full members were chosen: A. B. Aristov, N. I. Beliaev, N. G. Ignatov, F. R. Kozlov and the old-time Finnish Communist, Otto Kuusinen.[5] Several new candidate members were also named, including A. N. Kosygin (from 1949 to 1952 a full member).

Malenkov, Kaganovich, Molotov, and Shepilov were publicly stigmatized as an "anti-Party group," from which Khrushchëv claimed to have saved the Party and country. It appeared that he owed part of his victory to the backing of Marshal Zhukov and the army; certainly Zhukov was the first fighting general (as distinguished from such political generals as Bulganin and Voroshilov) to become a full member of the highest Party body. However, his eminence lasted only a few months. In October he was dismissed from the defense ministry and shortly afterward from both the Presidium and Central Committee, having been denounced for fostering his own "cult of personality" in the armed forces.

Khrushchëv's ascendancy seemed secure. He had a hand-picked majority in the Presidium. With Zhukov out of the way, he had dispensed with the need to show the generals special favor; with Malenkov exiled to a remote installation in Central Asia and the personnel of the ministries sent out of Moscow in May, control by Khrushchëv's *apparatchiki* had been assured; with Molotov gone (to Mongolia as ambassador), the way was clear to further "de-Stalinization." Plainly he had more power than any one man had had since Stalin's death, and when he deposed Bulganin and himself assumed the office of premier in March 1958, he held the top posts in both Party and government as Stalin had done.

The Sino-Soviet Dispute

If the Stalinist diehards who made up part of Khrushchëv's opposition were now in the political discard in the USSR, they were in the saddle in China. Since Stalin's death Mao Zedong had struggled with the problem of how simultaneously to keep fidelity to Stalin's heritage in Beijing, for his own reasons, and to maintain good relations with Stalin's successors in Moscow, who appeared disturbingly

---

[5] In December 1957 Mukhitdinov, an Uzbek, was made a full member of the Presidium.

ambivalent on the subject of the dead leader. As Mao moved into the period of "Second Revolution" (see p. 344) in China, the relevance of Stalin's writings and methods—indeed, of his entire image—to Chinese Communist policies became more and more direct. Khrushchëv's criticism of Stalin in the "secret speech" nettled the Chinese leaders; Mao was far senior to Khrushchëv as a first-rank Communist leader, and, aside from whatever personal jealousies Mao may have felt, considerations of prestige, vital to any totalitarian regime, had to be reckoned with. If domestic liberalization even in such mild degree as that being tried in the USSR had any attractions for Mao, his experiment of early 1957 dispelled them: In the aftermath of the Polish and Hungarian events, in February and March, Mao used the slogan, "Let one hundred flowers bloom, let one hundred schools of thought contend," in speeches appearing to invite open criticism. The resultant uproar was so vehement that a crackdown soon ensued. Khrushchëv might be able to manage the USSR in its current stage of development by some use of the carrot, but in China, where the process of creating a new society and a new economy was under way, the stick had to be Mao's main device for some time.

Thus Khrushchëv and Mao responded differently to the tremendous soar in Soviet prestige produced by the launching of Sputnik I and Sputnik II in October and November 1957, months before the U.S. was able to match the feat. Mao thought the world Communist offensive might now be pressed with more open brandishment of weapons; Khrushchëv believed that the need for open aggressiveness was less pressing. The result was such moves as the Rapacki Plan for a "denuclearized zone" in Central Europe, offered in October 1957 by the Polish foreign minister with Soviet support. In November Khrushchëv summoned two consecutive conferences in Moscow: The first included twelve Communist and workers' parties in power; the second, sixty-four parties from all parts of the world. Both meetings approved the Moscow line of re-emphasizing "peaceful coexistence."

The USSR had moved into the field of "economic aid," paying the United States the compliment of imitation, by an offer to build a steel plant in India after the Khrushchëv-Bulganin tour of 1955. In 1958, after Secretary Dulles refused Nasser's request for aid in building an Aswan High Dam, the USSR loaned Egypt a sum sufficient to undertake the project. A new Middle East crisis in July, provoked by General Abdul Karim Kassem's leftist coup in Iraq, led to the landing of American Marines in Lebanon. Khrushchëv's response was to propose a new summit meeting of the Big Four with India added but China absent, thereby perpetrating a grave slight to Mao.

Mao had returned home from Moscow to develop his own spectacular plans. More or less simultaneously he prepared to attack the offshore island of Quemoy and to push his "Second Revolution" into a greatly accelerated phase. Apparently the Soviets assented to a probing operation against Quemoy but insisted on drawing back when U.S. forces showed themselves ready to fight, and Quemoy remained in the hands of the Nationalist government on Taiwan. On the domestic front, Mao raised "three red flags": "the general line," the "people's communes," and "the great leap forward." Within a few months it was claimed that over 99% of the Chinese peasants had joined the communes, in which private property and the family nearly disappeared. By the autumn of 1958 the Chinese countryside was thrown into chaos similar to that of the early months of 1930 in the USSR. However, there soon came a retreat reminiscent of Stalin's "Dizziness From Success" statement: in December 1958 the Central Committee called for a temporary let-up in the drive for communes, and Mao Zedong resigned as chairman of the government. Initially the Soviets had praised the achievements of the "Great Leap," but as its pace mounted, their tone changed, for the Chinese Communists were claiming that they were moving through socialism in the direction of pure communism, thus jumping ahead of the USSR. Khrushchëv, Mikoyan, and other Soviet leaders did not conceal their belief that the offensive was bound to fail; moreover, they correctly perceived a Chinese challenge to the Soviet leadership of the whole Communist movement.

The XXI Party Congress

The result was the XXI Special Party Congress, which met against a background of successes for Khrushchëv. He had consolidated his victory over the "anti-Party group" by removing Bulganin from the Presidium in September 1958; in December he had named as new chief of the KGB A. N. Shelepin. Khrushchëv had other reasons for feeling confident. In 1958 the USSR had had the best harvest in its history. In November 1958 his threat to hand Berlin over to the East Germans within six months had spread alarm in all Western capitals—though he did not carry through the threat. In January 1959 Fidel Castro had seized Cuba with strong Communist support, and thereafter identified himself with Communism and the USSR.

There had also been several significant domestic innovations of Khrushchëv's. In April 1958, just as the American clamor for imitation of Soviet schools was reaching its height, he severely criticized the educational system for failing to meet the needs of socialist construction and called for greater emphasis on physical labor and actual part-time work in factories as part of the curricular pattern; such a program was enacted in December. (Actually the program was soon a dead letter, except for the limitation of compulsory schooling to eight years and in consequence the abandonment of the 1956 decision to extend full secondary education to all.) Another important step in agriculture was taken by the abolition of the Machine-Tractor Stations (see p. 204), which act the *kolkhozy* welcomed because it turned over farm machinery to them, but the results were dubious because they had to assume the great financial burden of paying for it and because complex equipment could not be properly maintained on most collective farms. At the same time a number of collective farms were being converted into state farms—*sovkhozy* in 1957 embraced over 25% of the land as against 10% in 1952—despite a Central Committee warning in February 1958 that conversion should not be too hasty.[6] The old Khrushchëv notion of the *agrogorod* (see p. 357), which he discussed again in a speech in his native village in October 1958, remained on the Soviet agenda as a distant objective. Such developments in the Soviet countryside, pointing in the same direction as the Chinese "people's communes," suggested that the dispute between Khrushchëv and Mao was less about goals than about whether the USSR was to be recognized as leading the way there.

The XXI Congress, in January-February 1959, represented Khrushchëv's attempt to reassert this claim against Mao's challenge. Ostensibly its task was merely to adopt an ambitious Seven-Year Plan, to run from 1959 to 1965, replacing the last two years of the Sixth Five-Year Plan which had more modest targets. Actually the aim was to demonstrate Khrushchëv's supremacy in the USSR and the USSR's primacy in the international Communist movement. Speech after speech attacked Bulganin, Pervukhin, and Saburov as members of the "anti-Party group" and lauded the leadership of Comrade Nikita Sergeevich. Nevertheless the remaining limitations on Khrushchëv's power were shown by the fact that Voroshilov remained a full member and Pervukhin a candidate member of the Presidium.[7] Perhaps the most significant event at the Congress was Zhou Enlai's speech, in which he renewed the same kind of acknowledgment of Soviet primacy as the Chinese had made at the 1957 meeting of Communist parties, without hinting that in the meantime Mao had challenged the Soviet position unsuccessfully. Doubtless Zhou found the speech somewhat easier to give in consequence of a new Soviet grant of 5 billion rubles' worth of aid to China, announced just after the Congress.

Khrushchëv's sixty-fifth birthday was commemorated in the Soviet press in April 1959, but so was Stalin's eightieth anniversary in December—for the first time in years. The new *History of the Communist Party of the Soviet Union,* published in 1959, contained criticism of Stalin, but of a much milder kind than to be found in the "secret speech."

One noteworthy development of 1959 was the extension of extrajudicial methods of compulsion and punishment. In April 1956 the Soviet worker had been relieved of some of the direst penalties of the Stalin era: prosecutions for absenteeism were stopped, compulsory transfer of workers from one plant to another was ended, the prohibition of unauthorized change of job was repealed. To be sure, the plant manager still had at his disposition all sorts of instruments to keep

---

[6] Meanwhile, especially in the first half of 1960, collectivization was "in the main completed" in most East European states. Collectives and state farms together reached 97% of the arable in Bulgaria, 91% in Albania, 86% in Czechoslovakia, 82% in Romania. By the beginning of 1961 Hungary reported 82%. Only Poland and Yugoslavia failed to match these figures.

[7] There were no changes in the roster of full members at the Congress, which remained the same as in June 1957 except for Bulganin's removal and Mukhitdinov's elevation—fourteen in all.

workers working: the labor book and passport still recorded the circumstances of change of job, and various economic privileges could still be denied the laggard. In 1959 a device long intermittently used was energetically revived: the comrades' courts, in which one's neighbors and fellow-workers might mete out certain punishments for social delinquency. New volunteer squads called *druzhiny* were also encouraged to form and act as guardians of public order and good conduct, hauling suspicious persons out of public places for questioning and combating "hooliganism." Labor discipline was the direct concern of a new series of judicial enactments, the "anti-parasite" laws passed in several republics in the late 1950's and in RSFSR in May 1961. Their vague provisions made it difficult for a dissident or critic, if charged under such laws, to show he was not a "parasite." At the XXI Congress Khrushchëv had claimed that no "political prisoners" were left in the USSR. However, only weeks before, in December 1958, a law had extended the death penalty as a maximum punishment for a variety of "crimes against the state," and in May 1961 such provisions were further broadened. Under such legislation several hundred people were executed and many more sent to detention, often for "economic crimes." The prominence of priests, Jews, and medium-rank Party officials among the victims, however, suggested that the laws were being used as political weapons. An especially clear example was the arrest of Olga Ivinskaia, close friend of Boris Pasternak, within weeks of the latter's death, nominally for financial misconduct.

Cultural Policy, 1956–1964

In the aftermath of the "secret speech," a few Soviet writers (and publishers) began to take risks by bringing out novels about Soviet society as it was, not as it was ideally supposed to be currently or to become in the future. Vladimir Dudintsëv's book *Not by Bread Alone,* for example, was sharply attacked by official spokesmen in a public discussion held in May 1957, but his defenders bluntly retorted, and no punishment was inflicted on him.

Boris Pasternak's great novel, *Doctor Zhivago,* was a quite different sort of work. Published in Italy in November 1957 despite reversal of an earlier Soviet decision to publish simultaneously in the USSR, it rapidly earned world-wide admiration. In the book Pasternak depicted a man who comes from the intelligentsia, is caught up in the Revolution, Civil War, and the building of the Soviet system, but retains his own system of human values and is destroyed because of them. Rather than an attempted depiction of Soviet reality, the work is a prose poem about the meaning of life: "Reshaping life! People who can say that have never understood a thing about life ... life is never a material, a substance to be molded ... it is constantly renewing and remaking and changing and transfiguring itself, it is infinitely beyond your or my obtuse theories about it." Although Zhivago dies, his spirit triumphs. The Christian that Pasternak had become shows in the last stanza of the poems with which this thoroughly poetic work closes:

> I shall descend into my grave. And on the third day rise again,
> And, even as rafts float down a river,
> So shall the centuries drift, trailing like a caravan,
> Coming for judgment, out of the dark, to me.[8]

After Zhivago's death, his beloved Lara disappears into a concentration camp; the Soviet regime faithfully fulfilled this prophecy by arresting Ivinskaia. Only in 1958 did the novel enter public discussion in the USSR when Pasternak was awarded the Nobel Prize and Khrushchëv compelled him to refuse it in exchange for being allowed to remain in the Soviet Union, where he died in 1960.

The post-Hungary freeze during which *Zhivago* had been condemned was followed by a mild thaw after 1959. Evgeni Evtushenko, one of the more popular young dissident poets, published "Babii Yar," a poem referring to a mass murder of Jews by the Nazis near Kiev as a means of striking at Soviet anti-Semitism. In November 1962 the boldest novel yet to be published in the USSR appeared, Alexander Solzhenitsyn's *One Day in the Life of Ivan Denisovich*. It was a narrative of life in one of Stalin's concentration camps, published on the authority of Khrushchëv himself. Later in the same month, however, someone persuaded the First Secretary to visit two exhibitions of modern art in Moscow, and he reacted with gutter language and brutal threats delivered on the spot to artists accompanying him. At a closed meeting in the Kremlin in March 1963, Khrushchëv denounced abstract art and literary experimentation in the strongest terms, sharply criticized Ehrenburg and Evtushenko, and declared that "the moldy idea of absolute freedom" would never find a place in Soviet life. In a few cases, dissident writers such as Valery Tarsis and Alexander Esenin-Volpin (son of the peasant poet of the twenties) were seized and confined on the grounds of "mental instability," thus recalling Nicholas I's treatment of Peter Chaadaev in 1836. A few others, such as Joseph Brodsky, were exiled under the "anti-parasite laws." For the most part, however, Khrushchëv's regime confined itself to verbal warnings and refusals to publish or exhibit, and the limits of the permissible, though fluctuating, were certainly broader than before Stalin's death.

Some of the dissident writers and artists—notably Pasternak and Solzhenitsyn—had religious convictions, and there was enough of a revival of interest in religion among Soviet youth to provoke a campaign of repression beginning in 1959. During the next five years perhaps half of the remaining 20,000 Or-

---

[8] Boris Pasternak, *Doctor Zhivago*, trans., Random House, 1958, p. 559. Reprinted by permission of the publisher.

thodox churches and all of the monasteries except for perhaps fifteen were closed. In June 1960 the first show trial of an Orthodox clergyman since 1927 was held; the defendant, the archbishop of Kazan, was sentenced to prison. Apparently because he refused to cooperate in the new crackdown, Metropolitan Nicholas of Krutitsy, the long-time mainstay of church collaboration with the regime, fell from favor, was deprived of his offices in 1960, and died mysteriously the following year. The beginning of resistance to religious repression appeared in 1961 in the formation of the Initiative Group (*Initsiativniki*) within the Baptist-Evangelical Christian Council. Repeated statements by high Party officials reminded their hearers that to be a Communist was to be an atheist, but even some of the rank-and-file showed disturbing hesitation on that apparently obvious point.

The XXII Party Congress

Khrushchëv had tried to follow up Chinese submission at the XXI Congress with action. Indications are that in July 1959 Marshal Peng Dehuai and others, with Soviet backing, tried to remove Mao as chairman of the Chinese Party. They failed, and Peng was purged. But the Chinese internal offensive had brought the economy near collapse, and Mao was unable to press a counterattack. His regime faced a full-scale revolution in Tibet in March 1959 that required months to put down. Though neither the U.N. nor any of the Western powers could be persuaded to take perceptible interest in the Tibetan blood bath, the result was unfavorable publicity aboard and intensive domestic precautions lest an echo of the rising appear within China proper.

The Chinese were enraged when Khrushchëv, after test visits by Mikoyan and then Kozlov, visited President Eisenhower, and became the first head of any Russian government to set foot in the United States. Talks at the President's mountain hideaway produced the "Camp David spirit," which served chiefly to pave the way for a planned summit meeting in the spring of 1960. It never took place. Khrushchëv announced that an American high-flying reconnaissance plane, or U-2, had been brought down over the USSR; arriving in Paris for the summit, he demanded an apology. Eisenhower, ignoring the ancient precedent that spies are not acknowledged when caught by the enemy, first denied the flight and then admitted it, but refused to apologize. The summit meeting was promptly called off. In September Khrushchëv appeared at a U.N. General Assembly meeting, making news by a fraternal meeting with Fidel Castro and by the astonishing act of taking off his shoe and pounding the table with it to show disapproval of a U.N. speaker.

Returning from these travels, the Soviet leader convened a meeting of eighty-one Communist parties in Moscow in November-December 1960. In June at the Bucharest congress of the Romanian party—the first such conclave in the Communist world for over thirty years to witness serious debate—Khrushchëv had spoken of the Chinese as "madmen" who were ready "to unleash war," and in July had withdrawn all Soviet economic and military technicians and advisers from China. Soviet trade with China was plummeting. At the Moscow meeting Beijing's delegates yielded to such pressure and signed the conference manifesto stating that the Soviet Communist Party was the "universally recognized vanguard" of the international movement. The Chinese did manage one minor achievement: they detached Enver Hoxha's Albania from the Soviet camp. For a time it was tacitly agreed that when Beijing attacked "revisionism" it mentioned Yugoslavia and not the USSR; when Moscow attacked "dogmatism," it gave Albania and not China as its example. The Sino-Soviet dispute would still publicly observe a few amenities.

During the next few months Khrushchëv did not press further toward *détente* with the West. Despite Soviet approval of the cease-fire in Laos in May 1961 and subsequent agreement at Geneva to reconfirm Laotian neutrality, Khrushchëv had used brutal language in his message to President Kennedy over the ill-fated attempt to overthrow Castro at the Bay of Pigs in April. At the meeting of the two leaders in Vienna in June he convinced the new President that he was ready to provoke a new U.S.-USSR confrontation, and followed up tough talk with the erection of the Berlin Wall and resumption of nuclear testing.

Khrushchëv was riding high. He sought to buttress the Soviet claim to be "vanguard," and did so by preparing for the "transition to communism." In July 1961 a new Party program and a new set of Party rules were published. The program envisaged completion of the "transition" by 1980, opening the way to the building of full communism thereafter. Among the delights that Soviet citizens were promised by 1980 were separate apartments for every urban family, "including newly-weds," and "conveniences"—that is, indoor toilets—for most peasant families. The earthly paradise was therefore still somewhat remote. As for the new Party rules, they provided for compulsory rotation of offices; in future elections, one-third of every party committee from the Presidium on down would have to be replaced by new people, with few exceptions. By this provision Khrushchëv may have signed his own (political) death warrant.

Against such a background the XXII Congress met in October. It had been preceded by a large-scale shake-up of Party cadres.[9] Of the 9,746,000 members and candidates, more than one-third had joined since the XX Congress (1956); of the 4,813 delegates to the Congress, 19% had joined since then and over 41% since World War II. One full member was added to the Presidium: G. I. Voronov, who had been credited with increasing agricultural production in the RSFSR. Four

---

[9] The only change among full members of the Presidium since the XXI Congress had occurred in May 1960 with the removal of three men—Kirichenko and Beliaev, previously identified as clients of Khrushchëv, and Voroshilov, a known enemy of his—and their replacement by Kosygin, N. V. Podgorny, and D. S. Poliansky. Voroshilov was also replaced as titular head of state, by Brezhnev, who in turn yielded the position in July 1964 to Mikoyan.

were removed: Aristov, Furtseva, Ignatov, and Mukhitdinov. In the smallest Presidium since 1953, eleven remained.[10]

The keynote of the Congress was further de-Stalinization. The ancient Madame Lazurkina, a Party member since 1902, told of communing with Lenin's shade: "It was as if he stood alive before me, and he said: 'it is unpleasant for me to lie side by side with Stalin, who brought so much harm to the party.'" Following this spiritualist report to the materialist Congress, Stalin's body was removed from the mausoleum in Red Square, though not before Zhou Enlai managed to place a wreath there in his memory. A number of speakers publicly eulogized Khrushchëv, added details of Stalin's crimes to those given in the 1956 "secret speech," and made an effort to associate the "anti-Party group" with Stalin's offenses. After the Congress, Stalinsk was renamed Donetsk; Stalinabad, Diushambe (its original name); and most traumatic of all, Stalingrad, Volgograd. A Soviet quip had it that the dead leader sent a message to the Congress acknowledging the correctness of all its decisions, signing it "Joseph Vissarionovich Volgin." Anti-Stalinist developments in foreign affairs came when relations were broken with Albania in December 1961 and when amity was restored in Soviet-Yugoslav relations in the fall of 1962. Khrushchëv's de-Stalinization line and his personal ascendancy, however, were still not completely secure; for example, not one of those denounced as criminals during the Congress was thereafter brought to trial for his alleged crimes.

Khrushchëv's Last Days in Power

Apparently misjudging both Kennedy and the United States, Khrushchëv installed Soviet missiles in Cuba, while offering bland assurances that he was not doing so. He was apparently surprised and certainly alarmed when President Kennedy, in October 1962, responded with a virtual ultimatum, to which the First Secretary yielded by withdrawing the missiles. Probably the world had not been so close to war since 1945. Soviet technology was certainly advancing in a spectacular way; Yuri Gagarin orbited the earth in April 1961, while John Glenn matched this feat only in February 1962. But the Soviets did not wish for war, however advanced their technology. In fact Khrushchëv did his best to convert his diplomatic humiliation over Cuba into a victory, and aside from his boast that he had preserved peace, he had gains to show: the United States, by being brought to confine its objective to the withdrawal of Soviet missiles, scrapped the Monroe Doctrine, and Cuba remained both free from the threat of invasion and intact as a base for Communist subversion throughout the Western Hemisphere. Khrushchëv's

---

[10] A. P. Kirilenko, after being dropped from candidate membership at the Congress, was suddenly elected full member in April 1962, making a total of twelve.

newly pacific posture (or resumption of the policy of *détente*) was reinforced in August 1963 by the installation of a Washington-Moscow "hot line" and by the signing of a treaty among the USSR, Britain, and the U.S.A. (to which many countries later added their signatures), banning further nuclear tests except under ground.

As a result of the Cuban crisis Soviet relations with the PRC worsened. The Soviets implied disapproval of the Chinese offensive against India that had just been launched when President Kennedy made his dramatic speech to Americans on the missiles in Cuba. During the Cuban crisis, Beijing supported the Soviets, but once it was over, there were ample taunts about both the adventurist unwisdom of placing the missiles in Cuba to begin with and the capitulationism involved in withdrawing them. The Chinese denounced the nuclear test-ban treaty, and polemics on both sides became overt, no longer using the surrogate targets of Yugoslavia and Albania. When the U.N. General Assembly convened in the fall, for the first time Albania, not the USSR, presented the perennial demand for the seating of the PRC in place of the Nationalist Government. Sino-Soviet relations deteriorated still further. Mao told some Japanese socialist visitors in August 1964 that the USSR was an imperialist state, that "the Russians took everything they could" in Eastern Europe and in Northeastern Asia, and that the Kurile islands should be returned immediately to Japan. The previous month the Soviets had laid plans for an international Communist conclave to condemn China.

If foreign affairs were not going well, neither were domestic affairs. Dissatisfaction with food shortages and the low standard of living led to a shocking event that the regime managed to hush up for several years. It began with a strike in Novocherkassk, provoked by a decree published in June 1962 raising meat and butter prices and a simultaneous lowering of wages for workers at a large locomotive plant. Arrests on the first day of the strike were followed by a large but peaceful demonstration that was fired on by troops, killing 70 or 80.[11] Many were arrested, some sentenced to death; a few officials were demoted. There followed disturbances in several other cities.

In November 1962 a division of the party was announced into industrial and agricultural sections, but no one knew how to make this work, especially after the *sovnarkhozy* were made much larger by being reduced in number to forty-seven early in 1963. A bad harvest in 1963 resulted in the humiliation of having to import grain. Restrictions on the private plots, decline of private livestock holdings, and conversions of *kolkhozy* into *sovkhozy* produced agrarian stagnation. Corn, "virgin lands," and other expedients had not worked. A better idea, if still no panacea, was being bruited by Khrushchëv at the very end: large-scale increase of fertilizer production. But his colleagues had lost patience. He returned from a vacation in

---

[11] Alexander Solzhenitsyn, *The Gulag Archipelago,* trans., Harper & Row, III, 1978, pp. 507–515, esp. p. 510.

the Crimea to be greeted on October 14, 1964, with the news that his resignation had been accepted. The next day *Pravda* reported the news and denounced "hare-brained schemes; half-baked conclusions and hasty decisions and actions, divorced from reality; bragging and bluster; attraction to rule by fiat; unwillingness to take into account what science and practical experience have already discovered. ..." Thus ran the political obituary of the colorful and crude little man who had brought the world to the verge of war and yet tried to further "peaceful co-existence" with the West; who had been brutal enough in his time but in the course of "de-Stalinization" freed millions of prisoners from the Gulag, posthumously rehabilitated millions of others, and permitted the return of survivors of the North Caucasian peoples exiled by Stalin; and who tightened the screws on the Soviet peasant while at the same time he offered the Soviet consumer visions of "goulash Communism." Overnight Khrushchëv disappeared into retirement, and the world gasped in astonishment.

26

The Brezhnev Regime
1964–1982

First Steps of the New Government

Bertram D. Wolfe facetiously formulated a "law of diminishing dictators" to explain changes in the top Soviet leadership: Lenin was a commanding personality in all respects; Stalin was intellectually limited but all-powerful; Khrushchëv had much less power, despite high visibility; Brezhnev "is not there at all." Although there was some truth in Wolfe's "law," Brezhnev was of course "there"; and the Brezhnev years even saw a partial reversion to Stalinism.

Born in 1906 in the small river port of Kamenskoe (later Dneprodzerzhinsk) near Ekaterinoslav, evidently the son of a Russian metal worker, Brezhnev finished the course at a technical institute in Kursk in 1927. After three years in land surveying work, he went to Moscow in 1930 for a year of study at the Agricultural Institute and became a party member. Returning to Dneprodzerzhinsk, he studied metallurgy and worked as an engineer. Following service in the army, in 1938 he became a full-time party worker and official in his home town and in 1939 became first secretary of the region. He spent the war as a high political officer. After 1945 he served in Chernovtsy, the Dnieper area, and in 1950–1952 in Moldavia. From there he was recalled to Moscow and became a member of the Central Committee (and also from October 1952 to Stalin's death a candidate member of the Presidium). Apparently attaching his fortunes to Khrushchëv's, he became the latter's viceroy in Kazakhstan (1954–1956) and had important responsibilities for the "virgin lands" scheme. In February 1956 he returned to Moscow and again became a candidate member of the Presidium; in June 1957 he reached full membership. From May 1960 he also served as chief of state until July 1964, when Mikoyan took over the position.

It seems that the first choice of the leaders of Khrushchëv's overthrow for first secretary was Alexander Shelepin. The nomenklatura, or party elite who also ran the government, balked at his ideological intensity and evident hankering for Stalin's methods and supported a safer alternative: Leonid Brezhnev. His contributions to Marxist-Leninist theory were imperceptible; his political or economic skills undemonstrated. An authoritative assessment has it, however, that he "had the one talent indispensable for a party leader, the ability to lead: to issue orders on virtually every subject, without being a specialist in anything."[1] He seemed unlikely to create a "cult of personality" of his own and apt to be willing to accept what came to be called "stability of cadres." So he was chosen, and Alexei Kosygin became prime minister, with the reputation of a mild modernizer. Shelepin became a full member of the Presidium, along with P. E. Shelest; Kozlov, clearly ill, was removed and soon died, as did the aged Kuusinen. In March 1965 Mazurov became a full member, and in December Podgorny replaced Mikoyan as titular chief of state.

To the new regime the problem of China appeared the most urgent. On the very day after Khrushchëv's fall was reported, China announced that it had exploded its first nuclear device. A preliminary meeting of twenty-six parties had been scheduled for December, whose business was to prepare for an international Communist conference condemning China. It was promptly postponed. Beijing welcomed the fall of Khrushchëv as just punishment for his ideological sins and awaited developments; for about six months polemics were suspended. The new regime relaxed restrictions on the private plots and private livestock holding, raised agricultural prices, and in general made clear that it was going to take a different line from Khrushchëv's in agriculture. It also ended the 1962 division of the party into agricultural and industrial branches. Most important, the provision of the 1961 rules was repealed that had required replacement of one third of all committees. Brodsky and Ivinskaia were released from prison and Lysenko fell for good.

In October 1965 the long-discussed proposals of Professor Evsei Liberman of Kharkov University were implemented in an economic reform of some proportions.[2] Under these proposals individual enterprises were to be given the power to plan and produce in a way related to sales contracts, and profit was to be the basis

---

[1] Mikhail Heller and Aleksandr Nekrich, *Utopia in Power,* trans. Summit Books, 1986, p. 606.

[2] Some of the East European Communist states—the term "satellites" was no longer applicable to these countries in view of the range of changes in foreign and domestic policy that had been affecting the region—had acted first. Economic "reforms" of the type described were enacted in East Germany already in 1963; they were adopted in Czechoslovakia in January 1965, Poland in July 1965, Hungary in November 1965, Bulgaria in December 1965. Yugoslavia was already far in advance. Only Romania and Albania failed to follow suit. In the USSR another line of economic innovation was being pursued: the attempt by such economists as Kantorovich and Novozhilov to optimize solutions using computer programming techniques, and Soviet economics rapidly became an arena wherein the investigation of real questions replaced the repetition of Marxian aphorisms.

of evaluation of performance. In mid-1964 these ideas had been tried out in two clothing factories, Bolshevichka and Maiak, with initially good results. The *sovnarkhozy* were simultaneously abolished and replaced by ministries of the pre-1957 type, so that conversion to the new system was to proceed within the ministerial framework. However, it moved slowly, and was at length swallowed up in the old system. More or less simultaneously, in mid-1966 guaranteed monthly pay in cash and kind was introduced for collective farmers.

From March 29 to April 8, 1966, the XXIII Party Congress was held, and the Five-Year Plan for 1966–1970 was outlined, providing for the first time a higher percentage rise in consumer goods than in producers' goods; mention was made of color television and of private automobiles—for construction of which a contract was soon thereafter signed with the Italian Fiat company to build a plant at the newly renamed Soviet city of Togliatti. Nevertheless the Party Program adopted in 1961 was tacitly abandoned; the question of "transition to communism" was shelved for more urgent goals than indoor toilets for 1980.

The Stalinists had made various warning noises. In April 1965 *Pravda* had criticized the "one-sided" treatment of historical events and personalities—read "denigration of Stalin"—and in January 1966 had questioned the use of the phrase "cult of personality." Nevertheless the satisfaction the XXIII Congress granted the Stalinists was mainly symbolic: the Presidium resumed its old name of Politburo, the First Secretary's title became again General Secretary, as in Stalin's day. After the Congress Shvernik and Mikoyan were dropped as full members of the Politburo; the old Latvian Communist Pelshe was added. The membership of eleven—Brezhnev, Kosygin, Kirilenko, Mazurov, Pelshe, Podgorny, Poliansky, Shelepin, Shelest, Suslov, and Voronov—did not change for the next five years; for the Politburo, that was great stability.

The Vietnam War and Relations with China

The new regime faced both challenges and opportunities in foreign policy, and in Asia both claimed Soviet attention. Under Khrushchëv the USSR had kept a low profile in the troubles of Indo-China, and according to the Chinese the First Secretary even "concocted the slander" that the Tonkin Gulf incident (August 1964, in which the U.S. retaliated against North Vietnamese torpedo boat action by air strikes, and which brought U.S. Congressional authorization for greater executive involvement in Vietnam) was provoked by China. In January 1965 the USSR announced a forthcoming visit by Kosygin to Hanoi and simultaneously (and secretly) transmitted to North Vietnam a U.S. plea to stop supporting the Vietcong in South Vietnam. While Kosygin was in Hanoi, President Johnson ordered American air raids on the north. As a result of the bombing, a period of cooler U.S.-Soviet relations set in.

Doubtless Washington's policy-makers considered that U.S. intervention in Vietnam carried with it the peril of lessening or ending the Sino-Soviet dispute. However, in fact the opposite happened. The delayed meeting of twenty-six Communist Parties (only eighteen showed up) was held in Moscow in March 1965. In China's eyes, the main need was help for North Vietnam; but the Soviet leaders wanted to discuss Communist "unity," by which they meant Beijing's sins against it. The result was fury in China as well as the astonishing spectacle of the March 4 attack by Chinese students and others on the U.S. embassy in Moscow, which was repulsed by Soviet police and soldiers. As for North Vietnam, her pro-Beijing attitude of the previous period was replaced by increased friendliness to Moscow as Soviet aid followed Kosygin's visit.

In the new situation produced by escalation of the war in Vietnam, Moscow tried to undermine Mao's anti-Soviet position in every way possible by encouraging Mao's opponents within China. Mao, perceiving that revolutionary fervor in his sixteen-year-old regime was weakening as a desire for material improvements increased, was prepared to shake it up from top to bottom, but he encountered much opposition within the party. As a result, one authority declares, "where Stalin had purged the CPSU from within, secretly and using the party apparatus, Mao purged the CCP from without, publicly and using mass organizations, such as the Red Guard youth."[3] Mao's action to purge his critics led Moscow to resume polemics with Beijing, after a thirteen-month hiatus, in November 1965. In August 1966, with the unleashing of the Red Guards, came the Great Proletarian Cultural Revolution. All secondary schools and colleges in the country were closed. Formal Moscow-Beijing relations almost ceased; for three months the Soviet embassy was under siege. The Soviet press seemed to enjoy recounting the absurdities of the GPCR—Mao's thoughts were claimed to help sell rotten watermelons—and its horrors—the bones in pianists' hands were crushed, books burned, and art treasures destroyed—and published anti-Chinese poems by such writers as Evtushenko and Voznesensky. Border clashes erupted, and finally those over an island in the Ussuri River in March 1969 were reported in the Soviet press. In September Victor Louis, a Moscow correspondent for London newspapers whose relations with the Soviet regime were very close, published not very veiled threats of a Soviet nuclear strike on Lop Nor (China's nuclear testing site) as well as invocation of the Brezhnev Doctrine as justification for Soviet "fraternal help" to China.

Under such pressure, the Chinese rulers decided to conclude the domestic upheaval. In June 1969 another international conference to discuss Communist unity brought 75 parties to Moscow, though not all signed the ambiguous communiqué. In September Kosygin stopped in Beijing en route home from Ho Chi Minh's funeral in Hanoi, and intergovernmental talks began.

---

[3] John King Fairbank, *The United States and China*, Harvard U. Press, 4th ed., 1983, p. 436.

The Six-Day War and
the Invasion of Czechoslovakia

On the heels of Arab troop concentrations and rumors of war, on June 5, 1967 the Israelis attacked Egypt, Jordan, and Syria, utterly defeating all three in the "Six-Day War." The Soviets could do nothing for their Arab clients except sever relations with Israel (which the East European states except for Romania did also) and begin to equip the shattered Arab armies and air forces. Ostensibly to summon Israel to evacuate the territory it had conquered, Kosygin made a pilgrimage to the U.N. and at that time met President Lyndon Johnson at Glassboro, New Jersey (halfway between New York and Washington), without much result. The sudden death of Nasser in September 1970 left the Soviets stuck in Middle Eastern mud without the benefit of a charismatic ally.

Another crisis erupted after the 1967 war. Following 1956 it was plain to Eastern Europe that the way out of Stalinist repression and stagnation was not armed revolt Hungarian style. For a time Gomulka in Poland was thought to be a possible model, since he had avoided Soviet intervention in 1956, but after riots in the north he was removed as leader in December 1970. Romania seemed to offer a possible alternative when it declined in 1962 to accept Khrushchëv's plan to revive Comecon and turn it into an agency for "international division of labor" (more agriculture and less industry for Romania). In 1965 Nicolae Ceauşescu succeeded Gheorghe Gheorghiu-Dej, and he developed further the latter's talent for self-assertion without provoking Moscow to sharp reaction. He even managed to hint that Bessarabia ought not to have been annexed by the USSR. Gheorghiu-Dej had released some political prisoners, but in general the regime did not experiment with freedom; it merely clung to Romanian independence of action, and demonstrated it by refusal to break with Israel after the Six-Day War.

In Czechoslovakia the economy was in grim straits, and dissidents among the writers voiced an embarrassing amount of discontent. In October 1967 Alexander Dubček, first secretary of the Slovak party, openly challenged the hard-line rule of Antonin Novotný. Moscow consented to the appointment of Dubček in his place in January 1968. Then events got out of hand. Virtual press freedom developed in fact and then civil liberties were proclaimed; in June the "coalition" of parties that made up the National Front was interpreted to be a real one. Moscow's alarm mounted. During July 29 to August 1 almost the entire politburos of the USSR and Czechoslovakia met at the border village of Čierna nad Tisou, with a follow-up meeting in Bratislava August 3 with the leaders of East Germany, Poland, Hungary, and Bulgaria. All seemed to accept the "Prague Spring," and Tito and Ceauşescu visited the capital to encourage the Czechoslovaks.

Then, suddenly, on the night of August 20, Soviet and other Warsaw Pact troops invaded Czechoslovakia. Inexplicably they had, however, failed to set up a political body which they could install in power and which they could then claim to be the agency that summoned "fraternal help" from abroad to save socialism.

Dubček and Svoboda were roughly hauled off to Moscow, but the Brezhnev regime was not prepared simply to impose Soviet administration on the country, and felt compelled to let them return. There was almost no violence, but the Czechoslovak people showed their hatred of the occupiers very clearly. In the U.N. the Czechoslovak delegate denied to their face the Soviets' account of what had happened. The Soviets were prepared to wait; within a few months Dubček had been replaced by Gustav Husák and expelled from the party, and the "Prague Spring" came to a decisive end. In October Kosygin came to Prague to sign a treaty by which Soviet troops would stay in the country indefinitely.

In September a statement in *Pravda*, expanded by Brezhnev himself before the Polish party congress in November, codified the meaning of the Soviet action in Czechoslovakia. Although, to be sure, Brezhnev was "resolutely opposed to interference in the affairs of any states," he declared that "when a threat arises to the cause of socialism" in a given Communist country, it becomes "also a general problem, the concern of all socialist countries." This "Brezhnev Doctrine," as it was promptly dubbed, thus asserted that Soviet forces might cross the border of any Communist country when it was deemed necessary to do so. The threat to invoke it in China's case has been mentioned; for many months the Romanians and Yugoslavs thought hard about what the Brezhnev Doctrine might mean to them, but the Soviets were not immediately to repeat the Czechoslovak invasion. A predictable storm of criticism arose abroad, but once again, as in the case of Hungary, the Soviet leadership rightly counted on the virtual certainty that nothing worse than words would be hurled at them by the West and that world opinion would soon find other problems with which to occupy itself.

It was reasonable to expect that the Czechoslovak crisis would have an impact on the top Soviet leadership, as the Hungarian crisis of 1956 had had. The army had done a technically brilliant job in carrying out the occupation; the party had fumbled the political side of it completely. What went on behind the scenes remains unclear, though there were a few puzzling signs that the military was in trouble, perhaps because the invasion had been *too* successful: a startling number of generals died in the first half of 1969, many of them in unspecified "tragic circumstances"; the May Day military parade of 1969 was abruptly cancelled only a few days before it was to be held. But conflict, if there was any, did not break into the open.

Dissent, Repressed and Unrepressed

Soon after the Soviet invasion of Czechoslovakia a handful of people led by Pavel Litvinov, grandson of the foreign minister of the 1930's, had demonstrated in Red Square in protest. This incident, lasting but a few minutes, was insignificant in itself, interesting as part of a larger pattern of events.

The Brezhnev regime first seemed to continue Khrushchëv's gentleness in deed (despite harshness in word) with intellectuals indifferent or even hostile to Marxism-Leninism. Hopes for more "thaw" in cultural policy were raised by the honors shown Anna Akhmatova on her seventy-fifth birthday in 1964, the rehabilitation of Sergei Esenin on his seventieth anniversary in 1965, and even the publication in June 1965 of a book of Pasternak's poems with a laudatory introduction by the critic Andrei Siniavsky. However, a murmur of disapproval of underground journals and officially published criticism was also growing, and a mild attempt in September 1965 by A. M. Rumiantsev, editor of *Pravda*, to defend those who helped to expose and correct abuses in Soviet society backfired and blew him out the editorship.

In that same month Siniavsky was arrested and in February 1966 was tried, along with Yuli Daniel. The two men had published abroad works critical of the USSR under the pseudonyms Abram Tertz and N. Arzhak. They were sentenced to seven and five years' hard labor. The sentences were widely recognized as a turning point, the first significant instance of penal action against the intellectuals since the death of Stalin. Michael Sholokhov, who had become the drink-sodden favorite of the regime, but who had himself just received the Nobel Prize in 1965, spoke in support of the punishment of Siniavsky and Daniel, but many Soviet and foreign writers sharply criticized the sentences and Sholokhov for his approval of them. Also in February 1966, however, another approach to the problem of controlling dissidence was tried; Valery Tarsis, an outspoken writer who had been confined in a mental ward, was permitted to go abroad—where he chose to remain.

Within the next few years dissent became something that can be termed a movement, or, more precisely, in three overlapping areas appeared a spectrum of protest ranging from what was officially tolerated to what was officially proscribed and persecuted. Those areas were literary-ideological, ethnic, and religious. Literary-ideological dissent was the best publicized, at least abroad, and yet embraced perhaps the fewest persons of the three areas. Perhaps 2,000 people identified more or less with the "democratic movement" wrote letters and petitions in support of the rights of dissidents who were being tried for this or that. Each trial seemed to provoke protests by distinguished Soviet intellectuals, which in turn led to more arrests and trials. In January 1967 four writers—Iu. Galanskov, A. Ginzburg, A. Dobrovolsky, and V. Lashkova—were arrested; in September V. Bukovsky and two others were tried for demonstrating for release of the four. The astonishing underground publication, *Chronicle of Current Events*, undertook to report the salient facts about dissidence and repression. The practice of *samizdat* ("self-publication") was transformed from a means of informal circulation of manuscripts that had not yet been published or had been rejected by official presses into something like an opposition press. A variety of modest-sized committees were formed to defend human rights, characteristically seeking, at least ostensibly, not to overthrow the Soviet regime or to change its laws but rather to enforce them. Academician Andrei Sakharov, a crucial contributor to the production of a Soviet atomic bomb, was a prominent "legalist." Then there were people who identified themselves as "Leninists" seeking to remove Stalinist blemishes on the Soviet socialist landscape; an example was Roy Medvedev, whose book *Let History Judge* was published abroad. The third group, loosely called Slavophiles, was more interested in the Russian past and promoting identification with it in one form or another than they were in establishing a kinship with the Slavophiles of the nineteenth century. At least part of this trend was not opposed by the regime. In 1966 a Society for Preservation of Ancient Monuments was launched, with government support, to arrest further deterioration of churches, monasteries, and the like as part of the artistic (not religious) heritage of the country. Vladimir Soloukhin and others wrote moving accounts of the surviving beauties of the Russian countryside, both natural and historical. To be sure, such interest in the artistic past, which happened to be almost exclusively religious in Russia, did not satisfy some religious persons: Iu. Stefanov wrote a poem called "A Lament for the Church of the Intercession" which declared his love for an ugly nineteenth-century church which did not deserve saving on its artistic merits but, he implied, ought to be preserved simply as a house of worship.

The most renowned of the literary-ideological dissidents and the man who attracted more attention in the West than any Russian oppositionist since the time of Alexander Herzen was Alexander Solzhenitsyn. Born in Kislovodsk in 1918, Solzhenitsyn had served in the army as an artillery captain against the Nazis, but had been sentenced to a concentration camp and then exile for making critical remarks about Stalin ("the man with the moustache"). In 1956 he had been allowed to return to European Russia, and in 1962 his novel *One Day in the Life of Ivan Denisovich* (see p. 379) had been published in the USSR. But by 1965 his works could no longer hope for publication within Soviet borders, and in 1969 he was expelled from the Writers' Union. Especially in recognition of his novels *The First Circle* and *The Cancer Ward,* he was awarded the Nobel Prize in the fall of 1970, but he was not permitted to receive it, though unlike Pasternak he was not willing to refuse it. As *August 1914* and the first volume of his first lengthy nonfictional work, *The Gulag Archipelago,* were issued, and praised, abroad, he became a thorn in the side of the regime which was finally extracted when he was forcibly exiled to the West in February 1974. The device of forcible exile was new, but seemed to work well, since Solzhenitsyn rather rapidly ceased to make headlines and in the eyes of the Western press became just another Soviet émigré. (Perhaps the experience of Svetlana Allilueva, Stalin's daughter, whose sensational defection to the West in April 1967 had been soon followed by a loss of interest in her by the mass media, encouraged the Soviet rulers to compel their most embarrassing subject to take the same path.) As Solzhenitsyn increasingly identified himself as a Christian and a Russian Orthodox believer, his position diverged from that of the Western-oriented quasi-liberal Sakharov. But by 1973 Sakharov himself had moved from "legalism" to a position of giving up hope for within-system changes.

Soviet response to the literary-ideological dissidents was uneven. No. 27 of the *Chronicle of Current Events* appeared in October 1972—and then no other issue until May 1974, then seven more up to early 1975. In 1972 Piotr Yakir and Victor Krasin were arrested; in September 1973 those who remembered Stalin's purge trials were chilled by the spectacle of Yakir's and Krasin's being presented to the press for public statements of recantation of their dissident views. By 1975 the "democratic movement" was in disarray.

Defense of ethnic groups was still another area of the protest movement. The appearance of spokesmen for the ethnic minorities who were willing to take risks was a novel phenomenon. In April 1966 two Ukrainian writers, one of them named Ivan Dziuba, were arrested. In his manuscript *Internationalism or Russification?*, which was published in the West, Dziuba asked indirectly why Russian dissidents did not support the cause of non-Russian groups. (Perhaps such questions helped to prompt Solzhenitsyn and Sakharov later to suggest that Russia free the borderlands.) There were other arrests and trials due to ethnic protest, against which Viacheslav Chornovil protested in essays that were also published abroad. In November 1967, he was sentenced to forced labor; released in February 1969, he was rearrested in January 1972, and in March 1973 he was sentenced to twelve years' imprisonment and exile. The issue of alleged Ukrainian nationalism reached beyond a handful of dissidents at least once or twice. The removal of Kirichenko in 1960 (see p. 381) and Shelest in 1973 from the Politburo may in both cases have been connected with their efforts to slow Russian immigration into the Ukraine and to refrain from unnecessarily repressive measures against Ukrainian consciousness or pride. Other minority areas, notably in the Baltic and Caucasus, also experienced covert or overt disputes and tensions over the position of the indigenous people vis-à-vis Russians. In a few cases dissidents from one nationality took open risks in order to help dissidents of another. A notable example was Major General P. G. Grigorenko, who was arrested in May 1969 in Tashkent, where he had gone to try to help eleven Crimean Tatars being tried there, and in February 1970 was declared legally insane. He was released from a mental hospital the day before Nixon arrived in Moscow in June 1974.

In the field of religion the Brezhnev regime permitted about five hundred churches to be reopened out of the approximately ten thousand closed during the previous five years, and acceded in some minor respects to petitions from the Evangelical Christians and others for clarification of the laws on religion and the conformity of practice with law. However, there was in 1966–1967 a sharp crackdown on proselytization by the Baptists and Evangelicals.

A new element of the period was a disposition for self-defense on the part of the Russian Orthodox. A number were especially troubled by a decision taken by an irregularly summoned council of bishops in 1961 declaring the *dvadtsatka* (the group of twenty parishioners who sign the parish contract with local authorities) to be the governing body instead of the assembly of all parishioners; the state Council on Russian Orthodox Church Affairs was exploiting this decision to make control more effective. In the summer of 1965 a group of eight bishops led by Ermogen of Kaluga petitioned Patriarch Alexii to summon a new council to reverse the decision, and in November and December two priests, N. I. Eshliman and G. P. Yakunin, protested in similar vein. The patriarch suspended the two priests from their functions, but many supported them, including Anatoly Levitin (who wrote under the pseudonym Krasnov), perhaps foremost among those who had been producing a new Christian literature. (Levitin was arrested for "anti-Soviet activity" in September 1969.) As for Ermogen, he was requested by the patriarch to retire to a monastery and await a new episcopal vacancy; two years later he protested that he had been passed over when such vacancies occurred.

There was some marginal convergence of the literary-ideological dissidence and religious protest: Levitin testified at the Galanskov trial, and in the Leningrad underground there was discovered an All-Russian Social-Christian Union for the Liberation of the People, desiring the establishment of parliamentary democracy and full freedom for the Russian Orthodox Church, whose members were influenced by the ideas of Berdiaev and others. The dissidents in the Orthodox Church archived few results. When the aged patriarch Alexii died and a successor was to be named, the choice fell on Metropolitan Pimen of Krutitsy and Kolomna, elected at a council in May–June 1971 at Zagorsk. He was known for his activity with church choirs and his passivity in regard to the regime.

The Muslims continued to be a problem for the Soviet government whose ethnic and religious identities were closely intertwined. By the 1980's the Islamic peoples of the USSR numbered about 50 million, their rate of increase vastly exceeding that of the Great Russians. The line between dissidence and expression of Muslim national consciousness was readily crossed. It was easier for the rulers to find and control official spokesmen for Islam than it was to bring the actual religion of the Muslim peoples under their control, and the growth of national feelings tended to drive the intellectuals among such peoples closer to Islam and away from the atheism that some of them had been brought to profess in their childhood and youth.

About 1970 the successive Middle Eastern crises and the danger they posed to Israeli achievements or even existence combined with the emergence into the open of a Jewish component of dissent in the USSR. Increased Western concern with the desire of Soviet Jews to emigrate and with dismissals of educated Jews in the professions from their jobs helped to swell the totals of Jews who were issued exit visas; in 1973 the figure reached 35,000, declining somewhat to 20,000 in 1974. The so-called Jackson-Vanik Amendment, hinging most-favored-nation treatment for the USSR in U.S. trade to free emigration from the Soviet Union, may well have contributed to the increased Jewish emigration while it was only a threat and a bargaining point between Washington and Moscow.

Détente

If the Brezhnev regime first appeared to repudiate Khrushchëv's objectives, it soon seemed to return to the pursuit of some of them—notably "goulash Communism" and what would soon be called *détente*. The consumption goals of the Five-Year Plan for 1966–1970 were achieved, for the first time in Soviet history. The Soviets' gross national product declined slowly but steadily in the 60's compared to the 50's, and in the early 70's in comparison with the 60's; in 1972 the worst crop failure since 1963 might have created a serious food crisis—if the USSR had not made major wheat purchases in the U.S.

The wheat deal came in the course of other improvements in relations between the USSR and the U.S. as well as other Western powers. Already before the Czechoslovak crisis, in June 1968, the Soviets agreed to the Strategic Arms Limitation Talks (SALT), and they were in fact begun in November 1969. In August 1970 the West German Chancellor, Willy Brandt, signed a goodwill treaty with the USSR and went on to sign another with Poland accepting the Oder-Neisse frontier. Brandt made clear, however, that ratification of the Soviet treaty might depend on a four-power agreement guaranteeing access to West Berlin. Such an agreement was reached in September 1971. In May 1968 on the initiative of President Johnson, but certainly with Soviet acquiescence, talks had begun in Paris seeking to end the war in Vietnam.

In July 1971 came the sensational announcement by President Nixon that U.S. Secretary of State Kissinger had secretly visited Beijing and that he himself would shortly go there. Nixon did so in February 1972. It was made clear, however, that the U.S. would pursue closer relations with both Moscow and Beijing without allying itself with either against the other.

On that tacit understanding Brezhnev received Nixon in Moscow in May 1972. There the first phase of the SALT talks was concluded with the signing of a treaty restricting deployment of antiballistic missile systems and an interim agreement to limit strategic offensive arms. Evidently Kissinger obtained consent of both Soviet and Chinese Communist leaders to the main lines of a Vietnam settlement. In order to hasten agreement the U.S. bombed Hanoi and mined Haiphong. In October 1972 what appeared to be agreement was temporarily disrupted by South Vietnam's refusal to accept the terms worked out by Kissinger and Hanoi's Le Duc Tho; once again North Vietnam hesitated, and the U.S. responded by the Christmas bombing of the north. On January 27, 1973, a cease-fire agreement was signed in Paris. The U.S. proceeded to withdraw all its armed forces from Vietnam, though sporadic fighting continued. In April 1972 more than 70 nations including the U.S. and the USSR signed a treaty outlawing biological weapons and requiring destruction of stocks of such weapons. In October 1972 U.S.-Soviet agreements were reached on trade, Lend-Lease, and credits; during 1973 Soviet trade with the "capitalist" world increased by more than 40%. Other summit meetings were held in Washington in June 1973 and Moscow in June 1974. *Détente* came to be widely recognized as at least an official description of the goals of both American and Soviet leaders,and perhaps as something more.

The Yom Kippur war of October 1973, which started with surprise Arab attacks on the Jewish holiday, ended in setbacks to Soviet influence. After a few days in which the Arabs made headway against Israeli forces, Israel rallied and dealt counterblows the full force of which were blunted by a cease-fire imposed by the two superpowers. In ensuing diplomatic moves Secretary of State Kissinger helped to arrange disengagement agreements between Israel and both Egypt and Syria, and what appeared to the Arabs as a more "even-handed" U.S. policy achieved a success whose counterpart was Egyptian coolness toward Moscow. So-viet-U.S. relations survived the Yom Kippur war without significant damage.

As the second phase of the SALT talks went forward, the new U.S. president, Gerald Ford, and Brezhnev met in Vladivostok in November 1974 and reached agreement on a basis for negotiating a limitation on strategic offensive weapons systems. In January 1975 the U.S. Congress passed and the president signed a trade act which included the so-called Jackson-Vanik Amendment (trade status in re-turn for less restriction of Soviet Jews), as well as the Stevenson Amendment, which placed restrictions on the credits on which expanded Soviet-American trade depended. The USSR promptly informed Washington that it would not rat-ify the 1972 trade agreement. Apparently what might have been acceptable to the Soviets by way of oral understanding was unacceptable when written into U.S. law by Congress, and for the moment U.S.-Soviet commercial relations were at an im-passe.

In the spring of 1975 the Paris agreement on Vietnam became a dead letter as the anti-Communist governments of Cambodia and South Vietnam collapsed. Long-surrounded Phnom Penh was captured by the Khmer Rouge. South Viet-namese withdrawals quickly turned into a rout. With unexpected speed the Viet Cong swept down the coast, and on April 30, 1975, Saigon surrendered. Moscow may have regarded the Communist triumphs as a mixed blessing, for Beijing's in-fluence on the Cambodian Communists was great and on the Communists of North and South Vietnam substantial though not dominant.

Domestic Developments

The complexities of the new triangular relationship between Washington, Mos-cow, and Beijing affected the Soviet domestic situation. On the eve of the XXIV Congress (March 30–April 9, 1971) of the Soviet Communist Party in Moscow, Beijing celebrated the centennial of the Paris Commune by a bitter attack on the "bourgeois renegade" regime of Brezhnev for abandoning Marxism-Leninism-Stalinism and for oppressing smaller people in Europe and Asia. Astounding the world by their invitation to the U.S. ping-pong team to visit the mainland, the

Chinese leaders entertained Americans in Beijing while the Soviet party Congress was taking place Moscow with no Chinese present.

In the main report to the XXIV Congress Brezhnev, after surveying foreign affairs with some satisfaction, turned to the domestic scene. The Ninth Five-Year Plan, for 1971–1975, was given the "main task" of ensuring "a substantial upswing in the people's material and cultural living standard. ..." Verbally, the consumer was placed first. Agriculture, the weak link in the Soviet economy, was promised a total of investment for the next five years exceeding that of the previous ten. Not a single full member of the Politburo was dropped from the roster, and four new ones were added: V. V. Grishin, leader of the Moscow city party; F. D. Kulakov, known as a specialist on agriculture; D. A. Kunaev, the first representative of the Central Asians on the Politburo in a decade; and V. V. Shcherbitsky, premier of Ukraine. No full member of the Politburo was under fifty. It was both a dull and aging party that was mirrored in the XXIV Congress.

At the XXIV Congress Brezhnev was spotlighted and praised, but not idolized. Although the four newly added Politburo members were reputed to be his protégés, there may also have been a few of his critics left in the highest levels of leadership, and he seemed to make headway in getting rid of them. In May 1972, on the eve of the Nixon-Brezhnev summit, occurred the first sign of his success: P. E. Shelest, who may have lacked enthusiasm for *détente* and undoubtedly was gentler with Ukrainian nationalism than Brezhnev wished, was dismissed as leader of the Ukrainian party and replaced by Shcherbitsky. However, it was not until the Central Committee plenum of April 1973 that Shelest and also G. I. Voronov were removed as full members of the Politburo. At that time three more were added: Yuri V. Andropov, chief of the KGB, Foreign Minister Gromyko, and Defense Minister Grechko. It seemed likely that the person Brezhnev's colleagues wished most to promote was Andropov, but since no active secret policeman had been on the Politburo since Beria in 1953, it was thought best to minimize possible domestic or foreign concern by placing alongside him two other state officials—a diplomat much less influential than Molotov in 1947, and a professional soldier less popular than Zhukov in 1957. In April 1975 A. N. Shelepin was relieved of his positions, first of Politburo membership and next of his leadership of Soviet trade unions. He was thought to have been the chief critic of Brezhnev remaining on the Politburo.

The XXV Party Congress

A decade of the Brezhnev regime suggested that, in some respects, it had continued Khrushchëv's objectives—for example, the stress on performance rather than rhetoric, the effort to raise the standard of living, the relegation to the background of party doctrine in the natural sciences (and to a lesser extent the social sciences), and the avoidance of mass terror. Though continuing to encourage material incentives, Brezhnev's government shifted its emphasis from collective to individual rewards, and relieved the pressure Khrushchëv had placed on the private sector in agriculture. So far Brezhnev seemed the more "liberal" of the two. However, there were even more powerful countercurrents; Khrushchëv's calls for debureaucratization, mass participation, and "trust in society" as a whole were followed under Brezhnev by more frequent summonses to "discipline" and greater stability of cadres. A computation in 1979 indicated that of those who had held the key post of *obkom* first secretary in the various local party organizations and had left it, about half had been demoted under Khrushchëv, whereas since 1964 that proportion had fallen significantly in the major republics (except Ukraine).[4] The party elite was aging and less willing to innovate or take risks.

The Ninth Five-Year Plan, 1971–1975, fell far short of its targets. Probably it counted on massive infusions of Western technology. Rapid growth in commercial importation of such items began in 1970, but although total Soviet-U.S. trade more than doubled from 1972 to 1973, it failed to reach the level needed (and after 1975 it was to sag markedly). There were also two substantial crop failures—1972 and 1975 (the worst in over a decade)—and the USSR had to buy over 5 million tons of grain from the United States in those years. The increasing importance of the so-called second economy, as Western students of the Soviet scene came to call it, attracted attention during the 1970's. Late in the decade the legal private sector accounted for about 10% of the gross national product, and the illegal private sector was certainly an additional noteworthy phenomenon—though its size could only be guessed.[5] In 1972 there was a serious effort to limit illegal private economic activity in Georgia, which geography and climate helped to make the easiest haven for profiteers. However, stealing from the state, bribery, *prinoshenie* (giving gifts to authorities without the expectation of specific favors), and other aspects of the "second economy" were often deeply intertwined with successes in industrial production—and it was risky to attack them too sharply. The "economic reform" of 1965 had been sufficiently pared down in its application—largely by its opponents—to disappoint the hopes of its supporters. Gross value of output, as the former single indicator, had been supposed to be supplemented by sales and profits. Planning was to have been partially decentralized and the industrial supply system reformed. The existing system resisted the changes, however.

The XXV Congress of the party, held February 24 to March 5 in 1976, attempted to wrestle with these and other problems. The membership of the Politburo had

---

[4] Table 6, p. 36, in Robert E. Blackwell, Jr., "Cadres Policy in the Brezhnev Era," *Problems of Communism,* March–April 1979.

[5] Gregory Grossman, "The 'Second Economy' of the USSR," *Problems of Communism*, September–October 1977.

for some time been quite stable. Changes made at the Congress were few: Poliansky was dismissed from full membership and a few days later from the ministry of agriculture as well; he was sent to Tokyo as ambassador. Gregory V. Romanov, first secretary of the Leningrad *obkom* (and at 53 becoming the youngest full member) and Dmitry Ustinov were both promoted to full membership. Marshal Grechko died a few weeks after the Congress. (In May 1977 Podgorny was dismissed from the Politburo and then in June from the chairmanship of the Presidium or titular headship of the state—a post often called "President" in the Western press. He was succeeded in that capacity by Brezhnev.)

The Tenth Five-Year Plan, 1976–1980, was announced without any such promise as was made (and not kept) for the Ninth; namely, that the output of consumer goods would rise faster than that of producer goods. Agriculture remained a substantial employer; about 25% of the Soviet labor force was still employed on the land (as against 4% in the U.S.). Private plots, aggregating 3% of the tilled area, continued to produce more than one quarter of the gross output of Soviet agriculture, including 64% of its potatoes and 33% of its vegetables.

In 1977, after prolonged discussion and many proposals of amendments, a new Soviet Constitution replaced the one of 1936. Adopted by the Supreme Soviet on October 7, the new constitution was described as one of a "developed socialist society," as distinguished from the Stalin Constitution's claim to have reflected the building of "socialism" (without a modifier). It was said to "make it possible to set about building communism"—without reference to Khrushchëv's promise of 1961 that the "transition to communism" would be complete by 1980. The day of adoption, "Constitution Day," was made a new national holiday. Few provisions were new. One that was noteworthy, however, legalized the "individual labor activity" of laborers and their families in all economic areas, thus recognizing and attempting to deal with some of the problems of the "second economy" mentioned above.

Changes in the Politburo included F. D. Kulakov, who died in July of 1978 and was not replaced. In November Konstantin U. Chernenko was made a full member, replacing K. T. Mazurov, who departed without explanation. The number of full members reached fifteen when Nikolai A. Tikhonov (December 1979) and M. S. Gorbachev (October 1980) were given such status. In late October of 1980 Kosygin resigned, apparently for reasons genuinely relating to his health. He was succeeded as prime minister by Tikhonov, whose career had been linked with the organization of heavy industry and who had been an associate of Brezhnev since the 1930's in Ukraine.

Growing Soviet Influence in Asia and Africa

At the time of the XXV Congress the international picture was on the whole brightening for the USSR—despite various setbacks. In Europe there were disappointed hopes, especially in Portugal. After the coup of April 1974, which opened up Portuguese politics following a long period of dictatorship, the Communist party under Alvaro Cunhal had made significant gains. The suppression of the leftist coup in November 1975, however, had reduced any immediate prospect of a gain in influence for the party. An effort to mobilize European Communist parties had been made at a conference in Karlovy Vary in April 1967 and was boycotted by the Albanians, Yugoslavs, Romanians, Dutch, Icelanders, and Norwegians—but with those present acknowledging Soviet leadership. A second conference was held in East Berlin in June 1976, a year behind schedule, after obvious difficulties in preparation. The spotlight was occupied by the three leaders of what had become recognized as "Eurocommunism": Enrico Berlinguer of Italy, Santiago Carrillo of Spain, and George Marchais of France. Carrillo called for the withdrawal of troops by socialist states from foreign countries; Berlinguer depicted a socialist society of the future with multiple parties, alternating governmental majorities, and freedom in all areas. Such remarks certainly threatened Soviet domination of European Communism; on the other hand, they may have led many voters—not only in the three countries concerned—to give Communists a new benefit of the doubt, in turn yielding advantages to Moscow. Somewhat comparably, the agreement of the Helsinki Conference on Security and Cooperation in Europe, signed in August 1975, provided clear benefits to the USSR. It confirmed East European borders and made less likely any future revival of the Eisenhower administration's talk of "liberation," but it assured continued embarrassment, as calls for real enforcement of the rights affirmed at Helsinki were promptly issued in both Communist and non-Communist countries by a variety of "Helsinki Watch" groups.

In Asia the main Soviet antagonist remained China. Negotiations between the two governments continued off and on during most of the 1970's, without any apparent result whatever. Mao Zedong died in September 1976, after visible signs that the end was near, and was replaced by Hua Guofeng. The death of Zhou Enlai in January 1976 had clearly evoked more genuine popular grief than Mao's. It was the line of muting ideological fanaticism and stressing technological and economic improvement (associated with Zhou), which was to grow in strength after Mao's death—rather than the leftism associated with the "Gang of Four," which had been headed by Jiang Qing (Mao's widow, but not identified in the Chinese press as such), and plainly supported—if not led—by her husband. ("Mao makes five," as one foreign quip had it.)

In March 1978, the PRC adopted a new constitution (the first since 1954), declaring China a "socialist state," almost as if in response to the new Soviet constitution but advancing no claims—as had been done in 1958—of being ahead of the USSR. China's only ally, Albania, now broke with Beijing. In December 1978 President Carter realized the expectations raised by Nixon's Shanghai communiqué six years earlier and recognized the PRC, breaking relations with the Republic of China on Taiwan abruptly and abrogating the mutual defense treaty between

Washington and Taipei—nominally with a year's notice. This was followed by a spectacular visit of Vice-Premier Deng Xiaoping to the United States—which helped to diminish hopes on both sides for U.S.-Soviet détente and for U.S. technological transfer to the USSR.

Fighting between the two Communist states of Cambodia (Kampuchea) and Vietnam had escalated gradually, and in January 1978 President Carter's national security adviser, Zbigniew Brzezinski, termed it a "proxy war" between Moscow and Beijing. In November 1978 the USSR and the newly unified Socialist Republic of Vietnam signed a treaty of friendship and cooperation, indicating that Moscow had emerged the clear victor in the long tug-of-war with Beijing for influence in Hanoi. In January 1979 Phnom Penh fell to Vietnamese troops and a new government was established, dependent on Hanoi and supported by Moscow. In February-March 1979, ostensibly to teach Vietnam a "lesson" for the mass expulsion and other harsh treatment of its own citizens of Chinese origin, the Chinese army launched a brief invasion, which fell short of demonstrating Beijing's superior military prowess. Thousands of refugees from Communist Vietnam, Cambodia, and Laos fled into adjoining Communist and non-Communist countries or took to the sea—where many drowned. The USSR emerged as the chief ally and mentor of all three Indochinese governments. It seemed indeed as if U.S. casualties in the Vietnam War—45,000 combat deaths and over 300,000 wounded from 1965 to 1973—had been entirely in vain, while for the USSR, substantial weapon shipments and some advisers, with negligible casualties, had yielded an influence possessed by none other in the peninsula.

A much-ridiculed assertion by U.S. governmental circles during the Vietnam War had been that the fall of South Vietnam would be followed by Communist takeover of several other states—in effect, toppling like a row of dominoes ("the domino theory"). The three Indochinese states did become fully Communist, and several other countries in Asia and Africa came close to being so. The USSR successfully used the device of the twenty-year treaty of friendship and cooperation in a number of cases. Such treaties were made with India, Egypt, Iraq, and Somalia from 1971 to 1974, and then from 1976 to 1979 with six additional states. Two of the ten, Egypt and Somalia, tore up the treaties, but Somalia remained Marxist-Leninist all the same. One, Vietnam, was clearly Communist; five, Afghanistan, Angola, Mozambique, Ethiopia, and South Yemen, were Marxist-Leninist and closely linked to Moscow; and two, Iraq and India, retained their own independent policy. The five came to constitute, along with the Congo and a few other small African states, a new category of Soviet foreign influence that had no exact historical precedents in earlier Soviet history.

In the meantime the Muslim world seethed with economic problems, religious reaction, and dissension on how to handle Israel. In March 1976 Sadat's Egypt abrogated its five-year-old Soviet friendship treaty and expelled Soviet advisers. The Sudan did the same in May 1977. Sadat felt it possible to visit Jerusalem in November 1977, in a startling initiative that led to the Camp David settlement in September of the following year by Sadat, Prime Minister Menachem Begin of Israel, and President Carter. The USSR opposed the Israeli-Egyptian agreement but could do little about it. However, Moscow continued its efforts to penetrate Arab countries and had greatest success in South Yemen, with which a friendship treaty was concluded in October 1979.

The Soviets carried out an amazing maneuver in the Horn of Africa, starting with the treaty with Somalia (1974) that granted the use of port facilities. Somalia was engaged in conflict with Ethiopia, whose southern territories were inhabited by Somalis. After the U.S. suspended aid to Ethiopia the ruler, Lieutenant Colonel Mengisthu Haile Mariam, promptly visited Moscow, securing a sharp increase in Soviet aid and the entrance of Cuban troops into the conflict. In November 1977 Somalia abrogated the 1974 treaty with the USSR and broke relations with Cuba; a Soviet-Ethiopian treaty of friendship and cooperation in November 1978 cemented the shift. In May 1977 the London *Economist* reported that Cuban troops, often along with Soviet and East German advisers, were to be found in nine African nations: Angola (where a Marxist party won a civil war), Congo, Mozambique, Tanzania, Somalia, Ethiopia, Guinea, Guinea-Bissau, and Equatorial Guinea. The USSR had found a powerful surrogate in the Cubans, partly descended from Africans and somehow not subject to charges of "imperialist intervention." No Russians had ever enjoyed such influence in Africa.

More important events, however, were occurring in Afghanistan and Iran. The government of the Afghan republic was overthrown in April 1978 by Nur Mohammed Taraki, with Soviet support, who established a quasi-Communist regime. Taraki was liquidated by his prime minister, Hafizullah Amin, who in turn was overthrown by Soviet intervention in December 1979 and replaced by Babrak Karmal. President Carter responded by declaring the Soviet invasion the greatest danger to peace since World War II, announced a grain embargo and a boycott of the Moscow Olympics, and threatened war if the Soviets moved into the Persian Gulf. The Soviets circumvented the grain embargo, but it cost them perhaps $1 billion to do so. The overthrow of the Shah of Iran by a Muslim fundamentalist republic headed by the Ayatollah Ruhollah Khomeini and seizure of 53 American hostages humiliated the United States and helped lead to Carter's defeat at the polls in 1980, but the USSR managed to avoid any immediate damage to its relations with Muslims in and out of its territory.

Dissent and Détente Become Entangled

Given the domestic turmoil and wave of isolationist feeling in the U.S. that accompanied the Watergate affair (frankly puzzling to the Communist regimes as well as worldly West Europeans) and the fiasco of U.S. policy in southeast Asia, *détente* receded to the background in the Ford administration. The inauguration of President Carter in January 1977 provided the opportunity for a fresh start in

U.S.-Soviet relations. Carter's twin efforts to carry forward arms control in the Strategic Arms Limitation Talks (SALT) and simultaneously to make strong statements on "human rights" soon proved impossible to pursue together. His public letter to Andrei Sakharov, the chief remaining Soviet dissenter, and other utterances were followed by an abrupt freeze in Moscow's attitude to Washington. By summer Carter publicly admitted his surprise at the sharpness of Soviet reaction. Exactly the contrary of what the Jackson-Vanik Amendment hoped to achieve, the number of Soviet Jews permitted to emigrate fell sharply after it was passed, in 1979 rose somewhat, then fell almost to zero in Brezhnev's last years.[6]

The formation of Helsinki Watch groups in several Soviet cities may have strengthened both domestic dissent and the demand to emigrate. Several prominent dissenters were allowed or in some cases, such as Alexander Ginzburg and Alexander Solzhenitsyn, deported against their will. A number prominent in Helsinki Watch groups were arrested: from 1976 to 1980 Ginzburg, Yuri Orlov, Anatolii Shcharansky; later, Orthodox activists including Fr. Gleb Yakunin, Lev Regelson, Fr. Dmitri Dudko. In 1979 a Western visitor enumerated the losses to Andrei Sakharov; he quietly replied, "Others come forward to take their place." Hitherto having enjoyed some protection by award of the Nobel Peace Prize in 1975 and Carter's letter, Sakharov himself was exiled to Gorky in January 1980 and stripped of his honors after he publicly condemned the Soviet invasion of Afghanistan.

The number of active dissenters remained small—but there were not many Decembrists in 1824 or Bolsheviks in 1903 either. In the early 1980's, as before, dissent had overlapping religious, ethnic, and artistic-literary components. Yuri Trifonov (d. 1981), author of such works as *The House on the Embankment,* insisted on the reexamination of the Stalin period; Chingiz Aitmatov, the Kirgiz writer, as well as the "village writers" (*derevenshchiki*) Vasilii Shukshin (d. 1974) and Valentin Rasputin, won many admirers. Some artists and writers, without wishing to become dissenters, ran afoul of cultural controls. An unofficial exhibition of modernist painting in Moscow was destroyed by bulldozers in 1974, but the worldwide outcry led authorities to permit another soon afterward. In January 1979, twenty-three Soviet writers, having been refused permission to publish previously censored but nonpolitical writings, issued a compendium called *Metropol'.* One of them, Vasily Aksionov, declared, *"Metropol'* was the bulldozer exhibition of Soviet literature." In December 1979 and January 1980 he and several others resigned from the Union in protest, and in July 1980 Aksionov left the USSR. Others who

---

[6] For example, 1974, 20,628; 1975, 13,221; 1979, 51,320; 1982, 2,688. It rose and became a flood (1990, 186,815; 1991, 179,720), still continuing in 1994, that threatened to extinguish Jewish identity in the former USSR. By September 1993, 845,125 had left (from 1968 on). Figures include only those going to Israel or the United States, but these were by far the most popular destinations. *Source:* National Conference on Soviet Jewry, New York.

did likewise included the writers Vladimir Voinovich (one of the funniest of Russian writers of any period) and Lev Kopelev in 1980, and the musician Maxim Shostakovich, son of the great composer Dmitry, in 1981. The Ukrainian dissident Vladimir Chornovil, just completing nine years of imprisonment and exile, was sentenced to five more years in a labor camp; the device of rewarding the serving of a lengthy sentence by an immediate additional sentence came to be a favorite technique in dealing with dissidents. In preparing for the 1980 Olympics, the KGB had arrested over 250 who were thought to be potential sources of embarrassment but apparently preferred to intimidate and silence many others without arresting them. Close to half of those arrested were Christians of various denominations.

The End of the Brezhnev Era

Brezhnev's boast of "stability of cadres" and his own advancing age and declining health seemed to advertise an arteriosclerotic regime in which old men (very few women had reached anywhere near the ruling level) resisted change of all sorts.[7] At the XXVI Party Congress in February-March 1981 no changes at all took place in the Politburo or Secretariat. Brezhnev announced that a new party program was being prepared and promised that nonindigenous nationalities in all fifteen republics (rather than only the RSFSR, as before) would be permitted their own schools, press, and cultural life—a move seen as designed to help persuade Muslims to move to the Slavic areas where their labor was needed and Slavic labor was in short supply. It was a congress at which Brezhnev was praised more resoundingly than he had been five years before. He was strongly critical of industrial performance and deprecated low labor productivity but was unable to suggest any significant remedies. Food, said Brezhnev, was the central problem of the Five-Year Plan just ahead.

In 1981 the Soviets suffered the third failure of the harvest in a row; 1982 would be a fourth failure—about 185 million metric tons of grain as against a planned 239 million. In 1978, Soviet agricultural performance had reached a high point, with a 230-million-ton harvest. Brezhnev had pushed the raising of state subsidies to agriculture, without raising the prices of staples (prices of bread, meat, and other staples had remained frozen for twenty years); in 1982 the agricultural subsidies exceeded 27 billion rubles, and still the Soviets could not feed themselves. In May 1982 the government announced a large-scale program to increase farm output not merely by direct investment but also by making the countryside more attractive and thus deterring able youths from leaving.

---

[7] And not only among the rulers. A perceptive and witty colleague, who had never visited the USSR before, appeared on a morning early in his visit in 1991 to announce that he had figured out what was wrong with the country: "everybody has tenure." The observation was illuminating about the Soviets, even if it unfairly implied academic sloth in the U.S.

In the area of foreign relations, earlier Communist gains had been followed by an increasing accumulation of problems. The invasion of Afghanistan in December 1979 had been followed by regular General Assembly votes of overwhelming and virtually unchanging majorities to demand withdrawal of Soviet troops; in November 1981 the count was 116 yes, 23 no, 12 abstaining. Talks with China, begun in October 1979, foundered over the invasion, and the first official reports since 1969 came in of shooting on the Sino-Soviet border.

The Iranian revolution, from which Moscow had hoped ultimately to profit, yielded no benefits, partly because of the proximity of Afghanistan. Even the Italian and Spanish Communist parties criticized the Soviet attack. Foreign reaction was so hostile that it was not until almost two years had passed, in November 1981, that Brezhnev ventured his first foreign visit since the invasion, to West Germany.

In October 1982 Deputy Foreign Minister Leonid Ilichev traveled to Beijing to attempt to resuscitate communication. However, the Chinese demanded some Soviet concessions on the so-called "three obstacles": the presence of Soviet troops in Afghanistan, Soviet assistance to Vietnam in its occupation of Cambodia, and the size of Soviet forces in Mongolia and elsewhere near the frontier with the People's Republic of China. Moscow was unwilling to make any.

The assassination of Anwar el-Sadat in October pleased—indeed was doubtless planned and carried out by—the USSR's radical clients among the Arabs, whichever specific groups were responsible; but it came on the heels of expulsion of Soviet diplomats from Egypt. In May 1981 another treaty of friendship and cooperation was added to the list, but it was only with the minor African state of the Congo.

Arms control had by the 1970's come to embody a professed goal of the two superpowers rather than the clearly more remote and less attainable disarmament—disarmament of any sort, let alone "general and complete," which were frequent Soviet qualifiers. Carter and Brezhnev had signed the SALT II agreement in Vienna in June 1979, but the Afghan invasion had induced Carter to refrain from trying to obtain Senate ratification. In December 1979 NATO decided to deploy cruise and Pershing II missiles as a way of rectifying a balance upset, in their view, by Soviet deployment of SS-20's. Ronald Reagan became president in January 1981. During the campaign he had criticized Carter's foreign policy, used harsh words about the USSR and Communism, and denounced SALT II. Nevertheless, as president he continued to adhere to its provisions, and in June 1982 he agreed with the Soviets to resume arms control talks under a new rubric, Strategic Arms Reduction Talks (START), after a three-year lapse.

What then seemed one of many problems—Poland—was to become the curtain-raiser on the drama of the fall of Communism itself. Gomułka, earlier symbol of national resistance, used violent reprisals against workers protesting price rises in December 1970 and was forced out. He was succeeded by Edward Gierek, who vowed close links with the workers. There were more strikes, and a Workers' Defense Committee, with a strong component of intellectuals, was formed; it supported the workers' strike of summer 1980 in Gdansk, and by fall there spontaneously appeared Solidarity (Solidarnošč), the first trade union to appear in a Communist country in decades. Now Gierek fell; General Wojciech Jaruzelski, prime minister since February, became first secretary of the Polish United Workers' Party in October 1981 and proclaimed martial law in December. Despite foreign denunciations, it transpired before long that this measure was taken to avoid Soviet intervention, and Jaruzelski, far from being a puppet of Moscow, was soon to prove a pivot of change throughout Eastern Europe.

The end of the Brezhnev regime came in a flurry of intrigue reminiscent of earlier times. When Brezhnev was felled by a stroke in 1975, Mikhail Suslov and Andrei Kirilenko apparently served as joint replacements. The next year, however, Kirilenko faded from the scene, though he remained on the Politburo until after Brezhnev died, and Konstantin Chernenko took his place as Brezhnev's close associate. Suslov's departure was attended by mystery and scandal. In January 1982 Yuri Andropov, then chief of the KGB, reported to Suslov that General Semen Tsvigun was implicated in an investigation of corruption that was taking place against a background of mounting press attention to the problem throughout the Soviet system. Tsvigun, reputedly a close associate of Brezhnev, then had a confrontation with Suslov. Within a few days of that scene, Tsvigun committed suicide and Suslov died of a stroke.

Suslov, thought to have turned down the position of leader of the party in 1964, before and after that the *éminence grise* of Brezhnev, seems to have been the last barrier to the challenge being mounted by Andropov. The KGB chief saw to it that foreign correspondents were informed that Brezhnev's own daughter, along with a shadowy character from the Moscow circus known as Boris the Gypsy, had been involved in a diamond-smuggling enterprise. Brezhnev experienced a second stroke in March 1982. By May he was back but could not stop Andropov from being chosen as Suslov's successor (in his capacity as chief ideologist). Andropov also joined the Secretariat and gave up his KGB position. Brezhnev's growing feebleness was evident even in what the Soviet television audience was shown. To counter efforts to publicize his weakness, he appeared on the rostrum in bitter cold for the November 7 anniversary of the Revolution. Three days later he was dead.

Brezhnev's departure from power, and from life, came after several years of a plainly faltering grip on the reins. During the eighteen years in which he was the foremost Soviet leader, however, the USSR had made substantial progress. The nation was a clearly recognized superpower; under Brezhnev, equality in nuclear arms with the United States had not only been achieved but had been accepted by the U.S. government and much of the American public, as well as by other countries. The Soviet navy had grown from a minor force to one of worldwide importance. Industrial output had continued to increase, though since 1978 economic growth had remained at an annual level of less than 2%.

Nevertheless, rising expectations were a problem for the regime, though Brezhnev had done his best to improve the supply of food and other consumer goods. Marxism-Leninism had invaded several widely scattered countries in Asia and Africa and seemed poised to spread in Latin America. The Soviet people seemed increasingly indifferent to these gains of "fraternal" forces in the world, and Soviet youth showed a disturbing decrease in enthusiasm for Communist ideology at home. Thus the death of Brezhnev was received without great emotion, either grief at his loss or hope for his successor.

27

The Venture of Gorbachëv

Andropov, the Abortive Reformer

Yuri Andropov was born the son of a railway worker in Nagutskoe in the north Caucasus in 1914. He was chosen as general secretary in a meeting of the enlarged Politburo on November 10, 1982. In that meeting he was nominated by Defense Minister Marshal Dmitrii Ustinov; the support of the military establishment helped to offset the known wish of Brezhnev for Chernenko to succeed him.[1] The full Central Committee ratified the choice two days later. Andropov gave signs of having not merely engineered the eclipse of Brezhnev by himself, but also of having the energy to introduce substantial reforms in an apparently immobilized economy. In fact, at 68, Andropov was the oldest man to lead the Party thus far, and he was far from healthy; he suffered from kidney disease and diabetes.

Nevertheless he acted rapidly and dramatically to attack inefficiency, absenteeism, and corruption (the issue on which he had done much to bring down Brezhnev). The ordinary police (*militsiia*) were put to work checking whether people visiting stores, theaters, and bathhouses were supposed to be at work in offices or factories. A few weeks earlier, Geidar Aliev, who had reduced and punished corruption in Azerbaijan, had been named full member of the Politburo and first deputy premier. More clearly identified as Andropov appointees were Viktor Chebrikov, who became head of the KGB in December 1982 and candidate member of the Politburo a year later; Mikhail Solomentsev, premier of the RSFSR and Vitalii Vorotnikov, first secretary of the Krasnodar party, both of whom became full members of the Politburo in December 1983; and Egor Ligachëv, whose background was in the KGB, like Andropov's, and who was named to the Secretariat in December. Also in May, Andropov himself was confirmed as chairman of the State Defense Council, a rather mysterious body whose very existence was revealed only in the mid-1970's when Brezhnev was announced as its chairman. In

---

[1] Zhores A. Medvedev, *Andropov,* Penguin, 1984, p. 21.

June Andropov became chairman of the presidium of the Supreme Soviet, or "president" of the USSR. This designation gave him the "triple crown" that Brezhnev had gained only after thirteen years in power.

Andropov's efforts to improve economic performance by simply improving labor discipline yielded discernible but modest results. In August 1983 a remarkable memorandum was leaked to the press from Novosibirsk. Composed by Academician Tatiana Zaslavskaia, the memorandum declared that although the organization of industry had once been an appropriate reflection of conditions, this had ceased to be the case. She called for greater decentralization of management and more attention to economic considerations. Whatever Andropov's wishes were in regard to the reforms Zaslavskaia suggested, the magazine *Kommunist,* organ of the Central Committee, promptly countered with an article reaffirming the primacy of political factors and invoking Leninist scriptures against those who would challenge it. What happened, in fact, was that a bit of decentralization of decision making was tried in a few plants, and that was all.

It seemed that Andropov lacked enthusiasm for the Brezhnev agricultural reforms, which had been announced with much fanfare a few months before Brezhnev's death. Under Andropov, they were not pursued very energetically. In August a new Soviet-U.S. pact for the purchase of grain was concluded, whereby the USSR was to import at least 9 million metric tons annually for five years. There were food shortages, but they were partly the result of problems in transporting food to the right places and especially of a dearth of refrigerator cars. Reports of badly planned transport multiplied. In 1970, it was said, the average trip of a reinforced concrete block from the factory to the place of use was 500 kilometers; in 1981 it was 842 kilometers. The former was bad enough; the latter was intolerable.

Under Andropov there was little perceptible change in cultural or religious policy. Georgii Vladimov, who had the reputation of being the last significant dissident writer left in the USSR, was allowed to leave the country in May 1983; the Siberian Seven, the Pentecostals who had spent several years in the basement of the U.S. Embassy in Moscow, were given exist visas in July. Jewish emigration was reduced to a trickle, and "refuseniks," people who had sought to leave and had been denied permission to do so, were harshly treated, deprived of their professional employment and other jobs, harassed, and forced to watch their families suffer. The use of psychiatric methods to make well minds sick instead of vice versa received enough publicity abroad so that in February 1983 the All-Union Scientific Medical Society of Neuropathologists and Psychiatrists withdrew from the World Psychiatric Association to avoid expulsion.

In June, the first properly ordained rabbi to function in Latvia for a generation was permitted to begin his service there. Roman Catholic Bishop Vincentas Sladkevicius was allowed to return from an exile of twenty-five years to resume his see in Lithuania, and a new bishop was consecrated to occupy a see vacant since 1975. In February, the pope raised Bishop Julijans Vaivods to become the first cardinal in Soviet history, but the predominantly Catholic Lithuanians were not overcome with pleasure at the naming of a Latvian cardinal, whereas the Protestant majority of Latvians also felt limited enthusiasm over the choice. However, four Lithuanian bishops were permitted in May to visit the Vatican; this decision may well have been an upshot of this complex episode. The assignment of the oldest monastery in the USSR—St. Daniel, near Moscow—as the new administrative center of the Russian Orthodox Church, replacing Zagorsk, was clearly a step looking ahead to the celebration of the millennium of the "baptism of Rus," the conversion of the Eastern Slavs to Christianity in 988.

The Soviet campaign in Afghanistan continued. A stream of coffins flowed back from that unhappy country to the USSR of young men who had died doing their "international duty," a phrase that did not fully assuage the grief of many relatives. The condemnation of the Soviet military presence in Afghanistan by the U.N. General Assembly continued—in 1980 there were 111 votes demanding Soviet withdrawal; in 1985 there were 122. Relations with the United States continued to be bad, despite grain sales. A new low was struck when, in September 1983, the Soviet air force shot down KAL Flight 007, killing 269 people, with a heat-seeking missile after the plane had strayed over Kamchatka, far off course. The act received universal condemnation. The unprecedented press conference held by then Chief of General Staff Nikolai Ogarkov did little to improve the situation, and a number of aspects of Soviet relations with Western countries went into temporary deep freeze.

NATO had decided in December 1979 to deploy both cruise and Pershing II missiles, in response to the Soviet deployment of SS-20's. In 1983 there was a frantic Soviet effort to prevent NATO from carrying out its decision, with the assistance of a wide range of antinuclear and pacifist groups in Europe and North America. When it became clear that the effort had failed, the Soviet delegates walked out of the INF (Intermediate Nuclear Force) talks in Geneva in November.

In the Middle East, in Iran the (pro-Soviet) Tudeh Party was banned in May 1983; its leader, Nureddin Kianuri, was arrested and, after who knows what treatment by Ayatollah Khomeini's police, confessed to having been a Soviet spy since 1945. Relations with several Arab countries improved, however, and those with China seemed marginally warmer, or at least less frigid.

The doctor in charge revealed later that from February 1983 Andropov's kidneys had ceased to function, and that only dialysis by machine had kept him alive for the last year of his life. During that time it appears that he worked through Mikhail Gorbachëv and Egor Ligachëv and, despite his physical disability, managed to replace almost one-fifth of all *obkom*[2] party secretaries. It seems that Andropov did much to make the second secretary of the Central Committee the

---

[2] *Obkom* is an abbreviation for *oblastnyi komitet,* the party committee of the local administrative unit or "region."

second leader of the country, a sort of vice president in a land without a real presidency. The post was occupied by Chernenko. With the certain approach of Andropov's death, it would pass to Gorbachëv, who was obviously Andropov's ally in reform and his heir in policy matters. Chernenko was Brezhnev's close associate, the man of the Old Guard and the flag-bearer of "stability of cadres"—*quieta non movere,* let sleeping dogs lie. Many of the dogs seemed sleepy indeed, and many of them were very old. Andropov had done a good deal to disturb them. On February 9, 1984, Andropov died. His wife—such a person not even having been known to exist before the funeral—was observed making the sign of the cross over the coffin.

Chernenko, the Living Corpse

Chernenko was chosen general secretary on February 13, after a bit of horse-trading behind the scenes. Gorbachëv was the candidate of the Andropovite, reformist forces; Chernenko, of the Brezhnevite old guard. A deadlock in the Politburo would have sent the decision to the Central Committee, whose membership of 319 was dominated by the old guard. Gorbachëv yielded, becoming second secretary and receiving a commitment from the old guard to approve Andropov's reformist line.

Chernenko was born in 1911 to a peasant family in the village of Bolshaia Tes in the Krasnoiarsk region. He claimed to have left his mother (his father's whereabouts were not specified) at a young age; at twelve he went to work for a "wealthy master" and at fifteen joined the Komsomol. Only after meeting Brezhnev in Moldavia in 1948 did he acquire a patron who believed him worthy of promotion and who was finally willing to make him his *alter ego.* At his accession to the top leadership he was seventy-two—and thus broke Andropov's record as the oldest Soviet Party leader—and was plainly ill. He delivered gasping and stumbling speeches, probably suffered from emphysema, and was the target of much scorn and ridicule, even from highly placed Soviet officials. Chernenko did not try to reverse Andropov's reforms, though he may have lacked the energy and probably lacked the motivation to accelerate them or expand their scope.

Chernenko acquired the "triple crown"—president, chairman of the State Defense Council, and general secretary—before the end of April, an unprecedented achievement that had little to do with his power or skill in Kremlin high politics; it was as if no one feared him or sought to hold back honors from him, as his career was all too evidently to be short.

Some interesting changes in personnel occurred in the military leadership. The chief of the general staff, Marshal Ogarkov, was dismissed from that position in September 1984 and replaced by his deputy, Marshal Sergei Akhromeev. Apparently the KAL 007 affair, either the decision to shoot the plane down or the extraordinary press conference by which Ogarkov had sought to justify the action, had damaged his reputation. Perhaps also the interview with Ogarkov published in *Krasnaia Zvezda* in May, wherein he had argued for change in military tactics to give greater weight to high technology, flexibility, and mobility, had aroused opposition among other high brass or civilian concern that his proposals would require greatly increased military expenditures. The highest military official, Defense Minister Marshal Dmitrii Ustinov (not a fighting general; the only one ever to be on the Politburo was Georgii Zhukov, who lasted only a few months there), fell ill, failed to make the expected speech on November 7 commemorating the Revolution, and died in December. Marshal Sergei Sokolov, his first deputy minister, had given the speech in his stead and succeeded him at his death.

Chernenko was certainly not responsible for a series of social problems that received increased attention from the press during 1984, but his administration had to try to come to grips with them. In June 1983, the ministry of health admitted that the number of abortions in the country was *twice* the live births, or about 6 million per year. The divorce rate stood at about 50%, and every fourth adult lived alone. In 1983, the official figures for consumption of alcohol had reached an annual per capita level of 4.2 liters (1.1 gallons), but these figures covered only state-produced and state-sold alcohol, and the amount of homemade moonshine, or *samogon,* would have substantially added to the total. It was reported that, over the past decade, the time spent shopping—usually by women—had increased 25%. That time was considerable and produced frustration and fatigue on a very large scale. Possibly it was increased foreign attention to these problems that contributed to heightened penalties for contacts with foreigners. A law was passed making it a crime to transmit any information gained through one's profession or job to a foreigner; another prescribed a fine of 50 rubles for any instance in which a foreigner stayed overnight in a Soviet home without being reported to the police.

The industrial side of the economy continued to grow, even a trifle ahead of planned targets, but again the harvest was bitterly disappointing—Western specialists estimated 170 million metric tons. *Pravda* reported that the breadbasket, or black-earth, territory had in thirty or forty years lost one-third of its humus and 4–6 inches (10–15 centimeters) of fertile soil. Still another new expedient was proposed; the Central Committee decided to add 30 million acres of newly irrigated or drained land by the year 2000. The problem of transportation continued to bedevil the planners. One-third of all Soviet trucks were estimated to be out of service at any one time, and the trucks that were operating often did things that were unnecessary or wrong.

Foreign policy was an area of gloom. In September 1984 TASS declared that relations between the U.S. and the USSR had reached the lowest point in their entire history. In May, the Soviets had given tit for tat by announcing their withdrawal from the summer Olympic Games, held in Los Angeles, though not many other countries followed their lead. Nevertheless, in that same month Foreign Minister Gromyko visited Washington, D.C., in addition to making an appearance at the

U.N. in New York, and reported Soviet willingness to resume arms control talks. Moscow's previous demand that the cruise and Pershing II missiles not be deployed, or be withdrawn after deployment, before any reopening of talks could occur was simply forgotten. Following the reelection of Ronald Reagan as president in November 1984, agreement was reached that Gromyko and Secretary of State George Shultz would meet in January 1985 to prepare the ground for full-scale negotiations. If this was a modest beginning in improvement in relations with Washington, an even more modest opening to China took place when First Deputy Premier Ivan Arkhipov visited Beijing in December 1984.

The lot of dissidents did not improve. Jewish emigration fell considerably below 1,000 for the year, and for those who wished to leave but could not there was the unpleasant new spectacle of an Anti-Zionist Committee, founded in April 1983 to agitate against Israel and to propagandize the equating, with ample help from the controlled press, of Zionism with Fascism and fifth-column activity. In the autumn of 1984, two noteworthy re-defectors returned to the USSR. In September, a prominent journalist, Oleg Bitov, reappeared in Russia one year after defecting in London, with a story of kidnapping and pressure exerted on him by English authorities. In October, Svetlana Allilueva, Stalin's daughter, after spending seventeen years in the West, returned with her daughter to the Soviet Union, which restored Soviet citizenship to her and conferred it on her daughter, Olga. (She was to return once again to the United States in April 1986.)

But in the same year the USSR also lost two greater talents than those. Yuri Liubimov was for several years director of the avant-garde (by restricted Moscow standards) theater, the Taganka. In 1977 he was bold enough to produce Mikhail Bulgakov's *The Master and Margarita,* in which the author, who died in 1940, had counterpoised freedom and repression. In 1984 Liubimov went abroad to produce a play and was forced into remaining there. One of the best young film directors, Andrei Tarkovsky, in 1966 made one of the finest films in Soviet history, *Andrei Rublëv;* the subject was the fifteenth century rather than Rublëv himself, for almost nothing is known about the man who was perhaps the greatest of medieval Russian icon painters. The film had to be withdrawn and reworked, and subsequent films by Tarkovsky were the object of harassment. In the summer of 1984 he emigrated.

Chernenko attended Ustinov's funeral in December 1984 but looked far from robust. He was seen in public no more; two appearances on Soviet television may actually have been staged in a hospital. On March 10, 1985, he died.

Gorbachëv's Attempted Revolution from Above

At a March 11 meeting of the Politburo, it seems that Grigorii Romanov proposed Viktor Grishin as general secretary; no one seconded the motion. Gromyko then nominated Mikhail Gorbachëv, and the choice was made unanimous.

Gorbachëv was born March 2, 1931, at Privolnoe in the Stavropol region. His parents and grandparents were peasants, as were Chernenko's. He worked on a state farm for a time and as a promising Komsomolets was sent to Moscow State University, where he took a law degree. He became a member of the Party in 1952. After rising in the Stavropol city and regional Party organizations, he was elected to the Central Committee in 1971; in 1979 he became a candidate member of the Politburo and in 1980 a full member. He was identified with Andropov, to the extent that he became Andropov's virtually sole channel of communication with the outside world. When Gorbachëv became general secretary in 1985, he first strove to emphasize the continuity between the 1982–1984 period and his government. He became general secretary at fifty-four, which was young by comparison with his predecessors, though both Lenin and Stalin had come to power in their forties, and he was the youngest member of the Politburo when he was elevated to the post.

Soon after the Chernenko funeral, Gorbachëv began to project an image different from that of his predecessors; he had already been innovative by taking his wife with him on a trip to England in December 1984. (His innovativeness did not include bringing women into ruling circles, although Raisa Gorbachëva soon gained considerable influence in cultural matters.) Now he began to appear in public in the USSR, visiting factories and inspecting outlying regions. For the first year or so he reverted to the Andropovite devices of sending the militia to pull people out of queues and send them back to their jobs, trying to reduce vodka consumption, and generally trying to make the system work—as it was clearly not doing; Soviet economic growth came to a complete halt from 1978 to 1985 as the USSR sought to match the Western arms buildup.[3] The antivodka campaign was launched in May; production was cut, public drunkenness was to be fined, the hours and number of liquor stores reduced, the drinking age raised from 18 to 21. Everyone recognized the seriousness of the alcohol problem; many remembered how prohibition during World War I had immediately raised productivity by 7 to 10% (alcohol was restored only in 1927 to bolster state revenues). Nevertheless, what happened was reminiscent of the experience of U.S. prohibition. The economist Nikolai Shmelëv estimated in early 1988 that previously two-thirds of revenues from alcohol went to the state and one-third went to moonshiners, but that since May 1985 the figures were simply reversed; alcohol consumption had not decreased. Sugar (essential in making *samogon*) disappeared from the stores and had to be rationed, and the effects on the state budget were horrendous, as revenues fell by 45 billion rubles.

But in the last months of 1985 and early 1986 Gorbachëv shifted to a broader attack on the problems of the country. Two slogans were invoked: *glasnost'* (publicity) and *perestroika* (restructuring); soon to be added were two more:

---

[3] Anders Åslund, *Gorbachev's Struggle For Economic Reform*, Cornell U. Press, 1989, pp. 14–15.

demokratizatsiia (democratization) and *novoe myshlenie* (new thinking, a phrase used chiefly in regard to foreign affairs). In February 1986 the XXVII Party Congress was held, the first since Brezhnev's death. Gorbachëv's speech, which lasted almost six hours and called for "radical reform," evoked aspects of NEP and thus was linked to the hallowed name of Lenin. A high rate of investment was envisaged. Capital stock badly needed renovation, so that reequipment of existing plants was to rise from one-third to one-half of all state investment in the new Twelfth Five-Year Plan (1986–1990). But Gorbachëv hinted that more was needed. In a speech at Khabarovsk in July 1986 he declared, "None of us can continue living in the old way"; before the June 1987 CC plenum he asserted that the USSR was in a "pre-crisis situation."

What many around Gorbachëv called the "era of stagnation" (under Brezhnev) had seen the formation of three more or less distinct economies: the legal one, based on central planning and dictation; the "second economy" (as Western economists called it), extralegal and illegal, which simply circumvented the orders and requirements of the first; and the military economy, run by the government but with sufficient care and capital so that it achieved results, of a sort. Horrible examples of the first economy abounded: the Kurgan bus factory, where workers took trucks from the Gorky truck factory, smashed them with sledgehammers, then put buses on truck chassis—because the All-Union Standards Bureau (GOST) decreed that trucks must be made complete, and it was harder to change GOST than to swing sledgehammers. Or, out of 3 million tractors in the USSR (1989), 250,000 were out of commission at any given moment—because each repair shop was assigned a target for the year, but since repairs needed and requested amounted to only 56% of target, shops compelled *kolkhozy* to send tractors for repairs they did not need.[4]

Gorbachëv now attempted to shake up the first economy and diminish the extent of the second, starting with the Law on Individual Labor Activity (May 1987); it was calculated that previously 50% of all shoe repair, 45% of house repair, and 80% of consumer services in rural areas were performed extralegally by private persons. The goal was to reduce or end the black market for such small-scale part-time work, estimated at a level of 16 billion rubles per year. But to make them legal was to make them taxable, so that much extralegal moonlighting continued. The Law on State Enterprises (June 1987) was designed to make them self-financing so that they could bargain with suppliers and use surplus profit for wages and benefits; but the law was undermined by the primacy given "state orders" over production for market. A third and for a time spectacularly successful measure was the Law on Cooperatives (May 1988), which sought to make private ownership a reality by permitting several persons, or one family having three adult members, to operate a cooperative and hire other workers on contract. In early 1989, however,

---

[4] According to the Soviet economist Nikolai Shmelëv; *The Economist*, November 25, 1989, p. 101.

its scope was severely limited. Banned activities included the sale of jewelry containing precious metals, the manufacture of icons and religious objects, publication of scholarly or artistic material, and film or video production. Out of 4,500 private clinics, which had sprung up to bypass the horrendously backward medical care system, 30% were promptly driven out of business. There was not only legal retreat from the path Gorbachёv had taken, but a good deal of popular resistance to private profit from a population long indoctrinated to regard it as immoral. An illustrative story: Ivan finds a bottle containing a genie, who grants him a wish. Ivan complains that Vasya has a cow and makes a profit from selling its milk and butter. The genie asks if Ivan wants a cow like Vasya's; Ivan replies, "No, I want you to kill Vasya's cow."

The "second economy" was nevertheless achieving amazing results. People bringing produce from Georgia to Moscow by air could get rich in a relatively short time. A different phenomenon featured conscientious managers, who sought only to do what the state asked of them (but made it difficult for them to do it) yet had to bribe and use a variety of illegal methods to produce their quota. One former manager reported, "my director and I … figured out that we [had] earned at least 200 years in jail each, without ever doing anything for our personal gain."[5]

Gorbachёv's measures had only a modest effect on the economy. (Some said he ought to have started with [virtual] land ownership, as did Deng Xiaoping; but he shied away from that.) He did, however, manage to do better on the political front. He got rid of a few opponents or rivals on the Politburo, starting with Grigorii Romanov, head of the Leningrad party organization—a post that had been disastrous for several past leaders: Zinoviev, Kirov, Zhdanov. Rumors had been circulating of Romanov's misbehavior, including an especially colorful one that he had borrowed from the Hermitage, for the wedding party of his son, Catherine the Great's china, which the drunken guests then smashed. Next to go was Grishin; he was replaced as Moscow party leader by a newcomer from Sverdlovsk, Boris Yeltsin, who became a candidate member of the Politburo when Grishin was removed from that body. Gromyko was kicked upstairs to become president; Tikhonov retired. New Politburo members were, or seemed then, to be Gorbachёv's own men: Eduard Shevardnadze, who had combatted corruption in Georgia and also became foreign minister; Viktor Chebrikov, head of the KGB; Egor Ligachёv, who became "second secretary"; Nikolai Ryzhkov, a technocrat who replaced Tikhonov as premier in September 1985; and at the time of the XXVII Party Congress in February 1986, Lev Zaikov.

In April 1986 plans for rapid domestic change suffered from the worst nuclear accident in history, when an explosion occurred in the fourth reactor at the nuclear power station at Chernobyl, near Kiev. The explosion was followed by a fire,

---

[5] Presentation by L. Khotin at the Kennan Institute for Advanced Russian Studies, Washington, D.C., May 1988.

and much radioactivity was released. As many as 100,000 people were reportedly evacuated from the vicinity. In the first few weeks 299 were hospitalized and 26 died; debate continued regarding the number of deaths expected to result in the longer run. Soviet authorities were criticized for holding back the news and then releasing it only partially and grudgingly; they were criticized as well for the mismanagement alleged to have caused the accident, which affected several European countries.

Foreign Relations: Gains and Losses

If the KAL 007 tragedy had carried relations with the United States to a low point, another incident in March 1985 suggested no increased Soviet regard for human life: U.S. Major Arthur Nicolson was shot by a Soviet guard in East Germany and was then denied medical care while he bled to death—the first fatality in forty years of U.S. liaison with the Soviet army. Minor espionage charges were also exchanged. In November 1985, however, a summit meeting was held in Geneva between the new general secretary and President Reagan. The two leaders announced their agreement that a nuclear war must not be fought and could not be won, and that neither side would seek military superiority. It was decided that air service would be resumed between the two countries and that new consulates—a Soviet one in New York and a U.S. one in Kiev—would be opened. But the chief result was resumption of talks on arms control.

In August 1985, meanwhile, a Soviet trade delegation visited Beijing for the first time in twenty years. Less-than-summit-level political talks with PRC representatives continued, but by spring 1989 anticipations of a Gorbachëv-Deng meeting had begun to surface. Liberia broke relations in July 1985 (they were restored a year later), but minor diplomatic successes were scored through the establishment of relations with Oman in September 1985 and with the United Arab Emirates in November. A new target for Soviet foreign policy was the Pacific islands; in June 1986 relations were opened with Vanuatu, followed by a fisheries cooperation agreement. Finally, the late 1980's witnessed a steady flow of Third World leaders on official visits to Moscow and of high- and low-level Soviet delegations to their capitals. At the XXVII Congress the heads of state of Communist-ruled Afghanistan, Mongolia, Laos, Kampuchea, Vietnam, Ethiopia, Angola, and Cuba were present, along with senior officials of other client states: Benin, Burundi, Burkina Faso, Cape Verde, Congo, Ghana, Guinea, Guinea-Bissau, Guyana, Libya, Madagascar, Mali, Mozambique, North Korea, Nicaragua, São Tomé e Principe, Seychelles, South Yemen, Syria, and Zimbabwe. Some of these governments were Communist, some not, and not all were equally tied to Moscow; but the list was still impressive.

In 1986 and early 1987 the course of Soviet-U.S. relations was a bumpy one. The arrest of a Soviet spy was promptly countered by the seizure of American correspondent Nicholas Daniloff on a trumped-up charge in August 1986. Daniloff was released after thirteen days in jail, and in October a "pre-summit" meeting was held at Reykjavík in Iceland, where a dramatic agreement narrowly missed being concluded. A startling plan to reduce nuclear arsenals and, after a time, to destroy them was set aside when President Reagan refused General Secretary Gorbachëv's demand to postpone the Strategic Defense Initiative (colloquially known as "Star Wars"). In November it was revealed that U.S. arms had been sold to Iran and the proceeds allotted to the "contras" seeking to overthrow the Sandinista government of Nicaragua. The resultant public furor in Washington, D.C., took the spotlight for a time.

In December 1987 came Gorbachëv's most outstanding success in foreign relations thus far (and Reagan's, too, to be sure), when, at the Washington summit, the Intermediate Nuclear Forces (INF) agreement was signed, calling for destruction of 1,752 Soviet and 852 U.S. missiles and providing for strict verification procedures. (The agreement may also have had domestic causes and effects, inasmuch as it implied cuts in spending.) In May–June 1988 another summit, in Moscow, saw exchange of ratification documents for the INF treaty and work on a draft treaty reducing strategic weapons by 50%. The general secretary's visit to the United States on the eve of President George Bush's inauguration produced a three-way display of amity, including Reagan.

On July 25 Foreign Minister Shevardnadze declared that peaceful coexistence should not be regarded as a form of class struggle; "the struggle between the two opposing systems is no longer the defining tendency of the present era." The way was open for what Yeltsin would later call simply a "normal" foreign policy, including friendly relations with the U.S. and Western Europe. The Bush administration reciprocated—so much so that it would be slow to recognize the setting of Gorbachëv's star and the rise of Yeltsin's.

An Uphill Battle for Reform

In May 1987 a young West German named Mathias Rust landed a small plane in Red Square, thus making a laughingstock of Soviet air defenses. Gorbachëv immediately replaced several high-ranking officers, including Marshal Sergei Sokolov as minister of defense; his successor was Army General Dmitri Yazov.

But this episode was only a minor distraction from a conflict that was taking shape between the reformers and the hardliners in the leadership. After a series of reformist decisions from a plenum of June, in which Nikolai Sliunkov, Alexander Yakovlev, and Viktor Nikonov became full members of the Politburo, a period of uncertainty ensued. The general secretary took a vacation lasting fifty-two days. While he was away, hardliners pushed through a ban on demonstrations in Moscow, and Chebrikov attacked the "demagogy and nihilism" of certain writers and artists. Minority discontent, simmering in several areas, erupted in the Baltic with a demonstration to honor Stalin's victims and a demand for separate citizenship for Estonia. After Gorbachëv finally returned on September 27 there were sharp exchanges, and a showdown came at a plenum in October. Yeltsin, head of the Moscow city party, made a speech declaring that *perestroika* had amounted to very little, attacked Ligachëv as the chief opponent of reform, and resigned from the Politburo; he also lost his headship of the Moscow party.[6] Less than three weeks later Yeltsin collapsed and was hospitalized. Gorbachëv had failed to defend him, and the mildness of the attack he delivered on Stalinism in his speech commemorating the October Revolution (November 2, 1987) also disheartened the reformers.

It was rumored that the hardliners first defeated the Law on Cooperatives in Gorbachëv's absence before he achieved a reversal; in any case they were not ready to give up. *Pravda* sharply attacked Michael Shatrov's play entitled *Onward ... Onward ... Onward,* which gave a revisionist view of the leadership around 1921. However, such attacks were termed Stalinist by eight leaders of the Soviet theater, and the play opened in Tomsk in March 1988.

In the same month the most powerful blow yet was struck by the hardliners. A letter headed "I Cannot Betray My Principles," written by a Leningrad chemistry teacher named Nina Andreeva, was published in the newspaper *Sovetskaia Rossiia,* reportedly after being approved by Ligachëv. Redolent of "anti-Semitism, patriotic xenophobia, and nostalgia for Stalinism,"[7] the letter was immediately followed by instructions from TASS to local newspapers to reprint it (an order defied by a courageous editor in Tambov!). For three uncomfortable weeks the reformers were silenced. Then Gorbachëv and Yakovlev returned, this time from Yugoslavia, and *Pravda* carried a sharp rejoinder apparently composed by Yakovlev. The reformers breathed a sigh of relief. Ligachëv was clearly worsted but not silenced. In August he made a speech opposing reliance on the market and improving relations with capitalist countries.

From June 28 to July 1, 1988, the Nineteenth Party Conference was held—the first such meeting since 1941. According to one estimate, 40% of the members of the Central Committee, 90 of the 157 *obkom* first secretaries, 8 of 15 of the Soviet republics, 72 of 101 ministers, 10 of 12 members of the Secretariat, and 8 of 14 Politburo members had been removed under Gorbachëv. At the Conference—which nevertheless had unanticipated conservative strength—a decision was made to form a new 2,250-member Congress of People's Deputies. Of that total, by universal and secret suffrage 750 would be chosen by nationality and 750 by territory, whereas 750 seats would be allotted to deputies nominated by "social organs" (the party, labor unions, veterans, the Academy of Sciences, etc.). The Congress would in turn elect a president and a two-chamber Supreme Soviet of 542 members (as against the 1,500 belonging to the previous body by that name) that would be in

---

[6] John Morrison, *Boris Yeltsin: From Bolshevik to Democrat,* Dutton, 1991, pp. 60–63.

[7] *Radio Liberty Research Bulletin,* as quoted in Ben Eklof, *Soviet Briefing,* Westview, 1989, p. 29.

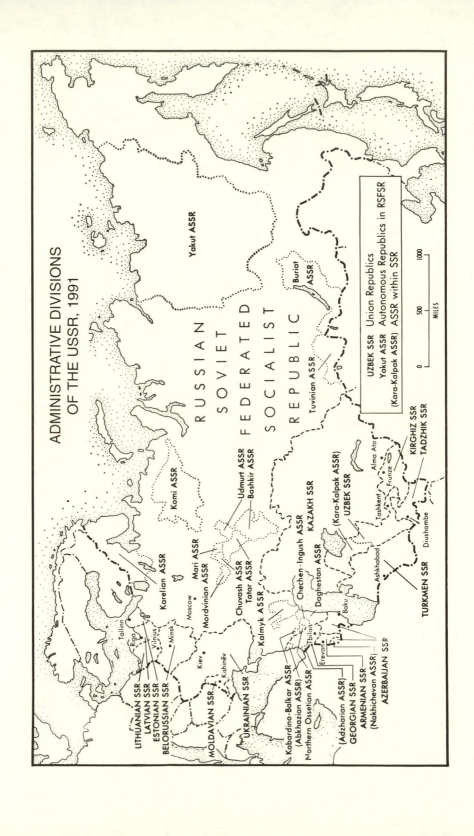

ADMINISTRATIVE DIVISIONS
OF THE USSR, 1991

RUSSIAN SOVIET FEDERATED SOCIALIST REPUBLIC

Yakut ASSR

Buriat ASSR

Tuvinian ASSR

Komi ASSR

Karelian ASSR

Udmurt ASSR
Bashkir ASSR

Mari ASSR
Mordvinian ASSR

Chuvash ASSR
Tatar ASSR

Kalmyk ASSR

Chechen-Ingush ASSR
Daghestan ASSR

(Kara-Kalpak ASSR)
UZBEK SSR

KAZAKH SSR

KIRGHIZ SSR
TADZHIK SSR

TURKMEN SSR

Moscow
Tallinn
Riga
Vilnius
Minsk
Kiev
Kishinëv
Tbilisi
Erevan
Baku
Tashkent
Alma Ata
Frunze
Diushambe
Ashkhabad

LITHUANIAN SSR
LATVIAN SSR
ESTONIAN SSR
BELORUSSIAN SSR

MOLDAVIAN SSR

UKRAINIAN SSR

Kabardino-Balkar ASSR
(Abkhazian ASSR)
Northern Ossetian ASSR

(Adzharian ASSR)
GEORGIAN SSR
ARMENIAN SSR
(Nakhichevan ASSR)
AZERBAIJAN SSR

UZBEK SSR Union Republics
Yakut ASSR Autonomous Republics in RSFSR
(Kara-Kalpak ASSR) ASSR within SSR

0   500   1000
MILES

almost continuous session and would have legislative and executive functions. Elections to the new Congress—the first genuine elections since those of 1917 to the Constituent Assembly—were held in March 1989, and they produced startling results. To take two examples out of many: Boris Yeltsin, ousted Moscow party chief, polled more than 89% of the vote against a stodgy opponent; Yuri Soloviëv, party boss of the Leningrad region, was defeated although he had actually run unopposed. (In part, he was defeated precisely because he was the sole candidate—a deeply ingrained practice that the voters were clearly rejecting.) Opposed and defeated were the mayor of Moscow, the president and prime minister of Lithuania, the party chief of Minsk, the admiral of the Pacific fleet, and the head of the Estonian KGB. Initially eliminated from the ballot, the reformer Andrei Sakharov, the former space czar Roald Sagdeev, and the economist Nikolai Shmelëv were triumphantly elected by the Academy of Sciences.

The Restless Non-Russians

Some observers have pointed to ethnic unrest rather than to the grumblings of the hardliners in the top leadership as the greatest danger to *perestroika*. As before, some Jews sought simply to leave rather than to improve their lot, and 8,011 were permitted to emigrate in 1987 (the largest number since 1979). But others wanted to stay and enjoy some kind of cultural life of their own; for them a Jewish cultural center, named for the great actor murdered by Stalin, Solomon Mikhoels, was established in Moscow in February 1989.

The first signs of real trouble came with the riots in Alma Ata in December 1986. These riots attended the firing of Dinmukhamed Kunaev and his replacement as leader of the Kazakh party by a Russian, Gennady Kolbin; 200 were said to be injured and more than 1,000 were arrested. The rapidly growing Muslim population—perhaps 50 million, having doubled in a quarter-century—was clearly vulnerable to certain influences from south of the Soviet frontier. The Kazakhs, along with the Kirgiz, Tadzhiks, Turkmens, and Uzbeks, are Sunnite like the great majority in the Muslim world; by contrast, Azerbaijan is three-quarters Shi'ite—the same variety as is dominant in Iran, where Khomeini's fundamentalist revolution was centered. Without doubt, a desire to minimize the influence of Khomeini (whose portrait was carried by demonstrators in Baku in November 1988) and, in general, unnecessary involvement with foreign Muslims were major factors in the decision to withdraw Soviet troops from the prolonged war in Afghanistan, a process that began on May 15, 1988, and was announced as completed on schedule on February 15, 1989. Babrak Karmal had been replaced as leader in May 1986 by Najibullah, former head of the security services, but in consequence the struggle had gone no better, and the prognosis for survival of the Communist government of Kabul without Soviet help was very poor. Approval for limited resettlement of the unhappy Crimean Tatars, unrehabilitated alone (except for the Volga Germans) among Stalin's deported peoples, was announced in June 1988.

Under Stalin, autonomy of the republics was an almost total sham, and the USSR was one of the most centralized states that ever existed. After 1953 not only did Russians continue to rule, but a gradual extension of Russification occurred; simultaneously, however, a good deal of "affirmative action" (to use the American term, which refers to preferential treatment in higher education and jobs for the indigenous population) benefited the secular-minded and party-member local elites. In 1978 a decree required study of the Russian language in all Soviet elementary schools. Gorbachëv initially paid little attention to the nationality issue. A plenum of the Central Committee devoted to the problem was announced for 1987 but was postponed twice, until the summer of 1989. In 1987 minority-nationality demonstrations were dispersed by force and their organizers deported; however, the following year Moscow changed its policy dramatically and, from mid-1988, adopted a much more conciliatory stance.

In February 1988 came the start of the "most serious ethnic unrest ever experienced in peacetime in the Soviet Union"[8]—in Armenia and Azerbaijan. The heavily Armenian Nagorno-Karabakh, an autonomous region (since June 1923) surrounded by the Azerbaijan SSR and included administratively within it since July 1921, was the scene of rioting and the occasion for demonstrations in Erevan. In May the party leaders of the two republics were replaced, without any noteworthy result. By September a state of emergency was declared in Karabakh, and troops and tanks were sent into Erevan to enforce a ban on street gatherings.

The great earthquake of December 1988 brought new misery to Armenia—about 25,000 people were killed and half a million rendered homeless. When Gorbachëv visited the scene of the disaster, he met a partly hostile reception. The Armenians, long loyal to Moscow as their safeguard against the Turks, were clearly swinging away from such sentiments. Armenia demanded to have Karabakh attached to it; Azerbaijan refused: Moscow was changing no boundaries.

The politically most daring and yet adroitly conducted campaigning was to be found in the Baltic republics. During the second half of 1988, the first secretaries of all three republics were replaced. All three proclaimed their indigenous languages and the pre-1940 flags to be official. Lithuania actually announced that it would compensate those arrested and deported between 1940 and 1953—a move that Leon Aron has termed "the first such action in Soviet history." Estonia, the most advanced of the republics, was restless with central dictation and its demonstrated ability to do better than the other fourteen in many respects. On October 1 occurred the inaugural conference of an Estonian Popular Front in Support of

---

[8] The phrase is taken from *Keesing's Record of World Events*, XXXIV:36033.

Perestroika, and similar bodies were formed in Latvia (October 9) and Lithuania (October 23). In the Supreme Soviet[9] in November, Estonia demanded "sovereignty," Armenia and Azerbaijan denounced each other, and almost everyone criticized Estonia. In a speech Gorbachëv announced changes in the electoral law and proposed amendments to the constitution to give the republics more power. Such promises satisfied few in the borderlands.

In comparison with the Baltics and the Caucasus, Ukraine remained fairly quiet under the iron hand of Vladimir Shcherbitsky, the only remaining Brezhnev appointee in charge of the party in a republic. Gorbachëv apparently left Shcherbitsky in Kiev as a guarantee against trouble: In February he told a group of coal miners, "You can only imagine what would happen if there were disorder in Ukraine." Nevertheless, several Ukrainian cultural societies were organized in 1988, announcing as their goal support of Gorbachëv's slogans but also advocating autonomy and more scope for Ukrainian language and culture.

The various national democratic movements showed a propensity to coalesce. In January 1989 a conference (billed as the fifth) of the representatives of such movements from Estonia, Latvia, Lithuania, Belorussia, Ukraine, Georgia, and Armenia met in Vilnius, capital of Lithuania, and adopted a Freedom Charter declaring that continued existence within the Soviet empire is "unacceptable for the peoples that we represent."[10] What that pregnant phrase might mean in practice was shown in April, when demonstrations in Tbilisi demanding Georgian independence went on for several days and were put down by army troops, with twenty dead. The party leader of the republic was replaced by the KGB chief, Givi Gumbaridze, and other heads rolled. Clearly the issue of nationality remained a dangerous one for the Moscow leadership.

More Political and Economic Changes

In September–October 1988 a plenum removed Gromyko and Solomentsev as full members of the Politburo and two candidate members; added were Vadim Medvedev as a full member and three candidate members including Alexandra Biriukova, the first woman on the Politburo for twenty-seven years (but still not a full member, as Ekaterina Furtseva had been). Two puzzling personnel changes were made: Ligachëv was stripped of responsibility for ideology (which passed to Medvedev) and was instead put in charge of agricultural policy in the Secretariat;

---

[9] On October 28 thirty-one deputies in the Supreme Soviet made history by voting against a proposed law (increasing the powers of the militia to control street demonstrations); such negative votes had not been cast for many decades.

[10] *Novoe russkoe slovo,* February 21, 1989.

and Chebrikov was deprived of his headship of the KGB (which was transferred to Colonel General Vladimir Kriuchkov) but was entrusted with legal policy. Gromyko, too, was retired from the presidency, a title that Gorbachëv also took— and one slated soon to become rather more important.

On October 12, 1988, one of the most potentially dramatic changes in the economy was signaled. The Central Committee evaluated the progress of agrarian lease teams thus far, such teams having been authorized on a trial basis only; it also discussed the prospect of extending the system to the whole country, with leases lasting fifty years. Gorbachëv declared that the USSR had turned the peasant into a wage laborer (an action he clearly intended to label as a mistake) and proclaimed the "need to make the people full-fledged masters of the land again." This astonishing statement was followed by a plenum of the Central Committee in March 1989 that approved a plan to permit peasants to lease land for "five to fifty years and more," in the words of Ligachëv, and to transfer leases to their children. Certainly new policies were being adopted; but the reaction of the Soviet peasantry to them was uncertain, inasmuch as one poll showed that only 5% of farmers were prepared to take advantage of private leasing.

In December 1988 a serious effort was made to broaden the scope of foreign trade. Previously every co-op had the right to a license to engage in foreign trade, but out of about 50,000 only 4 had successfully carried applications through the bureaucracy. Now many enterprises were to be allowed to trade directly (i.e., not through the centralized trading system).

A "Cultural Revolution"

The position of dissidents, religious groups, writers, and artists began a gradual improvement. In February 1986 Anatoly Shcharansky was released in exchange for five other people; he had been imprisoned since 1978 on trumped-up charges of high treason and espionage. In December 1986 the most renowned dissenter remaining in the USSR, Andrei Sakharov, was released from internal exile; he and his wife Elena Bonner, who had just been allowed to visit the United States for medical treatment, were permitted to leave Gorky and return to Moscow. Bonner also received a pardon for her conviction on charges of anti-Soviet activity in 1984.

Surprising scenes occurred at the congress of the Writer's Union in June 1986. Andrei Voznesensky called for the publication of Boris Pasternak's novel *Doctor Zhivago,* and Evgeni Evtushenko presented a petition requesting that the late writer's home in Peredelkino be made into a museum. Works by Nicholas Gumilëv, shot in 1921 for alleged counterrevolutionary activity, had been appearing in journals.

Before long, the trickle of works long banned but now permitted to be published became, if not a torrent, at least a flowing stream. In January 1987 a literary commission was appointed to examine the works of Pasternak (a step required before a book could pass into print); this and other such measures reputedly owed much to Raisa Gorbachëva. In *Knizhnoe obozrenie,* No. 38, 1988, appeared a list of 200 books scheduled to be reissued before the year 2000 that included works by tsarist official, White, liberal, Socialist Revolutionary, Menshevik, anarchist, and purged Bolshevik (Bukharin and Rykov) writers, Michael Pokrovsky's *Brief History of Russia* (denounced by Stalin), the Marquis de Custine's *Russia in 1839,* and the works of the chief Slavophile writers of the mid-nineteenth century, Constantine Leontiev, Nicholas Berdiaev, Vladimir Soloviev, and Father Paul Florensky. Long anathema to the censors, the classic anti-totalitarian novels were reissued: Eugene Zamiatin's *We,* Orwell's *1984,* Koestler's *Darkness at Noon,* Kafka's *The Castle.* A few writers were still banned, but those published made up an astonishing list. Sergei Zalygin, the reformist editor of *Novyi Mir* (perhaps the premier Soviet literary journal), announced that the back cover of November 1988 issue would carry word of an agreement with Alexander Solzhenitsyn to publish certain works of his. However, Vadim Medvedev, the Politburo member in charge of ideology, stopped it and forced the reprinting of the cover that would have capped the climax of *glasnost'* by heralding the publication of parts of *The Gulag Archipelago* in the USSR. Nevertheless, Solzhenitsyn's 70th birthday was commemorated in Moscow in December 1988, and an émigré journal published a letter signed by seventy Soviet (not émigré) writers and academics urging his rehabilitation.

Roy Medvedev (no relation to Vadim), the dissident who continued to call himself a Leninist, was justified in declaring in September that the USSR was undergoing a "cultural revolution"—not, it should be added, one of universal devastation as in China earlier, but one of an opposite kind—under the banner of literary freedom and recovery of Russia's cultural past. Writers long silenced were published again and honored: Vladimir Dudintsev's *White Robes (Belye odezhdy),* on Lysenkoist persecution of genuine geneticists, received a USSR State Prize.[11] Both dead and living émigré authors were published, including Joseph Brodsky, the Nobel laureate for literature in 1987; the late Ivan Bunin, the winner for 1933; and Vladimir Nabokov (d. 1977), who had written that he hated "the world of tyranny and torture, of Fascists and Bolshevists, of Philistine thinkers and jack-booted baboons." In October 1988 the decree condemning Anna Akhmatova and Michael Zoshchenko, the signal flag of the Zhdanovshchina in 1946, was revoked.

The new blossoming of literature (though, it was noted, not much writing from new authors) was paralleled by a revising of history and an ever-closer ap-

---

[11] Dudintsev's *Not by Bread Alone* had resulted in the firing of the renowned Konstantin Simonov as editor of *Novyi Mir,* and Dudintsev was thereafter unable to publish fiction for thirty years. Julia Wishnevsky writes that the two episodes show the difference between Khrushchëv's thaw and Gorbachëv's *glasnost'.*

proach to the truth. In February 1988 Bukharin was exonerated of the false charges placed against him, and in the spring he was posthumously reinstated as a party member. Following that came the rehabilitation of Zinoviev, Kamenev, and Rykov—as well as that of Trotsky's son but not Trotsky himself.

In January 1988 Michael Shatrov's sensational play *Onward ... Onward ... Onward* portrayed Alexander Kerensky positively and accused Stalin of murdering both Sergei Kirov and Trotsky. The historian Roy Medvedev wrote that 50 million "unnatural deaths" occurred between 1917 and 1953. In September the leading Soviet specialist on collectivization of agriculture, Victor Danilov, stated that a new book of which he was co-author would label the famine of 1932–1933 as "Stalin's most terrible crime." Yuri Afanasiev, director of the Historical Archival Institute, vigorously attacked Stalin's misdeeds; though the target of conservative counter-attack himself, he returned to the assault in 1988. The startling film of Tengiz Abuladze, *Repentance (Pokaianie),* veiled its indictment of Stalin only slightly by giving its villain some traits of Mussolini, Hitler, and Beria.

A generation of history students was thoroughly confused, and in June 1988 the authorities canceled the final examinations in history for all secondary school pupils. There was indecision in high places about how to respond to all this: In March snowplows were used to disperse demonstrators in favor of a monument to Stalin's victims, but in July the Politburo announced plans for precisely such a monument.

One of the most striking areas of innovation came in regard to religious policy. On April 29 Gorbachëv met, chatted amicably, and was photographed with Patriarch Pimen of the Russian Orthodox Church, the first such meeting since 1943. In June the 1,000-year anniversary of the conversion of Rus was officially celebrated, with Soviet officials present at several ceremonies. (One wag observed that it was a good thing that Prince Vladimir of Kiev had not converted a year or two earlier, or the government would not have permitted the millennium of conversion to be commemorated at all.) Three monasteries were returned to the church:[12] the famed Monastery of the Caves in Kiev, the Optina Pustyn in the Kaluga region, and one in Yaroslavl. A new church was promised to replace Moscow's old Church of the Savior, which had been razed by Stalin to permit the building of a Palace of Soviets—but since repeated efforts to build it had failed, a large outdoor swimming pool had been constructed instead. A council of the Orthodox Church held at Zagorsk canonized nine saints of the past as far back as the Middle Ages. In October 1989 the 400th anniversary of the Russian patriarchate was celebrated, and two of the patriarchs including Tikhon (elected in 1917) were canonized in the first church service in the Kremlin in seventy years.

---

[12] Earlier the Monastery of St. Daniel had been returned and replaced Zagorsk as headquarters of the patriarch.

On December 1 Gorbachëv visited Pope John Paul II in Rome, and at the same time the Uniat (or Ukrainian Catholic) Church was legalized. In May 1990 the aged Patriarch Pimen died, and the metropolitan of Leningrad was chosen to succeed him as Alexii II. After a period in which older laws on religion were simply not enforced, on October 1, 1990 the Supreme Soviet passed a law on religious freedom, giving churches clear legal status (not quite possessed earlier by the *dvadtsatka* [group of twenty] entitled to represent a parish) and the right to conduct charitable work and religious education, and also authorized conscientious objection to military service on religious grounds. A darker side of events still existed: Fr. Alexander Men, an Orthodox priest outstanding in his saintliness, was murdered, probably by the KGB, in September 1990. The death of Andrei Sakharov, the most promising leader of Russia's democrats, in December 1989, had been natural, but it was also a great loss.

The Fall of Gorbachëv

Andrei Gromyko once told a visiting foreign minister: "You know how it is—a bit like the Bermuda Triangle. From time to time, one of us disappears." After the new parliamentary institutions created at the 19th Conference met, and Gorbachëv, in March 1990, appointed a Presidential Council intended to supersede the Politburo as the main policy-making organ (to be followed by other such bodies), the former importance of Kremlinology—study of changes in the leadership of the party—diminished sharply. In September 1988 Solomentsev was dropped from the Politburo, and Gromyko himself was retired from both the Politburo and the presidency, an office Gorbachëv took over; in September 1989 another plenum removed Shcherbitsky, Chebrikov, and Nikonov; at the XXVIII Party Congress in July 1990 Vorotnikov and Sliunkov, along with candidate member Biryukova, followed them. (It proved to be the last Party Congress.) A new, larger Politburo was named, consisting of twenty-four people, but clearly it did not have the power of earlier times. The reformers thought they might be in the saddle, and in September Gorbachëv endorsed a "500-day plan" for "shock therapy" in the economy, proposed by academician Stanislav Shatalin.

But then the president stepped back and turned to the right. He killed the Shatalin plan by withdrawing his support under pressure from the hardliners. He went on to appoint several of them to high positions, chiefly Boris Pugo as head of the MVD and Gennadii Yanayev as vice-president. Shevardnadze had just resigned, warning of possible dictatorship—and he evidently did not mean Gorbachëv but a hardliner regime. In January 1991 an attempted putsch occurred in the Baltic region. Fourteen were killed and hundreds injured in an attack on the Vilnius radio-TV center, and it was announced that power in Lithuania had passed into the hands of a National Salvation Front. A similar attempt was made in Latvia but was abortive. Western reaction and his own abhorrence of large-scale bloodshed led Gorbachëv to call off the security forces, and the Baltic putsch failed.

But curiously, as the Soviet leadership moved to the right,[13] events in Eastern Europe were gaining momentum in the opposite direction. The story begins in Poland, where the workers, spontaneously organized in the union called Solidarity, pushed a strike into a virtual uprising; in July 1989 the party accepted a compromise by which General Wojciech Jaruzelski, secretary of the Communist party (PUWP), became president but a non-Communist cabinet took over. Events soon acquired a momentum of their own. In September Hungary opened its border with Austria, so that fleeing East Germans flooded across it; Czechoslovakia and Poland followed. In October Hungary discarded the name "People's Republic." On November 11 the Berlin Wall abruptly was breached (the following August East and West Germany were reunited). In December a Romanian uprising overthrew the government, and Ceauşescu and wife were executed. Four days later, on December 29, the recently imprisoned Vaclav Havel was elected president of Czechoslovakia. The major steps had been taken toward ending Communism in Eastern Europe. It all could not have happened—at least peacefully or easily—if it had not been for Gorbachëv's refusal to try to resist the changes by sending in Soviet troops and tanks. Evidence suggests that what he wanted was not what had happened but rather a reformist Leninism (whether or not warranted by Lenin's ideas or writings). Soviet spokesmen, asked what the difference between the Prague Spring of 1968 and the events of 1989 was, replied simply, twenty years (or twenty-one)—that is to say, the aim of both Dubcek and Gorbachëv was "socialism with a human face" but not abandonment of socialism. But the decay of the system, and the force of public opinion, had developed beyond the point where "socialism" could be saved. The emergence of civil society, "the ensemble of grassroots, spontaneous, nongovernmental (although not necessarily anti-governmental) initiatives from below" meant no turning back.[14]

In the USSR itself civil society had begun to make an appearance. By the beginning of 1989 the country had an estimated 40,000 voluntary organizations, and they continued to multiply. Several new democratic organizations took shape. In January 1990 a Democratic Russia vowed to follow the "ideas of Sakharov," and in the period 1988–1991 comparable groups were being formed right and left. In the March 1990 RSFSR elections the DR elected mayors in both Moscow and Leningrad. Pressure from workers, especially miners, forced the RSFSR Congress to grant emergency powers to Yeltsin and hold a popular election for an RSFSR pres-

---

[13] The terminology is confusing. In earlier Soviet usage "rightist" meant movement away from Stalin and toward reform; "leftist" meant hardliner. Now the meanings were reversed; some scholar will doubtless trace exactly when and how it happened.

[14] Vladimir Tismaneanu, *Reinventing Politics: Eastern Europe From Stalin to Havel,* Free Press, 1992, pp. 170–171.

ident in June 1991; Yeltsin received a heavy majority (see p. 434). One leader of the democrats declared: "We need what humanity has worked out over the past thousand years"—namely democracy and a market economy, and many followed the same path.[15]

In August 1991 an attempted coup by rightist forces occurred, while Gorbachëv was vacationing in the Crimea. Formation of a State Committee for the State of Emergency (GKChP was the Russian acronym) was announced; the organizer was KGB Chairman Kriuchkov, the figurehead was Vice President Yanayev, proclaimed acting president; six others made up the committee. Yeltsin rallied the opposition; at one point he climbed up on a tank and delivered a fiery speech; at another, he escaped arrest by one unit sent to apprehend him by ten minutes.

The leaders of the military-industrial complex and party hardliners faced a loose grouping of clergy, secular reformers, and ordinary people, more than 50,000 of whom tried to protect the White House, Yeltsin's stronghold; close to 200,000 demonstrated against the coup in Leningrad. Army units sent by the GKChP wavered and went over to Yeltsin. The Committee dithered and demonstrated incompetence in many ways. After three uncertain days, the coup collapsed and Gorbachëv returned in what ought to have been triumph to Moscow. But it was not. He had appointed several of the plotters—one, Boris Pugo, committed suicide; the other seven were arrested. He was accused of sympathy with them, or of preparing to join them if they won.

In the immediate aftermath of the failed coup, Russia recognized the independence of the Baltic states; Gorbachëv was virtually forced to abolish the Communist Party of the Soviet Union; he appointed the reformer Vadim Bakatin head of the KGB, suspended the USSR Congress of People's Deputies, and ordered "departification" of all USSR agencies from the army and the KGB on down.[16] Although Yeltsin first appeared confused and uncertain, after a doctor-prescribed seventeen-day vacation in the Crimea he returned in October to take the helm more firmly. He agreed with Gorbachëv to dissolve the USSR by January 1, 1992, and replace it by a new Commonwealth of Independent States. On the evening of December 25 the red flag was lowered from the Kremlin and replaced by the Russian tricolor.

Gorbachëv was now without a party or a country. One assessment was that he "was a great man with great promise that was never fulfilled. In the end he was too weak, too ambitious, and too indecisive to make big political decisions."[17] He remained a socialist and clung to the notion of supporting Lenin's heritage, but he favored democracy of a sort and tried to "restructure" the Soviet economy so that

---

[15] John B. Dunlop, *The Rise of Russia and the Fall of the Soviet Empire*, Princeton U. Press, 1993, p. 114.

[16] Ibid., p. 265.

[17] Maj. Gen. Oleg Kalugin, quoted ibid., p. 276.

it functioned, in doing so introducing elements of the market. Above all, he refused to use the massive force he still commanded in order to prevent the victory
of democracy and the end of Communism in the USSR and the Soviet sphere in
Europe—it survived, for the time being, in East Asia and Cuba, but quickly dissolved elsewhere, as in Africa and West Asia. That constitutes his great service to
humanity; it was he who enabled the peaceful dismantling of what Reagan called
"the evil empire," thus sparing mankind what might have been untold suffering.
Annelise Anderson wrote that a short time before there seemed to be "no peaceful
path, no evolutionary road, for making this transition. How wrong we were."
From one point of view it could be argued that George Kennan's containment
policy worked; from another, that Communism simply imploded and collapsed
of itself. But it was Gorbachëv who made it all possible, by action and inaction.

28

The Revolution of 1991
and After

The Failed Coup

Events had begun to move rapidly in Gorbachëv's last years of power. Several in-stitutions that had been by Stalin's intention fraudulent or impotent came to life in amazing fashion: the "republics" of perhaps the most highly centralized system on earth; the soviets chosen by charades rather than elections, a constitution many of whose provisions were dead letters from the start; a "presidency" with-out power. A large segment of Soviet people who were not supposed to under-stand genuine political life became enamored of and enthusiastic participants in one or more of its aspects. But it was the failed coup of August 1991 that precipi-tated what deserves to be called a revolution: the end of Communism in the USSR and Eastern Europe; the abolition of the Communist Party of the Soviet Union (though that was to be partially undone); the end of the USSR itself, with inde-pendence for all fifteen republics, even though efforts were made to put twelve of them (without the Baltics) back together in a new, looser form; and the end of the Cold War. To be sure, the effects, the habits, and the institutions created by sev-enty-four years of Communist rule could not be removed instantly, or within a year or two. What many observers found surprising was how little violence at-tended the changes that had occurred (by early 1994); although little wars broke out on or beyond the southern borders of Russia, few died in Russia itself, even in the October 1993 violence, in comparison to such revolutionary changes else-where.

Yeltsin Before the Coup

The leader in these events was Boris Yeltsin. He tells us that he almost drowned at the time of his baptism; a drunken Orthodox priest dropped him and his mother fished him out. Without question he subsequently had some narrow escapes, fateful for Russia itself as well as for him. Born and raised near Sverdlovsk in a village and then in a barracks in a town in Perm province, he and his family suffered from the extreme poverty to which Stalin reduced so many of the country's peasants and workers and also from the political repression he carried out—Yeltsin's father was arrested, for unclear reasons, when he was six. He did well as a student but got into mischief, on one occasion losing two fingers trying to take apart an army grenade he had filched from a local armory. Graduating in 1955 from school in Sverdlovsk, he went into building construction. His success led to party membership, and in 1976 he became First Secretary for Sverdlovsk. In April 1985, shortly after Gorbachëv became General Secretary, he was summoned to Moscow by none other than Egor Ligachëv, former First Secretary in Tomsk, who had come to know and admire Yeltsin as a hard worker who was not corrupt.[1]

Before the end of the year he was chosen to replace Viktor Grishin as party chief of Moscow city. There he won popularity by visiting streets and shops and attacking abuse of power on the part of the *apparatchiki*. He came to Moscow still believing that reform could be achieved by appointing new people instead of getting rid of the system. Experience with the center of power, however, was changing his mind. Alienated from Ligachëv and then Gorbachëv, frustrated at every turn, he resigned from the Moscow first secretaryship and candidate membership in the Politburo in November 1987, after an unpleasant scene in the Central Committee to attend which he had been brutally routed out of a hospital bed after a heart attack.

It looked as if Yeltsin was finished. But in June 1988 he was able to challenge Ligachëv effectively at the 19th Conference (see p. 419); in September Gorbachëv reorganized the party leadership, transferring Ligachëv and retiring Gromyko and other elders, as Yeltsin had wished. In March 1989 Yeltsin himself, standing in Moscow rather than his home base of Sverdlovsk,was triumphantly elected to the new USSR Congress of People's Deputies with 89.6% of the vote. As the Congress met, its proceedings, televised live in totally unprecedented fashion, captured the attention of almost all Soviet citizens. Yeltsin was then elected to the Supreme Soviet, and became a leader of a new reformist faction called the Interregional Group. Previously he had been outside the Communist orbit only twice, to West Germany; in September he made a private lecture tour of the U.S., and was dazzled—above all by a ten-minute visit to a supermarket, a sure-fire trauma for a Soviet citizen.[2] There were rumors (then and later) about his drinking, and a mysterious incident in which he fell or was pushed into a river was never explained.

---

[1] John Morrison, *Boris Yeltsin*, p. 42.
[2] Ibid., p. 105.

In March 1990 elections Yeltsin won more than 80% of the vote for a seat on the RSFSR Congress of People's Deputies; elsewhere reformers did so well that the USSR CPD repealed Article 6 of the Constitution, thereby abolishing the Communist Party's monopoly of power. When the XXVIII Congress was held in July, Yeltsin demonstratively resigned from the party altogether. He had been (with difficulty, and perhaps by dint of reaction against Gorbachëv's opposition) elected chairman of the presidium of the Supreme Soviet ("president") of the RSFSR. The reformers now controlled the White House (*Belyi Dom*), the Brezhnev-built headquarters of the RSFSR government.

The increasing autonomy of Russia was paralleled by similar, or stronger, demands from the other republics. By now a "war of laws" had broken out, pitting the central against republican and other local authorities as each issued decrees claiming precedence. After resisting pressure for a new Union Treaty (replacing the one of 1922), Gorbachëv yielded in mid-1990; a working group was established, but already the three Baltic republics were bent on independence and took no part, and Moldavia, Georgia, and Armenia soon dropped out, leaving nine. The republics' hand was much strengthened by elections held in 1990. After a humiliating confrontation with an army delegation in November, Gorbachëv swung to the right again with the resignation of Shevardnadze and the abortive crackdown in Vilnius and Riga. He abolished the Presidential Council, upgraded the Federation Council, and created a new Security Council in which the army and KGB would have a clear part in policymaking. He also decreed creation of a new vice-presidency and replacement of the Council of Ministers by a new and smaller Cabinet of Ministers. Finally, he published a draft Union Treaty. The Baltic fiasco stopped negotiations, and when they resumed in the spring events threatened to overtake them. Yeltsin took the republics' side, and in particular the Baltics'. Russia signed treaties with Estonia and Latvia in January 1991 and Lithuania in July.

In September Yeltsin had another mysterious accident, this time in a car, following an injury he had suffered in an emergency landing of a plane in Spain in April. Suspicions arose that the KGB was seeking to get rid of him; certainly the hardliners were waging a feverish campaign with the same aim. In February 1991 Yeltsin counterattacked by calling for Gorbachëv's resignation, and then managed to add to the ballot that Gorbachëv had ordered for the whole USSR on the Union Treaty a proposal for a directly elected presidency of the Russian republic only. A 76% majority was reported to have approved keeping the USSR together—in the nine republics that took part in the referendum, that is. (The Baltic states had already voted to approve [but not enact] independence.) In Russia 70% voted for a directly elected presidency. An April miners' strike undermined Gorbachëv's position further. In the same month Yeltsin went along with Gorbachëv in a "nine-plus-one" agreement of the USSR with Russia, Ukraine, Belarus (as it now called itself), Azerbaijan, and the five Central Asian republics, an agreement that was thought to have assured the future of at least part of the Union. At that point the reformers around Yeltsin regarded it as wise to support Gorbachëv as a barrier to someone worse. In June Yeltsin ran in such an election, having chosen as running mate the hero of the Afghan war Alexander Rutskoi, against five other candidates including former prime minister Nikolai Ryzhkov, candidate of the old guard, and won 57.4% of the vote. At his inauguration Gorbachëv was present—as was Patriarch Alexii II.

During the spring and summer of 1991 Gorbachëv once again shifted policy in a reformist direction, sending the economist Gregory Yavlinsky to Harvard University to plan a "Grand Bargain" to structure reform with U.S. help. But he left in place the hardliners he had appointed a few months earlier. In August they struck (see p. 429). Yeltsin survived as president of Russia; the USSR did not survive, so there was no longer a presidency for Gorbachëv to occupy.

Yeltsin in Power

In the aftermath of the coup the Communist Party was banned (though the ban was later declared invalid) and its property confiscated. To dismiss parliament, hold elections, and pass a new constitution would have taken time, and democrats were in a hurry to ride momentum to economic change.[3] In January 1992 Yeltsin and Prime Minister Gaidar launched shock therapy in the form of freeing prices and began a drive to privatize industry.

The non-Russian republics went their own way. Ukraine declared independence on December 1, 1991, and the rest of the republics followed. On December 8 Russia, Ukraine, and Belarus decided to form a Commonwealth of Independent States (*Sodruzhestvo Nezavisimykh Gosudarstv*), with headquarters in Minsk. Other republics protested, and in December eleven of them at a meeting in Alma Ata "refounded" CIS. It remained a shadowy body having little in common with the unified and centralized state it succeeded.

The end of the USSR, and of Communism there and in Eastern Europe, led to the formation of several small and shifting political groups, each striving to become the nucleus of a larger party. In November Democratic Russia (see p. 428) split into two groups; one included Fr. Gleb Yakunin and Yuri Afanasiev and was prepared to be gentle with minorities, the other was under Nikolai Travkin, Viktor Aksyuchits, and Mikhail Astafiev (heads of the Democratic Party of Russia, Christian Democrats, and Constitutional Democrats respectively), who were "democratic statists" and centralizers, but Aksyuchits and Astafiev then moved far to the right.[4] In June 1992 a Civic Union was formed, uniting Travkin's group with Arkady Volsky's Union of Industrialists and Entrepreneurs and Rutskoi's People's Party of Free Russia.

---

[3] Martin Malia, "The End," *New Republic,* October 18, 1993.
[4] Dunlop, *Rise of Russia,* pp. 184–185, 278.

Acting (Yeltsin was still keeping the title) Prime Minister Egor Gaidar managed to reduce monthly inflation to 9% in July. "Stability seemed within the government's grasp. But defeat was snatched from the jaws of victory when the central bank suddenly relaxed monetary policy in order to rescue Russia's industrial dinosaurs from collapse."[5] The big state-owned enterprises had done nothing after prices were unfrozen, and went on using energy, taking raw materials and actually reducing their value by converting them into products no one wanted. "Russia would be better off if much of its heavy industry went bankrupt and workers and capital were deployed elsewhere," as *The Economist* put it; but too many people had long operated under a system in which volume of production was all that mattered. Moreover, unemployment had long been thought shameful, and only in 1991 had it ceased to be a crime.

In four months Viktor Gerashchenko, head of the Central Bank, had increased the money supply threefold; savings were being destroyed, and the country teetered on the edge of hyperinflation. In December Yeltsin sacrificed Gaidar to try to hold centrist support; his replacement as prime minister was Viktor Chernomyrdin, a former manager who held an intermediate position between reformers and hardliners. There were also proto-fascists, notably Viktor Zhirinovsky, who declared he would pile nuclear waste on the frontiers of the Baltic states, turn on fans, and let radioactivity kill their peoples. He ran for president of Russia against Yeltsin and came in third—but with only 7% of the vote.

The tension between reformers and hardliners brought continual clashes between the president and the parliament—both the Congress of People's Deputies and the smaller body it elected, the two-chamber Supreme Soviet headed by Ruslan Khasbulatov. He was a Chechen who had been a close associate of Yeltsin at the time of the August 1991 coup, but turned against him. It was finally agreed to hold a referendum in April at which four questions were asked of all citizens of the Russian Federation (the official name as of April 1992): Do you trust the president of the RF? Do you approve the policy of the executive since 1992? Do you deem it necessary to hold early presidential elections? Early parliamentary elections? Yeltsin emerged with an improved position: over half the eligible voters said yes to the first two questions, no to the last two; but only 31.7% wished early presidential elections while 43.1% desired early parliamentary elections—which Yeltsin was trying to move toward. However, the momentum that the referendum might have generated was lost by inaction.

The Supreme Soviet, elected in March 1990 when the Communists could still dictate the outcome, fell into the hands of the so-called red-brown alliance—which linked ex-Communists (red), who were not very ex and who wished to recover the security they had once had and to keep the power some of them retained, with the extreme rightists (brown), who lamented the demise of the USSR

---

[5] *The Economist*, December 11, 1993, p. 24.

along with the loss of Russian power and prestige and explained them by imaginary conspiracies of Jews, Masons, and the West (despite the aid it was giving—admittedly clumsily and slowly).

The parliament did its best to ignore the referendum, get rid of reformer appointees of Yeltsin's, and block every move he made toward political or economic change. The Central Bank under Gerashchenko obeyed parliament's orders. The new Constitutional Court, chaired by Valery Zorkin, increasingly supported parliament, applying the Brezhnev Constitution of 1977 (amended some 300 times since, often self-contradictorily), sometimes declaring invalid Yeltsin's actions when they were only oral and not yet reduced to paper. A draft of a new constitution, drawn up by a Constitutional Assembly convened for the purpose, in July was sent to the republics and regions for comment. By then it was reported that one-third of all enterprises in Russia had been privatized, over half of the small ones. In August all Russian troops officially had left Lithuania.

After the executive had managed to reduce inflation somewhat, parliament passed a budget that tripled the deficit for the year, and the Bank followed up with the stupid July 19 withdrawal of all rubles printed before 1993—a measure then limited by executive action but not rescinded. On September 16 Gaidar was recalled as deputy premier.

On September 21 Yeltsin dissolved both the Congress of People's Deputies and the Supreme Soviet and set December 11–12 for elections to a Federal Assembly, to consist of a Federation Council made up of two representatives from each of the 88 republics and regions, totaling 176, and a State Duma to have 450 seats, half single-seat constituencies and half chosen from proportional representation by parties. Evidently by the design of Vice-President Rutskoi (though he was suspended from office by Yeltsin on September 1) and Chairman of Parliament Khasbulatov, on the afternoon of October 3 a group of red-brown opponents of Yeltsin broke through a police cordon into the White House (where a rump of the parliament still sat), seized the mayor's office, and attacked and took part of the chief TV station. On the night of October 4 government troops put down the attempted rebellion with 137 dead and 549 hospitalized during the whole affair. President Havel of the Czech Republic declared that what had occurred in Moscow was not a power struggle but instead a fight between democracy and totalitarianism.

Rutskoi and Khasbulatov were arrested; Zorkin resigned as chairman of the Constitutional Court and Yeltsin suspended the Court for bringing Russia to "the verge of civil war." Eight parties and organizations were excluded from the December elections. On October 9 Yeltsin decreed dissolution of all soviets at the local level and urged regional soviets to disband; two weeks later he ordered new elections by March 1994 for all soviets at the regional level and lower. A new civil code was approved by the government. On October 27 a decree provided for the first time for full ownership of land, including sale and purchase.

In the December 12, 1993, elections damage was done to the prospects of democracy by the poor showing of reformist parties, which had squabbled among themselves, failed to cooperate, and conducted a lackluster campaign. The red-browns had done better by unbridled demagogy but also shrewd handling of the media. Yeltsin distanced himself from the election except for the issue of the constitution, for which he campaigned hard. It was approved; 54% of eligible voters voted, and 58.4% of those voting cast ballots for it. The results were, for the reformers: Gaidar's party, Russia's Choice, won 76 seats in the Duma; the "Yabloko" (YA + B + L; it is a pun on the word "apple") bloc headed by Yavlinsky, Boldyrev, and Lukin elected 20; Sergei Shakhrai's Party of Unity and Concord, 30. For the red-browns: the misnamed Liberal Democrats, headed by Zhirinovsky, won 63; the Communist Party, 45 seats; the Agrarians, a creation of kolkhoz chairmen who wished to keep collective farming, 55. Thus reformers had 131 seats out of the 444 "registered members"; red-browns, 163. The centrist Democratic Party of Russia, led by Nikolai Travkin, won 15 seats; a new party called Women of Russia gained 23. Independents numbered 112, 65 of whom formed a group called New Regional Policy.[6]

Meanwhile Zhirinovsky proved himself either mad or dangerous by declaring that Russia should regain lost territories from Finland to Alaska; Germany (where he had former Nazi friends) and Russia should divide up Poland; and Romania was an artificial state peopled by "Italian gypsies." He threatened both Japan and Germany (*sic*) with nuclear attack. Many compared him with Hitler. But his party polled only 22.8% of the vote, and the likelihood of its duplicating the feat of the Nazis in seizing power seemed remote.

More serious was the flight of Russian reformers from Chernomyrdin's government: Egor Gaidar and Boris Fëdorov, and Western advisers: Jeffrey Sachs and Anders Åslund. Viktor Gerashchenko, whose scalp the reformers had demanded in vain, remained as head of the Central Bank to print rubles and make loans to near-bankrupt state factories, thus feeding inflation, in turn deterring foreign investment and making difficult the receipt of foreign assistance to the floundering economy.

Russia and the Former USSR in 1994

The end of Soviet Communism had seemed to come suddenly, but in fact a crisis had been visible on the horizon for some time. Gorbachëv had announced in February 1988 that Soviet economic growth (only 2 to 3% annually) since 1975 had been achieved almost entirely through high world prices of oil and increases in re-

---

[6] Official listings given in Steven Erlanger story in *New York Times* of January 15, 1994; Serge Schmemann story in the January 14 issue.

tail sales of alcohol. Economic problems had deepened since then. The government kept raising a minimum wage and a pension floor; inflation had risen without passing into hyperinflation. As Russia lost the borderlands, many industries and natural resources went with them—not that they brought prosperity to the newly independent states of the "near abroad" (the non-Russian former Soviet republics).

The Baltic states were making progress despite friction with their Russian minorities, but the other newly independent republics faced daunting problems. Ukraine's economy was in worse shape than Russia's; monthly inflation in Russia for December 1993 was 12%, in Ukraine almost 100%. Such political problems as the control of the Black Sea fleet and ownership of the Crimea (given to Ukraine in 1954 but coveted by many Russians) had taken precedence over any kind of serious economic reform. Belarus and Georgia seemed to be slipping back into Moscow's grasp. Moldova was rent by hardliner-Russian secessionists in the "Dnieper republic" and faced unrest in its Gagauz area. Armenia and Azerbaijan's struggle over Nagorno-Karabakh dragged on. Tajikistan suffered from civil strife. And these were not the only crises.

In the "near abroad" there lived an estimated 25 million Russians. The USSR had upward of 50 million Muslims; even after losing Central Asia and Azerbaijan, Russia had 20 million left. Non-Russians made up 19% of the population of the Russian Federation.[7] Few, however, wished to reopen boundary questions.

Before the coup of 1991 serious difficulties had beset the society of the USSR, and many of them remained with Russia: housing remained in very short supply; infant mortality exceeded 30 per 1,000 live births; the average Russian woman had six to eight abortions during her childbearing years; life expectancy for males, uniquely among industrialized countries, declined from seventy in the 1960's to sixty-two in 1979 before rising again a bit.[8] Dreams of gigantic projects such as the reversing of the flow of great Siberian rivers had been laid aside; the Baikal-Amur Mainline (BAM) railway, paralleling to the north a stretch of the Trans-Siberian, was "completed" but still unusable because of auxiliary needs. The state of the farms was lamentable, though an ever-smaller percentage of the population lived on them. In 1961 one-half of the population lived on farms, in 1990 only one-third. Almost all villages (where Russian peasants lived, like most peasants throughout the world) had electricity and television, but the overwhelming majority lacked running water, for which villagers had to go to the town pump, and only a tiny fraction had sewer systems. Two-thirds of the farms were still served by

---

[7] See Appendixes C and D for percentages of Russians living in the "near abroad" and in the Russian Federation itself.

[8] Murray Feshbach and Alfred Friendly, Jr., *Ecocide in the USSR*, Basic Books, 1992. The book gathers shocking information about Soviet demography and the environment. In March 1994 male life expectancy was reported to have declined again to 60 (actually lower than 50 in some areas), while female life expectancy held steady at 72. Michael Specter article in *New York Times*, March 6, 1994, p. 4.

unpaved roads. One collective farmer fed 7 to 9 people, whereas a Dutch farmer fed 112.

The fate of nuclear arms, which once consumed so much of the time of diplomats and on which the fears of millions were fixated, remained undecided. No one feared that Washington or Moscow would fire missiles at the other, but disposition of them languished because of lack of funds in Russia, Ukraine, and Kazakhstan (the three nuclear nations of the former USSR) and distrust of the biggest republic. President Clinton's visit to the area in January 1994 produced an agreement among Russia, Ukraine, and the U.S. for destruction of nuclear weapons, but its ratification and implementation remained uncertain.

Ordinary Russian citizens had lost the economic security of sorts that Communism had given them. Though health care was unspeakable in quality and housing ranged from dilapidated to derelict, they had been (and often remained) free of charge or nearly so; food was monotonous and required standing hours in lines after tiring working days, but it had been cheap. Thus in 1992 thousands of people stood elbow to elbow at metro stations or central squares selling anything they could find to cover the necessities of life. What was loosely called the Mafia (this one not Italian) had gained control of much economic activity, and street crime was a newly troublesome phenomenon.

However, there were hopeful economic signs. It was reported that from 3 to 4% of Russian industry was being privatized every month. In 1993 real incomes were 10% higher than in 1992; in January 1994 it took 40% of the average weekly wage to buy a standard basket of food; Russia had a $20 billion trade surplus in 1993.[9] Western advisers and Russian reformers urged cutting subsidies to loss-making big enterprises and using money directly for a safety net for the poor, and persuasive arguments were made for a currency board, which would link the money it issues to a reserve of hard currency (to be obtained from the IMF or other sources with natural resources as collateral).[10] Unfortunately those in power in February 1994 seemed more inclined to regress to the stable Brezhnev era than to court the uncertainties of reform.

The "cultural revolution" of the late 1980's had spent much of its force. Writers were no longer compelled to seek Aesopian ways of eluding state controls or painters to risk their careers by defying the canons of socialist realism. Religion was adjusting to a sudden liberation that brought both benefits and costs. It was thought appropriate for the patriarch of the Orthodox Church to attempt to mediate the conflict between Yeltsin and the parliament in October 1993 (though he failed), and only lack of funds was hindering the restoration of church buildings and monasteries that had been returned to the Church. The actions of young Protestant evangelists from the West were widely regarded as a nuisance, since

---

[9] *The Economist*, January 22, 1994, p. 52.

[10] For example, Boyden Gray in the *New York Times*, December 29, 1993, p. A11.

they did not seem to understand that the Russians had already been Christians for a thousand years, but they were not the only Westerners in Russia with a shaky grasp of the Russian past and present. The outflow of Jews to Israel had decreased somewhat, and those remaining could worship more easily but were also often exposed to ignorant and stupid anti-Semitic charges both oral and written. Russia's Muslims were slower to feel the greater scope for religious activity.

It was of course difficult to place all the complexities of 1994 into the perspective of the almost-finished century. In her powerful poem "Requiem" Anna Akhmatova had written, "I should like to call you all by name/But they have lost the lists"—that is to say, so much individual agony had accompanied the mass misery inflicted by Stalin, Lenin and other Communists, as well as resulted from wars and natural disasters throughout much of the twentieth century, that it became impossible for one writer, or many, to begin to record or even comprehend it all. The oppression of the tsarist period, relieved by increasing Russian entrance into the world community economically, culturally, and even politically, had yielded to the upheavals of the revolution, which brought hopes for liberation of Russia and all mankind—hopes dashed by the sufferings and cruelties of Communism. They in turn had ended, to the amazement of the world mostly peacefully, and the possibility was open for a country immensely rich in natural resources and the capacities of its peoples to create prosperity as well as democracy—perhaps in the twenty-first century if not the remaining years of the twentieth.

Appendix A

Russian Rulers Since Ivan III

TSARDOM OF MUSCOVY

HOUSE OF RIURIK

Ivan III	1462–1505	Fëdor I	1584–1598
Basil III	1505–1533	Boris Godunov	1598–1605
Ivan IV	1533–1584	"The Time of Troubles"	1604–1613

HOUSE OF ROMANOV

Michael	1613–1645	Ivan V (co-tsar)	1682–1696
Alexis	1645–1676	Peter I	1682–1725
Fëdor II	1676–1682		

RUSSIAN EMPIRE

HOUSE OF ROMANOV

Peter I	1682–1725	Catherine II	1762–1796
(after 1721 Emperor)		Paul	1796–1801
Catherine I	1725–1727	Alexander I	1801–1825
Peter II	1727–1730	Nicholas I	1825–1855
Anna	1730–1740	Alexander II	1855–1881
Ivan VI	1740–1741	Alexander III	1881–1894
Elizabeth	1741–1761	Nicholas II	1894–1917
Peter III	1761–1762		

PROVISIONAL GOVERNMENT

PRIME MINISTERS

G. E. Lvov	Mar.–July 1917	A. F. Kerensky	July–Nov. 1917

RSFSR, LATER USSR

CHAIRMEN OF THE COUNCIL OF PEOPLE'S COMMISSARS, AFTER 1946 PRIME MINISTERS

V. I. Lenin	1917–1924	N. A. Bulganin	1955–1958
A. I. Rykov	1924–1930	N. S. Khrushchëv	1958–1964
V. M. Molotov	1930–1941	A. N. Kosygin	1964–1980
J. V. Stalin	1941–1953	N. A. Tikhonov	1980–1985
G. M. Malenkov	1953–1955	N. I. Ryzhkov	1985–1990
	V. S. Pavlov	1990–1991	

RSFSR, LATER RUSSIAN FEDERATION

PRIME MINISTERS

I. S. Silayev	1990–Sept. 1991
B. N. Yeltsin	Oct. 1991–June 1992
E. T. Gaidar (Acting)	June–Dec. 1992
V. S. Chernomyrdin	Dec. 1992–

PRESIDENT

B. N. Yeltsin	July 1991–

Appendix B

Congresses of the
Russian Social Democratic Labor Party,
Later Bolshevik, Later Communist,
Later All-Union Communist Party

R.S.D.L.P.	I *Congress*	MINSK	March 1–3, 1898 (Old Style)
"	II *Congress*	BRUSSELS & LONDON	July 17–Aug. 10, 1903
" (Bolsheviks only)	III *Congress*	LONDON	April 12–27, 1905
" ("Unification Congress")	IV *Congress*	STOCKHOLM	April 10–25, 1906
"	V *Congress*	LONDON	April 30–May 19, 1907
R.S.D.L.P.(B.)	VI *Congress*	PETROGRAD	July 26–Aug. 3, 1917
R.C.P.(B.)	VII *Congress*	PETROGRAD	March 6–8, 1918 (New Style)
"	VIII *Congress*	MOSCOW	March 18–23, 1919
"	IX *Congress*	"	March 29–April 5, 1920
"	X *Congress*	"	March 8–16, 1921
"	XI *Congress*	"	March 27–April 2, 1922
"	XII *Congress*	"	April 17–25, 1923
"	XIII *Congress*	"	May 23–31, 1924
ALL-UNION C.P.(B.)	XIV *Congress*	"	Dec. 18–31, 1925
"	XV *Congress*	"	Dec. 2–19, 1927
"	XVI *Congress*	"	June 26–July 13, 1930

"	XVII *Congress*	"	Jan. 26–Feb. 10, 1934
"	XVIII *Congress*	"	March 10–21, 1939

ALL-UNION

C.P.	XIX *Congress*	"	Oct. 5–15, 1952
"	XX *Congress*	"	Feb. 14–25, 1956
"	XXI *Congress*	"	Jan. 27–Feb. 5, 1959
"	XXII *Congress*	"	Oct. 17–31, 1961
"	XXIII *Congress*	"	March 29–April 8, 1966
"	XXIV *Congress*	"	March 30–April 9, 1971
"	XXV *Congress*	"	Feb. 24–March 5, 1976
"	XXVI *Congress*	"	Feb. 23–March 3, 1981
"	XXVII *Congress*	"	Feb. 25–March 6, 1986
"	XXVIII *Congress*	"	July 2–13, 1990

Appendix C

Nationalities of the RSFSR
and then Russian Federation[1]

In thousands	1989	Increases (Decreases Shown with Minus Sign), 1959–1989, in Percent
GROUPS WITH ETHNIC HOMELANDS IN RUSSIA		
NORTH EUROPEAN RUSSIA		
1. Karelians	125	−24
2. Mordva	1073	−11
3. Chuvash	1774	23
4. Mari	644	29
5. Tatars	5522	36
6. Udmurts	725	16
7. Bashkirs	1345	41
8. Komi-Permyak	147	3
9. Komi	336	19
NORTH CAUCASUS		
10. Adygei	123	56
11a. Karachay	150	113
11b. Cherkess	51	74
12a. Kabards	386	92
12b. Balkar	78	122
13. Ossetians	402	62
14a. Chechens	899	244
14b. Ingush	215	285
15a. Avars	544	118
15b. Darghins	353	132

[1] Adapted from Table 1, Chauncy D. Harris, "A Geographic Analysis of Non-Russian Minorities in Russia and Its Ethnic Homelands," *Post-Soviet Geography,* November 1993.

15c. Lezghins	257	125
15d. Kumyks	277	109
15e. Laks	106	82
16. Kalmyks	166	65

SIBERIA

17. Altay	69	55
18. Khakass	78	40
19. Tuva/Tyva	206	106
20. Buryats	417	66
24. Yakuts/Sakha	380	61

PEOPLES OF THE NORTH

25-26. Nentsy	34	9
27a. Khanty	22	16
27b. Mansi	8	31
28. Dolgans	7	78
29. Evenki	30	22
30. Chukchi	15	29
31. Koryaks	9	45

GROUPS WITH ETHNIC HOMELANDS
IN NEAR-ABROAD COUNTRIES

Ukrainians	4363	30
Belarusians	1206	43
Kazakhs	636	66
Armenians	532	108
Azeris	336	373
Moldavians	173	177
Georgians	131	127
Uzbeks	127	330

GROUPS WITHOUT ETHNIC HOMELANDS
IN FORMER USSR

Germans	842	3
Jews	537	−39
Gypsies	153	111
Koreans	107	17
Poles	95	−20
Finns	47	−35
Crimean Tatars	21	—
TOTAL, RUSSIAN FEDERATION	147,022	25
RUSSIANS	119,866	22
NON-RUSSIANS	27,156	38

Appendix D

Russians and Non-Russians
in Successor Republics to USSR[1]

The most numerous group in the "Others" category, when available, is given in parentheses.

Republic	1989, in Thousands	Change, 1959–1989, in Percent
RUSSIAN FEDERATION		
Russians	119,866	−1.8
Non-Russians	27,156	+1.8
Total	147,022	
ESTONIA		
Estonians	963	−13.1
Russians	475	+10.2
Others (Ukrainians)	127	+2.8
Total	1,566	
LATVIA		
Latvians	1,388	−10.0
Russians	906	+7.4
Others (Belarusians)	373	+2.6
Total	2,667	
LITHUANIA		
Lithuanians	2,924	+0.3
Russians	344	+0.9
Others (Poles)	406	−1.2
Total	3,675	
BELARUS		
Belarusians	7,905	−3.2
Russians	1,342	+5.0

---

[1] Adapted from Table 1, Chauncy D. Harris, "The New Russian Minorities: A Statistical Overview," *Post-Soviet Geography,* January 1993.

| Others (Poles) | 905 | −1.8 |
| Total | 10,152 | |

UKRAINE

Ukrainians	37,419	−4.1
Russians	11,356	+5.2
Others (Jews)	2,677	−1.1
Total	51,452	

MOLDOVA

Moldavians	2,795	−0.9
Russians	562	+2.8
Others (Ukrainians)	978	−1.8
Total	4,335	

GEORGIA

Georgians	3,787	+5.8
Russians	341	−3.8
Others	1,273	−2.0
Total	5,401	

ARMENIA

Armenians	3,084	+5.3
Russians	52	−1.6
Others	169	−3.7
Total	3,305	

AZERBAIJAN

Azerbaijanis	5,805	+15.2
Russians	392	−8.0
Others	824	−7.2
Total	7,021	

KAZAKHSTAN

Kazakhs	6,535	+9.7
Russians	6,228	−4.9
Others (Germans)	3,702	−4.8
Total	16,464	

KYRGYZSTAN

Kirgiz	2,230	+11.9
Russians	917	−8.7
Others (Ukrainians)	1,111	−2.2
Total	4,258	

UZBEKISTAN

Uzbeks	14,142	+9.2
Russians	1,653	−5.2
Others	4,015	−3.8
Total	19,810	

TURKMENISTAN

Turkmens	1,537	+11.1
Russians	334	−7.8
Others (Uzbeks)	652	−3.3
Total	3,523	

TAJIKISTAN

Tajiks	3,172	+9.2
Russians	388	−5.7
Others	1,533	−3.5
Total	5,093	

A Selection of Materials
for Further Reading

The materials that follow are chosen for the general reader, teacher, or student who wishes to investigate further topics discussed in this volume. Mainly English-language materials are listed, with a few exceptions. The arrangement follows the sequence of chapters and topics as they appear in the book.

Reference material is found in the *Modern Encyclopedia of Russia and Soviet History,* 55 vols., 1976–1993, which contains many minor errors but is extensive and meaty; also consult the *Modern Encyclopedia of East Slavic, Baltic and Central Asian Literatures,* 9 vols. to date, 1977–1989 (A-Ho), and *Modern Encyclopedia of Religions in Russia and the Soviet Union,* 5 vols., 1988–1993, all three by Academic International Press. Generally reliable on facts, apt to be tendentious in interpretation: what will doubtless be its last edition, *Bol'shaia Sovetskaia Entsiklopedia,* 3rd ed., Moscow, 30 vols. plus index vol., 1970–1981; Macmillan has published an English translation as *Great Soviet Encyclopedia,* 31 vols. plus index vol. 1973–1983.

Introduction: Into Totalitarianism and Out of It

Introductions to the geography of Russia and the USSR: Leslie Symons, ed., *The Soviet Union: A Systematic Geography,* Barnes & Noble, 1983; Paul E. Lydolph, *Geography of the USSR,* 3rd ed., Wiley, 1977; S.S. Balzak, ed., *Economic Geography of the USSR,* trans. Macmillan, 1949. An attempt to explain the origins of the modern Russian state in patrimonialism is Richard Pipes, *Russia Under the Old Regime,* Charles Scribner's Sons, 1974. The proper interpretation of Russian absolutism is discussed by several authorities in Part 4 of Donald W. Treadgold, ed., *The Development of the USSR,* U. of Washington Press, 1964. Two important studies that attempt to explain changes within tsarist society are Victor Leontovitsch's fine if mistitled *Geschichte des Liberalismus in Russland,* Frankfurt-am-Main, Vittorio Klostermann, 1957, and Jacob Walkin, *The Rise of Democracy in Pre-Revolutionary Russia,* Praeger, 1962. Standard works are Carl J. Friedrich and Zbigniew Brzezinski, *Totalitarian Dictatorship and Autocracy,* 2d ed., revised by Carl J. Friedrich, Praeger, 1966, and Leonard Schapiro, *Totalitarianism,* Praeger, 1972. Critical treatments of the concept appeared subsequently in various articles and books not easily found in concise form.

1. The Russian People

The most detailed and authoritative history of Russia in English (although its treatment of the pre-Petrine period is relatively brief) remains Michael T. Florinsky, *Russia: A History and an Interpretation,* 2 vols., Macmillan, 1953. The best one-volume text is Nicholas V. Riasanovsky, *A History of Russia,* 5th ed., Oxford U. Press, 1993. A brilliant analysis of modern Russia up to the beginning of the twentieth century is Paul Miliukov, *Russian and Its Crisis,* Collier Books, 1962. Surveys of topics covering much of the imperial period or longer include: Dietrich Geyer, *Russian Imperialism: The Interaction of Domestic and Foreign Policy 1860–1914,* trans., Yale U. Press, 1987; Barbara Jelavich, *St. Petersburg and Moscow: Tsarist and Soviet Foreign Policy, 1814–1974,* Indiana U. Press, 1974; Jerome Blum, *Lord and Peasant in Russia From the Ninth to the Nineteenth Century,* Princeton, 1961; Donald W. Treadgold, *The West in Russia and China: Religious and Secular Thought in Modern Times,* 2 vols., Westview reprint, 1985, Vol. 1, *Russia, 1472–1917;* Andrzej Walicki, *A History of Russian Thought From the Enlightenment to Marxism,* Stanford U. Press, 1979. An idiosyncratic but challenging book is James H. Billington, *The Icon and the Axe: An Interpretive History of Russian Culture,* Knopf, 1966; the luminous essay of Wladimir Weidle, *Russia: Absent and Present,* Vintage paperback, 1961, is recommended.

Treatments of the nineteenth and early twentieth centuries only: Sergei Pushkarev, *The Emergence of Modern Russia, 1801–1917,* Holt, Rinehart and Winston, 1963, and Hugh Seton-Watson, *The Russian Empire, 1801–1917,* Oxford at the Clarendon Press, 1967. The distaff side is explored with skill in Richard Stites, *The Women's Liberation Movement in Russia: Feminism, Nihilism, and Bolshevism, 1860–1930,* Princeton U. Press, 1978; Lazar Volin, *A Century of Russian Agriculture: From Alexander II to Khrushchev,* Harvard U. Press, 1970 (about one-fourth deals with the pre-1918 period); George Yaney, *The Urge to Mobilize: Agrarian Reform in Russia, 1861–1930,* U. of Illinois Press, 1982; Dorothy Atkinson, *The End of the Russian Land Commune, 1905–1930,* Stanford U. Press, 1983.

Studies of the non-Russian peoples: the fine Hoover Institution Press Studies of Nationalities include Toivo Raun, *Estonia and the Estonians* and Martha Brill Olcott, *The Kazakhs,* both 1987; Edward A. Allworth, *The Modern Uzbeks,* 1990; and Audrey L. Altstadt, *The Azerbaijani Turks,* 1992. Some other titles: Georg von Rauch, *The Baltic States: The Years of Independence, 1917–1940,* trans., U. of California Press, 1974; Romuald J. Misiunas and Rein Taagepera, *The Baltic States: Years of Dependence, 1940–1990,* Expanded ed., U. of California Press, 1993; Anatol Lieven, *The Baltic Revolution: Estonia, Latvia, Lithuania and the Path to Independence,* Yale U. Press, 1993; David Marshall Lang, *The Armenians: A People in Exile,* London, Unwin Paperback, 1988; Ronald Grigor Suny, *The Making of the Georgian Nation,* Indiana U. Press, 1988. Introductions to the Muslims of Russia and the USSR as a whole: Alexandre Benningsen and Chantal Lemercier-Quelquejay, *Islam in the Soviet Union,* London, Pall Mall Press, 1967, and Hélène Carrère d'Encausse, *Islam and the Russian Empire: Reform and Revolution in Central Asia,* trans., U. of California Press, 1989. See also listing for Chapter 16.

A general introduction to Eastern Orthodoxy is provided by Timothy Ware (now Bishop Kallistos Ware), *The Orthodox Church,* Penguin Books, 1963, and Nicolas Zernov, *Eastern Christendom,* G. P. Putnam's Sons, 1961. On the Russian Church under the Empire, see Robert L. Nichols and Theofanis G. Stavrou, eds., *Russian Orthodoxy Under the Old Regime,* U. of Minnesota Press, 1978. On Islam and Judaism, see above.

2. Marxism Comes to Russia

The origins of the international (chiefly European, including Russian) revolutionary movement are traced in James H. Billington, *Fire in the Minds of Men,* Basic Books, 1980. V. V. Zenkovsky, *A History of Russian Philosophy,* trans. 2 vols., Columbia U. Press, 1953, has not been superseded. Non-Marxist socialism is the subject of Franco Venturi, *Roots of Revolution: A History of the Populist and Socialist Movements in Nineteenth Century Russia,* Knopf, 1960. Good political biographies are Martin Malia, *Alexander Herzen and the Birth of Russian Socialism, 1812–1855,* Harvard U. Press, 1961; Philip Pomper, *Peter Lavrov and the Russian Revolutionary Movement,* U. of Chicago Press, 1972; and James H. Billington, *Mikhailovsky and Russian Populism,* Oxford at the Clarendon Press, 1958.

No single biography of Marx is fully satisfactory. Useful, however, are David McLellan, *Karl Marx: His Life and Thought,* Harper & Row, 1974; Franz Mehring, *Karl Marx,* U. of Michigan Press, 1962; and Isaiah Berlin, *Karl Marx, His Life and Environment,* 2d ed., Oxford U. Press, 1959. On his partner, W. O. Henderson, *The Life of Friedrich Engels,* 2 vols., London, Frank Cass, 1976. A justly popular essay is Edmund Wilson, *To the Finland Station,* Farrar, Straus and Giroux, 1972. A magisterial work by a major thinker is Leszek Kolakowski, *Main Currents of Marxism: Its Rise, Growth, & Dissolution,* 3 vols., Oxford U. Press, 1978. All three Internationals are examined in Julius Braunthal, *History of the International,* trans., 2 vols., Praeger, 1967.

A good curtain-raiser to our story is Norman M. Naimark, *Terrorists and Social Democrats: The Russian Revolutionary Movement Under Alexander III,* Harvard U. Press, 1983. On the relations and differences among liberals, Socialist Revolutionaries and Social Democrats see Donald W. Treadgold, *Lenin and His Rivals,* Greenwood Press reprint, 1976. On the liberals who became the Kadets: George Fischer, *Russian Liberalism,* Harvard U. Press, 1958; Richard Pipes, *Struve: Liberal on the Left, 1870–1905,* and *Liberal on the Right, 1905–1944,* both Harvard U. Press, 1970–1980; Thomas Riha, *A Russian European: Paul Miliukov in Russian Politics,* Notre Dame U. Press, 1969; and Shmuel Galai, *The Liberation Movement in Russia, 1900–1905,* Cambridge U. Press, 1973; William G. Rosenberg, *Liberals in the Russian Revolution: The Constitutional Democratic Party, 1917–1921,* Princeton U. Press, 1974. On the early S.R.'s: Christopher Rice, *Russian Workers and the Socialist-Revolutionary Party Through the Revolution of 1905–1907,* St. Martin's Press, 1988; and M. Perrie, *The Agrarian Policy of the Russian Socialist-Revolutionary Party from its Origins Through the Revolution of 1905–1907,* Cambridge U. Press, 1976.

There are many studies of early Russian Marxism; a few good ones are: Bertram D. Wolfe, *Three Who Made a Revolution,* Dial Press, 1958; J.L.H. Keep, *The Rise of Social Democracy in Russia,* Oxford at the Clarendon Press, 1963; Allan K. Wildman, *The Making of a Workers' Revolution: Russian Social Democracy, 1891–1903,* U. of Chicago Press, 1967; Samuel H. Baron, *Plekhanov: The Father of Russian Marxism,* Stanford U. Press, 1963; Israel Getzler, *Martov: A Political Biography of a Russian Social Democrat,* Cambridge U. Press, 1967; Abraham Ascher, *Pavel Axelrod and the Development of Menshevism,* Harvard U. Press, 1972; Jay Bergman, *Vera Zasulich: A Biography,* Stanford U. Press, 1983. Definitive on the politics and theology of Russian Jewish socialism is Jonathan Frankel, *Prophecy and Politics; Socialism, Nationalism, and the Russian Jews, 1862–1917,* Cambridge U. Press, 1981. An excellent history of the Social Democrats from the beginning 1958 is Leonard Schapiro, *The Communist Party of the Soviet Union,* Random House, 1959.

Alfred G. Meyer's *Leninism,* Harvard U. Press, 1957, analyzes Lenin's ideas carefully. The best biography is Adam Ulam's misleadingly titled *The Bolsheviks,* Macmillan, 1965; a recent biographical trilogy, 2 vols. of which have been published (1985, 1991), is Robert Service, *Lenin: A Political Life,* Macmillan (they cover 1870–March 1918). See also Robert C. Williams, *The Other Bolsheviks: Lenin and His Critics, 1904–1914,* Indiana U. Press, 1986. The 5th Russian edition of Lenin's works is in 56 vols., 1958–1966; the only complete English edition is by the Foreign Languages Publishing House, Moscow, 45 vols., 1970. A useful documentary collection is Robert H. McNeal, ed., *Resolutions and Decisions of the Communist Party of the Soviet Union, 1898–1964,* 4 vols., U. of Toronto Press, 1974.

3. The Last Tsar: Reaction and the Revolution of 1905

On the Imperial central government, a controversial but challenging treatment is George L. Yaney, *The Systematization of Russian Government: Social Evolution in the Domestic Administration of Imperial Russia, 1711–1905,* U. of Illinois Press, 1973. Detailed and comprehensive information is provided in Erik Amburger, *Geschichte der Behördenorganisation Russlands von Peter dem Grossen bis 1917,* Leiden, Brill, 1966, and N. P. Eroshkin, *Ocherki istorii gosudarstvennykh uchrezhdennii dorevoliutsionnoi Rossii,* 2d ed., Moscow, 1968, which includes useful diagrams. Two volumes in the important Carnegie Endowment for International Peace's Russian Series of the Economic and Social History of the World War (Yale U. Press) are especially relevant: N. I. Astrov and P. P. Gronsky, *The War and the Russian Government,* 1929, and T. I. Polner, *Russian Local Government During the War and the Union of Zemstvos,* 1930.

On Nicholas II as tsar, the best work is Dominic Lieven, *Nicholas II: Emperor of all the Russias,* London, John Murray, 1993. A fine biography of the imperial couple is Robert K. Massie, *Nicholas and Alexandra,* Atheneum, 1967. A few monographs on aspects and periods of the reign: David A. J. Macey, *Government and Peasant in Russia, 1861–1906: The Prehistory of the Stolypin Reforms,* Northern Illinois U. Press, 1987; Jeremiah Schneiderman, *Sergei Zubatov and Revolutionary Marxism,* Cornell U. Press, 1976; Victoria E. Bonnell, *Roots of Rebellion: Workers' Politics and Organizations in St. Petersburg and Moscow, 1900–1914,* U. of California Press, 1983; G. M. Hamburg, *Politics of the Russian Nobility, 1881–1905,* Rutgers U. Press, 1984; Steven G. Marks, *Road to Power: The Trans-Siberian Railroad and the Colonization of Asian Russia, 1850–1917,* Cornell U. Press, 1991; Denis and Peggy Warner, *The Tide at Sunrise: A History of the Russo-Japanese War, 1904–1905,* Charterhouse Publishers, 1974.

Abraham Ascher's *The Revolution of 1905* is an excellent two-volume study from Stanford U. Press; subtitles are *Russia in Disarray,* 1988, and *Authority Restored,* 1992. See also Howard D. Mehlinger and John M. Thompson, *Count Witte and the Tsarist Government in the 1905 Revolution,* Indiana U. Press, 1972; Terence Emmons, *The Formation of Political Parties and the First National Elections in Russia,* Harvard U. Press, 1983; and Marc Szeftel, *The Russian Constitution of April 23, 1906: Political Institutions of the Duma Monarchy,* Peter Lang, 1982.

4. The "Silver Age" of the Arts

There are two superb surveys of literature: Victor Terras, *A History of Russian Literature,* Yale U. Press, 1991, marred by sloppy publishing, and D. S. Mirsky, *A History of Russian Lit-*

erature, Vintage paperback, 1958. On other arts, see George H. Hamilton, *The Art and Architecture of Russia,* Penguin, 1954; Tamara Talbot Rice, *A Concise History of Russian Art,* Praeger, 1963; William C. Brumfield and Milos M. Velimirovich, eds., *Christianity and the Arts in Russia,* Cambridge U. Press, 1991; Richard A. Leonard, *A History of Russian Music,* Macmillan, 1957; Marc L. Slonim, *Russian Theater From the Empire to the Soviets,* World Publishing Co., 1961; Serge Lifar, *A History of Russian Ballet From Its Origins to the Present Day,* trans., Roy, 1954; Jay Leyda, *Kino: A History of the Russian and Soviet Film,* Macmillan, 1960.

Studies dealing partly or wholly with the Silver Age: on literature, Renato Poggioli, *The Poets of Russia, 1890–1930,* Harvard U. Press, 1960; Martin P. Rice, *Valery Briusov and the Rise of Russian Symbolism,* Ardis, 1975; Oleg Maslenikov, *The Frenzied Poets: Andrey Biely and the Russian Symbolists,* U. of California Press, 1952; Leonid I. Strakhovsky, *Craftsmen of the Word,* Harvard U. Press, 1949, on the Acmeists; Vladimir Markov, *Russian Futurism: A History,* U. of California Press, 1968.

On painting, Elizabeth Valkenier, *Russian Realist Art—The State and Society—the Peredvizhniki and Their Tradition,* Ardis, 1977; John E. Bowlt, *The Silver Age: Russian Art of the Early Twentieth Century and the "World of Art" Group,* Oriental Research Partners, 1979; Robert G. Williams, *Artists in Revolution: Portraits of the Russian Avant-Garde, 1905–1925,* Indiana U. Press, 1977; Camilla Grey, *The Great Experiment: Russian Art, 1863–1922,* Harry N. Abrams, 1962; William Richardson, *"Zolotoe Runo" and Russian Modernism,* Ardis, 1986; William C. Brumfield, *The Origins of Modernism in Russian Architecture,* U. of California Press, 1991; Lynn Garafola, *Diaghilev's Ballets Russes,* Oxford U. Press, 1989.

On thought: *Vekhi,* referred to in the text as *Signposts,* is translated as *Landmarks,* Karz Howard, 1977. See George F. Putnam, *Russian Alternatives to Marxism: Christian Socialism and Idealistic Liberalism in Twentieth-Century Russia,* U. of Tennessee Press, 1977; Maria Carlson, *"No Religion Higher Than Truth": A History of the Theosophical Movement in Russia, 1875–1922,* Princeton U. Press, 1993; Alexander Vucinich, *Darwin in Russian Thought,* U. of California Press, 1988.

On Russian education and scholarship before (and sometimes after) 1917: Loren R. Graham, *Science in Russia and the Soviet Union,* Cambridge U. Press, 1993; Samuel D. Kassow, *Students, Professors and the State in Tsarist Russia,* U. of California Press, 1989; Jeffrey Brooks, *When Russia Learned to Read: Literacy and Popular Literature, 1861–1917,* Princeton U. Press, 1985; Ben Eklof, *Russian Peasant Schools: Officialdom, Village Culture, and Popular Pedagogy, 1861–1914,* U. of California Press, 1986.

5. Growth of the Russian Economy

Selected titles: Peter Gatrell, *The Tsarist Economy 1850–1917,* St. Martin's Press, 1986; Arcadius Kahan, *Russian Economic History: The Nineteenth Century,* U. of Chicago Press, 1989, includes material up to 1913; Paul R. Gregory, *Russian National Income, 1885–1913,* Cambridge U. Press, 1982; Alfred J. Rieber, *Merchants and Entrepreneurs in Imperial Russia,* U. of North Carolina Press, 1982; Theodore H. von Laue, *Sergei Witte and the Industrialization of Russia,* Columbia U. Press, 1963; Rose L. Glickman, *Russian Factory Women: Workplace and Society, 1880–1914,* U. of California Press, 1984. Alexander Gerschenkron, "The Rate of Industrial Growth in Russia Since 1885," *Journal of Economic History* 7 (1947), p. 144–174, is challenged in an interesting debate by Olga Crisp, *Studies in the Russian Econ-*

omy Before 1914, Barnes & Noble, 1976. Pre-revolutionary economic history still needs more study.

6. The Last Years of Tsarism

On the politics of the period 1906–1917: Geoffrey A. Hosking, *The Russian Constitutional Experiment: Government and Duma, 1907–1914*, Cambridge U. Press, 1973; Ben-Cion Pinchuk, *The Octobrists in the Third Duma, 1907–1912*, U. of Washington Press, 1974; Robert Edelman, *Gentry Politics On the Eve of the Russian Revolution: The Nationalist Party, 1907–1917*, Rutgers U. Press, 1980; George Tokmakoff, *P. A. Stolypin and The Third Duma*, U. Press of America, 1981; Raymond Pearson, *The Russian Moderates and the Crisis of Tsarism, 1914–1917*, Barnes & Noble, 1977.

On the military-diplomatic side: William C. Fuller, Jr., *Civil-Military Conflict in Imperial Russia, 1881–1914*, Princeton U. Press, 1985; George F. Kennan, *The Fateful Alliance: France, Russia, and the Coming of the First World War*, Manchester U. Press, 1984; D.C.B. Lieven, *Russia and the Origins of the First World War*, St. Martin's Press, 1983. On the war itself: Norman Stone, *The Eastern Front, 1914–1917*, Charles Scribner's Sons, 1975; N. N. Golovine, *The Russian Army in the World War*, 1931, and B. E. Nolde, *Russia in the Economic War*, 1928, both in the Carnegie Russian series; perhaps the best volume in the series is M. T. Florinsky, *The End of the Russian Empire*, 1931, sketching the background of the Revolution. Source collections are Frank A. Golder, ed., *Documents of Russian History, 1914–1917*, trans., Century, 1927, and Z.A.B. Zeman, ed., *Germany and the Revolution in Russia, 1915–1918*, Oxford U. Press, 1958.

7. The February Revolution

William Henry Chamberlin, *The Russian Revolution, 1917–1921*, reprint, 2 vols., Macmillan, 1952, retains its value, but Richard Pipes, *The Russian Revolution 1899–1919*, Knopf, 1990, is an important and seminal though controversial contribution. W. Bruce Lincoln's trilogy attempts a popular history of the entire revolutionary era: *In War's Dark Shadow*, Dial Press, 1983; *Passage Through Armageddon: The Russians in War and Revolution, 1914–1918*, 1986; and *Red Victory: A History of the Russian Civil War*, 1989, the last two by Simon and Schuster. On February: Tsuyoshi Hasegawa, *The February Revolution: Petrograd 1917*, U. of Washington Press, 1981; Bernard Pares, *The Fall of the Russian Monarchy*, Knopf, 1939; the factually careful, interpretively controversial George Katkov, *Russia 1917: The February Revolution*, Harper & Row, 1967; the courageous work of E. N. Burdzhalov, *Russia's Second Revolution: The February 1917 Uprising in Petrograd*, trans., Indiana U. Press, 1987.

Four works by significant participants: Leon Trotsky, *The History of the Russian Revolution*, trans., Yale U. Pres, 1936; Alexander Kerensky, *The Catastrophe: Kerensky's Own Story of the Russian Revolution*, Appleton-Century-Crofts, 1927; N. N. Sukhanov, *The Russian Revolution 1917: A Personal Record*, trans., Oxford U. Press, 1955; and V. M. Chernov, *The Great Russian Revolution*, trans. Yale U. Press, 1936. Subsequent months (or more) are treated in Allan K. Wildman, *The End of the Russian Imperial Army*, 2 vols., Princeton U. Press, 1980–1990; Alexander Rabinowitch, *Prelude to Revolution: The Petrograd Bolsheviks and the July Uprising*, Indiana U. Press, 1968; Oskar Anweiler, *The Soviets: The Russian Workers, Peasants, and Soldiers Councils, 1905–1921*, trans., Pantheon Books, 1974; Oliver H.

Radkey, *Agrarian Foes of Bolshevism* (on the SR's from March to October 1917), Columbia U. Press, 1958; Ziva Galili, *The Menshevik Leaders in the Russian Revolution,* Princeton U. Press, 1989; John D. Basil, *The Mensheviks in the Revolution of 1917,* Slavica, 1984. A useful documentary collection: Robert Paul Browder and Alexander F. Kerensky, ed., *The Russian Provisional Government, 1917,* 3 vols., Stanford U. Press, 1961.

On events in the borderlands: Richard Pipes, *The Formation of the Soviet Union: Communism and Nationalism, 1917–1923,* Harvard U. Press, 1954; Firuz Kazemzadeh, *The Struggle for Transcaucasia, 1917–1921,* Philosophical Library, 1951; and John S. Reshetar, Jr., *The Ukrainian Revolution, 1917–1920,* Princeton U. Press, 1952.

8. The October Revolution

Edward Hallett Carr's one-sided but valuable *A History of Soviet Russia* (Macmillan) reached fourteen books: *The Bolshevik Revolution, 1917–1923,* 3 vols., 1950–1953; *The Interregnum, 1923–1924,* 1954; *Socialism in One Country, 1926–1929,* 3 vols. in 4 pts., 1958–1964; *Foundations of a Planned Economy, 1926–1929,* 3 vols., in 6 pts., 1971–1977. Useful recent monographs include: John L. H. Keep, *The Russian Revolution: A Study in Mass Mobilization,* Norton, 1977; Alexander Rabinowitch, *The Bolsheviks Come to Power: The Revolution of 1917 in Petrograd,* Norton 1976; Diane Koenker, *Moscow Workers and the 1917 Revolution,* Princeton U. Press, 1981; Marc Ferro, *October 1917: A Social History of the Russian Revolution,* trans., Routledge & Kegan Paul, 1980; Graeme J. Gill, *Peasants and Government in the Russian Revolution,* Barnes & Noble Imports, 1979; S. A. Smith, *Red Petrograd: Revolution in the Factories, 1917–1918,* Cambridge U. Press, 1983; Rex A. Wade, *Red Guards and Worker's Militias in the Russian Revolution,* Stanford U. Press, 1984. Robert V. Daniels reassesses *Red October: The Bolshevik Revolution of 1917,* Charles Scribner's Sons, 1967, and explores differences among Communists in *The Conscience of the Revolution,* Harvard U. Press, 1960. A classic work by a historian, socialist, and participant is S. P. Melgunov, *The Bolshevik Seizure of Power,* ABC-Clio Press, 1972; a memorable eyewitness account by an American Communist is John Reed, *Ten Days That Shook the World,* International Publishers, 1919. Two recent independent leftist reevaluations: Stephen Cohen, *Rethinking the Soviet Experience: Politics and History Since 1917,* Oxford U. Press, 1985, and Roy A. Medvedev, *The October Revolution,* trans., Columbia U. Press, 1979.

On the early years of Soviet rule: Oliver H. Radkey's *Russia Goes to the Polls: The Elections to the All-Russian Constituent Assembly, 1917,* Cornell U. Press, 1990; and *The Sickle Under the Hammer: The Russian Socialist Revolutionaries in the Early Months of Soviet Rule,* Columbia U. Press, 1963; Vladimir Brovkin, *The Mensheviks After October: Socialist Opposition and the Rise of the Bolshevik Dictatorship,* Cornell U. Press, 1988; T. H. Rigby, *Lenin's Government: Sovnarkom 1917–1922,* Cambridge U. Press, 1979; Leonard Schapiro, *The Origin of the Communist Autocracy, 1917–1922,* Praeger, 1965, on Communist treatment of opposition parties (but not the Whites); Lennard G. Gerson, *The Secret Police in Lenin's Russia* (up to 1926), Temple U. Press, 1976; George Leggett, *The Cheka: Lenin's Political Police* (covers 1917–1922), Clarendon Press, 1981; Ronald I. Kowalski, *The Bolshevik Party in Conflict: The Left Communist Opposition of 1918,* Pittsburgh U. Press, 1991; J. W. Wheeler-Bennett, *The Forgotten Peace: Brest-Litovsk, March 1918,* Macmillan, 1939; Robert D. Warth, *The Allies and the Russian Revolution: From the Fall of the Monarchy to the Peace of Brest-Litovsk,* Duke U. Press, 1954. For sources: John Bunyan and H. H. Fisher, eds., *The Bolshevik Revolution, 1917–1918.* Stanford U. Press, 1934.

9. The Civil War (1917–1921)

On War Communism: Thomas Remington, *Building Socialism in Bolshevik Russia: Ideology and Industrial Organization, 1917–1921*, U. of Pittsburgh Press, 1984. A thorough account is Evan Mawdsley, *The Russian Civil War*, Allen & Unwin, 1987. See also George A. Brinkley, *The Volunteer Army and Allied Intervention in South Russia, 1917–1921*, Notre Dame U. Press, 1966; Peter Kenez's two books, *Civil War in South Russia, 1918*, 1971, and *Civil War in South Russia, 1919–1920*, 1977, both U. of California Press; J.F.N. Bradley, *Civil War in Russia, 1917–1920*, London, B. T. Batsford, 1975; Arthur E. Adams, *Bolsheviks in the Ukraine: The Second Campaign, 1918–1919*, Yale U. Press, 1963; Oleh S. Fedyshyn, *Germany's Drive to the East and the Ukrainian Revolution, 1917–1918*, Rutgers U. Press, 1971; Richard Luckett, *The White Generals*, Viking Press, 1917; and John M. Thompson, *Russia, Bolshevism, and the Versailles Peace*, Princeton U. Press, 1966.

On international relations and intervention: George F. Kennan, *Soviet-American Relations, 1917–1920*, Vol. 1, *Russia Leaves the War*, 1956, and Vol. 2, *The Decision to Intervene*, 1958, both Princeton U. Press; Richard H. Ullman, *Anglo-Soviet Relations, 1917–1921*, 3 vols., Princeton U. Press, 1916–1973; John Silverlight, *The Victors' Dilemma*, Weybright and Talley, 1970; Leonid I. Strakhovsky, *The Origins of American Intervention in North Russia*, 1937, and *Intervention at Archangel*, 1944, both Princeton U. Press, John A. White, *The Siberian Intervention*, Princeton U. Press, 1950; Betty M. Unterberger, *America's Siberian Expedition, 1918–1920*, Duke U. Press, 1956; James William Morley, *The Japanese Thrust Into Siberia, 1918*, Columbia U. Press, 1957; Michael Jabara Carley, *Revolution and Intervention: The French Government and the Russian Civil War, 1917–1920*, McGill-Queen's U. Press, 1983; John Swettenham, *Allied Intervention in Russia, 1918–1919, and the Part Played by Canada*, London, Allen and Unwin, 1967; Canfield F. Smith, *Vladivostok Under Red and White Rule: Revolution and Counterrevolution in the Russian Far East, 1920–1922*, U. of Washington Press, 1975.

On the internal unrest: Oliver H. Radkey, *The Unknown Civil War in Soviet Russia: A Study of the Green Movement in the Tambov Region, 1920–1921*, Hoover Institution Press, 1976; Orlando Figes, *Peasant Russia, Civil War: The Volga Countryside in Revolution, 1917–1921*, Oxford U. Press, 1989; Michael Palij, *The Anarchism of Nestor Makhno, 1918–1921*, U. of Washington Press, 1976. On the war with Poland: Piotr S. Wandycz, *Soviet-Polish Relations, 1917–1921*, Harvard U. Press, 1969; Thomas C. Fiddick, *Russia's Retreat From Poland, 1920*, St. Martin's Press, 1990. Of Serge A. Zenkovsky, *Pan-Turkism and Islam in Russia*, Harvard U. Press, 1960, over half deals with the period of the Revolution and Civil War.

For documents consult John Bunyan, ed. *Intervention, Civil War and Communism in Russia: April–December 1918*, Johns Hopkins Press, 1936, and Elena Varneck and H. H. Fisher, eds., *The Testimony of Kolchak and Other Siberian Materials*, Stanford U. Press, 1935. Portions of the memoirs of two other White generals are translated: Anton I. Denikin, *The Russian Turmoil*, London, Hutchinson, 1922 (on the period before October 1917) and *The White Army*, London, Jonathan Cape, 1930; *The Memoirs of General Wrangel*, Duffield, 1930. A biography of one of them is Dmitry V. Lehovich, *White Against Red: The Life of General Anton Denikin*, Norton, 1974.

10. Lenin and the New Economic Policy

What followed Lenin's death is dealt with in Nina Tumarkin, *Lenin Lives: The Lenin Cult in Soviet Russia*, Harvard U. Press, 1983. For what triggered NEP: Israel Getzler, *Kronstadt,*

1917–1921: The Fate of a Soviet Democracy, Cambridge U. Press, 1983; Paul Avrich, *Kronstadt, 1921,* Princeton U. Press, 1970. An attempt at a social history of NEP is Lewis H. Siegelbaum, *Soviet State and Society Between Revolutions, 1918–1929,* Cambridge U. Press, 1992; see also Benjamin M. Weissman, *Herbert Hoover and Famine Relief to Soviet Russia, 1921–1923,* Hoover Institution Press, 1974; Alan M. Ball, *Russia's Last Capitalists: The Nepmen, 1921–1929,* U. of California Press, 1988; Olga A. Narkiewicz, *The Making of the Soviet State Apparatus,* Manchester U. Press, 1970.

A good introduction to the way the Soviet economy worked is Alec Nove, *The Soviet Economic System,* 3d ed., Allen and Unwin, 1986. His *An Economic History of the USSR, 1917–1991,* Penguin, 1993, is authoritative. A revealing work is Naum Jasny, *Soviet Economists of the Twenties: Names To Be Remembered,* Cambridge U. Press, 1972. A useful work: Kendall Bailes, *Technology and Society Under Lenin and Stalin: Origins of the Soviet Technical Intelligentsia, 1917–1941,* Princeton U. Press, 1978. Arguing the crucial importance of Western assistance is the three-volume work of Anthony C. Sutton, *Western Technology and Soviet Economic Development, 1917–1930* and *1930–1945,* both 1971, and *1945–1965,* 1973, all from Hoover Institution Press. More favorable to East-West trade: Glen Alden Smith, *Soviet Foreign Trade: Organization, Operation, and Policy, 1918–1971,* Praeger, 1973. Instructive and sometimes shocking: Jovan Pavlevski, *Le niveau de vie en URSS de la révolution d'octobre à 1980,* Paris Economica, 1975.

The best account of Soviet government up to that time is Merle Fainsod, *How Russia Is Ruled,* rev. ed., Harvard U. Press, 1963; nominally a revision but really a new book is Jerry F. Hough and Merle Fainsod, *How the Soviet Union Is Governed,* Harvard U. Press, 1979. See also John S. Reshetar, *The Soviet Polity,* Harper & Row, 3rd ed., 1989, which inquires into the prerevolutionary background; and Robert J. Osborn, *The Evolution of Soviet Politics,* Dorsey Press, 1974, which covers the time from Lenin to Khrushchëv. On Soviet law: an overview is Harold J. Berman, *Justice in the USSR: An Interpretation of Soviet Law,* rev. ed., Harvard U. Press, 1963; John Hazard, *Law and Social Change in the USSR,* reprint ed., Hyperion Press, 1987, on the interwar period; F. J. M. Feldbrugge, *Russian Law,* Martinus Nijhoff, 1993, on the post-1991 scene.

Surveys of the whole Soviet period: Mikhail Heller and Aleksandr M. Nekrich, *Utopia in Power: The History of the Soviet Union From 1917 to the Present,* Summit Books, 1986, especially good on politics; John Löwenhardt, James Ozingas, and Erik van Ree, *The Rise and Fall of the Soviet Politburo,* St. Martin's Press, 1992, covering 1919–1990; on certain topics, Barbara Evans Clements, *Daughters of Revolution: A History of Women in the USSR,* Harlan Davidson, 1993; Robert Edelman, *Serious Fun: A History of Spectator Sports in the USSR,* Oxford U. Press, 1993; James Riordan, *Sport in Soviet Society,* Cambridge U. Press, 1977.

11. Stalin, Trotsky, and Bukharin

The best one-volume treatment of Stalin is Adam B. Ulam, *Stalin: The Man and His Era,* Viking, 1973. Two volumes of a psychologically oriented trilogy have appeared: Robert C. Tucker, *Stalin as Revolutionary, 1879–1929,* 1973, and *Stalin in Power: The Revolution From Above, 1928–1941,* 1990, both by Norton. See also Dmitry Volkogonov, *Stalin: Triumph and Tragedy,* trans., Grove Weidenfeld, 1991, and Robert H. McNeal, *Stalin: Man and Ruler,* New York U. Press, 1988. Isaac Deutscher's trilogy on Trotsky (Oxford U. Press) remains unsuperseded: *The Prophet Armed, 1879–1921,* 1954; *The Prophet Unarmed, 1921–1929,* 1959; and *The Prophet Outcast, 1929–1940,* 1963. Good biographies: Stephen F. Cohen, *Bukharin and the Bolshevik Revolution,* Knopf, 1973; Warren Lerner, *Karl Radek: The Last Internationalist,* Stanford University Press, 1970.

Monographs include: Moshe Lewin, *Political Undercurrents in Soviet Economic Debates: From Bukharin to the Modern Reformers,* Princeton U. Press, 1974; Alexander Erlich, *The Soviet Industrialization Debate, 1924–1928,* Harvard U. Press, 1960, which focuses on the debate between Bukharin and Preobrazhensky; and Stephan Merl, *Der Agrarmarkt und die Neue Okonomische Politik: Die Anfänge staatlicher Lenkung der Landwirtschaft in der Sowjetunion, 1925–1928,* München and Wien, Oldenbourg Verlag, 1981, a solid study depicting a strong Soviet agriculture on the eve of a collectivization. Journalistic accounts including this period, favorable to the Soviets: Maurice Hindus, *Humanity Uprooted,* London, Jonathan Cape, 1931, and Walter Duranty, *I Write as I Please,* London, Hamish Hamilton, 1937; unfavorable, Eugene Lyons, *Assignment in Utopia,* London, George G. Harrap & Co., 1983. Trotsky's own *The Real Situation in Russia,* Harcourt, Brace, 1928, and *The Revolution Betrayed,* Doubleday, 1937, both trans., are useful.

12. Finding a Soviet Foreign Policy (1917–1927)

The vast literature on the subject up to that point is evaluated in Thomas T. Hammond, ed., *Soviet Foreign Relations and World Communism: A Selected, Annotated Bibliography of 7,000 Books in 30 Languages,* Princeton U. Press, 1965. The best single-volume treatment is Adam B. Ulam, *Expansion and Coexistence: Soviet Foreign Policy, 1917–1973,* 2d ed., Praeger, 1974. See also George F. Kennan, *Russia and the West Under Lenin and Stalin,* Little, Brown, 1961, and Louis Fischer, *Russia's Road From Peace to War: Soviet Foreign Relations, 1917–1941,* Harper & Row, 1969. On the first year: Richard K. Debo, *Revolution and Survival: The Foreign Policy of Soviet Russia, 1917–1918,* U. of Toronto Press, 1979.

On the history of world Communism: Hugh Seton-Watson's careful survey, *From Lenin to Khrushchëv,* Praeger, 1960; the beginnings are treated in Branko Lazitch and Milorad M. Drachkovitch, *Lenin and the Comintern,* Vol. 1, Hoover Institution Press, 1972, and James W. Hulse, *The Forming of the Communist International,* Stanford U. Press, 1964. An excellent study: Theodore Draper, *American Communism and Soviet Russia,* Viking, 1960.

On activity in East Asia: David J. Dallin's *The Rise of Russia in Asia,* 1949 (up to 1931), and *Soviet Russia and the Far East,* 1948 (treats 1931–1949), both Yale U. Press; and Peter S. H. Tang, *Russian and Soviet Policy in Manchuria and Outer Mongolia, 1911–1931,* Duke U. Press, 1959; Allen S. Whiting, *Soviet Policies in China, 1917–1924,* Columbia U. Press, 1954; Conrad Brandt, *Stalin's Failure in China, 1924–1927,* Harvard U. Press, 1959; George Alexander Lensen, *The Damned Inheritance: The Soviet Union and the Manchurian Crises, 1924–1935,* Diplomatic Press, 1974. The Chinese Communist Party before takeover is the subject of Jacques Guillermaz, *A History of the Chinese Communist Party, 1921–1949,* trans., Random House, 1972; its whole history, James Pinckney Harrison, *The Long March to Power: A History of the Chinese Communist Party, 1921–1972,* Praeger, 1972; and Stephen Uhalley, Jr., *A History of the Chinese Communist Party* (through 1987), Hoover Institution Press, 1988.

On the Soviets and Western Europe: Stephen White, *The Origins of Detente: The Genoa Conference and Soviet-Western Relations, 1921–1922,* Cambridge U. Press, 1985; Albert S. Lindemann, *The "Red Years": European Socialism Versus Bolshevism, 1919–1921,* U. of California Press, 1974; Gabriel Gorodetsky, *The Precarious Truce: Anglo-Soviet Relations, 1924–1927,* Cambridge U. Press, 1977; Ronald Tiersky, *French Communism, 1920–1972,* Columbia U. Press, 1974; Werner T. Angress, *Stillborn Revolution: The Communist Bid for Power in*

Germany, 1921–1923, Princeton U. Press, 1963; Ruth Fischer's classic *Stalin and German Communism,* Harvard U. Press, 1948, which stops at 1929; and Gerald Freund, *Unholy Alliance: Russo-German Relations from the Treaty of Brest-Litovsk to the Treaty of Berlin,* Harcourt, Brace, and World, 1957.

13. The Revolution, the Arts, and the Church (1917–1927)

A fine study of the arts Russia lost by revolution: Marc Raeff, *Russia Abroad: A Cultural History of the Russian Emigration, 1919–1939,* Oxford U. Press, 1990. For what she kept, at least for a time: two books by Richard Stites, *Revolutionary Dreams: Utopian Vision and Experimental Life in the Russian Revolution,* Oxford U. Press, 1989, and *Russian Popular Culture: Entertainment and Society Since 1990,* Cambridge U. Press, 1992; Christopher Read, *Culture and Power in Revolutionary Russia,* St. Martin's Press, 1990; Lynn Mally, *Culture of the Future: The Proletkult Movement in Revolutionary Russia,* U. of California Press, 1990; Halina Stephan, *"LEF" and the Left Front of Arts,* Munich, Otto Sagner, 1981; Kurt London, *The Seven Soviet Arts,* Yale U. Press, 1938; Peter Kenez, *Cinema and Soviet Society, 1917–1953,* Cambridge U. Press, 1992; Richard Taylor, *The Politics of the Soviet Cinema, 1917–1929,* Cambridge U. Press, 1979.

The best survey of literature in the Soviet period is Edward J. Brown, *Russian Literature Since the Revolution,* rev. ed., Harvard U. Press, 1982 (but note errors, *Slavic Review,* Winter 1983, pp. 724–725); see also Gleb Struve, *Russian Literature Under Lenin and Stalin, 1917–1953,* U. of Oklahoma Press, 1971. Two works relating literature to its milieu: Ronald Hingley, *Russian Writers and Soviet Society, 1917–1958,* Random House, 1979, and Boris Thomson, *The Premature Revolution: Russian Literature and Society, 1917–1946,* London, Weidenfeld and Nicolson, 1972. Studies of limited aspects: Robert A. Maguire, *Red Virgin Soil: Soviet Literature in the 1920's,* Princeton U. Press, 1968; Milton Ehre, *Babel,* Twayne, 1986; Simon Karlinsky, *Marina Tsvetaeva: The Woman, Her Worlds and Her Poetry,* Cambridge U. Press, 1985. Of special interest: Leon Trotsky, *Literature and Revolution,* trans., reprinted, U. of Michigan Press, 1960, and Max Eastman, *Artists in Uniform,* London, Allen & Unwin, 1934. Two studies of a critic active in the 1920's (though he lived until 1975) but influential in the West only recently: Katerina Clark and Michael Holquist, *Mikhail Bakhtin,* Harvard U. Press, 1986, and Tzvetan Todorov, *Mikhail Bakhtin: The Dialogical Principle,* trans., U. of Minnesota Press, 1986. On art: John Milner, *Vladimir Tatlin and the Russian Avant-Garde,* Yale U. Press, 1983; on music, Boris Schwarz, *Music and Musical Life in Soviet Russia, 1917–1981,* enlarged ed., Indiana U. Press, 1983, and S. Frederick Starr, *Red and Hot: The Fate of Jazz in the Soviet Union, 1917–1980,* Oxford U. Press, 1983. On scholarship: Alexander S. Vucinich, *Empire of Knowledge: The Academy of Sciences of the USSR, 1917–1970,* U. of California Press, 1984, and Loren R. Graham, *Science and Philosophy in the Soviet Union,* Knopf, 1972. Sheila Fitzpatrick studies *Education and Social Mobility in the Soviet Union, 1921–1934,* Cambridge U. Press, 1979, and official policy toward culture in *The Commissariat of Enlightenment,* Cambridge U. Press, 1971; see also Timothy E. O'Connor, *The Politics of Soviet Culture: Anatolii Lunacharskii,* UMI Research, 1983.

On the church, the best single work is Dimitry Pospielovsky, *The Russian Church Under the Soviet Regime, 1917–1982,* 2 vols., St. Vladimir's Seminary Press, 1984; see also his *A History of Soviet Atheism in Theory and Practice, and the Believer,* 3 vols., St. Martin's Press, 1987–1988; Richard H. Marshall, Jr., Thomas E. Bird, and Andrew Q. Blane, eds. *Aspects of*

Religion in the Soviet Union, 1917–1967, U. of Chicago Press, 1971, and John S. Curtiss, *The Russian Church and the Soviet State, 1917–1950,* Little, Brown, 1953.

14. Stalin and the First Five-Year Plan (1928–1932)

A Leninist critique of Stalinism is Roy A. Medvedev, *Let History Judge: The Origins and Consequences of Stalinism,* Knopf, 1972; an illuminating memoir by an intellectual survivor of the Stalin era is Nadezhda Mandelstam, *Hope Against Hope,* Atheneum, 1970; *Hope Abandoned,* Macmillan, 1981. On industry: Michal Reiman, *The Birth of Stalinism: The USSR on the Eve of the "Second Revolution,"* trans., Indiana U. Press, 1987; Hiroaki Kuromiya, *Stalin's Industrial Revolution,* Cambridge U. Press, 1988; Naum Jasny, *Soviet Industrialization, 1928–1952,* U. of Chicago Press, 1961; Abram Bergson, *The Real National Income of Soviet Russia Since 1982,* Harvard U. Press, 1961, and G. Warren Nutter, *The Growth of Industrial Production in The Soviet Union,* Princeton U. Press, 1962. Eyewitness accounts include W. H. Chamberlin, *Russia's Iron Age,* London, Duckworth, 1935, and John Scott, *Behind the Urals,* Houghton Mifflin, 1942.

On the Cheka and its successors: Ronald Hingley, *The Russian Secret Police: Muscovite, Imperial Russian and Soviet Political Security Operations, 1565–1970,* London, Hutchinson, 1970; Boris Levytsky, *The Uses of Terror: The Soviet Secret Police, 1917–1970,* Coward, McCann and Geoghegan, 1972; and Amy W. Knight, *The KGB: Police and Politics in the Soviet Union,* Unwin Hyman, 1988. On the trade unions, for the pre-1941 period see Solomon M. Schwartz, *Labor in the Soviet Union,* Praeger, 1952; for the period following, Emily Clark Brown, *Soviet Trade Unions and Labor Relations,* Harvard U. Press, 1966. On the armed forces, see Malcolm Mackintosh, *Juggernaut: A History of the Soviet Armed Forces,* London, Secker & Warburg, 1967; John Erickson, *The Soviet High Command: A Military-Political History, 1918–1942,* St. Martin's Press, 1962; and Roman Kolkowicz, *The Soviet Military and the Communist Party,* Princeton U. Press, 1967.

On the concentration camps: Michael Jakobson, *Origins of the Gulag: The Soviet Prison-Camp System, 1917–1934,* U. Press of Kentucky, 1992; Robert Conquest, *Kolyma: The Arctic Death Camps,* Viking, 1978; the book that brought popular comprehension of the phenomenon to the West: Aleksandr Solzhenitsyn, *The Gulag Archipelago, 1918–1956,* 3 vols., Harper & Row, 1974–1979; David J. Dallin and Boris I. Nicolaevsky, *Forced Labor in Soviet Russia,* Yale U. Press, 1947.

The most authoritative treatment of collectivization to date is Robert Conquest, *Harvest of Sorrow: Soviet Collectivization and the Terror Famine,* Oxford U. Press, 1986. See also Sheila Fitzpatrick, *Stalin's Peasants: Resistance and Survival in the Russian Village After Collectivization,* Oxford U. Press, 1994; M. Lewin, *Russian Peasants and Soviet Power: A Study of Collectivization,* trans., Northwestern U. Press, 1968; Naum Jasny, *The Socialized Agriculture of the USSR,* Stanford U. Press, 1949; and Roy D. Laird, *Collective Farming in Russia: A Political Study of Soviet Kolkhozy,* U. of Kansas Publications, 1958. A remarkable personal account is Fedor Belov, *A History of a Soviet Collective Farm,* Praeger, 1955. Authoritative for the period is Franklyn D. Holzman, *Soviet Taxation,* Harvard U. Press, 1955.

15. The Consolidation of Totalitarianism (1933–1941)

A judicious study is John A. Armstrong, *The Politics of Totalitarianism: The Communist Party of the Soviet Union from 1934 to the Present,* Random House, 1961; a somewhat different appraisal is given in Alec Nove, *Stalinism and After*, London, Allen & Unwin, 1975; more detailed is Lewis H. Siegelbaum, *Stakhanovism and the Politics of Productivity in the USSR, 1935–1941*, Cambridge U. Press, 1988. On the Komsomol, see Ralph T. Fisher, Jr., *Pattern for Soviet Youth*, Columbia U. Press, 1959. A work based on captured local archives is Merle Fainsod, *Smolensk Under Soviet Rule*, Harvard U. Press, 1958. Two books based on the Harvard refugee interview project: Raymond A. Bauer, Alex Inkeles, and Clyde Kluckhohn, *How the Soviet System Works*, and Inkeles and Bauer, *The Soviet Citizen*, Harvard U. Press, 1956 and 1960. Useful accounts by former Communists include Victor Serge, *Memoirs of a Revolutionary, 1901–1941*, trans., Oxford U. Press, 1963, and Boris Souvarine, *Stalin: A Critical Survey of Bolshevism*, Alliance Book Co., 1939.

On the purges, see the two books by Robert Conquest, *The Great Terror: A Reassessment*, Oxford U. Press, 1991, and *Inside Stalin's Secret Police: NKVD Politics, 1936–1939*, Hoover Institution Press, 1985; Alex Weissberg, *The Accused*, trans., Simon and Schuster, 1951; Anna Larina, *This I Cannot Forget: The Memoirs of Bukharin's Widow*, Norton, 1993; and Amy Knight, *Beria: Stalin's First Lieutenant*, Princeton U. Press, 1993. Famous novelistic treatments of the purges are Arthur Koestler, *Darkness at Noon*, Bantam, 1966, and Victor Serge, *The Case of Comrade Tulayev*, Anchor, 1963; of the Soviet system in general, Eugene Zamiatin, *We*, Dutton, 1959, and George Orwell, *1984*, New American Library, 1983.

16. Lenin, Stalin, and the Non-Russians

The potential for disruption among the minorities is the subject of Hélène Carrère d'Encausse, *Decline of an Empire: The Soviet Socialist Republics in Revolt*, trans., Newsweek Books, 1979. Systematic introductory information is found in Ronald Wixman, *The Peoples of the USSR: An Ethnographic Handbook*, M. E. Sharpe, 1984. Soviet treatment of minorities is surveyed in Bogdan Nahaylo and Victor Swoboda, *Soviet Disunion: A History of the Nationalities Problem in the USSR*, Free Press, 1990. Stalin's wartime genocide is studied in Robert Conquest, *The Nation Killers*, Macmillan, 1970.

On Ukraine: Robert S. Sullivant, *Soviet Politics and the Ukraine, 1917–1957*, Columbia U. Press, 1962; Basil Dmytryshyn, *Moscow and the Ukraine, 1918–1953*, Bookman Associates, 1956; Alexander J. Motyl, *The Turn to the Right: The Ideological Origins and Development of Ukrainian Nationalism, 1919–1929*, East European Monographs, 1980; Hryhory Kostiuk, *Stalinist Rule in the Ukraine: A Study of the Decade of Mass Terror, 1929–1939*, Munich, Institute for the Study of the USSR, 1960; and John A. Armstrong, *Ukrainian Nationalism, 1939–1945*, Columbia U. Press, 1955.

On other areas: Ivan S. Lubachko, *Belorussia Under Soviet Rule, 1917–1957*, U. of Kentucky Press, 1972; Alexandre Benningsen and S. Enders Wimbush, *Muslims of the Soviet Empire: A Guide*, Indiana U. Press, 1986; Olaf Caroe, *Soviet Empire: The Turks of Central Asia and Stalinism*, 2d ed., St. Martin's Press, 1967; Geoffrey Wheeler, *The Modern History of Soviet Central Asia*, Praeger, 1964; Wayne S. Vucinich, ed., *Russia and Asia: Essays on the Influence of Russia on the Asian Peoples*, Hoover Institution Press, 1972; Ingeborg Fleischhauer and Benjamin Pinkus, *The Soviet Germans: Past and Present*, St. Martin's Press, 1986; David Marshall Lang, *A Modern History of Soviet Georgia*, Grove Press, 1962; Mary Kilbourne Matossian, *The Impact of Soviet Policies on Armenia*, Leiden, Brill, 1962.

On the Jews: Salo Baron, *The Russian Jew Under Tsars and Soviets*, 2d ed., Schocken Books, 1987; Yehoshua Gilboa, *The Black Years of Soviet Jewry, 1939–1953*, trans., Little, Brown, 1971; Zvi Y. Gitelman, *Jewish Nationality and Soviet Politics: The Jewish Sections of the CPSU, 1917–1930*, Princeton U. Press, 1972; and Lionel Kochan, ed., *The Jews in Soviet Russia Since 1917*, Oxford U. Press, 1970. See also listing for Chapter 1.

17 and 18. Stalin's Diplomacy and World Communism (1927–1935 and 1936–1941)

Chapters on two foreign commissars, Chicherin and Litvinov, are included in Gordon Craig and Felix Gilbert, eds., *The Diplomats, 1919–1939*, Princeton U. Press, 1953. On U.S. recognition of the USSR: Robert P. Browder, *The Origins of Soviet-American Diplomacy*, Princeton U. Press, 1953; Thomas R. Maddux, *Years of Estrangement: American Relations with the Soviet Union, 1933–1941*, U. Presses of Florida, 1980; and Hugh De Santis, *The Diplomacy of Silence: The American Foreign Service, the Soviet Union, and the Cold War, 1933–1947*, U. of Chicago Press, 1980.

On other aspects of the period: E. H. Carr, *Twilight of the Comintern, 1930–1935*, Pantheon, 1983; Richard C. Thornton, *China, the Struggle for Power, 1917–1972*, Indiana U. Press, 1973; Charles B. McLane, *Soviet Policy and the Chinese Communists, 1931–1946*, Columbia U. Press, 1959; David T. Cattell's *Communism and the Spanish Civil War* and *Soviet Diplomacy and the Spanish Civil War*, U. of California Press, 1955 and 1957; Jonathan Maslam, *The Soviet Union and the Threat From the East, 1933–1941*, U. of Pittsburgh Press, 1992; Alvin D. Coox, *Nomonhan: Japan Against Russia*, 2 vols. (mammoth study of the fighting of May 1939), Stanford U. Press, 1985; Jiri Hochman, *The Soviet Union and the Failure of Collective Security, 1934–1938*, Cornell U. Press, 1984; Gerhard Weinberg, *Germany and the Soviet Union 1939–1941*, Leiden, Brill, 1954; Allen F. Chew, *The White Death* (on the Winter War with Finland), Michigan State U. Press, 1971; Keith Sword, ed., *The Soviet Takeover of the Polish Eastern Provinces, 1939–1941*, St. Martin's Press, 1991.

For sources: Xenia J. Eudin and Robert M. Slusser, *Soviet Foreign Policy, 1928–1934: Documents and Materials*, Pennsylvania U. Press, 1967; and Raymond J. Sontag and James S. Beddie, eds., *Nazi-Soviet Relations, 1938–1941: Documents from the Archives of the German Foreign Office*, U.S. Department of State, 1948. (See also listing for Chapter 12.)

19. Stalin's Cultural Policy (1927–1945)

For the RAPP period of literary policy: Edward J. Brown, *The Proletarian Episode in Russian Literature, 1928–1932*, Columbia U. Press, 1953. A longer period in a single republic is treated in George S. N. Luckyj, *Literary Politics in the Soviet Ukraine, 1917–1934*, Columbia U. Press, 1956. See also Sheila Fitzpatrick, ed., *Cultural Revolution in Russia, 1928–1931*, Indiana U. Press, 1978; Vera Dunham, *In Stalin's Time: Middleclass Values in Soviet Fiction*, Cambridge U. Press, 1976; Victor Erlich, *Russian Formalism: History—Doctrine*, The Hague, Mouton, 1955; and Ernest J. Simmons, *Russian Fiction and Soviet Ideology: An Introduction to Fedin, Leonov and Sholokhov*, Columbia U. Press, 1958; Stanley D. Krebs, *Soviet Composers and the Development of Soviet Music*, Norton, 1970.

On Soviet education: Oskar Anweiler, *Geschichte der Schule und Pädagogik in Russland, vom Ende des Zarenreiches bis zum Beginn der Stalin-Ära*, Heidelberg, Quelle & Meyer, 1964; Nicholas DeWitt, *Education and Professional Employment in the USSR*, National Science Foundation, 1961; and Merwyn Matthews, *Education in the Soviet Union: Policies and Institutions Since Stalin*, Allen & Unwin, 1982. On Soviet philosophy: Gustav Wetter, *Dialec-*

tical Materialism; A Historical and Systematic Survey of Philosophy in the Soviet Union, Greenwood Press, 1973; Innocentius M. Bochenski, *Soviet Russian Dialectical Materialism,* Dordrecht, Reidel, 1963; Henri Chambre, *From Marx to Mao Tse-tung,* trans. Kennedy, 1963. (See also listing for Chapter 2.)

20 and 21. The USSR in World War II: The Military Crisis (1941–1943) and Political Successes (1943–1945)

Two excellent recent books survey the entire war: John Keegan, *The Second World War,* Viking, 1990, and Martin Gilbert, *The Second World War: A Complete History,* H. Holt, 1989. A fine one-volume treatment of the Soviet part is Albert Seaton, *The Russo-German War, 1941–1945,* Praeger, 1971; admirable are John Erickson's *The Road to Stalingrad,* Harper & Row, 1975, and *The Road to Berlin,* Westview, 1983. On the internal impact: John Barber and Mark Harrison, *The Soviet Home Front 1941–1945: A Social and Economic History of the USSR in World War II,* Longman, 1991; Alexander Dallin, *German Rule in Russia, 1941–1945,* rev. ed., Westview, 1981. On certain regions, cities, and institutions: Ihor Kamenetsky, *Hitler's Occupation of the Ukraine, 1941–1944,* Marquette U. Press, 1956; Leon Gouré and Herbert S. Dinerstein, *Moscow in Crisis,* Free Press, 1955; Leon Gouré, *The Siege of Leningrad,* Stanford U. Press, 1962; Harrison Salisbury, *The 900 Days: The Siege of Leningrad,* Harper & Row, 1969; Wassilij Alexeev and Theofanis G. Stavrou, *The Great Revival: The Russian Church Under German Occupation,* Burgess Publishing Co., 1976, and, on the same subject, Harvey Fireside, *Icon and Swastika,* Harvard U. Press, 1971. On the Vlasov movement: Up-to-date, judicious studies are Catherine Andreyev, *Vlasov and the Russian Liberation Movement: Soviet Reality and Émigré Theories,* Cambridge U. Press, 1987, and Joachim Hoffman, *Die Geschichte der Wlassow-Armee,* Freiburg, Rombach, 1984; see also Wilfred Strik-Strikfeldt, *Against Stalin and Hitler,* John Day Co., 1973. A good military analysis is Edgar M. Howell, *The Soviet Partisan Movement, 1941–1944,* U.S. Department of the Army, 1956. On the Katyn murders: Allen Paul, *Katyn: The Untold Story of Stalin's Polish Massacre,* Scribner's, 1991, and J. K. Zawodny, *Death in the Forest,* Notre Dame U. Press, 1962.

On Soviet relations with the Poles, see Edward J. Rozek, *Allied Wartime Diplomacy: A Pattern in Poland,* Wiley, 1958, and Jan M. Ciechanowski, *The Warsaw Rising of 1944,* Cambridge U. Press, 1974. On diplomacy with the Allies: William Taubman, *Stalin's American Policy: From Entente to Detente to Cold War,* Norton, 1984; R. F. Fenno, Jr., ed., *The Yalta Conference,* D. C. Heath, 1955; John L. Snell, ed., *The Meaning of Yalta,* Louisiana State U. Press, 1956; Herbert Feis, *Churchill—Roosevelt—Stalin* and *Between War and Peace: The Potsdam Conference,* both Princeton U. Press, 1957 and 1960. George Alexander Lensen studies *The Strange Neutrality: Soviet-Japanese Relations During the Second World War, 1941–1945,* Diplomatic Press, 1972.

22. Communist Expansion in Europe (1945–1953)

The masterwork is Hugh Seton-Watson, *The East European Revolution,* 3rd ed., Praeger, 1956, which covers the period 1939–1955 with a sure touch.

On the individual countries: Paul E. Zinner, *Communist Strategy and Tactics in Czechoslovakia, 1918–1948,* Praeger, 1963; Joseph Korbel, *The Communist Subversion of Czechoslo-*

vakia, 1938–1948, Princeton U. Press, 1959; M. K. Dziewanowski, *The Communist Party of Poland,* 2d ed., Harvard U. Press, 1976; Richard F. Staar, *Poland, 1944–1962: The Sovietization of a Captive People,* Louisiana State U. Press, 1962; Stanley M. Max, *The United States, Great Britain, and the Sovietization of Hungary, 1945–1948,* East European Monographs, 1985; Henry Krisch, *German Politics Under Soviet Occupation* (i.e., East Germany), Columbia U. Press, 1974; David Childs, *The GDR: Moscow's German Ally,* Allen & Unwin, 1983; J. F. Brown, *Bulgaria Under Communist Rule,* Praeger, 1970; Kenneth Jowitt, *Revolutionary Breakthroughs and National Development: The Case of Romania, 1944–1965,* U. of California Press, 1971; Stephen Fischer-Galati, *The New Rumania: From People's Democracy to Socialist Republic,* MIT Press, 1967; Paul Lendvai, *Eagles in Cobwebs: Nationalism and Communism in the Balkans,* Doubleday, 1969; Walter R. Roberts, *Tito, Mihailovic and the Allies, 1941–1945,* Rutgers U. Press, 1973; Phyllis Auty, *Tito: A Biography,* McGraw-Hill, 1970; an insider's view is found in Vladimir Dedijer, *Tito,* Simon and Schuster, 1953, and Milovan Djilas, *The New Class,* Praeger, 1957 (a classic dealing with Communism in general); Adam B. Ulam, *Titoism and the Cominform,* Harvard U. Press, 1952.

On countries where Communism did not win: D. G. Kousoulas, *Revolution and Defeat: The Story of the Greek Communist Party,* Oxford U. Press, 1965; John Louis Hondros, *Occupation and Resistance: The Greek Agony 1941–1944,* Pella Publishing Co., 1983; Roy Allison, *Finland's Relations with the Soviet Union, 1944–1984,* Macmillan, 1985.

On Soviet foreign relations in general during these years: Roy Douglas, *From War to Cold War, 1942–1948,* St. Martin's Press, 1981; Joseph L. Nogee and Robert H. Donaldson, *Soviet Foreign Policy Since World War II,* Pergamon Press, 1982; Alvin A. Rubinstein, *Soviet Foreign Policy Since World War II,* Winthrop Publishers, 1981. Much has been published on Soviet-U.S. relations and the Cold War, a good deal of it weakened by the authors' lack of knowledge of the USSR and Eastern Europe. Recommended: Adam B. Ulam, *The Rivals: America and Russia Since World War II,* Penguin, 1976, and *The Communists: The Story of Power and Lost Illusions, 1948–1991,* Charles Scribner's Sons, 1992; Lynn Etheridge Davis, *The Cold War Begins: Soviet-American Conflict over Eastern Europe,* Princeton U. Press, 1974; John L. Gaddis, *The United States and the Origins of the Cold War, 1941–1947,* Columbia U. Press, 1972; Hugh Thomas, *Armed Truce; The Beginnings of the Cold War 1945–46,* Atheneum, 1987; on the historiography rather than the history, Robert J. Maddox, *The New Left and the Origins of the Cold War,* Princeton U. Press, 1973. Useful is Bruce D. Porter, *The USSR in Third World Conflicts: Soviet Arms and Diplomacy in Local Wars, 1945–1980,* Cambridge U. Press, 1984.

23. Communist Expansion in Asia (1945–1956)

On China: Herbert Feis, *The China Tangle,* Princeton U. Press, 1953; Tang Tsou, *America's Failure in China, 1941–1950,* U. of Chicago Press, 1963; the U.S. State Department White Paper, *United States Relations with China, 1949,* concentrates on the period 1944–1949; Suzanne Pepper, *Civil War in China: The Political Struggle, 1945–1949,* U. of California Press, 1977; Richard L. Walker, *China Under Communism: The First Five Years,* Yale U. Press, 1955; Doak Barnett, *Communist China: The Early Years 1949–1955,* Praeger, 1964; Jurgen Domes's two books, *The Internal Politics of China, 1949–1972,* Praeger, 1973, and *Socialism in the Chinese Countryside: Rural Societal Policies in the People's Republic of China, 1949–1979,* McGill-Queen's U. Press, 1980; Roderick MacFarquhar's three volumes, *The Hundred Flow-*

ers Campaign and the Chinese Intellectuals, Praeger, 1960, and *The Origins of the Cultural Revolution*, 2 vols., Columbia U. Press, 1974 and 1983; Stuart Schram, *Mao Tse-tung*, rev. ed., Simon and Schuster, 1969.

On other Asian countries: Rodger Swearingen and Paul Langer, *Red Flag in Japan: International Communism in Action, 1919–1951*, Harvard U. Press, 1952; Robert A. Scalapino, *The Japanese Communist Movement, 1920–1966*, U. of California Press, 1967; Scalapino and Chong-Sik Lee, *Communism in Korea*, 2 vols., U of California Press, 1972; Galia Golan, *Soviet Policies in the Middle East: From World War II to Gorbachev*, Cambridge U. Press, 1990; Frank N. Trager, *Marxism in Southeast Asia*, Stanford U. Press, 1959; Robert F. Turner, *Vietnamese Communism: Its Origins and Development*, Hoover Institution Press, 1975; Donald Hindley, *The Communist Party of Indonesia, 1951–1963*, U. of California Press, 1964; David N. Druhe, *Soviet Russian and Indian Communism, 1917–1947*, Bookman Associates, 1959; Arthur Stein, *India and the Soviet Union: The Nehru Era*, U. of Chicago Press, 1969. Broader treatments: Charles B. McLane, *Soviet Strategies in Southeast Asia*, Princeton U. Press, 1966, and Russell D. Buhite, *Soviet-American Relations in Asia, 1945–1954*, U. of Oklahoma Press, 1981.

24. Stalin's Retrenchment (1945–1953)

On forced repatriation, see especially Mark R. Elliott, *Pawns of Yalta: Soviet Refugees and America's Role in Their Repatriation*, U. of Illinois Press, 1982 and Nikolai Tolstoy, *Victims of Yalta*, Hodder and Stoughton, London, 1977; on the spy network, see David J. Dallin, *Soviet Espionage*, Yale U. Press, 1955, and Otto Heilbrunn, *The Soviet Secret Services*, Praeger, 1956.

General treatments of the period: Timothy Dunmore, *Soviet Politics, 1945–1953*, and *The Stalinist Command Economy: The Soviet State Apparatus and Economic Policy, 1945–1953*, both St. Martin's Press, 1984 and 1980. On the Zhdanovshchina and related developments: Werner G. Hahn, *The Fall of Zhdanov and the Defeat of Moderation, 1946–1953*, Cornell U. Press, 1982, and George S. Counts and Nucia Lodge, *The Country of the Blind*, Houghton Mifflin, 1959. David Joravsky provides a careful account of *The Lysenko Affair*, Harvard U. Press, 1970. On other aspects of the period: C. E. Black, ed., *Rewriting Russian History*, Praeger, 1956; Robert C. Stuart, *The Collective Farm in Soviet Agriculture*, Lexington Books, 1972; Marshall D. Shulman, *Stalin's Foreign Policy Reappraised*, Harvard U. Press, 1963; Yakov Rapoport, *The Doctors' Plot of 1953*, Harvard U. Press, 1991, contains fascinating memoir and other material.

25. The Rise and Ascendancy of Khrushchëv (1953–1964)

The Khrushchëv period is the focus of Yosef Avidar, *The Party and the Army in the Soviet Union*, Jerusalem, Magnes, 1983. Fascinating in what they reveal of the author's attitudes, unreliable in detail: *Khrushchev Remembers* and *Khrushchev Remembers: The Last Testament*, Little, Brown, 1970 and 1974. Closest to a satisfactory political biography to date: Roy A. Medvedev, *Khrushchev*, Anchor, 1984. See also Edward Crankshaw, *Khrushchev: A Career*, Viking 1966; Carl A. Linden, *Khrushchev and the Soviet Leadership, 1957–1964*, Oxford U. Press, 1967; Michel Tatu, *Power in the Kremlin: From Khrushchev to Kosygin*, trans., Viking, 1969; William Hyland and Richard W. Shryock, *The Fall of Khrushchev* (on 1962–1964), Funk & Wagnalls, 1969; Thomas W. Wolfe, *Soviet Power and Europe, 1945–1970*, Johns

Hopkins U. Press, 1970; Wolfgang Leonhard, *The Kremlin Since Stalin*, trans., Praeger, 1962. On the revolts: Rainer Hildebrandt, *The Explosion* (on Berlin), trans., Duell, Sloan & Pearce, 1955; Stefan Brant, *The East German Rising*, Praeger, 1957; and Joseph Scholmer, *Vorkuta*, Holt, 1955.

On the Sino-Soviet dispute: Donald S. Zagoria, *The Sino-Soviet Conflict, 1955–1961*, Princeton U. Press, 1962; William E. Griffith, *Albania and the Sino-Soviet Rift*, MIT Press, 1963, and *The Sino-Soviet Rift*, Allen & Unwin, 1964; Herbert J. Ellison, ed., *The Sino-Soviet Conflict*, U. of Washington Press, 1982; Chin O. Chung, *Pyongyang Between Peking and Moscow: North Korea's Involvement in the Sino-Soviet Dispute, 1958–1975*, U. of Alabama Press, 1978. On the "secret speech": Bertram D. Wolfe, *Khrushchev and Stalin's Ghost*, Praeger, 1957. On the Polish and Hungarian events: Konrad Syrop, *Spring in October: The Polish Revolution of 1956*, Praeger, 1958; Paul E. Zinner, *Revolution in Hungary*, Columbia U. Press, 1962; Ferenc A. Vali, *Rift and Revolt in Hungary*, Harvard U. Press, 1961.

On certain aspects of the period: Kenneth C. Farmer, *Ukrainian Nationalism in the Post-Stalin Era*, The Hague, Nijhoff, 1980; William Taubman, *The View From Lenin Hills: Soviet Youth in Ferment*, Coward-McCann, 1967; Harold Swayze, *Political Control of Literature in the USSR, 1946–1959*, Harvard U. Press, 1962; George Gibian, *Interval of Freedom: Soviet Literature During the Thaw, 1954–1957*, U. of Minnesota Press, 1960; Robert Conquest, *The Pasternak Affair*, Lippincott, 1962; Deming Brown, *Soviet Russian Literature Since Stalin*, Cambridge U. Press, 1978; Priscilla Johnson, ed., *Khrushchev and the Arts: The Politics of Soviet Culture, 1962–1964*, MIT Press, 1965; Val S. Golovskoy, with John Rimberg, *Behind the Soviet Screen: The Motion Picture Industry in the USSR 1972–1982*, Ardis, 1986; Martin McCauley, *Khrushchev and the Development of Soviet Agriculture: The Virgin Lands Programme, 1953–1964*, Holmes and Meier, 1976; Richard T. DeGeorge, *The New Marxism: Soviet and East European Marxism since 1956*, Pegasus, 1968; Robert M. Slusser, *The Berlin Crisis of 1961*, Johns Hopkins U. Press, 1973; Herbert S. Dinerstein, *The Making of a Missile Crisis, October 1962*, Johns Hopkins U. Press, 1976; David J. Dallin, *Soviet Foreign Policy After Stalin*, Lippincott, 1961; Helen Desfosses Cohn, *Soviet Policy Toward Black Africa*, Praeger, 1972; William E. Ratliff, *Castroism and Communism in Latin America, 1959–1976*, American Enterprise Institute, 1976; Jacques Levesque, *The USSR and the Cuban Revolution: Soviet Ideological and Strategic Perspectives, 1959–1977*, Praeger, 1978; and Michael R. Beschloss, *Mayday: Eisenhower, Khrushchev, and the U-2 Affair*, Harper & Row, 1986.

26. The Brezhnev Regime (1964–1982)

On the leader: John Dornberg, *Brezhnev: The Masks of Power*, Basic Books, 1974. On the domestic political and economic scene: Harry Gelman, *The Brezhnev Politburo and the Decline of Detente*, Cornell U. Press, 1984; Michael Vozlensky, *Nomenklatura: The Soviet Ruling Class*, Doubleday, 1984; Marshall I. Goldman, *U.S.S.R. in Crisis: The Failure of an Economic System*, Norton, 1983; Abraham Katz, *The Politics of Economic Reform in the Soviet Union* (on the post-1965 reforms), Praeger, 1972; Werner G. Hahn, *The Politics of Soviet Agriculture, 1960–1970*, John Hopkins U. Press, 1972; Karl-Eugen Wädekin, *The Private Sector in Soviet Agriculture*, U. of California Press, 1973; Robert Sharlet, *The New Soviet Constitution of 1977*, King's Court Communications, 1978; John Barron, *KGB*, Readers' Digest Press, 1974; John E. Moore, *The Soviet Navy Today*, London, Macdonald and Jane's, 1975; and David Holloway, *The Soviet Union and the Arms Race*, 2d ed., Yale U. Press, 1984.

Problems the USSR shared more or less with other countries are explored in: Walter D. Connor, *Deviance in Soviet Society,* Columbia U. Press, 1972; Michael Kaser, *Health Care in the Soviet Union and Eastern Europe,* Westview, 1976; Philip R. Pryde, *Conservation in the Soviet Union,* Cambridge U. Press, 1972; Marshall I. Goldman, *The Spoils of Progress: Environmental Pollution in the Soviet Union,* MIT Press, 1972; Michael P. Sacks, *Women's Work in Soviet Russia,* Praeger, 1976; Alfred J. DiMaio, Jr., *Soviet Urban Housing,* Praeger, 1974; William Taubman, *Governing Soviet Cities,* Praeger, 1973; Olimpiad S. Ioffe, *Soviet Law and Soviet Reality,* Martinus Nijhoff (Dordrecht), 1985; and Olimpiad S. Ioffe and Peter B. Maggs, *Soviet Law in Theory and Practice,* London, Oceana Publications, 1983.

On foreign relations: Thomas B. Larson, *Soviet-American Rivalry,* Norton, 1978; Adam B. Ulam, *Dangerous Relations: The Soviet Union in World Politics, 1970–1982,* Oxford U. Press, 1983; Robin Edmonds, *Soviet Foreign Policy: The Brezhnev Years,* Oxford U. Press, 1983; John R. Thomas, *Natural Resources in Soviet Foreign Policy,* National Strategy Information Center, 1985; Herbert J. Ellison, ed., *Soviet Policy Toward Western Europe,* U. of Washington Press, 1983; John Barth Urban, *Moscow and the Italian Communist Party,* Cornell U. Press, 1986; Neil McInnes, *The Communist Parties of Western Europe,* Oxford U. Press, 1975; Robert H. Donaldson, ed., *The Soviet Union in the Third World: Successes and Failures,* Westview, 1980; Stephen T. Hosmer and Thomas W. Wolfe, *Soviet Policy and Practice Toward Third World Conflicts,* Lexington Books, 1982; David E. Albright, ed., *Communism in Africa,* Indiana U. Press, 1980; R. Craig Nation and Mark V. Kauppi, eds., *The Soviet Impact in Africa,* D. C. Heath, 1984; Arthur Jay Klinghoffer, *The Angolan War: A Study in Soviet Policy in the Third World,* Westview, 1980; Mark N. Katz, *Russia and Arabia: Soviet Foreign Policy Toward the Arabian Peninsula,* Johns Hopkins U. Press, 1986; Stephen Page, *The Soviet Union and the Yemens: Influence in Asymmetrical Relationships,* Praeger, 1985; Robert O. Freedman, *Soviet Policy Toward the Middle East Since 1970,* Praeger, 1975; Galia Golan, *Yom Kippur and After: The Soviet Union and the Middle East Crisis,* Cambridge U. Press, 1977; Robert H. Donaldson, *Soviet Policy Toward India,* Harvard U. Press, 1974.

On Chinese events and their implications for the USSR: Robert S. Elegant, *Mao's Great Revolution,* World, 1971, and C. L. Chiou, *Maoism in Action, The Cultural Revolution,* St. Lucia, U. of Queensland Press, 1974. On 1968: Karen Dawisha, *The Kremlin and the Prague Spring,* U. of California Press, 1984; H. Gordon Skilling, *Czechoslovakia's Interrupted Revolution,* Princeton U. Press, 1976; Jiri Valenta, *Soviet Intervention in Czechoslovakia, 1968,* Johns Hopkins U. Press, 1981. On Vietnam: William J. Duiker, *The Communist Road to Power in Vietnam,* Westview, 1981; Nguyen Van Canh, *Vietnam Under Communism, 1975–1982,* Hoover Institution Press, 1983.

In the cultural realm: Rudolf L. Tokes, ed., *Dissent in the USSR,* Johns Hopkins U. Press, 1975; Liudmilla Alexeyeva, *Soviet Dissent: Contemporary Movements for National, Religious, and Human Rights,* Wesleyan U. Press, 1985; Joshua Rubenstein, *Soviet Dissidents: Their Struggle for Human Rights,* 2d ed., Beacon Press, 1985; Frederick C. Barghoorn, *Detente and the Democratic Movement in the USSR,* Free Press, 1976; Sidney Bloch and Peter Reddaway, *Psychiatric Terror: How Psychiatry Is Used to Suppress Dissent,* Basic Books, 1977; George Saunders, ed., *Samizdat: Voices of the Soviet Opposition,* Monad, 1974; Klaus Mehnert, *The Russians and Their Favorite Books,* Hoover Institution Press, 1983. The best biography of Solzhenitsyn so far is Michael Scammel, *Solzhenitsyn: A Biography,* Norton, 1984, though weak on the religious side; see also John B. Dunlop et al., eds., *Aleksandr Solzhenitsyn: Critical Essays and Documentary Materials,* 2d ed., Collier Books, 1975, and Edward E. Ericson,

Jr., *Solzhenitsyn and the Modern World*, Regnery Gateway, 1993. By the chief dissident who did not emigrate: Andrei D. Sakharov, *My Country and the World*, Knopf, 1975.

On religion: Robert Conquest, ed., *Religion in the USSR*, London, Bodley Head, 1968; Nikita Struve, *Christians in Contemporary Russia*, trans. Charles Scribner's sons, 1967; Gerhard Simon, *Church, State and Opposition in the USSR*, U. of California Press, 1974; William C. Fletcher, *Soviet Believers: The Religious Sector of the Population*, Regents Press of Kansas, 1981; Leonard Schroeter, *The Last Exodus*, rev. ed., U. of Washington Press, 1979 (on Jewish consciousness and emigration). Hilarious and yet sobering is Paul Hollander, *Political Pilgrims: Travels of Western Intellectuals to the Soviet Union, China and Cuba 1928–1978*. Oxford U. Press, 1981.

27. The Venture of Gorbachëv

On the leaders of the 1982–1991 period: Zhores A. Medvedev, *Andropov: His Life and Death*, Oxford, Blackwell, 1984, and *Gorbachev*, Norton, 1986; Ilya Zemtsov, *Andropov: Policy Dilemmas and the Struggle for Power*, IRICS Publishers, 1983, and *Chernenko: A Return to the Past*, HERO Books, 1985; Dusko Doder and Louise Branson, *Gorbachev: Heretic in the Kremlin*, Penguin, 1991; Ilya Zemtsov and John Farrar, *Gorbachev: The Man and the System*, Transaction Publishers, 1989; Editors of *Time* Magazine, *Mikhail S. Gorbachev*, Time, 1988. Dusko Doder, *Shadows and Whispers: Power Politics Inside the Kremlin From Brezhnev to Gorbachev*, Random House, 1987, gives a Kremlinological overview. Summary treatments of his years in power: Robert G. Kaiser, *Why Gorbachev Happened*, Simon and Schuster, 1991, and Rachel Walker, *Six Years That Shook the World*, St. Martin's Press, 1993. On his policies: Anders Åslund, *Gorbachev's Struggle for Economic Reform: The Soviet Reform Process, 1985–1988*, Cornell U. Press, 1989; Mikhail Gorbachev, *Perestroika: New Thinking for Our Country and the World*, Harper & Row, 1987; Marshall I. Goldman, *What Went Wrong with Perestroika*, Norton, 1992; Ben Eklof, *Soviet Briefing: Gorbachev and the Reform Period*, Westview, 1989; Thane Gustafson, *Crisis Amid Plenty: The Politics of Soviet Energy Under Brezhnev and Gorbachev*, Princeton U. Press, 1989; Coit D. Blacker, *Hostage to Revolution: Gorbachev and Soviet Security Policy, 1985–1991*, Council on Foreign Relations, 1993. Tatyana Zaslavskaya, *The Second Socialist Revolution*, Indiana U. Press, 1990, is a call for restructuring rather than a study of it. On specific aspects of the period: Yuri Shcherbak, *Chernobyl*, London, Macmillan, 1989; E. A. Rees, ed., *The Soviet Communist Party in Disarray: The XXVIII Congress of the Communist Party of the Soviet Union*, St. Martin's Press, 1992; a sample of what Soviet citizens began to learn about their past is Walter Laqueur, *Stalin: The Glasnost Revelations*, Charles Scribner's Sons, 1990; Alec Nove, *Glasnost in Action: Cultural Renaissance in Russia*, Unwin Hyman, 1989; David Lowe, *Russian Writing Since 1953: A Critical Survey*, Ungar, 1987; Geoffrey A. Hosking, Jonathan Aves and Peter J. S. Duncan, *The Road to Post-Communism: Independent Political Movements in the Soviet Union*, Pinter, 1992; R. W. Davies, *Soviet History in the Gorbachev Revolution*, Indiana U. Press, 1989; Alexander Dallin and Bert Patenaude, *Soviet Scholarship Under Gorbachev*, Stanford U. Press, 1988; Robert Conquest, ed., *The Last Empire: Nationality and the Soviet Future*, Hoover Institution Press, 1986; Murray Feshbach and Alfred Friendly, Jr., *Ecocide in the USSR: Health and Nature Under Siege*, Basic Books, 1992; Philip R. Pryde, *Environmental Management in the Soviet Union*, Cambridge U. Press, 1991. On religion: Jane Ellis, *The Russian Orthodox Church: A Contemporary History*, Indiana U. Press, 1986; Kent R. Hill, *The Soviet Union on the Brink: An Inside Look at Christianity & Glasnost*, Multnomah, 1991.

On foreign policy; Jerry F. Hough, *The Struggle for the Third World: Soviet Debates and American Options,* Brookings Institution, 1986; Francis Fukuyama, *Moscow's Post-Brezhnev Assessment of the Third World,* Rand Corporation, 1986; Michael Radu and Arthur Jay Klinghoffer, *The Dynamics of Soviet Policy in Sub-Saharan Africa,* Holmes & Meier, 1991; Douglas Pike, *Vietnam and the Soviet Union,* Westview, 1987; Douglas M. Payne, *The Democratic Mask: The Consolidation of the Sandinista Revolution,* Freedom House, 1986; Jiri Valenta and Herbert J. Ellison, eds., *Grenada and Soviet/Cuban Policy,* Westview, 1986. Two remarkable assessments of the Soviet system as it slid toward oblivion: Seweryn Bialer, *The Soviet Paradox: External Expansion, Internal Decline,* Knopf, 1986, and Richard Pipes, *Survival is Not Enough,* Simon and Schuster, 1984. A journalist's last look: Hedrick Smith, *The New Russians,* Random House, 1990.

28. The Revolution of 1991 and After

One biography has appeared: John Morrison, *Boris Yeltsin: From Brezhnev to Democrat,* Dutton, 1991; his account of himself is Boris Yeltsin, *Against the Grain: An Autobiography,* Summit Books, 1990. Accounts of the end of the USSR and the beginnings of something new: James H. Billington, *Russia Transformed—Breakthrough to Hope: Moscow, August 1991,* Free Press, 1992; David Remnick, *Lenin's Tomb: The Last Days of the Soviet Empire,* Random House, 1993; John B. Dunlop, *The Rise of Russia and the Fall of the Soviet Empire,* Princeton U. Press, 1993; Vladimir Tismaneanu, *Reinventing Politics: Eastern Europe From Stalin to Havel,* Free Press, 1992. On the most populous non-Russian republic: Roman Solchanyk, *Ukraine: The Road to Independence,* St. Martin's Press, 1993. A look at current problems: Darrell Hammer, *Russian Nationalism and Soviet Politics,* Westview, 1994. A poignant testimonial of one of Yeltsin's closest associates who turned against him (after the book was written): Ruslan Khasbulatov, *The Struggle for Russia: Power and Change in the Democratic Revolution,* Routledge, 1993.

About the Book and Author

This classic work stands as the fullest, most comprehensive text available on twentieth-century Russian history. Donald Treadgold traces the wrenching transformations of Russian Society in the opening decades of this century, marking the emergence of Russian Marxism from an obscure radical movement and chronicling its success as a vehicle for the seizure and maintenance of political power. He then examines the development of the policy and practice of the Soviet government over the course of its seventy-year history. Revised and updated to include an account of the countries of the former Soviet Union since the collapse of communism. *Twentieth Century Russia* presents a seasoned scholar's interpretation of modern Russian history.

Although it centers on Russia's political changes throughout the century, this important work also examines developments in the economy, literature, arts, foreign affairs, and religion. The eighth edition is revised from beginning to end and attempts to reflect the massive published research of recent years. It carries the Russian epic into 1994: the Brezhnev era, the Gorbachёv interlude, the reemergence of nations of the former Soviet empire. The author adds vital new material to the introduction and provides updated analysis of the prerevolutionary economy and political scene. He also gives in-depth examinations of the attempted coup of August 1991, Boris Yeltsin's rise to power, and the extraordinarily complex economic and political problems facing post-Communist Russia. He concludes with a look into the future, evaluating the prospects for Russian democracy and economic reforms.

This newly revised edition of a classic account of Russian history is appropriate as the main text for courses on twentieth-century Russian history or Soviet history, or as a supplemental text for courses on Soviet foreign policy.

Donald W. Treadgold is professor emeritus of Russian history at the Henry M. Jackson School of International Studies and Department of History at the University of Washington, Seattle.

Index

Dates of reigns are given for monarchs; for others, dates of birth and death.